THE FRENCH ATLANTIC TRIANGLE

THE
FRENCH
ATLANTIC
TRIANGLE

→ Literature and Culture of the Slave Trade ←

Christopher L. Miller

Duke University Press

DURHAM & LONDON 2008

Duke University Press gratefully acknowledges the support of two organizations that provided funds toward the production of this book:

THE FLORENCE GOULD FOUNDATION

THE JOHN SIMON GUGGENHEIM MEMORIAL FOUNDATION

Printed in the United States of America
on acid-free paper ∞
Designed by Jennifer Hill
Typeset in Fournier by Tseng Information Systems, Inc.

Library of Congress Cataloging-in-Publication Data
appear on the last printed page of this book.

For Christopher Rivers

⤞ CONTENTS ⤝

viii

The French slave trade forced more than one million Africans across the Atlantic to the islands of the Caribbean. No one knows exactly how many, nor do we know how many died in the process—in Africa, on the ocean, or thereafter. This triangular trade defined relations between France, Africa, and the New World and allowed France to establish the richest single colony on Earth (Saint-Domingue, later Haiti). Yet the impact of the French slave trade on the wider culture of France and its colonies has remained gravely underexamined. This book is, first and foremost, about the French Atlantic slave trade, its representations and its aftermath, in literature and film from France, Africa, and the Caribbean. The subject proves difficult to contain: by its nature it spans the oceans and creates ripple effects in both time and space. I have tried to follow those ripples wherever they may flow, around the ocean and through the centuries. The broader consequences of the slave trade, both visible and invisible, are found today all around the Atlantic, in representations ranging from the historically explicit to the explicitly fictional. This study seeks, insofar as is possible, to cover that range, with a principal emphasis on the contributions of creative fiction.

As a subject of inquiry the slave trade cannot help but cast a horrific, negative light on the vogue in postcolonial studies for the celebration of encounter, movement, and hybridity. In the context of the slave trade, encounter meant war and capture; movement was a forced march in chains and a Middle Passage without return; hybridity came from rape. In this case the field of intercultural inquiry—the study of how cultures define themselves in relation to each other—is inarguably built on a foundation of radical inequality and exploitation unto death. My goal in this study is not, however, to make any particular point about theory; rather it is to read history, literature, and film together.

During the period of the slave trade, French literature, understood here in the largest sense of the term, manifested every possible attitude toward a problem that was increasingly difficult to ignore: from blithe ignorance (Rousseau), through ironic, somewhat hypocritical critique (Voltaire), to outright protest (Olympe de Gouges). Literature was one of the most important battlegrounds for the debate on slavery, race, and trade. For lack of authentic slave narratives in French (there were none), writers made them up. To read the broader *littérature négrière* now—some of it well known, some obscure—is, to a large extent, to marvel at the ability of France to keep the problem of slavery out of sight and out of mind. The struggle to bring down the wall of ignorance, to make the plight of the slaves real to metropolitan French people, was the nearly impossible task of the abolitionists. But abolitionism in metropolitan France was, more often than not, tinged with irony and ambivalence; after all, it was England—perfidious Albion—that was so obsessed with abolishing the slave trade. The French literary texts examined in this study will show the full span of that ambivalence, as well as the anemic nature of French abolitionist thought, which followed a twisted path, full of switchbacks, roughly from 1748 (the publication of Montesquieu's *Spirit of the Laws*) to 1848 (the final abolition of slavery in the French colonies).

The French Atlantic Triangle flows from a desire to consider metropolitan France and the "Francophone" polities that used to constitute the French Empire within the same analytical field; to break down the barrier that has tended to treat the literatures produced in these different spheres as if they were of separate "species."[1] Although it has been common to discuss literature of the former colonies as an outgrowth of French culture, and although the Negritude movement worked to rebuild the broken link between Africa and the Caribbean, it has been very rare for critics to look at the French Atlantic as a whole. That is my intent. The Atlantic slave trade and plantation colonialism brought Europe and Africa together, and the spawn of these two parents—the Creole cultures of the New World—have had plenty to say about both the slave trade and the Old World since then. As much as possible, then, this book is structured to reflect a broad, "circum-Atlantic" view, thus bringing Mérimée into dialogue with Boubacar Boris Diop and Dorothy Dandridge; Madame de Duras with Edouard Glissant; and Voltaire with Césaire. *The French Atlantic Triangle* is organized around a roughly chronological progression but with comparative flashes forward and backward in time.

The state of scholarship about the French slave trade has improved considerably during the years of my research, which began in 2000. Even before that, plenty of information was available but only in specialized contexts; it was not widely circulated or considered. The word *taboo* continues to be invoked almost unanimously by those who venture into this subject matter. France's general culture—so steeped in certain specific versions of its own history and so committed to the celebration of the Republic and its universal values—continues to display considerable ignorance about its own past. A few quick illustrations make this clear. In 2005 the well-meaning, left-of-center newspaper *Libération* published an article on the reluctance of the city of Bordeaux to acknowledge its slave-trading past—thereby documenting the type of repression of memory that I am discussing here. But the article also stated as fact that slaves purchased in Africa "passed through," or "transited" through, the port cities of Bordeaux (150,000 of them) and Nantes (450,000).[2] As if the French Atlantic slave trade had worked by systematically bringing slaves first to France and then to the New World; this is utterly false.[3] That such an error could find its way into print in a leading national newspaper is a reflection of a larger problem.

To take a different example: Pierre Nora's monumental set of seven tomes on French historical memory, *Les Lieux de mémoire*, published in 1984, contains not one essay about the slave trade or slavery—both being, in effect, *lieux d'oubli*. Marking some progress, the eight hundred pages of Marc Ferro's *Le Livre noir du colonialisme* (2003), include thirty pages on the slave trade and slavery, although about half are devoted to the American South.[4] The French government's official recognition of slavery and the slave trade as crimes in 2001 certainly reflects a leap forward, and the first annual day for the commemoration of slavery and the slave trade in 2006 brought forth significant discussion and observance. Still, despite the good intentions of many and the hard work of certain scholars and activists, France has much to do to overcome the most influential and lingering factor in its (mis)understanding of the history of its own empire: the colonies and the slaves were out of sight and out of mind.[5]

Part 1 of this book is intended to be a work of critical synthesis. It provides an overview of the French slave trade for readers who have not studied this history. It represents a reading of the history and the historiography of the French slave trade, thus relying on both original sources and the work of historians. In addition, I found it necessary to delve into certain problems that called for closer examination—certain blind spots, myths, and riddles

xi

pertaining to the French slave trade, its vocabulary, its origins, and its representations.

Part 2 was originally intended to be a short critique of an important critical anthology edited by Doris Y. Kadish and Françoise Massardier-Kenney, *Translating Slavery*, which proposes a feminist interpretation of abolitionism in France, working through the lens of "translation." My engagement with that book and with the authors it covered (and did not cover) grew in size and complexity as an interwoven set of problems emerged. The three authors anthologized in *Translating Slavery*—Olympe de Gouges, Germaine de Staël, and Claire de Duras—are key figures in the history of French *littérature négrière*, as my chapters on them will attempt to show. Most significant, I argue, we must recognize the slave trade as itself an act of translation, and we should continually question the role of gender.

Part 3, by contrast, deals with male authors of the French Restoration who, coincidentally or not, were less sympathetic toward the victims of the slave trade than the female authors discussed in part 2. Although I differ from Doris Kadish and the other contributors to *Translating Slavery* in my interpretation of this gendered shift, I do not hesitate to place it within the context that Margaret Cohen has described as a "hostile takeover" of sentimental literature by men. The other thread that runs through both parts 2 and 3 is that of the remarkable economic and social ties that linked these authors to each other and often linked their families to the slave trade. Having organized these two parts along gender lines, I was still somewhat surprised to discover the extent to which questions of sexuality and homosociality imposed themselves as preoccupations among male authors like Eugène Sue and Edouard Corbière.

Part 4 leaps forward to the post-slave-trade era of the twentieth century and the rise of Francophone literature and film. Now the other points on the triangle—Africa and the Caribbean—are heard from, but the result is neither a perfect symmetry of literary "replies" nor a complete rectification of history. Césaire responds to Mérimée but goes far beyond him; Maryse Condé, in *Hérémakhonon*, describes an Atlantic vision that is both derived from the slave trade and truly a product of its own postcolonial times. Still, African and Caribbean writers have not been able to tell the story of the slave trade fully or transparently. The presence of signs of this history in Africa and the Caribbean—on Gorée Island or in the memorials of Martinique—does not mean that everything about it can be known and disclosed. Glissant more than anyone is at pains to remind us that the captives' experience exceeds the outer limits of representability. The alleged "silence" of African writers — a silence that is in fact rather noisy — concludes this study.

↢↣

To save space and gain room for analysis, I have, with regret, eliminated most of the original French quotations in this book. All translations from French are mine unless otherwise indicated. I have marked "AT" (altered translation) the published translations that I have found necessary to alter.

An abridged version of chapter 8 appears in the volume *Approaches to Teaching Duras's "Ourika"* (New York: Modern Language Association, forthcoming).

Chapter 10 is based on a paper delivered at the conference "Les Antilles littéraires: Représentation des Antilles, de la traite et de l'esclavage chez les écrivains et les voyageurs du XIXe siècle," Pointe-à-Pitre, Guadeloupe, March 20–21, 1998. An article version was published under the title, "Forget Haiti: Baron Roger and the New Africa," in *Yale French Studies* 107 (spring 2005).

I regret that timing did not allow me to include references to a book that is closely related to this one: *Claims to Memory: Beyond Slavery and Emancipation in the French Caribbean* by Catherine A. Reinhardt (New York: Berghahn Books, 2006). Reinhardt deals with questions of slavery and emancipation in the second half of the eighteenth century, organized as a series of "realms of memory." Her last chapter examines the memorialization of slavery in the contemporary French Caribbean.

ACKNOWLEDGMENTS

The wide historical, cultural, and geographical span of this study induced me to rely on the kindness of many friends and strangers. Advice, pointers, tips, corrections, and valued help of various kinds came from Jean-Loup Amselle, Ora Avni, David Bellos, Zara Bennett, Philip Boucher, Vilashini Cooppan, Raina Croff, Charlotte Daniels, Daniel Delas, Elizabeth Dillon, Kelly Duke, Catherine Labio, Farid Laroussi, John Logan, Kenneth Loiselle, Bill Marshall, Sue Peabody, J. Ryan Poynter, Julia Prest, Alyssa Goldstein Sepinwall, Alan Thomas, Françoise Vergès, Elliot Visconsi, and Richard Watts. Laure Marcellesi provided superb assistance with my research in its early stages. And Mary Litch helped with screen captures. Those who read parts of this manuscript along the way and offered invaluable comments include Ian Baucom, Chris Bongie, Kamari Clarke, Samba Gadjigo, Peter Hallward, Robert Harms, and Dominic Thomas. Gregory S. Brown generously aided my work on Olympe de Gouges. Olivier Barlet provided indispensable help with films. I am grateful to my students, who have helped me find my way through this subject and have shed so much light on it. And thanks to Ned Duval, who told me I had to write another book.

This book was much improved by the thoughtful and expert readings it received from Laurent Dubois and Deborah Jenson. I am deeply grateful to them. At Duke University Press, I thank Ken Wissoker, Courtney Berger, and Mark Mastromarino for all their help and patience with this long manuscript; and copy editor Joe Abbott for his speed and precision.

I am indebted to the organizers and participants of several colloquia: the 1998 memorial conference "Les Antilles littéraires: Représentation des Antilles, de la traite et de l'esclavage chez les écrivains et les voyageurs du XIXe siècle," organized by Maryse Condé at Pointe-à-Pitre, Guadeloupe; "Migration, Memory, and Trace: Writing in French Outside the Hexagon," at the Graduate Center of CUNY and New York University, organized by Francesca Canadé Sautman; "Concatenations," at the University of Pittsburgh, convened by Yves Citton and Philip Watts; and the colloquium "Intertextualité et adaptation dans les littératures francophones," at the Université du Québec à Montréal and the Université de Montréal. I am also grateful to David Ellison for inviting me to give a keynote address at the Twentieth and Twenty-First Centuries French Studies Colloquium at the University of Miami in 2006. For offering many helpful comments after listening to my lectures, I am also grateful to hosts and audiences at Colby College, Dartmouth College, Princeton University, the University of Wisconsin, the University of Miami, and UCLA.

The breadth of this study was enabled by support I received from a John Simon Guggenheim Memorial Fellowship and a National Endowment for the Humanities Fellowship. K. Anthony Appiah, Chris Bongie, Eileen Julien, and Mireille Rosello kindly supported my grant applications. Institutional support came from Yale University, where I owe much gratitude to Chip Long.

Most important, I am grateful to my partner and legally married spouse, Chris Rivers, who contributed to my thinking in all aspects of this project and offered indispensable advice. I thank him for his insight, support, and love.

⤞ ABBREVIATIONS ⤝

A	*Alzire, ou les Américains*
AG	Eugène Sue, *Atar-Gull* (1993 Laffont edition)
AT	"Altered Translation"
	[indicates author's alteration of a published translation]
C	Liliane Crété, *La Traite des nègres sous l'ancien régime*
D	Serge Daget, *La Traite des Noirs*
DBD1	David Brion Davis, *The Problem of Slavery in Western Culture*
DBD2	David Brion Davis, *The Problem of Slavery in the Age of Revolution*
DBD3	David Brion Davis, *Slavery and Human Progress*
DN	Ousmane Sembene, *Le Docker noir*
E	David Eltis, *The Rise of African Slavery in the Americas*
EN	Olympe de Gouges, *L'Esclavage des Noirs, ou l'heureux naufrage*
EP	Olympe de Gouges, *Écrits politiques, 1788–1791*
FH	Gregory S. Brown, *A Field of Honor*
H	Maryse Condé, *Hérémakhonon*
K	Jacques-François Roger, *Kelédor*
LI	Edouard Glissant, *Les Indes*
MJM	Olivier Pétré-Grenouilleau, ed., *Moi, Joseph Mosneron, armateur négrier nantais (1748–1833)*
N	Edouard Corbière, *Le Négrier* (Baudinière edition, 1979 [conforms to the 1834 edition])
N 1832	Edouard Corbière, *Le Négrier* (first edition, 1832 [2 vols.])
N 1834	Edouard Corbière, *Le Négrier* (Dénain and Delamare edition, 1834 [4 vols.])

N 1990   Edouard Corbière, *Le Négrier* (Klincksieck edition, 1990)

ODG   Olivier Blanc, *Olympe de Gouges*

OE   Olaudah Equiano, *The Interesting Narrative of the Life of Olaudah Equiano*

OJ   Madame de Staël, *Oeuvres de jeunesse*

PG   Olivier Pétré-Grenouilleau, *La Traite des Noirs*

PM   Prosper Mérimée, *Théâtre de Clara Gazul, romans et nouvelles* (Pléiade edition, 1978)

PS   G. W. F. Hegel, *Phenomenology of Spirit*

QS   Edouard Glissant, *Le Quatrième siècle*

RMD   Madame la Baronne Staël de Holstein, *Recueil de morceaux détachés*

S   Robert Louis Stein, *The French Slave Trade in the Eighteenth Century*

SAL   Patrick Manning, *Slavery and African Life*

Sar   Edouard Glissant, *Sartorius*

SAST   Boubacar Barry, *Senegambia and the Atlantic Slave Trade*

SOC   *Oeuvres complètes de Madame la Baronne de Staël-Holstein* (Slatkine edition, 1967)

T   Hugh Thomas, *The Slave Trade*

TS   Doris Y. Kadish and Françoise Massardier-Kenney, eds., *Translating Slavery*

VOC   Voltaire, *Oeuvres complètes*

WC   William B. Cohen, *The French Encounter with Africans*

ZM   Olympe de Gouges, *Zamore et Mirza, ou l'heureux naufrage*

I

THE FRENCH ATLANTIC

INTRODUCTION

Examine the situations of all the peoples of the universe. They are set up in such a way that they appear to depend on nothing, yet they depend on everything. Everything is a cog, a pulley, a cord, a spring in this immense machine. In the physical universe it is the same. A wind that blows from the depths of Africa and from the southern seas brings with it a part of the African atmosphere, which falls as rain in the valleys of the Alps; those rains enrich our lands; and our northern wind in its turn sends our vapors to the Negroes. *We do good to Guinea, and Guinea does good to us. The chain stretches from one end of the universe to the other.*
—VOLTAIRE, "Chaîne ou génération des événements" (1764)

Man is born free, yet everywhere lives in chains.
—ROUSSEAU, *Du Contrat social* (1762)

THE SLAVE TRADE AND ITS BORDERS

The Atlantic triangle was invented by a system of trades, following a certain pattern. The French version of the Atlantic, perhaps more than any other, was triangular in its configuration. The Atlantic triangle was traced onto the earth and into world culture by men and women and ships, moving goods to Africa, captive Africans to the New World, and colonial products back to the mother countries. The forced migration of more than eleven million Africans to the New World presents a tremendous challenge to memory—but not only to memory: to ethics, politics, and, most of all, justice. The effects of the triangle are inscribed on the ground of Gorée

Island in Senegal, in the remains of the plantations of Martinique and Haiti, on the luxurious facades of Nantes and Bordeaux—and in the economic inequities of the postcolonial world. The impact of the slave trade remains with us today in more ways than one can count, for it truly created a "new world."

My goal in this book is to think about what I will call the French Atlantic: France, parts of Africa, and the French islands of the Caribbean, with occasional references beyond, to Louisiana and to the Indian Ocean.[1] I want to think of this as a whole in which the various parts are interpreted in relation to each other: France in relation to Africa, Africa in relation to the Caribbean, and so on. These multiple relations are reflected and refracted in literary texts, images, films, and a variety of other documents ranging from the seventeenth century to the twentieth. My hypothesis is that the infamous, slave-based "triangular trade" created a powerful sweep of forces moving around the Atlantic and that traces of those forces have survived abolitions, independences, and "departmentalizations." At the same time, the figure of the triangle is not all-encompassing: as a mercantilist plan it could not be fully enforced over time and space, and as a projection of the French nation-state it invited resistance from within, below, and outside. So considerable attention is due to the individuals, groups, modes of thought, and political forces that escaped the logic of the triangle and the state—or tried to. Through a reading of numerous texts, emanating from different points of the French (and Francophone) Atlantic, I hope to shed light both on the reality of the triangular system and on modes and moments of its undoing.

→──◄

That the *official* French slave trade was predominantly triangular is a matter of both historical record and geographical inevitability. Any vessel leaving France to move slaves from Africa to the Caribbean, once it returned home, would have traced a rough triangle spanning the Atlantic from north to south, from east to west, and then back. We will see that the mercantilist doctrine of the *Exclusif* established by Colbert, banning trade with other empires, solidified the triangle and made it the only legitimate pattern of trade. Herbert S. Klein warns against the "myth" of the triangular trade, but what he dismisses is the idea that each slave-trading vessel completed the full triangle in economic terms, perfectly balancing its books and possibly turning a profit. That is indeed a myth. But the triangle, we will see, remains both a fact on the ground (on the ocean) and an internalized cultural logic. There were other triangles (Newport–West Africa–Barbados; the cod-fish triangle France–Newfoundland–Mediterranean) and other polygons (as when the Atlantic triangle was illegally made into a quadrilateral by trade between the French planters of the Caribbean and British North America). The Atlantic could be constructed according to other, multidirectional or "crosshatched," logics, in which meanings might "circulat[e] promiscuously"; the French Atlantic in the time of the slave trade did not tend to be one of those.[2] It will be important here to pay attention to various mitigations of the triangle but equally important to recognize its forms of predominance. The phrase *commerce triangulaire* (or *trafic triangulaire*), referring to the Atlantic economy based on the slave trade, is commonplace in French.[3]

The triangle will therefore be not only the dominant figure here but, perhaps inevitably, a figure of dominance itself. The triangle is a sign of power — and of the direct contestation of power; it is the shape both of the slave trade and — to take a leap that cannot be avoided — of the Oedipus complex. It suggests a logic of ineluctable, "eternal" relationships: father, mother, offspring — terms that in the cultural logic of colonialism translate into Europe, Africa, and the New World. The history of colonialism is rife with metaphors casting Europe in the role of father, Africa as mother (an idea supported by the ideology of Negritude), and the new *creole* (from Spanish *criar*, to breed, to raise) colonies as children.[4] Aimé Césaire wrote of the West Indian as "the bastard of Europe and Africa, torn between this father who denies him and this mother he denies."[5] That triangulated family romance — set up by the slave trade — is at the heart of our concerns here.

But the very persistence of the triangle has incited certain artists to think outside its lines and to seek other logics. In a text that informs the basis of this project, Césaire's *Cahier d'un retour au pays natal* (*Notebook of a Return to My Native Land*), the triangle is plainly evident — the inescapable armature of thought about relations between Europe, Africa, and the Caribbean in the wake of the slave trade and slavery. The "negritude" that Césaire invented in that poem — an idea that is often misrepresented these days as a simplistic vision of a lost African paradise — was partially (but not entirely) an attempt to renegotiate a triangle that appeared to be so powerful that it could never be imagined out of existence. Césaire sought to renavigate the triangle according to a logic of indirect return (to Africa, but via France, its institutions, its language, and its literature). That reinvented triangle — Caribbean, France, Africa — is often represented as an ideological formula,

5

a prescription on Césaire's part, and certain passages of the *Cahier* seem to support this. Yet there is another logic at work in the poem: the thought of a spiral that spins and rises above the triangle, culminating in the final word of the poem, *verrition*. A neologism rooted in the Latin *verri* or *vertere*, to sweep, to spin or (most relevantly) to scan, *veerition* (as it has been translated) encapsulates the logic of escape, of the marooned slave who finds refuge in the forest.[6] Yet this word also conjures thoughts of sweeping away the triangle and of escaping into a wholly different logic, free from the violently imposed relationships of the triangle. *Vertere* also means to overturn, overthrow, destroy, so it is in a sense an act of veerition when the captives in the hold of the slave ship, at the dramatic climax of the poem, rise up in revolt and free themselves. "Veerition" might be that other logic: a spiral rising above the triangle, leaving it behind. As we will see later in this study, that would be consistent with Césaire's reinvention of Mérimée's "Tamango," a key tale of revolt on a slave ship.[7]

Too bad that Césaire only offers the possibility of escape within a mind-boggling oxymoron: it is not simply "veerition" that he gives us at the very end of the *Cahier*—sweeping us into redemption—but "*immobile* veerition." He leaves us to wonder if there is any real escape from the triangle, whether there is any viable alternative. It may turn out that the logic of the triangle and that of "veerition" are implicit in each other. Later in this study, the task of my chapter on the *Cahier* will be to read Césaire's interpretations of the inherited logic of the slave trade and to explore his mixed feelings about the possibility of escape.

→►◄←

At its most basic, this book is concerned with interpretations of space as they have evolved through time. Apprehensions of geographical space both help to explain history and affect what is done to create history.[8] European powers created the Atlantic system, putting in place what was in effect a vast triangular machine in which slave labor played an essential role. Their ability to shape the Atlantic came from their prowess as mariners, and it allowed them to see what they wanted to see. This selective vision in turn made it thinkable to base their new Atlantic economy on servitude and slavery—even as some within the European seats of power began to undermine philosophically the basis of slavery. My epigraphs from Voltaire and Rousseau illustrate this tension. These two thinkers loom large over any attempt to understand how the French eighteenth century could be, on the one hand, so deeply involved in the slave trade and, on the other, so productive of the ideas that would later abolish that trade, produce revolutions, and enable, as Giovanni Arrighi puts it, "a thorough transformation of ruler-subject relations throughout the Americas and in most of Europe"[9]—and later, less thoroughly, lead to decolonization in Africa.

It was during the eighteenth century that the majority of slaves were exported from Africa. Slavery and servitude had always been a part of the social order in both Europe and Africa in one form or another. It was in fact one of those "wheels, pulleys, ropes, and springs"—in Voltaire's words—that held the world together. In "Chaîne ou génération des événements" Voltaire celebrates what we might now call globalization: the amazing interdependence of far-flung elements. Voltaire's cheerful invocation of Africa as a place that is linked to France is very strange, and I don't believe he was really thinking of the weather. He knew perfectly well that it was not the weather but the slave trade that was the "pulley" bringing Africa and Europe together in an "immense machine." His metaphor, a chain, to suggest the links between peoples throughout the world, is a singularly unhappy choice. For in Voltaire's times (and, for a time, with his investments) some were more enchained than others. In his enthusiasm for global connectedness Voltaire shows his ability to ignore the inconvenient fact of African servitude.[10] He is typical of his era: the idea of a "Great Chain of Beings" was commonplace in the eighteenth century, while great chains were being applied to hundreds of thousands of Africans.[11]

Rousseau, in the epigraph, sounds like he recognizes the evil of slavery in this famous opening of the *Social Contract*, yet he too ignores the Atlantic slave trade, as he does throughout his vast writings, with one tiny exception. He makes slavery a metaphor for the condition of man in *modern* (which means European) society. This gesture dominates the Enlightenment's treatment of the theme of slavery, and the technique of "making-metaphorical" will require further examination. Those who are *literally* enchained do not enter his thinking here. Both Voltaire and Rousseau, even as they struggled to think their way out of various forms of oppressive dogma, were, each in his own way, barely interested in African slavery. Their indifference must be considered representative of one of the conditions that allowed for the turning of the machine of enslavement around and around the Atlantic in their times. Perhaps, to follow Orlando Patterson's general theory about slavery and freedom, the enslavement of Africans by Europeans was not simply a blind spot in the minds of the philosophes; perhaps "the joint rise

7

of slavery [for Africans] and cultivation of freedom [for Europeans] was no accident."[12] What I will call an *economy* held slavery and freedom together in a compromising tangle of relationships. Rousseau himself puzzled over this in the *Social Contract*: "Could it be that freedom is only maintained through the support of servitude? Perhaps. The two extremes meet."[13]

→ ←

Among the methodological hunches that I am making about the French Atlantic is the idea of following the money. As we will see, it was rarely cash that flowed around the ocean, but exchanges of valued objects—of everything from cloths and cowry shells to human beings—created the Atlantic. To follow the flow of those values is to see the emergence of a vast system that defied all borders. What were the boundaries of the slave trade? Where did its reach end? Trade goods produced in Europe were exchanged for captives in Africa. Cowries—the "shell money of the slave trade"—were taken from the Maldive Islands in the Indian Ocean to Europe as ballast, then shipped to Africa and used as currency for buying slaves; circulated widely in Africa and incorporated into ritual practices, some of those shells now adorn African art, which itself now circulates throughout the world.[14] If, as Patrick Manning asserts, "all of African society, not just a privileged elite, was compromised in the slave trade"—because everyone relied on the various forms of currency or trade goods that the trade brought in—and if, as Boubacar Barry writes, "The entire [Senegambian] society was intimately involved in the slave holding system," does the same model of general permeability not apply to European society, and American?[15] If those statements are true, then the Atlantic triangle looks like a conspiracy in which the elites of Europe, Africa, and the Americas collaborated (unequally) to exploit the labor of enslaved Africans.

The Atlantic slave trade was connected to the Arab or "Oriental" slave trade (both across the Sahara and east to the Indian Ocean), and both exporting systems fed on the trade in slaves that took place among sub-Saharan Africans themselves.[16] Ships plying the direct route back and forth between France and the Caribbean on the *commerce en droiture*, although they were not carrying slaves, were part of an economy that was wholly dependent on slavery, and those ships, as I will explain, were necessary to recuperate the full value of the slaves brought to the New World. This was a "world system."[17]

These are the pulleys, ropes, and springs of the Atlantic economy, and

8

they obviously reach far into Europe, Africa, and the New World. Money—
value in general—is fungible, and the wealth created by the slave trade
flowed far and wide at the time of the trade, beyond anyone's ability to
trace; it drove the Atlantic triangle but also sometimes defied it by flowing
in illegitimate directions. The *Exclusif*, a doctrine of the centralized French
state, sought to enforce a logic of *centripetal trade*—which is something of
an oxymoron. An initial, centrifugal gesture disperses capital outward (to
Africa and across the Atlantic to the New World) but within triangular paths
sanctioned by the central State. Everything flows around and eventually returns to the center: that is mercantilism, the pattern dictated by the *Exclusif*. As Ian Baucom writes, "Expansion contracts . . . [and] contraction
enriches."[18] In other words, the expansion of European power makes the
world smaller, which in turn helps to propel the return of capital and profits
to Europe. We know, however, that such logics can rarely maintain complete power or consistent profitability: the triangular trade did *not* always
bring the returns it was supposed to (and was capable of, particularly in the
early years). A healthy illegal trade—the *interlope*—was practiced outside
the lines of the official triangle. Expansion did not always "contract" the
way that Colbert, for example, wanted it to. Braudel describes how money
can work: "The economy, all-invading, mingling together currencies and
commodities, tended to promote unity [or perhaps promiscuity?] of a kind
in a world where everything else seemed to be conspiring to create clearly-
distinguished blocs."[19] In other words, money has a perverse centrifugal
power even as an imperial nation-state might try to control its flow centrip-
etally. So where are the boundaries of the slave trade? They cannot be demarcated, and this is consequently a subject without neat borders.

9

One of the porous boundaries that defines this subject is the one between
the slave trade and slavery itself. Some historians insist that the two "must
not be confused."[20] They are indeed different systems, and they were abolished separately: early abolitionists strategically advocated banning the
trade alone, as a first step. Yet, in an excess of methodological purity, to
ignore slavery in a study of the slave trade would be to shut out the most
important determinant. There could be no slave trade without slavery, yet
slavery continued after the end of the slave trade. Clearly the two institutions or systems were inseparable, since each fed and perpetuated the other.
And, as I will discuss below, what we know and don't know about the trade,

from the slaves' perspective especially, comes to us through the institution of slavery and particularly its control of literacy. Often in the course of this study it will be necessary to discuss French slavery in order to understand the French slave trade.

The general problem of borderlessness also has consequences for the interpretation of the literature and film. The frame of analysis — often established as a set of criteria from which various judgments can then flow (national, racial, ethnic, or sexual identity, to cite the most obvious examples) — in this case is highly fluid. We are contemplating the attempt of a nation-state to control the transnational flow of value, to keep that flow within a pattern that would benefit the French state: the triangle. The works that we will read here will both adhere to and undermine that effort. The challenge will therefore be to read these texts "Atlantically," or perhaps (in Joseph Roach's phrase) "circum-Atlantically," placing them in, as much as possible, the full context of their time and in their proper, highly complex, place(s). This will therefore be an exercise in *intercultural* interpretation.[21]

What do literature and money have in common? They are both figures of desire — as a force for transformation and transmigration, desire to have something (or something more) or to be somewhere else. The slave trade combined these two: traders had to go somewhere (or send others, their agents) in order to (they hoped) get rich. Capitalist greed, romantic longing, and exoticist esthetics all reflect a quest and a desire. For the slave traders the object was money; for the Africans they brought to the New World the object was their lost native land and the thirst for return, often expressed in literature.

Contemplating the literature of the slave trade and its economies of desire, we might do well to keep in mind Deleuze's and Guattari's critique of desire as lack, which they say is characteristic of something they happen to call a "slave morality" — reactive and antilife. If lack (*manque*) is "created, planned and organized through social production," then it is obvious that the slave trade itself was, to say the least, a machine for creating this negative type of desire.[22] But, following a philosophical tradition that we will see in Rousseau, Deleuze and Guattari stigmatize the slave as they deploy the *metaphor* of slavery for a problem that they conceive within the bounds of Western thought. Readers of Deleuze and Guattari are called on to set aside the shackles of "slave morality" and free themselves from desire-as-lack in favor of desire-as-affirmation.[23] In this study I want to ask about the literal slaves themselves within the context of an economy that was not simply non-life-affirming but actually built on death: what were *their* desires, as they labored for the fulfillment of the desires of those who claimed to own them? The flow and interchange of desire around the Atlantic — the "economy" of desire — as lack, affirmation, or ambivalence will be the object of this study.[24]

TRAITE AND TRADE

What are we saying when we use the word *trade* or, in French, *traite*? The French term defining the relations among the different parts and places in this scheme has no exact equivalent in English, although in *traite des Noirs*, *traite négrière*, or *traite des nègres*, it translates easily enough as "trade." But the French term contains important ambiguities that should not be ignored. The slave trade was the principal motor that propelled ships, persons, and values around the Atlantic. The word *traite*, even standing alone, came to be associated with the Atlantic slave trade at an early date; Furetière gave as one definition of *traitte* in 1690: "Traffic, commerce with Savages. . . . One goes to Senegal for the *trade* in Negroes" (*Dictionnaire universel*). The etymology of the noun *traite* contains a significant surprise: its appearance suggests that it must come from the verb *traiter*, meaning to treat or to deal with; slave traders in fact used that verb to describe the action of trading. But *traite* derived originally from another verb, *traire*, meaning to draw out, to extract, or to milk (*Robert* dictionary, 1985).[25] Etymologically, *traite* in the sense of milking suggests a transaction requiring two parties, one of which is the active partner taking from the other; desire or the ability to realize desire (that is to say, the power) is all on one side. Historian Joseph Miller identifies the years from 1500 to 1800 as the "extraction-based" period in the history of the Atlantic slave trade.[26]

Trade in English suggests something more reciprocal ("the buying and selling or exchange of commodities for profit" [*OED*]). The early slave trader Jean (or John) Barbot (himself both French and English) judged the Africans he encountered on the coast according to whether or not they were *traitables*: tractable, manageable, accommodating; people he could do business with.[27] The economics of *traite* (extraction) are far different from those of trade: the early-twentieth-century colonial exploitation of Africa is cited as an example of a "milking economy," and extraction is of course associated with the quest for oil in today's global economy.[28] However, etymology is not history. Historians now believe that *la traite des esclaves* did in fact work as a trade, as an economy of exchange according to "rational" sets of prices, and not as a pure extraction or theft of Africans from Africa by Europeans. This is not to say that the slave trade was an *equal* exchange by any reckoning that makes sense to us now—far from it. But pure extraction or theft was not its usual method.

So the phrase *traite des Noirs* contains ambiguities about the nature of the business that went on in the slave trade, and I would suggest that those ambiguities constitute a problem of desire as it relates to power. Who was able to realize their desires, to *draw out* the objects of their desire—and according to what framework of power?[29] And to what extent did an economy of exchange impinge on a desire for extraction?

The title-page engraving in Le Sieur Froger's travel account of 1695 to 1697 (see figure 1) depicts the ambiguities of power and exchange that Europeans and Africans must have felt in each other's presence in the early years. An imposing African leader reclines, at ease but armed, as a European approaches solicitously with offerings (no doubt the *coutume* that was required before trade could open). The African in the middle holds a bolt of checkered cloth, from which his shirt has been fashioned: it could be a West African kente type cloth, or it could be a European imitation thereof known as "Guinea cloth," purchased from an earlier visitor. Some single garments could be used to purchase one prime male slave (T, 322, 319). But no slaves are in sight here: the most valued commodity in the African-European trade is left out. This engraving idealizes "trade" as fair exchange. Yet in the bay lurks a sign of inequality, a European weapon of mass destruction: a ship.

The other significant implication of the word *traite* is movement: the word is used in expressions describing uninterrupted movement: *aller d'une traite, lire d'une seule traite*.[30] The French Atlantic was established and built around the slave trade, as a basically triangular set of *traites*: of trajectories, of things and people drawn across the space of the ocean. Within the vastness of that universe of exchanges, trades, and *traites*, my focus will be on impulses of desire that reach across the Atlantic and around the triangle, and, when possible, on texts that rather explicitly contemplate the broadest implications of the slave trade. The subject itself has no borders and cannot be fully apprehended or treated exhaustively, but printed texts and films that deal with the subject can be read, analyzed, and compared. The principal ar-

1 A French view of trade on the coast of Africa in the seventeenth century. From Le Sieur Froger, *Relation du voyage de Mr. De Gennes au detroit de Magellan* (Paris: Chez N. de Fer, 1698). Detail of title page. Beinecke Rare Book and Manuscript Library, Yale University.

tifacts that I will examine in this study will all reflect a transatlantic desire, a sense of place that is inflected or haunted by another place: this is the culture created by the Creole societies of the New World, with their sense of an origin located across the sea, in either continent of the Old World. France, Africa, and the Caribbean came to be joined in a web of interlocking desires—negative, affirmative, and ambiguous by turns and in constant flux. This cannot be analyzed *d'une seule traite*.

THE EMERGENCE OF THE
ATLANTIC TRIANGLE

The eighteenth century was the heyday of the Atlantic slave trade. Two-thirds of all slaves were brought to the New World in that century; 80 percent of all French slave-trading voyages took place in that period.[31] But the origins of the triangle are much older. In a sense it was Columbus, the "inventor" of the Atlantic, who laid the groundwork for the triangular trade:

he had sailed to Africa—on routes already well established by the Portuguese—in 1482. When he went to the Americas and returned to Europe, he was thus already completing a triangle.[32] By 1460, sugar was being produced by African slave labor on the Atlantic island of Madeira—where Columbus lived for more than ten years (T, 70, 87; DBD3, 62). The combination of slaves and sugar that would transform the Caribbean and drive the triangular trade had already been formulated on the Atlantic islands, which David Brion Davis calls "crucibles of New World institutions" (DBD3, 61). Columbus took sugar plants with him to his new world—and by that gesture literally planted the seeds of slavery. And if it is true that he took enslaved Africans to the West Indies as well, he can be said to have transferred the mode of production in which slaves were used to produce sugar from one side of the Atlantic to the other himself.[33] When Columbus came along, then, the Atlantic was ready for a commerce based on the exchange of enslaved human beings—at least two hundred years before that commerce reached its "perfected" form. Thus, as W. E. B. Du Bois put it, "the rape of Africa began and transformed the world."[34]

In Giovanni Arrighi's analysis of mercantilism there are three components: "settler colonialism, capitalist slavery, and economic nationalism," and slavery was "partly a condition and partly a result of the success of settler colonialism."[35] Settlers in the Americas and slaves from Africa went together—as part of a *triangulated* strategy that supported the third component, the nationalism of the European metropoles. Barbara L. Solow writes: "Firm and enduring trade links between Europe and America were not forged without and until the introduction of slavery. . . . Colonial development was strongly associated with slavery."[36] In other words, the Americas were not developed in a dyadic relationship with their respective "mother" countries; there was a triangular formation that constituted the key to successful colonization. To view the history of the New World this way is to fully acknowledge the importance of slavery and of Africa and to redress the systematic erasure of the New World's debt to Africa.[37]

The need for labor in the Caribbean stimulated the first imports of African slaves—from Iberia at first, then, more efficiently, directly from Africa (T, 92). By 1530 most slaves were being brought directly from Africa to the New World. At first they worked alongside European indentured servants, but that form of servitude was abandoned—for reasons that are often falsely cited as "climactic" according to Eric Williams; the lovely climate of the Caribbean islands is never as oppressive as South Carolina (nor even New Jersey) in the summer: African labor was simply "cheapest and best."[38] *Pace* Williams, racism played its part, at least as a rationale that emerged alongside of economic considerations and as an increasingly potent ideological support for the enslavement of Africans. With the rise of racism white slavery became unacceptable.[39] Somehow, agriculture paralleled race: on the French islands tobacco fell as sugar rose, and simultaneously, as if necessarily, indentured white labor was replaced by enslaved black labor.[40] Slavery became essential to the Atlantic system and to the establishment and functioning of the New World; David Eltis writes, "No one [between the middle of the sixteenth century and the late eighteenth century] . . . seriously contemplated an America without the enslavement of non-Europeans" (E, 27). From the moment it was decided that those non-Europeans would be Africans, the triangular Atlantic system was established, with Africa as an integral part of the relation between Europe and the Americas.

Eltis also shows how Africa itself narrowly escaped the "plantation complex" — the imposition of a large-scale, slave-powered agricultural system — thereby escaping European colonization for another three hundred years. The system that was invented in the Atlantic islands almost came ashore, but in the early sixteenth century its movement shifted toward the New World, paradoxically far from the supply of labor. As Eltis puts it, simply, "Europeans did not have the power to move into West Africa" (E, 146). They were unable to move beyond the coast: epidemiology played some part in this, but the strength of African states is at least as important. Africans controlled Africa and did not fall to European colonization until the late nineteenth century. Africans, as John Thornton puts it, "were active participants in the Atlantic world [and] controlled the nature of their interactions with Europe . . . including the slave trade."[41] They would sell captives to Europeans — thus setting up the pattern of the Atlantic trade — but they would not surrender control of their land for the establishment of European plantations. That would have to wait. (As we will see, the idea of setting up plantations in Africa was common among abolitionists in the late eighteenth century and the early nineteenth.) From this Eltis draws the interesting conclusion that "the slave trade was a symptom of African strength, not weakness" (E, 149).

15

VALUES

Underpinning the Atlantic triangle is the idea of value and the desire to increase value by transporting goods and human beings around the ocean. Arthur L. Stinchcombe explains the simple principles behind the triangular trade: "profits were due to the successful sailing of a ship with a valuable cargo from a place where the cargo was less valuable to a place where it was more valuable, to return with one that was more valuable yet."[42] The slave trade was predicated on the relatively low price put on human lives (for reasons that must be contemplated) in Africa, which enabled European traders to buy low, move across the Atlantic, and sell high—so high that the ships plying the Middle Passage from Africa to the Caribbean could not possibly carry enough Caribbean products home to equal the value of the captives they had sold; it took anywhere from two to four ships carrying sugar to equal that amount.[43] Cash payment would obviously have made this complicated system unnecessary, but for a variety of reasons cash was unavailable in the colonies (5, 52).[44] The system worked by barter and without any "common measure."[45] Especially in the early years in the islands, sugar (along with other commodities) *was* money: when the proprietor of a cabaret in Martinique was fined for selling brandy to slaves during a Sunday mass in 1689, his penalty was three hundred pounds of sugar.[46]

What is a person worth? Olaudah Equiano said that he was sold by one African merchant to another for 172 cowries.[47] What must it have been like to live in Africa at the height of the slave trade, when, as Manning points out, every encounter, particularly with a stranger, must have been haunted by the question, How much could you be sold for?[48] (The film *Adanggaman*, discussed in chapter 14, captures some of that feeling.) Questions of value—and of commercial desire for other humans—cannot be any more troubling than that. Le Sieur de La Courbe, a late-seventeenth-century trader and administrator in Senegal, reports that a Moor whom he met assessed the value of one horse as worth twenty-five captives or slaves; through the power of the Atlantic triangle, a captive sold into slavery was worth nine thousand pounds of sugar in the same time period—but only once that captive was transported across the Atlantic.[49] (And that of course is before said captive is put to work.) From one twenty-fifth of a horse—even in Senegal, where horses were highly valued[50]—to nine thousand pounds of sugar, the slave trade is full of bizarre calculations of the value of human life. The monstrosity of making such assessments in the first place is compounded by the prevalence of deception and cheating in all aspects of the slave trade.[51] But there can be no doubt that the force behind the rise of the slave trade was, in the early years, the general doubling (or more) of the value of a slave after crossing the Atlantic (T, 103).

Enticement for early French settlement in the Antilles came from Jean-Baptiste Du Tertre, a missionary priest in the mid-seventeenth century, who deplored the sale of young white men "as slaves" (his characterization of indentured labor) on the islands, which he called a "detestable" and a "shameful commerce." Du Tertre, however, optimistically reported that a settler owning "two good Negroes" can live "well at ease and honorably" because the slaves can produce "1700 or 1800 pounds of tobacco, not counting the food they grow."[52]

For the European slave traders the transformation of value by displacement was almost a miracle. At the height of the trade the businessmen of Nantes could hardly believe their good fortune: "We have in our State no . . . commerce as precious as the commerce with Guinea [Africa], and one can hardly do enough to protect it. What other commerce could be compared to this one, which results in obtaining men in exchange for merchandise?"[53] Despite their "slip" in admitting that slaves are "men," the question is a good one.

17

Value was thus transformed, and space was defined by the desire to increase wealth — at the expense of lives. Patrick Manning has produced the most compelling — and chilling — explanation of the inner logic of the Atlantic triangle: in simplified form his thesis is that human lives were worth more, monetarily, in the New World than they were in Africa because environmental factors (the persistence of certain diseases) and technological factors (dependence on the hoe, which cannot produce as much as a plow can) lowered the productivity of workers in Africa. A person removed from Africa and transported to a quasi-industrial plantation in the Caribbean was able to produce far more value: "The logic of African supply of slaves depends . . . on the notion that slaves in the New World were more productive than free producers in Africa, with a margin large enough that New World slave owners could pay for the costs of transportation, mortality, and seasoning of their slaves" (SAL, 33). This imbalance of values kept the triangle turning, as Europeans continually sought to increase their wealth by turning, spinning, and sweeping around the Atlantic. The profit motive is taken to be a rational mode of thought; its complicity with enslavement and genocide, as Paul Gilroy has pointed out, needs to be examined.[54] Abolition comes about only when an ex-slave appears to be more profitable to the system than a slave; only then is the triangle altered.

LOUIS XIII AND THE "ORIGIN" OF THE FRENCH SLAVE TRADE

The French entered an Atlantic slave trade that had been established and dominated by the Iberians. So it is fitting that it was a French captain (often mistaken for Portuguese) who may have been one of the first to make a triangular voyage around the Atlantic: Jean Alfonce Fontenau "de Saintonge" is reported to have sailed to the Grain Coast of Africa for pepper—and possibly for slaves as well—in the 1540s, crossing the Atlantic to "La France Antarctique" (a short-lived French foothold in Brazil).[55] But that foreshadowing is not the real origin of the French slave trade.

Nor, I think, is there much substance in the most-repeated tale of the origin of the French slave trade. It goes like this: in a decree of 1642 Louis XIII supposedly authorized the trade, expressing his wish that enslavement would save the souls of Africans. This narrative is widely accepted and often repeated when the press mentions the slave trade.[56] Its respectability is no doubt due to the fact that Montesquieu, the philosopher at the origin of French abolitionism, gave it credence and prominence in *The Spirit of the Laws* (1748). He wrote that Louis XIII "was extremely pained by the law making slaves of the Negroes in his colonies, but when it had been brought fully to his mind that this was the surest way to convert them, he consented to it."[57] And where did Montesquieu get this information about the king's state of mind? Not from any authentic document, nor from any authority on the reign of Louis XIII (who died in 1643, forty-six years before Montesquieu was born), but rather, his footnote indicates, from Jean-Baptiste Labat (1663–1738), a notorious, slave-trading, swashbuckling "pirate" priest of the Dominican order who was also a prolific (and plagiarizing) writer of travel accounts. Labat left his imprint all over the French Atlantic.[58] Labat, invoking what we will see to be the French "freedom principle," wrote in his *Nouveau voyage aux isles* in 1722:

> It is a very ancient law, that lands under the control of the kings of France render free all those who can reach them. That is why King Louis XIII, of glorious

18

memory, as pious as he was wise, had all the trouble in the world [*toutes les peines du monde*] consenting to the first settlers of the Islands owning slaves, and only gave in to the insistent solicitations that were made to him to grant this permission because it was argued to him that this was an infallible way—and the only means available—to inspire the worship of the true God in the Africans, to remove them from idolatry, and to keep them until death in the Christian religion that would be instilled in them [*qu'on leur feroit embrasser*].[59]

Labat cites no source for this anecdote, and before him the trail disappears; no one cites any textual evidence preceding Labat, and the existence of the putative edict cannot be verified. Without any further shred of support, however, this story has been perpetuated in French historiography. Historians should have paid more attention to Joseph Morenas, an abolitionist who refuted the myth in 1828.[60] There is a glaring anomaly here: Louis XIII's authorization of the slave trade is often repeated in the historiography of the French slave trade, but works on the king make no mention of it. The supposed role of Louis the Just in originating the French branch of a murderous enterprise is not mentioned in modern biographies and studies of him.[61]

The anecdote itself is a highly significant artifact: it connects the image of a precise, written, original authorization of the French slave trade to an inflection of moral ambivalence. Two tendencies in French culture—the *esclavagiste* and the abolitionist—are thus reflected in this historiographical mystery. Slavery *is* salvation, yet it brings moral "pain" to those who enslave others. This story, apparently made up, perhaps based on oral history, maybe by the slave-driving priest Labat himself, is a microcosm of French attitudes toward slavery and the slave trade. Its purpose shifts from outright justification of the slave trade in Labat to an increasing emphasis, beginning in Montesquieu, on the morally dubious nature of enslavement itself.

The origins of the French slave trade were in all likelihood less clear and more detached from moral qualms than Labat's story would have us believe. What Louis XIII authorized in his edict of March 1642 was the colonization of the Antilles.[62] The last decade of the reign of Louis XIII began to establish the French Atlantic triangle, and various decrees by the king regulated this process. Richelieu granted a monopoly on the Senegal trade to a group from Dieppe and Rouen in 1633; there were slaves on Saint-Christophe as early as 1626; a French slave trade began to supply that island in 1633.[63] Piecemeal authorizations for the importation of slaves from Africa were issued over the next several decades. Then, in 1664, Colbert established the

Compagnie des Indes Occidentales, designed to conduct a triangular trade that included the transportation of enslaved Africans to the Antilles.[64] This was the beginning of the real French slave trade, within a scheme of "exclusive" mercantilism that we will examine presently.

The French took possession of Guadeloupe and Martinique in 1635, of Guyane (definitively) in 1663, and of Saint-Domingue (officially) in 1697. Adopting the plantation system from the Iberians, and learning the art of refining sugar from Dutch-Jewish settlers who had been exiled from Brazil, the French established a slave society very quickly.[65] Du Tertre's descriptions and illustrations of 1667 already resemble (and in some ways surpass) what the *Encyclopédie* will depict one hundred years later (see figure 2).[66] Across the Atlantic France established itself in Senegal at Saint-Louis in 1659 and took Gorée Island in 1677. With these outposts scattered around the Atlantic, the French triangle was prepared. Already in the 1630s the first *lettres patentes* permitted trade in Africa with a direct connection to the Antilles — undoubtedly including slaves.[67]

If any moral scruples impaired the French entry into the trade — for example, those that made for a ban on the sale of slaves in Bordeaux in the 1570s — by the time labor was called for by Caribbean planters in the second quarter of the seventeenth century, everything moral and material was in place.[68] There could not have been great obstacles, since forms of slavery (serfdom and galley slavery, for example), still existed in France itself. The Church not only did not object but, in the person of Bossuet, encouraged slavery.[69]

But the moral and legal context in France was complex. Conditions of slavery and servitude were offset by what Sue Peabody calls the Freedom Principle: the notion, supported by a decree of Louis X in 1315, that "France" signifies freedom and that any slave setting foot on what we now call the hexagon should be freed. There was in fact a tradition of freeing slaves, and it remained influential, if often undercut, during the time of the Atlantic slave trade.[70] That principle made France's negotiation of the slave trade slightly more complicated, posing ethical and legal hurdles along the way. Which was the "real" France — the slave trader or the liberator? That debate animates much of the literature that will be studied in this book. In fact France would often seek to have it both ways, by asserting that enslavement saved (freed) the *soul* of the slave: that is what Labat's tale of Louis XIII manages to convey in a few words. Throughout colonial and postcolo-

20

1. Moulin   2. Fourneaux   3. Formes   4. Vinaigrens   5. Cannes   SVCRERIE   6. Gros   7. Latanir   8. Pazomirinha   9. Choux   10. Casse   11. Figuir. est

2   "Sugar Mill." From Jean-Baptiste Du Tertre, *Histoire générale des Antilles habitées par les François* (Paris: Thomas Iolly, 1667), 1:122. Beinecke Rare Book and Manuscript Library, Yale University.

21

nial history France will often be torn between its magnanimous, liberal impulses (religious at first, then humanitarian) and its desire to dominate and profit.[71]

Indentured servitude of Europeans was a step on the way toward race-based slavery. The French experimented seriously with *engagés à temps* in the New World, in what Crété calls a "temporary slavery" that generally lasted three years. Some were masons, coopers, tailors, or even surgeons; many were unskilled laborers working in tobacco fields, sometimes along with African slaves. *Engagés* could be bought and sold during the time of their contract, and by some accounts there was a veritable *traite des blancs*, complete with *marronnage* and rewards for recapture.[72] At the end of their indenture the laborers were paid in tobacco or sugar, and, most important, they were free to either stay or go home to France. The rise of sugar in the islands brought with it a demand for labor that seemed only possible to meet by the importation of African slaves. Sugar required a massive supply of labor that could not be provided by meager numbers of workers who would be set free soon after acquiring the expertise that sugar cultivation required. Sugar "needed" slaves, and sugar consumed slaves.

THE EXCLUSIVE TRIANGLE

Direct trade from our Colonies to the coasts of Africa is prohibited
for the sole purpose of reserving the advantages of that trade to the
commerce of the Kingdom.

"Lettre du Ministre à M. de Reynaud" (1784)

By 1656 the aboriginal people of Guadeloupe were eradicated and three
thousand enslaved Africans worked on the island, in the presence of twelve
thousand French people, some of whom were indentured laborers. In 1664
Colbert created the Compagnie des Indes with a short-lived monopoly on
the trade bringing slaves to the New World; in 1670 he exempted the slave
trade from tariffs to stimulate the importation of labor to the island. In 1716
the trade in "Negroes, gold powder, and all other merchandise that they
can draw from the Coasts of Africa" was opened to all traders, provided
that they operated out of Rouen, La Rochelle, Bordeaux, or Nantes; later,
Le Havre would replace Rouen. The acts of that year constitute a veritable
"code of the triangular trade."[73] One historian dates the emergence of the
French Atlantic to "the watershed year of 1713," when the War of Spanish
Succession ended and colonial investment was relaunched.[74]

Between 1640 and 1700 the French took 75,000 slaves into their colonies;
from 1700 to 1760, 388,000. The prodigious rise of Saint-Domingue began
in the 1730s, marked by huge importations of slaves, producing the richest
colony on Earth. French slave exports from Africa peaked in the years leading up to the Revolution, with an average of twenty-seven thousand slaves
transported per year between 1781 and 1790. At the end of the eighteenth
century the nations of Europe and the United States were collectively forcing eighty thousand captives per year on the Middle Passage; the total for
the whole century was more than six million.[75] During the entire period of
the slave trade, the French exported 1.1 million Africans (slightly more than
one million of which were traded in the eighteenth century alone) in 3,649
recorded voyages.[76] Extrapolating from all available data, David Geggus
concludes that "French carriers must have been responsible for about one-
eighth of the total [Atlantic] traffic."[77] The three French Caribbean island
colonies ranked third as an importer of slaves to the New World, taking in
17 percent of the total—the same number as was taken in by all of Spanish
America.[78] For perspective one should take onboard this fact, as stated by
Michel-Rolph Trouillot: "Martinique, a tiny territory less than one-fourth

22

the size of Long Island, imported more slaves than all the U.S. states combined" (excluding Louisiana).[79]

The grand scheme of the triangle was perfection itself; as shown by maps of the winds sweeping across the Atlantic, they trace the triangular trade.[80] When the Chevalier de Boufflers, governor of Senegal, tried to return directly to France in 1786 (bringing with him the "little captive" Ourika as a gift for his aunt and uncle), he found the winds "contrary," and some onboard suggested that they just go to America, "where the wind would lead us directly," and from there to France. The best heading the ship could get pointed them toward Newfoundland; they finally put in at the Azores, halfway across the Atlantic, before they were able (barely) to make a course for La Rochelle.[81] They might as well have gone to the Antilles and followed the triangle. Early in his correspondence, in fact, the governor complained that his letters to his mistress could only get to France via Saint-Domingue (129).[82] The Antilles were a "stopover" on the trip from Africa back to France.[83]

The winds may thus have encouraged the logic and economics of the triangle; the French state did the rest. For a variety of reasons, then, the triangle was set up as a one-way pattern.[84] Slave traders sailed out of French ports, went to Africa, then to the Caribbean, then home; there was little variation from that itinerary. This was especially true in the classical period of the trade, the eighteenth century. Few departures were recorded (and none that have left a narrative trace that I have found) from the French Caribbean bound for Africa.[85] That route was forbidden and almost totally closed off. Edouard Glissant writes in *Le Quatrième siècle* of that experience, from the point of view of those who had been enslaved: "They came on the ocean, and when they saw the new land, there was no hope; they were not permitted to go back [*de revenir en arrière*]."[86]

The simplicity of the triangular system was just as the Abbé Raynal puts it in the title to book 11 of his *Histoire des deux Indes*: "Europeans go to Africa to buy farm laborers [*cultivateurs*] for the West Indies."[87] Yet within that formula and within the Atlantic system itself, there was a fundamental irony of huge proportions. The triangle brought the workers to the work; only the products and profits returned home. The massive and paradoxical inefficiency of a system that moves labor across an entire ocean under hideous conditions—to cultivate crops that they might grow back in Africa—is a question that will occur to various observers over the centuries and a question to which I will return in my chapter on Baron Roger. The perceived

23

need to displace Africans in order to make the Americas productive created the Atlantic as we know it.

There were many exceptions to the classic triangular itinerary, and a healthy commerce *en droiture* (direct trade between Europe and the Caribbean) was necessary to supply the islands and bring home the excess value created by the import of slaves (that is, the two or three extra shiploads required to make up the value of one load of slaves).[88] The triangular trade and the commerce *en droiture* were inseparable parts of the same Atlantic economy. Colbert worked to ensure the rigidity of the triangle: his doctrine of the *Exclusif* did not allow trade that deviated from the lines of the French Atlantic triangle; trade with other empires — possibly creating webs of interwoven triangles — was not permitted (which doesn't mean it did not happen). The *Exclusif* had begun as a form of monopoly granted to French companies against each other but in 1674 assumed its classic form: the exclusion of non-French traders from the French Atlantic triangle. With the end of the monopoly companies, commerce was opened to all Frenchmen, while at the same time "foreign" trade (that is, outside the bounds of the French Atlantic triangle) was banned. Foreign ships were not to enter French colonial ports, and French colonial products were not to be shipped anywhere but to France. As Montesquieu described the *Exclusif* in *The Spirit of the Laws*, "the metropole alone may trade [*négocier*] with the colonies."[89] Enforcement — a nearly impossible task — may have been most rigorous from 1703 to 1715.[90] For Colbert the colonies were children; they should do what they were told; they did not even need (and did not have) money (T, 189). The mercantilist laws of the *Exclusif* demanded that it be so: the colonies were subject to "the most austere prohibitions favoring the metropole."[91] By this system of supports and encouragements, taxes and tax breaks, France institutionalized the triangle. The fall of state monopoly companies like the Compagnie des Indes and the rise of private enterprise in the slave trade (still regulated by the state) did not alter the basic functions of the triangle: trade goods still went to Africa, captives were transported to the islands, and colonial products returned to France. Social networks reinforced the triangle: by the late eighteenth century, writes Laurent Dubois, "many merchant houses in France's major port towns . . . owned plantations [and therefore slaves] in Saint-Domingue" and the other French islands; the Caribbean became "the main destination for Frenchmen seeking their fortunes in the Americas" after the loss of Canada.[92] The *Exclusif*, part real monopoly, part "program," and part "ideal,"[93] remained a force throughout most of the eighteenth century, until the American Revolution gave France a new reason to trade with North America. From that point on, the *Exclusif* lost its force, and the triangle was consequently altered—although it was substantially revived in its traditional form during the Restoration, between 1814 and 1830. In the nineteenth century some (now illegal) French slave traders set out from the Antilles bound for Africa, thus engaging in bilateral trade, revolutionizing the pattern that had been in place.[94]

It is important to the overall thrust of this book to note the lingering effects of the *Exclusif*. French Guyanese legislator Christiane Taubira makes this point eloquently: "We of France 'overseas' know what it is to run up against the vestiges of the colonial *Exclusif*, which link the former colonies to their former metropoles, from South to North, without facilitating contacts with neighboring countries, without the possibility of regional contacts. We know why migratory patterns follow the paths of languages and old dominations. We know the cost of trying to transgress the ban on industrialization formulated by Colbert ('not one nail should come out of the colonies')."[95]

Beginning in 1715, a "sugar revolution" took place in the Antilles: sugar production in Martinique quadrupled between 1717 and 1753, and the number of slaves increased by the same factor, from 14,500 to 65,000. Saint-Domingue took the lead in importing slaves and producing sugar in the mid-eighteenth century, with an estimated slave population of five hundred thousand or six hundred thousand in 1789, feeding six hundred sugar mills (C, 189). The direct relation between the number of slaves and the production of sugar has been well demonstrated.[96] Sidney Mintz's analysis of the triangle reflects mostly on Britain, where sugar had the most profound impact on diet, but the French islands in fact began to rival the British islands in the 1720s in sugar production and took the lead in 1767.[97]

As Mintz shows in *Sweetness and Power*, there was (and is, as everyone knows) a clear synergy of taste among the leading alimentary *denrées coloniales* (colonial products): sugar, coffee, chocolate, and tea: sugar is needed to sweeten the bitter tropical liquids, and all are stimulants, likely to produce cravings—a desire for more (see also T, 189–90). Sugar was needed or at least wanted "as work schedules were quickening . . . and as the factory system was taking shape and spreading" (in other words, as literal fuel for the labor of the industrial revolution).[98] In the upper echelons of society colonial products were not only found to be delicious and stimulating; they also connoted imperial power. Blackburn points out the symbolic value at

25

Versailles of colonial accessories and elaborate confections made of sugar. The rising craving for sweetness and stimulation in Europe — in all the leading colonial nations and at several levels of society — played a large role in the enslavement and forced migration of Africans, through the workings of the Atlantic triangle. As an early French abolitionist put it, with scathing irony: "We are wrong, but we need sugar."[99] Some sugar reached Africa: the fruit of the labor of Africans (who could not themselves return to Africa) returned to complete the triangular circuit.[100]

Other commodities drove the triangular trade as well, perhaps none as "perfectly" as cotton. As one of the principal goods traded for slaves in Africa, cotton cloths, initially imported from India, then manufactured in Europe (*les indiennes*, as they were and are called in France), paid for slaves, who would go to the colonies to produce raw cotton, which would go to Europe to make more cloth.[101]

The triangle was driven partly by cravings in Europe — for sweetness and the energy of caffeine but also more generally for wealth; and it was enabled by the cooperation of African elites, who, also motivated by a desire for enrichment or in order to punish criminals or enemies, sold their captives — thereby accounting for two points of the triangle. The whole scheme, however, depended on the Caribbean, and the New World more generally, as a place of both production and destruction. For the eighteenth century the figures on the productivity and thus the value of the Antilles to France are powerful. Guadeloupe, Martinique, and Saint-Domingue — three relatively small territories, with a combined area roughly equivalent to Massachusetts and Delaware together, and almost exactly the size of Normandy in France — produced value radically out of proportion to their size, all of it driven by slave labor and the continued operation of the slave trade. On the eve of the Revolution France's islands led the world in the production of sugar. Martinique became a large exporter of coffee — the second Antillean *denrée* — in the 1730s. Guadeloupe, under British control from 1759 to 1763, became the most productive of the British islands (only to go back to the French in 1763) (c, 7, 29, 190, 191). Saint-Domingue (which doubled its production between 1783 and 1789) alone accounted for two-thirds of France's overseas trade and was "the most profitable colony the world had ever known." C. L. R. James sees in that assertion one support for his controversial theory that "slavery and the slave trade were the economic basis of the French Revolution."[102] Thanks to the *Exclusif* and to *dirigisme* in general, all of this productivity was, in principle, aimed at the metropole alone.

Most dramatically, the real value of the Antilles to France was demonstrated by the Treaty of Paris, which ended the Seven Years' War in 1763: France gave up Senegal—its oldest and most significant foothold south of the Sahara (while retaining Gorée Island) and its part of Canada in order to regain Martinique and Guadeloupe. Voltaire famously quipped about this treaty: "I am like the public. I love peace much more than I love Canada, and I think that France can be happy without Quebec."[103] His reaction contains an implicit preference for one mode of colonization—the Caribbean version, based on slavery—over the Canadian version, based on settlement and trade (in the sense of exchange more than extraction) between free peoples. The twenty-five-year period from the Treaty of Paris to the French Revolution was the apogee of the triangular, slave-based economy: the slave trade churned, the plantations worked slaves to death, and the colonial products of their labor brought heaps of wealth to the planters and the slave traders.[104]

ON THE ISLANDS

So the hunger and greed of the metropole spurred the planters of the Antilles, who in turn spurred their slaves. The productivity of the islands was entirely conditioned on slavery and the continuation of the slave trade. The trade was necessary not only for the expansion of industrial agriculture but simply for its maintenance, because slavery killed slaves before, during, and after the Middle Passage. Demographics show that the destruction of human lives during the crossing and on the plantations of the Caribbean was a significant stimulus to the slave trade. Death created demand within the system and kept the triangle turning. It was found to be cheaper to keep importing slaves from Africa—in spite of the expense and danger of the African trade—than to raise slave children to working age; slaves were expendable.[105] Du Tertre reported from the islands simply: "An infinite number of Negroes die."[106] A century later, Raynal claimed that the 140,000 or 150,000 slaves present in the European colonies of the New World were the "unfortunate leftovers" of eight or nine million brought over from Africa.[107] The plantation system, as Robin Blackburn puts it, broke with "any geographical constraint" and displayed an "unquenchable thirst for slave labour and slave lives."[108] A dreadful arithmetic fills discussions of the slave trade, all of it uncertain yet certainly appalling. No one knows how many lives were lost in Africa in the violent process of taking captives for the slave trade; in 1915 W. E. B. Du Bois said that five Africans died for every one taken captive; Patrick Manning suggests it was five million who died in capture operations between 1700 and 1850.[109] Estimates of mortality during the Middle Passage generally vary between 10 and 20 percent and may average around 13 percent, but of course there were cases of a 100 percent death rate.[110] Robert Stein says that 150,000 captives died in French ships "either along the [African] coast or while crossing the Atlantic" in the eighteenth century (S, 99). French seaman Robert Durand recorded the deaths of captives on his ship, *Le Diligent*, with a skull (see figure 3), those of French crew members with a cross. Using historians' current best estimates, there is a chilling shortfall between the number of Africans put on ships and those who arrived in the New World: roughly 1.5 million died on the Atlantic crossing.[111]

French planters of the Antilles were known internationally as efficient taskmasters, yielding 25 percent more sugar per acre than their Jamaican counterparts (WC, 56). The *Code Noir* of 1685 attempted to regulate the entire institution of slavery as part of an effort by the central state to gain greater control over the slaveholding colonies. The order of prescriptions in the Code is significant: in article 1 Jews are expulsed from the colonies; in article 2 it is ordered that all slaves be baptized and instructed as Roman Catholics; in article 3 the exercise of all other religions is banned.[112] This was, after all, the year of the Revocation of the Edict of Nantes. The Code provided for certain minimal rights of slaves: they could not be married against their will (article 11); if baptized, they were to be buried in consecrated ground (article 14); each slave was entitled to a prescribed minimum of food (article 22) and to two sets of clothing per year (article 25). But owners were barely punished for violating slaves' meager entitlements, while actual atrocities were prescribed by the Code against slaves who attempted escape or committed other offenses: for maroons, branding with a fleur-de-lis, cutting the hamstring, or, after the third escape, death. These prescriptions were precise and legal, making "rational" what Du Tertre had twenty years earlier deplored as a system of "arbitrary punishments . . . at the discretion of [the] Masters."[113] Thus the Code enlisted rationality in the practice of violence. Louis Sala-Molins describes the Code as a spectacular "theoretical performance" allowing France to pronounce simulta-

3 Skull indicating death of a captive. Robert Durand, *Journal de bord d'un négrier* (1731), 93. Beinecke Rare Book and Manuscript Library, Yale University.

neously "slavery" and "law," "enslavement" and "code"—to have it both ways; the Code is one of the most spectacular instances of what Paul Gilroy calls "the complicity of rationality and ethnocidal terror."[114] Perhaps more important than anything, the Code's article 44 declared slaves to be *meubles* (possessions, "furniture," as it were) that could be treated as "sums of money" (*deniers*) and "other movable things" (article 45). Through these legal mechanisms slaves were subjected to the control of the French state. As Joseph Roach puts it, the Code set up "the partial incorporation of hundreds of thousands and eventually millions of Africans into the body politic of the Ancien Régime and its sucessors."[115] But the body metaphor is not completely successful here, because these enslaved, black members of the French body politic—perhaps one or two individuals for every ten thousand in the years leading up to the Revolution[116]—were kept largely out of sight (four thousand miles away) and out of mind. This brings us to an important point about the Code Noir, raised by Cilas Kemedjio: where did the slaves in this code come from? The Code "left the slave trade itself in the shadows."[117] The effects of the Code Noir have endured.[118]

The general context of cruelty in which the Code intervened can be discerned from an upbeat passage in Froger's relation of his time in Martinique during his triangular voyage:

I knew a planter of Martinique, who out of some kind of compassion was unable to order the leg cut off one of his Slaves, who had already deserted four or five times. So as to not risk losing him entirely, he [the planter] devised to rig the Slave up with a chain strung along his back between his neck and his foot, as shown in the Figure [see figure 4]. His nerves so shortened in this posture that after two or three years it was impossible for this Slave to use his leg. Thus with-

4 "Invention d'un François de la Marti-
nique" [Invention of a Frenchman of
Martinique]. From Le Sieur Froger,
Relation du voyage de Mr. De Gennes
(1698), 150. Detail. Beinecke Rare
Book and Manuscript Library, Yale
University.

30

out risking the life of this wretch, and *without causing him any pain* [*sans lui faire aucun mal*], the means of fleeing were taken away from him.[119]

Conditions were anything but conducive to human reproduction. In 1765 there were two hundred thousand slaves in Saint-Domingue, and "it was generally assumed that fifteen thousand slaves had to be introduced every year just to maintain the labor force at the right level"; imports to Saint-Domingue in fact rose to forty thousand per year (T, 277, 285). The traffic was so intense, and the birthrate among slaves was so low, that in 1750, two-thirds of all the slaves in Saint-Domingue had been born in Africa.[120] Olaudah Equiano's *The Interesting Narrative* speaks of a direct relation between cruelty in the Caribbean and the continuation of the slave trade: Barbados "requires 1,000 negroes annually to keep up the original stock, which is only 80,000" (OE, 79).

Looking at the entire history of the Atlantic slave trade, we see that certain statistics, as organized by Patrick Manning, reveal a horrific truth: ten million Africans were brought to the New World by 1820, while only two million Europeans came (thus five times more blacks than whites); yet in 1820 there were twelve million whites in the New World and half that number of blacks (*SAL*, 37). In 1600 Africa held 30 percent of the combined population of the New World, Europe, the Middle East, and Africa; two hundred years later that share had fallen to 20 percent (*SAL*, 171). Death drove the slave trade and kept it going.

The Atlantic slave trade continued its dreadful traffic — and passed as the "normal" scheme of things (T, 14) — until petering out in the nineteenth century, many decades after enlightened abolitionists began their work. The British and the United States banned the slave trade in 1807, and France did so partially in the period of the Bourbon Restoration, but interdiction — along with the industrial revolution, which lowered the price of the *mise hors* (T, 677) — only increased the profitability of the triangle. French slave-trading voyages doubled in 1819, and there may have been five hundred French slave-trading voyages between 1818 and 1831 (T, 621, 625).[121] This late, illegal trade by the French was the object of considerable "romance" in literature, as we will see: numerous accounts and fictions emphasized the "adventures" of French slave traders dodging British warships. This period of illegal trade during the Restoration will in fact be the central focus of both French and Francophone writers, as much of this study will show. The French slave trade only faded away after three different laws were passed, the last one with genuine enforcement, in 1831. Still, with slavery a legal institution in the French islands until 1848, some trade persisted. By the most recent count, 11,062,000 Africans were transported across the Atlantic as slaves, about 1,456,400 by the French, but these cold and rough numbers can hardly begin to establish an understanding of what happened (E, 42).[122]

31

INTERLOPING

My attention thus far has been devoted almost exclusively to the centripetal forces of the French Atlantic triangle. The illegal, clandestine, potentially revolutionary activities of those who worked outside the *Exclusif* are, by definition, harder to find in the written record. Historians have naturally tended to analyze what is documented more than what is undocumented. And, by definition, no one can say what proportion of the trade was conducted clandestinely outside the official paths. Was there in the French Atlantic economy anything like the remarkable "Many-Headed Hydra" described by Peter Linebaugh and Marcus Rediker in their book of that name? Or is French historiography (to borrow their terms) a "captive of the nation-state" — thereby suggesting that the *Exclusif* and the triangle are figments of a "largely unquestioned framework of analysis"?[123]

This intriguing possibility is somewhat vitiated from the start when applied to the French Atlantic triangle for the simple reason that the three islands that dominated this economy were among the most accessible and best-controlled of France's overseas territories. Martinique, Guadeloupe, and Saint-Domingue "offered far better opportunities for regular contact and for state influence than Canada and especially Louisiana."[124]

Even so, enforcement of the *Exclusif* was irregular and often corrupted; there were constant violations by regular traders as well as by pirates and freebooters. *Interlope* is the term used to describe "a vast and complex system of illegal exchanges" in the Caribbean and more generally within the New World (but *not*, significantly, with Africa).[125] The *interlope* was a logical "corollary" of the strictness of the *Exclusif*.[126] Illegal trade rose and fell depending on the ability of the French state to control both the seas and its own colonies. During the American War of Independence patterns were altered and disturbed, but from 1783 to 1792 the triangle regained strength: more than 1,100 French ships took 370,000 captives across the Atlantic, almost all to Saint-Domingue (c, 245).

But interloping trade among white people is only one part of the many different types of forces that resisted the control of the *Exclusif*. The slaves themselves were of course not merely passive recipients of the forces that we have seen here; they actively resisted, engaging in uncountable forms of *marronnage* (escape) as well as numerous open revolts. The ultimate form of rebellion was the Haitian Revolution, which irrevocably altered the French Atlantic triangle and caused its most basic assumptions to be rethought. But more subtle, less famous acts of resistance took place earlier and elsewhere. Those slaves who were reported to have fled Guadeloupe and Martinique for Puerto Rico and Trinidad in the mid-eighteenth century revealed "leaks" in the supposedly watertight system of the French slave trade and slave-labor economy.[127] Their ability to island-hop and cross the boundaries of the French, Spanish, and British empires raises important questions about official and antiofficial activity. So the question of resistance to the triangle is not, in this study, to be understood simply as a matter of shipping and trading either inside or outside of certain lines. Even if trade on the ground and on the seas had been absolutely limited to the triangle, some would have been able to *think* outside its lines.

My survey thus far has already encountered a number of epistemological and historical ambiguities. Before we go any further in establishing a context for the interpretation of literature and film about the French slave trade, I want to pause for a moment to consider *how* we know what we know (and do not know) about this entire subject.

SILENCES, LITERACIES, AND ABSENT NARRATIVES (WHY IS THERE NO FRANCOPHONE EQUIANO?)

The European side of this encounter is well documented by certain of the traders themselves (Jean Barbot, John Hawkins, Willem Bosman, and Pruneau de Pommegorge are often cited) and by observers such as the priests Jean-Baptiste Labat (who said he never left his ship on the African coast) and the Abbé Demanet (famous for his slave trading and his libertinism). Later, antislavery writings will document the horrors of the trade. In the late eighteenth century and the nineteenth abolitionist writings include both fictive and testimonial reflections on the trade—many of which will be discussed in this study. But the African side of the larger question—what might have been going on in the mind of African elites as they sold their captives, and the lived experience of those who were taken and enslaved—is more elusive and largely lost. Sources are "extremely rare" but "not inexistent."[128] Olaudah Equiano's *The Interesting Narrative* (1789) is the most frequently cited account of the Middle Passage and of slavery in the Atlantic world of the eighteenth century. Recent doubts about its authenticity, related to questions about Equiano's birthplace, compound the problem of silence considerably; the *Narrative* must now be read with caution and with awareness that at least some of the text may result from fabrication, embellishment, or indirect reporting taken from oral or written sources (all of which is far from a complete discrediting of the narrative).[129] As I will suggest in chapter 10, the possible fictivity of Equiano's narrative brings it into the same analytical field as some more obviously fictional texts, like the Baron Roger's *Kelédor*; it also narrows the gap between the discourse of the Anglo-American Atlantic, influenced by slave narratives, and that of the French Atlantic, without those texts as such.[130]

Another "interesting narrative," the *Biography of Mahommah G. Baquaqua* (1854) is not as well known; "written and revised from [Baquaqua's] own words" by Samuel Moore, a Unitarian minister and abolitionist, the text zigzags between third-person biography and first-person autobiography, lead-

33

ing its editors to ask, rightly, "Whose voice are we in fact hearing?"[131] The African point of view on the slave trade and direct eyewitness accounts of the Middle Passage do not come without a price of refraction and ambiguity.[132]

Among other sources of testimony about the slave trade from the slaves' perspective are those gathered in Philip Curtin's volume *Africa Remembered*. But there are few direct *African* representations and accounts of the sale of slaves *by Africans*—and almost nothing told from the point of view of an African Atlantic slave trader. Quobna Ottobah Cugoano, another rare source, states, "I must own, to the shame of my own countrymen, that I was first kid-napped and betrayed by some of my own complexion, who were the first cause of my exile and slavery."[133]

Cugoano, Equiano, and Baquaqua all tell how they were captured and sold, but their African captors remain silent. There are very few representations of the African slave traders' point of view and thus little chance for gaining insight into their motivations. There are small exceptions, in oral history, some reportedly recorded on tape in Nigeria (D, 13); a king of Asante speaks of his motivations in a journal by Joseph Dupuis published in 1824.[134] King Agaja of Dahomey sent a letter to King George I of England in 1726 that shed light on his motivations for trading in slaves: as Robert Harms describes it, Agaja needed cowry shells, gunpowder, and cloth— "the cowry shells for the common people, like the silk cloth for the royal wives and the gunpowder for the army, could be obtained only through the slave trade."[135] (Agaja is discussed in Maryse Condé's novel *Hérémakhonon* and in the film *Middle Passage*.)

In the English-speaking world, and especially in the United States, the problem of silence is significantly offset by testimonies and narratives, beginning with Equiano's. But in French the problem is far more serious, for *there are no real slave narratives in French*—not as we know them in the Anglophone Atlantic, not that have yet been discovered. That absence, for now at least, haunts any inquiry into the history of slavery. The slave narratives that emerged in the United States were in fact the exception; only one narrative, from Cuba, written by a slave during the time of slavery, came out of the entire Caribbean.[136] (Toussaint Louverture was "the first of the black memorialists" in French, but his memoirs are concerned with his actions as a general; they contain no recollections of Toussaint's life as a slave, so they are not a slave narrative as such.)[137] When abolitionists in France began their work and wanted the words of slaves to support their arguments, they either made them up — as is perhaps the case of Lecointe-Marsillac's *Le More-Lack* (1789) — or got them from English.[138] Thus the Abbé Prévost, in what Roger Mercier calls one of the "first traces of compassion" for African slaves, published in *Le Pour et le contre* the translation from English of a speech by Jamaican rebel slave Moses bom Saam — a text that was an early benchmark in the emergence of the "noble Negro."[139] Significantly, Prévost prefaces the text with elaborate skepticism, as an example of a work "of dubious authority," but the power of the speech comes through nonetheless.[140] The voice of the revolted slave thus emerges from a limbo between fiction and authenticity, thus precisely as *literature*.

With regard to the situation in French, Louis Sala-Molins writes, "We have at our disposal not a single written testimony on the reality of slavery coming from a slave."[141] This is *almost* literally true. The slave plantations of the Caribbean were anything but writerly places, and although the Code Noir mandated that slaves be instructed in religion, hardly any education happened, slave literacy was scarce, and no slave narratives were apparently written.[142] It seems clear that under the regime of slavery from the time of the Code Noir until abolition, "instruction" was seen as instruction in religion only, as catechism; that it was *oral*, with no attempt to impart literacy; and that very little of it took place.[143] Instruction required both free time for the slaves and their ability to assemble; it was therefore perceived as a risk of insurrection. Fénelon, the governor of Martinique in 1764, wrote, "Education . . . is a duty for the principles of holy religion, but wise policy [*la saine politique*] and human considerations are against it. . . . *The safety of the Whites demands that we keep the Negroes in the profoundest ignorance*."[144] Exceptional schools that gave any instruction to slaves were clearly seen as dangerous in an order issued in Martinique at the time of the Revolution: "It would therefore be a very dangerous imprudence to continue to tolerate schools for Negroes and people of color in this colony."[145] This phrasing of course suggests that in fact some slaves were receiving instruction, and this important point — the exceptional instances of slave literacy in the French islands — is addressed in a remarkable book by Haitian historian Jean Fouchard, *Les Marrons du syllabaire* (1953).[146]

Fouchard provides a wealth of information both on the interdiction of literacy in the French islands and on "miraculous" escapes into literacy on the part of slaves — the maroons of the title. The spelling book (*syllabaire*)

35

was forbidden to slaves (63, 67, 72) — and we need look no further for an explanation of the absence of slave narratives. But this does not mean that there was no literacy among slaves. Among the frequent and numerous notices of runaway slaves published in newspapers were some warning that the slave in question was literate and might be bearing a false pass that he or she had written. As Fouchard makes clear, we simply do not know how these slaves acquired the ability to read or write — but they did manage, and that is remarkable.[147] To Fouchard's research I can add one other sign of the nearly paranoid controls on literacy exercised by the slaveholding class of Saint-Domingue, this notice published in the daily newspaper *La Gazette du jour* (November 15, 1790): "N.B. Our honorable Subscribers are kindly asked to provide their Negro servant with a card, showing their name, when they send them to pick up the *Gazette du Jour*. The newspaper will be delivered only to those bearing such cards or to the Subscribers themselves." A newspaper in the hands of a slave was obviously a dangerous thing. But in all that Fouchard offers in his book, nothing is as startling as his observation that the slave's first contact with literacy, in many cases, was when he or she was *branded*; the initials of the buyer were the first spelling book (97).

Fouchard also reproduces a few exceptional documents that should be kept in mind: letters from slaves in Saint-Domingue, perhaps corrected by scribes, but in all probability authentic. In 1792 a slave named Polisson or Lapierre wrote to his master: "I implore your sympathy to have my master give me my freedom."[148] The controls on literacy and the suppression of the slave's rise to and through literacy take on a new weight when one sees the fears of the authorities realized, for example, in a letter from the slave leader Casimir to the governor of Martinique in August 1789. Casimir eloquently declared that the "entire Nation of black slaves, united" in one "cry," desired only independence and freedom.[149] This is the *cri* that Césaire will have to reinvent in his *Cahier*. It was in Haiti, not Martinique, Césaire tells us in the *Cahier*, that "Negritude stood up for the first time," but here, in his own Martinique in 1789, we see that cry in literate form and something beyond what Césaire himself would stand up for: independence.

Still, these letters, as compelling and moving as they are, cannot compete with the comprehensive value of the slave narratives published in the United States in the nineteenth century. The letters interrupt but do not overcome the "silence" or, to put it more precisely, the deficit of direct testimony in written form. What would African American history and historiography be without the testimonies of Olaudah Equiano, Frederick Douglass, Harriet

Jacobs, or the dozens of narratives of former slaves? That is the condition of the African diaspora in the French Atlantic.

→→←←

The problem of silences about the slave trade touches all points of the triangle and constitutes a veritable complex. The slave-trading ports of Europe (Liverpool excepted) have shown little inclination to acknowledge this part of their past: the elites of the slave-trading cities prefer to keep their "little green boxes" of family secrets secret; in this milieu the slave trade simply "must not be discussed publicly."[150] Renault and Daget compare the "muteness" of these families in France to that of Africans who guard oral traditions bearing on the slave trade.[151] There are no fitting memorials in the former slave-trading cities of Europe (except Liverpool) to the millions deported from Africa for the profit of the metropole. Until the appearance of the Martinican Guy Deslauriers's *Middle Passage* (from a script written by Patrick Chamoiseau) in 2001, no French film had really dealt with the Atlantic slave trade, although, for better or for worse, there are several *bandes dessinées*.[152] Most important for our purposes here, there is no French *Uncle Tom's Cabin*, no singularly influential literary work from which abolitionism gathered strength in its own times and which can serve as a compelling *aide-mémoire* now.[153]

37

The Committee for the Memory of Slavery chaired by Maryse Condé with a mandate to "repair" the forgetting of slavery and the slave trade, defined the problem: "Rare are the French people who know that, for nearly four centuries, their country was a great enslaving power [*une grande puissance esclavagiste*]."[154] In a recent novel Edouard Glissant evokes the condition that underpins France's forgetfulness: the absence of slaves on French soil, a fact of the triangular trade. "The former slave-trading cities of Europe," Glissant writes, "did not know the crowds of piled-up and festering slaves, nor the shouting markets nor the shitholes, the din and the public whippings, which haunt the atmosphere of the port cities of the Americas, of the Caribbean or of Brazil. . . . We look in vain for the stigmata of the Trade: the odor has not remained in the air; there was never any odor; no noise left a trace." What remains behind in Nantes and Bordeaux are yachts: "the exaltation of hot climates, . . . so many pure Atlantic pleasures."[155]

The fate of a monument project in Nantes is instructive. On April 25, 1998, a statue commemorating the abolition of slavery 150 years earlier was dedicated on the Quai de la Fosse in Nantes—the very site of outfitting and embarkation for hundreds of slave-trading expeditions. Six days later the statue was vandalized; a photograph of the statue stood on the empty pedestal years later, while funds were being raised for a new statue.[156] The government-sponsored organization Maison d'Outre-Mer and the association Les Anneaux de la mémoire (which sponsored an important exhibition in 1992) are working in Nantes toward the creation of a new monument.[157]

As Serge Daget said, the real monuments to this crime against humanity are the Sahara Desert, the Atlantic and Indian oceans themselves.[158] For a long time the slave trade was practically a "taboo" subject among French historians (C, 8). That has changed somewhat in recent years, since the commemorations of abolition in 1998 and the passing of a law that declared slavery and the slave trade to be crimes against humanity in 2001.[159] In April 2005 the French Committee for the Memory of Slavery, chaired by Maryse Condé, presented a report calling on the Republic to "contemplate this shameful page of its history" and proposing an array of measures aimed at "historical reparation." The committee called for the establishment of May 10 as an annual day of commemoration.[160] Still, the weight of centuries and decades of silence blocks memory, which itself should not be fetishized as a panacea for the crimes of history. As I will argue later, justice that needs to be done in the present should not be filibustered by arguments about injustice in the past; if some eighteenth-century Africans profited from the slave trade, it does not mean that general economic justice is not due to Africa now. But memory would seem an indispensable precondition to justice — whether justice implies reparations (as is currently being debated) or other actions.

In Africa there is an understandable reluctance to assume a share of the blame for the Atlantic slave trade, coupled with reticence about slavery in Africa itself; an outsider making inquiries may get answers that are "terse, surly and not very informative."[161] Discourse about slavery in Africa is, according to Manning, all too often characterized by half-truths designed to protect the reputations of slave sellers (SAL, 102). Numerous African scholars have in turn voiced resistance to the dominance of white Western historians in this field and the suspiciously concomitant scaling back of earlier assumptions about the total extent of the Atlantic slave trade (from, for example, W. E. B. Du Bois's "perhaps 15,000,000 in all" to Curtin's 9,566,000).[162] Debates on the numbers of slaves exported are plagued by conflicting assumptions about the relative importance of memory (for Africans) and accuracy (for Westerners).[163] In African literature the panegyric oral tradition, carried over into written forms, encourages "silencing that which is to be silenced."[164] In the French Caribbean, as in the United States, the remains of a society organized around slavery are everywhere, and the Francophone literature is full of allusions to slavery, but there is still a certain silence about the slave trade, stemming from the nature of the Middle Passage itself. Glissant wrote in *Le Quatrième siècle*: "Suffering found itself mute, as did hatred. Death, mute. Mute also the tragedy [*drame*] hatched in the delirium of the hold."[165] And forty years later Chamoiseau makes this observation about French Antillean culture: "Stories of slavery do not fascinate us. Little literature is devoted to it. However, here, in these bitter lands of sugar, we feel submerged by this web of memories which scorch us with things forgotten and screaming presences."[166]

39

AROUND THE TRIANGLE

What exactly were the links that joined France, Africa, and the Caribbean together to make the French Atlantic? In this chapter I will consider some of the practical factors that characterized each of the three journeys constituting the triangular trade, factors that raise in concrete terms some of the symbolic and cultural issues that will be the object of the rest of this study (because these factors created those issues).

From European ports ships set forth loaded with trade goods—cloth (*les indiennes*), bars of iron, pots and pans, alcohol, firearms, and the *pacotille* (countless fine but compact items like crystal, jewelry, and silks).[1] The preparation and outfitting of a slave-trading vessel cost a fortune—by one estimate, this *mise hors* was roughly equivalent to the price of a private palace on the rue Saint-Honoré: two hundred thousand to three hundred thousand *livres*.[2] The main slave-trading ports in France were Nantes (by far the leading city, with 42 percent of the French slave trade), Bordeaux, La Rochelle, and Le Havre. Many of the *négriers* were cosmopolitan Protestants, who formed an endogamous commercial elite. As costs increased in the eighteenth century, it was necessary for a larger number of merchants to invest in the outfitting of a single ship. But each expedition was an independent enterprise, in effect a floating, temporary, intercontinental corporation (C, 44–46, 56; D, 108–9).

The typical French slave-trading vessel of the eighteenth century was eighty or ninety feet long. The ships were not specially built for the triangular trade; they generally had three masts and three decks, the *entrepont* being reserved for cargo and slaves. Ships were often named so as to profess a clear conscience—*Notre-Dame-de-la-Pitié*, *Marie-Joseph*—or to display up-to-date Enlightenment credentials: *Le Jean-Jacques*, *Le Franklin*, *Le Voltaire* (a ship that will be seen in the next chapter), and even *Le Contrat social*.[3] I will return in the next chapter to the vexed relations between these two accomplishments of the eighteenth century, the Enlightenment and the slave trade.

The captain was in charge of the entire commercial operation once the ship left home; he had a financial stake in the success of the voyage and could possibly get very rich after only two or three successful triangular voyages (C, 64). The voyage from France to Africa took ninety to one hundred days (C, 110). European traders were not able to venture far from the coast into the African interior. As David Eltis points out, since the Europeans could not go inside Africa, and the African traders could not (and would not have wanted to) cross the Atlantic, only the captives crossed the boundary represented by the African littoral (E, 154). They alone would see the full reality of two worlds; they would ultimately tie those worlds together.

The time spent buying slaves on the coasts was dangerous and had to be kept to a minimum, lest supplies run out and diseases be contracted. Shipboard rebellions "were most common while the ships were anchored off the coast, waiting to complete their cargo" (SAL, 111). The popular image of the slave trade is of a European ship docking at a European fort on the coast of Africa and loading large numbers of captives all at once. The symbolic power of a building such as the Slave House on Gorée Island in Senegal—with its infamous "Door of No Return" overlooking the water—is overwhelming.[4] But the historical record makes clear that such European points of concentration rarely held large numbers of captives who could be bought at one time (C, 118). Captains bought slaves as best they could, day by day, at various points up and down the coasts of Africa. It could easily take six months to fill a ship with captives.[5]

A vessel called the *Suzanne-Marguerite* left La Rochelle in December of 1774 and traded on the coast of Africa through the following October. Taking on as many as seventy-one captives in a single day, the ship nonetheless could go for two weeks without a single new captive; it took nearly eight months to accumulate 566 captives in the hold, meaning that some of those people were held prisoner on the ship for all those months before beginning the torture of the Middle Passage.[6] Olaudah Equiano tells us exactly what it was like during that time: "The stench of the hold while we were on the coast was so intolerably loathsome, that it was dangerous to remain there for any time. . . . The shrieks of the women, and the groans of the dy-

41

ing, rendered the whole a scene of horror almost inconceivable" (OE, 40–41). Baquaqua describes how "the loathsomeness and filth of that horrible place [the hold of the slave ship] will never be erased from my memory."[7]

SLAVERY IN AFRICA
AND THE ATLANTIC CONSENSUS

Before returning to the practical aspects of the trade and describing the second stage of the triangle, I would like to consider some of the motivations and cultural factors that governed the slave-trading encounters that took place between Europeans and Africans on the coast of Africa. It was in bargaining over the sale of captives that Europeans and Africans formed relationships and developed impressions of each other; this trade had profound effects on each side, corrupting any potential that might have existed for nonviolent and equitable relations between the continents. Still, the slave trade was a *trade*, in all senses of that ambiguous term: a transaction in which two parties collaborated (Europeans and Africans), yet in which one "milked" the other, and a movement from one place to another.

42 Olaudah Equiano reveals much about attitudes toward slavery on all points of the Atlantic triangle, and of course his bestselling book was designed to alter those attitudes. Equiano says that he was born to a slave-owning family in what is now part of Nigeria, then kidnapped and enslaved in Africa around 1756 before being sold across the Atlantic. *The Interesting Narrative of the Life of Olaudah Equiano, or Gustavus Vassa, the African* was first published in England in 1789; it is "one of the first points of contact between African narrative and Western print culture" and an indispensable source of insight.[8] Equiano provides a dual perspective, speaking in defense of slavery in Africa (until it happens to him), then bearing witness to the horror of the Middle Passage. Equiano's autobiography reveals certain aspects of the consensus about slavery that dominated the Atlantic world until the late eighteenth century, even as he sheds light on the feelings of those who were victimized by this system. His narrative both explains and helps to unravel the consensus.

First he defends the Ibo people's practice of selling slaves: "Sometimes, indeed, we sold slaves to ["Oye-Eboe" traders], but they were only prisoners of war, or such among us as had been convicted of kidnapping, or adultery, and some other crimes, which we esteemed heinous" (OE, 24). So enslavement of prisoners of war and criminals is justified in Equiano's mind, and this is the classic description of enslavement in Africa. But kidnapping (one of the crimes Equiano names) was itself one of the principal means of enslavement. Orlando Patterson makes the startling argument that we should distrust any suggestion of a neat distinction in eighteenth-century West Africa between "wars" and "kidnappings." Most wars, he says, were merely "sordid kidnapping expeditions" designed to feed the slave trade (OE, 119).⁹ So if we read Equiano's reference to the crime of kidnapping as the crime of dealing in slaves, the underlying suggestion is that slaving (by means of kidnapping), in his mind, justifies . . . enslavement. The slave trafficker deserves to be enslaved, thus perpetuating a slave trade. This African rationale dovetailed perfectly with European thinking about slavery and the enslavement of Africans: it was frequently argued that (as the Abbé Raynal put it in his free-indirect paraphrase of common defenses of slavery, each of which he refuted): "But these slaves were captured in war, and without us they would have been executed. . . . But they were criminals worthy of death or the most hideous torture, and they were condemned to slavery in their own country. . . . But in Europe as in America, peoples are enslaved."¹⁰

Equiano's thinking reveals something of an Atlantic consensus on enslavement. As David Eltis writes: "Initial African enslavers and European slave traders had identical attitudes toward the people they enslaved and shipped. . . . The idea that it was inappropriate or immoral to enslave anyone did not exist anywhere in the world during the expansionary phase of the transatlantic slave trade" (E, 150). Johannes Capitein, an African who had been enslaved as a child in Africa, then educated in the Netherlands, defended slavery based on his reading of the Bible, in a treatise of 1742: the "New Covenant demands only *spiritual* freedom . . . not necessarily *external* freedom. . . . Slavery in no way contradicts Christian freedom."¹¹ The ideology of slavery flowed effortlessly around the Atlantic. Through this general meeting of minds, as Boubacar Barry puts it, "Europe imposed the slave trade as a permanent reality, with the complicity of the region's [Africa's] reigning aristocracies."¹² Maryse Condé has made the same point: slavery in African societies—whatever its form—was one condition of possibility for the Atlantic slave trade.¹³ One French defender of slavery glibly stated that it was impossible to take freedom *away* from Africans because they had none.¹⁴

Equiano envisions no abolition of slavery in Africa. But alongside his

43

defense of African slavery, Equiano raises trenchant questions about the motivations of those Africans who sold their neighbors into slavery. He discusses "invasions" of "one little state or district into another, to obtain prisoners or booty" — in other words, wars that are in effect the "sordid kidnapping expeditions" that Patterson describes. Equiano writes:

> Perhaps they were incited to this by those traders who brought the European goods which I mentioned amongst us. Such a mode of obtaining slaves in Africa is common; and I believe more are procured in this way, and by kidnapping, than in any other. When a trader wants slaves, he applies to a chief for them, and tempts him with his wares. It is not extraordinary, if on this occasion he yields to the temptation with as little firmness, and accepts the price of his fellow creatures [*sic*] liberty with as little reluctance as the enlightened merchant. (OE, 25)

These lines are some of the few — and some of the most powerful written by a contemporary African — about African motivations in the slave trade.

Slavery had existed for centuries in Africa. In a context where land was communally owned, "slaves were the only form of private, revenue-producing property."[15] Slavery in Africa has until recently been described as a relatively benign, *domestic* institution, characterized by relationships that enfold slaves within a family structure. But one must read such depictions carefully and fairly. Equiano offers an early version of a benign picture that will be reproduced by anthropologists in the early twentieth century and repeated by those defending African participation in the slave trade. But Equiano appears to contradict himself about slavery in Africa:

> Those prisoners which were not sold or redeemed we kept as slaves: but how different was their condition from that of the slaves in the West Indies! With us they do [no] more work than other members of the community, even their masters; their food, clothing, and lodging were nearly the same as theirs, (except that they were not permitted to eat with those who were free-born); and there was scarce any other difference between them, than a superior degree of importance which the head of a family possesses in our state, and that authority which, as such, he exercises over every part of his household. Some of these slaves have even slaves under them as their own property, and for their own use. (OE, 26)[16]

But at the point in Equiano's narrative when he is himself enslaved and forced to work within those exact conditions, he is overcome by "grief" and "love of liberty," "strengthened by the mortifying circumference of not daring to eat with the free-born children [also African], although I was mostly their companion" (OE, 33–34). Now that he is on the other side of the equation, he thinks only of escape, from the same conditions that he described as so mild in his father's household. The grief to which he attests at this moment should provoke skepticism among those who hold to the image of slavery within Africa as an entirely benign, domestic institution and of African slaves as wholly "integrated" members of the communities that owned them. The young Equiano was *mostly* their companion, and apparently treated well, but certainly not equal and not free. Slavery in Africa was not the same as slavery in the Americas, but it was, often, slavery.[17] Thus there was resistance both to the Atlantic slave trade and to internal enslavement.[18]

Reporting what he felt after subsequently being sold to white men, Equiano makes his preference clear: "Indeed such were the horrors of my views and fears at the moment, that, if ten thousand worlds had been my own, I would have freely parted with them all to have exchanged my condition with that of the meanest slave in my own country. . . . I even wished for my former slavery, in preference to my present situation" (OE, 38–39). Reflecting back from a point of view that knows full well the horrors of the Middle Passage and of plantation slavery, Equiano is clear about which slavery he would choose: Africa's. Equiano (or his semifictional self in the narrative) thus *lived* through three experiences of slavery in the Atlantic world: first as a slave owner, then as a domestic slave in African society, and finally as a chattel slave sold across the ocean.[19]

Patrick Manning's *Slavery and African Life* offers a broad and startling view of slavery in Africa, describing the rise of something like a real slave mode of production in the Western Sudan in the second half of the nineteenth century, complete with "plantations" that fed an "expanded African leisure class" in brilliant urban centers.[20] His analysis tends to undercut what most observers have assumed to be a complete contrast between slavery in Africa and in the New World, while suggesting that slavery in Africa may have responded to pressure from the slave trade and its abolition by expanding large-scale plantations—to such an extent that there were more slaves in Africa in the late nineteenth century than there were in the New World (SAL, 142–47, 23). Paul E. Lovejoy argues that slavery in "west-central Africa must be seen in conjunction with the development of planta-

45

tion slavery in the Americas," which stimulated slavery *in Africa* through the mechanism of the European slave trade: "the integration of Africa into an international network of slavery occurred because Africa was an area of slave supply." Thus in Africa *slave societies* arose where previously there had only been "a few slaves in society."[21]

But the slave-plantation model of production may actually have deeper roots in West Africa, if a passage from the Sieur de La Courbe is to be believed. Writing of Senegal as he saw it in the course of his administrative work there in the late seventeenth century, La Courbe describes a scene that evokes a plantation of the American South, complete with an armed overseer and work songs: "I found Jean Bare" (a Wolof aristocrat) in his fields, holding a saber and a spear, with sixty of "his people," all naked (a clear indication of their slave status), all hoeing the soil to the "cadence of an enraged music made by six guiriots" (griots).[22]

If this passage in La Courbe suggests the presence of organized and fairly large-scale agricultural slave labor in Senegal in the late seventeenth century, we should not leap from this evidence to a false equivalency — sociological or moral — between slavery in Africa and slavery in the New World. Institutions and customs of slavery in Africa did not match the brutality of New World plantation conditions in any sense. Slavery was a more porous institution in a context where the ideology of race did not apply. And as slavery was gradually suppressed by the colonizing powers, "slaves did indeed become, more than ever, part of the family"; early anthropologists saw this and concluded that this attenuated form of slavery was both benign and centuries old.[23]

The existence of slavery in precontact Africa was a condition of possibility of the slave trade; if slavery and slave trading had not existed in Africa, Africans would not have been willing to deal in slaves with Europeans. But both did exist, and as a consequence nearly all the captives sold across the Atlantic were delivered to European traders by African traders for prices that were mutually agreeable.[24] The trans-Saharan and "Oriental" trades in slaves for the Arab world preceded the Atlantic trade by centuries and is estimated to have deported "anywhere from 3.5 to 10 million Africans" before the Portuguese even began and as many as 17 million from the seventh century through the twentieth.[25] The first Europeans to trade in Africa enmeshed themselves in the practices of existing Muslim systems.[26] Over the centuries the expansion and increased brutality of slavery within sub-Saharan Africa was a response both to the Atlantic and trans-Sahara slave trades and to the abolition of the former. Both slave trades caused a huge expansion in the institution of slavery in Africa.[27]

Africa was, in the eighteenth and nineteenth centuries, in effect, a commercial center in which Europe and the Middle East were intensely interested, the crossroads of several different exploitative schemes—all because of slavery and the desire of the outside world to make Africans work for them. Africa was desired by France (and other European powers) but only in response to a lack or need—for slave labor in the New World. This would seem to epitomize that negative type of desire described by Deleuze and Guattari; Europe's embrace of Africa was a kiss of death. The triangulation of desire also appears as a negative here: the *mise en valeur* by the dominant point of the triangle (France) of one subordinate point (the Antilles) is effected through the exploitation *by extraction* of the third point (Africa).

Yet it is safe to say that Africa was at that time much higher on the list of the world's priorities than it is now. Negative desire meant lots of attention. As a result of the lucrative workings of the Atlantic triangle, French foreign minister Choiseul was able to say in the mid-eighteenth century: "I look upon this trade [with Africa] as *the motor of all others*"—a sentiment that reflected the interests of the slave traders of Nantes and other cities.[28] Without the slave trade the city of La Rochelle thought it would have to give up all its trade with the Americas.[29] This feeling of dependence on slavery was echoed by Napoleon in 1803, determined to get back the richest French colony after its slaves had rebelled and become independent: "Nothing is of greater interest to the nation than the island of Saint-Domingue, this vast and beautiful colony which is the object of the attention and the hopes of *all our commerce*."[30] Has a French leader said anything like that about Africa or the Caribbean since the eighteenth century, even at the height of colonialism? Has Africa ever been as close to the center of the world's attention as it was during the time of the slave trade? As far as Europe is concerned, the answer to that question must be sought in the afterlife of the Atlantic triangle, in the history of colonialism and postcolonialism, subjects that I will broach at a later stage. But before leaving these questions in suspension, one should take note of the fact that Choiseul's vision of Africa as central to the world's needs is completely predicated on the Atlantic triangle—it is only as a source of slave labor for the Antilles (which actually produced the cash crops) that Africa is useful—and that Napoleon's thirst for Haiti reflects his desire for preservation of that lucrative system.

→►◄←

The existence of slavery in Africa, coupled with the willingness of African elites to sell people, lent continuing justification to a commerce that at first needed none (since slavery existed in Europe as well at the time of Columbus)[31] and then, increasingly, needed plenty. Jacques Savary urged potential traders to console themselves with the thought that they would actually be rescuing their captives from "a cruel slavery" and taking them into "a milder form of servitude" (*une servitude plus douce*). The successive editions of his highly popular *Le Parfait negociant* would continue to issue this same assurance through its last edition in 1777.[32] (Above we saw the same argument reversed by Olaudah Equiano, to defend the African institution of slavery as milder than that which was practiced in the New World.) One French captain summed up the cozy complicity between European slave traders and African leaders trafficking in captives: "As this king [the Damel of Kayor, Senegal] pillages his own subjects at will, it is not surprising to see that he [is] able to furnish us with many Blacks."[33]

The priest Labat says there are four types of captives who are purchased on the African coast: criminals, prisoners of war, household slaves of princes, and (the largest group) those who are kidnapped (by *voleurs de nègres*) expressly for the slave trade.[34] The bargaining was full of deceptions and cheating.[35] The African traders were not about to be fooled, however, and sometimes threatened attack if they sensed a swindle. But the general dishonesty surrounding the slave trade complicates any calculation of value in the overall. Record keeping was generally mediocre. But most fundamentally, underlying the whole process of trade on the African coast was the perversity of assigning a value to a human life. How many shirts from Flanders would buy a man, a woman, or a child? How many guns? How much brandy? How many *onces de traite* or *livres-tournois*? Elaborate systems of conversion among all these values had to be made.[36] Nonetheless, retrospective analysis has shown that "rational" (that is, consistent) pricing was the general rule. Although Europeans liked to represent Africans as irrational and "so in thrall to fetishistic notions that they would part with slaves for baubles," in fact "consistent and systematic equivalencies" prevailed.[37] (Don't try to pass cheap rum off as brandy, Labat warns; African traders won't be fooled.)[38] Otherwise the *mise hors* would not have been so costly.

The true perversity of the trade is revealed in anecdotes. Jacques Proa, the French sailor, tells how African traders vaunted their human merchandise to him, bragging that the slave he was buying had been in his own village that very morning—fresh off the vine like produce.[39] The European traders were careful not to buy sorcerers for fear of a spell being cast over their entire capture.[40]

The newly purchased captives were stripped, handcuffed, and chained before boarding, clothed only in a bit of fabric. At this point, both eyewitness and retrospective sources agree, there was one traumatic fear that terrorized the captives: the idea of cannibalism. As Equiano put it: "When I looked round the ship . . . and saw a large furnace or copper boiling and a multitude of black people . . . I no longer doubted of my fate."[41] The moment of departure from the coast of Africa was much discussed and of concern to the captains, who were warned by Jacques Savary to sail away from the coast as quickly as possible, since the "slaves have such a great love for their homeland [*patrie*] that they despair when they see that they are leaving it forever, which pain causes many deaths." Many jump overboard, Savary says, while some beat their heads against the walls, and others try to suffocate or starve themselves to death. But once Africa is out of sight, they can be cheered up by the playing of music.[42] The departure is a continuing source of attention—Labat repeats this warning about "the sight of the homeland"[43]—and served as a focal point for abolitionist literature.

THE MIDDLE PASSAGE

The Middle Passage thus begins with the African captives deprived of their last glimpse of their homeland, and this imposed blindness takes on tremendous symbolic weight. Much of the remainder of this study will be devoted to reading that rupture, the afterlife of a forced migration. This crossing, endured by so many million Africans, is (or should be) one of the prime figures in the collective memory of the modern world.

The phrase *Middle Passage* seems to have been coined by British abolitionists in the late eighteenth century; Thomas Clarkson wrote in 1788, "The captain of a slave ship, then on the middle passage, had lost a considerable number of his slaves by death."[44] It has never had an equivalent in French, and the English phrase has come into use among French-language historians and writers. The rise of this phrase marks abolitionists' new attention to horrors that had simply been ignored previously. Eighteenth-century French slave traders' accounts of the crossing have little to report except winds (unless, of course, there was a revolt).[45]

Given the preeminence of the term *Middle Passage*, it is surprising that little attention is given to its first meaning, referring to the second stage in the three-stage triangular circuit that we have been examining (not, as one might think, to the mid-Atlantic). This phrase, defining the original African American experience and trauma, in itself reveals the global and globalizing scheme of the triangle from a point of view that beholds and experiences the entire three-part journey — the point of view of the European traders, not the captives. The crossing of the Atlantic from Africa to the New World is the "middle" passage for the slave traders *only*, a necessary step in what they hope will be a richly profitable enterprise — the middle is theirs to define. Since the Middle Passage was for the captives not merely a stage in a profitable scheme but the imposition of permanent exile, its legacy has made it hard to reinvent a "middle" that is valid and true for everyone. The contemporary vogue for in-betweenness and hybridity in cultural studies has had little to say about this experience of inelegant horror and Manichaean difference. Edouard Glissant writes that the slave ship "had only two possibilities: the hold and the deck."[46]

In spite of its dangers, this stage is already an improvement for the slave traders. In the view of the eighteenth-century French trader and memorialist Joseph Mosneron, it leaves the "hell on earth" of Africa behind and takes him to "an enchanted island" (*MJM*, 76, 78). After a scenic stopover in the islands of the Caribbean, within a matter of weeks or months the traders will complete their triangle and find themselves *home*.

For their captives the Middle Passage is something completely different: an uprooting experience of pure loss, creating a transatlantic void that later generations will labor to fill. In economic and demographic terms, as Herbert S. Klein puts it, "the loss of these young workers was total for Africa, with no inflow of savings possible."[47] The efforts of Césaire's Negritude and other New World cultural movements will reflect attempts to complete a circuit — triangular or direct, there is a question — and recover what has been lost: *home*, "the native country." The most explicit of these would be back-to-Africa initiatives like Marcus Garvey's Black Star Line.

The triangular trade put onboard the same ships, therefore, making the same passage, two groups with radically opposed interests: one with everything to lose from the voyage and one with everything to gain — directly from the sale of those they claimed to "own." Needless to say, that primal experience of *transmigration with racial differentiation* remains with us today, in a New World that has yet to overcome the heritage of slavery — and in a

French metropole that is only now beginning to acknowledge the consequences of the triangular trade and other forms of colonialism.[48] The primal difference of the Middle Passage—best represented by the segregation of the races, with free and white on top and enslaved blacks below, in the hold, *yet both sailing together*—is prefigured in the architecture of the Slave House at Gorée Island in Senegal. In buildings like this one slave traders lived directly above the cells in which captives were being held. There the races lived "together" yet were separated by the widest possible gulf in status: this is where the "intimacy" of slavery begins.[49]

➤➤◄◄

The distance from Africa to the Antilles was anywhere from thirty-two hundred miles (from Senegambia) to six thousand miles (from Angola); the crossing could take as little as twenty-five days or as much as nine months; the average French crossing took seventy days.[50] The captives were boarded naked and without possessions, as if to enforce their "social death" as Africans and future rebirth as slaves in the New World. They wore only chains. Their bodies were the focus of various attentions: first, the shipboard "surgeon" tattooed or branded the captives with a trademark or crude insignia—thus was ownership established. During the crossing, the captives were given food (rice, beans, manioc) once or twice a day, made to exercise on the deck once a day if conditions permitted, and forced to dance as a drum or other instrument was played. These shipboard dances were part of a general strategy on the part of the slave traders, who used such "mind-and-body" tactics to keep their precious cargo both presentable and as docile as possible. Such measures are not to be mistaken as humanitarian but rather as calculated attempts to preserve and enhance a capital investment.[51] In the cold words of the sailor Jacques Proa: "The better they are treated, the greater the number of them that are presented safe and sound in America, and the more money we receive."[52]

The men and women were held in separate compartments. Each captive typically had a space below decks approximately six feet long by sixteen inches wide by two feet seven inches high.[53] They were stacked, according to one captain, "like books upon a shelf."[54] One French source reports that captives had to lie on their side so that they would take up less room.[55] The reality of these conditions was made famous in a diagram of the British slave ship *Brookes*; the diagram was circulated by antislavery groups and has become one of the most infamous images of the slave trade. A French equiva-

5 Engraving from *L'Affaire de "La Vigilante": Batiment négrier de Nantes*
(Paris: Imprimerie de Crapelet, 1823), 9. Detail. Bibliothèque Nationale de France.

lent was published in 1823, showing the plan for packing slaves into an ill-fated ship named *La Vigilante* (see figure 5). With as many as six hundred or seven hundred captives crammed into a ship, with little air and minimal hygiene, deaths were inevitable; epidemics included dysentery, yellow fever, smallpox, and—most symbolically—opthalmia.[56] The latter disease caused blindness, which only literalized the curtain that was being closed on Africa for the captives—what Wilson Harris calls the "traumatic eclipse"[57]—and consequently the challenge to memory.

Mortality, as I discussed earlier, was a key factor in the triangular economy. On the French voyages of the eighteenth century death took an average of 13 percent of the captives.[58] As many as one-fifth of the crew could die as well (T, 311). Herbert Klein cites an overall figure, for all nations, of 5 or 10 percent, then rightly compares such apparently "low" estimates of death during a thirty-day to fifty-day voyage to an epidemic: "These rates still represented extraordinarily high death rate figures for such a specially selected healthy young adult population."[59]

On French ships there was on average one revolt in every twenty-five voyages, but revolt was of course the constant fear of the traders.[60] La Courbe, who left Senegal for the Antilles in 1687 on a ship carrying slaves, warns that with the crew outnumbered ten to one, "you have to watch out that they don't revolt during the crossing, which happens very often when captains don't take enough precautions." His solution was "to kill many of them, until the others surrender."[61] During a revolt onboard the *Affricain* nine captives were killed; afterward many were whipped, and the leader was tortured to death (C, 133). Aboard the *Diligent* a single slave who revolted was strung up and then shot to death "as an example to all the others," according to the officer Robert Durand.[62] Such accounts are abundant. In 1774 male captives aboard the *Diamant* broke down the partition separating them from the women captives and succeeded in taking over the vessel; the crew abandoned ship and was enslaved by Africans until a Dutch captain redeemed them (C, 134–35). In 1771 another ship arrived in the Antilles with only six whites onboard; the rest of the crew and all of the captives had been killed in an insurrection.[63]

As for the actual day-to-day experience of the crossing, many of the slave traders are quite blasé, giving it little attention in their accounts. La Courbe says only, "Nothing extraordinary happened to us on our route. . . . We saw certain birds."[64] Would any of the captives onboard have felt that "nothing extraordinary" had happened?[65] Traders of course hoped for an uneventful crossing; for some it was almost a matter of routine.

For Joseph Mosneron, a sailor from Nantes who would later prosper as an *armateur* of slave-trading vessels, the captives in the hold hardly exist as he crosses the Atlantic. In the narrative that Mosneron left behind — which I will discuss at some length here — Africans are heard to speak only when plotting a revolt: "I heard low talking near me. . . . Three Negroes . . . were discussing an upcoming revolt." The captives don't realize that Mosneron understands their language (what language? and when did he learn it?) and continue their discussion; Mosneron denounces them to the captain, and they are "punished" in some unspecified way.[66] After that, like La Courbe, Mosneron sees nothing extraordinary: "The rest of the crossing went by without anything remarkable happening" (*rien de remarquable*) (MJM, 140). When, at the end of his memoir, one sees the phrase "pile-up of men" (*entassement d'hommes*) (MJM, 237), one thinks that the reality of the Middle Passage has finally dawned on him; but he is merely complaining about the "unclean air" that he was forced to breathe and its ill effects on his health. The "barbarous compression of men" that he mentions in the same paragraph is simply those captains and other superiors who have mistreated him.

The near-"silence" of the captives in the hold — that is, more accurately, the absence of their testimony in the *written* historical record — is an epistemological challenge.[67] The slave traders were indifferent to the humanity of their cargo and were hardly interested in documenting the lives of those in the bowels of their ships. But that experience is not without direct testimony, and again Equiano is the most compelling African informant: he tells

53

of the "hardships which are inseparable from this accursed trade," such that captives threw themselves into the sea (OE, 41–42).

On arrival in the islands the captives were often quarantined, then bathed and rubbed with oil to make their skin appear more robust. Men, women, and children were brought naked before potential buyers and subjected to close inspection. Captains wanted to sell their captives as quickly as possible, but it could take a long time — for example, seventeen days to sell 377 slaves to one hundred buyers (C, 211, 214). Taxes were due, and bribes were often required. The captain, as the manager of the entire operation, was responsible for the challenge of translating the value of the human beings he sold into forms of value that could *return* to the point of origin, the apex of the triangle: the metropole. As I pointed out earlier, there was no colonial product that could complete this "return" in the hold of a single ship (since gold was not available). What returned to France, then, was a combination of *credit* and *partial payment* in the form of sugar, cotton, indigo, or tobacco; the outstanding credit was to be made up by other shiploads in the *commerce en droiture*. Crété explains how one captain sent his ship back to France and remained in Martinique to oversee the return of 342,952 *livres américaines* worth of tropical products.[68]

The captive Africans were sold, and those that survived lived on as slaves on the plantations of the Caribbean islands. I will return to the question of their experience later in this study, by the portal that literature makes available to us. But one of the cruel ironies of the Atlantic triangle is that it completed itself by "realizing" the value of these human lives beyond their reach, in Europe. Their persons stayed in the islands, while the profits from selling them *and* the products of their labor both traveled back to the point of the scheme's origin — there to be reinvested in products that would be traded for the enslavement of more Africans, and so on, and so on.

RETURN AND RETURNS

We should pause at this point to consider again the divergence in perspective that the triangle created. From this, the Caribbean point on the figure, the concept of "return" splits. For the Europeans engaged in the slave trade and making the Atlantic system work, return means completion of the triangle by traveling northeast to Europe. But for the new slaves, return is, of course, return to Africa, which is impossible; the way is barred. Half of all European immigrants to the New World returned to Europe; for Africans this was not an option.[69] According to the *Exclusif*, direct commerce between the French Caribbean and Africa, along the base of the triangle, was not permitted; everything had to pass through the apex, the metropole.[70] (It still does.) So even if slaves were manumitted, they could not return to Africa. Very few exceptions to this rule occurred in the French Atlantic triangle (as opposed, for example, to the back-and-forth flow between Brazil and Africa).

Consequently, when later generations like that of Aimé Césaire come to consider their situation, return—that is, return to Africa—will be *the* question. And how could there be any other question? Equiano already stated this central tragedy of enslavement in the Atlantic system, in words that Césaire will echo exactly 150 years later: "The blacks who brought me on board [the ship] went off, and left me abandoned to despair. I now saw myself deprived of all chance of *returning to my native country*" (OE, 39; emphasis added). The notion of return will become central in Caribbean thought— even if many will eventually conclude with Maryse Condé, "Just as a river doesn't flow back to its source, the Middle Passage can only be navigated once."[71] Glissant describes the Antilles as *irreversibly* cut off from "the original land of Africa" (and broken off from the France they dream of, as well).[72] The impossibility of return defines *diaspora*.[73]

For the French traders, return is banal and totally expected (except for those sailors who, finding the islands so delightful, desert and stay there, in "libertinage," disrupting the triangular trade).[74] But the word *retour* has a particular resonance here that is amplified by its contrast to the meaning of return for Africans in the New World. *Retour* (the singular) refers simply to the journey home to France; but *retours* (plural) bears another meaning, which is closely associated with the triangular trade. *Retours* was used constantly to indicate the merchandise brought back from the islands; the "returns" on the original investment made by the armateurs months or even years earlier. The *Dictionnaire de l'Académie Française* of 1798 may be the first to describe this: "It is said in the terminology of maritime Commerce, the returns [*les retours*] of a vessel, meaning the merchandise that it brought back in exchange for those it took out."[75] The 1835 edition of the same dictionary adds to the definition: "and the profits that result therefrom." *Retours* were therefore, on the one hand, sugar, cotton, indigo, and other colonial commodities but, on the other hand, the value or cash that those products represented to the investors. The chamber of commerce of Nantes summed up the importance of "returns" to the triangle as a whole

55

when it declared in 1767 that "the Profit is not determined only by the sale of the Blacks. . . . It is prepared by the economy with which goods are purchased in Europe and with which the vessel is outfitted, by the advantages of good trading [*une bonne traite*] on the coast, by good sailing to America; but it depends truly on the liquidation of the return in France" (C, 252). That was how the triangle was supposed to work.

While bearing in mind that the African captives are now in the hands of their new masters, cut off from their home and family and stuck in this "new world" of slavery—one might consider the sheer joy of the French sailor Jacques Proa, as he anticipates his "return" to France and the "returns" on his investment of time and labor: "Having lost only five Negroes during the crossing . . . with what delight I found myself arriving on this island! We were all equally joyous: we were going to sell the Negroes, get our money, then reload the ship with sugar, coffee, cotton, and indigo, for our return to France. The stay on Saint-Domingue, when one arrives from the Guinea coast, is very pleasant because one can refresh and relax."[76] Proa's guileless words reveal the human economics of the triangle on the most basic level: the Africans' loss is the Europeans' gain—in money, happiness, and freedom. The question of the profitability of the slave trade is hotly debated among historians, as is the question of its overall importance within the French and larger European economies. But Proa's eyewitness account of Saint-Domingue in 1777 should tell us something—that some group at least was getting rich: "This city [Cap Français] is as big as La Rochelle and is the finest and the most commercial one on the whole island. There are many rich French traders [*négotiants*]; there is much wealth and a lot of luxury. The *mulâtresses* and the *négresses* who serve as governesses to many Whites of the land are richly clothed and covered with jewels."[77]

In these passages from Jacques Proa one sees some validation of an idea that goes back to Plato and Aristotle, is discussed by Rousseau in *Du Contrat social* (cited earlier in this study), and has been recently analyzed by Orlando Patterson: the notion that one person's freedom is amplified by another's enslavement, that there is, in effect, an economy of exchange between freedom and slavery. Proa returns to France with more property and (therefore) more freedom—upward mobility—than he had when he left; his profit results directly from the deprivation of freedom and property from those he has helped to enslave. Patterson writes: "The idea of freedom and the concept of property were both intimately bound up with the rise of slavery, their very antithesis. . . . The joint rise of slavery and cultivation of freedom was no accident."[78] This idea certainly applies to the slave societies of the New World and their ties to their respective mother countries. Later in this chapter, we will see how a family of slave traders in Nantes, the Mosnerons, were able to devote their time to reading the works of Rousseau, nourished by their profits from enslavement. But the equation is not limited to those two points on the Atlantic triangle. According to Boubacar Barry's analysis of the Senegambia, "Slavery . . . gave free men, especially the class of Muslim clerics, the leisure to devote themselves entirely to the study of the Koran. . . . For slave labor *freed the aristocracy* to take its hand off productive work, concentrating wholeheartedly on politics and slave raiding along with the study and explanation of holy scripture, while nurturing the social groups needed to shore up its domination and to perpetuate it."[79]

Thus the Atlantic slave trade and its economy "freed up" the time of one class by enslaving another—and it apparently did this equally well in the Senegambia; in Fort de France, Martinique; in New Orleans; and in Nantes. But we should bear in mind that this idea of an economy of freedom and slavery can and will be reversed, as Patterson points out in his conclusion: true freedom will emerge out of slavery: "The first men and women to struggle for freedom, the first to think of themselves as free in the only meaningful sense of the term, were freedmen."[80] Some of the slaves sold by Jacques Proa at Port-au-Prince in 1777 may well have been among those who rose up in 1791 and eventually made themselves free in an independent Haiti.

The splitting in the significance of the word *return*, along racial lines, is a key to understanding the largest consequences of the triangle—and to seeing the unmistakable link between the triangle and the question of freedom. Europeans are free to return and to collect their returns. For Africans, return becomes an impossible dream—and their freedom to return is sacrificed so that Europeans can enjoy both return and returns.[81]

The return of the ship to France makes the circuit complete. Daget is wrong to say that this trajectory is not part of the slave trade (D, 217): the "return" is intrinsic to the trade—even if, as was sometimes the case, the slave-trading vessel returned with nothing but ballast, leaving the recuperation of the value of the slaves to other, larger ships.[82] The ships, propelled by west winds and the Gulf Stream, make their way back to Europe in one and a half or two months. It may have been fifteen or eighteen months or more since the ship left on its triangular journey.[83]

The economics of profit were, despite the self-interested claims of the

57

Nantes Chamber of Commerce, uncertain. The triangular trade was a high-risk undertaking, and fortunes could be either made or lost; payments were often subject to long delays, so the full realization of an expedition could take many years. During the course of the eighteenth century the price of slaves in Africa inflated, ending the huge profitability (which I referred to earlier, the transformation of value from 1/26 of a horse to five thousand pounds of sugar) that had motivated the expansion of the slave trade. European traders in 1780 had to pay ten times what they had paid a hundred years earlier. In his *Essai sur les mœurs* Voltaire attacked both the morality of slavery and, with some irony, the inflation of prices: "Thirty years ago you could get a fine Negro for fifty *livres*; that was about five times less than a fat steer. This human merchandise, now in 1772, costs around fifteen hundred *livres*."[84] "Cattle," "chattel," and "capital" all come from the same Latin root. The comparisons to horses and cattle are thus to be expected.

In the years leading up to the Revolution, fewer than half of the traders in Nantes made profits, although six of them made huge profits; by contrast, in the early eighteenth century, profits of 50 to 100 percent were typical (T, 443–44). Overall profits for the entire trade are a source of controversy and extremely hard to calculate: Reynolds suggests that the average would be around 30 percent. But it is clear that, if high profits were possible— the "ideal" was 500 percent—the slave trade was always a high-risk enterprise.[85] The actual, numerical contribution of profits from the slave trade to the enrichment of France remains a subject of controversy.

Whatever the final outcome of that debate might be, it seems reasonable to suggest that the slave trade made a considerable mark on the port cities of France and that its economic impact reached far into the kingdom. The slave traders themselves proclaimed this loudly, of course, if only in defense of their livelihood. Choiseul, cited above, seemed to believe what French historians confirm: that the colonies, driven by both the slave trade and the products of slave labor, were responsible for the positive balance of trade that France enjoyed at the end of the Ancien Régime.[86] C. L. R. James's thesis (which runs parallel to that of Eric Williams)—that "the slave trade and slavery were the economic basis of the French Revolution"—while perhaps difficult to prove with numbers, takes on its full moral significance in the quotation from Jean Jaurès that James offers: "The fortunes created at Bordeaux, at Nantes, by the slave trade, gave to the bourgeoisie that pride which needed liberty and contributed to human emancipation."[87] So again, there is an economic relation: the rising freedom of a class in France was

purchased with the sale of the freedom of Africans and the sale of the products of their labor.

The profits of the trade are still standing in Nantes, Bordeaux, and the
other slave-trading cities. Robert L. Stein says that the slave traders of
Nantes were collectively worth about fifty million livres on the eve of the
Revolution; they had by that point built their city into a gem with wide
streets, white façades, and splendid *mascarons* (some depicting smiling Africans).[88] At the height of the slave trade Nantes was "cosmopolitan, splendid,
and gleaming with white houses that the slave trade had built."[89] The armateurs' neighborhood in Nantes was the Ile Feydeau; there one can still see
the houses they built.[90] Many of the "great slavers" had succeeded in getting
themselves ennobled and were "among the most active and most prosper-
ous merchants in eighteenth-century France" — even if their fortunes might
have been larger on paper than in reality (s, 187, 189). At the funeral of one
armateur in 1774, eighty Africans carried torches.[91] But such displays were
rare; the traders remained for the most part truly bourgeois, not aristocratic;
if they bought a vineyard, it was so that they could send wine to Africa for
the purchase of slaves (s, 192).

The other reason why such displays were rare is more significant: there
were "no slaves in France." It was a risky proposition to bring a slave to
France; consequently, few Africans ever saw the metropole that controlled
the Atlantic triangle. The exceptions are of course fascinating—the cases
studied by Sue Peabody in her book *"There Are No Slaves in France."*[92]
Some came from the islands to learn a trade; some were brought by force to
the port cities as nominally free "servants."[93] But those exceptions should
not distort the dominant fact: Africans did not circulate freely around the
French Atlantic triangle. The idea that contact with French soil would set
a slave free was one motive for keeping slaves out; fear of miscegenation
did the rest. In 1738 a three-year limit was put on slaves' sojourns in France
(wc, 110). Even small numbers were so worrisome to the regime that an
outright ban on persons of color was enacted in 1777.[94] There was no large
African population in France in the eighteenth century: only some number between one thousand and five thousand were likely present at any
one time.[95] The products and profits from the labors of Africans returned
to France, but Africans did not. As the armateurs of Nantes and Bordeaux
went about their daily business, the effects of their participation in the slave
trade were thousands of miles away, out of sight and out of mind. The citizens of France could see the ships and trade goods going out and the colo-

nial products coming back, in blissful ignorance of what was happening on (and between) the two other points on the triangle. Any Africans they did see were "servants," not field slaves. With the exception of those slaves who were brought from the islands to France under severe restrictions, slave-trading sailors were the only people to actually see the totality of the triangle, the only ones known to travel all the way around the Atlantic.

The small number of Africans in France and the distance of the plantation colonies were important conditions of possibility for the whole system. It was easy for French people to think of "slavery" as a metaphor for intra-European oppression, since real slavery was nowhere to be *seen*. But there is another demographic that needs to be taken into account here. It seems that, in the years from 1738 to 1787, a high proportion of those registering for marriage at Nantes were born in the Americas: about 20 percent of the women and slightly more than half of the men.[96] In other words, there were very considerable numbers of residents of Nantes who were in fact Creoles: whites born in the colonies. The left-hand side of the triangle was thus fortified by family ties that shuttled back and forth along the route of the *commerce en droiture*. In Nantes and in the other slave-trading cities there was therefore fairly widespread knowledge of two points of the triangle: but again, only the seamen and those slaves who were brought to France saw all three points.

Awareness of Nantes as a hub of the slave trade has lingered in Haiti for centuries after independence. Gloria Bigot-Legros reports that a child slow to return from an errand might be asked, "Ou t'al Nantes?" — "Are you back from Nantes?" In the Haitian imaginary, "Nantes occupies a place that is equivalent [and equidistant] to Guinea."[97] The latter is the mythic Africa to which souls return after death; Nantes, the port of return for the French, is for Haitians synonymous with distance itself, with the unreachable.

In completing this survey of the Atlantic triangle in its French version, we should not forget the extent to which it was a perpetual-motion machine, with each point of the figure feeding the next. C. L. R. James goes so far as to say that "nearly all the industries which developed in France during the eighteenth century had their origin in goods or commodities destined either for the coast of Guinea [Africa] or for America."[98] His argument dovetails with that of the colonial lobby and may be somewhat distorted by its slant. In 1790 the Constituent Assembly was told that five million Frenchmen depended on colonial trade for their living and that "both the slave trade and West Indian slavery were essential for the prosperity of

France" (T, 522). French industries had adapted themselves to the trade and were producing goods, like the famous *indiennes*, that pleased the African market. Even if new historians are now calling into question the proportions of the slave trade's impact on European industrialization, it is important to remember, in a context where cultural issues are the prime focus, that the *claim* of slavery's importance was made and widely believed in France at the time. The economic importance of slavery and the slave trade was taken for granted.[99]

In turn, we must not forget that the Atlantic triangle (along with the Eastern slave trade) stimulated the slave market in Africa, which in turn spread the social mayhem of war, kidnapping, and depopulation ever deeper into the continent and, according to Barry, "blocked" and "frustrated" all possibility of progress in Africa.[100]

THE SLAVE TRADE
IN THE ENLIGHTENMENT

CULTIVATION AND CULTURE

The return to France of the wealth generated by the slave trade enabled the outfitters and their partners to indulge in the luxuries of high culture, to decorate their shelves with the works of the Enlightenment, and even perhaps to read them. But through books and theater, slave traders risked exposing themselves to ideas that could undermine their clear conscience and their livelihood. In this chapter I will examine an instance of exceptional performative contact between the slave trade and Enlightenment culture.

The slave merchants were "cultivated" people.[1] In Nantes the *négriers* established six *chambres de lecture* and helped to establish the music academy. Robert Louis Stein describes what could be found in their libraries: "nonfiction, particularly geography, history, and languages. Religious works occupied but a small corner, and the classics were poorly represented" (S, 193). The culture of the slave traders resembles the "practical," businesslike point of view known in the United States as Babbitry: there is no taste for fiction here.[2] Fortunes were not made by reading *Julie* or *Manon Lescaut* — nor even the *Encyclopédie*. After all, the Enlightenment worked for liberation and against slavery, didn't it?[3] Yet some slave traders had surprising titles on their shelves: the complete works of Voltaire and Rousseau, the *Histoire des deux Indes* by Raynal.[4] Were they just like modern-day nouveaux riches who allegedly buy books by the yard as long as they have nice bindings? What happens when a slave trader actually reads Voltaire and Rousseau?

The memoirs of Joseph Mosneron, the sailor who later became an *armateur*, raise interesting questions about the relation of French slave traders to the canons of eighteenth-century French literature and culture. Recently published as a book, these memoirs are an extremely rare document of the slave trade. The relation of the Mosneron family to French high culture and literature deserves to be seen in the context of the Atlantic economy of slavery and freedom discussed earlier. Like the African aristocrats whose leisure to study the Koran derived from their enslavement of others, Joseph Mosneron and (even more so) his brother, the "philosopher" Jean-Baptiste, could devote themselves to the finer things in life because of the profits from the family's trade in slaves.

Born in 1748 — thus with the clock beginning a one-hundred-year countdown to the final abolition of French slavery — Joseph Mosneron was the third son of an armateur in Nantes. He came home from his second slave-trading voyage in 1767 to discover that he was *inculte* (especially compared to his older brother Jean-Baptiste, who had literary ambitions, spent time in Paris, and wrote plays): "I was, as far as knowledge of moral ideas was concerned, a man coming out of the hands of nature, opening his eyes for the first time *to the light*. . . . I took it upon myself to find the parcels of genius in our language among my selected readings of good French authors" (*MJM*, 161; emphasis added; see also 100). To the retrospective reader, the mention of *idées morales* by a returning slave trader evokes hopes of moral reform, of repentance for the evil he has done. But no such thoughts occur to Joseph Mosneron.

In 1767, readings in French could already have raised some serious questions about the slave trade as an honest way to make a living. It would have been possible for Joseph Mosneron to read, for example, the Chevalier de Jaucourt's article on the slave trade in the *Encyclopédie*, published in 1755; there he would have been told, "This buying of Negroes in order to reduce them to slavery is a trade which violates religion, morals, natural law, and all the rights of man's nature."[5] Apparently he did not read that or any of the other mid-eighteenth-century texts that called slavery into question. By that point, as David Brion Davis says, "the classical justifications for slavery, already discredited by Montesquieu and Hutcheson, were being demolished by the arguments of Rousseau, Diderot, and other philosophes."[6] Mosneron would have heard about these ideas, which threatened his livelihood, and clearly he chose to ignore them, but I will argue that it was not terribly hard for him to do so; the "demolition" was limited and often couched in irony. As E. D. Seeber puts it, among the philosophes "there is a danger of finding negro slavery treated only in a spirit of levity and indif-

63

ference."[7] Levity is found both in Voltaire and Montesquieu, indifference in Rousseau.

Montesquieu, as Mercier points out, was one of the first French authors to write about Africa in creative literature based on the information that was available to him (largely from Labat).[8] In the *Persian Letters* (1721) slavery is denounced but via an approach that Rousseau will use later: the denunciation of the slave as a "vile" and debased creature, cowardly and without virtue.[9] Later in the letters, through his Oriental spokesman, Usbek, Montesquieu proffered one very startling passage about the slave trade:

> Let us go on to Africa. We can discuss scarcely any of it except the coastal regions, the interior being unknown. . . . As for the Guinea coast, it must have been terribly depleted over the two hundred years during which the petty kings, or village chiefs, have been selling their subjects to European rulers, for transportation to their American colonies. The odd thing is that America, where new inhabitants arrive every year, is desolate itself, and fails to profit from Africa's continual losses. These slaves, having been transported to another climate, perish there in thousands; and working in the mines, which employ natives as well as imported labor all the time, destroys them inexorably. . . . Nothing is more absurd than to cause the death of countless thousands of men so as to get gold and silver out of the depths of the earth.[10]

This vision of the Atlantic slave business corresponds closely to the idea of a death machine, and it was certainly a departure for its times. But by focusing only on labor in the gold and silver mines, Montesquieu implicitly critiques Spanish America, not the French islands. He remains silent on the close link between sugar and slave mortality, and he steps around the fact that France, in 1721 and always, was much more heavily and directly involved in the Atlantic slave trade than Spain was.[11] So this, the first significant attack on the slave trade in French literature, is a leap forward, but it is also partly a diversion. We will see in Voltaire's play *Alzire* a similar movement of partial sidestep.

Montesquieu's *Spirit of the Laws* was published the year that Joseph Mosneron was born, 1748. It contains the seeds of abolitionism and is most often cited in that vein. Yet the text is full of ironies on numerous levels. Montesquieu begins by making a distinction that will be essential during the rest of the Enlightenment: between "political slavery" and "civil slavery" — in other words, political oppression of various forms on the one hand and chattel slavery on the other. This "political slavery" is a *metaphor*, reflecting real

forms of oppression, of course, but not slavery itself. The very metaphoricity of this usage—the predominance of political "slavery" in European discourse—becomes an obstacle to the Enlightenment's consideration of *real* slavery.

An important gesture that Montesquieu makes in his consideration of slavery has, I believe, escaped attention. I would like to return to the passage in which the philosopher describes Louis XIII's supposed authorization of the slave trade. Montesquieu describes this as "the law making slaves of the Negroes *in his colonies*."[12] This wording elides the reality of the slave trade by mentioning slaves as if they were *already* in the colonies. But what was in question was the slave *trade*: the purchasing of captives in Africa, where France had no real "colonies" (only *établissements*, outposts), and their transportation to the West Indies and enslavement there. Montesquieu's gesture of sidestepping the Atlantic triangle will become familiar. As Madeleine Dobie explains, this is part of a large pattern in French literature and culture of the eighteenth century, a general "displacement" away from "France's *interests* in its New World colonies, and, by extension, . . . a repression of France's involvement in the Atlantic slave trade." We will see examples here of the problem Dobie (following Hoffmann) describes: how the Orient serves as "symptom" of that displacement—what I would also call an alibi.[13]

The most famous passage of *The Spirit of the Laws* is the one in which Montesquieu unleashes the full power of his acerbic irony on the justifications of slavery that were current in his times. His mock defense of slavery—whose irony has on occasion been missed, thus backfiring[14]—seems to ridicule the hypocrisy of Christians enslaving Africans just because they have a differently shaped nose. Slavery at that point seems to be completely discredited, as long as the reader fully appreciates Montesquieu's irony. But two pages later, he appears to rejustify the institution of slavery elsewhere, outside Europe, based on his theory of climates: "as all men are born equal, one must say that slavery [*l'esclavage*] is against nature, although in certain countries it is founded on a natural reason." "Therefore, natural slavery [*la servitude naturelle*] must be limited to certain particular countries of the world."[15] In tropical climates, where the natural inclination would be to indolence, slavery is natural; slavery was part of the "esprit général" of the Americas; coercion and force were therefore justified. And in any case, Montesquieu went on to argue, there could be no question of a sudden, massive emancipation.[16]

What Montesquieu did, in effect, was banish slavery from the top point on the Atlantic triangle while justifying its existence at the other two points, in Africa and the Caribbean. In modern terms, he allowed for slavery in the nations of the South, while making it unthinkable in the North. His division of the world works on the other, East/West axis just as well: slavery will of course persist in lands of Oriental despotism but not in the West.

Voltaire admired the "humorous" treatment of slavery by Montesquieu, the way that he "painted Negro slavery with the brush of Molière."[17] What remains beyond question is that Montesquieu opened the door to a debate about slavery in France that would, very slowly, ultimately lead to abolition. But as David Brion Davis puts it, "Even in an age of sparkling wit, there was risk in saying that Negroes had such black skins and squashed noses that it was almost impossible to pity them" (DBD1, 403). Ironies pile on top of ironies as one considers, in turn, Voltaire's entangled positions with regard to slavery and his investments in the trade.

I will review abolitionist literature in later sections of this book. At this point I would simply like to note that the terms of early protests against the slave trade often seemed to reflect so badly on Africa and Africans that slave traders could find threads of self-justification in the same arguments. The Abbé Pluche wrote in 1735 what has been called the first unambiguous protest against the slave trade (although we saw a passage in the *Persian Letters* that condemned the Spanish slave trade in 1721). Pluche describes a "depraved" (*dénaturée*) African mother "calmly selling her daughter to a stranger for a sum of cowry shells" and a pair of sons selling the father that they have "surprised and garroted." Pluche says that the European buyers "wounded my eyes as much as those who make these abominable sales," but the depraved indifference that he attributes to Africans makes this protest, in fact, ambiguous.[18]

Throughout the eighteenth century the climate in France was not terribly uncomfortable for the slave traders, even as abolitionist notions and principles began to take shape. Joseph Mosneron and other slave traders might well have known, for example, that "the subtle baron" Montesquieu — whose critique of slavery, as we have seen, was less than complete — was president of the parliament of Bordeaux, a slave-trading port, and sold his wines to the slaveholders of the Antilles, thus participating in the Atlantic triangle.[19] The armateurs of Nantes — the class to which Mosneron belonged — must have been well aware of such complicities.

By the time Mosneron wrote his memoirs in 1804, a Revolution based

on liberty, equality, and fraternity had happened; abolition had come (in 1794) and then gone (in 1802); and Haiti had revolted and become independent. Yet after all that ferment, no qualms about slavery or the trade, nor any sign that abolition had even been a question, disturb his memories. In 1767, when Joseph Mosneron undertook his self-education, he mainly studied navigation, although he was strongly attracted to "works of sentiment" and to travel accounts (*MJM*, 163). His brother Jean-Baptiste, the "philosopher" and future politician of the family, was stricken with smallpox and blinded; he asked Joseph to read Rousseau aloud to him. Joseph finds in this exercise an entire moral education, exactly what he was seeking (and one should bear in mind that Mosneron wrote this memoir specifically for his children, for *their* moral instruction):

> I read *Emile* and *Julie ou la nouvelle Héloïse* to him. The salutary morals [*la saine morale*] which reign in these works made more of an impression on me than the voluptuous sentiments that are painted with magic and warmth by this illustrious writer. I followed up by studiously rereading these works, in order to identify for myself the principles worthy of being adhered to, and I am certain that I owe to Rousseau certain virtues which he reinforced in me: the application of duties to render to the author of my life; and within my family he made me sensitive to the value of friendship, of unity and of the reciprocal care that one should take in commerce of the world and society. He allowed me to see the necessity of living in peace with men, of tolerating their faults, of disdaining their vices in silence. (*MJM*, 166)

With all this learning going on, Mosneron doesn't mention the part in *Julie, ou La Nouvelle Héloïse* where Saint-Preux tells of his four-year voyage around the "four parts of the world," in which he discovered the horrors of European domination, including slavery: "I have seen those vast and unfortunate countries that seem destined only to cover the earth with herds of slaves. At their lowly appearance [*vil aspect*] I turned aside my eyes in contempt, horror, and pity, and seeing the fourth part of my fellow men turned into beasts for the service of others, I bemoaned being a man [*j'ai gémi d'être homme*]."[20]

This—the only condemnation of the contemporary European enslavement of Africans that Rousseau seems to have made—would have been easy for Mosneron to miss or ignore; this concern about a distant one-fourth of humanity rapidly disappears in the vast fabric of European sentiments that is *La Nouvelle Héloïse*.[21] As Saint-Preux says, he turned his eyes away, and

67

that is exactly what Rousseau did: starting from "contempt," pity produces aversion. The enslavement of Africans is of no further interest to Rousseau; the political servitude of citizens in Europe is his preoccupation. An *anthropology* is of course behind this act of turning away: Africans are different. In *Emile* one encounters the usual eighteenth-century thought about Africans, which can only soften any guilt about the slave trade: "Negroes don't have the sense [*le sens*] of Europeans."[22]

Still, what did the Mosneron brothers say to each other, if anything, when Joseph read that passage aloud? Did they roll their eyes, scoff? We will see later in this study that at the time of the Revolution, Jean-Baptiste Mosneron "de l'Auney" (as he called himself) became an ardent defender of the slave trade and of the plantation system that had made the family's fortune (*MJM*, 18).

The information about Africa that was available to the philosophes was deplorable, and it of course played a large role in determining their anthropology of the world. But as Roger Mercier suggests, they *might* have found a way to apply their prodigious critical faculties to such sources as Father Labat, whose book on Africa was "the essential source for the philosophes' knowledge about Africa"—although Labat (as he put it himself) "never set foot there."[23] Labat, meanwhile, wanted to convert Africans to Christianity and had no particular objection to the slave trade. On Martinique, where he ran a sugar plantation and mill, he was concerned with productivity. When Labat looked at Africans, it was as a potential buyer and consumer more than anything else.[24] Another prominent source, the debauched and drunken priest Demanet, was himself a particularly greedy slave trader, who incorporated a business with four hundred thousand *livres* of capital on Gorée in 1772.

Information from sources like these underpins all the pronouncements about the non-European world made by Rousseau, Voltaire, and other philosophes.[25] Knowledge about Africa was in fact held hostage by the slave trade: until the late eighteenth century almost everyone who went to Africa and wrote about Africans was involved in it.[26] An abolitionist, Frossard, made this observation as early as 1789: "We owe most of the details that we have about the inhabitants of Guinea to travelers with a direct or indirect interest in the slave trade."[27]

Many of the philosophes made it rather easy to feel enlightened—to make ironic remarks or even morally resounding condemnations of slavery and the trade—while remaining complicit with the trade in slaves, as we have already seen briefly from the example of Montesquieu. Rousseau is a more complex case. On the one hand, he is the most categorical in his condemnation of slavery. Joseph Mosneron apparently did not read *Du Contrat social*, in which Rousseau wrote: "The right to enslave is null, not only because it is illegitimate, but because it is absurd and means nothing. The words slavery and right [*droit*] are contradictory and mutually exclusive."²⁸ But there are two problems with Rousseau's treatment of slavery and (non)treatment of the slave trade. The first is that his condemnation of slavery betrays a total disdain and contempt for anyone who has been enslaved. Slaves in Rousseau's writings are almost always characterized as "vile" and "groveling"; "obedience" is "the only virtue left to slaves."²⁹ The slave is "nothing" and "loves [his] servitude."³⁰ This characterization of slaves *almost* rationalizes — by twisted logic — an institution that Rousseau detests.³¹

The second and more serious problem is that Rousseau, the philosopher of liberty, remains almost completely aloof to the Atlantic slave trade — nearing its high point as he wrote *Du Contrat social*, in 1762, soon after the sugar revolution had radically increased the number of enslaved Africans in the French islands. He never mentions the trade itself; slavery in the ancient world is his referent.³² For Rousseau as for Montesquieu, slavery is a metaphor for the debased condition of man in society *in general*, that is to say, in Europe: "Man is born free but everywhere lives in chains"; modern man is "chained by our institutions."³³ This is what Montesquieu called political slavery (but at least Montesquieu discussed chattel slavery separately, acknowledging its existence, if only to justify it in tropical climates). For Rousseau the metaphorical chains that hinder the white European force him to live "outside of himself" (as opposed to the "savage" who lives "within himself").³⁴ These are the chains that occupy Rousseau's attention. As did Voltaire in the epigraph to my first chapter, Rousseau ignores the literal chains being used against black Africans in his time. The specific institution for buying and selling Africans by the millions — which was having a significant impact on France in Rousseau's day — is barely mentioned.³⁵

In the middle of *The Social Contract*, in a passage that seems to have escaped scrutiny, Rousseau reveals the extent of his indifference to actual slavery, as he assesses the regrettable symbiosis between servitude and freedom: "Modern peoples, you *have no slaves, but you are slaves*" ("Pour vous, peuples modernes, *vous n'avez point d'esclaves, mais vous l'êtes*" [*Du contrat social*, 303]). Rousseau's real concern in this passage is with representation: peoples who give themselves over to representatives are no longer free. But by way of making that argument, in which slavery serves as a *metaphor*, he literally denies the existence of real slavery in his own times. The modern people of France in 1762 *did* have slaves, thousands of them, but elsewhere, out of sight and out of Rousseau's mind, in the colonies. It would have been easy for Mosneron to miss Rousseau's general, theoretical condemnation of slavery in *The Social Contract* (if he had read it), and no attack on the Atlantic slave trade would have troubled his sleep. He, like most of Rousseau's other readers in Europe, seeing the word *slavery*, would have understood perfectly well what it referred to: political injustice among Europeans.

In all the grand lessons that Mosneron learned from Jean-Jacques, there is no glimmer of a doubt about the morality of trafficking in human lives, which Mosneron continues to do as a sailor (although his last voyage is *en droiture* to Saint-Domingue and back) and then as an important armateur. Nothing that he read in Rousseau in 1767 prevented him from pursuing this career.[36] Along with the other members of the slave-trading bourgeoisie, Mosneron knew how to take from Rousseau and other writers of the Enlightenment only what was useful and supportive of his worldview (see *MJM*, 20). Mosneron's Rousseau is thus a prop for family values, religion, and, in effect, good business sense—how to influence people (something Rousseau may not be famous for).[37]

A moral narcissism affects Mosneron, Rousseau, and the Chevalier de Boufflers, the governor of Senegal mentioned earlier. The spectacle of Africans being tortured and killed is a problem *for these observers*. We saw how Saint-Preux's reaction to the sight of slavery turned him back on his own fate as a man. Mosneron echoes this gesture in this sentence reflecting back on his first voyage: "The poisoned air that one breathes and the pestilential stench coming off the Blacks piled up in the ship affected *my* lungs" (*MJM*, 95; emphasis added). The Chevalier de Boufflers complains of a similar occupational hazard that comes with his lodgings on Gorée: "Sea air is always and everywhere the healthiest, and in this weather the air of Senegal is the worst of all. Imagine if you can that we smell from our rooms, and especially from mine, the stench of the bodies of captives who die by the dozens in their dungeons; and the merchants, to save money, throw them in the water at night with cannonballs tied to their feet."[38] In each case the assault on the observer's nose (or more general sensibility) is more of a concern than the suffering of those who are being contemplated. This is, to say the least, a failure of what we will see Rousseau describe as *morale sensitive*.

VOLTAIRE AND THE THEATER OF SLAVERY

At another point in his narration, during his second voyage to Africa, Joseph Mosneron reveals a different link between Enlightenment culture and the slave trade, this time through Voltaire. I would like to devote some more extensive attention to this curious moment of intertextuality, in which French literature suddenly irrupts on the coast of Africa, and the circum-Atlantic economy of desire and slavery becomes visible.

Onboard the slave-trading vessel the *Comte d'Hérouville*, on a date between June 11 and August 26, 1766, Mosneron finds himself at Gorée Island, and the crew has time on its hands. So they put on a play. The following passage is Mosneron's complete commentary on this episode, so we can only speculate about questions that he does not address: "The first time in my life that I saw live theater, it was in Africa. *Alzire* was performed, and my very uninitiated eyes were very pleased by this spectacle, in which all the roles were filled by men. You have to be truly carried away by the illusion in order to go along with the sight of a grenadier dressed up as Alzire, declaiming in a booming voice and with the gestures of a vigorous Hercules the melodious verses of one of Voltaire's masterpieces" (*MJM*, 118). Here is an extraordinary exception to the rule that Edouard Glissant describes: on the slave ship the only writing is in the account book.[39] *Alzire, ou les Américains: Tragédie en cinq actes et en vers* was first performed in Paris in 1736; the play is set in Lima, Peru, and is directly concerned with conquest, colonialism, and slavery. *Alzire* has been seen as one of Voltaire's most important plays and, erroneously, as "the first on the French stage to utilize the theme of primitivism"—the first French play to represent native Americans.[40] His "desolate tragic muse," said Voltaire, had traveled "among the Americans." The play's premiere was accelerated when Voltaire learned that the marquis and playwright Le Franc de Pompignan had proposed a play on the same theme, *Zoraïde*; Voltaire accused Le Franc (the putative father of Olympe de Gouges) of plagiarism.[41] *Alzire* opened and eventually earned more than fifty-three thousand livres, which the author gave to the actors.[42]

In this play Voltaire—the philosophe with by far the most vexed relation to the slave trade—seems to have in mind a question that would later be posed in a prize essay contest organized by the Abbé Raynal: "Was the discovery of America useful or harmful to mankind?"[43] In his *Essai sur les mœurs*, Voltaire, citing Las Casas and Garcilasso de La Vega, will describe precolonial Peru as "the most civilized [*policée*] and industrious nation in the New World" and as "perhaps the mildest on the entire globe."[44]

In *Alzire* Don Alvarez, the former governor, is saved by an "American," and he sees Indians as noble, if savage, and Spaniards "alone" as "the barbarians."[45] His son Gusman, the current governor, sees the Indians differently: "The wild American is a savage monster / Who champs and pulls against slavery's bit" ("L'Américain farouche est un monstre sauvage / Qui mord en frémissant le frein de l'esclavage" [*A*, 387/6–7, AT]). Father and son debate what should happen to a group of enslaved Indians being held hostage by the son. Gusman is in love with Alzire, an Indian princess whose waverings have made the Spanish governor her "slave"; her conversion to Catholicism will be a model, and their marriage will be "the knot that ties together the two worlds" (*A*, 389–90/9). But Alzire stills burns with love for Zamore, the virile Indian hero (whom she believes dead for three years and who was the hope of "this oppressed world" [*A*, 395/this line is missing from the translation, 16]). Alzire declaims: "I owe my country, and I must obey; but remember, sir, / How dreadful it is, and tremble at the thought / Of such unnatural, such detested bonds" ("Mon pays le demande; il le faut, j'obéis: / Mais tremblez en formant ces noeuds mal assortis" [*A*, 393/14, AT]).

Meanwhile, the fate of the slave hostages hangs in the balance: Gusman will let them remain free so long as his marriage to Alzire is forthcoming. Zamore, who turns out to be alive, describes Alzire's father, the collaborationist King Montèze, as a "slave" (*A*, 397/17); Zamore calls for the vengeance of his defeated people and the end of their *enslavement*. He and his rebels will "perish beneath these walls, or avenge America" (*A*, 402/23, AT). Alzire marries Gusman, who sees her as a "slave" (*A*, 419/43) and who, nonetheless, plans to execute the slave hostages—including Zamore. Alzire must then choose between her marriage vows to a brutal oppressor and her love for the resistance leader. Zamore attacks and nearly kills Gusman, and Alzire is thought to be an accomplice. Zamore will be spared if he converts, but both he and Alzire are eager to fulfill their destinies in a horrible death. In a sudden, formulaic, and nearly preposterous conclusion, Gusman rises from his deathbed to grant clemency and reestablish harmony: "Live and hate me not, / Restore your country's ruined walls, and bless / My memory" (*A*, 435/61). After all, Gusman declares, "Christians are born to give laws to [Americans]" (*A*, 434/60, AT). Zamore is utterly disarmed and conquered by such "grandeur d'âme"; he is utterly seduced, if not wholly "converted" by

72

Christian "law."[46] Gusman's death is convenient, clearing the way for Alzire to marry a pacified Zamore and for the play to end in a "Christian" state of forgiveness and equilibrium. (Voltaire admitted that his goal in this play was to "reconcile myself with some of the pious.")[47] To use a partially facetious, presentist vocabulary: the nationalist (Zamore), the collaborationist (Montèze), the relativist (Alvarez), and the imperialist (Gusman) are reconciled; and Alzire, the allegorical American, can live in peace.

In *Alzire* — which has been called the best expression of Voltaire's views on an improved, "humanitarian" Christian religion[48] — the natural rightness of Christians to colonize others, without brutality, is therefore upheld. In the end Christian "law" must govern because of its sheer virtue. This would be in line with Voltaire's view of slavery, according to Michèle Duchet: that it should be reformed and improved, stripped of its cruelties, but not questioned in its very principles — for Duchet, a perfect illustration of the "bad conscience" of the philosophes.[49]

Perhaps most important in *Alzire* is the fact of Voltaire's talking so much about slavery while eliding and avoiding the transatlantic trade in Africans going on under his nose and supported by his investments. Voltaire knew that there was African slavery in Peru; he wrote in *Essai sur les mœurs*: "To those slaves [the Incas] were added Negroes purchased in Africa and transported to Peru like animals meant to serve humans. Neither these Negroes nor the inhabitants of the New World were treated like a human species."[50] (We should note that his language allows for the possibility of more than one "human species.") He concludes the chapter by noting with approval that the "Americans" "are today *subordinated subjects [sujets soumis]* and not slaves" (VOC, 402; emphasis added). Braun describes *Alzire* as "a fine play, one of Voltaire's very best . . . [in spite of] the shoddy poetry"; in it he sees Voltaire "preach[ing] his message of tolerance, forgiveness and humanitarianism, which is the main theme of the play." But if Voltaire "attempts to preach tolerance and humanity" in *Alzire*, and is according to Braun "anthropologically and sociologically correct" about sixteenth-century Peru, I would say that it is nonetheless within a context of assumed and unapologetic imperialism, an attack on "slavery" perhaps but also a defense of the submission of subject peoples.[51] And, by predicating his sympathy for the colonized on the "civilized" quality of the Incas, Voltaire allows himself to keep sympathy for Africans at bay.

Back to Gorée in 1766. As Mosneron and his shipmates listened to the passion of Alzire and her struggle against enslavement, they could tell

73

```
                        France
```

Peru   Orientalized Slavery
Alzire   *Le Blanc et le Noir*

French Atlantic Triangle:
acknowledged in:
Candide
Essai sur les moeurs
Dictionnaire philosophique

6   Voltaire and the French Atlantic.

themselves that these Peruvians—so "civilized" and "gentle"—had nothing in common with the Africans that they were about to buy and sell. That displacement of the subject of slavery—pushing it into an exotic, often Oriental realm in order to keep discussion away from the reality of the triangular trade and plantation slavery in the West Indies—is characteristic of the eighteenth century. Léon-François Hoffmann showed how French literature in this period often transposed African slaves into an Oriental decor.[52] In those texts it is as if the slave trade from Africa to the Middle East were the only one, as if the Atlantic trade had never begun. Voltaire's Orientalist tale *Le Blanc et le Noir* (1764), featuring an African slave named Ebène in the province of "Candahar," fits this pattern.[53]

In *Alzire* the gesture that Voltaire makes is somewhat different. There is certainly a displacement away from direct comment on France's own colonialism and slave trade. Avoiding the reality of the French Atlantic triangle by moving to the West and South instead of the more customary Orientalist East (see figure 6), Voltaire nonetheless completely elides African slavery in *Alzire*.

Alzire debuted only fourteen years after Voltaire had stated in a letter that a good part of his wealth was invested in the Compagnie des Indes, which traded in slaves (and I will return to this question). Voltaire knew that

there was massive African slavery in Peru, where he chose to set his play. He clearly wanted to comment on the European colonization of the New World; but by eliding the Atlantic slave trade, French participation in that trade, and African enslavement in Peru, he clearly chose, for whatever reason, to stop short of an attack on the Atlantic triangular system. Among the possible reasons he did this we should allow for the idea of Peru as an allegory for French colonialism: an indirect expression of reservations that Voltaire may have had—within his complex mixture of evolving thoughts—about slavery, the slave trade, and colonialism. Even as he held on to those investments.

→→←←

Voltaire could pass and can be seen as an in-principle opponent of slavery, based on certain of his utterances. For example:

> In 1757 French Saint-Domingue had about thirty thousand *persons* and one hundred thousand Negro and mulatto *slaves* [note the distinction], working in the sugar mills, the indigo and cocoa plantations, who were shortening their lives in order to flatter our new appetites, filling new needs that our fathers did not have. . . . This commerce does not enrich a nation; on the contrary it makes men perish and causes disasters; it is not for the good. But since men have made up new needs for themselves, France cannot, at a higher price, buy from foreigners a trifle that has become a necessity [*un superflu devenu nécessaire*].[54]

75

This passage then leads into the discussion of prices that I cited earlier; at that point, knowing that Voltaire had a financial interest in the slave trade, one can't help but see some ambiguity in his concerns. We must look further for Voltaire's purer condemnations of slavery. In his *Dictionnaire philosophique* he wrote: "Those who call themselves white buy Negroes at low prices, selling them higher in America. . . . Ask the lowest manual laborer clothed in rags . . . if he would like to be a slave who is fed, clothed, and housed better. . . . He will respond by recoiling in horror. . . . Then ask a slave if he would like to be emancipated, and you will see his response. That alone decides the question."[55] And of course there is the famous passage in *Candide* (1759) where a slave who has been mutilated according to the prescriptions of the *Code Noir* tells Candide, "It is at this price that you eat sugar in Europe" (VOC, 21:180). Is this the same Voltaire who seemed to justify slavery and the trade anthropologically?

The fact is that Voltaire has no single position on slavery: he is against it in principle, and he subjected it to numerous ironic critiques without ever calling outright and loudly for its abolition. His actual political struggle was against lingering serfdom in France, but his view of the world left room for various forms of subordination.[56] It is easier to justify slavery if you believe that "each type of being is a different mode."[57] Voltaire's sense of *singularités*, essential differences among peoples, justifies a hierarchy that includes enslavement of lower peoples by higher ones: "Nature has by this principle subordinated different degrees of genius and character among the nations, which are rarely seen to change. . . . *That is why the Negroes are the slaves of other men.*"[58] In his *Commentaire sur "L'Esprit des lois"* (1777) Voltaire praises Montesquieu's work against the idea of slavery but shows far more concern about continuing servitude in France than about the enslavement of Africans.[59]

→→←←

The treatment of slavery in *Alzire* is a complicated issue: the word is used frequently, but in most cases it seems to refer to the general condition of colonial subjugation.[60] For a play written in 1736 — if one makes allowances for its formulaic plot — *Alzire* is remarkably prescient about the tensions between colonizer and colonized. Most surprising, the play is filled with sympathy for the colonized and enslaved, given voice through Zamore and Alzire; here Alzire speaks:

> Je vis tomber l'empire où régnaient mes ancêtres ;
> Tout changea sur la terre ; et je connus des maîtres. (*A*, 414)
>
> . . .
>
> Tu vois de ces tyrans la fureur despotique,
> Ils pensent que pour eux le ciel fit l'Amérique . . . (*A*, 422)[61]
>
> . . .
>
> Ce peuple de vainqueurs armé de son tonnerre,
> A-t-il le droit affreux de dépeupler la terre ? (*A*, 429)

> I saw the ruin of the empire of my ancestors;
> All on earth changed; and I had masters.
>
> . . .
>
> These tyrants think the world was made for them,
> That they were born the sovereigns of America . . .

. . .

This all-conquering nation,

Shall they depopulate the earth, destroy my race? (39 AT, 46, 54)

The poetry of *Alzire* may be wooden, but the play raises serious questions that might have made an impression on those sailors at Gorée in 1766. It may not have occurred either to Voltaire—who famously (if indirectly) invested in the Atlantic slave trade,[62] even while critiquing the institution of slavery (a slave trader's ship was named for him, with his "delighted" consent: *Le Voltaire*)[63]—or to the slave-trading sailors putting on and watching the play, that the horror of enslavement expressed in rhyme by Zamore and Alzire might be *felt* by the Africans in the hold of the ship and in the dungeons of Gorée a few yards away. Did none of them think of making the connection between Peru at the time of the Spanish Conquest and Africa *now*, subjected to the French slave trade?[64]

Joseph Mosneron reports no particular reaction to *Alzire*. He sees nothing that merits comment except the amusing fact that the role of Alzire is performed in drag by a burly sailor. The sailors, including Mosneron—and I would say Voltaire as well—all appear able to "compartmentalize" issues to such an extent that they can emote over the fate of a Peruvian princess while, inches under their feet, Africans are in chains awaiting the Middle Passage and, if they survive, a life of bondage.

The ambiguous entanglements of the French Atlantic are further symbolized by a small fact that emerges later in Mosneron's memoirs. Leaving Nantes on his last voyage, which is *en droiture* to Saint-Domingue, on August 17, 1768, Mosneron reports seeing a ship named *Le Voltaire* also on its way to the islands (*MJM*, 186). This must be the ship owned by Jean Gabriel Montaudoin, named with Voltaire's blessing, as I mentioned earlier. This fortuitous crossing of paths of the sailor and a "work" (if we can call it that) of the greatest author of his day, again, two years after Mosneron saw *Alzire* at Gorée, is a sign of how connected the French Atlantic was and how bound it was to issues of slavery.

→→←←

The play *Alzire* had a circum-Atlantic life. Within its diegesis the history and ethics of colonialism were opened up for the scrutiny of French and French-speaking spectators. Beginning in Paris in 1736, the history of the performance of *Alzire* retraces the Atlantic triangle, and at each stage we

77

might consider its contextual meaning. Its fortuitous performance at Gorée takes the ethical question of slavery back to the source, to the most sensitive *lieu de mémoire* in the French Atlantic. For us at least, this location heightens the drama of slavery, although we have seen that Joseph Mosneron showed no awareness of it. To complete the picture, *Alzire* had in fact been performed in Saint-Domingue in June of 1765 — thus just a few months before the *Comte d'Hérouville* put it on at Gorée — and it would be performed at least six more times in Saint-Domingue between 1769 and 1782. It was one of the most popular plays of one of the most popular authors in the very rich and varied theater of the island.[65]

The phenomenon of theater in the richest colony on Earth is not what one might expect of this tinderbox of a slave society. Theater in Saint-Domingue included people of color both on the stage and in the audience. There was theater in Saint-Domingue at least as early as 1740, and we know that mulattoes and blacks were allowed to attend, sitting in the rear, at least from 1766.[66] According to the meticulous observer Moreau de Saint-Méry, the glorious theater at Le Cap Français in 1784 reserved "ten boxes in the back of the third row, seven for *mulâtresses* and three for *négresses*."[67] S. J. Ducoeur-Joly, writing an already-obsolete *Manuel des habitans de Saint-Domingue* in 1802, says the theater on the island is quite good and that free people of color are seated in the second balcony.[68]

So blacks, mulattoes, and free people of color were not cut off from the currents of thought that swept through French theater and, through that repertoire, traveled around the Atlantic, in the mid- to late eighteenth century. Plays like *Alzire* and *La Mort de César* by Voltaire, *Le Mariage de Figaro* by Beaumarchais (by reputation "the play that started the French Revolution"), Rousseau's opera *Le Devin du village*, and numerous plays by Louis-Sébastien Mercier exposed Saint-Domingue audiences to the ideas of the Enlightenment. Works by French authors including Voltaire and Rousseau were translated into Creole, parodied, and adapted.[69]

With this context in mind I would like to repeat the question I asked earlier about the performance of *Alzire* at Gorée, but with a difference. This time we can be certain that people of color, whether free or not, heard and understood Voltaire's play. What did *they* think when *they* heard: "You see the despotic furor of these tyrants / They think that heaven made America just for them"? It was one thing for Mosneron and his shipmates to ignore the relevance of these lines, but for the audiences of Saint-Domingue, in an America, between 1765 and 1782 — especially those in servitude or close to it—it must have been quite another. It is hard to imagine that *Alzire* did not raise questions and make people think; that it did not, in spite of its limitations and in spite of its author's prevarications, contribute in some small way to the thinking that would eventually rise up against the "despotic terror" of real slavery.

As we will see in chapter 4, it is part of the national historical mythology of Haiti to say that Toussaint read Raynal and answered his call for a black Spartacus. The resonance of Alzire and Zamore and other voices of the Enlightenment onstage in Saint-Domingue is part of a larger movement of texts and ideas, a circulation of words and ideas around the Atlantic and across barriers of color and servitude. Once in motion, those ideas could not be stopped.[70]

A note on the afterlife of *Alzire* in the Western Hemisphere before traveling back to France: *The Afro-Louisiana Historical and Genealogical Database* reports records of twenty-four female slaves named Alzire and one named Alzir between 1778 and 1820.[71]

To complete the triangular peregrinations of *Alzire*, we can assume, in light of the popularity of the play, that it was performed numerous times in Nantes, the slave-trading capital and home of Joseph Mosneron, with a theater "twice the size of Drury Lane and five times more magnificent."[72] In 1770 Joseph's father joined a group of merchants devoted to "spectacles" who backed a new theater troupe; the theater was the "rage" in Nantes and often overflowed the seating capacity.[73] Before the Revolution, the slave trade made Nantes one of France's richest cities, and its theater "found powerful protectors among our capitalists," writes one historian.[74] Fouchard says that the repertoire of Saint-Domingue and that of Nantes were "curiously identical."[75] And we can assume that the audiences in Nantes understood "slavery" in the play in the political, metaphorical sense that was so current in the Enlightenment—the sense that isolated slave traders from the inhumanity of their business.[76] Diderot diagnosed the problem in 1780, when he described how Europe had been filled for a century with "the sublime maxims of moralism" and how "even imaginary misfortunes make our tears flow in the silence of our reading rooms and *especially in our theaters*." But, Diderot wrote, "only the deadly fate of the wretched Negroes fails to arouse our interest."[77]

Meanwhile, back in Grenoble, Rousseau was said to be so moved by a production of *Alzire* that he found himself short of breath and shaken by palpitations.[78] This would appear to be a moment of perfect *morale sensi-*

79

tive — a hybrid of the mind and the body working together; Rousseau called this "the faculty of attaching our affections to beings who are foreign to us."[79] For an instant this bodily reaction seems to collapse the distances of the Atlantic triangle, and Peru — itself possibly an allegory of African slavery in the French West Indies — is present in Grenoble. Rousseau's reaction completes the circum-Atlantic journey of *Alzire*, in a moment that symbolically disturbs the normal Atlantic economy of desire — an economy that relies on distance and absence. It is important to note that this is less an intellectual experience than a physical sensation. Rousseau's body acts out a revolt against real, non-European slavery, even if his mind and his pen do not follow.[80]

→ ←

Going back to Gorée for a moment, we can only wonder what Mosneron would have thought if the play his crewmates put on had been some adaptation of a novella written by Voltaire in 1756: *Histoire des voyages de Scarmentado*. Taking off on the theme of Marivaux's famous *L'Ile des esclaves* (1725), in which masters and servants reverse roles, and perhaps inspired by real incidents in which slave traders were enslaved, Voltaire turns the tables on European slave traders in Africa.[81] A crew is itself enslaved by Africans. What would the crew of the *Comte d'Hérouville* have thought, as they sat anchored off of Gorée, if they had listened to these lines, spoken by the African pirate captain to his European captives? — "You buy us in the markets of Guinea like beasts of burden, to make us perform all manner of tasks, as painful as they are ridiculous. . . . So when we meet you [here in Africa], where we are the stronger ones, we make you cultivate our fields, or else we'll cut off your nose and ears."[82] These remarks are not amplified in any way in the short novella *Scarmentado*; they seem to bear little weight for Voltaire. The famous Voltairean wit makes this reversal of oppression seem a clever twist, nothing more. There is no real "combat" here, nor elsewhere in Voltaire's writings, for the abolition of slavery, the slave trade, or imperialism.

Joseph Mosneron's memoirs, and particularly his remarks on the great writers of his time, have provided a window into the complex interminglings of Enlightenment culture and the Atlantic slave trade. This glimpse of slave-traders' culture illustrates how *bonne conscience* tends to follow economic self-interest. A brief look at what we might call, with apologies to David Brion Davis, "the problem of *culture* in Western slavery" may be helpful at this point.

We have already seen the extent to which culture was implicated in the slave trade. The Enlightenment led to revolutions based on liberty and equality even as some of its leading lights (Montesquieu, Voltaire, Rousseau) viewed the slave trade of their own times with indifference, irony, or ambivalence. Yet the complexities and contradictions of their philosophical writings have much to teach us about the conditions that allowed the slave trade to flourish in the French Empire for so long. At bottom, the object of our consideration here must be the twisted link between two senses of the word *culture* (in French): on the one hand culture as we call it in English, and on the other, *culture* in French as the cultivation of plants and crops: agriculture. The question is, How did French culture at home in France, at the apex of the triangle, allow for and tolerate the establishment of a vast machine—working with those pulleys and ropes that Voltaire admired—subject the other two points on the triangle to a violent scheme, covering the entire Atlantic and devoted to culture (agriculture) based on slavery and the slave trade?[83]

The difference between those two senses of the word *culture* echoes the radical divergence of perspective between the crew of the slave ship and the captives during the Middle Passage. Joseph Mosneron returned to France and submerged himself in French culture by reading Rousseau. The Africans that he sold remained in the islands, enslaved to the other sense of culture.

The traders were able to justify themselves for every minute of the three hundred years that the triangular trade operated out of French port cities. A clear conscience was constructed and maintained, even while reading Rousseau on liberty, and certainly while performing a play by Voltaire. The most prominent philosophes—with some exceptions to be seen in the next part of this study—did not trouble the slave trade too much: Rousseau, focusing on European problems, ignored it almost entirely, and Voltaire actually invested in it, while making witty and ironic comments on the inhumanity of it all. The application of Enlightenment notions of liberty and self-determination to Africa would have to wait a lot longer, until independence movements seized the idea of self-determination and made it their own in the twentieth century. In the eighteenth century the slave trade and slavery persisted for the profit of a class that considered itself cultivated.

Atlantic Crossings: Voltaire, Rousseau, and the Mosnerons

1736 (January 27): Voltaire's *Alzire* first performed, Paris

1737: Rousseau sees *Alzire*, has palpitations and shortness of breath

1756: Voltaire, *Histoire des voyages de Scarmentado*

1762: Rousseau, *Du Contrat social*

1765 (June): *Alzire* performed at Saint-Domingue

1766–67: Joseph Mosneron's second triangular voyage, starting on the *Comte d'Hérouville*

1766 (August): *Alzire* performed at Gorée by crew of *Comte d'Hérouville*

1767: Joseph Mosneron reads Rousseau to his brother Jean-Baptiste

1768 (June 2): Voltaire writes to Jean Gabriel Montaudoin, accepting naming of vessel *Le Voltaire*

1768 (August 17): Joseph Mosneron sees the vessel *Le Voltaire* offshore from Nantes, apparently heading for the Antilles

1769–82: *Alzire* performed six more times in Saint-Domingue

1770: Mosneron (likely Joseph's father, Jean) along with other traders including Graslin, all "amateurs de spectacles," form a corporation to support a new theater troupe, devoted to tragedy, French and Italian comedy, and opera[84]

1775: In Nantes a "Madame Mosneron" (perhaps Joseph's sister-in-law) sings the role of Colette in Rousseau's opera *Le Devin du village*[85]

1789: Jean-Baptiste Mosneron de l'Aunay (Joseph's brother) reports "alarming news" from Saint-Domingue in the *Journal de Paris* (Dec. 28): a slave revolt has broken out; the colonies are the "destiny" of France and provide the livelihood of "innumerable" Frenchmen

1804: Joseph Mosneron writes his memoir

THE VEERITIONS OF HISTORY

ABOLITIONS AND THE DISRUPTION
OF THE TRIANGLE

Studies of slavery and the slave trade tend to be teleological, plotting backward from the moments of abolition that fulfill and conclude their narrative arc. Thinking teleologically, one inevitably looks for prefigurations. Signs that foretell the satisfying conclusion that we know is coming are deemed "abolitionist." This pattern is inevitable, and I will use it extensively in the remainder of my book, even though, in the context of the French Atlantic, it is undermined by a fundamental weakness and an array of ironies.

In the Anglo-American Atlantic, teleology works more smoothly than it does in the French Atlantic. Britain and the United States both abolished their Atlantic slave trades in 1807; Britain freed all slaves in the empire in 1838; and the United States finally abolished slavery in 1865. Those four respective acts of abolition provide relatively neat delineations and points of arrival; such is not the case with France. In French history various factors complicate analysis and storytelling: the fact that France abolished slavery twice (in 1794 and 1848), having reestablished it in the interim (in 1802); the fact that France feinted, delayed, and prevaricated on its path toward finally ending its own slave trade in 1831. Those who would depict abolition as the simple realization of an ideal born in the Enlightenment—which of course it was to a certain extent—have a twisted path to walk, roughly between 1748 (the publication of *L'Esprit des lois*) and 1848 (the second and final abolition of slavery). The narrative would be much simpler if the abolition of 1794 had not been reversed by Napoleon in 1802. Many hesitations and reversals complicate the narrative. Abolition veered and lurched its way toward an outcome — the demotion of the Caribbean and the colonization of Africa — that was less than perfect. We will see that, along the way, judgments about what was "abolitionist" cannot be straightforward. The related question of how abolitionism was gendered is the subject of my next chapter.

If, in the previous chapters, I emphasized the shortcomings of certain major Enlightenment figures in confronting the reality of the slave trade, it is nonetheless true that a rising chorus of voices eventually destroyed the moral foundations of slavery. But was it philosophy that led to abolition, or was it economics? Some combination of the two, no doubt; Michèle Duchet sees the philosophes' resistance to slavery as precisely a defense of the interests of the metropolitan bourgeoisie; the physiocrats had made this point rather explicitly during the eighteenth century.[1] It should be kept in mind that there were two distinct issues: abolition of the slave trade and abolition of slavery itself.

In Britain in the eighteenth century and the early nineteenth a genuine and very modern mass movement united intellectuals, clergy, and hundreds of thousands of ordinary people in opposition to slavery and the slave trade. No such thing happened in France, where a relatively small and elite group had a limited impact.[2] France would be the first of the principal Western powers to abolish slavery but also the first to reinstate it.

Mirabeau's *Ami des hommes* (1756) was one of the first economic arguments against slavery;[3] Helvétius observed in 1758 that there was not one barrel of sugar that arrived in Europe untainted by the blood of slaves;[4] a few articles in the *Encyclopédie* savaged the idea of slavery and the trade, while other entries left slavery undisturbed.[5] The Abbé Raynal, particularly in the early editions of his *Histoire des deux Indes*, was more reformist than abolitionist — calling, for example, for a "softening" of slavery through an increased use of music in slaves' lives. But he famously raised (if only as a warning to the planters) the *possibility* of a black Spartacus who would rise and save his race, in a passage he plagiarized from Louis-Sébastien Mercier: "All the Negroes lack is a leader courageous enough to lead them into vengeance and carnage. Where is he, this great man that Nature owes to her children?"[6] Toussaint Louverture, according to tradition, heard and answered this call.[7] Diderot dismissed the religious defense of slavery and went beyond his contemporaries, including Raynal, whose *Histoire des deux Indes* he amended (and perhaps ghostwrote); Diderot went so far as to question the right to colonize as well as enslave.[8] Condorcet's *Réflexions sur l'esclavage des nègres* (1781) stated its radical position in the title to chapter 7: "The slavery of Negroes must be destroyed, and their masters must demand no indemnification."[9] Jacques Necker, a one-time trustee of the Compagnie des Indes, finance minister to Louis XVI, and father of Madame de Staël, attacked the barbarity underpinning the French economy; in 1789 he proposed abolishing the slave trade.[10]

One landmark nonfictional text, Pruneau de Pommegorge's *Description de la Nigritie* (1789), is particularly significant for its use of quotations of enslaved Africans; this practice was rising in French literature of all kinds. A former slave trader himself, Pruneau wrote this volume partly to confess his sins and partly to provide precious information about Africa. He gives considerable attention to the speech of the slave leaders when he describes how a revolt among five hundred captives (that he himself had "traded") was suppressed at Gorée: "The two chiefs, far from denying the facts or trying to dissemble, answered with boldness and courage: nothing was more true; they had planned to take the lives of all the whites of the island, not out of hatred for them, but so that they would not be able to stand in the way of their escape. . . . They preferred death to captivity. To this truly Roman response, all the other captives shouted in one voice: '*Dé gue la, dé gue la*' — that is true, that is true."[11] I do not know if there is an earlier quotation of an African language in French writings; Pruneau appends a Wolof glossary to his book. So not only did he portray African rebels as noble; he let them speak in their own language. His work, printed in the year of the Revolution, marks a shift not only toward sympathetic and abolitionist views of the African but also toward real firsthand information about the continent from a point of view that is disinterested (or "postinterested," since he was a slave trader when he was in Africa but was no longer when he was writing).

The rising chorus of opposition to slavery and the trade was finally organized into the Société des Amis des Noirs in 1788, counting Lafayette, the Abbés Sieyès and Grégoire, Volney, Mirabeau, and Condorcet among its members; both Bernardin de Saint-Pierre and Thomas Jefferson declined to join.[12] But the French abolitionist movement — characterized by a "politics of pity . . . maintained through the elaboration of plans for future action"[13] — cannot claim to have imposed itself successfully by the sheer power of its ideas or the effectiveness of its actions. Abolitions came slowly in France, with reversals, foot-dragging, and great reluctance.

The first French abolition was of uneven effectiveness. The Revolution had sparked rebellions among slaves, mulattos, and free people of color in Martinique and Guadeloupe, and in Saint-Domingue civil war broke out.

85

The slaves of Saint-Domingue largely freed themselves: even before abolition was declared in Paris, the Jacobin commissioner on the island, Léger-
Félicité Sonthonax, in August 1793 declared the freedom of slaves, many of
whom who were already free.[14] The import of these facts can too easily escape notice: the most important "abolitionists" in the French Atlantic were
these slaves who freed themselves in massive numbers before anyone could
"emancipate" them with a written decree. Further references to abolitionism in this study should be read with this in mind: intellectual abolitionism
in France in the nineteenth century was preceded and driven by the self-
liberation of the slaves of Haiti.[15]

It was not until the sixth year of the Revolution, on February 4, 1794, that
the Convention abolished slavery and accorded French citizenship to all,
regardless of color. The potential for narcissism, even in so great a gesture
as this first abolition, is revealed in the iconography of this abolition. In one
engraving a crowd of French people hail the decree, which is proclaimed
and inscribed from on high, while only one black man and one black woman
look on. This embodies what will become the official view of abolition: that
it came from France exclusively, both times, and that slaves were its passive
recipients and beneficiaries.[16] (Fanon, reflecting the historiography of his
times and forgetting Haiti, accepts this image of the slaves' passive emancipation, even as he deplores its consequences.)[17]

The abolition of 1794 ratified what was largely a fact in Saint-Domingue,
but it also liberated thousands of slaves in Guadeloupe and Guyane. However, there were limitations on the applicability of the declaration: at that
moment Martinique was in British hands, so there was no emancipation
there; and in the Mascarene Islands of the Indian Ocean, abolition was
simply ignored by the commissioners of the Republic.[18] Freedom would be
permanent only in Haiti (c, 267, 274). And, importantly, the decree of 1794
said nothing about the slave trade. This was ironic, since the Société des
Amis des Noirs had taken the abolition of the trade rather than slavery itself
as its first objective; but the elite société had been devastated by the Revolution.[19] The Jacobins and the Assembly were told "that five [some said six]
million Frenchmen depended on the colonial commerce" and on the slave
trade for their livelihood (T, 522). Families like the Mosnerons exercised all
their influence to preserve slavery and the slave trade. The trade was allowed—even subsidized until 1793; in 1790 Nantes had its best year ever
(T, 522). Then in 1793–94 the slave trade was stopped by a combination of
factors that of course included the abolition of slavery itself. Whether this

constitutes a genuine "abolition" of the French slave trade or an accidental consequence (of war with Britain, for example) is a matter for interpretation; in any case the interruption was effective.

With the coming of Napoleon, abolitionism was suppressed, slavery was reestablished in 1802 — in a "brutal withdrawal of freedom" for Guadeloupe and Guyane[20] — and a French force attempted to reimpose the old order on Saint-Domingue (resulting in French defeat and the establishment of independent Haiti in 1804). For a time, all the intellectual progress of the eighteenth century seemed to have been without value for those who were, again, enslaved; and simultaneously "public opinion ceased to be interested in Africa."[21] The French slave trade continued even after British and American interdiction efforts began in 1807 — although there was serious disruption of the economies of the slave-trading ports and, consequently, effects rippling throughout the rest of France.[22] The workings of the triangle had been threatened and disrupted for decades. The Atlantic system was regularly interrupted by wars during the entire eighteenth century, only to bounce back each time.

The rest of this story, with its remaining abolitions, will unfold in the upcoming chapters of this book. The final telos, the ultimate abolition of slavery itself, came in 1848, after another revolution. The movement that produced this abolition was "elitist, legalistic, [and] hierarchical"; it did not resort to "antigovernment or popular based strategies in its cautious confrontation with slavery"; in fact, "there was no disciplined French anti-slavery force in the modern sense."[23] Official French iconography represents the abolitionist Victor Schoelcher magnanimously bestowing emancipation on a kneeling slave; Glissant describes Schoelcher as "the new 'father,' a sublimated substitute for the colonizer."[24] Lamartine congratulated himself effusively for signing the proclamation. Officially, freedom came again from on high, from Paris, the dominant point on the triangle, and as the realization of a *philosophy*. Some economic historians support this view, contending that slavery was profitable to the very end, that it did not collapse or decay, and that abolition was purely an act of the metropole.[25] But resistance, insurrections, and revolts had all been increasing in the final decades of slavery. On April 27, 1848, abolition was declared in Paris, but the great news — carried across the Atlantic by commissioners — would not arrive in the Caribbean colonies until the beginning of June. In the interim, with the abolition still unknown in the colonies, slaves "below" in Martinique took matters into their own hands and wrested freedom from their masters: a rebellion on

May 22–23, 1848, resulted in a local declaration of emancipation on May 23, eleven days before news of the abolition decree arrived from Paris.[26] Joseph Zobel, in his novel *Rue Cases-Nègres* (1950); Aimé Césaire, in his 1948 introduction to Schoelcher's *Esclavage et colonisation*; and Daniel Boukman, in his play *Les Négriers* (1971), all assert the simultaneity of revolt from below and emancipation from above in Martinique. Determinations of sequence and causality are controversial, but it seems fair to say that emancipation resulted from a combination of the "high" (politics in the metropole) and the "low" (rebellion in the colonies). As Daniel Maximin puts it, abolition was "the result of a dialectic between the African slave resistors on the one hand, and the struggle in Europe for the rights of man."[27]

The sluggishness, sidesteps, and reversals of French abolition, coupled with the economic history, thus support certain historians' claims that abolition in France resulted less from the triumph of an idea, propelled by intellectual leaders, than from a waning mode of production.[28] The details and the overview offered by historians such as Olivier Pétré-Grenouilleau, Dale W. Tomich, and Liliane Crété are far more convincing than Hugh Thomas's simple assertion that abolition came about "because of the work of individuals, with writers such as Montesquieu playing an essential part."[29]

The first half of the nineteenth century saw the progressive waning of the triangular trade. France's relation to both Africa and its few remaining possessions in the New World would never be the same. The transition from slave to free labor in the Caribbean brought about "a dramatic and protracted deterioration in exports."[30] The dynamics would slowly shift, and, most significant, France would ultimately follow Baron Roger's plan, redirecting the power of its attention from the Caribbean to Africa. The relative importance of the Caribbean — so disproportionately huge in the glory days of sugar in the eighteenth century — would shrink to a condition that was often described by Caribbean intellectuals of the twentieth century as "nothingness."

The most powerful statement of this condition is the opening of Césaire's *Cahier*, with its evocation of a volcano that has "forgotten" how to blow up, of a crowd that doesn't know how to be a crowd, and of an "inert" city, unable to express itself in a "true cry." Derek Walcott, in his Nobel Prize address, describes the Antilles as "fragments, echoes, shards . . . a brilliant vacuity"; V. S. Naipaul sees "nothing"; and Glissant describes his people as glued onto a "canvas of nothingness."[31]

It is not right to attribute all power to France, at the apex of the triangle, but we cannot pretend that the condition described by these writers does not flow from the colonial policies of France and Britain and to their loss of interest in the islands in the wake of abolition. The Caribbean became all but *valueless* in their eyes.[32] The long-term condition of the French Caribbean was therefore transformed. The remaining islands, along with Guyane on the South American mainland, would remain utterly dependent on "la mère patrie."[33] The ultimate outcome of this ongoing erasure and devaluation is the act of *départementalisation* of 1946, orchestrated as a solution to the problem of nothingness, by Aimé Césaire.

The general *devaluation* of the Caribbean (and of the other "old" slave colonies in the Indian Ocean) is both dramatized and made literal by one little-known fact: that emancipation was construed in the nineteenth century as a *debt* that blacks owed to whites.[34] After all, indemnification was owed to the planters who had lost their "property." We will see how that debt was exacted out of Haiti in chapter 10—how value was extracted.

At this point we should remind ourselves that it was the transportation of *value* that established the Atlantic triangle. Moving a captive across the ocean increased his or her value, stimulating the further transformation of other values. After 1848, the miracle of the Atlantic triangle no longer worked, yet the Atlantic had been formed into an economy. Value would have to be generated elsewhere, and, it was suggested, the deep colonization—the *mise en valeur* as they called it—of Africa was a possible solution.

What could Africa be to France as the slave trade faded away? Obviously the continent would no longer have the importance that Choiseul had attributed to it in the mid-eighteenth century, as the "motor" of all commerce. The interior of Africa remained largely inaccessible and unknown to Europeans until the very late nineteenth century. Any exploitation of Africa seemed to face enormous obstacles: diseases threatened the ability of Europeans to survive, and African states, which had never surrendered their sovereignty to European power (certainly not during the slave trade), would have to be subdued by force.

The dream of shifting enormously profitable agricultural operations from one side of the Atlantic back to the other side, from the Antilles to West Africa, was thus one motivation for the colonization of Africa. But other factors, both material and ideological, made it possible. Among the material factors were improvements in medicine and weapons. And high on the list of ideological conditions of possibility for the European colonization of Africa was, with supreme irony, the abolition of slavery and the re-maining "Arab" trade in slaves. Europeans were now shocked, shocked, to see slavery persisting in Africa. Colonialism, reinvented for a new era in the wake of the Berlin Conference in the 1880s, would allow European powers finally to realize Baron Roger's dream: to abolish slavery (but in Africa this time) and exploit the interior of the continent in a vast *mise en valeur.*

There was a linkage between France's policies in Africa and in the Carib-bean; a general economy held them together, and any change in one part of the system would affect the other parts. So Africa's "gain" — if it can be called that — would be the Antilles' loss. This reversal would not be the last. In the course of this study I will try to follow a certain number of these shifts and reversals. But through it all the traces of the slave trade and Atlantic tri-angle are continually visible. The forced migration of ten to twelve million Africans (one million in the French trade alone) cannot be easily erased or forgotten.

THE SLAVE TRADE
AND GLOBALIZATION

> For four hundred years, from 1450 to 1850, European civilization
> carried on a systematic trade in human beings of such tremendous
> proportions that the physical, economic, and moral effects are still
> plainly to be remarked throughout the world.
> — W. E. B. DU BOIS, *The Negro*

The history of the Atlantic is full of reversals, some of which I will attempt to follow in this study. In the eighteenth century a handful of islands were worth more to France than all of Canada; with the end of slavery those is-lands were left adrift as attention turned to the colonization of Africa. But in our times, the end of statutory colonialism and of the cold war, along with the rise of "globalization," is leaving Africa outside the sphere of invest-ment and Western interest once again, while the Caribbean plantations — emptied of their inhabitants — are reborn for tourism. This is the premise of Daniel Boukman's play *Les Négriers.*

Globalization, it is now commonplace to observe, began with Columbus. The slave trade itself has been called "the globalization of forced labor" (*SAL*; see also PG, 27). A single slave-trading voyage starting from France moved capital all around the Atlantic. The voyages of discovery, the slave trade, and the colonization of the New World were all related parts of a process of expanding power and contracting distances. Europe came to dominate the Atlantic precisely through the ability of its ships to cross distances efficiently.

It is in those linked but opposed movements that one can see the value of a comparison between today's globalization and the emergence of the Atlantic starting more than five hundred years ago. Globalization, as we saw, is characterized by two things happening at once: on the one hand the expansion of multinational power, either corporate or governmental, and on the other hand the shrinking of space by communications and information technology; "expansion contracts," and "contraction enriches." Before, it was ships driving a global economy; now it is computers and airplanes. In each case some form of servitude is essential. The clothing industry—which was essential to the Atlantic slave trade in the form of *indiennes*—has moved into zones of cheap labor like Mauritius, where the descendants of the slaves and indentured laborers manufacture clothes for France, the United States, and the rest of the consuming market. In the Caribbean some of those descendants of slaves who have not emigrated to France have a chance to wait on tables in tourist facilities, many of which are renovated plantations. In Martinique, at the Leyritz Plantation, the slave cabins themselves have been converted into tourist bungalows. It is no coincidence that tourism brings people from the North to places in the South where slaves used to labor. The sun is a *denrée tropicale* that cannot be exported, so jets bring tan-seekers to the islands in a perverse, reverse Middle Passage.

The inequality may be quite different from what it was 150 years ago and may take quite different (and certainly more benign) forms, but no one could believe that the injustice created by the Atlantic triangle has been erased. What remains are postmodern funhouse refractions of the horrors of earlier times—the slave market is now a quaint mall for tourists (this is the case in Charleston, South Carolina). At the Gorée Slave House groups of French tourists sometimes barely listen as the director Joseph N'Diaye tells the story of what went on nearby; African American groups listen with reverence.

The world economy is the only "road to salvation," but Africa—with 11 percent of the world's population—has only a 1.5 percent share in that economy; aid from the West fell by a third in the mid to late 1990s, and "Africa still attracts less than 5 percent of all investment in the *developing* world

91

at a time when it faces the severest health crisis with AIDS."[35] Howard W. French commented rightly in the *New York Times* in 2004: "Africa . . . has become the virtual stepchild of the international trade system, a mere footnote — or worse, simply unmentioned in discussions of global commerce."[36] In today's globalization, zones that are not profitable are left to starve.[37] When people in such places (like Rwanda or Darfur) start to kill each other, multinational powers do not overexert themselves.

TRAUMATIC ECLIPSE AND THE
LITERARY IMAGINATION

In planning the outlines of this study, I tried to think about the broadest implications of the slave trade and its afterlife in French and Francophone literature and culture. The overview of the triangular trade that I have given here obviously results from the work of historians. But all who study the slave trade are confronted with one enormous problem: the relative "silence" in the written record of those who were enslaved. Into that void imaginative literature and cinema have poured their speculations and reflections. What might a reading of literary texts add to the now considerable historiography on the slave trade?

There are many imaginations in the French Atlantic, and, I will suggest, the various imaginations at work on all points of the triangle need to be brought into dialogue in a way that has largely been lacking. What view of the slave trade can be found in French literature of the eighteenth and nineteenth centuries? How have writers in the twentieth-century Caribbean interpreted the remains of the trade, which established their societies? What have African literature and film contributed to a general reflection on the slave trade? And how do writers and filmmakers now, in the era of globalization, see the heritage of the slave trade and the Atlantic triangle? My goal in the rest of this study will be to evoke a dialogue among all three points of the French Atlantic triangle, by bringing together voices from all points and several different historical periods. Some of the texts under consideration here represent a single aspect of the triangular trade: a life, a voyage, a period; others reflect, explicitly or implicitly, on the triangle as a whole.

The discourses of literature and film offer a variety of different perspectives on the cold and horrendous facts that we have reviewed. The historiography itself, we have already seen, contains mysteries, questions, myths, and riddles. Novelists, poets, and filmmakers from all points on the triangle have—for centuries, not just in recent years—been willing to fill in the silence, to oppose myth with countermyth, and to speculate about the inner lives of those who were enslaved.[38] This process begins with the ventrilo-quism of the abolitionists: in order to end the slave trade and free the slaves, African slaves would have to "speak" in texts written by Europeans.

The preponderance of metropolitan French literature on this subject, in terms of the sheer number of texts, over writings from both Africa and the Caribbean, is of course one of the principal asymmetries of the triangle. It is an imbalance that I have not been able to fully overcome in this study. The sheer weight and breadth of the French paper trail has imposed itself. Acts of projection by French authors are certainly not uniformly abolition-ist, and their literariness is no guarantee of a stance against slavery or the trade. They by no means fill the historical void nor remedy the silence of the captive or the slave. But they try to, and their efforts sometimes merely *reflect*—although in a fascinating way—the agenda of European power (Roger's *Kelédor* is such a text). But in other cases the intervention of lit-erature results in an utterly surprising *refraction* of the moral and economic questions that underpin slavery (Sue's *Atar-Gull* is a case in point). In both cases literature has surprising perspectives to add to the questions that his-tory raises.

In the Caribbean the impossibility of return made return the obvious preoccupation, the central trope of, for example, Negritude. Wilson Harris says that "an act of imagination [can] open gateways between civilizations" and reconnect "dispossessions."[39] Caribbean writers of the twentieth cen-tury went far toward accomplishing their goal: the imaginative way back to Africa has been charted, if only to be rejected, and the recuperation of Africa at least begun—even if it can never be finished.[40] The project of "re-turn" has now been supplanted and called into question as a new paradigm has come to dominate studies of the Francophone Caribbean: *créolité*. Even before, Edouard Glissant rejected the idea of the triangle and the paradigm of return that it seemed to impose. But the rise of that school of thought should not diminish our appreciation of what was accomplished by an earlier generation. Césaire's *Cahier*, as we will see, remains one of the most important reflections on the Middle Passage and its aftermath—and one of the most significant rewritings of the French Atlantic.

The slave trade created the Atlantic triangle. It established patterns of transoceanic inequality that remain with us today. The slave system was in-trinsic to the rise of the New World, and millions of Americans trace their

93

ancestry to the Middle Passage and Africa. In light of all this, even as the institution of slavery lurks within most of the literature, there is surprisingly little attention to the slave trade in contemporary Francophone Caribbean literature and its criticism. I would like to look again at Chamoiseau's remark: "Stories of slavery do not fascinate us. Little literature is devoted to it. However, here, in these bitter lands of sugar, we feel submerged by this web of memories which scorch us with things forgotten and screaming presences."[41] His words are riddled with oxymorons (bitter/sugar, memory/things forgotten) reflecting the inerasable difficulty of the subject. The exceptions to Chamoiseau's rule ("peu de littérature") are of course the focus of this study: most important are those texts that consider the Atlantic triangle and the heritage of the slave trade in the broadest sense.

Of all points on the triangle, Africa may be the most reticent on the subject of slavery and the slave trade. In Francophone African literature the slave trades are rarely evoked. Although a certain number of works deal with internal forms of servitude, no Francophone African novel gives extensive attention to the Atlantic slave trade.[42] No Francophone text competes with the treatment that the subject receives in Ayi Kwei Armah's *Two Thousand Seasons* (1979). Matar Gueye attributes this "silence" to the bad conscience of African elites, "who have preferred to rely on the advantages of a partial and forgetful literature."[43] Under colonialism, in order for Africa to stake a claim to its own liberation, the slave trade had to be represented as purely the result of European action; in order for Africa to be wholly innocent, the continent had to be an entirely passive victim of the slave trade. Thus in Lamine Senghor's call to revolt, *La Violation d'un pays* (1927)—the first representation of the slave trade in Francophone African fiction—precolonial Africa is depicted as an idyllic land of "perfect harmony," where the very acts of buying and selling were unknown, with no servitude of any kind. A white man introduces capitalism and the slave trade all at once.[44]

Though many thousands of Africans in Francophone countries, particularly city dwellers, may be descended from people who were slaves of various kinds as recently as the early twentieth century, literature has had relatively little to say about internal African institutions of slavery.[45] Aminata Sow Fall, in *Le Jujubier du patriarche* (1993), mentions the survival of prejudice against the descendants of former slaves; and Ahmadou Kourouma, in *Monnè, outrages et défis* (1990), paints nineteenth-century African society as frankly "esclavagiste."[46] But this does not make a critical mass. In contrast, there has been relatively generous treatment of the status of "casted" persons (especially griots) in West Africa—not to be confused with slaves.[47]

The African texts and films that will be of interest in this study are those exceptional ones that do represent the Atlantic slave trade and its aftermath. The few novels concerned with slavery inside Africa, beginning with Félix Couchoro's *L'Esclave* (1929), will not be the main focus here.[48] Of greater interest will be texts like Sembene's *Le Docker noir*; his novella and film that share the title *La Noire de . . .* (1962 and 1966); and his film *Ceddo* (1976). These four works reflect a complex and profound engagement with the history of the slave trade and its impact in the colonial and postcolonial eras. In 1968 Yambo Ouologuem's infamous *Devoir de violence* shocked many readers for its full frontal attack on the theory of African innocence promulgated by Lamine Senghor; the work is no less controversial today. In Ouologuem's version of African history European colonizers were practically pawns in the hands of a much older African elite that had been dealing in slaves for centuries. In the novel, responsibility for the slave trade in the African "Nakem" empire lies squarely in the hands of its dynastic ruler, Saïf. The pages that Ouologuem wrote about the slave trade are immensely powerful. Ibrahima Ly's novel *Les Noctuelles vivent de larmes* (1988), although it does not attempt to represent the Atlantic, depicts the effects of the various slave trades on the peoples of the African interior, their experience of "social death." A recent, controversial African film, Roger Gnoan M'bala's *Adanggaman* (2000), dared to represent Africans enslaving and selling each other.[49] Tierno Monénembo provides a truly Atlantic perspective in *Pelourinho* (1995), the story of an African who sets off for Brazil in hopes of finding his lost brethren and of repairing the fractures of memory left in place by the slave trade. As I will argue in chapter 14, the "silence" of Francophone African literature has been interrupted by some rather significant noise.

→►-◄-

If Chamoiseau is right about the small amount of literature on slavery and the slave trade in the Caribbean (which is certainly true in Africa as well), criticism of Francophone literatures has not yet confronted the question either. Interpretive models used to seek the specificity of a certain society or place; now "migrancy" and even "migritude" are much discussed but with little if any reference to the forced migration that brought the Atlantic into existence. Various critics have alluded to the slave trade and its triangular form in passing or in studies of works that deal with the Atlantic, but there has been no sustained effort to bring knowledge about the trade to bear on the reading of the Francophone literatures created in its wake.[50] To fill that void, partially, is the purpose of this study.

But how can there be a "dialogue" ("trialogue"?) in the aftermath of the radical difference and inequality that the slave trade imposed? In undertaking such a project, do we risk reproducing the phony world machine so cheerfully described by Voltaire, with all its pulleys and springs concealing a condition of blatant inequality? Such happy-talk globalization is something that our times seem to share with his. In this context, is Harris's vision of global communications possible?

As I said at the beginning, Césaire's *Cahier*, which reflects the triangle of the Atlantic, also points the way toward another logic: that of an infinite, revolving motion. The *Cahier* forces its reader first to experience the oppressiveness of a triangular relationship built on a void and marked by total inertia, but, I will suggest, the poem offers two logics of escape. The first is through the triangle itself: one way *out* of the "eternal," messy, Oedipal triangle is to follow it to its extreme, to go to Africa by going to France (thus reproducing the *Exclusif*)—and to come back to the Caribbean only in revolt, "standing and free." The other logic is that of "veerition," the fluid motion of sweeping or scanning that defies the triangle and opens the door to an infinite number of other paradigms. Those two ways of thinking are not, we will see, divorced from each other but rather implicit in each other.

2

FRENCH
WOMEN
WRITERS

REVOLUTION, ABOLITIONIST

TRANSLATION, SENTIMENT

(1783–1823)

GENDERING ABOLITIONISM

The narrator of Paul Auster's recent novel *The Book of Illusions*, having lost his family in an accident, undertakes a project of translating Chateaubriand's *Mémoires d'outre-tombe*. He is struck (as I am) by a short passage in the memoir that manages to telescope into a few lines a period of immense turbulence in French history, from 1789 to 1815: "In three short sentences," the narrator says, "Chateaubriand travels twenty-six years." On a visit to Versailles in June of 1789 Chateaubriand (incidentally, the son of a slave trader) encounters Marie-Antoinette, as he recalled in his memoirs: "Casting a smiling look in my direction, she gave me the same gracious salute that I had received from her on the day of my presentation. I shall never forget that look of hers, which was soon to be no more. When Marie-Antoinette smiled, the shape of her mouth was so clear that (horrible thought!) the memory of that smile enabled me to recognize the jaw of this daughter of kings when the head of the unfortunate woman was discovered in the exhumations of 1815."[1]

This second part of *The French Atlantic Triangle* will span roughly the same period but not quite so quickly. The time from the Revolution to the Restoration was one of nearly complete upheaval for France and consequently for its Atlantic system. In these years the French slave trade rose to its all-time peak, collapsed, was outlawed, then resurrected. Slavery itself was abolished and then reestablished. From 1793 through 1815 tens of thousands of European soldiers—both British and French—were sent into the Caribbean to fight.[2] Islands changed hands; commerce was disrupted. Every factor underpinning the French Atlantic triangle was transformed and *translated* (a key term here) from one period to the next. Within the vortex of these changes I will attempt to follow the rise (if it can be called that) of French abolitionist discourse. There will be a few beheadings and exhumations along the way.

Gender and translation are key concepts in the emergence of abolitionist discourse. Certain women writers—most notably Olympe de Gouges, Germaine de Staël, and Claire de Duras—played highly significant roles in the rise of new reflections on the French Atlantic triangle, slavery, and the slave trade. Some years ago, an important volume brought these two issues together while anthologizing those three women authors: *Translating Slavery: Gender and Race in French Women's Writing, 1783–1823*, edited by Doris Y. Kadish and Françoise Massardier-Kenney. In this chapter I want to test and contest some of the assumptions about gender and abolitionism that animate that book. I will gratefully adopt the authors' idea of translation, which they apply to slavery, and I will *adapt* it to an interpretation of the slave trade. Then in the remaining chapters of part 2 I will branch out to comment more directly on Gouges, Staël, Duras, and their works. Because of the complexities implicit in the works and lives of these authors, the process of moving from the time just before the Revolution to the middle of the Restoration will take more than a few sentences. And the trajectory that I follow here will of necessity be spatial as well as temporal, moving around the Atlantic and even beyond it as we progress forward in time.

What is the privileged relation between gender and translation, and, for that matter, between women and translation? The project of *Translating Slavery* calls for a thorough examination of the ways in which gender, like any boundary, is a line of demarcation that can be crossed, tripped over, or even transcended through acts of translation. The other key element in this picture is race, another boundary that can be constructed or deconstructed by texts. All of the texts in *Translating Slavery*—the primary literary texts, the translations, and the criticism—bring questions of translation, race, and gender together. But certain exclusionary gestures that the editors make with regard to literary history are at odds with their stated antiessentialist philosophy. If gender is truly being "problematized," as Massardier-Kenney says (*TS*, 25), and if the editors "refused to consider gender as a factor overriding all others" (17), then why are physical females alone "women" here? Why are men who participated in the same intellectual project of abolitionist "translation" not considered as part of the same picture? I will nominate counterexamples: several men who conform to the intellectual definition of a "woman" that seems to be at work in *Translating Slavery*.

In France, efforts toward abolition of the slave trade and slavery (in that order) were largely *translated* from England and from English. Translation played an essential role in abolitionism (see Kadish in *TS*, 36). Much of the information used by French abolitionists, even in the nineteenth century, came from the 1789 translation of Thomas Clarkson's *Essay on the Slavery and Commerce of the Human Species*. The importance of translation will be confirmed throughout this part of my study. For these reasons I want to *adopt* the idea of "translating slavery."

But I also want to *adapt* that idea to the context of this study, with its focus more on the slave trade than on slavery itself. The "problem of slavery" *requires* translation and interpretation: the slave must be made to speak through mediating devices like literature. The slave trade, however, *is itself translation*, literally, according to the dictionary, in both French and English. The first definition of the infinitive *to translate* in the OED is "to bear, convey, or remove from one person, place or condition to another; to transfer, transport."[3] In French, *traduire* has meant, first, "to transfer from one place to another" — with reference to moving *persons only*.[4] The eighteenth-century slave trader Jean Pierre Plesse wrote in his journal, "The male captives are translated [*traduits*], attached at the wrists."[5] Translation suggests movement across a border — for example, an ocean. The movement implied in translation is thus naturally linked to the idea that we saw in the French word for "trade" (*traite*): extraction. Millions of Africans were extracted and translated, *trans*-Atlantically. The slave trade was the most massive act of forced physical translation ever committed; the Atlantic triangle was a vast system designed to translate value.

The Atlantic slave was a person who had been translated and who had to, as a consequence, translate. His or her translation thus begat others — all the linguistic and cultural transfers and conversions that flowed from the huge infusion of Africans into the Americas. Creole languages, vodun, Francophone literatures, and Caribbean forms of music all come to mind as active translations of African cultures in the New World. Clearly, such translations never stop — even if, as we have seen, the French Atlantic system blocked the flow of transfers along one of its axes, effectively preventing *return* to Africa, the single most meaningful potential act of "retranslation" in the wake of the slave trade.

The translations implicit in the texts by Gouges, Staël, and Duras that I will read here all take place within and around the French Atlantic triangle. They narrate the transfer of individuals — French, African, and native

American as well — from point to point within the Atlantic system, and they describe contact among these groups. (In addition, Gouges takes us, willy-nilly, into the Indian Ocean.) These texts reflect on and create various vectors of translation in the French Atlantic during a crucial period in its evolution. Reading these authors will take us from a time in which the slave trade was at its apogee, through the French Revolution, the Haitian Revolution, one abolition, the restoration of slavery, and the rise of a new abolitionist movement. The spatial and cultural translations that Gouges, Staël, and Duras create are thus compounded by these forward *and backward* movements of history.

There is a certain gendered division of labor in French literary discourse on slavery and the slave trade, even if it is not as neat as it appears to be in the pages of *Translating Slavery*. The distinction is real enough to have inspired my structuring of the two central parts of *The French Atlantic Triangle*, which follow a shift from female to male authors and from abolitionist (or para-abolitionist) representations to indifference. Thus is it largely true, as Massardier-Kenney writes, that "women authors of this period were, perhaps because of their cultural position, sensitive to the plight of Africans and opposed slavery textually in ways that their male counterparts (canonical writers such as Hugo or Mérimée) did not or could not" (*TS*, 14).[6]

But before embarking on a long journey through late-eighteenth- and early-nineteenth-century French literature, I want to partially deconstruct the gendered ground I am standing on. For, to put it simply, all abolitionists were not women, and it would be perverse, while attempting to give women authors their due respect, to ignore male authors who opposed slavery and the slave trade: Condorcet, the Abbé Grégoire, Brissot, Necker (Madame de Staël's father), Mirabeau — all leading up to the first abolition of slavery in 1794; and — after the reestablishment of slavery in 1802 — Grégoire again, Benjamin Frossard, Joseph Morenas, Auguste de Staël (Madame de Staël's son), the Duc de Broglie (her son-in-law), Baron Roger, and others.[7]

The issue here is *literary* history and its "gendering." By rather severely limiting the texts that they consider and by taking a narrowly feminist view, Massardier-Kenney and Kadish create a distorted impression of literary history and the role that gender played in it. French abolitionism, in literature and nonfiction alike, is not a glorious or crowded history, as we will see in upcoming chapters. Gouges, Staël, and Duras deserve recognition for their interventions and creative contributions to the cause of abolitionism; but the impression given in *Translating Slavery* about gender and abolitionism in France is quite misleading. Doris Kadish supports the "impression" that sympathy and abolitionism may be an exclusively female tradition.[8] By failing to test the gender specificity of this (gender-specific) thesis through actual comparison to the relevant male writers, *Translating Slavery* cannot sustain its own argument and creates an inaccurate impression about the literary history of abolitionism. I therefore want to introduce a note of caution about the role of gender within abolitionism.

Several (five) rapid examples will suffice to illustrate the type of comparison that is lacking in *Translating Slavery*. These are all fictional narrative or poetic texts (or groups of texts) written by French males in the period discussed by the authors of *Translating Slavery*. This quick review will serve both as a corrective to *Translating Slavery* and as a summary of texts that must at least be mentioned in a study of the French Atlantic and the literature of the slave trade.

Ziméo (1769), by Jean-François de Saint-Lambert, is a French descendant of Aphra Behn's *Oroonoko* (1688).[9] As one of the nine most-read English novels in France in the mid-eighteenth century, *Oroonoko* was, according to Edward D. Seeber, a "vital source of antislavery thought" in France and a "model for much of the subsequent *littérature négrophile* in France" —from authors of *both* genders.[10] Kadish mentions Saint-Lambert in passing (and the title of *Ziméo* in a footnote), as one of three French authors who "extended the vogue of stories about African slaves that [Behn] launched" (*TS*, 28, 320n8).[11] This is true, although it was a slow "vogue," with an eighty-one-year lag between *Oroonoko* and *Ziméo*. She claims that *Oroonoko* "contains a select but significant number of abolitionist and resistant elements which are typically not found in the works of those male writers" —"those male writers" being Saint-Lambert, Hugo, and Mérimée (*TS*, 28). The problem is that Kadish does not test that assertion through analysis of the relevant texts. The first question to ask about her statement is, What can be "typical" in a group of writers whose apposite works span a period from 1769 to 1829? And why were only those three authors chosen? An important distinction needs to be made between the single eighteenth-century author to be mentioned, Saint-Lambert, on the one hand, and the two nineteenth-century authors on the other. In the case of Hugo and Mérimée, as upcoming chapters of this study will show, Kadish and Massardier-Kenney are right: the "takeover" (my usage, not theirs) of the representation of Africans by these authors—in the wake of Gouges, Staël, Duras, and others—coincides with a decline of sympathy, sentiment, and emancipatory engagement.[12] But Saint-Lambert is something else.

Ziméo is a "triangular" text, representing the French Atlantic and its slave trade. Very much a descendant of Oroonoko and an ancestor of Hugo's Bug-Jargal, Ziméo is a well-educated prince of Benin, with an "air of grandeur" and Apollonian, "regular" features, taken as a slave by treacherous Portuguese traders. (His name, by the way, will be copied by Madame de Staël, spelled "Ximéo," as the name of her African chief in *Mirza*.) In an embedded narrative that is one of the first and most significant descriptions of the slave trade in French, Saint-Lambert's Ziméo speaks, recounting the horrors of captivity and of the Middle Passage. Sold to the French, he "resisted everything."[13] The tale ends with "some thoughts on Negroes" (in a section that is thus a precursor to Olympe de Gouges's *Réflexions sur les hommes nègres*). Saint-Lambert leaves no ambiguity here about the meaning of his tale: Africans are complicit in the slave trade but less guilty than the Europeans who buy them; Europe is corrupt. He issues a complete moral condemnation of the slave trade and of the stranglehold of slave traders on information about the Atlantic slave system: "The peoples of Europe are like many men who in a situation start by being unjust and finish by insulting the victims of their injustice. . . . The businessmen who trade in slaves, the settlers who hold them in bondage, do them too much wrong [ont de trop grands torts avec eux] to speak the truth about this. . . . You will realize that *your money cannot give you the right to hold a single man in slavery*" (21, 23; emphasis added).

The significance of this condemnation is amplified by the popularity of the text, which was reprinted seventeen times in twenty-eight years.[14] Clearly, *Ziméo* does many of the things that *Translating Slavery* credits only to female authors. It is "sensitive to the plight of Africans and oppose[s] slavery textually" (*TS*, 14); it, as much as the texts by Gouges, Staël, and Duras, "attempt[s] to make us hear colonized voices at a time when such voices were barely audible" (*TS*, 13); it "translates" African resistance to the slave trade into French. All of this is much more noteworthy for having been created fifteen years before Gouges wrote her first, unpublished and long-unperformed version of an antislavery play. "Abolitionist and resistant elements" are in plain evidence in *Ziméo*.[15] The most important point about Saint-Lambert, however, is simply that he is a male participant—hiding in

104

plain sight within *Translating Slavery*—in the exact tradition of resistance that *Translating Slavery* describes as exclusively female.

And he is far from alone. A few years before the publication of *Ziméo*, Gabriel Mailhol had written *Le Philosophe nègre*, another triangular text that gives voice to abolitionist discourse through the mouthpiece of an enslaved African prince, another noble descendant of Behn's *Oroonoko*.[16] His hero, Tintillo, is first sold to the English, who rub vinegar, salt, and pepper into his wounds, setting up a tirade that was obviously inspired by Montesquieu: "So this is how men who possess the fine advantage of reason treat men in this country, because . . . they are of a different color and don't have slender noses."[17] Sold to the French, Tintillo describes the Middle Passage with bitter Voltairean irony: "Some of my comrades learned the minuet, the *allemande*, and the *bourrée*; and in the course of the voyage only [*sic*] 189 of them were found to have stabbed themselves, suffocated, or hanged themselves. This small commerce, as you see, should give our peoples a charming idea of the sweetness of European manners, and of the humanity that directs our souls" (67–68). Because he learned French from a captive Frenchman in Africa (as Staël's Mirza will), Tintillo becomes the librarian of his new master in Martinique; he devours the works of the Enlightenment and becomes a "philosopher" (69). This allows him to *translate*: to shuttle back and forth between an African and a European perspective (both, of course, creations of Mailhol), in a work that spans the entire Atlantic triangle in order to condemn the slave trade. Although Tintillo is "at once a Prince, a Hero, a Man of Science, and reasonable," he is nonetheless "a Negro, without a state, without money, without a shirt" (110). This is a remarkably antiracist argument for 1764.

In the times of Gouges, Staël, and Duras several other works by male writers can fairly be described as contributions to the tradition of emancipatory literature. Bernardin de Saint-Pierre's *Paul et Virginie*, one of the most popular works of French fiction related to the colonies and to slavery, was first published in 1788, the same year as the publication of Olympe de Gouges's play *Zamore et Mirza* and her essay "Réflexions sur les hommes nègres." Saint-Pierre returned from a sojourn on the Ile de France (Mauritius) marked by his contact with the institution of slavery; he had also spent a year in Martinique in his youth. So, like Aphra Behn and (by some accounts) Claire de Duras, Saint-Pierre "lived in the colonies and responded favorably [as we will see below] to African women in [his] literary works"

(TS, 3). In 1784 Saint-Pierre worked a critique of the slave trade, echoing *Candide*, into his *Etudes de la nature*: "We don't worry in Paris if our sugar and our coffee cost Africa tears"; and he wondered if the slave trade had not caused as many ills in Europe as in Africa.[18] Unlike his mentor Rousseau, Saint-Pierre had seen slavery and the slave trade firsthand and could less easily ignore the subject: he had reportedly owned slaves himself on the Ile de France, and he refused to join the Société des Amis des Noirs.[19] When it came to *Paul et Virginie*, it seems as if he had a hard time fitting slavery into a novel that might otherwise have been an idyll, what Chris Bongie calls an "uncorrupted Rousseauesque nature free from the conflicts and ambivalent negotiations of colonial culture."[20] To the modern eye, Saint-Pierre's representation of Paul and Virginie's faithful slaves Domingue and Marie is dangerously close to his depiction of their dog, whose name is a word the author often uses to evoke the slaves: Fidèle.[21] But to Saint-Pierre's contemporary readers no such concerns would have come to mind. What grabbed their attention was a daring exposé of the cruelty of slavery, which the author dramatized in one episode of the novel. A marooned female slave, starving and clothed in rags, shows the scars left by her master's whip and begs for shelter; more important for our purposes, she speaks, testifying to the horrors of slavery: "Young lady, take pity on a poor runaway slave; for a month I have been wandering in these mountains, half dead from hunger, often pursued by hunters and their dogs" (62). Paul and Virginie naively return the slave to her master, who promises forgiveness. But later she is seen being tortured according to the prescriptions of the Code Noir. It was reported that this brief episode in *Paul et Virginie* was powerful enough to cause reforms on the Ile de France, improving the lives of slaves.[22] The full impact of the novel is hard to calculate, but the sympathy that initially produced reforms likely contributed to eventual abolition. Roger Mercier places this novel "at the origin of the movement that would lead [slaves] to freedom; the emotion stirred by a touching story had done more than the best-deduced reasonings."[23] Saint-Pierre's "weeping readers" would be open, if not to actual abolition, to the reform of colonial slavery.[24] *Paul et Virginie* was not literally the origin of abolitionist discourse in France, but it clearly propelled the idea forward. This male author, too, "translated slavery," based on his direct observation of it, and, despite his own compromises and racist views, gave "voice" to slaves. The fact that he attributed his success to women only makes the question of gender more interesting.[25]

Leaping forward to the second period of slave-trade abolitionism in

France, during the Restoration, we arrive at a year in which two important events took place. Duras's *Ourika* was first published in 1823 (and it caps the female tradition that the authors and editors of *Translating Slavery* have defined). But in that same year a literary event of massive proportions also took place: the poetry contest organized by the Académie Française on the theme "The Abolition of the Slave Trade."[26] Of the fifty-four submissions, I do not know if any were written by women.[27] I will discuss this poetry in a later chapter. What Hoffmann says is true: that the Africans in these poems are pure figments of the European imagination, defined exclusively as victims, in acts of "magnanimous" sympathy.[28] Yet, on a large scale, these poems "give voice" to slaves, putting hundreds of (mostly awful) verses in their mouths. The fact that this contest was organized by the "Immortals" of the Academy makes it all the more significant: at this point giving voice to slaves is no longer a marginalized gesture; it is quite fashionable.

The best example of a male who fully participated in and contributed to the supposedly female tradition described in *Translating Slavery* will be the subject of a later chapter here: the Baron Roger, who was governor of Senegal from 1821 to 1826. This author, who published his works at the end of the 1820s, was both a translator (of Wolof fables and of an epic that he claimed to have heard from an African narrator, his protagonist Kelédor) and an abolitionist. He too "revoiced the colonized." Ain't he, so to speak, a woman?

To sum up, my point is simple: abolitionism as a project of translation, including everything that is described within the pages of *Translating Slavery* as particularly or especially female, was a project to which both men and women contributed. To say this takes nothing away from Gouges, Staël, or Duras; as we will see in the following three chapters, their works occupy vital positions in the history of abolitionist literature. The examples I have brought forward here simply put these women authors in a less restrictive context, with more porous borders: gender itself is creolized. To represent the literary history otherwise, exclusively, is particularly ironic in light of Gouges's expressed belief in the complementarity and cooperativeness of the two sexes.[29]

Clearly, the special contribution of women writers to abolitionism is not that they *alone* were "sensitive to the plight of Africans and opposed slavery textually" (*TS*, 14) nor that they were necessarily more sensitive than everyone else. It is rather to be found, first, in the unique seminal influence of Aphra Behn's *Oroonoko* and, second, in perhaps the greater *proportion* of abolitionists among women writers than among men. But no other gender-based specificity can be demonstrated. The relation between the authors' gender and the texts they wrote cannot be said to be causal, not in light of this broader, if rapid, consideration of literary history. And any suggestion that there was ever a popular abolitionist movement of women (or men) in France is particularly unwelcome, given the belated, derivative, elitist, and generally anemic nature of the efforts that were made.[30]

Gender nonetheless remains a useful concept here, and I have employed it as a convenient organizational tool for the middle parts of this book. There is a difference between the female authors — Gouges, Staël, and Duras — and the male ones — Mérimée, Sue, and Corbière. (But Roger erases the distinction.) Gender and chronology work largely in tandem here: first the women, who seriously engage with questions of servitude and abolition on moral and sentimental grounds; then the men, who (except Roger) seem more interested in entertaining their readers with tales of the sea. How this shift from female to male also generates questions of sexuality — of homoeroticism and homosexuality — is a question to be taken up in part 3.

OLYMPE DE GOUGES,
"EARWITNESS
TO THE ILLS OF AMERICA"

A CONTESTED REPUTATION

If humanity ever triumphs over barbarism in the colonies, my name
will perhaps be cherished and revered in those places.
—OLYMPE DE GOUGES, *Ecrits politiques, 1788–1991*

One has to admire Olympe de Gouges, *née* Marie Gouze, officially the
daughter of a provincial butcher, whose real father may have been a
powerful marquis and playwright, Le Franc de Pompignan. (We saw previously that Voltaire accused Le Franc of plagiarizing *Alzire* in his play *Zora-
ide*.) With only rough literacy she struggled against all odds to make herself
a woman of letters and politics. Writing (actually, dictating to an amanuen-
sis) in a language that was not her native Occitan, Gouges pushed her way
into the almost exclusively male public sphere of theater, pamphleteering,
and political action during the dangerous years of the French Revolution.
It was a path that ultimately led her to the guillotine but not before she had
made herself heard on a plethora of social issues, including women's rights,
slavery, and the slave trade. After a long period of "neglect and disdain,"
the revival of interest in Gouges among critics and historians since the late
1980s has derived mainly from her significance in the history of feminism,
which is obvious and considerable: she was, after all, the author of the *Declaration of the Rights of Women* of 1791, as well as numerous plays and pam-

phlets.[1] The most influential reading of Gouges has been Joan Scott's essay on the author's elaborate acts of self-imagining and self-invention.[2] Gouges's engagement with the issues of slavery and the slave trade, in two related plays and several essays, logically positions her prominently in *Translating Slavery*: she seems actually to originate a tradition of female and feminist abolitionism in France. Kadish says that Gouges "sought the same kind of reconciliation, compromise, and mediation in the political realm as in the linguistic and literary arenas. She was an ardent abolitionist" (*TS*, 40).

But, as Marie-Pierre Le Hir argues, any characterization of Gouges as an "abolitionist" requires considerable qualification. Like many of her contemporaries, Gouges "seems to postpone the abolition of slavery to a not foreseeable future" (*TS*, 76). Gouges's abolitionism is also a moving target; her thinking evolves between the first draft of her play about slavery and the time of her death. Unfortunately, Le Hir does not discuss the precursor of *L'Esclavage des Noirs*, which was significantly different: *Zamore et Mirza*. Important issues arise in the transition from the first play to the second. Combating the tendency of criticism to reduce women writers to their biography, Le Hir purposefully avoids discussing Gouges's life (see *TS*, 323n1). Although understandable, this approach eliminates some of the most interesting acts of Gouges's creativity, the zigzags of her self-invention that Scott and Gregory S. Brown analyze. The other issue that Le Hir is at pains to confront is that of literary quality; she argues persuasively that the financial failure, under pressure from the colonial lobby, of Gouges's abolitionist play, and its unpopular political stance, have helped seal its reputation as an aesthetic failure as well: "the play failed, it was therefore a 'bad' play" (*TS*, 80). Le Hir is right to refute that logic, but she does not confront the danger of falling into the converse mistake: assuming that a play is "good" (by some definition) because it is on the right side of a moral issue; Le Hir's unexceptionable conclusion is that Gouges's plays "should be viewed as politically committed drama" (*TS*, 83). Questions of literary quality haunt both Gouges and another abolitionist woman writer, Sophie Doin, whom I will discuss later in this study. Gouges herself begged of her readers a "plenary indulgence" for her mistakes in French, in style, and in knowledge, while provoking their skepticism with tales of how quickly she wrote her plays—one in four hours, for example.[3] Gouges did not therefore "reject" the "aesthetic perspective" in regard to her works, as Le Hir claims; she simply requested understanding in light of the larger moral issues that were at stake.[4] Reading Gouges, we should consider her faults and weaknesses as integral parts of her theatrical work and of its significance, rather than sweeping them under the rug. We can analyze the badness—for example, her shaky command of geography—without being prisoners of a misogynist aestheticism.

Gregory S. Brown's work on Gouges comes as a corrective to those who might be misled by "any one of the images that she herself put forth or that were projected on her by her contemporaries or her critics, biographers, and historians." Brown wants to push back against the tendency of "feminist criticism and historiography to romanticize eighteenth-century women writers as socially marginal heroines."[5] (Brown does not say whom he is accusing of romanticism.) He insists on a Gouges who is very much a product of her times, a full participant in and manipulator of—rather than an outcast from—late-eighteenth-century codes of *honnêteté* or civility. He implies, without actually using the word, that Gouges was opportunistic in her "adoption of the identity of an antislavery writer."[6] Brown's Gouges, who "entered literary life from neither a position of social marginality nor intellectual dissidence," is less original, less honest, and more in step with her times than the heroic Gouges of other interpreters. In his interpretation her abolitionism comes across as much more of a pose than a moral engagement: "Gouges did not participate in [antislavery] discussions, nor did she become a member of the Société des Amis des Noirs."[7] But Gouges's only biographer, Olivier Blanc, claims otherwise, citing Brissot de Warville's unpublished memoirs. Brissot wrote that she was "admitted into our Society," and he praised her play.[8] So, whether she was a card-carrying member of the Amis or not, Gouges was apparently part of *some* wider conversation about abolition, and I think Brown's judgment needs to be recalibrated.

Central to Brown's revisionist reading of Gouges is his insistence on the importance of the first version of her play about slavery, entitled *Zamore et Mirza*, ignored by most critics, conflated with the final play *L'Esclavage des Noirs* by others, including both Le Hir and Scott.[9] *Zamore et Mirza* was written in 1783 or 1784 and submitted to the Comédie Française on April 17, 1784 (*FH* 5/117). Now that both plays are available for downloading via the Web site of the Bibliothèque Nationale de France, comparison of the two is both easy and necessary. Even though most of the basic elements of the two plays are the same, their differences are significant enough to merit attention. I think they should be seen as two distinct works.

Without "romanticizing," it seems fair to say that, as one of only a dozen female writers active in Paris in the period of the Revolution, and not a native speaker of French, Gouges, especially at the moment of her *entry* into the literary milieu of Paris, was to some extent "marginal." The existence of a current of abolitionist thought in her times does not make her position less than dissonant with the long dominant and powerful proslavery doxa. Between the putative feminist-abolitionist romantic heroine on the one hand, and the disingenuous self-fashioner on the other, perhaps we can find room to read Gouges's texts for what they say. I am less concerned with Gouges's personality—although she makes it impossible to ignore—than I am with her writings. I want to read Gouges's writings as interventions within, rather than merely echoes of, larger debates. While acknowledging the transitional, unstable nature of her intellectual progress and the debts that she owed (and sometimes denied), one can nonetheless give credit to the positions that she staked out and fixed in print along the way.

I am indebted to Brown's work, but my take on Gouges is somewhat different, as are my goals here. I am less concerned with Gouges's self-fashioning within and against the codes of late ancien régime *honnêteté* (Brown's topic) than I am with the tropes of her dawning (and perhaps self-serving, perhaps opportunistic) abolitionism and, most important, its imagined geography. Brown's topic is Gouges's "self-fashioning," while mine will be her "other-fashioning," how she builds images of race and servitude. If it was by the imagination that Gouges was able to overcome the blindness of her times, the figures of her literary imaginings deserve further scrutiny. What, then, is the geography of Gouges's theatrical vision, and how does it reflect on the world at the time of the French Revolution? How does she imagine the translation of slaves in the French Atlantic triangle, and how does she translate them to the French stage? How does her geography—a source of real confusion among her readers to this day—change between *Zamore et Mirza* (the two texts published in 1788) and *L'Esclavage des Noirs* (the text of 1792)? Within the transition from one play to the other, we will see the shift from an earlier (in fact archaic), soft-focus exoticism in the representation of slavery and the slave trade to a more timely and precise abolitionism. Her essays "Reflections on Negroes" and "Response to the American Champion," also included in *Translating Slavery*, as well as her "Declaration of the Rights of Women," will provide important evidence here.

THE *AFFAIRE* OF *L'ESCLAVAGE DES NOIRS*

Gouges's idea of theater was just right for a revolutionary period: didactic, uplifting, engaged, a veritable "school of morals."[10] Le Hir explains Gouges's idea (shared with Diderot and her friend Mercier) of a new theatrical genre, the *drame*, as a bridge between tragedy and comedy. *Zamore et Mirza* is labeled "drame indien" and *L'Esclavage des Noirs* "drame en trois actes." According to Gouges's friend, the playwright and abolitionist Louis-Sébastien Mercier, audiences should be made to *feel* again. *Drame* was therefore melodramatic, and melodrama was the language of politics (see *TS*, 67–68). For abolitionists melodrama would provide a language capable of collapsing the distances of the Atlantic triangle: French spectators would be made to *feel* the pain of distant slaves just as they could taste the sugar in their coffee. Theater would attempt to make distances disappear by stimulating "an immediate authentic compassion."[11] One could only hope that they would react like Rousseau, fainting at a performance of *Alzire*.

Gouges railed and revolted against the stranglehold exercised on French theater by the Comédie Française, which could and did hold plays hostage for years on end before performing them (or not). The repertoire was decided by the actors themselves, who thus exercised great power. Theater was the "royal road" to literary stature in this period, but it was also a "narrow door," fiercely guarded by the Comédie.[12] Not only did its actors choose what plays to put on, but they also gained exclusive rights over any play they accepted. If a play did not earn enough in entries once it was performed, it became the exclusive property of the Comédie forever. Women authors, numbering perhaps a dozen in the revolutionary period, were subjected to an "excessive strictness," commented Mercier.[13] The story of Gouges's misadventures with the Comédie and its actors is long and twisted; Gouges's "tempestuous" behavior throughout the process, and what it may or may not reveal about her character within the codes of society, is a matter that I leave to Blanc and Brown to debate. Gouges left a paper trail that made her own views quite plain: "No author has ever been mistreated as I have for the last eight [actually, it was four] years by the Comédie Française."[14]

One anecdotal coincidence is of some interest in the context of this chapter, however. Gouges was nearly thrown in jail at one point, at the behest of the Comédie's actors and by the order of a powerful duke, a marshal of France, "first gentleman of the King's Chamber," and supervisor of the royal

113

theaters: none other than the Duc de Duras. He was part of the colonial lobby and grandfather of the future husband of Claire de Duras.[15] (Gouges later referred to him as "the illustrious marshal of the menus, the formidable Duc de Duras [who] put himself at the head of a deputation from the actors' house of ill repute.")[16] Thus the workings of the Atlantic triangle and the influence of the planters at the highest levels of society nearly prevented Gouges's early literary protest against slavery from reaching an audience. It is an interesting marker of a certain evolution to see the elder Duc de Duras — who had been a trustee of the Compagnie des Indes in the 1760s, and for whom a slave-trading vessel was named *Le Duc de Duras*[17] — engaged in violent defense of the slave-based system, while his grandson's wife, herself indebted to colonial holdings, will create one of the most sympathetic portraits of an African in French literature. This reflects a shift in which a certain segment of the French elite, including members of the Staël and Duras families, becomes involved with the abolitionist cause. The network of Atlantic interests will become increasingly visible as we examine the lives and works of Gouges, Staël, and Duras.

Meanwhile, Gouges saved herself from the duke's order by pulling other social strings; she had been in Paris since 1767 and had cultivated many influential people.[18] After her play was delayed further, she violated the protocol that required *Zamore et Mirza*, like all other plays, to be held, unperformed and unpublished, until duly considered by the Comédie on a first-come, first-served basis. She suspected unfairness (rightly, since other plays had leapfrogged over hers) and did not hesitate to denounce what she saw as "the greatest of injustices," "the most indecent procedures," the "despotism," the "intrigue and the cabal," in short, the "conspiracy of the Comédie Française against my play."[19] In an act of literary revolt Gouges attempted to go "directly" to her audience, bypassing the bureaucracy of the Comédie: she published *Zamore et Mirza* in August of 1788 as a brochure and in September in a volume of her collected works. The latter included, in the preface, a claim that the play was "the Story of the Negroes . . . which the Comédie forced me to disfigure, in the costumes and the color, making me put Savages [American Indians] in their place" (*ZM2*, 21). As Brown points out, this claim is not supported by the text of the play that follows, but we'll come back to that later. Both editions of *Zamore et Mirza* end with "Réflexions sur les hommes nègres."

A year later, Gouges defended herself and her play against a different foe, the "abettors of American [i.e., French colonial] despotism."[20] After four years of complications, delays, and intrigue, on December 28, 1789, the revised play *L'Esclavage des Noirs* was performed at the Comédie Française, then called the Théâtre de la Nation. The play was greeted with catcalls and whistles by crowds of "agitators," who nearly prevented the performance from being completed. According to Gouges, *les Américains* — that is, the French colonists, absentee planters of the West Indies, and their allies — had threatened to cancel their subscriptions to the Comédie (*EP*, 1:141). Not to her credit, Gouges volunteered after the first performance to modify her play, most likely in order to temper its (already modest) abolitionist discourse. In fact Gouges had been downplaying the abolitionism of her play even before its debut: the day before, she wrote in the *Journal de Paris*, "In my Drama I have not developed any incendiary principles that might incite Europe against the Colonies."[21] Yet she wanted credit for having, over a period of nine years, "*alone . . .* raised my voice in favor of these men who are so unfortunate and so slandered," enslaved Africans.[22]

The Comédie preferred to see the play fail economically, which it did. Gouges nonetheless proposed another play, with the intriguing title *Le Marché des Noirs* to the Comédie, which refused it (the text was burned by revolutionaries in 1793).[23] After another important engagement with the topic of race and slavery in her *Déclaration des droits de la femme* in 1791, which we will examine below, Gouges's involvement seems to end with the publication of *L'Esclavage des Noirs* in 1792. (She was arrested and executed the following year.) In the preface to that edition she declares herself to be an "earwitness to the disastrous accounts of the ills of America" (*témoin auriculaire des récits désastreux des maux de l'Amérique*, *TS*, 87 AT/232). By claiming this role, Gouges places herself at the center of our concerns in this study. Again, a bodily, sensorial function (hearing) collapses the distances of the Atlantic triangle and enables sympathy. In reading Gouges's texts, I will highlight her frequent gestures that tend to dramatize or reveal the structure of the French Atlantic. We will see that, depending on the requirements of her various arguments, Gouges will either minimize or emphasize the distances of the Atlantic triangle. In the discourse of slave-trade abolitionist debates, the Atlantic will alternately dilate and contract, as proximity and distance are invoked to support different points of view.

Before proceeding, I would like to note a contextual fact that seems to have gone unnoticed within discussions of Gouges's antislavery plays. The actors of the Comédie, already so powerful before the Revolution, were at this precise moment flexing new muscles. Formerly outcasts without civil rights, they were socially emancipated and given full rights as citizens for the first time in December of 1789, the same month in which Gouges's play was performed at the Comédie Française.[24] (In that same month Gouges declared herself "the most decided royalist and the mortal enemy of slavery.")[25] The actors obviously saw no connection between themselves and slaves; the idea would have struck them as absurd. But, from the emancipation of actors (in 1789), to the emancipation of women (wishfully declared by Gouges in 1791), to the emancipation of Protestants in 1788 and Jews in 1791 (the latter two being groups that are tightly controlled in the Code Noir, by the way) — the doors of freedom were flying open on all sides. Condorcet is even reported to have said that "sodomy violates the right of no man."[26] Slaves (through the uprisings of 1790 and 1791 that began the Haitian Revolution and the emancipation that passed into law in 1794) would free themselves as well. So where would the movement of freedom stop? Could the entropy of emancipation be arrested? (It is of course Napoleon who will end the spread of emancipation and reestablish slavery, where he can, in 1802.)

116

Joan Scott brilliantly analyzes how Gouges's self-inventing, performative imagination was both the source of her originality and the cause of her demise under the guillotine of a Jacobin Truth. Imagination allowed this provincial named Marie Gouze to appear in Paris as "Olympe de Gouges," to claim the rights of Man for women, to "make herself a man for the country," and, most important here, to think through and alter the analogy between slavery and the oppression of European women. "This sex, too weak and too long oppressed, is ready to throw off the yoke of a shameful slavery," she wrote, using slavery in the extended or metaphorical sense that we know was so common in the Enlightenment.[27] Yet Gouges, we will see, went beyond the blindness of her times to make the connection to those who were actually chattel slaves, out of sight in the colonies. What Scott calls Gouges's "wanton disregard for reality" (47) enabled her to do this — to see things that were not right in front of her. (Those like Saint-Pierre, and, putatively, Duras, who *had* seen the reality of slavery and the slave trade, were sometimes compromised by it.)

"RÉFLEXIONS SUR LES HOMMES NÈGRES"
(FEBRUARY 1788)

Jamais il n'est entré dans l'idée d'un marin négrier qu'un noir fût
de la même espèce que lui. [It has never occurred to a slave-trading
sailor that a black might be of the same species as he.]
      —EDOUARD CORBIÈRE, *Elégies brésiliennes* (1823)

I want to begin my review of Gouges's relevant texts not with the play that
she wrote first, *Zamore et Mirza*, but with an essay that she authored four
years later, while she was still at loggerheads with the Comédie Française
and in the process of revising the play. I do this because her "Reflections on
the Negroes" posits a very intriguing, if perhaps fictive, point of origin for
her thoughts about race and slavery. This text was published as a postscript
to both of the 1788 printings of *Zamore et Mirza*. It was first and foremost a
plea addressed to the Comédie: "Ladies and Gentlemen, put my play on . . ."
(*TS*, 231/86, AT).[28]

But the essay begins far from Paris and far from the Comédie, in a representation of Gouges's childhood. The anecdote that grounds these "thoughts
on black men" may be a pure product of her imagination; we cannot know.
In the first paragraph she places racial otherness near the origin of her own
earliest awareness of the world: "I have always been interested in the deplorable fate of the Negro race/species [*l'espèce d'hommes nègres*]. I was just
beginning to develop an understanding of the world, at that age when children hardly think about anything, when I saw a Negress for the first time.
Seeing her made me wonder and ask questions about her color" (*TS*, 229/84,
AT).

Reading the passage (perhaps too) literally, this encounter would presumably have taken place in Montauban (in the southwest of France) where
Gouges grew up, around 1754 to 1758, assuming that Gouges was anywhere
from six to ten years old at the time. Considering that there may have been
fewer than one thousand blacks in all of France at that time — and presumably very few in a place like Montauban (far from any seaport) — the anecdote may or may not be apocryphal.[29] But the unlikeliness of the story only
serves to heighten its significance: Gouges begins her own intellectual biography here with a question about difference and what we would call "racial"
distinction. In her vocabulary and in ours the marker of this kind of differ-

117

ence is "color." What could it mean for a young girl in the French provinces to be "asking questions about color" in the 1750s—and for a woman in Paris to be writing about it in 1788? The most important fact, in my mind, is simply that Gouges created this narrative against the odds established by the Atlantic triangle, which prevented most French people from experiencing such encounters with the objects of the slave trade—and from raising questions about race, color, and slavery. Perhaps fictitiously (and more power to her if so), Gouges erases the distance of the Atlantic so that she may expose one of its "ills."

There is another possible dimension to this anecdote: as Brown suggests, Gouges may be trying to retrofit her own history as a writer.[30] But there is more going on in this text than the self-promotion on which Brown focuses. Coming four years after the first draft of *Zamore et Mirza*, and appended to both publications of the play in 1788, these "Reflections" project a stronger abolitionist agenda not only back onto her play but all the way back to her childhood. She who displayed (as we will see) such a wobbly command of race in *Zamore et Mirza* itself now makes blackness foundational to her apprehension of the world. Even as a self-promoting fiction, this is a remarkable gesture for 1788. It may have been a brazen act of self-fashioning, but it was also a significant act of "other-fashioning." In the sentences that follow, Gouges smoothly weaves this initial experience of difference into her intellectual and literary history. She "naturalizes" her abolitionist thought, making it indissociable from her evolution and identity as a writer.

Of course, by this gesture Gouges erases some steps in her own evolution and some elements of the intellectual debts that she owed. The question of the *color* of Africans, for one, had been a source of great general interest among European intellectuals; the Academy of Bordeaux had organized an essay competition on the subject in 1741, and the *Encyclopédie* gave the subject considerable attention in the article "Nègre."[31] But nowhere in those writings does one find anything like Gouges's moral engagement with the issue that defined Euro-African relations, the slave trade. Transfixed by blackness, the philosophers who wrote about its "causes" were indifferent to the enslavement of those who were black. If Gouges makes no mention of those writers in her "Réflexions," it serves them right.

The other, more pertinent, debt that Gouges incurs in this text is to her friend the Marquis de Condorcet and his "Réflexions sur l'esclavage des nègres" of 1776.[32] Condorcet argued that no defense of slavery could withstand moral scrutiny, that "black slavery hurts commercial interests as much

118

as it does justice," and that justice "requires the destruction of slavery," with no compensation to the slave masters.[33] Beyond the obvious similarity of the titles, and their shared abolitionist stance, the two texts differ considerably: in tone, length, and format. Condorcet offered a full program for "gradual" emancipation, whereas Gouges's remarks are more scattered and interwoven with reflections on her fate as a playwright. Still, there is a great harmony between the two: slavery is deplored; emancipation is called for, although it may be dangerous; in the meantime, both say, the slaves' conditions must be "softened." Both are concerned with the slaves' potential behavior in the wake of emancipation. So Condorcet assures his readers that "Before raising slaves to the ranks of free men, the law must ensure that with that new status they will not threaten the safety of citizens. . . . Negroes are naturally a mild, industrious, and sensitive people."[34] And Gouges writes, "They will cultivate freely their own land like the farmers of Europe and will not leave their fields to go to foreign Nations" (*TS*, 231/85). To allay fears, Gouges emphasizes the distances of the Atlantic triangle — which she had erased with her initial anecdote about meeting a black woman — as a source of safety, as if to say, Don't worry, they won't be coming here; they will stay where they are and keep producing sugar. Gouges allays the primal fears of slaves' revenge and colonial "blowback" that Eugène Sue will exploit so sensationally in *Atar-Gull*.

The articulation of distance is of course fundamental to exoticism. In Gouges's theater, costume and what she called "color" were essential vectors of distance and difference. In "Réflexions" this subject comes up twice. In the process of promoting her play Gouges (over)emphasizes its originality: "Several men had taken an interest in [the Negroes] and worked to lighten their burden; but none of them had thought of presenting them on stage *in their costume and their color* as I would have tried, if the Comédie Française had not been against it" (*TS*, 229/84; emphasis added). Later she finds her way back to this subject, advising the actors "to wear the color and the costume of the Negro race," for the Comédie will be "honored rather than dishonored by color" (*TS*, 86/231, AT). This plea comes in the middle of Gouges's efforts to "blacken" a play that had been submitted to the Comédie as an "Indian drama"; she was making it into "The Slavery of the *Blacks*." So "color" is a moving target in Gouges's discourse (and we will follow it from one text to another). But color is not a random signifier for Gouges; it is in fact the key for a moral understanding of the slave trade, as this passage reveals:

Buying and selling men! [*Un commerce d'hommes!*] Heavens! And Nature does not quake! If they are animals, are we not also like them? How are the Whites different from this race [*cette espèce*]? It is in the color. . . . Why do dull blonds not claim superiority over brunettes who look like Mulattoes? Why is the Mulatto not superior to the Negro? Like all the different types of animals, plants, and minerals that Nature has produced, the color of man is nuanced. . . . Everything is different, and herein lies the beauty of Nature. Why then destroy its Work? (*TS*, 230/85, AT)[35]

Color is thus a key to difference, and difference is key to ethics. If whites can trade blacks as slaves, why shouldn't blonds do the same to brunettes? Gouges deconstructs color, destroying it as a sign of dehumanizing and un-redeemable difference. This is part of an agenda that is very important to Gouges, well explained by Catherine Nesci: she wants to defuse and diminish *excessive* difference, like the kind that justifies slavery and the slave trade, so as to create a world in which selves and others are all part of the same "Work."[36] (Undoubtedly, this is where the rise of universalism coincides with the possibility of abolitionism.)

To more fully appreciate what Gouges is doing here, we should bear in mind that, even in supposedly enlightened French thought, as late as the 1780s, the idea that Africans were of a different *species* was widely entertained. Voltaire was a polygenist (if only to fly in the face of the Church).[37] The Abbé Raynal himself had written in the 1770 and 1774 editions of his highly popular *Histoire des deux Indes*: "The Negroes are a particular species [*espèce*] of men" (he, or perhaps his editor Diderot, later retracted his polygenism).[38] Polygenism did not necessarily make one proslavery, but seeing Africans as a different species certainly did not help the abolitionist cause. An antiabolitionist like Dominique-Harcourt Lamiral brandished the word *espèce* in defense of a color line that supposedly guarded France from total economic apocalypse.[39] On the other side, Diderot stated categorically: "Everything proves that the human genus [*le genre humain*] is *not* composed of essentially different species [*espèces*]."[40] When Gouges uses the word *espèce*, then, we should not conflate it with the nineteenth-century idea of race; there is an even more extreme version of difference lurking here, and that is what Gouges, like Diderot, is combating. Her "Réflexions" begins with the word *espèce*, while the rest of the essay works (starting with the very next word, *hommes*) to diminish the *literally radical* difference of "species" that that word implies, so that she can posit a shared humanity.[41] (The epigraph above, from Edouard Corbière, a novelist who was an eyewitness to and possibly a participant in the slave trade, lends a sense of what is at stake in the word *espèce*/species: much more than semantics.)

Yet if Gouges seems to argue *against* color and against difference, she nonetheless wants to conserve both as elements of her dramaturgy. Despite the abuse of color as a justification for the slave trade, color remains for her a sign of authenticity, including linguistic accuracy: thus she brags that "Mirza [in the play] had kept her native language [*son langage naturel*], and nothing was more touching" (*TS*, 229/84). It is hard to know what she meant by that; there is no difference of speech between Mirza's French and others' in the written texts. Color is a marker of Gouges's evolving awareness of the Atlantic triangle and of her increasing ability to distinguish one "Indie" from another. Before seeing how the trope of color is spun in Gouges's dramas, we should simply take note of the importance she attaches to color and costume as figures of *proximation*: color and costume bring distant points together, making slavery "real" on the stage and therefore serving the moral cause of abolition. That concept of color, as a vector of difference, foreshadows the practice that nineteenth-century writers like Mérimée will call *local color*.

121

WHY SO GREAT A DIFFERENCE?
ZAMORE ET MIRZA BETWEEN
INDIES (1788)

What is an "Indie"? Or, as Montesquieu might put it, How can one be Indian? Or "nègre" for that matter—on the stage in Paris in 1788? According to the title of the Abbé Raynal's influential *Histoire des deux Indes*, there were "two Indies." Obviously, that meant East (Asian) and West ("American," in the hemispheric sense). All "Indies" were in some sense colonial; the term was more or less synonymous with the colonized world except Africa. (Raynal's work commented on Africa—"Guinea"—but only in relation to the slave trade.)[42] In the earlier geographical imaginary of Europe, Africa and Asia were poorly, or not at all, differentiated: in Ptolemy's *Geography* they were connected.[43] A contemporary of Gouges, Charles-Jacques Rochette de La Morlière, published something called *Angola, histoire indienne* (aptly subtitled *Ouvrage sans vraisemblance*) in 1771. Columbus's designation of Native Americans as "Indians" has made the confusion of East and West permanent. The *Encyclopédie* explained the lexical situation trenchantly:

"Less excusable than the Ancients, Modern men have named *Indies* countries that are so different in their position and by their span on our globe, that, in order to solve part of the ambiguity, they have divided the Indies into East and West. . . . Then the latter name [West Indies] was *improperly extended to all of America*, and in a further abuse that can no longer be corrected, writers refer to Americans as Indians."[44] Some of this confusion carries over into the works of both Gouges and Staël, although there may be more coherence than meets the eye.[45]

The opening directions of *Zamore et Mirza* state that the play is set "first in an island, and then in a large City of the East Indies [des Indes Orientales]." The character Zamore is an "educated Indian," and the Frenchman Saint-Frémont is "Governor of a City and of a French Colony in India [dans l'Inde]." If we put those two indications together, there is no real ambiguity about the geographical context of the play: the Asian Indian subcontinent and an island near it—"only two leagues from one of the greatest cities of India," the play says.[46] A "French colony in India" in the eighteenth century, taken literally, could refer to a number of settlements on the coast of the subcontinent that were hotly contested with the British. The French lost all their substantial territories in India in the Treaty of Paris in 1763, later regaining a handful of "concessions." Their principal enclave was Pondicherry, a city on the east coast, and a former jewel in the crown of the Compagnie des Indes Orientales. Described by the *Encyclopédie* as having been "destroyed by the English" in 1760, Pondicherry happened to be an important source of *indiennes* (also known as *guinées*), the cloths that were used to trade for slaves on the coast of Africa.[47] But the coast of India was itself the object of a slave trade: a minority of slaves on the French islands of the Indian Ocean were from India.[48]

The European slave trade was not limited to the Atlantic but carried over into the Indian Ocean, where Bernardin de Saint-Pierre witnessed it. The Mascarene Islands of the Indian Ocean were, with the Antilles, part of "one great slave market," one economy.[49] Some ships left France for India, where they bought cloths, which they then traded for slaves on one coast of Africa or another, before crossing the Atlantic to complete the circuit. This extended triangle—actually a "quadrilateral," as Stein calls it—was a significant factor in the slave trade, although it was much less heavily traveled than the triangular West Indian–Atlantic trade.[50] Across these huge distances, it was still a small world. Incredibly, it seems that real-life slaves named Zamore and Azor, as in Gouges's play—from India but enslaved on Mauritius—once ran afoul of the law. Scarr reports (unfortunately without a date) on "a fatal argument between Indian slaves owned by coloured people"; one is named Zamore and the other Azor.[51] (Probably at the same time, as we will see below, Azor was a highly popular name for slaves in Louisiana.)

So it is not surprising to learn that Pondicherry or its environs may have been the original home of a slave named Zamor (or Zamore), given to Madame du Barry by Louis XV and used, as was the height of fashion, as her pet and servant (Gouges's friend Louis-Sébastien Mercier satirized this practice in his *Tableau de Paris*).[52] At court everyone wanted one. Although he was, by all accounts, from India, this Zamor was widely referred to as "le nègre de la du Barry," and some contemporary portraits represented him with African features.[53] He is seen in paintings of Du Barry, including one in which she is drinking chocolate; his darkness enhances her whiteness, making him the perfect accessory.[54] As Doris Kadish points out in *Translating Slavery* (49), Gouges likely took the name of her slave-hero from this real-life Zamor. But Madame du Barry (or the prince de Conti, who reportedly named him) got the name *Zamor* from a previous source, likely none other than the play by Voltaire that we examined earlier in this study, *Alzire* (first performed in 1736). Zamore was Voltaire's proud Inca nationalist. Life imitates art. There was some prophesy in this, since, during the Terror, Madame du Barry's Zamor, reportedly an avid reader of Rousseau, testified against her and helped send her to the guillotine in 1793.[55] This real Zamor was still part of Du Barry's household at the time when Gouges was writing *Zamore et Mirza*. His status as *nègre* shows that the "confusion" of Africans and Indians was not limited to Gouges and that eighteenth-century ideas of race were somewhat fluid.

123

Beyond the question of Du Barry's Zamor as an antecedent, Gouges's direct debts to Voltaire and to *Alzire* deserve attention that they have not received.[56] Voltaire, as we saw, was one of the first to bring the "color" of America to the French theater, in a play that expressed many reservations about slavery and colonialism. The common ground occupied by the two plays includes a shared purpose of diminishing difference: in both, the other—the Indian, the slave—is given voice and humanized. In light of many other things that Voltaire wrote, he makes a very strange bedfellow with Gouges, but these two plays speak a common language. Gouges in fact compared her dramaturgy to Voltaire's: "Like him, I have written plays—not tragedies, but good dramas, which could be compared to his masterpieces."[57]

Returning to the question of geography: Gouges takes both the name *Zamore* and the signifier "Indian" from *Alzire*, but she shifts "Indian" from one referent ("American" or Peruvian) to the other (Asian). Why does she do this? The play in fact has nothing to say about India or about the slave trade that was operating in the Indian Ocean at the time. She does not bother to work any Indian personal names, places, or other signs of local color into the play. Before the play was first performed, and by the time Gouges wrote her essays about the play ("Réflexions" and the 1792 preface), she had already transposed the setting, translating it from one *Inde* to the other. By that time, India disappeared, replaced by a still-vague but clearly American *Inde*. The play reads as if it were suspended between Indies.

In fact, trying to determine a precise geographical referent for *Zamore et Mirza* is, as the French say, like looking for noon at two in the afternoon. The play is too imprecise, with signifiers scattered throughout various Indies. *Zamore et Mirza* is a strange work, full of anomalies and lapses. Ethnic parsing of Gouges's characters is difficult. Yet I disagree with Brown when he says that "slavery and race are barely mentioned" in *Zamore et Mirza*: this play is very definitely about slavery and animated by a certain engagement with abolitionism, even if the racial and geographical markers are ambiguous.[58] Much of its discourse would appear to make sense only in reference to the plantation system of the West Indies, with its enslaved Africans, which is not the setting. There is in fact nothing African in the play. Zamore is an educated Indian slave; his lover, Mirza, is Indian. Both the "inhabitants" and the masses of slaves are Indian. There are many Indian "Habitants & Habitantes," a word that meant both inhabitant and colonist or planter.[59] Yet one Indian slave driver refers to slaves, including Zamore, as "this cursed *race*" (23), demonstrating that we must not project twenty-first-century (or even nineteenth-century) notions onto Gouges's vocabulary. It is as if slavery *were* race here. The preoccupation with difference that we saw in her "Réflexions" is voiced here, as a naive question from Mirza is obviously designed to undermine justifications of slavery: "We are men like them," she protests to Zamore. "Eh! *Why so great a difference* from their *species* to ours?" (ZM, 5; emphasis added).[60] In fact the play ignores racial lines in its protest against slavery: servitude alone makes people like Zamore and Mirza a different "species" (or "kind" as Maryann DeJulio rightly translates [TS, 91]) from

their fellow Indians, the privileged *Habitants*. "Slaves" and "Indians" are referred to as discrete groups, as are slaves and *Habitants* (see *ZM*, 31, 88).

Zamore and Mirza are to be executed because Zamore accidentally killed
the overseer, a "monster" who was pursuing Mirza (*ZM*, 20). Only the governor, Saint-Frémont, can spare their lives. The slaves are opposed to the impending execution of Zamore and Mirza and are on the brink of revolt; the
Indians want the execution to proceed (*ZM*, 31). Before he is apprehended,
Zamore saves the life of Sophie, who turns out to be the long-lost natural
daughter of Saint-Frémont. Zamore's "honesty and virtue" (*ZM*, 46) predis-
pose the governor to clemency; but the perceived "need" to be "barbaric"
in a context of slavery must be overcome (*ZM*, 48, 79). Sophie exercises
moral suasion on behalf of Zamore and Mirza; when she is revealed to be
Saint-Frémont's daughter, the balance tips in favor of pardon and reconciliation. Gouges thus invented a forum for discussion of two issues: slavery
and the birthrights of illegitimate offspring like herself. The "most generous
of men" is at the end (*ZM*, 88) both a noble slave master and a kind father.

Two characters in the play are intriguingly ambiguous: Azor and Betsi
(or Betzi), valet and chambermaid to Governor Saint-Frémont and his wife,
respectively. (Azor's name, nearly an anagram of Zamore's, suggests the
Atlantic and its Azore Islands, an important station on slave-trading voyages.) This servant couple parallels the slave couple of Zamore and Mirza and
seems to raise questions about their different types of servitude. Azor and
Betsi express sympathy for the plight of Zamore and Mirza and bear witness
to the sterling character of Monsieur and Madame de Saint-Frémont. Azor
and Betsi are not racially or ethnically labeled. In one dialogue they seem
to see themselves as neither French nor Indian, yet it is not clear what they
are supposed to be. Azor observes, "All the Frenchmen are the same. The
Indians are much crueler," to which Betsi responds, "I have heard that in
the earliest times we were not Slaves." Azor agrees and adds, "There are still
countries where the *Savages* [*les Sauvages*] are free in their climes." Betsi
concludes: "no one takes up our defense. We are even forbidden to pray for
our kind [*pour nos semblables*]" (*ZM*, 28; emphasis added).

Are Betsi and Azor therefore "savages"? That word, in the eighteenth
century, almost exclusively referred to *American* Indians; its presence in *Zamore et Mirza* contributes to the sense of suspension (or confusion) between
one *Inde* and the other.[61] But in the dialogue above, the word is clearly supposed to apply to many different nations. In *L'Esclavage des Noirs*, Gouges
will change the word *Sauvages* to *Nègres* (*TS*, 100/245), and these two char-

125

acters become Africans. "The slaves" as a group in the latter play will become "the Blacks."[62] In the earlier play the dialogue above would make perfect sense if the two characters were African, but the play never says that. Azor and Betsi are waiting to be "Africanized," which is exactly what Gouges will do to them. Meanwhile, in *Zamore et Mirza*, Azor and Betsi are suspended between races, as if waiting to be colored in. "Race" is written all over the play but between the lines and with confusion.

In 1784 or 1788 what does it mean to represent slavery without Africans? We saw that in Voltaire's *Alzire* no mention was made of the Atlantic slave trade or the enslavement of Africans in the New World; the slaves were American Indians. This seemed to be either a way of sidestepping the issue or of talking about it allegorically. It was one thing for Voltaire to represent slavery without Africans in the 1730s; it would be quite another for Gouges in the 1780s. With the enslavement of American Indians even further in the past (particularly in the French slave societies) and the enslavement of Africans so terribly active, a play of the 1780s in which slavery is anything but black seems timid, disingenuous, or egregiously ill-informed. Here Gouges's "wanton disregard for reality," the reality of the Atlantic slave trade, comes out of a long tradition of such disregard; it seems retrograde.

Still, we could allow for the possibility of allegory, as we did with *Alzire*. In that case India would be a screen for the West Indies, and words like *race* and *species* would be a covert invitation from Gouges to see through the screen and to look toward the abolition of Atlantic slavery. Allegorical or not, *Zamore et Mirza* is unambiguously abolitionist — in its fashion and for its times. The whole melodrama is built on the premise of sympathy for Zamore, who killed the intendant only because he had to, in order to defend Mirza. The Saint-Frémont couple are the mouthpieces of a liberal, reformist ideology that advocates better treatment of slaves; Madame de Saint-Frémont says, "My husband has found that by treating them with kindness, one can do with them anything one wants" (*zm*, 32). Her husband, the governor, argues with the judge who condemned Zamore, opposing his Creole cruelty with the governor's own form of pity: "the voice of humanity shouts within my heart: 'Be good, and sensitive to the lot of these wretches'" (*zm*, 42–43). His discourse contributes to the idea of abolition, even if he does not call for actual emancipation. Gouges amplified the abolitionism in converting *Zamore et Mirza* into *L'Esclavage des Noirs*; at this exact point in the text she added the following: "I know that my opinion must be displeasing to you. Europe, however, is at pains to justify my logic, and *I dare to hope that before long there will be no more slaves*. O Louis! O adored Monarch! If I could but *put before your eyes* the innocence of these unwanted men! By showing them mercy, you would grant liberty to men who have remained too long unknown" (*TS*, 252). It is interesting that Gouges, in this direct address to the king, seeks to make him an "eyewitness" to this ill of America, slavery. The slaves have remained "unknown" in France because of the Atlantic triangle and the "proscription" on slaves in France. Here we see in precise terms how abolitionist discourse had to conjure up absent slaves for the mind's eye of the public. The imagination alone—through the medium of theater, with blackface makeup—could close the distances of the Atlantic.

→→←←

One important element in Gouges's antislavery plays has been neglected by historians and critics: the *divertissement* that ends *Zamore et Mirza*, which is reduced to a simple *ballet* at the end of *L'Esclavage des Noirs* (inexplicably omitted from the text in *Translating Slavery*). In the first play the prose description of this coda (a common element in eighteenth-century opera and theater) fills a page and a half. A *divertissement* is a mix of dancing and singing, typically representing a fête or a wedding, with "public joy its only purpose."[63] The capstone of *Zamore et Mirza*, this ballet depicts the wedding of the title characters, surrounded by "savages and soldiers," with Madame de Saint-Frémont bringing up the end of the procession in a carriage drawn by "savages." The bride and groom are crowned by two "aged persons," and a dance ensues. But then cannon fire is heard, and the celebratory tone of the *divertissement* is violated: now "the Ballet is to depict the discovery of America." (What?) The sea is covered with ships and the "savages"— who are now clearly American Indians—are terrified. They surrender their women to the European soldiers and flee; then the women flee. At that moment a general intervenes and explains to the Indians that he has come to protect them, not to tyrannize them. "The Ballet ends with an admirable concord, and Indian music, which, mixed with military music, will create a new effect in the Theater" (*ZM*, 93–94). The righteous authority of the general, obviously reflecting Gouges's monarchism, thus resolves differences and instills harmony.

127

How do we account for the sudden—and suddenly unambiguous—intrusion of America and its Indians at the end of a play that was expressly set in the East Indies? It certainly suggests cognitive dissonance; there is no way to smooth over all the inconsistencies here. I would like to suggest that this apparent sloppiness—let's call it Gouges's poor control of geography—is itself meaningful. It reflects her carelessness of course and her lack of knowledge (as she admitted). In constructing her representation of *ethical* concord, quibbles about this or that *Inde* were of little consequence. Indians, Africans, Europeans, men, women—all are subjects, entitled to speak. Her general agenda of diminishing differences seems related to this *indifference* about the world and its divisions. She threw *Zamore et Mirza* and its coda together from whatever cultural signifiers came to mind. So if there is cognitive dissonance, there is also ethical harmony.

The geographical and racial confusion that we have seen in *Zamore et Mirza* is an example of the type of "flaw" in Gouges's writing that has been used in the past to dismiss her work. But Gouges's vagueness is also part of a more collective and historical phenomenon, reflecting the state of French literary exoticism in the earlier eighteenth century, before her time. This was an exoticism of vague displacements, in which a random collection of names created an all-purpose Orient. Africans had Asian names, Asians were *nègres*; American Indians were confused with Asians, and so on. The shift from *Zamore et Mirza* to *L'Esclavage des Noirs* reflects the transition toward the more focused evocations of the colonial world that abolitionism will attempt to produce. It is in the latter that a clearer picture of the Atlantic triangle emerges. In the messy transition from *Zamore et Mirza* to *L'Esclavage des Noirs* we see Gouges hastily turning the corner from the first type of exoticism to the second.

128

INTERVENTION BY FICTIONAL PROXY: *L'ESCLAVAGE DES NOIRS*

The second play gives the impression of being a hastily and partially Africanized version of the first one. I have already cited several representative examples of how Gouges sharpened the abolitionist thrust of her writing in the second play. By the time *L'Esclavage des Noirs* was performed, there was plenty for the defenders of slavery to jeer at. Still, as critics have noticed, anomalies remain. If she wanted to make a statement about the Atlantic slave trade and slavery, why did Gouges *not* make the lead characters Zamor and Mirza, her abolitionist mouthpieces, into Africans? Why did she keep the anachronism of "Indian" slaves, which, again, seems like a diversion from the Atlantic slave trade and the enslavement of Africans?

Why did she include anomalies like an Indian overseer of African slaves (see *TS*, 98/243)?

There is still a confusion of Indies in *L'Esclavage des Noirs*, as there was in *Zamore et Mirza*. The stated setting of the play has been changed from "the East Indies" to "the Indies," unspecified (*TS*, 90/235). Because of Gouges's newly Africanized slaves, interpreters have reasonably assumed that the new setting is therefore the *West* Indies.[64] But in the second play Saint-Frémont is still identified as governor of an island "in India" (*dans l'Inde*).[65] Although Zamor (whose name has now lost its final *e*) and Mirza are still "Indian" slaves, Mirza is referred to at one point as a "jolie Négresse" (*TS*, 95/241) — like the Zamor of the Comtesse du Barry. The masses of slaves who threaten to rise up in rebellion are now black.

How abolitionist is *L'Esclavage des Noirs*? Is the new play a "manifesto"?[66] Gouges herself did not hesitate to describe it as "the first hammer blow to strike against tyranny."[67] Several key passages added to the play make Gouges's conception of "abolition" clear, showing the transatlantic conditions and limitations to which it is subject. The most remarkable of these dialogues (act 1, scene 7) suggests a scenario in which one liberation will beget another. Saint-Frémont's natural daughter, Sophie, and her husband, Valère, discuss emancipation with Mirza. Valère has just commented on what a pretty *Négresse* Mirza is; he assures her that Frenchmen are "free in appearance" only. Thus they "have a horror of slavery. One day when they are freer, they will see to softening your lot. [*Plus libres un jour ils s'occuperont d'adoucir votre sort.*] . . . My people one day will break their chains" (*TS*, 96, AT/241).[68]

We should remember the colossal false statement made by Rousseau: "Modern peoples, you do not have slaves, but you are slaves." Unlike Rousseau, Gouges recognizes, on the one hand, that Frenchmen *do* have slaves and, on the other, that there is some relation between the political "enslavement" of the French and the enslavement of Africans by the French. Gouges has the merit, at least, of recognizing that there are two forms of "slavery," that they are distinct but comparable. Her idea of the relation between the two, however, maintains French priority: the French will free themselves first, *then* turn to a "softening" of chattel slavery. Gouges is less than totally revolutionary in her approach to both forms of servitude: she maintains her belief in monarchy for France, and she speaks of reform rather than outright abolition of slavery. The slaves will have to wait for the French people to take care of themselves; then "we'll see." Meanwhile, Gouges has stepped up the rhetoric of her protest. If she equivocates about the abolition of slavery itself, she is clearer about the slave trade, reproducing language from her "Réflexions":

> A Z O R : . . . And, in the bargain, they sell us like cattle at the market.
> B E T Z I : Buying and selling men! [*Un commerce d'hommes!*] O Heaven! Humanity is repulsive!
> A Z O R : It is quite true, my father and I were bought on the coast of Guinea.
> (*TS*, 101/246)

Sophie would appear to be Gouges's mouthpiece and alter ego in *L'Esclavage des Noirs*; the character recycles a line from "Reflections on the Negroes" ("Un commerce d'hommes!"). Sophie, like Gouges, is the natural daughter of a nobleman, the governor Saint-Frémont. She arrives on the island and gives voice to the horror that the metropolitan French feel before the reality of slavery. She intervenes in the arrest of Zamor, declaiming "with heroism": "This excess of cruelty gives me courage. (*She runs and places herself between Zamor and Mirza, takes them both by the hand, and says to the Judge*) Barbarian! Dare to have me assassinated with them; I shall not leave them; nothing can wrench them from my arms." The judge orders the major: "Sir, have this impudent woman [*cette femme audacieuse*] removed: you are not fulfilling your duty" (*TS*, 111/259).

To paraphrase Spivak: a white woman is trying to save brown people from white men.[69] The "impudent woman" is transparently the "tempestuous" Gouges, projecting herself across the Atlantic. Her intervention by fictional proxy brings the tensions of the Atlantic into view. In the colonies those French who are not directly involved in the slave economy are "foreigners" and not welcome; they must be kept "separate" from the slaves. The slave system's most basic organizing principle is stated by the judge in the next scene, as he argues for the violent repression of a slave uprising and the execution of Zamor and Mirza: "We are not in France here; we need examples" (*TS*, 115/260, AT). Governor Saint-Frémont has reluctantly recognized the "necessity" of brutality in a slave economy. The perpetuation of the plantation system requires that this distance *not* be collapsed. Gouges's (somewhat) emancipationist discourse works toward narrowing the gaps.

But in the transition from *Zamore et Mirza* to *L'Esclavage des Noirs* Gouges at other moments worked in the opposite direction, with increased emphasis on the distance between the colonies and the metropole. Under the accusations of the proslavery lobby she assured the Comédie and the public that her play was not the match that would light the powder keg on fire. Thus in her account of the affair of *L'Esclavage des Noirs* she argues, "The objection has been made to me that my drama is incendiary, that it could provoke an insurrection in the Colonies. 'Eh! Sirs, we are in Paris! It is not in front of Negroes that this play will be performed. I assure you that it would [in any case] only lead them to submission.'" [70] (There are "no slaves in France.")

The containment of change was in fact just as important to Gouges as change itself. A new "gentle and consoling morality" will revolutionize France but only under the continuing reign of Louis XVI, the "best of kings." The monarch must be protected from a "criminal populace" (*Les Comédiens démasqués*, ii). Gouges abhors the rabble in France and fears the "cruelty" of revolted slaves. Thus in *L'Esclavage des Noirs* much supports the claim that the author made in defense of her work: it does encourage submission, and it does tread softly on the question of actual abolition. We have seen examples of abolitionist rhetoric that Gouges added to the play, but at the same time she added passages designed to limit the entropy of the slaves' expectations: in French one could call these passages *garde-fous*. The most significant is Zamor's final speech, as he is poised to be executed: he advises the slaves to "fear rendering yourselves guilty by defending me" and to "Cherish this good Master [Governor de Saint-Frémont], this good father, with filial tenderness." (*TS*, 117/262–63). The door to actual abolition is opened, but slaves are asked not to push their way through. Respect for paternal order, represented by the governor, is more important than complete emancipation. The consistent thread running through Gouges's statements is a commitment to nonviolence: for her, no social change can or need be brought about through violence. [71] The result is far from a "radically new society, based on democratic principles." [72]

The violence of revolted slaves, for Gouges here as it will be for Duras in *Ourika*, is a line of demarcation, a limit of sympathy. Both authors turn away and withdraw their support when slaves rise up violently. Gouges's antiviolence, when applied to slavery and emancipation, seems caught within a certain web of assumptions. She included a long paragraph in the preface of 1792, addressed directly to the slaves, who at that point in Saint-Domingue had already begun a full revolution. She reproaches them for their "cruelty," adding these appalling remarks: "By imitating the tyrants, you justify them. . . . Men were not born for chains, [but] you are proving that they are nec-

131

essary" (*TS*, 88, AT/233–34). More important, she says, revolting slaves subvert the cause of abolition: "Ah! How you make them moan, they who wanted [note the past tense] to prepare you, by temperate means, a kinder fate" (*TS*, 88/234). In other words, *If you try to take it, we won't give it to you*: a curious thought (though typical of its times). Gouges assumes completely that emancipation will come from above and will not—should not—be *taken* from below. In Saint-Domingue the enslaved population had already made such thinking moot.

In *L'Esclavage des Noirs*, consistent with her life and death as a Girondist, Gouges leaves patriarchy and monarchy solidly in place.[73] Thus the governor, in his final speech, tells the slaves exactly what to expect in the way of emancipation: whatever he and his government, in their wisdom, see fit to grant them (see *TS*, 119/265). In the meantime, with abolition left in suspense, he proclaims, "My friends, my children, may a general fête be the happy portent of that sweet liberty" (*TS*, 119/265, AT). At that point, a *ballet* forms the important symbolic capstone of the play.

Gouges reduced the *divertissement* at the end of *Zamore et Mirza* to a short ballet in *L'Esclavage des Noirs*. I will quote the coda in its entirety, since it is omitted from *Translating Slavery*:

> The Show ends with a Ballet that is similar to the play. Zamor and Mirza are carried in on throne-chairs. There is a march of Negroes which will produce an interesting effect. The Comédie Française had perfectly imitated the folkways, the pastoral customs of America, and the ballet master had exactly fulfilled the intentions of the Author. The Theater that will put this play on should procure the musical score and the program of the ballet. No Show except the Opera could have produced this Celebration better than it was by the Comédie Française. I cannot praise too much the Composer of the music and the Master of the ballet. (*EN*, 91)

Bearing in mind that the stated purpose of the ballet-fête is to represent the "hope" of emancipation rather than emancipation itself, this description is interesting for the things it does not say. Only three sentences now describe the ballet. There is no mention of the wedding of the main characters, for example, although that can be inferred, nor of a minidrama representing the discovery of America.[74] All that is left is a march. Gouges quickly turns to uncharacteristic praise of the Comédie and its production.[75] It seems that the actors followed the advice Gouges gave in "Réflexions sur les hommes nègres," to "adopt Negro color and costume." In spite of the jeering colonists in the audience, the ballet was apparently delightful. Specifically, Gouges loved the "perfect imitation" of the manners of America, presumably of its black slaves. Remembering that she said this play would never be performed in front of (real) slaves, the (ersatz) slaves' dance onstage at the Comédie is one of those devices used to narrow the gap of the Atlantic for a specific purpose. Here the purpose is to seduce and delight with *color*, which includes music and dance. One can well imagine that the show was a toe-tapping delight like Rameau's *Indes galantes*. Still, it seems fair to ask, What are these "slaves" celebrating? Not emancipation, but emancipation deferred.

Everything we have seen about Gouges suggests that her abolitionism cannot be discussed as a yes-or-no choice. Gouges was an abolitionist but only within the limitations and with the qualifications that we have seen, which were typical of her period. After all, the Abbé Grégoire himself recalled that, at that time, "we were of the unanimous opinion that . . . as to the slaves, their emancipation should not be rushed, but they should be led gradually to the benefits of civil rights." The emancipation of 1794 was, he said, "a disastrous measure . . . in politics what a volcano is in nature."[76] That act of emancipation, by the way, ended slavery but said nothing about the slave trade.

"RÉPONSE AU CHAMPION AMÉRICAIN" (1790)

This short text by Gouges is one of the many salvos in the polemical war that surrounded the performance of *L'Esclavage des Noirs* at the Comédie Française. In another of the Atlantic coincidences that we keep encountering in this study, the "American champion" to whom Gouges addresses this essay was most likely Jean-Baptiste Mosneron "de L'Auney"—as he styled himself—the "philosopher" brother of the slave trader Joseph Mosneron, the brother to whom Joseph read aloud the works of Rousseau. As we know, the Mosneron family was "American" in the sense that it had interests in the Caribbean colonies (and in fact on all sides of the Atlantic triangle), including a branch that lived in Martinique. At the time of the revolutions in France and Saint-Domingue, the Mosnerons had huge colonial holdings: their losses in Saint-Domingue were reported to be 5.5 million livres.[77]

Jean-Baptiste had served as an ensign on one voyage to Saint-Domingue, before turning to law, theater, and politics. He wrote a reformist essay in 1788, stating his wish that the nobility would disappear in favor of the productive merchant bourgeoisie, his class. (In 1792 he helped the royal family flee from the Tuileries palace, for which he was made a baron in the Restoration, in 1822.)[78] At the moment when Gouges wrote her "Réponse," Jean-Baptiste was an elected deputy in the national assembly and a prominent voice in the colonial lobby. (These two had more in common than they may have realized: two plays by Mosneron were passed over by the Comédie Française.)[79]

On December 28, 1789, the *Journal de Paris* published an open letter (dated December 16), signed by Jean-Baptiste Mosneron and addressed to Condorcet. Mosneron defended "the men who make their living directly or indirectly from the Commerce of the Slave Trade [la Traite des Noirs] and from that of the Colonies . . . : These are excellent Citizens, good fathers, men full of humanity." A quarter of the population of France, he argued, would be jeopardized by any disruption of the slave system. In a postscript dated December 24 he reported the outbreak of revolt in the "sugar islands" including Saint-Domingue: "the Planters of this island may now be under the dagger of the revolting Negroes." For Mosneron, the spread of the idea of freedom from one hemisphere to the other, from France to the Caribbean, is perverse. He perceives and fears a causal link between the French Revolution and what will become the Haitian Revolution: "Perverse men are abusing your pure intentions, criminally interpreting the decrees of the National Assembly, and subjecting to their perfidious designs that which humanity and liberty have done, *on a different hemisphere*, for the happiness of citizens."[80] Let freedom *not* ring across the Atlantic, Mosneron is saying. In effect, he is asking Condorcet to arrest the entropy of liberation by limiting its application to white Frenchmen only. If liberation "perversely" crosses the Atlantic, "half of France" will be "plunged into mourning and misery."

That letter, announcing rebellion in Saint-Domingue, was published on the very day that *L'Esclavage des Noirs* opened at the Comédie.[81] This was a crucial time for the Atlantic system, which was simultaneously in grave danger and at its apogee: the slave trade was debated in the Constituent Assembly in March 1790, denounced with powerful eloquence by Mirabeau; but the Assembly did nothing, and the slave trade continued to receive government subsidies until 1793. In 1790, nineteen thousand Africans — a record number "for any American port"—arrived at the port of Le Cap Français in Saint-Domingue—and fifty thousand in all of Saint-Domingue—just in time for the Haitian Revolution![82] Nantes, the home of the Mosneron family, had its best year ever in the slave trade (T, 521, 522).

Jean-Baptiste Mosneron's entanglement with Olympe de Gouges began on December 25, 1789, when he—probably he—circulated an attack, denouncing her as a mouthpiece of the Amis des Noirs, signing his pamphlet only as "A colonist who is very easy to identify." (That signature is highly ironic, since positive attribution of the pamphlet has turned out to be elusive.)[83] Responding to Gouges's letter in the *Chronique de Paris* of December 20—in which she had attacked the "abettors of American despotism"—Mosneron, "in the name of all Colonists," but anonymously this time, lashes out at the Amis as "cowards and assassins, conspirators and public enemies," who "have people *butchered* in America while they *dissemble* in Paris."[84] He mocks the "modern" idea of equality by suggesting that "equal" numbers of Amis des Noirs and colonists show up for a sword battle, "to the death," in the fields on the outskirts of Paris.

In her response, dated January 18, 1790, Gouges addresses herself as if to the "colonist who is very easy to identify" alone but through him to the colonial lobby as a whole. Characteristically, she draws attention to herself, as she attempts carefully to control and modulate the perception of her play as abolitionist. She slaloms through a number of different ideological signposts, beginning with her relation to the Amis des Noirs. She who was apparently a member of that group, and who publicly associated her play with its cause at the time of its premiere, now holds the Amis at arm's length: "It is not the philosophers' cause, the cause of the Amis des noirs, that I undertake to defend; it is my own."[85] This rebuts what Mosneron had claimed: that the Amis had ignobly used a woman playwright as a mouthpiece to "provoke the colonists." Gouges innocently—disingenuously—asks, how could I be the "agent of men I know less than you [do]?" (*TS*, 121–22/267–68)—she was in fact a close friend of Condorcet's. She is a "royalist and a true patriot."[86] Still, echoing her own "Réflexions sur les hommes nègres," she writes: "Without knowing the history of America, this odious Negro slave trade [*traite des nègres*] has always stirred my soul, aroused my indignation. The first dramatic ideas that I set down on paper were on behalf of this species of men tyrannized with cruelty for so many centuries."[87] As for the Amis, that organization "did not exist when I conceived this subject"

135

(which is true); the "society is perhaps based on my drama" (which is dubious). In any case, her play is the thing, and her play is, *pace* Mosneron, not incendiary. If you'll just come see the play or perhaps *even have it performed in America*, she tells him, you'll see that "it will always bring black men back to their duties, while expecting [*en attendant*] from the colonists and the French nation the abolition of the slave trade and a happier fate" (*TS*, 123/270, AT). This is in fact a fair representation of the play's final message to the slaves: wait. The slave trade should be abolished, but slavery itself must wait.

Gouges's dare to Mosneron, to produce *L'Esclavage des Noirs* in the colonies, brings us to another moment of speculation about theater in the French Atlantic. What if Gouges's play had been performed in Saint-Domingue, as *Alzire* was? In that context the submissive final message would of course have resonated loudly, provoking a variety of reactions, no doubt, in the mixed audience. It is hard to imagine that any enslaved person listening to the end of the play would have simply acquiesced. And some of the earlier, more utopian and antislavery sections of the play would certainly have caused a ruckus (as they did in Paris). Unlike *Alzire*, *L'Esclavage des Noirs* directly discusses race-based slavery and could not be taken as purely a commentary on the political "slavery" of white French people. There is of course no evidence that the play was produced in (fast-waning) colonial Saint-Domingue, and it is no wonder.[88]

"DECLARATION OF THE RIGHTS OF WOMEN" (1791)

Gouges's "Declaration" is justifiably famous as one of the first manifestos of women's rights, "arguably the most comprehensive call for women's rights in this period," according to Scott (20). It was in this text that Gouges made her most explicit comparison between the status of women in Europe and the status of slaves. The Declaration offers a chance to examine the workings of slavery and the slave trade as analogies to domestic French forms of oppression and to ask who benefited from these comparisons.

Some feminist commentaries on this key text (including *Translating Slavery*) have failed to point out its debt to Choderlos de Laclos, who had already made the comparison between women and slaves with some vehemence in "Des Femmes et de leur éducation" in 1783: "O women! Come closer and hear me. . . . Come learn how, born as companions to men, you become their slaves. . . . Everywhere that slavery exists, there can be no education; in all societies, women are slaves; therefore women in society are not educable."[89] Laclos's anthropology of slavery (if we can call it that) is vague, but it definitely stems from an awareness of the enslavement of Africans by Europeans. As he says, the lot of women in early society must have been "scarcely better than that of the Blacks in our colonies" (420). That comparison cuts both ways but not with equal force: it is, on the one hand, a protest against the situation of women (who are presumed to be European), and, on the other hand, it establishes enslaved Africans in "our colonies" as a benchmark of the abject. But Laclos only invokes slaves in the colonies as the subordinate and static side of the analogy; the goal of the essay is to advance the education of (French) women, not the emancipation of the slaves. This leads to the question of whether the terms of Laclos's analogy could ever be recalibrated so that liberation would reach both sides of the equation.

I want to suggest that, taken in the context of Gouges's work against slavery, the "Declaration" does take Laclos's uneven analogy some distance down the road toward equity. (I do not know if Gouges—who bragged "I owe nothing to the knowledge of men: I am my own work, and when I compose there are only ink, paper and pens on my table"—ever read Laclos's essay.)[90] Whereas he considered only the liberation of French women, Gouges, after all, had already written about the emancipation of slaves. She was an "abolitionist" before she was a "feminist." If women in France were "like slaves," could slaves, like French women, "throw off the yoke of shameful slavery"?[91]

The "Declaration" is dedicated to Marie-Antoinette, who is urged in this "epoch of Liberty" to "defend this unfortunate sex" (204, 205).[92] Then, speaking to men, Gouges asks rhetorically, "Who gave you sovereign rule to oppress my sex?" (101). The seventeen articles of her declaration follow, in an "outraged imitation" of the Declaration of the Rights of Man, with no mention of slavery.[93] In the *Postambule*, addressed to women, slavery comes up immediately, but first as political or metaphorical "enslavement" of the French masses in the Ancien Régime: "Enslaved men multiplied their strengths by relying on yours [women's], in order to break their chains." Here Gouges, like Rousseau, borrows the chains of real enslaved Africans to use as a metaphor for politically oppressed Frenchmen and -women. She continues: "Freed, they [men] became unjust toward their companions" (106). The Revolution has done nothing for French women.

137

It is in an invocation of the slave trade that Gouges makes the leap from metaphorical or political slavery to real Atlantic slavery:

> The commerce of women was a type of industry that was accepted in the upper classes; from now on, it will have no more credit. . . . However, can reason conceal from itself that all other paths to fortune are closed to women, whom men buy *like slaves on the coasts of Africa? The difference is great, one knows.* The slave commands the master; but if the master gives her liberty without recompense, and at an age when the slave has lost all her charms, what becomes of the unfortunate slave? [*à un âge où l'esclave a perdu tous ses charmes, que devient cette infortunée?*] (108; emphasis added)

The trade in French women *like* chattel brings Gouges to speak of the slave trade on the coasts of Africa. Without putting too much emphasis on it, I think the phrase that follows the analogy is very important, for Gouges recognizes that the "difference" between the two terms of her analogy is "great." This suggests an awareness of the reality of the slave trade on its own terms, an awareness that we know she had. Still, in the last sentence above, woman and slave have become one, a *female* slave (*esclave = cette infortunée*). The difference between the two terms of the analogy is acknowledged, but they have nonetheless been melded.[94]

So it is not surprising that Gouges, after veering away, returns to the subject of slavery more explicitly in the long last paragraph of the declaration. This paragraph is not entirely clear, but I will venture an interpretation.[95] She begins by recoiling at the violence that is overtaking the islands: "Nature trembles in horror" (111). The instigators of these "fermentations," presumably including Mosneron, are to be found in the National Assembly. They spill the blood of their own natural offspring, the mulattoes, in defense of their economic profits. The colonies are caught in a double bind: violent repression will only increase resistance, and leaving slaves enchained will "bring all calamities to America" (112). The spread of liberty cannot be contained, Gouges writes, and it must be "equal for all." "A divine hand seems to be spreading man's endowment—*freedom*—everywhere. Law alone has the right to repress this freedom, if it degenerates into license; but freedom must be equal for all" (112). Here, flashing briefly in front of our eyes, is the equity that Laclos did not imagine: liberation spreading *equally* from North to South, and around the Atlantic triangle. What was a lopsided analogy in Laclos has become a genuinely universal *possibility* in Gouges's mind, even if, she startlingly admits, it spells "the loss of the French Empire" (112). She seems to be going much further here than she did in *L'Esclavage des Noirs*, where caution and patience seemed to suggest the indefinite postponement of emancipation, with no thought of decolonization. She has crossed the line and now suggests exactly what the colonial lobby most feared. Here Gouges *approaches* the radicalism of the encyclopedist Jaucourt, echoed by both Diderot and Robespierre—all of whom declared that the colonies should "perish" rather than impose the stain of slavery on the French Revolution and inscribe it in the constitution (as the United States had done).[96] Gouges's paragraph is too cryptic to be taken as a new, radically anticolonial and antislavery statement on her part; she remains "stuck" within the bounds of "meliorist" thinking that is based, ultimately, on a sense of inequality.[97] It was Gouges, after all, who in 1789 warned the Third Estate that too much of "an awful equality" would make for "a horrible anarchy."[98] Nonetheless, a hint of a rupture with that kind of thinking can be seen here.

We need not even consider the fact that hardly anyone paid attention to this "Declaration" at the time.[99] It is generally true, as we have seen, that Gouges worked toward the diminution of differences based on gender, race, "color," and servitude. Propelled by imagination, she "made herself a man for the country" so that she could intervene in the problem of gender difference.[100] Sexual difference should be made "irrelevant for politics"—so how about slaves' difference?[101] Did she attempt any such intervention in the problem of race and slavery? Only those that we have seen, which I do not discount. If an ethical imperative linked women and slaves, the difference nonetheless remained "great." Her thoughts about color as a sign of difference reflect attempts to diminish and destigmatize otherness, but her definitive work on the subject of slavery, *L'Esclavage des Noirs*, severely limited the prospects of change. The slightly enigmatic universalism of the end of the "Declaration of the Rights of Women" seems to suggest something much more revolutionary, but it leads nowhere. After all, Gouges published the text of *L'Esclavage des Noirs*, with all its constraints on emancipation, in 1792, after the "Declaration."[102]

What one sees in Gouges's texts is still a compelling and imaginative intervention in the debate on slavery, the slave trade, and gender. While those around her were using slavery either as a pure metaphor for the oppression of French people (as in Marat's *Les Chaînes de l'esclavage*) or (as in Laclos) as a real but secondary and unchangeable element in an analogy, she came close to imagining the Atlantic world as a place in which change could take place "equally" on all sides. Gouges was executed during the Terror, on

139

November 3, 1793, three months before the first abolition of slavery. That abolition came ironically—"disastrously," Grégoire said—after the Amis had either fled or been guillotined; it was an "aberration" according to some appraisals, yet it, along with the Haitian Revolution, liberated the vast majority of slaves in the French Atlantic at that time.[103]

MADAME DE STAËL, MIRZA, AND PAULINE

Atlantic Memories

> Quelle gloire pour un siècle que l'abolissement [*sic*] de l'esclavage!
> [What glory for a century, the abolition of slavery!]
> —MADAME DE STAËL, *Correspondance générale* (1786)

Germaine de Staël (1766–1817) is a pivotal figure in the history of abolitionism in France. Her involvement was prolonged, profound, and effective, even if her contributions to the literature on the subject, paradoxically, are not copious. None of her canonical writings—including *De la littérature considérée dans ses rapports avec les institutions sociales* (1801), *Corinne, ou l'Italie* (1807), and *De l'Allemagne* (1813)—reflect her engagement with the antislavery movement.

Madame de Staël's life span takes us from the Enlightenment and the Revolution through to the rise of romanticism, with which she is intimately associated; simultaneously she takes us from one moment of abolitionism to another. The daughter of Louis XVI's on-again, off-again finance minister, Jacques Necker, and of Suzanne Curchod, both Swiss Protestants, Germaine grew up in the company of such visitors to her mother's salon as Grimm, Diderot, d'Alembert, and the Abbé Raynal. The family's Protestantism, as we will see in chapter 9, was linked to its abolitionism; yet the direct contact with these giants of the Enlightenment is obviously the other wellspring.

During the Revolution, Germaine de Staël evolved from a position of constitutional monarchism like that of Gouges to the liberal republicanism that some aristocrats came to favor. She followed her father to Switzerland when the Revolution became radicalized but went to England in January 1793, then back to Coppet. She rescued friends from the guillotine during the Terror. The "excesses of the French Revolution," she commented, "harmed the cause of the poor Negroes."[1] Madame de Staël spent many years in exile during the rule of Napoleon, whom she opposed and who despised her. Together with her son Auguste de Staël and her son-in-law Victor de Broglie, she worked toward the abolition of the slave trade in the early nineteenth century; we will thus see her again in chapter 9, which deals directly with that abolitionist movement.

THE NECKERS, THE STAËLS, AND THE ATLANTIC

The Necker family's social connections and its great wealth could not help but link it to the Atlantic system and the slave economy in several ways. The first link is substantive, while the others are anecdotal and incidental yet very intriguing. Jacques Necker was, starting in the 1760s, alongside the Duc de Duras, a reformer and great defender of the Compagnie des Indes; like Duras, Necker was a trustee (1765–67). It has been said that the basis of his great wealth came from his investments in the company.[2] As a trustee, Necker held on to the basic ideas of Colbert's mercantilism and defended state sponsorship of the Compagnie against those who favored free and private trade. In his plea he credited the company with having "changed two uncultivated and deserted islands into two mercantile [*commerçant*] and cultivated colonies" — those islands being Maurice (Ile de France) and Bourbon (Réunion) in the Indian Ocean: slave islands.[3] (He lost the debate, and the company's privilege was suspended in 1769, then reestablished in 1785.) The Compagnie ceased most of its trafficking in slaves as of 1744 but continued occasional slave trading between Africa and the Mascarenes, sending six more ships out from Lorient through 1756. Even after that direct participation ended, and notably during the time of Necker's involvement, the company's interests in the Mascarene Islands kept it in close association with the slave trade. Later, as minister to Louis XVI, Necker told Clarkson that "he dared not show the diagram of how slaves were transported on the ship *Brookes* of Liverpool" because "it would distress [the king] too much" (T, 13). With or without his permission several slave ships were named *Le Necker* at the time of the Revolution; this would have been a fashionable, progressive gesture. But the same Jacques Necker, in an economic treatise of 1784, deplored "how we preach humanity yet go every year to bind in chains twenty thousand inhabitants of Africa."[4] He argued for reducing the subsidy to slave traders and was reported to be opposed to the trade itself.[5] At one point he suggested the idea of an international maritime enforcement of a possible ban on the slave trade (D, 237). Necker was a liberal; his dismissal provoked the riots that brought down the Bastille. He was certainly not impervious to the ideas circulating in his wife's salon. In him we see the beginnings of a shift toward outright abolitionism, a cause that his daughter, grandson, and grandson-in-law will espouse and personify.

The other two links that I want to mention between the Necker family and the slave trade both stem from the curious history of Germaine's arranged marriage. The choice of a spouse for the richest heiress in Europe was considered a matter of state; her mother favored William Pitt, but Germaine refused. After years of negotiations, beginning when the girl was only twelve years old, a contract of marriage to Eric Magnus, the Swedish baron de Staël-Holstein, twenty-nine years old and Protestant, was finalized in 1785. Marie-Antoinette took an active role in the negotiations and signed the contract along with Louis XVI. The handsome, debt-ridden baron gained a fortune and social prominence in France, while the Neckers gained the classic prize for the upwardly mobile bourgeoisie: a title for their daughter. Also written into the contract was a guarantee that Germaine, a daddy's girl, would never have to leave Paris. But as part of the process of this negotiation, to prove that he was worthy of the position of ambassador for life, Eric got something from the French for the king of Sweden: the island of Saint-Barthélémy in the Caribbean. (The king wanted Tobago but was refused.) Approximately four hundred slaves and five hundred French settlers lived on Saint-Barthélémy at that time. After the transfer the new governor tried to set up a Swedish branch of the triangular slave trade, exploiting Swedish toeholds on the coast of Africa.[6]

This bit of biographical marginalia deserves far more attention than it has received. Looking back to the comparison that Gouges made in her "Declaration of the Rights of Women," between the "sale" of women in France and the sale of slaves, the Necker-Staël marriage transaction takes on an interesting symbolic weight. Germaine Necker was, first of all, an object of bargaining and trade, and she also was at least incidentally tied to the loss of one of France's colonial islands. Territory and slaves were traded in order to prepare for the marriage of the future mother of French abolitionism.

143

The irony of this did not escape her: the theme of the arranged marriage of a young girl, with direct consequences in the slave trade, frames one of the works that I will analyze here, *Histoire de Pauline*.

The second anecdotal connection between the wedding of Germaine Necker de Staël and the Atlantic system involves another axis of the triangle, the one linking France to Africa. The matchmaker in the negotiations between the Neckers and the Swedish court was Madame de Boufflers, who was close to the Neckers and to the king of Sweden and who was the wife of the Chevalier de Boufflers. The governor of Senegal who brought the little girl Ourika back to France as a gift to his aunt and uncle, Boufflers returned to Paris for several months in 1786, and Madame de Staël saw him at that time. That much is known; but perhaps she saw Ourika as well. It is clear that her father, Jacques Necker, knew Ourika; he sympathized with Madame de Beauvau when Ourika died at the age of sixteen in 1799.[7] It was in the wake of Boufflers's 1786 visit that Madame de Staël most likely wrote *Mirza*, which features a character named Ourika.[8] In a letter to the king of Sweden she wrote of Boufflers's admirable plans to establish free-labor sugar plantations in Africa: the theme of *Mirza* and the basis of an abolitionist agenda that we will examine in detail later in this study. She also told the king that Boufflers had given her "harrowing" details about the slave trade.[9] There can be little doubt that Germaine de Staël's ideas about Africa derived directly from her acquaintance with Boufflers. The first "Ourika" in French literature, in Staël's *Mirza* — much less famous than the one created by Madame de Duras in 1823 — could have resulted from actual contact with the real person of that name.

The Necker-Staël family tree thus grows — even more dramatically than the Duras' — from early entanglements and complicities with the slave system toward the struggle for abolition of the slave trade and of slavery itself. Still, compromises remained. In *Translating Slavery* Doris Kadish comments on some of these. Staël, she reports without documentation, may have owned a slave herself; her lover Narbonne's fortune derived from his own wife's holdings in the slave islands.[10] Yet later, during the Restoration, Germaine de Staël was the center of a swank abolitionist coterie, surrounded by her lover Benjamin Constant, her son, and her son-in-law.[11] Elite and probably elitist, this group nonetheless moved from sentiment to action.

In the reading that follows I will try to situate Staël's *Mirza* within the process of evolution that I just described. *Mirza* is the only *nouvelle* or short story by Madame de Staël that is thoroughly Africanist and abolitionist in its themes. But it was originally published within a largely forgotten collection that included two other novellas, one of which, *Histoire de Pauline*, is of great relevance here. Staël's *Recueil de morceux détachés* (1795) comprised a poem deploring the excesses of the Revolution, an "Essay on Fictions," a preface, and *Three Novellas*.[12] In her preface to the three stories Staël downplays their value, claiming they were all written before she was twenty — thus before 1786 (*TS*, 146, AT/271). Their only merit, she says, comes from "the depiction of a few sentiments of the heart." The Revolution has intervened, and she hopes the unhappiness it brought has made her capable of writing "more useful works." But she is not sure, for "the greatness of the events around us makes us feel the emptiness of general thoughts and the impotence of individual feelings." The two novellas that I will concentrate on here are indeed what Staël says they are, depictions of sentiment. By stating her goal so explicitly, Staël inscribes herself perfectly into the arc of French literary history that Margaret Cohen describes in *The Sentimental Education of the Novel*: Staël is one of the women writers whose product — sentiment — will be subject to a "hostile takeover" by realist male authors in the 1830s.[13]

But, despite what Staël says, there is more than sentiment in these stories; there is a dramatic social context. In both *Mirza* and *Histoire de Pauline* Staël staged the sentiments of her characters within a context of slavery and the slave trade — within evocations of the Atlantic triangle. Written before the French and Haitian revolutions, but published during both, and also one year after the first French abolition of slavery, these stories sit astride "great events." To what extent are those events reflected or anticipated in the stories?

MIRZA, "OU L'AFRIQUE"

Before looking at this novella, it might be useful to have an overview of the exotic names that have circulated among the characters we have been seeing (see table below).

These names span the Atlantic and Indian oceans, the boundary between fiction and reality, and the borders between various literary works and genres. Real children were named after fictional characters; the Chevalier de Boufflers seemed to find this particularly amusing, naming another of his "living souvenirs" from Africa "Vendredi."[14] In literature these names circulated among authors like borrowed pens. The slash of the *z* or the *x*,

Exotic Names Associated with Slavery

MIRZA[a]	ZAMOR(E)	ZIMEO/XIMEO	OURIKA
Montesquieu, *Les Lettres persanes* (1721)	Voltaire, *Alzire* (1736)		
	Madame du Barry's slave, 17??–1820	Saint-Lambert, *Ziméo* (1769)	
	A slave named Zamore on Mauritius (Scarr)		
	A slave "Zamor dit Azor" from Africa petitions for his freedom in France, 1781[b]		
Staël, *Mirza* (1786/1795)		Staël, *Mirza* (1786/1795)	Staël, *Mirza* (1786/1795)
Gouges, *Zamore et Mirza* (1788) and *L'Esclavage des Noirs* (1792)	Gouges, *Zamore et Mirza* (1788) and *L'Esclavage des Noirs* (1792)	A child named Ziméo is given by the Chevalier de Boufflers to Madame de Blot	Chevalier de Boufflers brings Ourika back from Senegal, 1786
40 slaves in Louisiana named Mirza, 1803–20[c]	In Verdi's opera *Alzira* (1845): "Zamoro"		Duras, *Ourika* (1823) and many imitations that it spawned

a Sir Richard F. Burton identifies the word *mirza* as "The Persian 'mister.'" *Personal Narrative of a Pilgrimage to El-Medinah and Meccah* (London: Longman, Brown, Green, and Longmans, 1855), 1:20n. Isbell writes, "Mirza is in fact a Persian man's name" ("Voices Lost?" 41).

b Léo Elisabeth, *La Société martiniquaise aux XVIIe et XVIIIe siècles: 1664–1789* (Paris: Karthala, 2003), 379.

c See *Afro-Louisiana History and Genealogy, 1719–1820* database, www.ibiblio.org/laslave.

and the sound it represents, in three of them, connoted strangeness (perfectly embedded in the French word *bizarre*). The juxtaposition of the *z* to an *A* (Alzire, Mirza, Zaga, Azor, Zaïre) seemed to accentuate the feeling of polarization and distance.[15] In all of these cases a sonorous exoticism was evoked.

→→←←

Staël's *Mirza, ou lettre d'un voyageur*, we saw above, is among the most generous users of these names.[16] Here "Ourika" enters French literature long before Duras made the name much more famous. (But Staël's Ourika stays in Africa and seems to owe nothing to the real Ourika.) *Mirza* is explicitly framed within the French Atlantic triangle and the slave trade. The male narrator's presentation of his anecdote is, according to Staël's footnote, "based on the circumstances of the slave trade, reported by travelers to Senegal."[17] Staël, who had not been to Africa, thus borrowed the eyewitness authority of someone who had, someone like the Chevalier de Boufflers. (The plural *travelers* is probably an exaggeration.) The narrator has just returned to France from Gorée:

> A month ago, at Gorée, I heard that the governor had persuaded a Negro family to come and live a few miles away so as to establish a plantation similar to the ones found on Saint-Domingue. He had imagined, surely, that such an example would incite the Africans to grow sugarcane, and that, by attracting the free trade of this commodity to their land, the Europeans would no longer take them away from their home to make them suffer under the hideous yoke of slavery. In vain have the most eloquent writers attempted to effect this revolution in the virtue of men. (*TS*, 146–47, AT/271–72)

147

The word *revolution* of course leaps off the page. But I will attempt to read this text as an artifact of 1786, of the prerevolutionary period in which it was supposedly written, before thinking about it as a reflection of 1795; it is both. What is suggested in these few lines is an idea that will, as I have said, receive fuller attention later in this study: the idea of reinventing the Atlantic slave-trade triangle by destroying it. Why enslave Africans and take them across the ocean, at a great cost in human life, to grow crops that they could grow at home? This rhetorical question became one of the abolitionists' main arguments. Reading referentially, the governor here is the Chevalier de Boufflers, who returned from one stint in Senegal in the summer of 1786 with his "little captive" Ourika, who was presented to his uncle, the prince Beauvau-Craon. Buying what appears to be a different two-year-old girl in February of that same year, Boufflers described himself as moved to tears "by the thought that this poor child was sold to me like a little lamb." While in Africa, Boufflers wrote home to his mistress of his plans for "millions" in "African riches" that would come from the cultivation of cotton and indigo.[18]

In the fiction of *Mirza* the salient factor is Staël's framing of her story within the broadest Atlantic context. France, Africa, and the Caribbean colonies are all in play here. More specifically, she has stated an openly abolitionist agenda. Then, after some racist remarks about Africans being unable to plan for the future, the story begins to turn from the general and political to the register that Staël told us was the only one in this collection: that of individuals and their sentiments. Thus: "One single African, freed from slavery through the generosity of the governor, had agreed to take part in his project. A prince in his own country, he had been followed by a few Negroes of a lower station [*subalterne*], who farmed his plantation [*habitation*] under his orders" (*TS*, 147, AT/272). This is Ximéo, and his wife is Ourika. Her beauty and hospitality charm the visitor-narrator; thus, Staël begins the process of humanizing and rehabilitating the image of the African. Typical of her times, she does this partly by de-Africanizing them, as Behn had done before her: Ximéo's "features had none of the defects of men of his color" (ibid., 147/272). In this he is like his namesake, Saint-Lambert's Ziméo, who had the "regular features" and "beautiful proportions" of an "Apollo."[19] As the visitor's perceptive gaze detects "soul" and "melancholy" in these Africans, the gap between France and Africa closes; *Mirza*, despite its exotic setting, now belongs to Staël's project of depicting "a few sentiments of the heart."

If Staël assimilates her Africans to European norms, can she be said to be practicing in *Mirza* the kind of "translation" that *Translating Slavery* valorizes? In her life and in much of her oeuvre, Staël may indeed, as Massardier-Kenney writes, "embod[y] the ideal of translation," but this early work seems a problematic example of the intercultural contact that Staël will later espouse and theorize. I am not sure that anything in the novella supports the claim that Staël is "engaged in the representation of different modes of thinking and speaking."[20] *Mirza* is, however, directly concerned with that other form of mass "translation," the slave trade.

Ximéo begins to speak, and his discourse at first intertwines sentiments with the economics of agriculture. His support for the abolitionist scheme of establishing plantations in Africa is unqualified: "When I realized that a product of our country, neglected by us, was the sole cause of the cruel suffering endured by these unfortunate Africans, I accepted the offer to give them the example of growing sugarcane" (*TS*, 149/274). But Ximéo's countenance conceals a troubled past, which he now unveils. At this point the abolitionist scheme fades from view for a time and is largely replaced by romance; we will have to ask what those two registers have to do with each other.

The romance of *Mirza* itself is set against another "general" problem, a background of war between two kingdoms of the Senegambia, the Jolof and the Cayor. For lack of indicators within the text, it is not possible to insert Staël's narrative very precisely within African history. Muslim revolutions took place in West Africa throughout the eighteenth century; they were connected to the Atlantic slave trade and in some cases involved resistance to it, as we will see in the chapter on Baron Roger later in this study.[21]

Ximéo is betrothed to his cousin Ourika but meets an enchanting and mysterious girl, Mirza, who tells him she has been schooled by an expatriate Frenchman. From him she has learned all the philosophy that Europeans "abuse." Mirza is many things. She is a female Rousseau in Africa and, alternatively, a genuine feminist. She is a poet and a genius, a precursor of Staël's more famous heroine in *Corinne, ou l'Italie*.[22] She is also, as a descendant of Staël's called her, a "blue-stocking."[23] In other words, Madame de Staël in blackface, a fictional proxy like Gouges's Sophie. A critic writes: "Staël thus launches her Romantic career by seeing herself as African."[24] The figure of the African who has learned everything from a Frenchman and become a rustic philosopher is clearly derived from Mailhol's *Le Philosophe nègre*, which we saw earlier.[25] Mirza is *une négresse philosophe*. She is the figure of the translator in this story: she represents the hinge between France and Africa. But she is a purely *virtual* translator, in reality speaking French philosophy back to French readers in a closed circuit that only pretends to involve Africans. Virtual translation is not nothing; the gesture is admirable and compelling, particularly within the context of France in both 1786 and 1795. But virtual translation is not exactly the same as the genuine "representation of different modes of thinking and speaking." Mirza is thus a paradoxical figure: when she speaks out against slavery later in the story, we are hearing African resistance to the slave trade, but only as it is imagined by French philosophy.

Mirza teaches Ximéo everything, including writing. Passion arises between the two, despite the fact that they are from warring nations. An intense interplay of sentiments ensues, but Ximéo's passion fades for reasons he does not understand. As in the other novellas in this collection, sentiment is at odds with circumstances and is impossible to control. The war intrudes, and Ximéo turns back to Ourika, whom he marries. He tells Mirza he wants to be "friends," and she calls him a "barbarian." He is then injured and taken prisoner by Mirza's countrymen.

As a captive, Ximéo sees firsthand and reports (as will his successor, the Baron Roger's Kelédor) how Africans collaborate with the European slave trade: the Jolof, "serving our common enemies," are selling their prisoners to white traders (*TS*, 154/278). Determined to drown himself, Ximéo hears Mirza's voice; the romantic and the abolitionist coincide as she both saves her lover and denounces the slave trade:

> "Europeans," she said, "it is to cultivate your land that you condemn us to slavery; it is your interest which undoubtedly makes our misfortune necessary to you; you do not seem to be evil gods, and making us suffer is not the goal of the pains to which you condemn us. Look at this young man, weakened by his wounds: he will neither be able to withstand the long voyage nor the work that you will require of him. Yet look at me, see my strength and my youth; my sex has not sapped my courage; let me be a slave in Ximéo's place. . . . I shall no longer think slavery degrading. . . . I do not love anyone in this world; I may depart from it without leaving any void in a heart that would feel that I no longer exist." (*TS*, 154, AT/279)[26]

150

The last gesture is obviously designed to punish Ximéo for spurning her. With great efficiency Mirza reduces her listeners—both the slave traders and her former lover—to a state of combined "admiration and shame."[27] The perfidious European traders, however, want to take both of them as captives; the governor intervenes, "like an angel of light," and frees them. The personal and the political are both resolved, as the governor says, "I return you to your country and to your love. So much nobility of soul [*tant de grandeur d'âme*] would have shamed the European who would have called you his slaves" (*TS*, 155, AT/280). Staël's governor, like Gouges's, is wholly benevolent. There is no discussion of the fact that he must have been overseeing the sale of slaves from Africans to Europeans.

But if the Atlantic triangle has been interrupted—since this slave-trade transaction has been cancelled—the romantic triangle involving Ximéo,

Mirza, and Ourika remains to be resolved. This is quickly taken care of: Mirza, disconsolate because Ximéo had denied her his love, stabs herself to death. As will be the case in *Histoire de Pauline*, the problem for Mirza is posed as a torment of inerasable memory: "I would have believed that I had dreamed your fickleness; but now, *to destroy this memory*, I have to cut through the heart *from which nothing has been able to erase it*" (*TS*, 156, AT, emphasis added/280).[28]

This sets Ximéo up to live out the rest of his days in romantic melancholy, even as he simultaneously becomes the personification of the abolitionists' plan for agriculture in Africa. Part of his time is spent "prostrate before [Mirza's] tomb," feeling "the enjoyment of grief, the full feeling of its sorrows." But we know from having read the beginning of the story that this does not take too much time away from his duties as overseer of a plantation, with "subaltern" blacks under his command. These two functions that Ximéo fills at the end of the narrative together form a remarkable picture, an abolitionist utopia that derives exactly half of its seductiveness from the romantic discourse of sentiment. Later, Staël and others will expand on the idea of a post-slave-trade utopian colonization and evangelization of Africa: in her 1814 "Appeal to the Sovereigns Convened in Paris" she asks for the abolition of the slave trade "so that this humanitarian act might persuade the hearts of those [in Asia and Africa] to whom the Gospel is to be preached" (*TS*, 159/283).

In *Mirza* the project that Staël shared with all her fellow abolitionists, of humanizing Africans so that they will appear "worthy" of emancipation, does not limit itself to questions of appearance or nobility of birth. Her Africans work two jobs: as romantic souls and as happy, "free" producers of sugar cane. The moral economics of sugar and slavery are therefore altered, in effect removing the "price" at which "you eat sugar in Europe" (as Voltaire put it in *Candide*). In retrospect, Staël's preface looks somewhat sneaky. The "depiction of a few sentiments of the heart" is clearly not the only "merit" or the only purpose of *Mirza*. Abolitionism enters French literature in romantic garb. Or, it has to be said, sugarcoated. In this we should see a parallel to what Massardier-Kenney describes as Staël's strategy: "seeming to obey the paternal injunction not to write . . . while nonetheless engaging in the act of writing." This was part of a larger pattern by which Staël controlled her works "so that she would avoid being silenced the way women like Gouges had been" (*TS*, 137).

ADÉLAÏDE ET THÉODORE

So when we turn to the next story in the *Recueil*, entirely set in France among French people, what is the effect? Does the reader's retina hold on to some of the melanin of the previous characters? Are Adélaïde and Théodore Africanized at all by their proximity to Ximéo, Ourika, and Mirza? Sandwiched between two colonial tales, *Adélaïde et Théodore* is nonetheless entirely metropolitan, with no allusion to the world outside France. Staël plays on the register of private passions and sentiments alone in this story, with no hint of great events. More than either of the other novellas, *Adélaïde et Théodore* conforms to the expectation that Staël created in the preface.

The eponymous lovers, here too, are divided by their station in life, which forces them into a secret marriage. Ximéo kept his marriage to Ourika secret from Mirza for a time; now Théodore cannot tell his mother, the Princesse de Rostain. But it is Théodore's jealousy of Adélaïde that ultimately kills him and pushes her to suicide. As in *Mirza*, the misery here is delicious and is savored by the characters: Théodore has an "avidity for unhappiness" that prevents him from clearing things up with his wife (*OJ*, 188; *RMD*, 121). Adélaïde gives birth to their son, takes opium, and kills herself. The novella hovers between romanticism and melodrama, as Staël plays the register of sentiment with a very heavy hand.

There is of course nothing "African" about these characters; since there was nothing African about those in *Mirza*, why should there be? What is intriguing, in these three novellas taken together, is Staël's idea of placing all these characters from around the Atlantic on the same plane of analysis. In that sense even *Adélaïde et Théodore* is part of an abolitionist agenda.

HISTOIRE DE PAULINE AND COLONIAL BLOWBACK

Histoire de Pauline takes the reader back across the ocean and deep into the colonial world. But this will be a very different location on the Atlantic triangle. The story begins in Saint-Domingue before the Haitian Revolution: "in those scorching climates where men, solely occupied by barbaric commerce and profit, seem mostly to have lost the ideas and sentiments that might make them recoil before such things."[29] The lack of sentiment—that gendered commodity in the history of French literature—is part of the depraved moral frame. The characters in the story are Creoles, *Américains*, as they would have been called at the time. Pauline de Gercourt is a twelve-year-old orphan (the same age as Germaine Necker) when she is contracted to marry a planter who thinks only of his business. The sentence describing the economic terms of the marriage will be striking to readers of Gouges: "He married because, at that time, he needed a large sum of money in order to make a significant purchase of Negroes [*un achat considérable de Nègres*]; Pauline's dowry gave him the means" (*OJ*, 199).[30] With this efficient gesture Staël not only suggests the comparison between (white) women and slaves; she also sets up a narrative in which one kind of trade is the direct consequence of the other. Pauline's "enslavement" (my word, not Staël's) to a loveless husband is the result of a purely economic intention, a desire for profit on his part. In turn that transaction enables the husband to enslave, literally, more Africans. Values are calculated and exchanged across the lines of gender and race: one white woman for so many slaves; in turn the slaves will produce values within the Atlantic economy. What is interesting here is that, because of the dowry system, the husband *gains* all of this for nothing; it is pure profit. Both Pauline and the unnamed slaves are pawns within a scheme that makes profits only for white males like her husband. What we see here is therefore not "trade" in the sense of exchange—for all the value flows toward the planter-husband; it is *traite* in the etymological sense of extraction. He alone *draws* the values of his woman and his slaves.

But at this point we reach a fork in the narrative road: the comparison between women and slaves having been made, they now go their separate ways. Pauline—and by implication, white women as a whole—remains the focus of the story, while the slaves recede into utter invisibility. Staël's Pauline is not Gouges's audacious Sophie, who, in *L'Esclavage des Noirs*, intervenes on an island of slave plantations in order to give voice to an abolitionist sentiment. Nor is there a Mirza in sight.

Between the lines there is another dimension to the comparison between Pauline and the slaves. Pauline enters into the marriage "without knowing the *value* of the commitment [*engagement*] she was making, without having thought about either the present or the future" (*OJ*, 199; emphasis added). These terms echo those used by the initial (French male) narrator in *Mirza* to describe the blacks of Africa, "who do not think of providing for their own future, are even more incapable of thinking about generations to come, and they refuse a present evil without comparing it to the fate from which it could free them" (*TS*, 147/272). (The word *engagement* also reminds the reader of the system of indentured labor.) Discursively, by this character-

153

ization, Pauline is racialized. By not understanding *value*, she becomes a passive object of trade.

Pauline's "nature" is fundamentally good, but the colonial world she grows up in is not. Naive Pauline is surrounded by rapacious and deceitful men, starting with the "depraved" libertine Monsieur de Meltin, who undertakes to "corrupt her." She falls in love with a friend of his, Théodore, a slightly better model of roué; but he fears the "slavery" of sentiment and runs away to France (*OJ*, 201). Real slavery thus fades from view so quickly in this novella that it can, after only a few pages, revert to its metaphorical usage as a condition of European sensibility. It is never mentioned again. Pauline remains caught within a web of false love, "the obligation of appearing to love" (*OJ*, 205). Her husband dies in a shipwreck, and Pauline inherits his fortune, his plantation—and therefore, though they are not mentioned, his slaves. Her wealth only makes her more irresistible to depraved suitors; she is "debased" (exactly how we don't learn) and considered to be not *fréquentable* by society women. She founders in the moral quagmire of the colony. But a virtuous older lady, Madame de Verseuil (who had wanted to marry Pauline's father many years before but was not allowed to), arrives and urges Pauline to return with her to France: "Follow me to another country; put the immensity of the seas and more, put a virtuous education between your childhood and your youth" (*OJ*, 208). The distances of the Atlantic are thus invoked for a moral purpose: the ocean will bury the secret of Pauline's past "forever" (*OJ*, 223). In the rest of the story there is no comment on the property, including slaves, that Pauline is also leaving behind. She will presumably be one of the numerous absentee planters of Saint-Domingue, like Claire de Duras with (at least for a time) her holdings in Martinique.[31]

Like Joseph Mosneron the young sailor, Pauline arrives out of an Atlantic world that is deeply involved in slavery, to find that she is uncultivated. She spends four years living in isolation with Madame de Verseuil outside of Le Havre, reading: "She acquired all forms of knowledge" (*elle acquit toutes les connaissances*). She is transformed into a heroine out of Rousseau, "pensive" and "wild"—her very face now has "a novelistic quality" (*OJ*, 210). But she is still wracked by guilt, tainted by the moral compromises of the island, which remain murky. So when she meets the perfect man, Count Edouard, she feels unworthy. "Remove from my heart," she implores, "these memories that degrade me" (*OJ*, 216). In spite of the "secret" of Pauline's past, Madame de Verseuil works to arrange her marriage to the Count "at any price" (OJ, 218). But Pauline can't bear the tension of her guilt and tells Edouard to go away forever. She then finds him on the brink of suicide; to save his life, she promises to marry him. Again — as with Germaine Necker herself and as with Pauline at the beginning of the story — a wedding results from bargaining. Her urge to confess is overpowered only by the joys of motherhood, and all goes well until Edouard dines with someone who has arrived from Saint-Domingue. He turns out to be the depraved Monsieur de Meltin; the Atlantic closes in on Pauline. She whom "the slightest mention of America . . . threw into despair" (OJ, 210) now has America coming back to haunt her. She confesses to Edouard that Meltin was "one of the objects the choice of which dishonors me; the other one died over there" (OJ, 226). Edouard still professes his love for Pauline, but there remains the problem of the duel he must fight with Meltin in order to defend her honor. He kills Meltin, which only casts another shadow of guilt over Pauline, who lapses into fever and delirium. What had been a guilty neurosis now deteriorates into psychosis. At this point, then, even if she is not in the attic, Pauline has followed the path that *Jane Eyre* will make famous: like Mr. Rochester's wife, Bertha Mason, Pauline is a Creole who has come out of her own Caribbean/Atlantic world of slavery to the mother country and madness. If it is indeed syphilis that afflicts Mrs. Rochester, then the comparison is even more appropriate.[32]

155

Pauline regains her senses just enough to describe her own death as the only equilibrium that her story can find: "Dying, I believe myself worthy of you; the excess of my passion is demonstrated to you" (OJ, 230). We are left with the image of the devoted and perfect husband turned widower. *Histoire de Pauline* is thus, to a large extent, one of those European stories that uses slavery and colonialism as a backdrop for the staging of European emotions. But what is striking is how clearly this novella reveals the process by which this happens. The relation between the "sale" of European women into marriage and the sale of slaves is, as we have seen, stated with unusual bluntness at the outset. Then real slavery disappears, and those so inclined could denounce the rest of the story as a bad-faith exploitation of the theme of slavery, used as mere decoration. But I do not think interpretation should stop at that point. *Histoire de Pauline* is more deeply engaged in the question of empire than, for example, works like Austen's *Mansfield Park*, in which, if Edward Said is correct, the colonies are merely alluded to and assumed to be "available for use."[33] All of the moral freight in this novella — the guilt that obsesses Pauline and ultimately takes her life — seems in some less tangible way to reflect not only on her personal background but on the colonial system from which she emerges. The stain of her past may not come only from her marriage and her relations with other men in Saint-Domingue; it may result from her contact with slavery. Words like *degradation*, *torture*, *crimes*, *shame*, and *barbaric*, which appear on nearly every page of *Histoire de Pauline*, were already the stock-in-trade of abolitionism.[34] When these stories were written, prior to 1786, the Société des Amis des Noirs had not yet been organized, but Condorcet's *Réflexions* was in print in 1781, and he deployed many of the same words in an argument against slavery.[35] And Staël herself had of course just used that vocabulary in *Mirza*, the first story in this 1795 collection. The vocabulary of moral reprobation forms a link between the personal-romantic and the political-abolitionist registers; the same terms are used in each. Thus in *Mirza* the slave trade is "the barbaric [*barbare*] scheme of men of your color," while Ximéo is denounced as a "barbarian" (*barbare*) for rejecting Mirza's love. "Torture" (*supplice*), "crime," and "shame" (*honte*) are all used in both registers.

Through the dual valence of this vocabulary, then, the comparison between Pauline and slaves that was made at the beginning of *Histoire de Pauline* seems to creep back into the story, subliminally. That interpretation is obviously easier with hindsight, but I think it is only *partly* retroactive to see a connection — which Staël may or may not have been aware of — between the two tracks: between the private emotions of the characters on the one hand and the political background, featuring the slaves that Pauline left behind, on the other hand. Reading this story after *Mirza* makes it almost impossible *not* to see that connection. It is in the interaction between those registers that, I would suggest, Staël's act of translation is to be found.

When the *Recueil* was published in 1795, the Haitian Revolution was well under way, and slavery had been abolished. As we saw in our readings of Gouges, the idea of the Atlantic closing in on the metropole, with consequences flowing from Saint-Domingue back to France — "blowback" — was a logical preoccupation in this period.[36] *Histoire de Pauline*, with all its emphasis on a burden of guilt that is brought back across the Atlantic to France, seems to reflect those concerns between its lines. More specifically, Madame de Staël's representation of the Creole as someone who has been morally compromised, in some unstated way, by the institution of slavery — if we may read *Histoire de Pauline* that way — is somewhat ahead of its time. Although the Creole was known as a strange "experimental subject"[37] in French culture at least since the time of *Paul et Virginie*, the solid stereotype comes later. It will become commonplace in the nineteenth century.[38] Furthermore, the "torment of memory" (*OJ*, 220) that tortures and kills Pauline (as it killed Mirza before her) evokes a problem that will plague France in the nineteenth century, after Saint-Domingue/Haiti has been definitively lost: how to "forget" Haiti, the subject of a chapter later in this book.

→→←←

Three Novellas thus begins and ends with narratives that are deeply, if ambiguously, involved in Atlantic issues and questions about slavery and the slave trade. Just as Germaine Necker herself was treated as an object of trade with implications for the Atlantic system, these early works of hers are entangled in questions of servitude, trade, and economics. When Staël framed the troubles of her heroines Mirza and Pauline in terms of pathological memory, she of course hit upon a theme that will have great importance later in history, when the descendants of the slave trade put pen to paper.

DURAS AND HER OURIKA, "THE ULTIMATE HOUSE SLAVE"

About *Ourika*: I just got a letter from Martinique saying, ". . . The clandestine trade in human flesh is flourishing; the colonials look on every recently-arrived Frenchman as a Negrophile, and the witty and generous author of *Ourika* is constantly accused here of having, in her detestable novel, made interesting a Negress who didn't even have the advantage of being creole." Isn't that amusing?

—ALEXANDER VON HUMBOLDT
to Claire de Duras (1825)

The duchess de Duras had imagination, and in her face a bit [of] the expression of Mme de Staël: one can judge her talent as an author by *Ourika*.

—CHATEAUBRIAND, *Mémoires d'outre-tombe* (1849–50)

It is hard to disagree with the notion that Duras, in *Ourika*, went "far deeper psychologically" than the "strictly surface portrait drawn by Madame de Staël" in *Mirza*.[1] And there is no point in deconstructing those terms of analysis, since depth, or more precisely depth-effect, is what Duras manages to create with remarkable power. The revival of this novella in recent years, with several new editions, and its frequent use in French literature courses in the United States are well justified. It is simply one of the most compelling short works of fiction in French and a startlingly modern commentary on race. My treatment of it here will be very limited. I want only to highlight its underappreciated Atlantic dimensions; I believe that what it actually says about slavery has been largely overlooked.

I have already reviewed the real-life facts on which Duras based her story: the Chevalier de Boufflers brought a Senegalese girl named Ourika back with him to France in 1786; and we have seen how Staël, who may have met Ourika, used the name. Claire de Duras, part of the same social set as both Staël and Boufflers (though younger, born in 1777), takes the story into new dimensions, making it into a critique of the prejudices of her own class. Framed by the recollections of a doctor who meets Ourika in a convent, the novella unfolds as a first-person narrative in Ourika's own powerful voice. First printed without the author's name and in a limited number of copies in 1823, *Ourika* quickly became a sensation. Later it lapsed into a period of obscurity that lasted until its recent revival, which has mostly been limited to the United States and Canada.[2]

FAMILY TIES

We have already seen some traces of the Durfort de Duras family's involvement in the slave trade and abolition. Even before her marriage to the Duc de Duras, the future author of *Ourika*, Claire de Kersaint, like Staël, had family ties to the Atlantic economy. But she was much more directly linked to the plantation-slave system. Claire's father, Guy-Armand-Simon de Coëtnempren, comte de Kersaint, was a lifelong naval officer and ultimately vice admiral. In 1792 he took a moderately abolitionist position, while admitting that he had owned slaves himself in the islands and that he maintained part of his fortune there.[3] (A Girondist, he was guillotined on December 5, 1793, one month after Olympe de Gouges.) The author's mother, *née* Claire d'Alesso d'Eragny, was, like Staël's character Pauline, a Creole, born in Martinique and owner of large holdings there. She was not just any *dame créole*. She was descended from one of the most illustrious families of the island: her great-great-grandfather was François d'Alesso, marquis d'Eragny and governor of the French islands of America in 1691 — whose remains are buried in the cathedral of Fort-de-France, marked by a plaque. He had just distinguished himself by chasing the English off the islands when he died of yellow fever; his son stayed on Martinique, and the family became important landowners.[4] The masters' house of their *habitation*, La Frégate, is (even now) one of the most impressive on the island.[5]

The author's parents met when the father was a young naval lieutenant assigned to the defense of Martinique. Claire was born at Brest in 1777 (thus twenty-nine years after Gouges and eleven years after Staël) and raised in

159

Parisian salon society "without a childhood." Her parents lived separate lives, and Claire entered an elite convent for her schooling. She was an "orphan" in a convent, like Ourika. In 1794, with the property of émigrés being confiscated by the revolutionary government, mother and daughter traveled to the New World to rescue their fortune. At the French consulate in Philadelphia they signed various legal documents by which Claire took ownership of her mother's estates in Martinique.[6] Philadelphia was at the time a sort of clearinghouse for refugees from France and the French islands (including Moreau de Saint-Méry, who published his famous *Description topographique, physique, civile, politique et historique de la partie française de l'isle Saint-Domingue* there in 1797). At this point a certain mystery arises.

Sainte-Beuve, writing in 1834, gave the version of events that has been repeated by most modern critics: "Mlle de Kersaint embarked for America with her mother, whose health was ruined and whose very reason was weakened by so many misfortunes. She was in Philadelphia first, *then in Martinique, where she managed her mother's estates [possessions]* with a prudence and an authority that were well in advance of her age. Now truly an orphan and a rich heiress despite confiscations in Europe, she went on to England, where she married the Duc de Duras."[7] This image of the future author of *Ourika* residing, for an indeterminate time, in Martinique has become widely accepted. Most of the recent works on Duras claim that the two women traveled from Philadelphia to Martinique.[8]

But neither of the two most significant biographical sources about Duras—Bardoux and Pailhès—says that Claire de Kersaint went to Martinique. Bardoux's narrative strongly suggests that mother and daughter went only to the United States, not to Martinique.[9] Pailhès's version is succinct: "The presence of the mother and the daughter is noted in Philadelphia on June 15, 1794; and after a stay in Switzerland, Claire and her aunt, Mme d'Ennery, meet up again in London, in 1795."[10] No mention of Martinique. There is reason to doubt that the Kersaint women went there. For one thing, the island was in the hands of the British at that time.[11] For another, the Kersaints are documented in Philadelphia in June of 1794; there would have been little time for Claire to "manage" a plantation in Martinique and still be in Switzerland, then England, later that same year or in 1795.[12] It is easy to see how the idea of Claire in Martinique could have arisen, since she went to Philadelphia, paradoxically, to claim property in Martinique. But Claire's trip to Martinique would appear to be a riddle. It cannot be dismissed, for how could one prove that she did *not* go? Yet no real evidence demonstrates that she did go.[13]

At the risk of falling down the rabbit hole of biographical criticism, I would like to devote some more attention to Sainte-Beuve's scenario, which, like other riddles that we have encountered in this study, invites both skepticism and reflection. If real, Claire's direct contact with the French colonial world would be a significant point of contrast between her and the two other authors with whom I have dealt in this part of my book. As an eyewitness to (not to mention stakeholder within) the slave-plantation system, she would have a different status, moral burden, and narrative authority. Her eyewitnessing would stand in marked contrast to Gouges's "earwitnessing" and to the inauthenticity of Staël's *Mirza* as well. Claire de Duras would be something nearly unique: an "abolitionist" author with direct knowledge of and a large financial stake in the slave system. Based on the assumption that Claire went there, one critic writes, logically, "Her experience in Martinique was no doubt related to her inspiration for the novel *Ourika*, whose heroine is a young black former slave."[14] Within the scenario of her visit to Martinique, Claire de Kersaint, at the age of sixteen, sees the colonial plantation system firsthand. She meets and interacts with the slaves whose very ownership she is there to claim—or perhaps to sell—along with the fruits of their labor. Following Sainte-Beuve's description, we imagine Claire issuing orders around the plantation, taking charge; perhaps ordering punishments like whippings, perhaps buying and selling slaves. Fighting adversity and rising out of defeat, plucky Claire becomes a crypto–Scarlett O'Hara (the comparison could be taken further: if she had been in Martinique at this time, Claire would in fact have been surrounded by British soldiers, the equivalent of the "Yankees" in *Gone with the Wind*). Or is that whole scenario false? For now, Duras's status in *Translating Slavery* as one of "those women writers—notably Aphra Behn and Claire de Duras—who *lived in the colonies*" (Kadish in *TS*, 3; emphasis added) should be viewed with skepticism.

Even setting aside the hypothesis of Claire's presence in Martinique, there are questions that persist: what became of her colonial holdings (or their profits) in later years, even near the end of her life, when she was writing *Ourika*? As she was creating one of the most sympathetic representations of an African in French literature, did she still hold title to hundreds of

African slaves in Martinique? Even if the plantation was sold at that point, as seems likely, Duras was living on the benefits it brought her, some of which may have allowed her to buy her château, Ussé, on the Loire.[15] The author of *Ourika* was, in any of these cases, in some sense a slave trader: she had owned and had likely sold human beings as chattel (or had them sold by others). With so much having been made of Voltaire's investments in the slave trade, and before we make Duras into the French Harriet Beecher Stowe, more attention to her involvements might be warranted.

The rest of Claire's life is well documented. After a stopover in Switzerland she went on to London in 1795, with plenty of money, and joined the aristocratic emigré community. There she met and married the Duc de Duras. They settled back in France definitively in 1808. The duc assumed his functions as Premier Gentilhomme de la Chambre with Louis XVIII, as his father (whom we encountered earlier) had with Louis XVI. The Duchesse de Duras became "queen of a society: surrounded, solicited, admired, adored, and envied for the brilliance of her salon," which was "the most famous of Paris."[16] Germaine de Staël was very much part of this circle. Sainte-Beuve says that Duras told the story of Ourika orally in her salon, and her delighted friends urged her to write it down: "The next day, in the morning, half of the novella was written." She reportedly completed *Ourika* between January and April of 1821. When published in 1823, the novella was hailed as "a pure and flawless piece of writing." Goethe supposedly said that the emotion of the novel was almost more than a man his age could stand.[17] It set off a veritable fad of Ourika imitations, translations, and adaptations in poetry and theater—even clothing.

162

DREAMS OF SLAVERY

Ourika is a text that reviews the period from the French Revolution to the Restoration with a concision approaching that of Chateaubriand's three sentences. One of the beauties of the novella is the sad grace with which its cloistered African narrator casts her eye on the turmoil of revolutions around the Atlantic during this time. Ourika's point of view on events is double: she consistently gives voice to the opinions of her aristocratic foster family, while adding her own views as a member of a "proscribed race." Duras approaches the questions of race and slavery differently from either Gouges or Staël, and she moves her players around the Atlantic in an original way. In contrast to the characters in Staël's three novellas, Duras has an African come to France (it is as if Staël's Mirza met Theodore). This placement of an African into French society has the psychological effects that Duras explores, but as a literary strategy it also allows the author to follow the adage of writing schools: write what you know. Unlike Gouges and Staël, Duras does not attempt to represent foreign climes about which she knows little or nothing—with one very important exception in *Ourika*, which we will study. She does not even mention her mother's native Martinique—not explicitly. Since Ourika is raised in France from the age of two, little remains of her African culture (except a dance that her body itself seems to remember), so her difference comes down to one element alone: color. Duras has freed herself from the burden of representing almost anything beyond the fact of blackness.[18]

Another aspect of the historical and geographical framework should be pointed out. Sainte-Beuve comments on Duras's role in society and as a writer within the context of the Restoration; he says that it all gives off "the feeling of great catastrophes in the background," of a fading "twilight glow" in the last days of the aristocracy ("Portraits littéraires," 1044, 1052). To make an African woman the voice of this feeling is a fascinating gesture, since her own life unfolds against the background of a great catastrophe: being ripped away from her family and sold. *Ourika*'s status as a "sentimental social novel" can be found in this duality between the distant and the intimate.[19] In this it resembles Staël's *Mirza* and *Histoire de Pauline*, in which registers of sentiment and society complemented each other.

163

Since *Ourika* is based on the well-documented, real existence of a young African girl brought to France, the narrative significance of this setup could escape the attention it deserves. For Duras's story is not only a fictional interpretation of real events; it also reflects the expansion of a narrative gesture that we have seen before. Writers like Mailhol in his *Philosophe nègre* and Staël in her *Mirza* have been at pains to make their Africans speak French. In both of those cases this was explained as a result of prior contact with a Frenchman. It was part of a broader imperative within abolitionist discourse, beginning with *Oroonoko*: the need to make the African an active spokesperson within the literature of his or her own liberation.[20] Apparently, this could only be imagined through gestures of assimilation, making the African noble, French-speaking, "enlightened," and so on. Now Duras takes the idea further. Unlike in those other narratives—in fact, all of those that we have seen in the second part of this book—Duras is only responsible for representing the amount of African culture that a two-year-old might remember. Her Ourika will be assimilated to France—and will thus be "the ultimate house slave"—in every way but skin color.[21]

The arrival of Ourika in France, where the slave trade, plantations, and the labor of slaves were all far from view, refracts the structure of the Atlantic triangle in a significant way. Ourika's initial status as chattel is made clear by the first verb of the novella ("je fus *rapportée*"), which is supposed to be used only for things, not people (*TS*, 196/295).[22] (The real Chevalier de Boufflers had used the same language when listing the "things" he was bringing back from Senegal, including Ourika.)[23] She is apparently in the very process of being dragged, protesting, onboard a slave-trading vessel when "Monsieur le chevalier de B." is moved to buy her: "He took pity on me one day when he saw slaves being taken aboard a slave ship which was about to leave the harbor: my mother was dead, and they were taking me onto the vessel, despite my cries" (*TS*, 196, AT/295). Ourika is *extracted* from Africa, extracted from the slave trade, and brought "back" (*rapportée*) to a place she has obviously never been. From the outset her point of view is partially someone else's.

164

Once in France and "given" to "Madame la maréchale de B." (the chevalier's aunt), Ourika is "rescued from slavery." Her status as an object officially ends, and she becomes (or will try to become) a person. France's traditional self-image as a space of freedom is thus preserved. Because Ourika's enslavement ends *nominally*, the story is no longer supposed to be about slavery, the slave trade, or the Atlantic; rather it is, and has mostly been read as, an allegory of race, a dramatization of the color bar. *Ourika* is, in the words of one early critic, "the first (and certainly one of the best) analysis by a white writer in French of the psychological effect of white racism on a black person."[24] In *Translating Slavery*, *Ourika* is said to "expose race prejudices," and Duras is said to "take racial equality as a given" (*TS*, 186, 193). Roger Little sees in *Ourika* a "female consciousness-taking that anticipates . . . both Negritude and feminism."[25] My fear is that critics, understandably impressed by Duras's pioneering psychological portrait of racism, have assumed too much about what she is actually saying about slavery and the slave trade—and what she is not saying. Thus Little asserts that *Ourika* "discretely sensitizes the reader of 1824, by means of art, to the barbaric effects of the slave trade" (x). Ourika is generally, if loosely, associated with abolitionism by many critics. We will see that Little's claim is dubious and that the relation of the tale to abolition needs to be scrutinized.

The passages in *Ourika* that interest me most are therefore those in which the Atlantic and questions of actual servitude—questions that were ostensibly *removed* from the frame so that a purified discussion of color alone could take place—sneak back into the narrative. The moments when Ourika reflects on the Atlantic and on her own place within it cast a new light on the context we have been reviewing in this chapter.[26] Slavery and the slave trade are mentioned only four times in the novella: at the beginning, when Ourika is saved from the slave ship (*TS*, 196/295); during the French Revolution, when the revolt in Saint-Domingue is discussed with revulsion (*TS*, 203/302); in one passing allusion to the slave ship from which she was removed (*TS*, 209/309); and near the end, when Ourika mentions the "vices of slavery" from which she was saved (*TS*, 216/315).

Ourika's experimental personhood fails of course; that is the point of the story. As Margaret Waller has rightly pointed out, Ourika "derives her sense of self from her value as an object of social exchange."[27] That value is completely destroyed by the obstacle of race—for, as a visiting sharp-tongued marquise puts it, "Who will ever want to marry a Negress?" (*TS*, 199/298). At that point Ourika's eyes are opened: the illustration from the 1826 edition makes this painfully literal (see figure 7). Separated from the two conversing French women by a screen, Ourika is instantly made aware of the barrier of color difference and its implications for her. Because she is barred from reproduction, she has no human value. In front of a mirror she sees her own hands as those of an ape; she feels "foreign to the entire human race!" (*TS*, 201, AT/300). It is no coincidence that the word *espèce*—which we saw as a potential marker of polygenism in Gouges—is used at this point in the narrative. Her color is an "incurable ill" (*TS*, 206–207/306); "Nobody needed her!" (*TS*, 211/310). Rescued from the slave trade and from slavery, Ourika nonetheless finds herself subjected to a ruthless "economic" system in which she loses all value merely because of the color of her skin. Only God, the ultimate equalizer, can save her and restore her value: "For Him there are no Negroes or whites; all hearts are equal in His eyes" (*TS*, 215, AT/314)—hence the convent, and death.

The realities of the Atlantic triangle frame the tale, while remaining *almost* completely removed from the main narrative. The French Revolution offers Ourika a brief moment of hope for some improved social status, but

7   Ourika at the screen. From Madame
    de Duras, *Ourika* (Paris: Ladvocat,
    1826). Courtesy of the Yale
    University Library.

the specter of the Haitian Revolution intervenes to reaffirm a sense of absolute difference:

> People were beginning to talk about freedom for Negroes: it was impossible
> for me not to be deeply affected by this question; it was an illusion that I still
> liked to cherish, that elsewhere, at least, there were people like me [*j'avais des
> semblables*]: Because they were unhappy, I thought them to be good, and I be-
> came interested in their condition. Alas! I promptly discovered my mistake! The
> Saint-Domingue massacres caused me a new, excruciating pain: Until then, I
> had been distressed at belonging to a proscribed race; now I was ashamed of be-
> longing to a race of barbarians and murderers. (*TS*, 203/302)

The word *elsewhere* casts Ourika's vision across the Atlantic and into the
maelstrom of another revolution, only to be repulsed. The Haitian Revolution is represented here from the point of view of French propaganda;
French atrocities are not mentioned.[28] And the *success* of the Haitian slaves
in liberating themselves is not even considered. For Ourika (and, one assumes, for Duras, as for Gouges), freedom that comes at the price of violence is not worth anything. Thus both revolutions are dead ends. (This is a
moment of "forgetting Haiti," to be explored later in this study.)

Hopeless in France and practically suicidal, Ourika cannot help but look toward the other point on the Atlantic triangle, her native Africa. But there, too, in a statement reflecting a condition of internalized oppression, she sees only "my barbarous fatherland" (*ma patrie barbare* [*TS*, 207/306]). At that point it would appear that glances outward and around the Atlantic would be completely over, but, very significantly, they are not. Near the end of the tale, Ourika reinvents her own life, imagining what it would have been if she had not been rescued from that slave ship. This passage—overlooked by critics and far more significant than its length suggests—can be seen as an act of translation:

> Why did they not let me follow my fate? So! I would be [*je serais*] the Negress slave of some rich colonist; burned by the sun, I would farm the land for another, but I would have my own humble hut to go back to at night; I would have a life's companion [*un compagnon de ma vie*] and children of my color who would call me "Mother!" They would press their little lips on my forehead without disgust; they would rest their head on my shoulder, and they would fall asleep in my arms! (*TS*, 212–13, AT/312)

Ourika translates her life into the present conditional (not the past conditional, as the translation in *Translating Slavery* has it), moving herself into a different sector of the Atlantic world, the plantations of the New World islands. The first thing to notice here is that the crossing of the Atlantic—the Middle Passage—is instantaneous, silent, and harmless; Ourika simply appears, years later, in the middle of a life that has already been well established. This is completely inconsistent with the abolitionist effect that Little attributes to *Ourika*: on the contrary, Duras covers up the horrors of the Atlantic crossing.

The passage goes on to suggest an emotional/economic calculus: for the small price of cultivating someone else's land during the day, a perfectly ordered and fulfilling life—replete with family values—is offered in return. It is very appealing. However, the slaves of Martinique might have taken exception to this representation of their lives. Would a female slave's existence have resembled this sentimental fantasy in any way?

Concerning women and slavery in the French islands, the insights of early observers and recent historians should be juxtaposed to this passage in *Ourika*. In the eighteenth century a governor of Martinique deplored the low birthrate among slaves and blamed it on abuse and overwork imposed by the planters, who in turn suspected slave women of inducing abortions. Pregnant slave women were worked until the moment of their delivery.[29]

The poor demographics among slaves of course drove the slave trac͏. torian Bernard Moitt finds that "the institution of slavery itself was antithetical to the promotion and development of strong family units" and that its burdens, including hard labor, "fell disproportionately upon slave women." Jennifer Morgan reports that slave owners cherished the idea of slaves' reproduction, even "in the face of sky-high mortality and dismal fertility rates" among slaves. "Black women," she writes, "found themselves on the bottom of the work pyramid on the sugar plantations." Despite the wishful thinking of the Code Noir (with its provisions for religious marriage, with the owner's consent), there were, Moitt reports, "few legal marriages among slaves" on the French islands. Slaves themselves seem to have resisted the institution. The truth about real but extralegal affective bonds among slaves is hard to extract from the writings of priests and slaveholders, who disapproved of African marriage practices among slaves in the islands. It would be a mistake to take at face value one priest's assertion that "there are no family ties" among slaves.[30]

In light of this, Duras's choice of the word *compagnon* (companion) instead of *mari* (husband) is intriguing. Period dictionaries do not suggest that *compagnon* was used to mean, in effect, common-law husband, but that is clearly what Duras implied with the phrase *compagnon de ma vie*.[31] In an otherwise emphatic portrait of close, monogamous, nuclear family bonds, why did the author choose this one slightly off-key word? I want to suggest that this may be a rare, perhaps unique, sign of Duras's actual knowledge about plantation life, information that her mother might have passed on to her. She may well have known that slaves were more likely to be "companions" to each other than spouses. In any case, the solid, lifelong bonds that Duras's Ourika dreams of in this passage would have been embedded within a context of immense hardship. It is difficult not to see in this passage by Duras an implied defense of her mother's Martinique and of the plantations that Duras herself may still have owned or profited from as she was writing *Ourika*.

Duras subtly conveys another comforting and insidious myth about slavery in this passage: an image of fertility. A proslavery manifesto argued that "the womb that bears children is the most productive part of slave property."[32] But, between "a negligible birthrate among slave women" and "a very high mortality rate," slaves on the French islands "did not reproduce themselves."[33] The absence of children was noted by observers. As one French medical doctor in Saint-Domingue concluded, "one could not expect live, healthy births from overworked, undernourished, and unhealthy slave women."[34] This was one factor that kept the slave trade in business. There were, Gautier writes, "few children on the plantations"; slave traders didn't favor children and sometimes threw them overboard.[35] As an unspecified number of children press their kisses onto Ourika's forehead, readers therefore receive a false and rosy impression about slave life. In this vignette one recognizes a common defense of slavery: here at least Africans live Christian lives; they are better off than they would be in Africa, and so on. No hardships, mutilating punishments, privations, or indignities are mentioned; no Code Noir, no cause for revolt. It is practically a sales pitch. (The fantasy is not unlike that in Randy Newman's song about the slave trade, "Sail Away.") Exceptionally for Duras, this passage is an instance of "optimistic" translation.[36]

I would like to propose two counternarratives that might productively be juxtaposed to Ourika's fantasy of a safe and fertile existence on a slave island. The first comes from history. On October 12 and 13, 1822—one year after Duras is supposed to have written *Ourika*, and before it was published—slaves on a coffee plantation in Morne Vert, Martinique, revolted with the aim of taking over the island's principal city, Saint-Pierre. The uprising was repressed by *milices de couleur* from Fort-Royal. The government exacted its vengeance on the rebellious slaves: twenty-one were mutilated and then executed; ten others were transported to France for a life sentence in the galleys.[37] The dissonance between this reflection of life on Martinique and Duras's contemporaneous fantasy could not be greater. If the Haitian Revolution was rejected with a shudder earlier in the story, the other slave islands return here as perfectly viable models. "Unfortunately" for Ourika, she *was* rescued from the fine existence that the slave trade would have sent her to, so she is left in France with no hope, begging God to remove her "from this world."

The second counternarrative reads almost like a refutation of Ourika's fantasy. It is found in Edouard Glissant's novel *La Case du commandeur*. Onboard a slave ship during the Middle Passage, a woman, whose name is never revealed, is raped repeatedly, along with two of her companions— "day after day and night after night"—by gangs of sailors. The memory of the last flower that she saw on the African continent "supported her body and her mind during this agony." She knows right away that she has been impregnated, but once on the island, she rejects the available option of abortion by means of herbs. She "offers herself" to dozens of male slaves every night in order to "ravage her body," but she wants to see her baby born.

Once it is born she kills the infant and herself. It is a horrendous example of a *grève du ventre* by means of infanticide and an utter rejection of the comforting image that Duras projected.[38]

It should be kept in mind that the passage of *Ourika* that I have been discussing is not a journalistic report on slave life in the islands; it is a reverie on Ourika's part, built into a novella, and thus doubly fictive. It is obviously intended by Duras to be both a product and a reflection of the despair that Ourika feels, not necessarily a realistic representation of plantation life. But, ultimately, Ourika's dream is Duras's creation, and nothing in the tale contradicts its images. It is Duras who fosters this image of a happy slave life on the islands, in a statement that leaves a powerful impression. Slavery itself remains nominally associated with "vices" at the end of the tale (*TS*, 216/315), but the image of happiness in bondage lingers. (Baron Roger will create a similar image in a part of *Kelédor*.)

So is *Ourika* abolitionist in any sense? Does Duras actually condemn slavery? When, at the end, Ourika says that God "rescued [her] from the vices of slavery" (*TS*, 216/315), it is not clear that the institution of slavery itself—slaveholding—is a vice. Instead, she sounds like Rousseau, stigmatizing the slave as a "vile" creature. The vices of slavery seem to include rising up in rebellion, as in Saint-Domingue; they seem to be vices of the slaves, not the slaveholders. The only sense in which this novella is abolitionist is an extremely loose one: by creating an extremely human portrait of the effects of racial exclusion, Duras contributed to the general project of sympathy for blacks, a precondition of abolition. But she goes no further than that. Servitude is of course implied every time Ourika refers to herself as a *négresse*, but the question of color (the other half of that word) overshadows any consideration of the institution of slavery in *Ourika*: we are, after all, in France, where the plantations are out of sight and out of mind (except in that one fantasy of Ourika's). You can remove a *négresse* from slavery, *Ourika* tells us, but you can't erase the problem of color. Duras found a way to write sympathetically about an African while tiptoeing around the problem of slavery.[39]

Ourika is a critique of racial prejudice. Yet the solution it seems to imply is simply for all individuals to stay in their place, on their own side of the color bar. Ourika "would have been" better off either in Africa or in the bosom of her imagined family on a plantation, on either of the two *other*, non-European points of the Atlantic triangle. The races cannot mix and should not be translated into each other's spaces. Culture is "instinct," which wells up in Ourika as she performs the "national dance of her country" (*mon pays*) to the delight of the assembled aristocrats (*TS*, 198/297). By bringing her into French society, Madame de B. has made Ourika "estranged from everything"; she cannot go back to her country, where no one, she says, would understand her (*TS*, 201/300); they are "savages" (*TS*, 207/306). Her "position was so false in the world" that she lost her "place in the [great] chain of beings" (*TS*, 207/306, 214/313).[40] The segregationist view is expressed by the hateful "Marquise de . . . ," who thinks that the "natural order of things" (*TS*, 199/298) has been broken by this social experiment, but nothing in the tale suggests that she is wrong or that there is any way to cross the color bar and survive.[41] It is sad, for sure — as Werner Sollors comments, "everybody could cry" — but there is no "third space," at least not on Earth.[42]

Ourika is the precursor of other tragic exiles in French colonialism, those punished for attempting to dwell between cultures. One thinks of Josephine Baker's Zouzou and of Fara in Ousmane Socé's novel *Mirages de Paris*, and we will see the spectacular example of Dorothy Dandridge's role in the film *Tamango*.[43] As Massardier-Kenney argues, this can be seen as a manifestation of "skepticism [about] translation as a viable cultural paradigm" on Duras's part: things and people are better off left where they were (*TS*, 185). Duras actually stated in a letter: "I am against translation" (*TS*, 188).

In the final analysis *Ourika* has at best a tenuous, perhaps "unconscious," relation to abolitionism.[44] On the one hand, Duras created an immensely powerful narrative on racial prejudice, thereby contributing to the pity and sympathy that were the building blocks of abolition. Hence the poor reception of the novella in Martinique as reported by Humboldt (see the epigraph above). But on the other hand, Duras, through Ourika's reverie, preserved the image of plantation slavery as a productive and reproductive way of life, thereby defending her mother's background and perhaps her own investments, transactions, and fortune. Duras translated the experience of race into French, but she also translated the justifications of her mother's (and her own) planter class into fiction.

171

EPILOGUE: THE *VIGILANTE* AND A FRENCH *ZONG*

I want to go back briefly to Duras's silence about the Middle Passage so that I can suggest, first, how she might have been able to see things differently and, second, how we might, with hindsight, disturb her silence.

Almost simultaneously with *Ourika*, another text appeared in France: a booklet entitled *L'Affaire de "La Vigilante," batiment négrier de Nantes*. This was a rare *untranslated*, original work in French documenting the slave trade—not merely reproducing and translating Clarkson or other English abolitionists—and it includes original engravings (previously mentioned; see figure 5). Arguing that the present laws against the slave trade were insufficient, the anonymous author recounts events that took place in April 1822—thus just as Duras was finishing *Ourika*. On the Bonny River (Nigeria) British cruisers apprehended a French slave ship, *La Vigilante*, with 345 captives onboard, along with several other slave-trading vessels. A battle ensued, and many captives were killed, jumped overboard, or were mutilated. The British lieutenant, with the poetic name of Mildmay, removed a ten-foot-long chain from a twelve-year-old slave girl and clamped it on the ankle of her captor, the French captain of *La Vigilante*. This parallel-universe Ourika was taken to Sierra Leone, the colony for liberated captives. There, the author says, the captives found, "with freedom, all the facilities necessary in order to instruct themselves about everything concerned with agriculture and trades."[45] This report on the slave trade thus leads to the subject of chapter 10, the "interests" of European slave-trade abolitionists in the development of Africa.

172

Another real-life incident should be mentioned here. The French slave ship *La Jeune Estelle* has not inspired a novel as the story of the British slave ship the *Zong* inspired Fred D'Aguiar's remarkable *Feeding the Ghosts*. It should have. In both cases African captives were murdered by slave traders on the high seas, although under different circumstances. The captain of the *Zong* ordered the drowning of 132 captives because the ship's food and water were running out, and he wanted to file a claim for "lost" goods with the ship's insurer.[46] On March 4, 1820, a French slave-trading vessel operating out of Martinique, *La Jeune Estelle*, was arrested by the British ship *Tartar*. The French captain stated that he had previously been apprehended and that he had only one captive left onboard. A British sailor heard muffled cries coming from inside a barrel. Opening it, the sailors found that two young African girls, perhaps twelve or fourteen years old, had been stuffed inside and had nearly suffocated. Again, Ourika in a different life. The British officers then recalled that they had seen "many barrels" being thrown off *La Jeune Estelle* as it was being pursued. The French crew had attempted to conceal the evidence of one crime, slave trading, by committing another, mass murder. Captain Olympe Sanguines defended himself by saying he knew forty other captains who had done the same. His punishment was forced retirement.

The atrocity of *La Jeune Estelle* was denounced in the Chamber of Deputies by Benjamin Constant, but he was "shouted down by fellow members, who accused him of calumniating the nation."[47] In 1822 enforcement of the ban on the slave trade was, after all, a preoccupation of perfidious Albion.

The scandals of both *La Vigilante* and *La Jeune Estelle* (most certainly the latter) could have made an impression on Claire de Duras and might have modulated her silence about the horror that we now call the Middle Passage. The fact that they did not takes nothing away from the achievement that *Ourika* represents in terms of intercultural understanding, but it does reveal how distant the problems of enslaved Africans must have seemed, even to a well-meaning and liberal elite in France at this time.

CONCLUSION TO
PART TWO

The works, lives, family histories, and *interests* (in all senses of that term) of these authors have crisscrossed with each other, and all have spanned the Atlantic many times over. The network of complicities and engagements that has been evoked here is too complex to schematize. On the one hand, Gouges, Staël, and Duras were part of a small world; the latter two in particular were part of the same elite, knew each other, and corresponded. Even Gouges crossed paths with a Duras. Yet on the other hand, the distances and consequences that we have seen here are vast, reaching far beyond the borders of the hexagon. In the lives of Staël and Duras we saw entanglements with the Atlantic slave economy. On the part of all three authors we saw literary gestures that reached out and around the Atlantic. With some awkwardness, and with varying interests at play, each author attempted to translate a certain concern about race and slavery. It is the next generation of the same elite, including Staël's son and son-in-law (but also including Germaine de Staël herself), who will engage abolition more directly and more effectively, as we will see in the next chapter.

Meanwhile, that other kind of translation, the French slave trade, continued until 1793. Between 1783 and 1792—thus the years in which Gouges was working on *Zamore et Mirza* and *L'Esclavage des Noirs*—the French slave trade was flourishing: more than 1,100 French ships plied the Atlantic triangle, taking more than 370,000 captives to the Antilles.[1] After that, the trade was interrupted by wars and did not renew itself until the peace of the Restoration. During the Napoleonic years France's slave colonies were in British hands, and Haiti gained its freedom, so the Atlantic triangle was broken. (One of the last expeditions to leave Nantes in this period was financed by Joseph Mosneron, forty-five-years old; *L'Eole* was prepared to take 450 captives but had only 68 onboard when it was chased away from the Gulf of Guinea by a British warship. Returning to France via Guadeloupe, the ship could not have turned much of a profit.)[2]

Turning away from the three women writers featured in this segment and toward a number of their male successors, I want to borrow from Margaret Cohen's analysis of the gender politics of nineteenth-century French literature. A "previously frivolous feminine form," the novel, was "masculinized" by the realists Balzac and Stendhal; this involved a "hostile takeover" of the sentimentality that women writers (including Staël and Duras) had previously practiced with great success. Realism would acquire the lion's share of cultural capital. In the chapters that follow I will not be tracing the "female" alternative thread, the history of the sentimental social novel, of which *Ourika* is an early example. Instead I will examine a different hostile takeover: of the representation of the slave trade by male authors. With the death of Staël in 1817 and of Duras in 1828, writers like Hugo, Mérimée, Corbière, Sue, and Dumas will rise to dominate the representation of Africans, of slavery, and of the slave trade. With the notable exception of Baron Roger, these male writers spelled the demise of abolitionist sentiment and the rise of other priorities like "adventure." The abhorrence for violence that Gouges, Staël, and Duras seemed to share will be replaced by a distinct taste for it. In terms of literary history, this corpus, like that of the sentimental social novel that Cohen explores, veers away from the dominant codes of realism, into a different *littérature hors d'usage*.[3] Representations of the slave trade will be associated with subordinate but highly popular genres like *littérature maritime* and the *roman feuilleton*.

3

FRENCH
MALE
WRITERS

RESTORATION,
ABOLITION,
ENTERTAINMENT

TAMANGO AROUND THE ATLANTIC

Concatenations of Revolt

C'est la chose la plus horrible dont on puisse se faire une idée qu'une révolte de Noirs. [A revolt of Blacks is the most horrible thing that can be imagined.]

—DOMINIQUE-HARCOURT LAMIRAL,
L'Affrique et le peuple affriquain (1789)

I t's a simple story, really: a crafty ship's captain; a dynamic African warrior who is taken captive; a beautiful African woman; a slave revolt on the high seas. Yet the combination of these elements in a short story called "Tamango," by Prosper Mérimée, produced one of the most compelling, influential, and pernicious representations of the slave trade in all of history. The Mérimée tale is one of the few texts on the theme of the slave trade that is closely associated with the French literary canon.[1] "Tamango" is the most important literary representation of the slave trade in French and perhaps the most influential representation of the French slave trade of any kind. Together with its sources and its intertexts (including works that respond to it), Mérimée's "Tamango" amounts to a compendium of thoughts and images related to the French slave trade at a particularly important moment, that of its official but incomplete abolition. It is a veritable master text.

"Tamango" is richly ambiguous and heavily ironic, especially when read in the context of its times and as a recombination of ideas and images that Mérimée must have gleaned from his readings. With characteristic economy, within the twenty or so pages of the story, Mérimée creates an indelible and, I will argue, invidious image of the revolted slaves' alleged inability to handle their freedom. The power of this story can be seen in its afterlife: in literary creations that it seems to have spawned in nineteenth-century France, and, of most interest to me here, in literary and filmic responses that the tale has provoked in Africa, the Caribbean, the United States, and France in more recent times. In this chapter I will attempt to find out where this paradigmatic narrative of a shipboard slave revolt came from, what its meanings might have been in its own time, and how it has been both refuted and reinvented by other artists since then. Doing this will necessitate tracing a transhistorical spiral around the Atlantic, as we follow the evolution of the Tamango figure through time and space.

I will thus begin in Mérimée's France, at the particular moment at the end of the Bourbon Restoration of the French monarchy, in 1829, when "Tamango" was first published. I will move backward to look at a few of Mérimée's possible sources, and then I will flash-forward to the twentieth century and to the twenty-first, with their replies to and reinventions of the tale: Césaire's *Cahier* (Martinique via France, 1939), John Berry's film *Tamango* (adapted, produced, and filmed in France by an American and French team, 1957), Boris Boubacar Diop's novel *Le Temps de Tamango* (Senegal, 1981), and Jean-Roké Patoudem's project for a new Tamango film. "Tamango" has become, and I will examine it as, a truly circum-Atlantic phenomenon.

At stake in this tale, in its interpretations, and in its reinventions are not only the questions about the slave trade, slavery, and abolition that cannot escape any reader but also larger issues of what I will call connectivity. Each Tamango narrative that I will examine here raises questions about how people come together and form (or fail to form) collective wholes — to "concatenate," as Spinoza would put it.[2] Or, as Césaire will write in his *Cahier*, to form a crowd (*faire foule*). To state it simply: in order for the slaves to revolt, they must come together and form a cohesive group, unified by a certain consciousness; then, if they win, they must decide what to do with their freedom. Each "Tamango" narrative will describe a rise of centripetal forces gathering around the leader, Tamango, and culminating in a revolt. At that point, however, versions of the tale diverge radically. To take the two versions that I will devote the most attention to here: in Mérimée's tale the concatenation of revolted slaves will be undone by centrifugal forces: ignorance of navigation, drift, and death; whereas in Berry's film a massacre of the revolted slaves by the slave traders will be converted into a symbol of black racial and political solidarity.

In the intellectual climate of the present day, to study these Tamango narratives as allegories of connectivity is inevitably to engage with models of postidentitarian thought such as hybridity, nomadology, diaspora, creolization, and so on. These models rose to preeminence in the 1990s as part of a larger paradigm shift away from essentialism (a shift that had begun with poststructuralism and deconstruction in the 1960s and 1970s). This movement was largely, rightly, and quite explicitly driven by an abhorrence of certain specters: colonialism in general with its politics of division, apartheid in South Africa, genocide in Rwanda, ethnic cleansing in the former Yugoslavia. Most generally, the work of this movement has been characterized by a critique of the nation-state, the consummate form of modern identity. In reaction against these various forms and consequences of separateness, postmodern thought has valorized linkages, in-betweenness, and hybridity. Yet within this line of thinking there is a fundamental paradox: *connections* are valorized, yet *collectivities* are viewed with suspicion. If the latter are too strong, they are suspected of "essentialism" — the cardinal sin of cultural studies. It is our distrust of hardened social formations now that marks our distance from the age of nationalism — an ideology that runs through the various twentieth-century versions of "Tamango." There are compelling reasons for this paradox, yet it leaves us without a clear roadmap for interpretation. How are we supposed to view connections — between individuals, first of all, and then collectivities? At what point do we think that things have congealed "too much" and that something dangerous has taken shape?

In more intuitive terms, why do we tend to assume that connections are a "good" thing? Linkages, connections, networks, and bridges are all intrinsically seen in a positive light, barring some other determinant like an evil purpose. The Panglossian quotation from Voltaire that I referred to early in this study, giving voice to a classic Enlightenment idea, invokes the air of optimism that so often surrounds the idea of connectivity: "Everything is a cog, a pulley, a rope, or a spring in this immense machine" (the universe). As we saw in the introduction, the (unmentioned) slave trade haunted that passage, in which Africa is mentioned only, and celebrated, as a source of rains that fertilize Europe. In the postmodern world that tendency to celebrate connectivity has colored the emerging field of Atlantic studies: when

181

the journal *Atlantic Studies* was launched in 2003, its editors' rhetoric echoed Voltaire's: "The Journal aims to *celebrate* the original Atlantic mappemonde: a highly critical space, centered not on a single nation or land mass but on a new cosmopolitan interchange of ships and peoples, cultures and texts, ideas and tools."[3] One can only ask, Since the slave trade was absolutely intrinsic to that "cosmopolitan interchange" in the "original Atlantic mappemonde," why should we necessarily celebrate it?

Whether in the language of postmodern theory or in the realm of intuition, the slave trade poses a challenge to ideas of connectivity. As we saw in the early pages of this study, the trade brought the Atlantic together in a triangular form of solidarity that was predicated on the abuse of human lives. The "solidarity" of the Atlantic system joined the elites of Europe, Africa, and the Creole New World together in an unholy concatenation that was entirely predicated on the repression of any counterconcatenation by those who were enslaved.[4] Revolts occurred on approximately one voyage in ten; if that figure sounds low, we should consider what David Richardson suggests: that, absent these revolts, one million more Africans might have been shipped across the Atlantic.[5] In the French trade there may have been one revolt for every twenty-five expeditions (T, 424). Revolts threatened the system and were a constant preoccupation of slave traders. Captives or slaves who joined together to "make a crowd" troubled both the clear conscience and the economic reality of the slave system. Because of its dramatic nature, because one's sense of justice cries out for resistance to oppression, revolt is the story that everyone wants to hear about the slave trade. Mérimée understood that. "Tamango," in all its versions, is the story of a revolt, and the story of a "crowd."

MÉRIMÉE'S "TAMANGO" AND
ABOLITIONISM

The Story of Tamango according to Mérimée

Ledoux, a wily and experienced sea captain who lost a hand in the battle of Trafalgar (1805), is bored with the peace that breaks out in 1814. Having proved himself as a corsair, Ledoux is a natural for the rejuvenated, illegal trade in slaves that follows interdiction in 1815. Eluding British cruisers will be his specialty. Ledoux brings innovative engineering to the trade, finding a way to fill "empty" space in the hold and accommodate ten extra captives on a ship; he oversees the construction of a state-of-the-art slave-trading vessel and names it *L'Espérance* (Hope). As for the captives, Ledoux allows, they are "men like white men," but "when they get to the colonies ... they'll spend more than enough time on their feet!"[6] An evening at the theater in Nantes, watching fat people squeeze themselves into their seats, teaches him about "the compressibility of the human body" (PM, 483/76). The port inspectors in Nantes don't take any notice of the excessive stores of water or of the trunks filled with chains and handcuffs; *L'Espérance* sails away unimpeded.

On the coast of Senegal, with no British cruisers in sight, Ledoux can begin his trade. His African counterpart is Tamango, "a celebrated warrior and dealer in men," garbed in an old and ill-fitting uniform that is described in detail (PM, 481/74). Tamango has no stated political status; he is never identified as either king or chief, only as a "warrior." Tamango and Ledoux meet, size each other up, and drink brandy. Tamango orders his merchandise to be paraded in front of Ledoux; each captive bears a yoke that is six feet long and links him or her to the next captive. Through an interpreter (a Frenchman who is described as a "humane man" — *un homme humain*),[7] the two men bargain, and they continue to drink; but the more Ledoux drinks, the cleverer he gets in his dealings, while the alcohol has the opposite effect on Tamango. In the end 160 slaves are sold for what Mérimée represents as a pittance: some cotton cloth, three barrels of brandy, fifty shoddy guns, and a few other items. But thirty captives are left; remembering his night at the theater in Nantes, Ledoux adds twenty of them, and three children, to his load, which is already full. Tamango threatens to kill those who are left unpurchased, and he promptly murders the mother of the three children that Ledoux has just bought. In his drunkenness Tamango gives away one of his two wives. She is pretty, and Ledoux says with heavy innuendo, "I'll manage to find room for her," thus setting off the sexual tension between this woman, who is named Ayché, and the captain (PM, 484/77).

Waking up the next morning, Tamango is horrified to find he has given Ayché away; he paddles out to the *Espérance*. Ledoux sees his chance to make an extra one thousand *écus* and trepans Tamango, despite "heroic resistance" (PM, 485/78).

The ship sails away from the African coast, setting its course for Martinique. Ayché is granted special status: she alone is unchained and elegantly dressed, as she serves the captain. "It was evident that she performed important services for the captain" (PM, 487/80). Seeing this, Tamango threatens Ayché with the sorcery of "Mama-Jumbo," which is explained to the captain (and the reader) by the interpreter. Mama-Jumbo (Mérimée's variant of Mumbo-Jumbo) is represented as a *hoax* (something Mérimée knew about, as we will see)—a bogeyman, actually "some joker dressed up in a white sheet" (PM, 488/80, AT)—designed to frighten wives who contemplate adultery. Ayché is duly "petrified." The captain brings her to his cabin, but she is neither consolable nor "tractable" (*traitable*, PM, 489/82, AT). That night, the following sounds are heard: a low and solemn chant; the "hideously shrill scream of a woman"; Ledoux shouting threats; the crack of a whip; then silence. The next day Tamango appears on deck with a "bruised face" (*la figure meurtrie*) but looking proud and resolute. Ayché begs for his forgiveness; Tamango responds by demanding that she get him a file.

Tamango exhorts his people in the hold of the ship. He promises that after a revolt he will, using "occult sciences," be able to get them back to Africa. They are persuaded and swear an oath of solidarity; the *conjurés* (conspirators, as they are now called) are ready to rise up at any time. Ayché provides a file to Tamango, concealed inside a biscuit. On the eve of the revolt Tamango performs a phony ritual investing the file with magical powers, and the "primitive" deceit succeeds among "men [who are] more primitive still" (PM, 491/84).

Some of the captives have filed their leg irons to the breaking point. As Tamango sings "the warrior chant of his family," the rebels position themselves, surrounding the sailors. On a command from Tamango, they break their chains, unlock their comrades and begin killing their guards—"the European crew was doomed" (PM, 492/85). Tamango and Ledoux fight ferociously until the African bites through the Frenchman's jugular and finishes him off with a saber. The remaining crew members are "pitilessly slaughtered" and hacked to pieces. Then, tellingly, the Africans raise their eyes to the sails, which are still filled with the wind that is still bearing them toward "the land of slavery" (PM, 493/86, AT). A hundred voices now call on Tamango to steer the ship. At the helm Tamango confronts technology of which he has no knowledge. He pretends to read the compass, moving his lips in a pantomime and striking a pensive pose for his audience. Finally he jerks the tiller wheel, and the ship, driven in opposite directions by the current and the wind, lurches violently to one side, catapulting several men overboard. The masts crash to the deck.

Angry slaves now surround Tamango and denounce him as an imposter (PM, 494/88). He sold them in the first place, then incited revolt with false assurances of his *knowledge* (*savoir*). Tamango takes Ayché to the bow and isolates himself, with food, behind a wall of barrels and planks. Some of the Africans surround the compass, "whose continual movement they admired," while others break out the ship's supply of brandy and begin to drink. The "orgy" lasts several days; some commit suicide.

Tamango finally emerges and proposes that the remaining group of eighty take the small boats that are aboard the *Espérance* and row away "toward our country" (*notre pays*). "Insane," comments the narrator: they can only "wander aimlessly" (*errer à l'aventure*), because they are "ignorant of the use of the compass and with no knowledge of the stars." In any case, the Africans believe that "Blacks own the land and Whites live on their vessels" (PM, 496/90). The wounded and infirm are either abandoned or killed. Two vessels of unequal seaworthiness set off: Tamango and Ayché take their places in the bigger one. But the launch is soon swamped by a wave and capsizes; only twelve, including Tamango and Ayché, survive and make it back to reboard the *Espérance*. Another vessel passes in the night; the next morning Ayché is dead.

A line of suspension points marks the rest of the story as an epilogue. An unspecified amount of time later, an English frigate finds Tamango unconscious and emaciated aboard the *Espérance*. He regains "perfect health" by the time he is deposited at Kingston, Jamaica. The governor (the second *homme humain* in the story) resists planters' pressure to hang Tamango, seeing in his revolt both legitimate self-defense (*légitime défense*) and the welcome killing of some Frenchmen (a touch of Voltairean humor on Mérimée's part). Tamango is "freed" — "that is, they had him work for the government" (a dig at abolitionist hypocrisy?). Still handsome, Tamango is pressed into service as a cymbal player in a regiment. He drinks to excess and dies in a hospital "of a chest infection" (PM, 499/92).

In a reduced version of "Tamango" that may or may not have been altered by Mérimée himself, published in 1837, one sentence was added to the end: "The principal facts reported in this narration are historical."[8]

→>—<←

At this point I want to raise only one question, before looking into the context of "Tamango" and then returning to the tale itself. Bearing in mind the crucial historical junction at which it was published — in 1829, on the eve of the final and effective suppression of the French slave trade — is this an abolitionist work? There is an enduring tradition of interpreting it as such: the eminent André Billy wrote in 1959 that Mérimée had in "Tamango" surrendered his customary "skepticism and detachment" so that he might "add a building-block to the work of liberation"[9]—a view that some critics espouse even today.[10] The latest of the widely distributed Petits Classiques Larousse editions, dated 2000, states: "*Tamango* constitutes undeniably an exhibit [*une pièce à conviction*] in the prosecution of slavery and the slave trade."[11] And the current English edition of Mérimée's stories labels "Tamango" as "abolitionist propaganda."[12] Yet for Mérimée's biographer, A. W. Raitt, it is "anything but abolitionist propaganda."[13] What accounts for this divergence of views? If, as Eric Gans states, "Tamango" "articulates with rigor a coherent vision of the human condition" (for Gans, "a plea against slavery"), how can readings of it be so contradictory?[14] And, whether "abolitionist" or not, what is the relation of this tale to the discourse of abolition?

Mérimée in 1829

His career and his temperament suggest that Mérimée was both preoccupied by and profoundly ambivalent about issues of authenticity and otherness (or "local color," in vocabulary of his times). I will sketch a quick portrait of him using those two ideas—which are rather conventional in Mérimée studies—as my starting point. Born in 1803, the year of the Louisiana Purchase and one year after the reestablishment by Napoleon of slavery in the colonies, Mérimée grew up in a liberal household. His background was very different from that of the other writers of the Restoration that we have already studied, Staël and Duras. The Mérimée family lived in the Ecole des Beaux-Arts in Paris after Léonor Mérimée was named as its Permanent Secretary. As the son of an artist and art instructor, Prosper imbibed a reverence for the monuments of the past; he eventually made himself into an archaeologist. Yet the family was Voltairean and anticlerical in outlook. In 1823 Mérimée received a law degree, while reading as a voracious dilettante in a variety of fields. The gerontocratical Bourbon Restoration—with a king Mérimée referred to as a "fat pig"[15]—governed France from the abdication of Napoleon in 1814 until the July Revolution of 1830—thus during the entire time of Mérimée's intellectual formation and emergence as a writer, one of the "generation of 1820," which was, according to Benjamin Constant, "distinguished by its thirst for knowledge, its love of scholarship, and its devotion to the truth."[16]

But if the Restoration was reactionary, it was nonetheless a constitutional monarchy with (at least under Louis XVIII if not under the more *ultra* Charles X) a certain level of freedom of expression.[17] New currents of opinion about slavery and the slave trade were influenced by the lingering question of Haiti and the debate leading up to the "emancipation" (that is, recognition) of Haiti by Charles X in 1825 (at a cost: 150 million francs of "indemnification" to be paid by Haiti to the former planters of Saint-Domingue).[18] In this period particularly, it is impossible to interpret France in isolation: after Waterloo, British abolitionism — translated into the acts of the Congress of Vienna and backed up by British power on the high seas — was all but irresistible. The abolition of the slave trade became, finally, an issue in France. This would be a period in which the slave trade, slavery, and the memory of the Haitian Revolution would be on the agenda for debate among intellectuals. A number of prominent literary works bear witness to this: Duras's *Ourika* (1823) of course; but also Sophie Doin's *La Famille noire* (1825), Charles de Rémusat's (unperformed and unpublished but influential) play *L'Habitation de Saint-Domingue, ou l'insurrection* (1825), Hugo's *Bug-Jargal* (1826 in its expanded version), Baron Roger's *Kelédor* (1828), and "Tamango" (1829).[19] The poetry competition organized by the Académie Française in 1823 shows the vogue: its theme was "The Abolition of the Slave Trade."[20]

187

The old men of the Restoration gave members of Mérimée's generation plenty to rebel against, and he rose to the challenge in a peculiar way. The Restoration defined its own authenticity as a turning back of the clock to 1788 or earlier. The regime literally exhumed the past: as we saw in the passage from Chateaubriand's memoirs, the bodies of the guillotined royals were dug up — as if they could be revived — in 1815. In one sense the young Mérimée was in tune with this program: he would seek his authenticity in the past (in the *Chronique du règne de Charles IX* of 1829, for example). But in other, more innovative, aspects of his work — those which have had by far the most lasting cultural impact — he reached out in *space*, in encounters with the Other and masquerades as the Other. It is obviously that spatial gesture, reaching out beyond the borders of contemporary France, that produced "Tamango." In this, Mérimée was creative, even as he was following fashion.[21]

Mérimée's early literary production has a promiscuous geography: Spaniards in Denmark, Cuba, and Peru; North African Muslims in Spain; Napoleon's soldiers in Russia; poetry supposedly from Dalmatia, Croatia, and Herzegovina ("Illyria"); Corsica; and of course the Atlantic Africa of "Tamango."[22] France is represented only by the sixteenth century of Charles IX.

The only exception, the only representation of contemporary France, seems to be those glimpses of the docks and the theater of Nantes that figure in "Tamango."[23] That exception is strange and significant. Mérimée exploited all of these exotic settings before 1830, before he had traveled to any country except England. Looking back on this period later in life, Mérimée described his state of mind in 1827 as "dying to go where [local color] still existed; but it isn't found everywhere."[24]

The actual literary debut that Mérimée staged for himself presents a complex brainteaser of (in)authenticity and cultural otherness. The future inspector of historic monuments—the guarantor and protector of France's authenticity, which he becomes only five years after writing "Tamango" and only nine years after his first publication—began his literary career as the perpetrator of hoaxes, as the author of two deliberately *inauthentic* texts. In 1825 he published *Le Théâtre de Clara Gazul*, as the work of a Spanish actress of that name. To add to the fun, Mérimée included a portrait of himself in drag as Clara Gazul and wrote the preface under the apt pseudonym "Joseph L'Estrange." The publication was a transgender and transnational masquerade, even if Mérimée was widely known to be the author and almost no one was fooled.[25] Two years later he promulgated another, more elaborate, hoax, the unsigned but falsely "Illyrian" ballads of *La Guzla* (which were exposed by Goethe in 1828). Both *Gazul* and *Guzla* work across a north/south divide within Europe.[26]

So it can be said that, for lack of direct contact with "local color" before his voyages began, Mérimée made it up—based on his readings. I am not sure that sufficient attention has been paid to this author's penchant for jokes and hoaxes. Even "Tamango," with its deadly serious subject matter, owes something to this aspect of Mérimée's imagination, and I will return to that idea later. At this stage, then, Mérimée's exoticism (let's call it that) *without* travel is about to end. He is about to go to Spain for the first time and enter into a more profound engagement with that culture. In 1839 he will go to Corsica, and I think it is important to note that contact with the real Corsica will induce him to "correct" his representation of the island in later editions of "Mateo Falcone."[27] There will be no trip to Africa, however, and no "correction" of "Tamango."

In 1829 Mérimée was a dandy of few words, a well-connected salon maven with no visible means of support. This would be his *année miracle* as a writer. During that year, according to the biographer A. W. Raitt, his literary talent found full and immediate success—a success that he would have difficulty matching in later life: "When Mérimée first tried his hand at the short story early in 1829, he achieved mastery at one stroke."[28] Mérimée believed that an author should "get on with the story" (conter son affaire).[29] With a concision rarely seen in French literature and with an avowed "antipathy for stylistic brilliance,"[30] laying out the facts efficiently in front of his readers in a spare style, Mérimée renewed the genre of the short story in French, and "he hasn't been equaled since."[31] His early stories often assault the reader with otherness.[32] The aesthetic of assault seems often to be linked in Mérimée's mind to cultural otherness and to what has to be called primitivism.

This was part of Mérimée's appeal to his contemporaries. Sainte-Beuve, the literary arbiter of the day, relished the "debris of early folkways," the retrogression in Mérimée's works—whether they took place in the sixteenth century, in Corsica, or in Africa: all contexts of "primitive savagery." This author "who erases himself," the "least Christian artist" of his day, "became at will [se faisait à volonté] Spanish, Corsican, Illyrian, [and] African." This was for Sainte-Beuve a delightful "ironic revenge on the [nineteenth] century, . . . our blasé and flat [nivelée] era."[33]

Mérimée had, as Raitt puts it, a greater interest in effects than in causes. Raitt's psychological profile of Mérimée describes someone who is generally detached, an author who withholds judgment and refuses to identify himself with any of his characters.[34] In the next section, I will take this analysis one step further with regard to the pressing question of a different kind of cause: the moral cause of abolitionism.

After the July Revolution of 1830, with amazing speed and in a purposeful effort to gain status, Mérimée became a consummate careerist and a pillar of the new bourgeois, liberal monarchy of Louis-Philippe. He had been true to his liberal beliefs, even during the last years of the Restoration, when he declined a government position; later he was rewarded by the new, more liberal order.[35] He was named Inspector of Historic Monuments for all of France in 1834, inducted into the Académie des Inscriptions in 1843, and made an "Immortal" of the Académie Française in 1844 (thus immortalized at the age of forty-one). His steady, avuncular friendship with the Empress Eugénie, whose family he had met in Spain in 1830, helped enhance his position during the Second Empire. He died a wealthy man in the year of France's great defeat, 1870.

Mérimée, "Francophone" Writer

Before pursuing the task of situating Mérimée within his historical context, I would like to interject a transhistorical observation about his writing. The concerns with authenticity and otherness that I mentioned above place Mérimée in an unexpected alignment with authors whose existence he could not have dreamed of: the Francophone writers of the colonial and postcolonial eras. Like Mérimée and other French exoticist writers, many of these authors, particularly the early ones, would struggle to render in French realities that are not congruent with the norms of that language. What Léon Laleau described in the mid-twentieth century as painful and nearly impossible—

> do you feel the suffering
> And this despair beyond all others
> To tame with words from France
> This heart that came to me from Senegal?[36]

—later Francophone writers (beginning in the 1960s with Ahmadou Kourouma and continuing with writers such as Sony Labou Tansi and Patrick Chamoiseau) will revel in, exuberantly scrambling the politics of language. All Francophone writers have had to come to terms with the fundamental condition underpinning the representation of the colonial and postcolonial worlds in French: diglossia, the presence of at least one other language that, unlike French, is "native" to the area being represented. And, more generally speaking, all will feel some burden to represent distant places and "other" cultures to readers who are presumed not to know about them.[37] So it is interesting to take note of two moments in Mérimée's life as an author when he dealt with these issues.

In the story that lends its name to a collection in which "Tamango" has often been published, "Mateo Falcone," first published five months before "Tamango," Mérimée depicts Corsica.[38] The original subtitle of the story— "Mœurs de la Corse" (Manners of Corsica)—makes the agenda of cultural representation explicit. In this process he engages with the Corsican language and "imports" some of it, assimilating it or "digesting" it into the body of the French language for the first time. What he does with the word *maquis* in the opening paragraph is exemplary: "on se trouve sur le bord d'un *mâquis* très étendu. Le mâquis est la patrie des bergers corses" (you come to the edge of a very extensive *maquis*. The maquis is the home of the Corsican shepherds [PM, 451/54, AT]). At this point a word that was foreign, the Corsican *macchia*, has been introduced in a French form, first marked by the standard indicator of foreignness, italics. But immediately, in the next sentence, the italics disappear: *maquis* has been naturalized; it has become French. This happens even before Mérimée has explained to his readers exactly what this Corsican phenomenon is; a few lines later, after describing how Corsicans burn sections of their landscape in order to gain bare, fertilized ground, he provides his definition of *maquis*. In the burnt areas that grow wild again, a profusion of vegetation reaches a height of seven or eight feet: "This kind of dense brushwood is known as *mâquis*."[39] *Maquis* will lose the circumflex with which Mérimée decorated it and go on to have a long history as a perfectly French word (notably referring to the French Resistance in World War II).[40]

That literary technique, by which linguistic and cultural difference is processed into French, is a sign of linguistic transnationalism or creolization, and it will run like a strong current through both colonial and postcolonial literatures. This is how English embraced *pyjama* and *khaki*, and how French took on *bled*, *kif-kif*, *maboul*, and many other words. All of this of course takes place within a context of imperialism and colonialism. While Mérimée shares with future Francophone writers a concern with the accurate representation of otherness, his attitude toward Corsica in "Mateo Falcone" is imbued with superiority and a design to shock the reader. He makes it clear that he sees the *maquis* as entirely a product of Corsican laziness.[41] The apparently neutral linkage between France and Corsica indicated by the linguistic processing of vocabulary needs to be seen as in fact part of a larger, less innocent scheme.

191

In fact, a more radical interpretation of the process of linguistic assimilation might be suggested by things we have learned about the slave trade. *Traite* means extraction; these words are, in a real sense, extracted from colonized territories and taken into ownership by the French language. It may seem forced to describe them as "enslaved," but the idea is written into the history of language and politics.[42]

Mérimée was a processor of exotic information, of what he called local color, synonymous in his vocabulary with manners (*mœurs*).[43] And if we see in this example from "Mateo Falcone" a literary technique that later colonial and Francophone writers will exploit frequently,[44] it is equally interesting to see how, later in life, Mérimée already saw the "creolization" of French, which he had helped to propel, as having gone too far. In *Djoûmane*, the last tale Mérimée wrote, published posthumously in 1873, he represents Algeria, which in his lifetime had gone from the rule of the deys, then through a process of violent conquest beginning in 1830, to absorption into the body of the French state by *départementalisation*. Algeria became part of France just as *maquis* and, not coincidentally, *bled* became part of the French language. In this dreamlike tale, Mérimée continues his practice of importing local color through foreign vocabulary: *bournous, colback, marabout* (PM, 1092), *cheyk* (PM, 1095), the title itself (meaning pearl or jewel), and other Arabic terms appear, in roman, not italic type. The relation of language to colonialism here is clearly implied by the annotation of the word *bournous* in the Pléiade edition: "The word was introduced in France following the [French] occupation of Algeria" (PM, 1654). The forced intimacy between France and "French" Algeria perhaps made italics seem superfluous.

In light of that linguistic practice, it is amusing to read in a letter by Mérimée that was published in 1871 the following sarcastic remarks about French journalists' writings on Algeria: "Je lisais, il y a peu de temps dans un journal, que 'le goum de Tlemcen réuni au maghzen avait fait une razzia sur les . . . à la suite de quoi une diffa avait été offerte au kaïd.' Franchement, il faut être un peu arabisant pour comprendre ce français-là" ("I was reading recently in a newspaper that 'the goum [native contingent] of Tlemcen had joined with the maghzen [cavalry] to stage a razzia [raid] on the . . . [,] following which a diffa [feast] had been offered to the kaïd [chief].' Frankly, you have to be quite a student of Arabic to understand that type of French."[45] Through his literary practice, then, Mérimée anticipated and, arguably, influenced the representation of the world beyond the hexagon in French-language writings. He was a proto-Francophone writer. But in this letter he evokes the fear of going too far, of an excess of foreign elements that could overwhelm French. And overwhelming the French is, of course, exactly what the captive Africans in "Tamango" do.

The linguistic politics of "Tamango" are quite different from those of "Mateo Falcone" or *Djoûmane*. The intimacy that characterized French relations with North Africa (and Corsica) will never be matched south of the Sahara; no territory of Black Africa will become a *département* of France, and fewer vocabulary words will be assimilated into French from sub-Saharan languages. So it is not surprising to see in "Tamango" in 1829, long before the height of the French presence in West Africa, few traces of African languages or cultures. Thus, although "Tamango" is nearly contemporaneous with Roger's *Kelédor*, Mérimée will of course show nothing like the knowledge of Africa that Roger was able to display. There are three linguistic exceptions in "Ta͟ngo": the word *guiriot* (one of the slaves that Tamango threatens to kill ᵈuring the bargaining process is identified as a griot [484]); *balafos* (a type o͟ᵈlophone that the interpreter says he has heard in Africa [488]); and the c͟e that the interpreter saw, referred to as the "*folgar*, as they say in their ͟ͅon" (488). These are all signs of Mérimée's limited but intrigued engageᵐᵉnt with the African cultural terms that were available to him. Mérimée probably picked up these terms from his reading of the *Nouvelle relation de l'Afrique occidentale*, which was one hundred years old, by the slave-trading priest Labat, whose works have crossed this study so many times already.⁴⁶ He may well have contemplated the illustration of the *balafo* in that book.⁴⁷ *Guiriot*, *balafos*, and *folgar* are italicized in "Tamango," and Mérimée offers contextual explanations or synonyms rather than annotations.⁴⁸ Most of the linguistic hurdles that Mérimée delights in throwing in front of the readers of "Tamango" are from a different domain, that of seafaring. As required by the genre of *littérature maritime*, the text bristles with nautical terms, which are not italicized: *aide-timonier*, *écubiers*, *lougre*, *vergues*, and others. Together with the African elements of local color, these are all signs of the authenticity and otherness that are the hallmarks of Mérimée's exoticism.

193

But the most important sign of Africanist local color that Mérimée exploits in "Tamango" is "Mama-Jumbo." The British explorer Mungo Park was the first to report to the Western world on many aspects of West African culture; his *Travels in the Interior Districts of Africa . . . in the Years 1795, 1796, and 1797* was one of the few works offering recent, firsthand information about Africa that were available in Europe in the early nineteenth century. The fact that Park traveled through West Africa with a slave-trading coffle—bonding with both "slatees" (captors) and captives and even making the Middle Passage, reporting on its horrors—made him an indispensable source for abolitionists. His work was translated into French immediately and was widely read and quoted. Two sections of Park's account seem to have made the greatest impression: one on "Mumbo-Jumbo," the other the tragic story of a captive African woman named Nealee (which was important to the abolitionists, as I will discuss below). "Mumbo-Jumbo," which had been described by previous travelers and reported in the *Encyclopédie*, was a practice allegedly used by husbands to control their wives.⁴⁹ Mérimée's reprise of this account is typical of the way he often worked, appropriating reports that were available to him, processing them into the local color that was essential to his narrative style. But of course it becomes more than that in "Tamango": Mérimée uses this for two main purposes. On the one hand, this rather long embedded tale told by the interpreter — who has seen the Mama-Jumbo hoax himself and seen *through* it — seems to be designed to substantiate one essential allegation: that Africans are stupid ("But the Blacks are simple-minded, they don't understand anything" [PM, 488/81, AT]). That idea will be essential to the unfolding of the plot because it "establishes" the inability of Africans to handle their own affairs. The other purpose of the Mama-Jumbo story is to propel the plot forward: it is the device used by Tamango to assert his lordship over Ayché, against his rival, Ledoux; and it leads directly to her procurement of the file that makes the revolt possible.

Mérimée's literary policy of local color thus had many effects. It led him to an engagement with the world outside contemporary France that was initially (as of 1829) based only on reading and research, not on firsthand observation. He "didn't need" to see Spain or Corsica or Africa in order to reveal their essential characteristics, as one biographer put it.[50] He mined otherness in texts. Hence the importance of sleuthing Mérimée's "sources" to shed light on his works, a topic to which I will return below. As we have seen, the practice of local color seems to have forced Mérimée to confront issues of cultural representation and diglossia that will later preoccupy Francophone writers. But the racist use that Mérimée makes of the Mumbo-Jumbo story shows that he was a creature of *certain aspects* of his own times, times that I now want to discuss in more detail.

Restoration and "Abolition"

What avenues of thought were available to Mérimée in the 1820s? In "Tamango" — the product of this author who "invented nothing" — are we seeing merely the involuntary imprint of his times? I do not think that it is that simple: there were numerous currents of thought about the slave trade and about Africans, and Mérimée obviously had his preferences.

The Bourbon Restoration (1814–30, with a brief interruption by Napoleon's Hundred Days in 1815) was the era during which the second French abolitionist movement arose — of necessity — organized itself, and gained a certain level of influence. Mérimée frequented intellectual salons where famous abolitionists (the Baron de Staël, Fanny Wright) were known to hold forth; he "was accustomed to hearing slave-trading indignantly condemned as a degrading and inhuman practice."[51] He may well have known Victor Schoelcher, whose first journey to slave-holding societies took place the year "Tamango" was published. A friend's father, Philippe Albert Stapfer, a Swiss Protestant pastor, was one of the founders of the Société de la Morale Chrétienne, the first organization in nineteenth-century France that was (partly) devoted to the abolition of the slave trade. Emerging from an unusual alliance of French Protestants and Catholics, the society took shape in 1821 and remained influential during the rest of the decade.[52] According to Lawrence C. Jennings, the membership of the society was a "veritable Who's Who of the leaders of the liberal opposition in the 1820's and of the future governing elite of the July Monarchy"—including the Duc de Broglie, Baron Auguste de Staël, Benjamin Constant, Adolphe Thiers, the husband of Sophie Doin, and even the future king, Louis-Philippe himself. Charles de Rémusat, the author of *L'Habitation de Saint Domingue*, was a leading member. The society "deigned not appeal to public opinion because of its own elitist orientation," but it "exercised considerable moral and political sway during the last decade of the Restoration."[53] (It is important to note that the Société de la Morale Chrétienne formed an anti-slave-trade committee, with Auguste de Staël at its head, in 1822, but added the abolition of slavery itself to its agenda only in 1829.)[54]

Does Mérimée's personal acquaintance with these personalities somehow make his text, "Tamango," abolitionist? Certain interpreters would have us believe this theory, according to which Mérimée's story, furthermore, seems almost magically to give impetus to the abolition of the French slave trade in 1831: *post hoc ergo propter hoc*.[55] I will examine the story itself in detail below, but for the moment I want to dispel the idea that its author had any credentials as an actual abolitionist (which is of course a separate issue).

In spite of liberal affinities he must have shared with many members of the Société de la Morale Chrétienne, there is no evidence that Mérimée ever joined.[56] He was, first of all, hardly of the *notable* class that filled the society's rosters with titles and *particules*. But another factor sets Mérimée apart from the abolitionists of his day—from Broglie, Staël, and Sophie Doin, not to mention Britons like Wilberforce: he was distinctly not religious and in fact "violently anticlerical."[57] There will be no preaching from Mérimée.

As for the French abolitionist movement during the Restoration, it is important to keep in mind, for starters, that the impetus for the abolition of the French slave trade came largely from Britain, which had defeated France at Waterloo, which had recently been an occupying power, and which held sway over France and influenced its newly restored monarchy. Britain's genuine *mass* protest movement put pressure on France. No such popular

195

movement or concatenation — flowing out of a participatory moral zeal that was distinctly Protestant — ever arose in France. The Abbé Henri Grégoire deplored this disequilibrium at the moment of the 1814 Treaty of Paris, when France obtained an extension on the slave trade: "Can one cite a single petition from a city or a guild opposed to the article of the treaty that relates to the slave trade, an article which, in England, stirred so many souls? Instead, we have the deplorable scandal of a petition that came from Nantes, asking for the continuation of the misfortunes of Africa, in order to enrich a few Europeans."[58] It was, indeed, three quarters of a million *Britons*, not French people, who signed petitions urging *French* abolition of the slave trade in 1814. "In France," lamented the abolitionist Duc de Broglie, "nothing of this sort took place."[59] Efforts led by the elite to produce similar petitions in France in the 1820s collected the signatures of only 42 Parisians in 1825, 130 Parisians in 1826, 49 merchants of Le Havre in 1826 — all "orchestrated" by the Société de la Morale Chrétienne.[60] It wasn't until 1844, in the lead-up to the final abolition of slavery itself, that a grander gesture, a petition for the abolition of slavery, was signed by seven thousand French workers ("guided" by one thousand intellectuals).[61] The intractable apathy of the French public toward the abolition of the slave trade may have been rooted, at least partially, in government censorship of antislavery publications (WC, 188). An abolitionist pamphlet of 1823 (*L'Affaire de "La Vigilante,"* which I discussed in the last chapter) suggested that "only ignorance of the facts can explain the tepid nature of [French] opinion on this question."[62] Anglophobia certainly played a role, as well. Abolition of the slave trade was, after all, associated in the minds of Frenchmen with Napoleon's defeat and with a British thirst for hegemony.[63] Abolitionism "had always been branded as an English plot."[64]

The abolitionist movement in France was an affair conducted by and among members of the elite, many of them royalists, unlike their predecessors in the first abolition of 1794, whose revolutionary names they could not mention. The Abbé Grégoire was the only survivor of the first movement who continued the struggle — but, as a "regicide," he was considered not *fréquentable* by the elite of the Restoration. Their ideology was generally inflected with a religious moralism that had direct ties to British and French Protestantism. Altogether, French abolitionism formed a "diffuse" movement that owed much to England.[65]

It is also essential to recall that "abolition" in the early nineteenth century was almost universally seen among slaveholding nations as, at best, a two-step process, with the elimination of the slave *trade* taking precedence over the actual and complete abolition of slavery as an institution. Hence the importance of the Restoration and the early 1830s to the subject of this book: the trade was question, under attack, and finally officially abolished. As we will see, much of the abolitionism that marked the period, while vehement in its opposition to the slave trade, assumed and accepted that slavery itself should be both "improved" and continued. The very humanity of Africans was still a matter for debate. It was thought that the condition of slaves should be softened; eventually they might become wage laborers. Cutting off the transatlantic supply of slaves might force better treatment of slaves already in the colonies. It was the horrors of the slave trade that preoccupied liberal consciences and imaginations in the 1820s. Thus the poetry competition of 1823 had as its prescribed subject the abolition of the slave *trade*, not the abolition of slavery. In the 1820s France was not yet ready to contemplate the abolition of slavery itself; the voices that dared raise this question were suppressed.[66]

It was during the Restoration that the slave trade would become, by fits and starts, officially illegal in the French Empire. But at the beginning of the regime, neither Louis XVIII nor his foreign minister, Talleyrand, viewed abolition with any enthusiasm. This may have been because, while moral ideology moved for abolition, political facts on the ground took a turn in a different direction. The ambiguity can be seen in the acts that followed the definitive fall of Napoleon. The Congress of Vienna condemned the slave trade in 1815 and began the process of its suppression, but in May 1814 the Treaty of Paris had already given France back its colonies and thereby *restored* the French Atlantic triangle. By giving Martinique, Guadeloupe, and Senegal (including Gorée) back to France, the treaty re-created the conditions of possibility of the French Atlantic economy, and the reality of a renewed, if illicit, slave trade was quick to follow. As the abolitionist Duc de Broglie said in 1822, "The renewal of peace in Europe [in 1814] rang in the renewal of the slave trade."[67]

While British moral and naval power militated for the abolition of the trade, the merchant class of Nantes urged the opposite. Talleyrand negotiated a five-year extension on the French slave trade, which Wilberforce denounced as the return of "the angel of death" (T, 584). After Waterloo, Louis XVIII and France were forced to be abolitionist. But this reluctant French abolition led to great ambivalence in France's posture and considerable ambiguity in its practices. As a forced "convert" to the abolition of

197

the trade, France was generally lax in enforcement—which the British were supposed to take care of anyway, according to the provisions of the Congress of Vienna. When the first French law prescribed enforcement of the ban on the slave trade, the punishment was less severe than for stealing a loaf of bread.[68]

Thus, a figure who sounds a lot like Mérimée's Captain Ledoux tested the waters of the trade in this new context of ambiguous illegality and found them quite navigable. Robert Surcouf was a famous *armateur* of Saint-Malo in this period; Hugh Thomas calls him "the father of this new stage of the French slave trade." During the Napoleonic Wars, like Ledoux, Surcouf was a *corsaire*; he captured many English vessels, which made him a national hero. Two months after Waterloo, in August 1815, when France was vacillating about the abolition of the slave trade, Surcouf sent his ship *L'Affriquain* to Angola, and the Ministry of Marine "had no idea what to do." According to Thomas, this signaled to all concerned that the slave trade was open again.[69]

The Duc de Broglie blew the whistle on this revival of the slave trade in 1822, in a speech to the Chambre des Pairs. The French slave trade, he asserted, "goes on without interruption, in broad daylight, almost without any need for disguise" ("Discours," 15–16). In the last ten months the trade had been renewed in Nantes, Le Havre, and Bordeaux (26). If slavery itself was "an evil for which immediate liberty is not the remedy, an evil from which we must, with lament, avert our eyes for many more years" (7), the slave trade was another matter. France, he thundered, was "the only state which has not sanctioned the abolition of the trade with serious corporal penalties. . . . We must follow the example of the nations that surround us" (72, 77).

France actually declared the trade illegal in 1818, but, as we have seen, this was only one of many incremental steps toward actual abolition. Thus in 1819, even as French *négriers* were being intercepted on the coast of Africa and in the Indian Ocean by both the British and the French navies, fifty-six slave-trading expeditions left French ports. This represents a radical increase over the previous year, in which twenty-nine voyages were outfitted. From 1814 to 1825, there were 472 French expeditions to Africa "suspected" of slave trading; from 1820 to 1826 the illegal trade was at its "apogee."[70] During the Restoration, 318 slave-trading ships sailed out of Nantes alone, 40 of them in the final years between 1827 and 1830; numerous others plied the "forbidden" route directly between the Antilles and Africa.[71] Among the ships of the French slave trade in 1819, two were named *L'Espérance*, one of which sailed from Nantes, making a triangular voyage to Africa, Cuba, and home.[72] The illegal trade made perfect material for a literature of seafaring adventures and contributed to a "vogue of the maritime novel."[73] We will see more of this in connection with Eugène Sue's *Atar-Gull* and Edouard Corbière's *Le Négrier*.

This period is thus one of many contradictions. Within it the French voices of abolition — the Baron de Staël, the Duc de Broglie — did their best to influence events, although they had nothing like the influence of their British counterparts and models, Wilberforce and Clarkson. When abolitionists like Broglie assume power under Louis-Philippe in 1830, things will change, and the French slave trade, though not slavery itself, will finally end.[74] In 1830, however, the French abolition of slavery is still eighteen long years away.

The Slave Trade and/as Piracy

If the slave trade is outlawed, only outlaws will trade in slaves: that is the logic of the connection between piracy and slave trading in nineteenth-century French maritime life and literature. Piracy and the slave trade had been intertwined since the seventeenth century: pirates infested both the Gulf of Guinea and the Caribbean; some slave traders turned pirate; and some pirates stole cargoes of slaves, which were a "particularly attractive quarry."[75] The "nomadism, errancy, and intemperance of the pirates" posed a threat to the working order of the *Exclusif* and colonial settlements.[76] With the interdiction(s) of the slave trade that followed Waterloo, the French slave trade entered a period of clandestine intrigue. The new illegality of the trade made slave traders *into* pirates; pirates therefore flocked to the slave trade. Seamen who happened to be expert at evading pursuit were in demand; corsairs and freebooters were perfectly qualified. Edouard Corbière, a former sea captain whose novel we will be reading, observed the prominence of former corsairs in the Restoration slave trade: "the slave-trading captains who inundated the Antilles after the peace of 1814 had almost all been corsairs in Europe during the war."[77] When *la course* (corsairing or maritime pillaging) was made illegal by France in 1825, even more corsairs turned to the slave trade.[78] Since British ships were enforcing the ban on the high seas, slave trading, for many in France, appeared as a form of insurgency and resistance to the hegemony of perfidious Albion.

The new, illegal French slave trade provided a rich context for the exploits of swashbuckling heroes like Mérimée's Ledoux, Sue's Brulart (in *Atar-Gull*), and Corbière's Léonard (in *Le Négrier*). This backdrop was conducive to the vogue of the maritime novel in the 1830s. In 1835, boulevard playwrights Desnoyers and Alboize created out of whole cloth a figure of which there is no historical record: a French naval officer who, ashamed of his complicity in the slave trade, turns into a slave-rescuing pirate, a sort of Robin Hood of the slave trade. The hero, named Léonard like the protagonist of Corbière's *Le Négrier*, declaims to his men, "Yes, I have made myself into a pirate, and I will take you anywhere that there are enemies to fight and slaves to set free, for a freebooter has his own glory and honor. . . . I swear, for my part, eternal war on the slave trade!"[79]

In the late 1820s and the 1830s both piracy and the French slave trade were in the process of fading away in real life; this was thus the perfect time to preserve them, together, in literature.

"Sources"

Critics of my generation were taught to smirk at the idea of literary sources and to put quotation marks around the term. The hunt for sources was thought to exclude critical thinking about texts themselves. (In a later section of this chapter we will see how the contemporary Senegalese novelist Boris Boubacar Diop mocks the "sourcing" of literature.) But the idea that literary ideas have genealogies—that texts are in part derived from previous texts—is too compelling and too important to give up. It would be sheer folly to read Mérimée, of all authors, without reference to the sources of his ideas and images, for he is said to have "invented nothing" in his writings. "Je crois qu'il a peu créé," sniffed one critic in 1853; another restated this enduring idea in 1933: "Mérimée had no imagination, . . . and never invented a story."[80] In 1829, the year of "Tamango," Mérimée stated, "What I love in history is only the anecdotes."[81] Although I will ultimately argue that Mérimée invented plenty in "Tamango," I would nonetheless like to look briefly at a few of his possible sources. These works are relevant not only to the fabric of this short story but also to the wider theme of this study. Mérimée's sources (works he most probably read) and intertexts (works that simply bear some resemblance to his, whether they were known to him or not) amount to a compendium of literature about the slave trade and its most dramatic theme, revolt. Where did the "anecdote" of "Tamango" come from, and what involvement with the Atlantic triangle is visible in Mérimée's intertexts?

Reading Mérimée in context has already taken us back into the history of representations of the slave trade and to the climate of restrained abolitionism in France of the 1820s. Mérimée's reputation as a reader who simply reinvents what he has read is of particular importance in the context of European knowledge about Africa. That body of knowledge was, as we have seen, largely held hostage in the eighteenth century by slave traders (virtually the only Europeans to see Africa).[82] In the early nineteenth century there could be no statements made about Africa in France that did not in some way derive from sources that were involved in the slave trade; Labat, one of Mérimée's apparent sources of Africanist local color, is the most compelling example.

During times of abolitionism the idea of Africa was hotly contested. The slave trade and slavery could only be abolished if Africa and Africans could be successfully represented as being worthy of such a "gift." During the period of gestation for "Tamango" this was being debated in France and England. Proslavery writers represented Africans as "brutal beasts," living in "the stupidest ignorance."[83] On the other side, Clarkson, in *The Cries of Africa*, defended the moral character of Africans (based on Mungo Park's accounts of their goodness and generosity, even in adversity) and argued that slave traders were "guilty of the crime of having retarded the civilisation of Africa for nearly three hundred years." And the Protestant Duc de Broglie, in his famous speech of 1822, invoked Africa as a place ripe for conversion to Christianity; what the British had already done in Sierra Leone for emancipated slaves could be reproduced elsewhere in Africa.[84] This gesture reflects in microcosm the double-edge sword of slave-trade abolitionism, which often called for the European colonization of Africa. Broglie's mother-in-law, Madame de Staël (also Protestant), had argued in 1814 that the abolition of the slave trade would "sway the hearts of those to whom the Gospel will be preached."[85] Thus the rationale that, according to legend, had been used by Louis XIII to justify the establishment of the French slave trade — the conversion of Africans — was now dusted off to support the abolition of the same slave trade. Proof that slave-trade abolitionism and the colonization of Africa were twins born from the same egg is found in this single sentence by Charles de Rémusat in an article about Sierra Leone in the journal of the Société de la Morale Chrétienne: "In order to destroy the slave trade, we see that it is necessary to advance the level of the civilization of whites, and to build the beginnings of the civilization of the blacks."[86]

The abolitionist poetry of the 1823 Academy contest traded on the image of a fallen, victimized Africa filled with, first and most important, *human* peoples, who also happen to be pacific; the noble savage got a new lease on life: "They are black, it is true, but is it by color that God measures the grandeur of his goodness?"[87] "God . . . did not say: Be born for slavery!"[88] "The Negro . . . dares to plant his field, dares to be a husband and a father."[89] "Thus these brotherly tribes lived in peace / When the monsters of Europe disembarked on their shores."[90] The pious sincerity of this poetry represents the polar opposite of Mérimée's narrative attitude in "Tamango." But, as we will see in more detail, Mérimée's rejection of this romantic sentimentalism goes beyond mere tone; his most notable Africans are not peaceable victims but also "monsters" themselves.

The key player in the abolitionist cast of characters was the African prince fallen into slavery; his status somehow allowed Europeans to identify with the suffering of Africans, thus creating moments of empathetic closure of the Atlantic triangle. The figure of the enslaved African prince reaches back to Aphra Behn's *Oroonoko*, and was current enough in Restoration France for the sixteen-year-old Victor Hugo to build his first *Bug-Jargal* around 1818.[91] J. J. V. Chauvet's *Abolition de la traite des Noirs*, the winner of the poetry contest, features an African heroine taken from the pages of Clarkson's *The Cries of Africa* (where she is imported, with acknowledgment, from Mungo Park). Chauvet's Néali, unlike Park's and Clarkson's (who dies in the interior of Africa), is found on a slave-trading ship, where she defends herself against the sexual violence of the captain, pronounces a stirring tirade against the slave trade, then defies the captain to torture her. In the hold a male captive named Sélim, hearing Néali's cries, leads a general uprising that ends in a massacre of the captives. The issue of a slave-trading captain's sexual assault on a female captive—specifically as a provocation for a slave revolt—is thus raised in 1823. That theme will loom large in Mérimée's "Tamango," as well as in Berry's film. But the plot of the film follows the story of Chauvet's poem, not that of Mérimée's tale, ending in a massacre of the revolted captives that is nonetheless a moral victory; the captives in Berry's film echo those in Chauvet's poem, who have "died for liberty."[92]

In a poem that was submitted for the contest but never published, we find one of the most important elements—perhaps the most indelible image—in Mérimée's "Tamango," the ship of revolted slaves, adrift in the Atlantic: "They found the magic, devouring water / Which pierces the heart with an intoxicating flame."[93] Mérimée, who must have read at least some of these poems, was not "buying" their discourse of pity—certainly not on its own terms. His representation of Africa and of Africans owes nothing more than superficial images to abolitionist discourse. He read the same sources that the abolitionist poets read (Clarkson, Park) and picked up some of the same figures; it seems highly likely that he read the poems of 1823 that were published (five out of the fifty-four poems). But he put the figures that he found in those and other sources, I will argue, to an essentially different and perverse use. He was immune to their passion and to the substance of the abolitionist cause. He pored over these documents, gleaning images, colors, sights, and sounds that he could cut and paste into "Tamango," but he left out the moral import.

I want to revie v the most significant of the sources of "Tamango" as quickly as possible 'n chronological order, and comment on Mérimée's use of them, including both the texts that are associated with abolitionism and those that are not. I will not include those that I have already discussed, such as Park and Clarkson.⁹⁴

Aphra Behn's *Oroonoko* is the recognized progenitor of abolitionist literary heroes. But in 1688 (as opposed to either 1829 or now) it may have been easier to accept the idea that Behn produced: that of an African *slave-trading* prince, who, like Tamango, is himself enslaved, but who, unlike Tamango, is converted into a mouthpiece for (very early, very limited) *anti-slavery* sentiment. The figure of Oroonoko was well known in France since the story's translation in 1745 and through subsequent adaptations. But in contrast to another Restoration writer who borrows from Behn — Hugo in *Bug-Jargal* — Mérimée attributes power alone, without nobility either of rank or of character, to his African protagonist. Tamango is a simple "warrior" and completely ignoble.⁹⁵

Daniel Defoe's novel *The Life, Adventures, and Piracies of the Famous Captain Singleton* is a remarkable artifact within the history of Africanist discourse and the history of slave-trade literature. It has been identified as a source of "Tamango" because of an episode in which Captain Singleton's vessel encounters a ship of six-hundred revolted slaves adrift off the coast of South America. "I was struck with horror at the sight," says the captain-narrator, "for immediately I concluded, as was partly the case, that these black devils had got loose, had murdered all the white men, and thrown them into the sea."⁹⁶ Singleton's mate William, a Quaker, relativizes the slaves' actions, persuading the crew not to kill the slaves summarily because it is only natural for slaves to revolt: "the negroes had really the highest injustice done to them, to be sold for slaves without their consent; and that the law of nature dictated it to them" (209). What ensues is a fascinating process by which Singleton and William eventually achieve communication with the slaves across a language barrier that is given careful attention and treated with respect; they teach English to some of the slaves in order to hear their story; punishment is suspended until the story can be told. At that point the emphasis shifts to the Africans' ignorance of navigation: "'They no understand; they no know what the sails do'" (218). Africans' ignorance of European vessels and tools of navigation emerges in this text as a theme that Mérimée will exploit to a far greater extent: this particular limitation of knowledge seems to be an insinuation of far deeper forms of ignorance. (Césaire will be very sensitive to this accusation and will respond.)

Haplessly, the revolted slaves in *Captain Singleton* only wanted to "go home to their own country again" (218). They have no singular leader: no Oroonoko, no Tamango. But, having given voice to abolitionist sentiments and having evinced a cross-cultural understanding of the Africans' point of view—including an acknowledgment of their languages—Defoe has his Quaker efficiently sell all the slaves for a tidy profit. "William passed for what he was—I mean, for a very honest fellow" (220). Here, then, is an "anecdote" for Mérimée. The story of a slave revolt gone adrift is reproduced, but the gestures of understanding between Europeans and Africans that Defoe sketched out are absent in "Tamango."

Count Louis-Marie-Joseph Ohier de Grandpré, a former slave trader himself, published *Voyage à la côte occidentale d'Afrique*, which included a "précis de la traite des Noirs." This may be the work from which Mérimée got his knowledge of the "fork" used to constrain captives by the neck. Grandpré's book contains an illustration in which the graceful posture of both captor and captive belie the violence that is being represented (see figure 8). The book amounts to a form of confession: Grandpré tells of having "traded" (*traité*) fifteen hundred slaves in 1787 alone and of having seen "often many cruelties." He estimates that millions of Africans have been sacrificed.[97] Here again we see Mérimée capture an image, a term—*fourche*—and its precise definition, from a source, while ignoring the abolitionist content and message of the earlier text.

Three years before the publication of "Tamango," Auguste de Staël renewed the challenge to France that his brother-in-law, Broglie, had launched in 1822. Staël traveled to Nantes personally and returned with proof of what many had suspected: that the slave trade went on. "A stay of forty-eight hours in Nantes was sufficient to offer in abundance the material proof that

8 "Noir au bois Mayombe" [A Black in the Forest of Mayombe (Congo)]. From Louis-Marie-Joseph Ohier de Grandpré, *Voyage à la Côte occidentale d'Afrique* (Paris: Dentu, 1801), 2:49. Detail. Courtesy of the Yale University Library.

205

I was looking for," he reported to the Société de la Morale Chrétienne. "The illusory law that prohibits the slave trade has only redoubled its horrors. They pile into the filthy holds of these ships a number of slaves that is triple that which the old ordinances allowed." A dramatic illustration is provided, showing a ship's hold in cross section, loaded with captives. Staël provided statistics and physical evidence, documenting the use of chains, handcuffs, and "an apparatus called the 'bar of justice' [*barre de justice*]," which appears in "Tamango." He appended an explanation by a Nantes blacksmith of how these devices worked, along with illustrations.[98] These allegations about the increased packing of captives in the illegal trade clearly underpin Mérimée's creation of Captain Ledoux and his clever ideas, and some of the vernacular language of the slave trade (*barre de justice*) evidently comes from Staël. This is yet another instance in which abolitionist discourse is mined for its information, its colorful terms and anecdotes, while its moral point is left behind.

One of the most remarkable documents from this period of the French slave trade, often cited as a source of "Tamango," is a treatise on insurance by Balthazard-Marie Emerigon. Insurance for losses associated with the slave trade was a crucial issue, particularly as abolitionist thought called into question the status of captives as property.[99] Emerigon's treatise navigates its way through these questions, finding in the Code Noir's declaration that slaves are moveable property justification for insuring captives.[100] But what to do in cases of revolt—are those losses covered? In the process of addressing this thorny issue, Emerigon narrates the anecdote that Mérimée exploited in "Tamango." It concerns a ship named the *Comte d'Estaing*, which set sail from the coast of Africa with thirty-three captives onboard, bound for the French islands. Its crew was weakened by fevers caught on the "deadly shores" of Africa (393). During the Middle Passage the captives revolted, and what ensued will be recognizable to readers of "Tamango": "The Negroes, freed from the presence of the French crew, for a while enjoyed the freedom that they had fought for. *But they were ignorant of the art of navigation.* The brigantine followed an uncertain course. It crashed onto the rocky shore of one of the Caicos Islands, where the Negroes took refuge. An English boat from Bermuda was in the area. The captain of this boat removed everything from the brigantine and set the ship on fire" (393). Emerigon ponders the question of whether this loss should be covered by insurance and makes this remarkable statement: "When one takes Negroes on board, they are one's enemies" ("Quand on embarque des nègres, ce sont des ennemis qu'on embarque") (394). In March 1776 the admiralty decided that a slave revolt is a "fortune of the sea" and is therefore insured.[101]

A final example: Joseph Elzéar Morenas was one of the few French slave-trade abolitionists who had any impact before the rise of the Société de la Morale Chrétienne in 1822; he was a genuine whistle-blower. Morenas worked as an "agriculteur-botaniste" in Senegal from August 1818 to October 1819 and observed firsthand the continuation of the illegal slave trade. He returned to France with what Serge Daget calls "dangerous information," capable of compromising the colonial governor, Schmaltz. He dined often with Grégoire while plotting his moves (a sign of his lack of powerful connections in the Restoration power structure).[102] Fired by the Ministry of the Marine in 1820, Morenas published an attack on the illegal French slave trade in a London newspaper, describing "shameful violations of the law and of justice that are being practiced in Senegal."[103] Then he filed his first petition with the Chambre des Députés, which "feigned to consider it as baseless."[104] He quickly followed it with a second petition, this time to the Chambre des Pairs as well; it too was rejected. Official France did not want to hear about the illegal slave trade in 1820 or 1821. Then in March 1822 the Duc de Broglie took over as the chief voice of French abolitionism, and in his famous speech he shamed the Chambre for having ignored Morenas's petition.[105] Broglie's social standing would carry the issue forward in a way that the impolitic Morenas could not.

But Morenas had not finished his work. In 1828 he published a remarkable compendium of his findings, which stands today as a rare *French* exposé of the illegal French slave trade, not based on information from British abolitionists—the first of its kind. Mérimée quite possibly read it as he wrote "Tamango." The *Précis historique de la traite des Noirs et de l'esclavage colonial* concludes what Morenas calls his "affaire de noirs." Claiming twenty years of experience in various colonies around the globe, Morenas aims to counter the accusation that critics of the slave trade are people who have "never left Europe."[106] The slave trade is a fundamental wrong with no basis in any religion, both a cause and a consequence of genocide. As I discussed earlier in this study, Morenas is the only voice in any century who refutes Labat's myth of Louis XIII and the authorization of the slave trade, asserting that there was no authorization until 1670, under Louis XIV (206). Louis XIII is for Morenas a "defender of the blacks" (94). Morenas proceeds into an economic argument for the abolition of the trade but, fitting the pattern of the 1820s, not of slavery itself: the slave trade is immoral (365), but it is also "impolitic because it is unproductive" (363). The trade feeds a system that kills slaves in the colonies; eliminate the trade and slavery will necessarily be "softened" and made more palatable; the slaves will flourish and multiply. Creole slaves are less likely to revolt (381). "Do you want gold? Then treat your slaves well, educate them, and they will earn it for you" (*Précis*, 351–55). (Morenas, like the Baron Roger, had big plans for colonizing Africa and establishing productive plantations there.) With the elimination of the trade the Code Noir, a "monument to the wisdom of Louis XIV and Colbert," could be put back in force (386)—a clear sign of how much separates the abolitionism of 1828 from that of 1848.[107]

What is the import of Morenas's book for a reading of "Tamango" and its context? The pattern here remains the same: there is reason to suspect that Mérimée used Morenas as a source of information, but again, the passionate moral thrust of the source disappears, replaced by irony. The mere fact of a continuing, illegal French slave trade is the main connection between Morenas's *Précis* and Mérimée's "Tamango": "His Majesty Charles X has manifested his royal will, the ministers have promulgated orders to put his

207

will into action, but the trade has nonetheless gone on under the *fleur de lys* standard, as if it were legally authorized" (*Précis*, 415). Furthermore, the association of illegal trade with the tight packing of captives (perfected by Ledoux) seems to owe something to this passage in Morenas's *Précis*: "Since the slave trade is being practiced now with fine sailing ships, the traders try to pack the maximum number of blacks into the smallest possible space" (406).

Navigation, Moralism, and Irony

> I thought a knowledge of navigation might be of use to me; for, though I did not intend to run away unless I should be ill used, yet, in such a case, if I understood navigation, I might attempt my escape in our sloop . . . and I could be at no loss for hands to join me.
>
> —OLAUDAH EQUIANO, *The Interesting Narrative*

My argument has been that Mérimée took only the superficial images from his sources—the local color—while eliding in "Tamango" the moral force of abolitionism. I now want to examine that theory more closely. The editors of the Pléiade edition note with approval that "there is in this narrative no display of false sensitivity, no ax to grind [*parti-pris*] in favor of the blacks" (PM, 1344). There is another dimension that needs to be acknowledged: the extent to which Mérimée's description of the cruelties of Ledoux, taken in isolation (and that is the key condition), *do* support an abolitionist agenda. To begin with, "Tamango" depicts the continuing illegal trade, which easily circumvents the inattentive authorities on the docks of Nantes. Ledoux's practices and state of mind, depicted with ironic relish, become the principal focus. His ship's design is calculatingly cruel, as described by Ledoux with sadistic humor: "When they get to the colonies . . . they'll spend more than enough time on their feet!" His bargaining with Tamango is cold, masterful, and dishonorable, even within the context of the slave trade. He has made Ayché into his sexual slave. These elements in the narrative—along with a lot of vague suppositions about Mérimée's personal associations and what they might imply—must be what impresses those who consider "Tamango" to be "undeniably" abolitionist.[108]

These elements do derive from abolitionist texts (as we have seen), and could even be taken to support abolitionism, but only when viewed outside

208

the larger framework of the story. Mérimée is an equal-opportunity ironist, and, as many have observed, no one escapes "Tamango" unscathed.[109] But in a context—that of the 1820s in France—where the slave trade remained an unresolved problem and a subject of urgent public debate, "equal" treatment of the two sides involved in the trade, African and European, with brutality and guilt shared indifferently, could only serve to support indifference. Why "concatenate" to help people who sell each other into slavery, have no civilization, and can't handle their freedom once they get it?

And, I would submit, the treatment is in fact not equal at all. Nothing that Ledoux does equals in depravity Tamango's cold-blooded murder of a female captive, the mother of three children, when bargaining does not go the way he wants: "'A little glass of brandy or I'll fire.' . . . The slave fell dead to the ground" (PM, 484/76). European civilization is subjected to an ironic poke in "Tamango"—the switch from wooden to iron collars for the slaves is "proof, if any were needed, of the manifest superiority of European civilization" (PM, 483/76, AT). But, despite that little wink to abolitionist sentiment, European civilization is not really scrutinized in "Tamango." Europe's slave trade is exploited as a backdrop for an exciting tale of the sea, but the (im)morality of the trade is nowhere near the center of attention. African civilization and the character of Africans, however, are subjected to considerable attention and ridicule. The first major evocation of Africa is the long description of Tamango's costume, written for laughs. Africa here is a pathetic imitation of Europe, in a cast-off uniform that Tamango has no idea how to wear and which reveals his naked blackness. The black race in general is in decline, according to Ledoux: "everything is degenerating" (PM, 482/75, AT).[110] In its viciousness, Mérimée's description of the famous slave dance on the deck of the ship foreshadows the images of American racism of the later nineteenth century: the sound of the violin changes their "expression of stupid despair" to a "broad grin" (PM, 487/80, AT).[111] The Mama-Jumbo passage then goes to considerable lengths to substantiate the idea that Africans are unintelligent: "Blacks are simple-minded; they don't understand anything" (PM, 488/81, AT). The slaves tremble in front of Tamango as he pronounces "unintelligible" words and makes "bizarre gestures" (PM, 490/83); everything suggests that Tamango does not even consider himself to be a master of the occult—that he is merely fooling his subjects. He is "less primitive than the others" but still primitive (*grossier*) (PM, 493/87). They all drink themselves into a stupor. And they all die, except Tamango, because of their ignorance of the sea. All of this seems designed to reflect not merely on the individuals involved, nor only on this particular group of captive Africans, but on Africans in general.

Mérimée does not simply ignore abolitionism; he actively negates it. The force of his irony blunts and stymies the arguments that were necessary for abolitionism in his times. He makes his Africans unworthy of liberation and unable to handle it once they get it. The contrast to the noble Africans who populate the anti-slave-trade poems of 1823 could not be more pronounced. To point this out is not to deny the right of literature to its own values (like irony) or to indulge in mere "political correctness" (as Francis Marcoin would have it): such considerations clearly must recede when a question like abolition is actually at stake, as it was in 1829.[112] Mérimée undercut and mocked the arguments for abolition of the slave trade at a crucial moment in the evolution of the debate.

Mérimée's principal metaphor for this purpose is navigation, the ultimate form of "know-how."[113] At sea, as the quote from Equiano above suggests, command of the esoteric science of navigation was a form of power and a safeguard against the mutiny of sailors and the rebellion of slaves. This knowledge belonged exclusively to the officers onboard. The narrator of Edouard Corbière's novel Le Négrier worries about "the grossest of men" acquiring "the means to steer themselves without the help of officers." He is referring to the lowly sailors, although what he is saying could go for the captives as well. Happily, crews are "forced to submit themselves, as to Providence, to the science that their officers possess."[114]

In "Tamango" the Africans' inability to handle the European technology of seafaring, and thereby to make their way home, is a key sign of the putative inferiority of African civilization.[115] What Mérimée does with this theme — the insistent emphasis that he puts on the idea of "ignorance" — harkens back to Defoe's Captain Singleton and to Emerigon's narration of the revolt on the Comte d'Estaing. The Africans who tell the story of their revolt in Defoe's novel are completely lost: they can't count days; they have no idea where they are or have been; and, most egregiously, "'They no understand; they no know what the sails do.'" This suggestion is perfectly plausible, since Africans from the interior of the continent would have no familiarity with the sea. But the idea could just as easily be called into question, in light of the extensive involvement in seafaring by many coastal Africans.[116] Black sailors could be found on many Atlantic vessels, including slave ships.[117] My question about the theme of navigation is one of emphasis. In Captain Singleton the slaves' ignorance of the sea condemns them to be resold, and the

episode is quickly concluded. In "Tamango," however, the theme of ignorance is greatly expanded. It becomes one of the principal thrusts of the narrative and seems to suggest far more than anecdotal information.

Things begin to go wrong for the slaves from the moment the revolt is
completed:

> When the corpse of the last white man had been dismembered, chopped up,
> and thrown into the sea, the blacks, their thirst for vengeance sated, raised their
> eyes towards the ship's sails, which were still filled by a fresh gale, and which,
> despite their victory, seemed still to be under orders from their oppressors, and
> to be bearing the victors away into the land of slavery. "We have achieved noth-
> ing," they thought sadly. "And will this great fetish of the white man still take
> us back to our country, now that we have shed the blood of its masters?" Some
> said Tamango would know how to make it obey. At once they called loudly for
> Tamango. (PM, 493/86, AT)

Attributing to Africans a view of European technology as a "fetish" is of
course an old trick in the arsenal of Africanist discourse (the idea carries
forward all the way to *Tintin au Congo* in the twentieth century). By representing Africans' cognition as fetishism, Europeans collapsed African
knowledge of the world into ignorance and represented Africans as devoid of practical sense: everything for them is a god, so all knowledge for
them must be occult. Technical mastery of the world replaces religion as the
principal wedge that Europeans will use to establish their superiority over
Africans, and seafaring, with the slave trade at its core, will be not just the
metaphor that it is in *Captain Singleton* and "Tamango," but also the means
by which dominance is achieved. Mérimée's use of the word *fetish* is a sign
of that process, showing how Europe claims to be leaving primitive Africa
behind. Therefore Mérimée's Africans "knelt before the compass, whose
ceaseless movement was a source of wonder to them, imploring it to take
them back to their homeland" (PM, 495/88) — they are stuck in a pretechni-
cal understanding of the world.

The pantomime that Tamango performs is a study in ignorance, with the
ship's compass as a prop: "Tamango examined the compass for a long time,
moving his lips as if reading the letters he could see inscribed on it. Then
he raised his hand to his forehead, adopting the pensive attitude of a man
engaged in some mental calculation. All the blacks were gathered around
him open-mouthed, their eyes starting from their heads, anxiously following his every movement. Finally, with the mingled fear and confidence that

211

ignorance confers, he gave a violent turn to the ship's wheel" (PM, 494/87; emphasis added). As the ship is laid flat on its side by the wind, just to make things perfectly clear, Mérimée refers to Tamango as the "ignorant helmsman" (*son pilote ignorant*).

But Mérimée does not stop at this. Acknowledging that Africans use boats in Africa, he has Tamango suggest to the group that the small launches aboard the *Espérance* "resemble those of our homeland, and we can control them as we wish" (PM, 496/90). But his ignorance of navigation condemns his plan, which is that "my master and yours will make [the wind] blow towards our country." Again Mérimée wants the point to be absolutely clear: "Never was there a more insane scheme. *Ignorant* of the use of the compass and with *no knowledge* of the stars, he was doomed to wander aimlessly" (*errer à l'aventure* [PM, 496/90, AT; emphasis added]). In a scene reminiscent of the shipwreck of the *Méduse*, the launches are swamped and the plan fails.

The tragedy of the *Méduse*, immortalized by Géricault's painting, is woven into this part of "Tamango" in another way, through another instance of intertextuality. As Tamango formulates his plan for escape in the small boats, "He believed that if he kept rowing straight ahead he would eventually come upon some land inhabited by black men; for black men possess the land, and white men live on their ships — so his mother had told him" (PM, 496/90). The words of a survivor of the *Méduse* are echoed in that passage. Gaspard Mollien was part of the mission, sent onboard the *Méduse* in June 1816, to reoccupy the French colonies of Senegal that had been regained (on paper) in the Treaty of Paris. But the captain of the ship reportedly had not sailed for many years, during the wars, and inadvertently steered the *Méduse* onto shoals off the coast of Senegal, where it sank. Mollien was one of the fifteen lucky survivors, finding his way to Saint-Louis and then back to France. He returned to Senegal in 1818 and set out to explore the interior, and then wrote a book, in which one reads: "Africans, like ignorant Europeans, are inclined to talk nonsense about things they don't know. These blacks [*ces nègres*] believed that Europeans live only on water, that they have no land, no houses, no livestock; they added that the rivers and the great bodies of water belonged to us, just as all lands were their birthright. They thought that, for this reason, whites should be forced to pay duties to the black kings [*rois nègres*] as do their own subjects."[118] This is another theme that Césaire will reprise. Underlying the entire question is the constant idea that Africans are more blinkered in their knowledge of the world than Europeans are. It is ironic, in light of what I have been saying, to find traces of the *Méduse* here in "Tamango," since that shipwreck represented a monumental failure of European, not African, navigation. *Pilote ignorant*, indeed.

Mérimée's treatment of the navigation issue is also haunted by another specter: the Haitian Revolution. Memories of that French defeat were fresh in the 1820s; the only truly successful slave revolt troubled abolitionists (this is visible in Duras's *Ourika*). Would legally emancipated slaves massacre whites as revolted slaves had done? They can set themselves free by violence, but they can't handle their freedom, the argument went. Raynal, less a friend of the slaves than he is reputed to be, said that "these stupid men, who would not have been prepared for a change of status, would be incapable of *directing themselves*" (*incapables de se conduire eux-mêmes*).[119] The image of Mérimée's revolted slaves, ignorant, drunk, and adrift on the Atlantic, is inescapably an allegory of Haiti. It is the image that the Abbé Grégoire had tried to refute in 1808 in his *De la littérature des Nègres*, the image that Hugo incorporates in his *Bug-Jargal* and Baron Roger in his *Kelédor*.[120] Even Madame de Duras, in *Ourika*, was obliged to have her black narrator recoil in horror and disassociate herself from her black brethren in Haiti. Narratives like that of the Saint-Janvier sisters, supposedly the last two white women to leave Saint-Domingue, continued to detail the gore of the revolution.[121] Mérimée, with his tale of a slave revolt that leads to nothing but chaos, suggested "Haiti" very clearly between his lines.[122]

I have suggested that Mérimée created a very powerful metaphor for political chaos and failed concatenation in "Tamango" and that the slaves' inability to navigate was central to this. One indication of the extent to which this metaphor made an impression on French culture comes up in a letter that Balzac wrote at the time of the 1848 revolution, thus twenty years after the publication of "Tamango." "What is to become of us?" he asked. "We are rereading Mérimée's novella *Tamango*."[123] In coded language Balzac was suggesting that the revolutionaries of 1848 were incapable of steering the ship of state that they had taken over.

Undoing Heroism

The most powerful and lasting irony of "Tamango" is to be found in the characterization of Tamango himself. While Mérimée's contemporaries had already exploited the theme of the black hero, Mérimée chose to deviate from that program. Hugo had inherited and re-created the figure of the *nègre généreux*. The traces of Hugo's *Bug-Jargal* are more than evident in

"Tamango," as is the clear difference of tone between the two texts. Hugo's narrator (of the first version, published in 1820) says of the generous black hero: "No man that I have met has matched him in nobility or originality" (114). Bug-Jargal is exactly the thing that Mérimée does not allow Tamango to become: a hero. Mérimée seems in fact to have been writing *against* the image of the *nègre généreux* that Hugo had taken up and reinvented—as if to destroy it. He goes to considerable lengths to make his Tamango *unheroic*, and I want to examine exactly how he does that.

The issue of heroism or of leadership is of obvious relevance for any possible concatenation. The hero-leader is the first link in the chain of revolt, pulling from below. In the eighteenth century Raynal had asked where the black Spartacus would come from; Toussaint had seemed to provide an answer. Tamango is no Toussaint. The description of his garb—an ill-fitting European uniform—consists of an amassing of details, each designed to connote foolishness. It is a corporal's uniform that the warrior wears so proudly on this special occasion; he has the epaulettes hanging the wrong way; he is shirtless, and the black skin of his stomach shows, "resembling a broad belt." In case the reader has somehow missed the point that is being conveyed, Mérimée ends the paragraph explicitly: "In this rig-out, the African warrior adjudged himself more elegant than the most consummate dandy [*petit-maître*] to be found in Paris or London" (PM, 481/74).[124] Thus it is not only Tamango's physical appearance that is supposed to be ridiculous; more important is his deluded state of mind: he "reveled in the impression he supposed himself to be making on the white man." From this point forward there is no need to dwell on Tamango's obvious failures as a leader of his people: after all, he is selling his own people into slavery, some for single glasses of liquor. (Mérimée helps to sustain the European myth of Africans selling each other for a pittance, as 160 captives are exchanged for "a few shoddy cotton goods, some gunpowder, some flints, three casks of brandy, and fifty dilapidated rifles" [PM, 483/76]).

Yet Tamango's actions, in the remainder of the story, seem to be very purposefully orchestrated so as to negate his potential heroism. The potential is actually suggested: Tamango's resistance to being trepanned is described as "heroic" (PM, 485/78), and Mérimée allows Tamango to lead an effective uprising; without that, there would be no plot. The concatenation takes the form of an oath sworn by the captives, "the conspirators, bound by a solemn oath" ("les *con*jurés, *liés* entre eux par un serment solennel" [PM, 491/84, AT]; emphasis added); this linkage is the product of Tamango's leadership—his "harangues" and his ability to procure, through Ayché, the file that makes the revolt possible. But at the point when the Africans find themselves alone onboard the *Espérance*, everything changes, and the downward arc of the story begins. Several key actions of Tamango's have not attracted sufficient attention. After his disastrous attempt to steer the ship, Tamango barricades himself, alone with Ayché, in isolation from the people he led into revolt: "he erected a kind of barricade out of empty barrels and planks; then he sat down in the middle of this sort of blockhouse, from which the bayonets of his two guns projected menacingly" (PM, 495/88). So much for the concatenation. The "crowd" is now something through which Tamango passes, and at which he aims his guns. The revolt had two stated purposes: vengeance and liberation ("le grand jour de vengeance et de liberté" [PM, 491/84]); Tamango has betrayed the oath of liberation, becoming a new oppressor.

Again, Mérimée is not going for subtlety. To make clear what kind of leader Tamango is, he is compared to Coriolanus. The Roman emperor, known to posterity (and perhaps to the anglophile Mérimée) through Shakespeare's play, was accused of starving his own people, against whom he waged war. Shakespeare's Coriolanus colorfully refers to the people as a "herd," a "rabble," and "the mutable, rank-scented many."[125] An old man approaches Tamango's blockhouse, but "Tamango was as inflexible as Coriolanus, and turned a deaf ear to his entreaties" (PM, 496/89). It all comes down to food. Tamango, unlike Coriolanus, is not so much indifferent to his people's hunger as he is careful to take care of himself. "During the night, amid the confusion, he had laid in a store of ship's biscuits and salt meat. He seemed determined to live alone in his retreat" (PM, 496/89, AT). Most of all he is determined to *live*. During the attempted escape in the smaller boats, Tamango and Ayché "take their places" in the larger of the two vessels, which has been more heavily laden with supplies; again they are looking out for themselves. But their selfishness backfires when the launch sinks; few survive, but Tamango and Ayché, perhaps with the benefit of their extra rations, are among them. Thus it is not by chance that Tamango is the only one to survive in the end, even if he is "emaciated" and "scrawny": at every turn he did all he could to ensure this outcome. By the time he reaches Jamaica, "Tamango [is] in perfect health"(PM, 498/92). In glaring contrast to the noble black heroes that Behn, Hugo, and others had produced, Mérimée created an *ignoble* black *anti*hero.

The most important effect of this is to demolish the black concatenation that was built in "Tamango." The *conjuration*, the conspiracy of slaves, is de-

215

stroyed by the intellectual and character flaws that Mérimée attributes to its leader. Tamango's ignominious survival, alone, and his desultory, mundane death in Jamaica seem to remove him from any links of solidarity with the people he led in revolt.[126]

"Tamango" was not and is not an abolitionist tale. The slave trade is much more of a backdrop for Mérimée's real agenda: literary entertainment. His depiction of Africans certainly could not have contributed to their emancipation. To explain the negativity of "Tamango" as the simple pasting-in of stereotypes — the reproduction of ready-made images that were somehow automatic in Mérimée's times — would be to discount the creativity of Mérimée's devastating imagination. He puts considerable energy into reinforcing the negative depiction of his African characters. As we have seen, in many cases he took "noble" images and anecdotes and debased them. The fact that this tale is still labeled abolitionist in its marketing (by Larousse and by Oxford University Press) is perhaps best understood as another of Mérimée's hoaxes, from beyond the grave; for "Tamango" is about as abolitionist as Mérimée was a Spanish actress or an Illyrian balladeer.

If "Tamango" "sets in parallel savagery and civilization, to the greater glory of neither,"[127] the stakes are much higher for those who might (later) see their race or their culture represented as "savage." "Civilization" (France) will quickly forget the slave trade and wrap itself in the flag of abolitionism as it invades Africa; but the subalterns, especially those in the New World, will not forget so easily. Which will bring us, in a moment, to Césaire.

Moralism and irony are very different commodities in the marketplace of literature. Most memorably expressed by Gide, the idea that noble sentiments make for bad literature is widely accepted. A relevant contrast can be drawn between, on the one hand, Mérimée's "Tamango" and, on the other, Sophie Doin's *La Famille noire* and other stories. Both emerged from the abolitionist context of the Restoration in the 1820s, and both deal with the slave trade. But "Tamango" is an amoral or at least morally ambiguous tale that seems to have been written for the pleasure of the writer and the reader; it became a classic, constantly available to and enjoyed by readers of French. On the other hand, Doin's engaged, sentimental literature, like the poems submitted to the French Academy in 1823, was well intentioned and noble in purpose but mediocre by any standard of literary quality. Even in her story "Le Négrier," which is supposed to be more "simple and direct" than her other, more florid writings, the forest of exclamation points (sometimes three or four at once) detracts from the very lessons that the author wants to emphasize.[128] Moralistic literature need not be dreck, notwithstanding the example provided by "Tamango" on the one hand and Sophie Doin's tales on the other. Duras's *Ourika*—which is both morally engaged and stylistically restrained, and therefore *effective*—has already demonstrated that point.

The Theater of Slavery Revisited

Before moving on, I must point out the remarkable reprise of a theme that arose earlier in this study, the intrusion of theater into the world of the slave trade. The abolitionist Morenas wrote that slave-trading ships are "the *theater* of barbarism" (*Précis*, 365). Francis Marcoin makes the following observation, which sums up the eerie relation between the slave trade and theater: "[In] *Tamango*, . . . the ship is nothing but a stage. We know that the vocabulary of the theater borrows from that of the sea: the scenes of battle and famine that Mérimée likes to render in the purest academic style take place on *boards* [*planches*] and under the raw light that cuts across the theatrical stage—with the possible intervention of painting (as in Diderot), since Mérimée's narrative can be linked to *The Raft of the 'Medusa.'*"[129] Earlier in this study, in a nonfictional context, we saw how Voltaire's *Alzire* circulated around the French Atlantic in the context of the slave trade. The thematics of slavery and colonialism in Voltaire's play resonated uncannily with the reality of the slave trade, in the midst of which the play was performed, at Gorée, in Saint-Domingue, and in France.

With that in mind it is interesting to look at Ledoux's flashback to the theater in Nantes (PM, 483/76). This synapse, collapsing Africa and France together, momentarily closes one distance of the Atlantic triangle. The play that Ledoux went to see was *Les Vêpres siciliennes*, by Casimir Delavigne, a popular work that opened in Paris on October 23, 1819. As in the case of Voltaire's *Alzire* being performed on a slave-trading vessel at Gorée, it happens here again—but this time in a fictional context—that the thematics of the play repeat the dramatic themes of the context in which it is performed. Thus the character Ledoux sits through a play that depicts a revolt against French oppression. Delavigne sets the play in Sicily under French (Angevin) occupation in the thirteenth century; in history the French were generally massacred in this anticolonial rebellion, which began with the tolling of the bells for vespers. Giving voice to the Sicilians, Delavigne uses the conventional Enlightenment metaphor for political oppression and occupation: slavery.[130]

So I must repeat the question that I asked about the various stagings of *Alzire*, but this time in a fictive context: what could Ledoux have (fictively) thought when he (fictively) listened to the following two lines in the play (among many others making a similar point): "Will you tell me after all, my lord, by what right / You oppress the weak and *defy the laws* [*braver les lois*]?"[131] Spoken by a Sicilian to the French governor, these lines seem remarkably apt for the context of the illegal slave trade in which Ledoux is about to embark.

As the play reaches its climax, the call to arms that is declaimed by the Sicilian leaders deploys the *exact* terms that Mérimée uses to describe the goals of the slave revolt in "Tamango": "vengeance et liberté!" (73). For French liberal audiences in 1819 (presumably including Mérimée), *Les Vêpres siciliennes* was a clear political allegory. Its rhetoric signaled a daring critique of the Bourbon Restoration: seeing themselves as the Sicilian rebels, the liberals associated the Bourbons with the former occupying power, the British, who had in fact helped establish the Bourbon Restoration. (The play escaped censorship because it was set so far in the past.)[132] If the fictive Ledoux sat through Delavigne's play thinking about French politics and not about slave revolts, he would be reproducing the pattern that we saw so much of in the eighteenth century: "slavery" is the political oppression of the French, not French exploitation of African slaves as chattel.

As with the buried reference to the *Méduse*, which deconstructs the myth of European technical superiority, this excursion into the interstices of Mérimée's text reveals ironies that go beyond those that he made so abundantly clear (Ledoux, *Espérance*, etc.). *Les Vêpres siciliennes* represents an explosive force within the text of "Tamango," the potential uprising of the repressed masses. It is no coincidence that both *Les Vêpres siciliennes* and Shakespeare's *Coriolanus* describe the revolt of oppressed peoples—of, to use Shakespeare's word, which is also Césaire's word, the *crowd*. This pattern harkens back to Voltaire's *Alzire*—another "liberal" play—and its curious circum-Atlantic history. (The fact that both *Alzire* and *Les Vêpres siciliennes* later became Verdi operas is intriguing.)

These allusions to *Les Vêpres siciliennes* and to *Coriolanus* within "Tamango" can in fact be taken as a way to salvage an abolitionist reading of the text. The frontal attack on tyranny, oppression, and "slavery" that Ledoux would have heard during his evening at the theater in Nantes acts as the repressed abolitionist conscience of the text (and perhaps of Mérimée himself; we cannot know).

CÉSAIRE AND "TAMANGO"

The image of revolted slaves that Mérimée created—drunk and ignorant, led by a corrupt tyrant, unable to control their own fate—remained as a toxin within the French canon. I want to suggest that, as that canon circulated around the world during the colonial times that so quickly followed the publication of "Tamango," this image was a particular irritant. The damaging effects of this image must have been exacerbated by the increased canonicity of Mérimée after the fiftieth anniversary of his death in 1920. A Mérimée "boom" ensued, with a wave of new editions (including two sets of his complete works), and a quadrupling of studies devoted to him. Interest in him remained high throughout the 1930s, and numerous editions of his works, including "Tamango," remained available.[133] If the effects of "Tamango" were not what I am suggesting here—that is, toxic—Aimé Césaire, one of the fathers of Negritude, would not have responded as he did in his epic poem *Cahier d'un retour au pays natal* (*Notebook of a Return to My Native Land*, 1939 in its first edition). The *Cahier* is one of the most important works of the literary French Atlantic, and I will return to it at greater length later in this study.

219

Writing 110 years after "Tamango" was first published and in the wake of the Mérimée boom, which occurred during Césaire's student years in Paris, Césaire takes up the image of the slave vessel on the Atlantic, and the allusion to Mérimée's "Tamango" is unmistakable. The specificity of the illegal trade during the French Restoration is evoked, and the allusion to Mérimée is fortified, when Césaire mentions (undoubtedly British) *frégates policières*, just like those that pursue *L'Espérance*.[134] In the *Cahier*, as in "Tamango," the central, transformative drama is a slave revolt and its aftermath. The outcome of that rebellion, the moment at which the slaves find themselves alone, facing the technology of navigation, is crucial in both texts. Césaire altered and augmented his massive poem significantly between its first, partial publication in 1939 and its "definitive" version of 1956, but the shipboard slaves' revolt, depicted in the verses quoted below, remains the same. This is the emotional and political climax of the poem in all its versions. Césaire's revolt is bloodless: the only violence mentioned in this passage (stanzas 162–67) is that of the ship's captain. Revolt is condensed into one word that symbolizes triumph: *debout* (standing). Césaire's vision of a revolt on a slave ship is both a direct refutation of Mérimée and a way of making the "Tamango" scenario irrelevant:

And the blackscum [*la négraille*] is standing

the seated blackscum

unexpectedly standing

standing in the hold

standing in the cabins

standing on deck

standing in the wind

standing under the sun

standing in blood

    standing

       and

          free

standing and not a poor madwoman in her maritime freedom and

destitution gyrating in perfect drift

standing at the helm

standing at the compass

standing at the chart

standing under the stars

    standing

       and

          free

and the lustral ship fearlessly advances [*s'avancer impavide*] on the

crumbling waters[135]

The key verses in French being:

debout et non point pauvre folle dans sa liberté et son

dénuement maritimes girant en la dérive parfaite

Standing is, visibly, one of the key terms of empowerment and autonomy in the *Cahier*: once the work of negritude has been undertaken, the narrator says: "nous sommes debout maintenant, mon pays et moi" ("we are standing now, my country and I" [28/77]). It is important to call to mind the physical environment of the slave ship, which Césaire chose as the setting for the climax of his poem: *standing up* is precisely the thing the captives *could not* do in the hold of a slave ship, because they were not given enough room. The famous engraving of the slave ship *Brookes*, which Césaire could have seen in an edition of "Tamango" published while he was in Paris, made this clear.[136] As Mérimée's Captain Ledoux mused: "Why should they need to stand? 'When they get to the colonies,' Ledoux used to say, 'They'll spend more than enough time on their feet!'" (PM, 480/73). Standing is the first act of self-liberation and thus a fitting symbol of the victory that is achieved in the *Cahier*.

Furthermore, the presence of the revolted slaves "standing at the helm . . . at the compass . . . at the chart" suggests their ability to face the technology of navigation—and all it implies—without fear or disorder. The explicit project of the captives in "Tamango" was the same as the dream that animates the *Cahier*, the dream of captive Africans that is expressed from the time of Equiano forward: return to the native land. The slaves on the *Espérance* wonder, "Will this great fetish of the white men still take us back to our country?" ("ce grand fétiche des Blancs voudra-t-il nous ramener dans notre pays?" [PM, 493/86]). (The phrase "ramener dans [notre] pays" occurs five times in "Tamango.") But Césaire's representation of this scenario is not as simple as a reversal of Mérimée's plot, whereby the revolted slaves are now somehow masters of navigation and sail off to their native land—no such Hollywood ending is suggested in the poem. The idea of return, as we will see, is not nearly that easy for Césaire. Instead, the slaves' triumph here will be political and moral. Césaire's answer to all the European calumnies about Africans not being masters of navigation is, simply and eloquently, that the ship advances, fearlessly. (Césaire said that the verb *s'avancer* was an "exclamative infinitive.")[137]

221

One verse in particular seems designed to throw the triumph of the masses into relief; it is also a verse that clearly alludes to "Tamango": "standing and *not* a poor madwoman in her maritime freedom and / destitution gyrating in perfect drift."[138] The phrases "maritime freedom and destitution" and "drift" (coming soon after the evocation of British cruisers policing the slave trade) show that "Tamango" is the subtext here. Césaire is invoking the essential elements of the revolted slaves' doomed situation in Mérimée's story. Freedom in "Tamango" led immediately to destitution and death because the slaves could not control their *maritime* situation; they were stuck in a "perfect" (that is, an absolute) "drift."[139] Césaire exorcizes that negative image—the "Tamango" scenario—with the powerful words *non point*. And he proceeds to substitute a positive reinterpretation of the scenario by simply asserting that the revolted slaves *are* in control, "standing" and, more important, free. Césaire also draws a significant contrast between the singular and the collective: the madwoman is alone; the "blackscum"—*la négraille*—that triumphs is a "crowd" that has found its "true cry"—a concatenation, Shakespeare's "many." Miraculously perhaps, the ship moves forward without fear.

But at that point Césaire abandons the "plot" of the slave ship and adjourns toward more spiritual questions: the *Cahier* is not only a counternarrative to "Tamango"; it comes also to counternarrative itself. What happens in the passage above, this transformation from one condition to another, is thus miraculous, in a way that is specific to the *Cahier*. The alchemy by which such a change can take place is a subject for a later chapter. For the moment I want only to mark this passage of the *Cahier* as an important sign of two things: first, the influence of Mérimée's "Tamango" on French colonial and postcolonial culture and, second, the ability of a Francophone writer to turn this paradigmatic tale of the slave trade on its head. Working intertextually, as he so often does in the *Cahier*, Césaire is able to recuperate and rehabilitate (the key verbs of Negritude) an image, that of a ship full of revolted slaves — restoring its value as a sign of solidarity for a people — rescuing the image from the corrosive, disabling irony with which Mérimée had covered it.

TAMANGO AND DECOLONIZATION ON FILM

Tamango in 1958

"Water-borne 'Uncle Tom's Cabin' tinged by sex . . ."
— *Kinematograph Weekly* (Jan. 14, 1960)

Twenty years after the first appearance of the *Cahier*, a new Tamango will enter the world, in a film that rewrites the tale for a context — in fact for a highly complex network of contexts *around the Atlantic* — with connections to the civil rights movement in the United States, decolonization in the French colonies, and the cold war. The changes that the Mérimée tale was subjected to will say a great deal about evolving views of the slave trade in France, in Africa, and in the United States. Created in France by a group of American refugees from McCarthyism and their French collaborators, this film tells a tale that is quite different from Mérimée's. But why would filmmakers of an obviously leftist persuasion use "Tamango" in the first place?

The film was made and released in separate French- and English-language versions, so its status as a transatlantic work is quite literal. In John Berry's *Tamango* Mérimée's tale involving the French and the Africans is further internationalized, both at the level of the film's production and, as we will see, within the story as it is remodeled.

The essential changes that were made begin with the character of Tamango: in this film he is not the slave-trading African chief (who is present as a different, overweight character); he is a young lion hunter, innocent of the slave trade and a captive himself onboard the ship, which is now called the *Esperanza*. The character of Ayché (Dorothy Dandridge) is also radically revised: in the film she is a biracial Creole African American (in the hemispheric sense), raised on a plantation, apparently in Cuba, although she makes it sound a lot like the American South. Ayché is the captain's mistress, and is desired by both the ship's doctor (Corot, a new character, played by Jean Servais) and Tamango. The captain (Curt Jurgens) and Tamango wage psychological war for Ayché's loyalty and sense of belonging. Ayché is undecided until the end. At the film's dramatic climax Ayché joins the captives' war chant and thus ends her in-between status. Then, in a complete change from Mérimée, the uprising is suppressed by a massacre of the slaves at the end of the film: the captain turns cannons filled with grapeshot down into the hold. The ship's name fills the last frames of the movie, and a strong message of solidarity, heroic martyrdom, and "hope" lingers as the credits roll.

From this brief summary alone, a provisional answer to my question should already be apparent: the filmmakers thoroughly highjacked Mérimée's story and remade it as a *nationalist* fable. But the film is, as we will see, far more complex than that simple characterization might suggest. In the almost nonexistent history of *le cinéma négrier*, this *Tamango* occupies a special place, for it is likely only the second film ever to depict captive Africans as they are loaded onto slave ships.[140]

Directed by John Berry, *Tamango* revolves around the incomparable Dorothy Dandridge as Ayché, in a vastly expanded role; she nearly overwhelms the movie with her sheer presence, her beauty, her status as a sex goddess, and her symbolic value as what Donald Bogle calls "the apotheosis of the tragic mulatto."[141] All of these qualities were used as commodities in her films. Dandridge was, as Robert Lightning explains, "the first black performer to attain certain specific signifiers of genuine Hollywood stardom (a glamorous and/or sexual image that functions as such *within* individual narratives [including *Tamango*], an Oscar nomination in the Best Actress category, star billing, the cover of *Life* magazine, etc." (Lightning, "Ruminations," 32). *Tamango* came four years after Dandridge's triumph in *Car-

223

men Jones (which was kept off French screens by a lawsuit),[142] and the film was clearly predicated on her star power. It is practically a vehicle for her.

Reactions to Dandridge's performance in *Tamango* were generally negative at the time. When the film was released in France on January 24, 1958, *Cahiers du cinéma* spoke derisively of "the grimaces of the late Carmen Jones."[143] The African critic (working in France) Paulin Vieyra agreed: Dandridge, "except at rare moments, was not able to bring to life the character of the slave who becomes the 'whore' of the white man, torn between the softness of her privileged material situation in the captain's service and the lamentable spectacle of her blood brothers."[144] John Berry later commented, "The French intellectuals kicked the shit out of that movie. First of all, because it was from a Mérimée story, then because it was very expensive to make; because I was an upstart American pissant—yes, maybe talented."[145]

Appraisals of Dandridge's acting have grown more favorable in recent years, as critics seem to take the context of her career more into consideration. The 1998 San Francisco International Film Festival described Dandridge's performance in *Tamango* as "among her very best."[146] Gwendolyn Audrey Foster goes so far as to claim that Dandridge—in *Tarzan's Peril* (1951), *Carmen Jones* (1954), and *Tamango*—created "triumphant performative displays of counter-hegemonics."[147] Still, in *Tamango* one cannot help but notice the strange diffidence that Dandridge exudes; her acting is oddly casual and peevish in the context of high drama that unfolds. Part of that effect is created by her language, which I will discuss below. But we should keep in mind that the whole premise of her character in this film is that she is caught between worlds, "adrift" between Manichean, racialized choices, unable to commit yet forced to choose.

The controversy about *Tamango* in France and in the United States was not limited to the quality of the acting or of the film's aesthetics. Released three years after Dien Bien Phu, in the middle of the Algerian war, and on the eve of African independences—and depicting a violent uprising of subalterns—*Tamango* ran headlong into French government censorship.[148] The end result was that the film was released in metropolitan France but banned in the French colonies: as Vieyra commented, "Without hesitation, the censors decided that Black Africans and Malagasies would not see the film. . . . Neither would Algeria." This was done in spite of protests from journalists, filmmakers, and writers (Vieyra, *Le Cinéma et l'Afrique*, 62). Presently I will examine the effects that censorship seems to have had on the writing and packaging of the film.

The American debut of *Tamango* took place on August 19, 1959, a year and a half after its French opening. American authorities had their own "colonial" problems to worry about, namely the civil rights movement; but here censorship would be exercised the good old American way: by the marketplace. Because of the rising civil rights movement, "no major American distributor would touch the film" (Bogle, *Dorothy Dandridge*, 454). *Jet Magazine* reported reactions apparently gathered from a largely African American public in Detroit: *Tamango* "evinces a variety of reactions. It has been called 'a welcome ally to the Negroes' fight for civil rights . . . an excellent motion picture that should do a good job for present-day civil liberties . . . good for integration.' Other previewers found the racial issue 'too strong,' felt the film 'too vividly portrays the brutality of the white man . . . radiates hostility' and 'would not create any goodwill.'"[149] Initially reporting a box office success in Detroit, *Tamango* withered away for lack of adequate distribution. Its militancy was a decade too early.

Curt Jurgens, in the role of the captain (who is nameless in the film but "Captain Reinker" in the credits), was at that time a popular European leading man; his performance is appropriately flinty. Jean Servais, then a well-known French actor, as the ship's doctor, seems to have replaced the interpreter of Mérimée's tale as the *homme humain*, the voice of conscience; this doctor fought for liberty in the Revolution, only to find himself working for the slave trade ("Look at me now," he laments). Roger Hanin, near the beginning of his long career, is a sailor. Most remarkably, the film "introduces" a young Martinican medical student named Alex Cressan in the role of Tamango. According to *Le Monde*, Cressan intended this to be his only role; he is almost universally recognized — and rightly so — as the best actor in the film.[150]

John Berry began working at Orson Welles's Mercury Theater at the age of seventeen. He was Billy Wilder's assistant on *Double Indemnity* and began a promising career as a director. Following his political convictions, Berry directed *The Hollywood Ten* (1951), which documented the anticommunist witch hunt. This attracted the unwelcome attention of the House Un-American Activities Committee, which identified him as a communist; he was subsequently blacklisted.[151] His career was, for the time being, over in the United States. He escaped from the FBI, literally, through a back window, and fled to France, where he relaunched his career and directed several movies before *Tamango*.[152] This new *Tamango* should be seen alongside other allegories (as I will argue) produced by blacklisted Americans, "black" works in which slavery and the slave trade stood in for contemporary forms of oppression.[153] Among these would be Howard Fast's *Spartacus* (1951).[154]

Tamango was written by a team, with Berry listed as one of four adapters along with Lee Gold, Tamara Hovey, and Georges Neveux. The English-language dialogues are credited to Earl Mills, who happened to be Dorothy Dandridge's manager, and the French dialogues were written by Neveux, a playwright. Among the other participants were cast members whose names bear witness to their West African origins: Assane Fall, Ababakar Samba, Cissé Karamoko, and Douta Seck, who would later play the old man Médouze in Euzhan Palcy's film *La Rue Cases-Nègres/Sugar Cane Alley*. The credits say that technical documentation came from two sources: "Tamango" (Mérimée's, obviously), and an intriguing book printed in 1957, *Journal de la traite des Noirs* (mistranslated in the English-language credits as *The Treaty [sic] of the Negroes*).[155]

The most significant anecdote about the making of *Tamango* is related to a shipboard "revolt" by Dorothy Dandridge. Sailing across the Atlantic onboard the *Queen Elizabeth*, bound for France to film *Tamango*, Dandridge reviewed the script, which she had just received. In a cover letter John Berry said that "all the changes have been made in order to get a great part for you" (quoted in DB, 379). But Dandridge was "incensed" by what she read: she found that the focus of the story had been shifted from a shipboard slave revolt to a shipboard "sex drama, tawdry and exploitative." Her manager Earl Mills cabled ahead to Berry: "Tamango script not approved. Surprised and shocked script not like treatment. Role as characterized will not be performed by Dorothy" (DB, 379). Contractually obliged to work with Dandridge's approval, Berry and his team were forced to make changes; presumably the film that we see is one that she approved.

Filming began at the Victorine Studios in Nice on April 27, 1957. Dandridge took up residence in a luxury suite at the Hôtel du Cap d'Antibes. (One might bear in mind that Antibes is the setting for Sembene's tale of colonial and postcolonial servitude, *La Noire de. . . .*) Her salary was $10,000 a week, for a total of $125,000 — plus $500 a week for expenses. A full-scale ship was built on pilings at the fishing village of Cros-de-Cagnes between Nice and Cannes.

In fact there are two *Tamango* films, one in French and one in English.

It appears that many scenes were shot twice so that Dorothy Dandridge and Curt Jurgens could recite their lines in both French and English. Berry stated that the bilingual shooting was "hysterical."[156] I have not detected any differences of photography or content between the two versions. The American version was rereleased in 1997 and is currently available as a commercial video; the film remains commercially unavailable in France.

Why "Tamango," then? Of all the tales that it was possible to tell and retell in the 1950s, why did this team of producers and writers, along with the director, choose Mérimée's story of the slave trade? Why the slave trade for a "black" (that is, blacklisted) picture? A quick overview of Mérimée's legacy should help to put that choice in context. His nineteenth-century preoccupation with the exotic — with otherness, local color — created a field of signifiers that has proved extremely fertile and open to revision. It would not be possible to count the number of artists who have re-created Mérimée's works in a variety of media, most notably in literature, opera, and film. Earlier we saw some indication of the stylistic groundwork that Mérimée established for Francophone literature. His literary exoticism, it turns out, could be appropriated by artists who actually called "exotic" (that is, colonial) locales their home; at that point exoticism is altered if not reversed. The network of threads connecting two distant cultural figures, Mérimée and Dandridge, reveal how this happens (quite aside from the connection in *Tamango*): Mérimée wrote *Carmen*, which became Bizet's opera and then, through Oscar Hammerstein and Otto Preminger, the film *Carmen Jones*, starring Dandridge. The Carmen story has also recently been adapted by a Senegalese filmmaker, Joseph Gaï Ramaka, in *Karmen Geï* (2001). That set of connections thus runs parallel to the "Tamango" phenomenon. Through a series of transformations, Mérimée's "Tamango," a tale that casts Africans in an extremely unfavorable light, could be transformed into a parable of African liberation on one side of the Atlantic and an anti-McCarthy, anti-racist fable on the other side.

The symbolic and practical meaning of France itself is also a major factor in the birth of this film. France was a haven for John Berry, a place where he could work without fear of anticommunist hysteria. Dorothy Dandridge's presence in France to participate in this film — which could not have been made in Hollywood because of the infamous Production Code and its influence — needs to be seen in the context of African American exile in France. Jack Johnson and, later, Richard Wright moved to France seeking escape from American racism; Josephine Baker had made a fabulous career there;

227

James Baldwin would follow.[157] Compared to the United States, France seemed, and often claimed to be, free of racism. But France was double-edged: on the one hand, the absence of a large black population meant that there was no Jim Crow, and liberal French traditions welcomed American black intellectuals and entertainers; but on the other hand, France was less than open and hospitable to immigrants from its own colonies. France's dualistic attitude is revealed by the fortunes of the film *Tamango*: its left-wing director and its African American star were welcomed, but the product of their labor was kept away from France's colonial subjects. These conflicting forces of liberalism and repression, exile and freedom, all come into play in the production and content of Berry's film in ways that I will examine. We should note that these tensions are revolving around an Atlantic triangle, this time with France, Africa, and the United States at its three points.

Tamango, it must be said, is no cinematic masterpiece; it comes across as a distinctly B picture. (*Cahiers du cinéma* claims that the houses of the Côte d'Azur can be seen in the background, but I have not been able to see that.) According to the *Village Voice*, *Tamango* "belongs to a group of 'progressive' protoblaxploitation films by black-listed directors."[158] We saw that it was connected to works by other blacklisted writers. It certainly belongs in comparisons to the great Hollywood melodrama of race, métissage, and passing from this period, Douglas Sirk's *Imitation of Life* (1959); and it also needs to be understood in relation to the pulp fiction of its day—paperbacks that exploited sex and violence.[159] The posters for *Tamango* and the box for its current video version maximize the film's "raciness": "Love as bold and daring as the casting!" "Savage Tamango—he brought revolt aboard a tyrant's slaveship!" "I've always hated your hands on me!" These affiliations leave *Tamango*, as the *Village Voice* put it, "suspended in the limbo between trash and truth" (Hoberman, "Tamango," 89).

I want to suggest that some of *Tamango*'s apparent imperfections and historical distortions are in fact signs of an international, heteroglot, circum-Atlantic agenda that the film seeks to convey. The Tamango story, derived from Mérimée, will now be radically revised, as new meanings are invested in it by creators coming from different points on the old Atlantic triangle.

Introducing Ayché

Berry's film is not constrained by the literary text on which it is based; it takes the story where it wants. I think one can view the film as a radical expansion of the following passage from Mérimée's "Tamango," an expansion that is entirely predicated on the star power of Dorothy Dandridge: "Beside [Ledoux] stood Ayché, wearing, not irons, but an elegant blue cotton dress, her feet clad in pretty morocco leather slippers, holding a tray laden with liquor, and ready to serve him a drink. It was evident that she performed important services for the captain [*elle remplissait de hautes fonctions auprès du capitaine*]" (PM, 487/80). It is of course the sight of his wife in this role that provokes Tamango to invoke Mumbo-Jumbo; when Ayché apologizes to him for her complicity with the captain, Tamango demands the file that makes the revolt possible. The triangle of desire linking the captain, Ayché, and Tamango propels the plot forward in this way.

But in the film things are very different. Tamango first sees Ayché, along with the audience, onboard the slave ship, through a process of teasing revelation. The first we see of her is a single (unchained) foot in a close-up; the camera rises but Ayché has turned and is walking away. Then she is partially perceived in silhouette through a gauzy curtain on the captain's cabin door, but we still don't see her face. Finally, after the ship has set sail with its captives onboard, we enter the captain's cabin, and the camera coyly reveals the star we have been waiting for. First she is shown from the back with her bare legs exposed, sitting on the floor in front of a bird cage; she turns and we finally see her face as she enters into conversation with Doctor Corot (see figure 9). The impact of Dorothy Dandridge's beauty and charisma is thus enhanced.

The symbolism of the bird cage is inescapable: she is a pretty bird trapped in servitude. This image rather clearly invites recollections of another famous African American woman, Josephine Baker, at the end of another film made in France, *Zouzou* (1934), singing in a giant bird cage. Corot is pressuring Ayché about her in-between status, with "white blood in your veins," but still a slave: "What do you feel when you see the blacks, *the blacks like you* chained and made slaves?" Her saucy reply, her first utterance in the film, speaks volumes, as she serves him coffee: "One lump of sugar or two?" In the context of the slave trade, sugar is of course not just any condiment; it is the most concise symbol of the trade itself. Ayché's question seems to have been written very purposefully, departing from the more standard phrase "One lump or two?" to make the implication clear. The heavy double entendres continue as Ayché asks Corot if he wants milk in his coffee (another *denrée coloniale*): "Half and half, your color," he replies, and in the French version, "Moitié-moitié, ta couleur."[160]

To focus on one detail that the short story and the film have in common:

229

9 Dorothy Dandridge as Ayché
in John Berry's *Tamango*.
First full view.

Ayché is not chained. She is, so to speak, "deconcatenated," detached from
the chains that bind the African captives together on the ship.[161] In Mérimée
this is a temporary state: she is taken over as a concubine by Ledoux, and
Tamango is for a time referred to as her "former husband" (MP, 489/82);
but she rejoins the concatenation, providing the file to Tamango, and she
kneels before him, kissing his hand, when the revolt is over. The film's Ayché, however, does not belong; like all tragic mulattoes, she is caught between two warring worlds, and her false consciousness (as we will see) is
the center of the film's drama.[162] Her first encounter with Tamango draws
the lines of debate. He is chained on deck as punishment for attempting to
attack the captain; when Ayché offers him water, he calls her "White man's
trash" ("Putain de l'homme blanc!"). She tells him he is no better than a
gun or other piece of cheap merchandise used to buy him, so, "Don't put on
airs with me." Her thesis statement follows: "A slave can never fight back!
Never! Never! Never!" Tamango spits in her face. Only at the end of the film
will the seemingly unbridgeable gap between these two characters — and
between the parts of the world they represent, African America and Africa — be closed.

A short scene that takes place on deck perfectly illustrates Ayché's half-
and-half status. A group of women captives sits in a circle with Ayché; all
are in the neatly tailored outfits that drew derisive remarks from some critics. They are all weaving baskets, and it is worth noting that basket weaving
is a craft that very directly links West Africa to the Americas; the same traditional baskets can be seen today in both South Carolina and Senegal. So
this craft suggests a cultural bond between the African American Ayché and
her African sisters. Yet the questions Ayché asks show that she is mainly an

230

outsider to their culture: they must explain betrothal practices and symbols to her, with some signs of impatience.

A lovers' quarrel with the captain provides the spark that leads Ayché down the path toward identification with the African captives. Corot tells her that the captain is preparing to marry another woman at home in Rotterdam; she confronts him, and he sends her to the hold with the captives. Tamango tells Ayché: "Your place is with us." Ayché makes no active contribution to the revolt until near the bitter end, even though she seems willing to try to procure the captain's keys.[163] Her most important contribution to the revolt is passive: she does not inform the captain that Tamango has procured a file; she is thus complicit with the revolt. (She also tells the revolted captives how they can hide the body of the sailor that Tamango has killed.) The battle for her identity is joined. When she says to the captain, "I belong to them" (the captives), he makes an impassioned yet cynical argument against concatenations of all sorts. In a speech that seems designed to reproach fence-straddlers, a speech that could have been scripted by Fanon if he were giving voice to those he characterizes in *The Wretched of the Earth* as "onlookers" (who are all "cowards or traitors"),[164] the captain says to Ayché: "Those people out there, they would die for their tribe. We don't want to die for anything. We, we want to live, for ourselves. Maybe it's not very great or noble, but that's the way we are, both of us. . . . You sold them all out. You became — what do the slaves call it? — white man's trash. You'll stay. I know you will." The solidarity that the captain offers is that of pure individualism. Born perhaps as a result of rape, Ayché has no white "family"; the white half of her "blood" is not available as an identity position. The captain's speech takes that absence of white identity and makes it into an ideological posture of accommodation and opportunism. What is elided from this entire picture is any sense of Ayché's belonging to an *African American* culture on its own terms; the third term, in this case a biracial Creole, is suppressed. (The very idea of biracialism or interraciality was not yet current in the 1950s.)

231

It is striking to see the extent to which critics of the film in the 1950s and, more strangely, now, go along with this logic and assume that biracial Ayché is, for all intents and purposes, "black" or African. Thus the phrase "her people" is constantly used to refer to the African captives: her "loyalty is torn between her passionate master and her own people down in the hold" (*New York Times*); she hears "her people's war chant" (*Monthly Film Bulletin*) and reverts to "her own people" (*Variety*); she "elects to die with her people" (*Motion Picture Herald*). Vieyra refers to the Africans as Ayché's "blood brothers," although the whites onboard are, in fact, just as likely candidates for that label (Vieyra, *Le Cinéma et l'Afrique*, 63). Such was racial thinking in the 1950s, the "cultural norm" that Werner Sollors explains: in the modern United States, "a 'Mulatto' is really (and does not have to be proved) 'black.' This norm has come to be shared by black and white alike."[165] This idea lives on. Gwendolyn Audrey Foster reproduces this pattern in 1999, taking Ayché as a symbol of "*Black* female subjectivity" and repeating the idea that Ayché "finally aligns herself with *her own people*."[166]

Ayché herself begins to contribute to this alignment near the end of the film but continues to send mixed signals. In her confrontation with the captain she declares, "I belong with them. . . . I am part of them." But to Tamango in the hold she says the opposite: "I'm not a slave any more. . . . I'm free. You have no right to keep me here. You can't win. He isn't going to take you back to Africa." When Ayché fails to steal the captain's keys, a woman captive tells Tamango, "Ayché isn't with us."

Two factors make that forced assumption of the mulatto into the black understandable (though still problematic). The first is particularly obvious in the context of the United States, the home of the "one-drop rule": to be partially black is to be black. Dorothy Dandridge herself, despite her status as "mixed American," was "marked as black."[167] The second factor is that race, around the Atlantic, has so often stood for servitude: the captives are indeed Ayché's "people" in the sense that she is a slave. That, more than race, is what draws her into the concatenation with them in this film. The story that the film is telling is therefore less about race per se than about servitude. Ayché's final alignment is more political than racial, even though it cannot be seen outside the complexities of race that the film dramatizes. Very much by design, this concatenation remains open to wider interpretations and extrapolations. Viewers are invited to consider widening categories of thought: from geography to race, from race to servitude, and from servitude, possibly, allegorically, to other forms of oppression.[168]

A phrase from Mérimée's "Tamango" might shed light on the situation of Ayché in both the tale and the film. After Tamango has threatened her with Mumbo-Jumbo, the captain tries to "console" Ayché, but neither "caresses" nor "blows" succeed in making "the beautiful Negress *tractable*" (PM, 489/82, AT). The word that Mérimée used was *traitable*, hardly a random term in the context of the slave trade. It refers generally to that which can be influenced or tamed, but significantly of course, like the verb *traire*, it refers to drawing out or extracting. Slave traders in their journals took

10   Ayché (Dorothy Dandridge)
      on the stairs (*Tamango*).

notes on the peoples of Africa as either *traitables* or not *traitables*.[169] Ayché is
used in the film, even more than in the short story, as a figure of tractability
itself: she literalizes and sexualizes the battle between the white man and the
black man. And we must not forget that this role makes her (as was so often
the case with Dorothy Dandridge's characters) an object of violence.[170] In
the film she appears nearly impervious to Tamango's influence until, following her conversion, she conveys the idea that even the most stubborn, intractable onlooker can eventually become part of the mass movement from
below. The significance of her final allegiance is increased by the strength
and duration of her resistance.

233

     In the final moments of the film Tamango takes Ayché hostage in the hold
of the ship: "We've got your woman down here," he tells the captain. "If we
have to, we'll kill her." The captain is forced to choose and decides to massacre his mistress along with the rest of the slaves. In the film's climax, as
the slaves chant, Tamango tells Ayché she is free to go. But on the stairs, literally suspended between worlds, Ayché looks up (see figure 10), then turns
and joins the chant and the concatenation it represents. The cannon is fired
as the camera remains discretely above deck; screams, then silence. Ayché
has perished with "her people." If Ayché is initially set up as a figure for the
lack of any sense of agency, her behavior does not ultimately bear such an
interpretation out. Instead she "speaks truth to power" by denouncing the
captain to his face ("Bas les pattes!" she screams in French—"I've always
hated your hands on me!"). In the end she opts for death in solidarity with
her fellow slaves—but *not* as an act of submission to the other alpha male,
Tamango (as Marguerite Rippy sees it). She has committed herself to the
group concatenation, not to any single man.

Tarzan Meets Fanon

The Tamango in Berry's film is a very modern figure. If Ayché's initial position is that slavery can never be resisted or escaped, that white power is implacable, Tamango's is exactly the opposite: "He [the captain] will never make a slave of me." Always a slave, or never a slave. As I said earlier, Mérimée's Tamango was "split" into two new characters for this film. An African king who, like Mérimée's Tamango, trades in slaves and has a taste for rum is present, but he is not Tamango. The film's Tamango is a young, virile, handsome lion hunter, sold by the king to the ship's captain. This splitting of Tamango is vital: without it, as in the Mérimée tale, Tamango is so complicit in the slave trade that he could hardly be transformed into a modern black nationalist hero. The modern sensibility can no longer accept what Aphra Behn offered in 1688 in *Oroonoko*—an African *slave-trading* prince, himself enslaved, who is converted into a mouthpiece for (very early) *antislavery* sentiment.[171] The film's Tamango hunts nothing but lions in Africa; he is noble like Tarzan (but black) and looks every bit as good in his loin cloth. He is ready to lead his people. Tarzan meets Fanon. (Unless we can think those two things at once, and operate in those two very different registers at once, we can't understand an artifact like this movie, which is both kitsch and a serious work of liberationist ideology.)

234

Alex Cressan's physical presence is a major factor in *Tamango* and a worthy match to the power of Dorothy Dandridge. Tamango is first seen when the captain is buying him, a "fine specimen." From his first encounter with his captors, this Tamango resists; he tries to attack the captain. For participating in a hunger strike, he is chained to the deck, lying on his back. Wearing only a loincloth, with his physique thus on full display as Ayché offers him water, the sexual and ideological tension between the two is launched. The ideological purity of nationalism is associated with his pure, masculine blackness, in counterpoint to the masculine whiteness of the captain, who is also sexualized in the film, in steamy, shirtless clinches with Ayché.

Such scenes could be filmed in France, far from the Hollywood Production Code (which would not be abandoned until ten years later). This is phallic nationalism, the "manliness of pure races."[172] Indecisiveness is represented as feminine and biracial. Tamango never wavers or shows any doubt about the course of action; Ayché does nothing but waver, until the end. Together with the captain they form a perfect triangle. The "love" triangle reflects the Atlantic slave-trade triangle: Europe (the captain), Africa (Tamango),

11 The Atlantic triangle personified: Tamango (Alex Cressan), Ayché (Dorothy Dandridge), and the Captain (Curt Jurgens) (*Tamango*).

and the New World (Ayché) (see figure 11). Standard Hollywood plotlines, especially in westerns, would require the two sexualized males to fight it out with their fists in order to collapse the untenable triangle; here of course that cannot happen because one is a slave. Direct physical engagement between the two men is ruled out by the cultural code. Therefore the confrontation will take place on a collective level, as Tamango leads his people—finally including Ayché—in revolt.

235

Tamango plots resistance and revolt from the beginning, vowing never to be a slave. As for those captives who are not warriors, "We'll make them into warriors." At one point he feigns submission to the captain as a ruse, and his dubbed speech in English is that of an Uncle Tom: "Yessir, mighty fine, mighty fine, giddy up." But soon he has a stolen file in hand; he kills Bibi, the bosun, who sees it. Soon after the captain's speech quoted above, as the final moment approaches, Tamango preaches the opposite view to Ayché and the others in the hold. With tears flowing down his face, Tamango says: "Give up if you want. They'll let you live. . . . Maybe not all of you, but most of you. Or we can all stay and fight. And *even if we die, we'll win* because they can sell living men, but you can't sell dead ones. Me, they won't sell me."[173] The captives, hearing this, immediately gather around Tamango and vow to fight, as they swear a blood oath: "Brothers in life, brothers in death." A woman captive tells Ayché, "The women are going to fight too." Tamango's leadership has formed this complete concatenation.

"Even if we die, we'll win" is the premise of the film's ending.[174] Within the diegesis the statement is true in the sense that the slaves will win by making the slave traders lose their potential profit. But considering the film's powers of representation and connotation, the implications of the statement are far broader; the idea is martyrdom. If they are massacred, they will become — and did become — figures of heroism onscreen, rousing audiences to tears and applause. And that is the effect that the film has had. At its Paris premiere, *Le Figaro* reported, the audience, including a Princess Sixte de Bourbon-Parme, cheered Ayché's conversion (Jan. 25, 1958). At the Film Forum in New York in 1997 Foster says that *Tamango* "evoked audience members to tears and shouting, and left the audience shattered by the grim ending" (*Captive Bodies*, 182).

The era of decolonization was rich with literary martyrs of nationalism, often a singular male hero dying for a cause that is then supposed to be propelled onward by his legacy. Jacques Roumain's novel of Haiti, *Gouverneurs de la rosée* (1944); Ferdinand Oyono's novel of Cameroon, *Une Vie de boy* (1956); and Sembene Ousmane's tale of Senegal, *O Pays, mon beau peuple!* (1957), itself derivative of the Roumain novel — all follow this pattern. (Sembene's first novel, *Le Docker noir*, is far more ambiguous about nationalist heroics, although it uses the slave trade as a central theme, as we will see in a later chapter.) Berry's *Tamango* calls on those who, like Ayché, lack commitment, to join the struggle for liberation. Ayché chooses the concatenation of the revolted slaves over continuing bondage and concubinage with the captain. We have seen that, if this is an allegory of liberation, it offers only *two* possibilities, a Manichean choice: the captain and Tamango. The in-between position is erased; Ayché is not allowed to remain on the stairs, suspended between white and black.

Mating

An important subplot throws the phallic nationalism of the film into relief. The bosun, Bibi (Roger Hanin), and his mate Dana have a *very* close relationship. This becomes evident when Bibi is killed and Dana consequently goes insane. He stabs a slave who he thinks killed the bosun, and as Dana repeats over and over, "He killed Bibi," the captain orders him to be put in irons. As the screen time devoted to Dana's grief goes on, its significance becomes inescapable: this is a lover's mourning. Dana speaks through his tears of Bibi as "my mate," a term that spans maritime and matrimonial usages in ways that were actually institutionalized onboard sailing ships (and on the islands of the Caribbean as well). I will explore this practice, called *matelotage*, in detail in the chapter on Corbière later in this study. This subplot is, I believe, a reflection of two things at once: first, the historical practice of sailors pairing themselves off as each other's mate or *matelot*; and second, the workings of the "celluloid closet," the coded ways in which homosexuality was depicted onscreen in the decades when it could not be discussed openly.[175]

But there is more to the homosexual subtext of *Tamango* than this one, apparently loving and consensual, relationship. Bibi is a sinister character. The male captive who accepts Tamango's charge to hide the file on deck hid himself underneath a tarpaulin, waiting for nightfall. In the dark he emerges and begins crawling across the deck. But Bibi appears, towering over him, cuffing him lightly on the head and gently kicking his buttocks as the captive scuttles further. Bibi then looks over his shoulder, to see if anyone is watching, before following the captive, who is still on all fours. As the scene cuts away, the suggestion of impending rape is clear. The next morning, the same captive is hanged on deck as all captives and crew look on; Bibi is there, sneering at the slaves.

Here is a taboo within a taboo: homosexual rape within the context of the slave trade, a subject that no historian or novelist has touched. Later, in Sue's *Atar-Gull* and Corbière's *Le Négrier*, and in another glance at Equiano's *The Interesting Narrative*, we will find traces of homosocial pairings across the color line but no suggestion of rape. The mere thought of sex of any kind between a male captive and a male sailor has the potential to disrupt the patterns of modern phallic nationalism that we examined. It is fascinating to see how Berry's film managed to include this disturbing subplot, discreetly and discretely. This thread does not, however, interrupt the forward motion of the film, nor the unfolding of its nationalist ideology.

Nationalism and Internationalism

I have been describing *Tamango* as a nationalist film. The term *nationalism* was used in the African context of the 1950s (and the African American context of the 1960s) not to suggest the defense of a preexisting nation, state, or even "tribe" — but rather the struggle against colonialism to be, first of all, *free*, perhaps then to attempt to create such a thing as a nation-state. This was *international* nationalism. In the 1950s nationalism was more centrifugal than centripetal, more concerned with opposing imperialism than with building nation-states.[176]

This film is an international phenomenon in numerous ways, beginning with its transatlantic genesis and bilingual production. With that in the background it is interesting to examine the ways in which *Tamango*, which had to be made in France, seems to have been deliberately "de-Frenchified."

In order for the film to pass through French government censorship, the story that it told had to be washed of Frenchness; French involvement in the slave trade—a taboo subject—had to be downplayed. In the Mérimée story the captain and crew are entirely French, and, true to history, they evade an English cruiser enforcing the ban on the slave trade. But in the film a bizarre array of transformations takes place, the effect of which is to muffle French involvement in the slave trade. The captain, whose name is not spoken, is apparently Dutch, since he refers to Rotterdam as home. He is played by a German actor who speaks English and French in the respective versions. If he had been played by, for example, Jean Servais or Jean Gabin, a great deal of Frenchness would have been implicated; that was avoided. The ship is not called the *Espérance* but the *Esperanza*, which is Spanish. This is a little odd, though not totally implausible. Since the Papal Bull of 1493 granting Africa to the Portuguese, the Spaniards were not major direct buyers of slaves on the coast of Africa; they worked through *asientos* granted to other European powers.[177] This situation changed somewhat in the early nineteenth century, but still, the idea of changing the ship's nationality from French to Spanish is a strange gesture, part of a pattern of flouting the "rules of evidence" that Natalie Zemon Davis would like to see respected in historical films. Staking out a position that we cannot ignore in the context of this study, Davis declares, "Historical films should let the past be the past" (precisely what *Tamango* does not do).[178] Those rules would suggest that, to avoid misrepresentation about the principal facts of the slave trade, the ship should more likely be French (or perhaps English or Portuguese) rather than Spanish.

There is reason to think, however, that the producers thought the word *esperanza* was Portuguese (although the Portuguese word for hope is *esperança*). When the ship sets sail, the captain gives the following orders: "If he [the lookout] spots a British cruiser, run up the French flag. If it's a French boat, hoist the Union Jack. If it's anything else, *keep it Portuguese*" (emphasis added).[179] This obscures the fact that, in 1820, a ban on the slave trade was being enforced almost entirely by the British and violated by French traders; French enforcement at that point was rare and ineffectual.[180]

None of this would have been a surprise to a well-informed viewer of the French version of the movie, which begins with an outrageous disclaimer: "It is to the honor of France that it was one of the first nations to abolish slavery, by a decree of the National Convention on February 4, 1794, and that its government rose up in 1815 against the slave trade" ("C'est l'honneur de la France, d'avoir été une des premières nations à abolir l'esclavage par un décret de la Convention nationale du 4 février 1794 et d'avoir vu en 1815, son Gouvernement s'élever contre la traite des Noirs"). French capitulation to English pressure in 1815 hardly qualifies as an uprising. Vieyra interprets this and the other gestures of "de-Frenchifying" in the film as pandering.[181] But with the benefit of hindsight it seems essential to reinterpret these transformations as measures that were necessary in order for the film to be made and distributed. For *Tamango* to be made in France—which was a refuge from American racism and American McCarthyism—France had to be exonerated; its history as the third-ranking nation in the Atlantic slave trade had to be obscured. That awkward fact will be erased by "de-Frenchifying" everyone and everything in the film except the doctor with the (slightly) complicated conscience.

It wasn't quite enough. The film was screened in France but banned in the colonies. Algerians, Africans, Malagasies would not be allowed to see it.[182] *Tamango*, in spite of its catering to French sensitivities, remained (and remains) an allegory of liberation and of nationalism—not what the French government wanted to be broadcasting in its tumultuous colonies. Even after breaking the "rules of evidence" and playing fast and loose with the facts of history, *Tamango* delivers an unmistakable message of liberation.

239

She Says "Tamango" and He Says "Tamahngo"

In the English-language version of the film all characters speak English from the beginning; in the French version all speak French. The captives who are brought onboard speak these languages from the beginning. The language barriers that were so much a part of the slave trade are magically suspended so that the nationalist allegory can proceed unfettered.[183] A huge suspension of disbelief is required.[184] It does not come, however, without some strange effects. Different versions of English cross-hatch the film, as some characters (including all of the Africans) are dubbed, some speak in European accents (including the captain), and Dorothy Dandridge, alone, inserts colloquial American English, creating what the *Monthly Film Bulletin* called a "What's cooking, you guys?" tonality. Thus she and the captain say "Tamango" and everyone else in the film says "Tamahngo." Some call the bosun Bibi, some Bébé. Some say Ayché, some Aycha. Thus underneath the smooth surface of the two universalized, colonizing languages (English and French), various centrifugal, heteroglot forces can be heard, pulling outward toward different points around the Atlantic. The French version is more uniform, although some of the African actors have slight accents;

and Dorothy Dandridge's spoken French is marked by a distinct American accent.

At the end the force of heteroglossia is made explicit. The one non-English, non-French utterance in the film (other than the name of the boat) comes at the film's climax and serves as the vehicle for Ayché's conversion. This is the final chant, in an indistinguishable language that is obviously intended to be "African."[185] The "true cry" of the "crowd," of the "many" — the voice of the concatenation — thus breaks away from the patent artificiality of universal English, which has propelled the narrative, in order to reach for a new *symbolic* language. If this other language is itself artificial, it nonetheless is meant to bear the burden of political, existential authenticity.

But although the African chant is represented as the true language of liberation in the film, it is not given the last word. The revolt is, after all, repressed by a massacre. The final frame is given over to a single word: ESPERANZA, the ship's name, which we read on a sign over the aft cabin. The screen at that point has two locutions on it THE END (or FIN) and ESPERANZA: the ending *is* "hope." In that word Mérimée's sneering irony can still be sensed: after all, the slaves are dead, so where is the hope? But that irony has itself been superseded by the message of solidarity that the film has prepared and produced. The toxin of Mérimée's anticoncatenating irony has been counteracted. The message is, again, clear: we are *not* to be discouraged by the death of the oppressed; rather we should find "hope" in their martyrdom. Being expressed in Spanish, this message effectively suspends us in an artificial Atlantic, where the French slave trade is absent. The film thus speaks of the French Atlantic slave trade "otherwise," in a language, Spanish, that was largely alien to it. This gesture thus fulfills the etymological idea of allegory, to speak "otherwise."

Tamango does not let the past be the past. Very purposefully, it insinuates the present into the past; the 1950s cast a complex network of shadows onto the 1820s, *distorting* the past. The film does this so that the present can speak — and get away with it. On one side of the Atlantic the Hollywood Production Code and the sensitivity of civil rights issues made *Tamango* an untouchable project; on the other side censorship and the specter of decolonization made it nearly so. (The idea of producing the film on the third point of the triangle, in colonized Africa, was of course not considered.) Caught within these constraints, *Tamango* compromised with the French so that the movie could be seen.

Tamango thus seems to offer a form of connectivity—and even a meta-phorization or allegory of the slave trade—to celebrate. But only within limits and not without a cost. We can look back with admiration at those who struggled for liberation in the 1950s—and before, or after. But closer examination of the choices they saw and imposed on their contemporaries may make us uncomfortable in our age of hybridity. The drama of Ayché—and of Dorothy Dandridge herself—is the erasure of third, middle terms when faced with an implacable binary opposition. The inability to *be* Ayché and to "survive the consequences" (which of course Dorothy Dandridge herself did not do)[186] is difficult to contemplate. When humanity is divided in this way, some do not survive.[187]

Perhaps the hopefulness of the film's ending requires that we stay in 1957, 1958, and 1959—when the film was produced and released. To go beyond that moment, at least in Africa, into the brave new world of paper independences and disillusionment, would be, potentially, to find ourselves again in a zero-sum game where the new nation-states wake up, caught in the old, *negative* concatenations of colonialism. Or perhaps we'd rather flash-forward and across the Atlantic again, to the Film Forum in 1997, where the audience found something to cheer about.

If nothing else, the film, like Césaire's *Cahier*, offers a stunning response to Mérimée. There *can* be a concatenation of revolted slaves, who *can* take control of their destiny, even if it is only to sacrifice their lives.

241

ANOTHER TIME OF TAMANGO

> *Le Temps de Tamango*—un titre qui ne veut rien dire. [*The Time of Tamango*—a title that means nothing.]
> —BOUBACAR BORIS DIOP, *Le Temps de Tamango*

A novel by Senegalese author Boubacar Boris Diop, *Le Temps de Tamango* (1981), takes the deliberate anachronism of Berry's film much further, in a reinvention of the Tamango tale that is wildly postmodern and not unlike the novels of Georges Perec in its pseudohistoriographical pseudoserious-ness.[188] It has been cited as the "first example of African meta-fiction."[189] But in fact, I would suggest that Ousmane Sembene's first novel, *Le Docker noir*, also contains elements of metafiction, if only because it contains a novel within a novel; and as it happens, the embedded novel (*Le Dernier voyage du négrier "Sirius"*) is concerned with the slave trade and constitutes another echo of Mérimée's "Tamango."[190]

Le Temps de Tamango actually has very little to do with the slave trade, and beyond the name, only a few pages are devoted to a reinvention of Mérimée's "Tamango."[191] Diop seems to have at least one clear goal: to mock the "sourcing" of literature as practiced by Mérimée and the sleuthing of sources by his critics.[192] "Tamango" in this novel is, first of all, the nom de guerre of the main character, N'Dongo Thiam, who lives from 1949 to 1986, and who is being discussed from the perspective of the 2060s. The "time" of Tamango is thus rather complex. The place is less ambiguous: Diop has brought Tamango "home" to Africa.

The Mérimée text first comes up as N'Dongo is on his way to a demonstration in Dakar, surrounded by a *crowd* that "does not seem to know where to go"—does not know, in Césaire's words, how to be a crowd (*faire foule*). The thematics of concatenation and the drama of the Tamango paradigm (complete with a ship that has gone adrift for lack of a competent helmsman) that we have been reviewing are fully engaged here, as N'Dongo muses: "'Neither did Tamango, the unchained slave, know which direction to take. After the revolt and the victory he had to let the boat drift [*voguer au hasard*]. That is what lost him. He did not know how to steer a boat [*conduire un navire*]. A fine subject for a novel.' N'Dongo does not write much but he feels that he has things to say" (31).

But the setup here does not produce the conventional results; this is no bildungsroman in which the hero, having perceived that his people are adrift, neatly rises to the occasion like the poet of Césaire's *Cahier*, Emmanuel in *Gouverneurs de la rosée*, or Oumar in *O Pays, mon beau peuple!* N'Dongo, to begin with, has a bad attitude, casting "a distracted and contemptuous gaze upon his contemporaries" (31). To produce a nationalist hero, realism—a firm belief in reality and confidence in its representations—must prevail. N'Dongo parallels—and even parodies—the trajectory of such a hero: he knows that he must "reach his people and emerge with them into the light"; the main character in this self-analyzing novel "will be called Tamango, the symbol of all revolts" (120). He assumes roles of false submissiveness to French power (like the film's Tamango at a certain moment, and like Toundi, the hero in *Une Vie de boy*, an expert in the art of feigning). The French people fail to grasp the revolutionary overtones of his name because they don't know African "history"—as if Tamango were historical (112). Like Diouana in Sembene's *La Noire de . . .*, "Tamango" is an invisible subal-

242

tern. His assignment is to avenge the death of a martyr of the resistance by killing a French general (111). All of this is consistent with a narrative of liberation. But the Fanonist paradigm is not fulfilled in this novel, which radically questions reality itself and leaves nothing certain. The reader is unsure what to believe in a novel that, at one point, mocks the idea of a Narrator ("A loser who . . . hides behind others in order to have them say whatever" [123]). N'Dongo seems to wind up living alone, talking to himself and to imaginary enemies, writing "incoherent" graffiti on the walls of the city (100–101). We are back to an ignominious ending for a "Tamango." He might as well be playing the cymbals in a regiment.[193]

Like a much more famous postmodern/postcolonial novel, Henri Lopes's *Le Pleurer-Rire* (1982), which also happens to be much more readable, *Le Temps de Tamango* alternates narration with commentary on the narration—what John Erickson calls the "pseudo-paratextual" practice of the novel ("Writing Double," 106). Within the final set of "notes" in the novel the Narrator is quoted, describing his efforts to find the "historical" Tamango. This turns into a reinvention of the Tamango story as a new postcolonial myth. But, true to postmodern form, it is precisely as a gesture of *demythification* that this new myth is created:

243

> The Narrator took particular care with the "notes" on Tamango. If it can be believed, numerous obstacles nearly made him give up on his research: "I had to investigate arduously and remain absolutely obstinate in order to maintain my belief that Tamango had actually existed in flesh and blood. At the beginning I had the impression that I was chasing a mirage. I first consulted all the important works of the twentieth century that dealt with the slave trade, and I didn't find the name Tamango anywhere. Going back into the nineteenth century, I didn't find anything either, except for a novella by a certain Prosper Mérimée, a French novelist of that period. . . . Indeed, if I couldn't prove the existence of Tamango in a convincing, even indubitable way, my work would have absolutely no meaning. . . . In spite of my doubts, I was convinced deep inside myself that it was impossible that Tamango never existed anywhere [*impossible que Tamango n'eût jamais existé nulle part*]. (133)

The Narrator's stated goal is to "restore to history a personage that has been almost entirely devoured by mythology" (134). In fact this personage is, ironically, himself a myth. The Narrator has a breakthrough when he finds a work by one W. T. Bennett entitled *Une Révolte d'esclaves au XVIIIe siècle*, whose bibliography leads to seventy-three other works. The kind of literary sleuthing that is being mocked here is, of course, precisely the type I was doing earlier in this chapter, working on Mérimée's sources.

The "true" Tamango emerges now for this Narrator, as Mérimée is dismissed (he "was only a novelist, that is, a gentleman authorized to say anything he wants [*n'importe quoi*] in the name of the imagination"): "Tamango was the chief of an important tribe that lived on the West coast of Africa in the eighteenth century" (135). On June 22, 1729, this Tamango takes his people to greet the first European ship to reach their coast, joyfully, for their founding ancestors had told them to expect white people who would bring happiness for 999 years and 33 days. Tamango sells his enemies to the captain, "Jean-Baptiste Delarose," for blue jeans and tape recorders. But things go sour in 1742 when Tamango (now following Mérimée), drunk, sells his wife, Léna, into slavery, and, attempting to rescue her, is trepanned himself.

For another moment the story follows Mérimée fairly closely: Tamango revolts, breaking his chains and killing the captain, whom he finds caressing a naked Léna. With the ship taken, Tamango lies to his compatriots, saying he knows how to sail the ship. Then we depart from Mérimée again: in spite of Tamango's ignorance the ship is "mastered" and reaches "the native land" (*la terre natale*) (138–39). Tamango becomes a powerful leader of resistance to the slave trade in Africa: "The slave trade quickly became impossible on an entire sector of the African Continent, and for that we are indebted to Tamango" (140). Erickson sees Diop's use of Tamango as "an intertextual metaphor for the neo-colonialist failure that substitutes one system for another while using the same instruments of control" ("Writing Double," 109). To this, one qualification must be added: Diop's Tamango *defeats* the slave trade and therefore has some claim to heroism.

Of course the joke is that history and fiction have been reversed within the novel: that which is presented as history, starting with the work by "W. T. Bennett," is pure fantasy. The follow-up to the indirect reporting on this pseudotrue Tamango hints at what may be Diop's purpose in (re)telling this story. In the era of the novel's narration, in the future, a communist government rules, speaking a hollow *langue de bois*; it is far from utopian.[194] The Commentator who is the author of the annotations (not to be confused with the Narrator) suggests that any denigration of Tamango as a leader who didn't care about his people (thus exactly my reading of Mérimée's "Tamango") should be reported to "our communist leaders" so that "our valiant youth" can have valid heroes (140). Communist or not, postcolonial authoritarianism of the 1980s is being targeted here, and at this point this highly unconventional novel approaches the mainstream of postcolonial Francophone African fiction.

To end his reinvention of Tamango on an appropriately perverse note, Diop's Narrator adds, "Léna never existed. . . . Gentlemen, Léna is simply a symbol. . . . 'Yes, but symbol of what?' Move on! Really move on!" Then, "the 'notes' end with a short appendix entitled *Tamango, Literary Myth*" (140). Myth and "history" have been thoroughly scrambled. We are no longer in the era of confident nationalism that was so readable in both Cés-aire's *Cahier* and Berry's *Tamango*. Now the artist, Diop, wants us to worry about what happens in the gap between a myth of concatenation and its en-forcement as state dogma. So we are back to an ironic Tamango, and in that sense we have come full circle. Tamango was rescued from Mérimée's cor-rosive irony by Césaire and Berry, pressed into service for the purposes of Negritude and nationalism. Diop's postcolonial Tamango now invites us to be skeptical about myths of leadership, representation, and concatenation. His ironic skepticism is, however, a long distance from Mérimée's; it is one of many warnings that postcolonial African writers have issued about the condition of their own continent.

245

A TAMANGO FOR THE NEW MILLENNIUM

In 2003 a Cameroonian filmmaker working in Paris, Jean-Roké Patoudem, discussed with me his project for a new film version of the Tamango story. Having done copious research into the history of the slave trade and on Mérimée and his sources, Patoudem was in the process of constructing a film that would bring Tamango "back" to Africa, inserting the story into the history of the continent for the first time.[195] Strongly disliking Berry's film, Patoudem wants to bring, in his view, gravely needed awareness of the slave trade to Africa.[196]

FORGET HAITI

Baron Roger and the New Africa

Saint-Domingue was lost to France forever. All that was left was
the *memory*; and during the Restoration and the Second Empire,
it was considered good form to have a grandmother who had returned from the islands.

—COMTESSE JEAN DE PANGE,
"Madame de Staël et les nègres" (1934)

THE TRIANGLE DISRUPTED

Cultural memory is a topic that has been much discussed in recent years,
and it is of great relevance in the context of this study. Memory is
nearly synonymous with studies of slavery and the slave trade. But what
of memory's other, forgetting? A nation, in Renan's famous formulation,
requires both remembering and forgetting; the same is true of a transnational construct like the Atlantic. The French Atlantic triangle was built on
and has left as its legacy a structure that combines memory and forgetting
in a complex web. I have already discussed at numerous points in this study
how the mercantile policy of France, the *Exclusif*, helped to enforce a ban
on "return" journeys to Africa from the islands, thereby imposing memory
loss and setting up the most important restorative task of African American cultures. This chapter will examine an important change in the Atlantic structure of memory and forgetting: how France attempted to come to
terms with the Haitian Revolution, long after it was over, through a calculated plan for forgetting.

The persistence of representations of the Haitian Revolution in French literature and in the nineteenth-century debates over the abolition of slavery, even many years after the revolution, showed that France was having a hard time forgetting its former colony and letting it go. The revolution was, as Michel-Rolph Trouillot puts it, "unthinkable even as it happened."[1] David Brion Davis describes it as "a turning point in history. Like the Hiroshima bomb, its meaning could be rationalized or repressed but never really forgotten."[2] Afterward, schemes for retaking Saint-Domingue (as the French still called it) were an "obsession."[3] Narratives of the "crimes, tortures, and devastations" of the revolution perpetuated a one-sided view of France as purely a victim in the Haitian Revolution, and "grim memories" of that revolution "constantly haunted" the planters of the remaining slave islands; Napoleon was so traumatized that he sold Louisiana, doubling the size of the United States for four cents an acre: "damn sugar, damn coffee, damn colonies!"[4] Around the Atlantic, images of the upheaval "hovered over the antislavery debates like a bloodstained ghost."[5] In the United States, "for thirty years every slave revolt was attributed to blacks from [Saint-Domingue]."[6] In France the memoir of the Saint-Janvier sisters' harrowing experiences and escape from the revolution was typical.[7] The hurried and traumatized allusion to Haiti in Duras's *Ourika* was a moment of involuntary memory (and a gesture of attempted forgetting), while Hugo's *Bug-Jargal* reflected the persistence of the images of violence and loss. When French abolitionism reorganized itself in the 1830s, its agenda was still "stained" with the blood of the planters of Saint-Domingue.[8] Even on the eve of the 1848 abolition, the memory of Haiti would be brought back as a specter: "Let us look back and *remember* the horrible disasters which took away from France forever its most beautiful, most flourishing, most productive colony . . . Saint-Domingue."[9] Françoise Vergès accurately diagnoses the cause of this mnemopsychosis: "The Haitian Revolution, its violence, and its excesses allow Europe to justify its role as ruler of the world."[10] Haiti will thus be forgotten only when its symbolic use value is exhausted and, incidentally, after its monetary "debt" to France (150 million francs of "indemnity") is paid.[11] In other words, Haiti is required to pay that ruinous sum in order to end French schemes of reinvasion and reenslavement. Haiti buys the right to be forgotten by France. Sure enough, following the emancipation law, "the wave of French publications about Haiti came to an end in 1826," and, with few exceptions, "interest in the country declined."[12] Exactly two hundred years later, after the coup d'état of March 2004 ended the presidency

247

of Jean-Bertrand Aristide—who had demanded reparations (or restitution) from France for the nineteenth-century payments Haiti had made—Defense Minister Michele Alliot-Marie became the first French minister to visit Haiti since independence. The new Haitian leader, Gérard Latortue, dropped the "ridiculous" demand for payback.[13]

The novel that I will analyze in this chapter, Baron Jacques-François Roger's *Kelédor, histoire africaine* (1828), suggests a strategy for forgetting Haiti and for dominating (a part of) the world (Africa). Everyone knows that the only way to get a persistent tune out of your head is to hum another one in its place; Roger's *Kelédor* methodically substitutes Africa for Haiti in hopes that France can change its colonial tune: end the slave trade, abolish slavery, forget the Antilles, and turn Africa into a productive "garden."

Colonial Saint-Domingue would prove hard to forget; it had been essential to the French Atlantic economy. As the recipient and consumer of the largest share of enslaved Africans, Saint-Domingue became the most productive colony ever known. Deaths on the lucrative plantations there fueled the slave trade, which in turn, as Roger dramatizes in his novel, fueled wars in Africa. The enslavement of subaltern Africans raised the living standard of elites in Europe, in Africa, and in the islands, thereby fueling desire for further investment in the slave trade and slave labor.[14] Thus the French Atlantic economy perpetuated itself. Out of sight in France, slavery was out of mind—even as the slave labor of Saint-Domingue in particular, according to the Creole observer from Saint-Domingue Moreau de Saint-Méry, "built in the Kingdom cities which astound by their magnificence."[15]

The Haitian Revolution of course brought most of that to an end. The French Atlantic slave system would limp along until the final abolition of slavery in 1848, but it would never be the same as it was at its peak in the late eighteenth century. Hugo described what was at stake in the Haitian Revolution: "a struggle of giants, with three worlds involved, Europe and Africa as the combatants and America as the battlefield."[16] As the revolution evolved into Haitian independence, it became clear that the French Atlantic was forever altered. This new opening of the question of the Atlantic brought to the fore doubts that had been raised about the wisdom of the entire triangular system almost from its inception. Was it really necessary to transport enslaved Africans all the way across the ocean?

As early as the seventeenth century, the extravagance of the Atlantic system was questioned. An African king, Agaja of Dahomey, considered trying to grow sugar cane himself, so that all of the profits of slave labor would not go to the Europeans; the English and the Dutch both mused about setting up plantations in Africa.[17] Louis Moreau de Chambonneau wrote in 1677 that Senegal could produce tobacco, indigo, sugar cane—in other words, the colonial products of the Antilles.[18] In 1762 the Abbé Roudaut put forth the idea that Africans should be left at home to cultivate sugar cane there; the result, he was sure, would be "a greater quantity of sugar cane, thicker, and more succulent, more delicious than that that we get" in the Antilles.[19] The physiocrats, who were in favor of colonialism, argued for the establishment of plantations in Africa based on free labor so that "we shall have perfected [Africans'] ways of life and ours."[20] A number of different French voices argued, from the middle of the eighteenth century forward, in favor of a rehabilitated image of the African continent that often emphasized its fertility and readiness for colonization.[21] Lafayette proposed conquering North Africa and establishing free-labor plantations that could make the Antilles obsolete.[22] The eighteenth-century abolitionist Louis-Sébastien Mercier wrote in his novel *L'An 2440*, which is set in a utopian future:

> We no longer carry [Africans] in filthy containers fifteen hundred leagues from their country in order to cultivate, under the lacerating whip of a cowardly owner, sugar canes that are much less fine than those grown right next to their paternal huts. You ravaged America so that you could then plant sugar cane, and you got both the cane and the Negroes from the African coast. Alas! You shouldn't have taken so much trouble, expenditure, and cruelty in order to have sugar. It would have been sufficient not to degrade men whom nature had placed next to sugar canes, in their home country.[23]

Raynal echoed this idea, stating plainly the connection between abolitionism and a new colonialism aimed at Africa: "It is not necessary to give up the products that habit has made so dear [sugar, rum, etc.]. You could get them from Africa itself."[24] In 1795 Condorcet argued in favor of planting sugar in Africa as the leading edge of a civilizing and *abolitionist* mission: bringing sugar plantations to Africa would, somewhat paradoxically, end the slave trade.[25] The Société des Amis des Noirs et des Colonies (1796) stated that the abolition of the slave trade should facilitate the opening up of Africa to salutary European commerce.[26] We saw how Madame de Staël, in her novella *Mirza* (1795), described plantations in Senegal that would equal those of Saint-Domingue, using free and "happy" labor.[27] And the former naval officer Ohier de Grandpré summed up the argument in 1801: "European greed went [to Africa] looking for men to cultivate the Antilles, islands that it would have been better not to depopulate. From [Congo] we insisted on transplanting these wretches to a foreign soil that killed them, when all the while, with less expenditure and more success, we could have cultivated their own soil."[28] According to this whole chorus of observers, colonies in Africa, without slavery, are the answer to the horrors of the Atlantic triangle. Implicit in all these observations was the idea that Europe should change its approach to the Atlantic economy: instead of bringing the workers (African slaves) to the work (in the Americas), it should bring the work (plantations) to the workers (in Africa).[29] This should be done in a spirit of utopian, egalitarian agrarianism. The radical alteration of the triangular Atlantic economy was implicit in this wish expressed in *Mirza*: "May free commerce be established between the *two* parts of the world"—between Europe and Africa bilaterally, America as the third term having been forgotten.[30]

In the Anglo-American Atlantic a "peculiar alliance of slaveholders and abolitionists" promoted the colonization of Africa.[31] These "colonizationists" founded Liberia in 1816, and the idea had considerable influence in France. So when Roger proposed, enacted, and "novelized" in *Kelédor* an abolitionist scheme for growing colonial products in Africa, he was far from original; he was giving new substance to an old idea and a "common abolitionist argument."[32] It is the different forms that Roger gave to this premise—on the ground and on paper—that give him a unique place in the history and the literary history of the French Atlantic.

ROGER: *ARRIVISTE, AFRICANISTE*

Jacques-François Roger is an intriguing figure. Born in 1787, the son of a lawyer, he studied law himself, but, with an impulse that was very rare in his times, he sought out "extraordinary things" by requesting a position in the colonies.[33] Through his good connections, he was made the first civilian governor of Senegal in 1821. Roger was "terribly ambitious" and "eager for accolades," with a taste for intrigue, according to the historian Georges Hardy; Roger succeeded in getting himself the title of baron in 1824.[34] He ended his term as governor in 1826 and was elected deputy—from the *département* of the Loiret, not from Senegal.[35] This "ambitious *parvenu* of the Restoration" leveraged himself socially and politically at home through his work in Africa.[36] But his legacy is not mere vanity; his engagement with

Africa was genuine and effective. In retrospect he appears as the prototype
of a new species of French administrator in Africa with a brilliant future,
the protoanthropologist. He was succeeded by a whole tradition, associated
with names like Faidherbe in the late nineteenth century, and Maurice Delafosse, M. J. Clozel, and Georges Hardy in the twentieth.[37] What characterizes this particular phenotype of administrator is "interest" in Africa—a
term that Roger uses often. The notion of *intérêt* is in fact full of ambiguity—connoting both engagement with the world and exploitation of it—
and will require examination here.

Roger's appointment as governor came during the Bourbon Restoration
in France, under Louis XVIII. As we have seen, turning back the hands
of time was the order of the day. With the Treaty of Paris and the restoration of the colonies, the slave trade became both illegal and feasible. During
the period when Roger, an abolitionist, was governor of Senegal, approximately 680 captives were exported from Senegal each year—thus upwards
of 3,400 during Roger's term, perhaps more.[38] Although this is not a huge
number within the larger scheme of the Atlantic slave trade, it is certainly
significant, especially for those enslaved.

One thing, however, could not be restored: Saint-Domingue. Thoughts
of taking Haiti back and reenslaving its population were ended in 1825 by
the "emancipation" law, in which Charles X "conceded" independence to
Haiti. This was while Roger was still governor of Senegal. In order to better
understand Roger's preoccupations of 1828, it is important to see how proximate these events and concerns were. At the beginning of the Restoration
in 1814, colonists had wondered how much could be "restored"—could the
old Saint-Domingue not be brought back? Several thousand "bitter, nostalgic, and vengeful" planters lived in France, forming a "powerful proslavery lobby."[39] Peace in Europe provoked thoughts of reconquering what
had been the richest island in the world, the jewel of the French Atlantic
economy. In 1814 a legislative committee recommended that Haiti be re-
invaded, an idea that was widely supported.[40] The concept of retaking and
reenslaving an island that had broken its chains twenty-three years earlier of
course had another facet: the resumption of the massive slave trade to Haiti.
The economist Sismondi, among others, denounced the whole idea as folly;
it was time to look forward to other models for the Atlantic economy.[41] But
the colonists did not give up agitating for intervention. Still in 1825, the
recognition of Haiti was hotly contested; it provoked furor among French
conservatives, and, Eugène Sue reported from Guadeloupe, it plunged the

planters of the other French slave islands into the "darkest anxiety."[42] A few poets praised the gesture as a manifestation of the king's generosity.[43] Some of those reacting to the recognition of Haiti were thinking Atlantically, predicting consequences in Africa: thus one of the poets asserted that the "emancipation" of Haiti would "facilitate the future civilizing of Africa."[44]

If the central motor of colonial wealth, Saint-Domingue, could not be restored, what model of Atlantic economy could France contemplate? What could the Atlantic be without Saint-Domingue? Roger has an answer, the answer foreshadowed by all those who had questioned the Atlantic triangle almost from its beginnings: forget Saint-Domingue; forget Haiti; turn to Africa.

Roger arrived in Senegal with enormous curiosity about the place and interest in its inhabitants. What made him different from his missionary, slave-trading, and military predecessors was his new type of respect for and interest in the people he encountered. As a European he was far ahead of his time in allowing for the possibility of culture and history among Africans. In Senegal Roger set about asking questions, "taking every opportunity to inform himself."[45] The results of his inquiries were two remarkable books published in 1828 and a linguistic-philosophical study that appeared a year later. *Fables sénégalaises* reflects one of the first attempts to "harvest" African oral arts, poems that Roger transcribed and translated into French.[46] In spite of the violence undoubtedly done to African poetry by Roger's florid versifications, and in spite of some offensive opinions he offers here and there, this work occupies an important place in the history of African literature, as a forerunner of many such encounters between the oral and the written.

The work that concerns me here is the other literary product of Roger's experience in Senegal, the novel entitled *Kelédor, histoire africaine*. Using an African mouthpiece in ways that I will examine, Roger created this text as a treatise garbed in narrative form, complemented by voluminous footnotes. The plan that emerges without subtlety maps out a new form of French colonialism in Africa, based on an agricultural economy using indentured laborers. It quickly becomes apparent that *Kelédor* is a brochure advertising something that Roger actually established in Senegal: a "garden" where the "colonial products" of the islands — sugar, cotton, indigo, coffee — could be grown by "free" laborers. *Kelédor* has been dismissed by some historians as mere expansionist propaganda, and it is that.[47] But in its generic complexities and its narrative strategies, *Kelédor* is more than that: it is a unique marker of the transition from the old colonialism of islands and slaves to a new colonialism of the African interior.

It is important to remember that Roger was not merely an observer in Senegal; he was a governor who created facts on the ground. He sought to realize the abolitionists' Africa. Roger abhorred the slave trade and slavery, and, as we will see, he represented Haiti as a dystopia. In *Kelédor* he denounced slavery as "the institution that is the most opposed to the laws of nature and reason."[48] As governor, in 1822, he established a colony called Richard-Toll (*tol* meaning garden in Wolof), the showpiece of Roger's new model, based on "des grandes cultures! des grandes cultures!"—the new source of "honor and profit" in Africa.[49] In fact his actions in Africa were part of a larger plan initiated from the moment France regained Senegal (on paper in 1814 and on the ground in 1817) under Governor Schmaltz and put in place in 1819: there would be a "series of plantation schemes in an effort to save the colony of Senegal, now reduced to living without its principal business, slave trading."[50] (Roger makes no mention of that broader effort, nor of Schmaltz's earlier attempt to set up a plantation at Dagana, upriver from Saint-Louis.)

As an abolitionist with a flair for public relations, Roger was at pains to break with the appearance and the vocabulary of the slave societies of the West Indies: thus there would be no "plantations" in his Senegal, only "gardens"; no one was to use the words *slave* or *captive* in reference to his *engagés à temps*, indentured laborers.[51] How much difference the politically correct vocabulary made to those workers is questionable. Roger recruited his workers from four principal sources: "men of color" deported from Martinique; captives redeemed from the slave trade in Africa and subsequently indentured for fourteen years; former slaves from Saint Louis du Sénégal; and free laborers "on loan." The system of indenture soon resulted in a new trade not unlike the slave trade; *engagés* were bought and sold.[52] Roger said that his policy resulted from equal portions of practicality and "humanity," and he issued rosy reports on the complete success of his "fine establishment."[53] His experiments in agriculture were extensive. Convinced of his own success, Roger resigned in 1826, citing health reasons. He continued to declare "mission accomplished," insisting that Richard-Toll had "succeeded as much as could have been hoped" and that it was "the realization on a small scale of a great idea."[54] But a government commission found otherwise: that Senegal "has only the appearance of fertility"; that Richard-

Toll was something of a Potemkin village; that Roger's whole experiment was a "*novel* that promoted the elevation of Baron Roger and which cost France two or three million francs."[55] The whole idea of growing the colonial products of the islands in West Africa, though it had been bruited about for many decades, was deeply flawed: the annual rainfall in Haiti is about fifty to sixty inches; in the northern sections of Senegal it can be twelve to fourteen inches. Richard-Toll was abandoned in 1829—at the end of the Restoration—and Roger's dream died.[56] The failure of this scheme, writes Boubacar Barry, "revealed the depth of the depression into which French commerce had slumped in its search for new ways of adjusting to the abolition of the slave trade" (*SAST*, 141). It will be some time before French colonialism finds the crop on which it will stake its claim in Senegal: peanuts.

As one historian has suggested, the failure of these early plantations was a lucky thing for Senegal, which reverted to its previous status as a mere trading post for the French, with twenty-seven governors between 1831 and 1854.[57] Senegal thereby escaped a regime of French settlement and exploitation that could have produced another Algeria: a colony dense with Europeans who claimed the land itself and resisted decolonization fiercely when the time came.[58] Looking back, we can see that the question about Roger's scheme revolves around issues of labor. To what extent did he attempt genuinely to break with the New World plantation regime; to what extent did he merely move it across the Atlantic, cloaked in euphemisms—in an attempt to create "a second Antille" (if not a "second France")?[59] His recourse to indentured labor—that is, "an indirect way of prolonging slaving practices" in a context where labor had been depleted by three centuries of the slave trade[60]—invites skepticism. It seems a fitting symbol of the gradual and partial abolitionism that was typical of the period. Abolition of the slave trade—and not of slavery itself, not yet—was the concern of abolitionists in France during the Restoration. It was only in 1829 that the main abolitionist organization in France, the Société de Morale Chrétienne, added the abolition of slavery to its agenda, which had included abolition of the slave trade since 1822.[61] Abolition in the 1820s was primarily a *maritime* issue: it was necessary to change the Atlantic economy, weaning it of the slave trade, and that is what Roger thought he was doing. Even if he did this by perpetuating exploitative labor, bringing new forms of servitude to Africa, with recourse to slavery in everything but the name (and we have to suspect that that was the case), Roger would no doubt have argued that his scheme nonetheless represented a complete break with the Atlantic slave trade and therefore constituted real progress.

Those Martinican workers brought to Senegal represent an important anomaly, one of the rare exceptions to the one-way nature of the French Atlantic triangle, for these men "returned" to Africa (although they were in all likelihood born in Martinique). Those two hundred free "men of color" were deported from Martinique for political reasons; they constituted in fact "the greater part of the free black elite of the island."[62] Their crime consisted of publishing demands not only for abolition but also for political enfranchisement. Their leader was Cyril-Auguste Bissette, an intriguing, protopostcolonial figure, an appropriate guardian angel for this exceptional, reverse transmigration.[63]

KELÉDOR BETWEEN HISTORY AND FICTION

The investigating commission's characterization of Roger's agricultural experiment—his work on the ground—as a "novel" is intriguing. Roger's decision to promote his ideas for colonization in a novel, *Kelédor*, throws that text into a strange relation with history, suspended between fact and fiction. On the one hand, the novelistic format of *Kelédor* is a thin veil over the baron's wishful representation of a certain reality; some readers have dismissed the literariness of the text as an insignificant formality. On the other hand, Roger's real experience in Senegal was itself nothing but a "novel." As we will see, the propagandistic aspects of the text are perfectly transparent. If fiction haunts both *Kelédor* and the reality it is trying to represent, the novel has nonetheless been cited by recent historians (Boubacar Barry and David Robinson) as a *nonfictional* source akin to transcribed oral histories.

Two other dimensions of the novel's discourse are perhaps more complex: its narrative structure, which anticipates certain aspects of the colonial and Francophone literatures of the twentieth century; and what would now be called its anthropological relativism, expressed as both a concern for accuracy and a posture of advocacy with regard to African culture. An enthusiastic reviewer, Edme-François Jomard, for the journal of the Société de Géographie (an organization of which Roger was a founding member in 1821 and of which Jomard was longtime president)[64] saw in Roger's novel a fine exemplification of what the new science of geography could be, that is, something with "newer and more accurate colors" than the old "arid geog-

255

raphy of nomenclature." The metaphor of color again asserts itself: as in Mérimée's version of literary exoticism, "color" is a sign of otherness, the fresh air of the outside world. Jomard also was pleased that Roger dared to write against the grain of dominant thought by providing "facts" that could help "respond to the detractors of the blacks." On this point the reviewer is both perspicacious and prescient: he argues that the "philosophical minds" of the day are increasingly "inclined to deduce from the differences among races not only an inferiority of intelligence and of the faculties, but also a sort of social incapability." It is true that scientific racism, as we would call it, was on the increase; the rise of physical anthropology and the perception of "inequality" among "races" seemed to go hand in hand.[65] Roger, along with very few others, dissented. To argue against slavery and the slave trade in 1828 was to be part of a certain small, elite movement; but to go further and militate against *all prejudice based on skin color*, in 1828, was a far lonelier position, with very few allies. To do this within a discourse that was heavily influenced by the scientism of Cuvier, Linné, and Buffon was perhaps even more remarkable.[66]

Jomard showed little curiosity, however, about the literary form that Roger had taken the trouble to concoct: "for this work is novelistic in form only." And although Jomard says he has discussed the work with Roger directly, he apparently failed to ask one of the most pertinent questions: Did this Kelédor person really exist?[67] Roger himself does nothing to bolster the reader's belief in Kelédor's existence: no mention of how Roger met him, nothing.

Kelédor is a "triangular" text, representing and reflecting on all three sides of the French Atlantic system that the slave trade made possible and calling for a reform if not an abandonment of the triangle itself. Roger wants to represent the West Indies and their plantations as corrupted by slavery and damned; and his new Africa — with its "gardens" and its "Negro workers flocking willingly from all the surrounding countries" (K, 201) — as the alternative. This willingness of Africans to participate is of course key to Roger's plan; without it he is little better than a slave driver. So it is not surprising to see him use a literary device that is closely analogous to his labor practices in Senegal: he builds his entire novel on the collaboration of one (apparently fictive) African subject: his "indentured" narrator, Kelédor.

The novel is presented, following convention, as through the voice of an authentic participant — as testimony. In his introduction Roger writes: "I decided to write this story, which is not without interest, in French. I could have and perhaps should have assumed the role of historian, thus not staging Kelédor so directly as the narrator of his adventures. But his story [*récit*] had made such a vivid impression on me that I feared sacrificing, through an intermediary, something of its color, its force, and its truth. It seemed preferable to confine my own role to that of a sort of translator" (*K*, xv). The title page thus presents *Kelédor* as a "history" that has been "recorded" or "taken down" (*recueillie et publiée par M le Baron Roger*), reflecting a transformation from oral text to written one in a direct, face-to-face encounter. Roger's gesture echoes eighteenth-century concerns with bolstering the authenticity and verisimilitude of the novel by presenting it as actual "found" discourse. But readers of twentieth-century African literature will also recognize this tactic: the writer claims to erase himself in the presence of an oral source such as a griot.[68] In the introduction to *Le Maître de la parole*, Camara Laye bills himself as "the modest transcriber and translator" of the griot Babou Condé; in *Soundjata ou l'épopée mandingue*, Djibril Tamsir Niane repeats the formula coined by Baron Roger: "I am only a translator."[69] The extensions of this type of encounter in anthropology are well known: the authority of the ethnography derives from the performance of the speaking subject, the native informant. The main text of *Kelédor* is supposed to represent the unmediated—merely transcribed and translated—voice of this African subject.

A few critics who have written about *Kelédor* have not hesitated to denounce the setup as a sham and Kelédor as a visibly literary figment of Roger's imagination and a transparent alter ego of the author himself.[70] Yet the historian David Robinson cites *Kelédor* as one of a handful of "important accounts" of the Cayor campaign led by the Almamy Abdul Kader Kane; he treats the text as if it were an authentic, transcribed oral history. Boubacar Barry, of Cheikh Anta Diop University of Dakar, also cites *Kelédor* as an accurate historical account.[71] In the absence of any documentary evidence we cannot know if Roger's interlocutor "Kelédor" ever existed nor exactly how this narrative came to be.[72] But there does not appear to be anything in the major outlines of Kelédor's epic life—his upbringing, his military experience leading to his enslavement, his survival of the Middle Passage, his life in Santo Domingo/Haiti, and even his return to Africa—that could *not* have happened.

It is important to take stock of Roger's gesture in a wider context. By

257

making an African "speak" this narrative, Roger created a *simulacrum* of
the exact thing that does not exist in the French Atlantic: a slave narrative
written in French (as discussed earlier in this study). His Kelédor is a sort of
French Atlantic Equiano. Questions that have been raised recently about the
actual origins of Olaudah Equiano can only serve to enfold *Kelédor* within
the same analytical field as Equiano's famous *Narrative*, with similar questions of authenticity.[73]

From the beginning of his introduction Roger appeals to the "curiosity"
of the European reader, raising the curtain on what he hopes will be a new
area of "interest": "Senegal is little known, and the few notions that we have
about this country are inaccurate or false. Senegal has, however, to the highest degree, everything that can prove to be of interest or advantageous [*tout
ce qui peut intéresser*]. Nothing there looks like anything in our Europe. . . .
Everything there makes an impression of deep originality on the observer,
who moves from surprise to surprise" (*κ*, v–vi). Africa is "a vast domain
open to the curiosity of all, to the meditations of the philosopher" (*κ*, xiv).
Declaring Africa to be both open (or blank) and full of interesting things,
Roger invites an influx of *interests*. His appeal is thus framed as a bringing
of French attention to Africa, with the potential for extracting, as we will
see, products from his "garden." The economy of "interest" is thus from the
beginning something that moves from France to Africa but with the potential to extract a profit. To be interested is to bring your attention to bear on
something outside yourself; but to be interested (*intéressé*) is also "to seek
above all one's personal advantage . . . [to be] greedy" (*Petit Robert*). Roger
combines the two.

Kelédor has a composite structure. Roger's eleven-page introduction is
followed by the main narrative—two hundred pages divided into eight
"books"—much of it in the first person from Kelédor's point of view. But
the main text is riddled with notes, which take up sixty-six pages at the end
of the book; some of the endnotes themselves have footnotes. In the endnotes, a rival narrator, the baron himself, expatiates, doubling Kelédor's
testimony with informative annotations, definitions, observations, and emphatic verifications. But the discursive authority of the notes surpasses that
of the main text. It is as if there were a one-way mirror between the two
narrators: Roger "hears" and comments on Kelédor's narration, but Kelédor of course has no awareness of Roger. This is not true dialogism. By
defining couscous, describing what a baobab looks like, characterizing the

Serer people, and explaining the horrors of the Middle Passage, Roger exercises knowledge that encompasses and transcends Kelédor's first-person account. All the while Roger insists on two things: the veracity of Kelédor's story and the relativism with which Roger wants it to be understood. Thus "everything [here] is of a rigorous truthfulness" (*K*, 217n18) and must be interpreted by comparison to Europe, for Africa belongs within the same *human* sphere of values: "This narrative [of a war in Africa] is of the most exact truthfulness. The facts are historical. . . . They would be admired if they were dressed in Greek or Latin names. But, for a long time to come, many people will have trouble getting used to seeing black figures create history. But we will have to come around to it" (*K*, 232n1). Roger's insistence on documentary veracity is significant: he is seeking to counter the "unreal Africa" that characterized earlier abolitionist representations (as in Staël's *Mirza*, for example).[74]

Roger is at pains to establish a perspective that would have been called "négrophile" in his times. In this passage he is nearly prophetic in foretelling the difficulties that the idea of African history would face in the West more than a century later. Describing the practice of war in Africa, he says: "Things take place just as they would in Europe in similar circumstances. These Negroes are almost as turbulent, as mad, and sometimes as cruel as if they had white faces" (*K*, 206n2). But Roger's defense and illustration of African cultures and peoples is made in the name of a *mission civilisatrice* that does not yet bear the name: Africa is *worthy* — of being *colonized*. As early as his fifth note, Roger describes the kind of project he is promoting:

259

> At Saint-Louis-du-Sénégal . . . colonization has been experimented with: more than forty *plantations* have been started; useful crops that are fit for the climate have been introduced. This territory already has all the earmarks of a great outpost [*établissement*], with great success, which *interests* not only France, but also the sciences and all of humanity. Now it is up to enlightened public opinion, to capital, and to the powerful industry of Europe to do the rest. Then culture, commerce and civilization will soon conquer the interior of Africa. (*K*, 210n5; emphasis added)

This footnote gives the solution to a problem that has not yet been fully posed to the reader: the problem of slavery and the slave trade. Roger's note lays down the teleology of the narrative that follows, and Kelédor's story has only to confirm that truth.

KELÉDOR AND ATLANTIC REVOLUTIONS

Kelédor opens in the wake of an African war that took place in 1796 — thus, in the wider Atlantic context, at the time of both the French and the Haitian revolutions. But West Africa, the Senegambia in particular, was having its own revolution: a Muslim theocratic revolution, which is the setting for the first parts of this novel. In both Haiti and West Africa these revolutions were of course related to the slave trade. Although certainly a minority in comparison to Africans from Kongo or Dahomey, Africans from the Senegambia who, like Kelédor, were veterans of the Muslim Revolution in West Africa could surely have been among the slaves who rose up and fought in the Haitian Revolution.[75] And both of these black revolutions were simultaneous with and connected to the French Revolution, with its complex and unresolved attitudes toward colonialism. I have found little attention to the connectivity of these circum-Atlantic revolutions among historians — that is, analysis that includes Africa.

As the narrative of *Kelédor* opens, the Almamy (from the word *imam*) of the Fouta-Toro, a zealous Muslim who sought to impose the Sharia in all his domains, is about to lead a holy war against the Damel of Cayor, whom he found to be deficient in religion. One of the Damel's crimes was selling Muslims to Christians as slaves (*K*, 6). Thus the slave trade and the Atlantic are, realistically, implicated in a war in the interior of Africa in this period. In Roger's version of events, the Islamic militancy of the Fouta-Toro is associated with resistance to the Atlantic slave trade, while the older African belief system of the Damel of Cayor (who surrounds himself with griots, wears *gris-gris*, and drinks brandy) is depicted as complicit with the trade (see *K*, 8–12).

Juxtaposing Roger's narrative to recent historians' versions of the same events produces little friction. This is not surprising, since at least two of these historians use *Kelédor*, as we saw earlier, as a nonfictional source. Boubacar Barry praises *Kelédor* as an "excellent account [*témoignage*] of the revolution . . . [that] shows well the religious fervor of the Fouta."[76] Barry's chapter "Muslim Revolutions in the Eighteenth Century," in *Senegambia and the Atlantic Slave Trade*, provides a fuller sense of the context that Roger evokes: the theocratic Almamy was part of the wider revolution that was sweeping through this region, in opposition to the secular *ceddo* regimes, represented by the Damel, Amari Ndeela, of Cayor.[77] The Almamy Abdul Kader Kane considered himself "Commander of the Faithful" and dreamed of hegemony over the Upper Senegal valley (*SAST*, 104). The Muslim revolution was in part a result of Atlantic events: "a reaction against the generalized violence and chaos caused by the slave trade" (*SAST*, 96).[78] Born out of resistance to the slave trade, this revolution nonetheless sometimes produced states that, "once consolidated, . . . made slave trading their exclusive business. . . . Islam became an excuse for slave raiding" (*SAST*, 98, 99). The reader of *Kelédor* could be forgiven for getting the impression that the war represented in its pages pitted a simply pro-slave-trade state (the Damel's Cayor) against a simply anti-slave-trade group (the Almamy's Fouta-Toro). In fact the situation was less clearly demarcated; the Almamy had no objection to the enslavement of non-Muslims.[79] Roger papers that over so that his readers' admiration for Africans might be increased and so that his story will be more closely aligned with European ideas of abolitionism.

When Kelédor is introduced as narrator at the beginning of book 2, he tells us that he was "no more than fourteen" years old at that time (thus born around 1782), living in a village of the Fouta-Toro (*K*, 22). Unlike so many African protagonists, from Behn's Oroonoko to Hugo's Bug-Jargal, Kelédor is not a prince or a king but a commoner: son of a "marabout who was zealous but uneducated" (*K*, 22). His father has aspirations of upward mobility for the son, hoping he will become "one of the leaders of the land," to whom "consideration, respect, influence, power, [and] benefits of all kinds" will flow (*K*, 23, 22). (In this, Kelédor is clearly an alter ego of Jacques-François Roger, the son of a lawyer who rises to be a governor, a baron, and a deputy.) So Kelédor is enrolled as the *talibé* (student) of a *serigne* (distinguished man of religion). The teacher's remuneration comes from his pupils' labor, or from the loan of a slave by the pupil's family (*K*, 23); slavery is part of the landscape. Rumors of the war reach the village and are greeted as the exciting prospect of "the success of religion" and of "universal domination" (*K*, 24–25). Kelédor marches off to war with the Almamy's forces, reported to be an army of thirty thousand men, women, and children (*SAST*, 104). His progress across the country provides Roger with ample opportunity to display before the reader's eyes, in discourse that owes much to Buffon and Cuvier, a catalogue of the flora, fauna, and folkways of Senegal.[80] His notes thus "prove the resources of the vegetation" and cry out for "well-managed farms" (*des cultures bien conduites*) (231).

But the Damel of Cayor, using a scorched-earth policy, defeats and enslaves his starry-eyed enemy. The captives are lined up as the Damel passes by, coolly deciding whom to give away and whom to keep (59). The Al-

261

mamy himself makes a passionate speech warning the Damel not to sell Muslims to Christians; the Damel is unmoved and declares that "few of my prisoners will see their fatherland [*leur patrie*] again" (62, 64). The stage is thus set for this narrative of the African interior to join the Atlantic and its narratives:

> We were all reduced to slavery, to be sold to Europeans. When the slave traders of Saint-Louis, Gorée, and Rufisque learned that a war was about to break out between Cayor and Fouta-Toro, they were delighted, for whoever should be the winner, the result could only be captives, and *the slave trade* could only gain from it. . . . As soon as our disasters were known, slave-trading agents visited the African prince to make new deals, to take advantage of the situation, and to oversee the delivery of slaves that were already due. . . . What was, therefore, in these unhappy times, the role played by these white men following black armies? Seeing them, how could we not think of hawks and vultures, behind a cloud of grasshoppers; of hyenas and jackals devouring bodies on a battlefield or on the path of voyagers lost in the desert? (κ, 66–67)

With this passage in particular, *Kelédor* joins abolitionist literature. As in Equiano's narrative, the impending separation from the native country, and the known impossibility of return, weigh heavily on Kelédor's mind as he awaits "rough slavery in a distant, unknown country, with no hope of seeing our dear homeland [*pays*] again" (κ, 69). Equiano had written: "I now saw myself deprived of all chance of *returning to my native country*."[81] But Roger's revision of the Atlantic triangle, as we will see, allowed for that which was, with rare exceptions, impossible for those enslaved in the French West Indies: return to the native land (*revoir mon pays natal*, 84). Both Equiano and Roger foreshadow—using the exact same phrase—the theme of "return to my native land" that Césaire will take up in the twentieth century.

The scene of separation from Africa and from loved ones and the theme of the impossible return were key in abolitionist literature. When Kariallah, the beloved of Kelédor's friend Niokhor, cries, "Separate us? Never! Never! It is impossible!" (κ, 70), and when Kelédor evokes "the sweet fatherland [*patrie*] that I would never see again" (κ, 74), they are echoing the rhetoric of the famous 1823 poetry contest organized by the Académie Française on the theme of the abolition of the slave trade,[82] as well as many other precursor texts. These include Mungo Park's story of Nealee, an African woman who "perished, and was probably devoured by wild beasts" after she failed to cooperate with her captors.[83] The story of Nealee was picked up by Thomas Clarkson and became emblematic of abolitionist discourse.

As Françoise Vergès rightly says, the key emotional trope of abolitionist rhetoric is pity.[84] We have seen, with Margaret Cohen's help, the importance of sentiment as an armature of French literature in the nineteenth century. As an abolitionist, Roger approximates the literary practice of (mostly) female precursors by appealing to sentiment at this point in *Kelédor*. He heightens the pathos of his novel as the moment of separation from Africa approaches: Kelédor's friend Niokhor kills his beloved Kariallah rather than let her face enslavement on foreign shores. As she expires on her blind grandfather's lap, the old man has a vision that outlines the rest of the novel:

> Children, calm your despair, and dry your tears. My eyes, which are closed off to the world around me, miraculously see into the future. . . . The time is approaching when the inhabitants of this part of Africa will get some respite. Like the sages of the Fouta-Toro, who prohibited the slave trade in their domain, the peoples of Europe, belatedly ashamed of their cruelties, will soon renounce their practice of devastating our lands with the slave trade. What do I see? In a country across the oceans, slaves, you will shake off the yoke, and in an unbelievable miracle, whites will be enslaved to blacks! (*k*, 80)

263

The Haitian Revolution, which Kelédor will witness, is thus foretold. But as the old man's vision continues, it shifts quickly back to Africa, where the "population will multiply" and "industry" will flourish. In this passage Roger neatly welds the familiar rhetoric of abolitionism, cited above, to his new plan for Africa. Here one sees in precise and condensed form the hinge between the old French colonialism in the islands and the new one in Africa:

> Now where am I? These must be the beloved shores of our Senegal! What change has taken place here? Who has raised these solid, elegant houses next to our old huts? Whence these fine and useful crops that nature had refused to us? . . . It is no illusion; I see them. Here are free men, flocking from the interior of the country, *cultivating, producing the same crops [denrées] as those African slaves who had been ripped out of Africa*. Blessed be the prince who works such marvels in the interests of humanity! *May the French prosper!* May God and His prophet look kindly on their noble enterprise! (*k*, 80–81; emphasis added)

The old man's vision thus provides, from the mouth of an African, complete sanction for Roger's plans as governor. The calls for an end to the inefficiency and brutality of the triangular trade are answered. As book 3 concludes, the old man further predicts Kelédor's return to Senegal to fulfill the prophecy. The rest of the novel is therefore predetermined, and the hero has only to go through his paces around the Atlantic. This device serves to accentuate the unnecessary nature of the horrors that the narrator is about to recount—the Middle Passage and the brutality of slavery in the islands; we have already been told that these things are obsolete.

HISPANIOLA: UTOPIA AND DYSTOPIA

What, then, can Roger say about these other shores of the Atlantic, which, unlike Senegal, he does not know through personal experience? In 1828 his depiction of the Middle Passage (*la traversée*) was neither original nor widely familiar: Wilberforce and Clarkson had been translated into French, and their documentation of the slave trade was used by French abolitionists. Reflecting English leadership in abolitionism, Roger cites reports made to the House of Commons (*K*, 242n5) and a French translation of Alexander Falconbridge's *Account of the Slave Trade on the Coast of Africa* of 1788 (246n9).[85] Roger uses many of the same sources that were perused by, for example, Mérimée for his depiction of the slave trade in "Tamango": Mungo Park, the Abbé Proyart, the botanist Michel Adanson, and the ubiquitous Father Labat (whom Roger reproaches for his failure to condemn the slave trade [*K*, 235–36n7]). When writing about Africa, Roger has the advantage of direct experience and asks his reader, in the endnotes, to take his word as an eyewitness (for example, *K*, 240n1). But that ends at the water's edge.

Perhaps for lack of any reliable information about the actual life of captives and slaves, Roger immediately steers his enslaved protagonist into the sphere of the whites. Kelédor becomes the prototypical house slave. This process begins from the first time the slave traders cast their eyes on Kelédor, mere seconds before he is to enter the hold of the ship with three hundred fellow captives. His ethnic physiognomy saves him: "When it was my turn to go down into that foul dungeon [the *entrepont*] . . . [a] mulatto of Gorée, who I believe was employed as a broker, said to the Europeans who were shoving me, 'This boy is not Peul; you have less to fear from him. Judging by his physiognomy'"(88). Based on this ethno-logic (which Roger critiques as inaccurate [241n3]), Kelédor becomes a valet to a lieutenant, and "thus I escaped the unimaginable tortures that my fellows in misfortune endured during the crossing" (*K*, 89). Kelédor therefore bears witness to the suffering of the captives, while remaining unscathed himself; he sees and reports on "these wretches laid out on planks, compressed and stuck one against the other, almost deprived of the air necessary for breathing" (K, 90–91). Have the most despised beasts been treated with such barbarism? he asks (K, 92). Kelédor's friend Niokhor throws himself into the sea, and "his example was followed by many of our compatriots" (K, 97). Illnesses break out, and the lieutenant is blinded by ophthalmia; Kelédor showers him with devoted attention, and the "master" (as he now calls him) seems to "take an interest" in his slave (K, 100). Kelédor's upward mobility will be driven by his "curiosity," the motor of his intelligence, which will lead him to marvel at, for example, the science of navigation. This fills him with enthusiasm for "the civilization of the Europeans" (K, 101).

The other captives are less enthralled. As the crossing nears its end, they revolt, and a general massacre ensues. Kelédor saves his master by hiding him. When the rebellion is over, in spectacular confirmation of his status as a sort of house slave, Kelédor (alone of all the Africans onboard) and seven Europeans are left on the deck, while sixty surviving captives are confined in the hold (K, 104–5). And in a twist on the theme that was popularized in Mérimée's "Tamango" one year later—the theme of revolted slaves adrift, unable to steer the ship they have taken—Kelédor and his seven Europeans are all "*equally incapable* of steering to port this ship, almost abandoned to the winds and the waves" (K, 104–5; emphasis added). Roger's depiction of this key theme stands in marked contrast to Mérimée's: Kelédor does not see the technology of navigation as a "fetish," and Africans are not the only ones unable to master it. Roger's statement of *equal* incapacity on the part of both races seems to have great symbolic weight. If the antihero Tamango's inability to navigate the *Espérance* was a derogatory allegory of the Haitian Revolution and a powerful metaphor for political chaos in general,[86] what are we to make of this *shared* impotence in *Kelédor*? In fact, not too much, for, as book 5 begins, the blind lieutenant emerges to supervise the safe passage of the ship into the Spanish port of Santo-Domingo: thus European know-how quickly regains supremacy. Kelédor is delighted by everything he sees and looks forward to a "smiling" future (K, 107) . . . until he is sold by his dear master to a Spanish planter. The lieutenant is going home to France, and as he explains to a tearful Kelédor, the triangle is not open on all sides to Africans: "It is impossible, Kelédor; it is not permitted to bring slaves into Europe" (K, 110).[87]

Representing the enslaved African narrator as a liminal figure, suspended

265

between black and white, slave and free, is not something that Roger invented. The African who can give voice to enlightened ideas better than any European goes back to Behn's *Oroonoko* and filters into French literature throughout the course of the eighteenth century. The most apposite precursor of Roger's Kelédor is the eponymous "philosophical Negro" in the novel by Gabriel Mailhol. In *Le Philosophe nègre* (1764) as in *Kelédor*, an African narrator tells his story to a Frenchman, who reports it. Tintillo is of course a prince, of "Mitombo." Like Staël's Mirza, he is educated in Africa by an expatriate Frenchman, Bellefont, an academician of Bordeaux who is enslaved in Mitombo. Bellefont teaches "everything" he knows, including the French language, to his master, Tintillo, who is later enslaved himself and sold across the Atlantic. In Martinique, Tintillo, because he knows French, is almost immediately promoted to a higher station. This places him between worlds: "Whereas my comrades were condemned to the most painful labors and treated like animals . . . my new Master made me his Librarian and Advisor. From his numerous books I drew extensive enlightenment [*des lumières étendues*] and all the reason that I am showing you now."[88] The culture of "enlightenment" brings the races together in dialogue, across the boundary of servitude; that fiction is central to abolitionist discourse. For the slave to participate in the literature of his or her own liberation, he or she must speak the language of enlightenment (and of the Enlightenment).

If Roger's Kelédor, like Mailhol's Tintillo, sets himself apart from the fate of his compatriots and therefore offers a skewed, perhaps hybrid, view of the slave trade (from an African captive who remains above deck), the novel effects another displacement of perspective once land is reached. For this French writer does not situate the American phase of his narrative in Saint-Domingue/Haiti but rather in the Spanish part of the same island, Hispaniola. This may appear to be a curious, self-defeating strategy on the part of a novelist who has made it clear that he wants to establish Haiti and its revolution as a negative model, the better to throw his new Africa into relief. But Roger was, in fact, rather clever in his representation of the Caribbean: by moving Kelédor to a Spanish colony, he was able, as we will see, to display Spanish practices of slavery as a model and as a reproach to the French planters; and then, by situating the story in the Spanish part of the island during the Haitian Revolution and during Toussaint's seizure of it, Roger was able to address the revolution directly.

Kelédor thus becomes the literal house slave of a Spanish planter, Don Péréyras, again because of his handsome appearance (*K*, 113). Again Kelédor's situation places him in the middle between masters and slaves: his position is "bearable," even "pleasant"; his chains are "light," and he can be happy (*K*, 129). This allows Roger to chime in with an endnote that holds Spanish slavery up for relative admiration: after having been "so cruel and so atrocious" to the indigenous peoples of America, the Spaniards, "through an inconceivable twist of the human mind, proved to be the softest of masters with regard to Africans." Their laws pertaining to slavery are a "model" that others should have followed. Roger here makes plain his belief that slavery can be "modified, rectified" (*K*, 253n1)—perhaps without absolute abolition, perhaps in the form of indenture. In one of his endnotes Roger makes it clear that resistance to the European slave trade is one thing, but actual abolition of slavery is another; the latter must be gradual and is best when earned by each individual slave.[89] (Roger will become an immediatist abolitionist only later.)

Don Péréyras and his family are "sweet, benevolent, and naturally human," and the master himself is "what one calls a philosopher." "Unity, peace, and order" rule his house (*K*, 127). He runs his plantation in an enlightened and efficient way, so "everything was in the only place it belonged, and every individual in his natural line of work." Slaves are well cared for and even encouraged to buy themselves out of slavery (*K*, 132). This "little republic" of slaves and masters is thus close to utopian, with strong echoes of Roger's vision of Senegal. In one passage Roger transparently evokes the image of himself ensconced at an idealized version of Richard-Toll: "I don't believe that any social position provides purer or surer joy than that known by the enlightened, sensible proprietor living as a wise man and a friend of humanity on a vast colonial domain, surrounded by three or four hundred individuals who depend on him entirely and whose happiness it is his ineffable pleasure . . . to ensure" (*K*, 132). A nearly feudal sense of propriety and order pervades these passages, in which one senses the authoritarian side of abolitionist discourse, concerned with the *enlightened* control of forces that might be unleashed by emancipation.[90] The Péréyras plantation is less a referential comment on Spanish slavery than it is a prescriptive vision of Roger's African utopia.[91]

These opinions and descriptions of the Péréyras plantation stand in contrast to other passages in the novel and the broader depiction of island life, where one sees a blistering, uncompromising condemnation of slavery. Traveling through the countryside, Kelédor sees the abuses to which other slaves are subjected: "I saw thousands of slaves fertilizing *foreign* soil with

267

the sweat of their brows, with no hope for any portion of the rich products they drew out of it" (κ, 125; emphasis added). If they were to do the same work, with the same crops, on their *native* soil, Roger implies, and if they received a share of the fruits of their labor, the problem would be solved. This passage builds into a tirade against European slavery in the Americas and borrows rhetoric from one of the most famous phrases of antislavery discourse — Voltaire's *Candide*: "It is at this price that you eat sugar in Europe . . ." — which Roger echoes: "It is at this execrable price that you consent to buy unnatural pleasures, a soft life, superfluous products. . . . These products [*denrées*] of the tropics, these liquors that you savor, do you know why they often poison you? It's because in them you are drinking the sweat, the tears, and the blood of your fellow men. . . . Your enlightenment? It is the light of a devouring forest fire" (κ, 127–28). This rhetoric collapses the distance and the absence that were fundamental to the organization of the Atlantic triangle: slaves and their suffering were invisible to French people, out of sight and out of mind. Voltaire's phrase, and Roger's after it, destroys that structure of *bonne conscience*. And Roger goes beyond standard abolitionist phrases here: by placing blame on European civilization itself, comparing its enlightenment to a destructive flame, Roger anticipates the rhetoric of twentieth-century Pan-African nationalism.[92]

268

The Americas cannot be the abolitionist utopia that Roger has in mind; that belongs back in Africa. So events work to expulse Kelédor from the Péréyras plantation. Ever accommodating, he converts to Christianity, is baptized Louis, and gets married. But then the son of Don Péréyras, Manuel, returns from schooling in Spain and casts a shadow over the happy plantation. He takes a fancy to Kelédor's wife, Mariette. Kelédor is sent on a horrendous "hunt" for marooned slaves (κ, 154) and returns to find Mariette in Manuel's arms.[93] Kelédor strikes Manuel, who appears to die (κ, 159). He must flee, so he joins the maroon community he had just returned from attacking. They welcome him, but he rejects their "sentiments of hatred and vengeance . . . their thirst for crimes which they call just reprisals" (κ, 167). So Kelédor joins the army of Toussaint Louverture, which has invaded the Spanish part of the island, and *Kelédor* joins the Haitian Revolution, in progress.

By hitching his story to the Haitian Revolution at this point in its evolution, Roger connects with a Toussaint who was at the height of his powers and ambitions, not only "the supreme authority" but "the only authority in the colony" at that point (late 1800 and early 1801).[94] Even Napoleon had to briefly recognize Toussaint's power by naming him captain-general (then rescinding the decision).[95] Within *Kelédor* the figure of Toussaint resonates across the Atlantic with that of the visionary African Almamy and his Muslim revolution in Senegal. But he also, curiously, bears some resemblance to Roger himself. Toussaint, like Roger, was an abolitionist of sorts but a social conservative who kept the plantation system intact "at all costs" and sought out white colonists as economic partners; his labor regime was almost as despised as slavery itself by his compatriots. His constitution of 1801 authorized the procurement of new slaves from Africa.[96] (Toussaint had been freed before 1776 and reportedly had owned a dozen slaves himself.)[97] If Toussaint's rural masses were "condemned to remain as 'salaried' workers under a 'slave-type' plantation regime," if his rural code "emptied [the workers'] freedom of any practical substantive meaning," the situation sounds a lot like Roger's scheme for African "gardens" and indentured labor.[98] Toussaint's representation, in his memoirs, of Saint-Domingue under his command sounds a lot like Roger's depictions of his Senegal: "The colony . . . enjoyed the greatest tranquility, [and] agriculture and commerce flourished; the island had achieved a level of splendor that it had never known before, and all of this was, if I may say so, my doing."[99] What Toussaint and Roger shared, then, was a general commitment to black freedom (in circumscribed forms), together with a continuing belief in the plantation system. The affinity is completed if one believes Victor Schoelcher's assertion that Toussaint dreamed of colonizing Africa in the name of France.[100]

None of that is mentioned in *Kelédor*, of course; the affinities between Roger and Toussaint remain unstated. Toussaint, already a hero of English romantic literature thanks to Wordsworth ("To Toussaint Louverture," sonnet, 1803), remains in the wings in Roger's novel and has no speaking role. The French public was not ready for Toussaint to join the ranks of idealized black heroes like Oroonoko, Bug-Jargal, or Kelédor (that will have to wait for Lamartine's *Toussaint Louverture* in 1850).[101]

Kelédor is swept up in the fervor of an all-black regiment marching to the cries of *liberté! égalité!* (*K*, 168). (The absence of interracial "fraternité" will turn out to be the fatal flaw.) But once they have reached Le Cap Français, rumors of Leclerc's invasion and the restoration of slavery begin to circulate. Roger represents Toussaint as giving the order "to burn everything in the path of the French, to leave nothing to them but ruins and dead bodies"

(*K*, 171). According to Carolyn Fick, it was Christophe who burned Le Cap, and without Toussaint's authorization.[102] The only source that Roger cites in his notes, the "unreliable" but interesting French general Pamphile de Lacroix's *Mémoires pour servir à l'histoire de la révolution de Saint-Domingue*, emphasizes allegations of Toussaint's "*ressentiment . . .* toward our color" and the "cold calculation of his unpitying policies," including massacres; he characterizes Toussaint as "the most impenetrable man on earth."[103] Lacroix's work no doubt contributed to Roger's characterization of Toussaint, which turns out to be a crucial element in the plot of *Kelédor.* Roger comments that "modern annals, before the fire of Moscow, have few examples of such a horrible disaster" (*K*, 261n9). Kelédor is horrified and repulsed by the joy that his companions take in watching the fire from the surrounding hills. European women and children are tortured and killed, and Kelédor ends his infatuation with the Haitian Revolution in these terms: "Liberty! Liberty! Is it only at this price that man may partake of your benefits?" (*K*, 172).[104] Thus the groundwork is laid for the protagonist to turn elsewhere in his quest for utopia, to look back across the Atlantic and to stage his *return.*

First he must slog through the rest of the revolution in Christophe's army. One day, the sight of white servants waiting on black officers produces "a total revolution" in Kelédor's head (*K*, 178). Back in Senegal the old man's vision had predicted this: "whites . . . enslaved to blacks," the world turned upside down. He experiences "involuntary" memories of Africa and begins to think — prefiguring Césaire — of the impossible, of "returning to my native land" (*mon pays natal*) (*K*, 178–79). But still, in order for Roger's scheme to be seen as completely necessary, the West Indies must be even more thoroughly repudiated. So Kelédor returns to the ruins of the Péréyras plantation, whose "dear masters" left more than twenty years earlier" and where the former slaves now live in "pain and misery" (*K*, 184). Traveling to Puerto Rico, he learns that Mariette is dead. Thus personally and politically, there is nothing left for him in the islands. War and abolition have produced chaos in their wake. He encounters men from Senegal who are planning their return to "the fields of Senegal" (*K*, 191), and Kelédor joins them, thus fulfilling the old man's prophecy. "The thoughts and emotions of Africa prevailed over those of Saint Domingue" (*K*, 191). But it is not just any Africa to which this group wishes to return; it is an Africa of "fields" that can be cultivated, the Africa of Roger's gardens.[105] The sacred nature of "native soil" is the supreme value.

The terms with which Roger/Kelédor sums up the experience of the West

Indies are revelatory: "Shores of the Antilles, lands of servitude, of which I had had such an awful idea, where *slavery had made me the happiest of men*, . . . I will not leave you without tenderness!" (*κ*, 192; emphasis added). If the institution of slavery as it was practiced in the West Indies has clearly been shown in *Kelédor* to have considerable faults, and if the West Indies as a whole are left in smoldering ruins, certain forms of servitude have not been ruled out by anything that Roger has written. Indentured labor remains distinctly permissible: How else can the native soil be made to turn a profit?

Every element in this novel has been calculated to come out at the precise endpoint that Roger has planned; everything leads to Richard-Toll in Senegal in the year 1822; everything supports his scheme for plantations. The chronology of Kelédor's life has been plotted so that he returns to Africa still young enough to be a happy laborer (Roger does the math on this in a note [259–60n5]) just as Richard-Toll is being organized. The statements about slavery throughout the novel have left plenty of room for indentured servitude as a desirable form of labor. The last book of *Kelédor* hastily inserts the protagonist into Roger's utopia, which fulfills the old man's vision pronounced at the beginning of the novel. Kelédor finds that his family has been dispersed by Moorish invasions, so he seeks protection "in the environs of the farms started by the French" (*κ*, 199). "Solid houses . . . which put our thatched, mud huts to shame," "a center of industry and civilization whose useful influence will gradually spread throughout this entire part of Africa" (*κ*, 200). Roger's revision of the Atlantic triangle is completed in these final passages, as the voices of Kelédor and Roger finally converge; Kelédor now joins Roger's drumbeat about the plantation scheme:

271

> I have seen these colonial farms [*ces cultures coloniales*], worked by the hands of free men! Senegal and Saint-Domingue together refute the prejudice that said that such projects were impossible (11). Here are working Negroes who have flocked voluntarily from all the surrounding countries . . . to hire out their time and their strengths! They are all thinking of one thing: the products manufactured in France that they can take home with them. . . . And what an indescribable pleasure it is to recognize here, already naturalized, almost all the useful and lovely plants that I had seen in the Antilles! . . . Hail to the garden of Richard-Tol! . . . May this *advantageous* [*intéressante*] and noble enterprise prosper! Lord! Hear my fervent wish: protect these projects, these efforts which pure and philanthropic intentions alone have inspired! Let these territories, finally delivered from the homicidal exactions of the slave trade, take their place

among civilized nations . . . and *let Europe gloriously expiate her crimes against Africa! [que l'Europe consomme glorieusement cette grande expiation de ses crimes envers l'Afrique!]* (201, 203; emphasis added)

The rhetoric is practically self-contradictory here: the scheme is pure and philanthropic, but it also happens to be advantageous—a coincidence that will be useful for the future of "enlightened" colonialism. Roger's expiation for the crime against humanity (as we now call it) of the slave trade consists of a profit-making scheme that places Africans in a new form of exploitation on their native soil. In the note numbered 11, Roger indignantly catalogues efforts made by slaveholding colonies to sabotage the "free-labor" experiment in Senegal. For him Saint-Domingue/Haiti on the one hand and his Senegal on the other stand as the twin pillars of an argument against slavery. "Forget Haiti" and "forget slavery" is the clear message; we will enter into a new relation with Africa, with no sacrifice of colonial products (Kelédor just told us he saw them growing in Senegal). His Africa will be *intéressante* in the sense of advantageous. France and Africa will find themselves in a new, bilateral alignment, to the advantage of France. The colonization of Africa, Roger tells us at the end, will be "built on a basis that is *entirely different* from that of the colonies of the Antilles" because Senegal will be filled with "free and numerous *consumers* . . . eager for our products" (269n12; emphasis added). This is all quite modern, and eerily prophetic of the future of French colonialism and postcolonialism in Africa, with France and its colonies or former colonies united in one economy.

In the short run things did not work out at all in the way that Roger wanted in Senegal: for all his prescience, his plan for literally transplanting the economy of the slave islands to Africa failed. Its basis was not, in fact, "entirely different," not different enough: the crops of the islands did not actually flourish in Senegal's soil. And genuinely free laborers simply did not show up. Roger's strategy for forgetting Haiti and forgetting slavery was undone by his failure to jettison the plantation system as a whole and the indentured labor on which it had been originally founded. France will have to pass through 1848 (the final abolition of slavery) and 1885 (the Congress of Berlin, which opened the path for deep colonization of Africa). Then and only then, as the nineteenth century concludes and the twentieth begins, France will indeed, as Roger predicted, "open a path for herself into the interior of Africa" (*K*, 270n12) and forge a new bilateral relationship with the continent. "La Françafrique" will be the result.[106] And Haiti will be long

272

since forgotten, surrendered to American domination and subject to the "silencing" of history.[107]

Roger's brand of "interest"—with all the ambiguities that we have seen in his usage of the term—may be his most lasting legacy. It is within a complex web of interests that "the colonization of Senegal" (tellingly, these are the last words of Roger's last endnote), and of Africa, will be founded.

EPILOGUE

To give Roger his due, we should leave him with full credit for his devotion to the abolition of slavery. This can be seen in another encounter with the baron, eight years after the publication of *Kelédor*. In 1836 the *Revue des colonies*, published by the Martinican gadfly Cyril-Auguste Bissette—whose deported disciples had been among Roger's laborers at Richard-Toll—published a transcription of a recent debate in the Chambre des Députés. And here we find Roger's voice among the participants. This reappearance of Roger thus reflects a curious reversal of the racial roles normally assigned to the oral and the written; now the European voice is being printed by the (part) African Bissette. Roger was a founding member of the Société Française pour l'Abolition de l'Esclavage in 1834. During a period when abolition was making little headway, as the Chambre des Députés was debating the status of the colonies, the baron forced its attention to a more urgent matter. If we are going to discuss the colonies, he argued, "it is a duty for the friends of humanity . . . to bring your attention back to the great question of the abolition of slavery. . . . Gentlemen, I wish only that our silence not be construed as an abandonment of the sacred cause to which we have devoted ourselves." He demanded a response from the minister of the colonies, in the "interest of the black slaves," as well as "of course" that of the French planters.[108] Roger's persistent "interest" in the abolition of slavery would have to wait twelve more years to be realized. Through his dual engagement—with both colonialism and abolitionism—Roger reveals how closely those two ideas were related in nineteenth-century France.

273

HOMOSOCIALITY, RECKONING, AND RECOGNITION IN EUGÈNE SUE'S *ATAR-GULL*

Who reads Eugène Sue?

— ALLAN NEVINS, introduction to James Fenimore Cooper,
The Leatherstocking Saga (1954)

SUE, THE SEA, AND THE NOVEL

He was part Charles Dickens and part William Randolph Hearst. Eugène Sue is recognized as an innovator of the serial novel and, along with Edouard Corbière, as an originator of the maritime novel in France. He was an instrumental figure in the popularization and commodification of the novel in France. Sainte-Beuve saluted him as the first to have "risked taking the French novel to sea" — long before he began creating "industrial literature."[1] Sue's *Mystères de Paris*, published serially from 1842 to 1843, was "the most popular novel of the century" and was "arguably the first French bestseller."[2] Readers wrote to him as the story unfolded from week to week, influencing his social vision and the substance of his novel. A capitalist marketing device, serialization, thus led to a "socialist" democratization of the novel, as working-class readers inserted their reality into Sue's pages.[3] Sue ultimately became "Europe's first press baron."[4] But all of that takes place at least a decade after the publication of the novel under consideration here, *Atar-Gull*, which was neither a serial nor a social(ist) novel. Still, parts of it were published in advance, and its preface, as we will see, expounded a theory of episodic literature.[5] If *Atar-Gull* was not a social novel in the way that Sue's later works would be, it was a rather peculiar *maritime* novel, perhaps the second of its genre in France, directly concerned with the slave trade and the French Atlantic triangle. It belongs to the early phase of Sue's work, marked by a humorously cynical misanthropy, before he was swayed toward reformist social optimism in the 1840s.

Sociologically, Sue and Mérimée had much in common. Sue's father, a medical doctor, occupied, like Mérimée's father, various prestigious positions during both the Empire and the Restoration, successfully negotiating the transition from one to the other. Jean-Joseph Sue had the good fortune to be Joséphine de Beauharnais's doctor. After she became empress, he asked to be made a baron but was only granted the title of chevalier by Napoleon; he used his title constantly. Eugène Sue was born in 1804 and baptized Marie-Joseph, with the empress as his godmother and her son Prince Eugène de Beauharnais as his godfather. Marie-Joseph would adopt the prince's first name as his own.

Born within a year of each other, Sue and Mérimée were both members of the "generation of 1820," famous for its *mal du siècle*. Sue had many friends in common with Mérimée, including Balzac, Dumas, and eventually Schoelcher, and they traveled in overlapping social circles, but these two writers do not seem to have been friends with each other. In the late 1820s both were dandies living *la dolce vita* in Paris. Sue was soon rich from his father's considerable estate; he managed to be one of the first writers allowed into the salons of the aristocrats. His mistress in 1830 was Olympe Pélissier, who received in her salon Balzac, Rossini, and the ubiquitous Duc de Duras (Claire's widower, now remarried).[6]

275

We saw how a certain exoticism was fundamental to Mérimée's creativity, even before he ventured anywhere but England. Sue's early experience was quite different. By the time of the July Monarchy, he had served six years in the navy as an assistant ship's surgeon. Sue *père* (like Baudelaire's stepfather later) thought that the sea and exotic climes would cure his son of his Parisian debauchery.[7] As a consequence Sue saw combat and did his share of amputations. He became intimately familiar with the sea, with sailors, their language, and their culture. In the 1840s he published a four-volume history of the French navy (which contains no chapter or subchapter on the slave trade).[8]

Sue visited the Antilles twice in his youth and saw how slavery and the slave trade worked. Later in life, influenced by his readers, Sue would be famous as a socialist and a reformer, but when his reports from the Antil-

les of the 1820s were published in the *Revue des deux mondes* (in 1830), they
sounded so much like an apology for slavery that the editors appended a
disclaimer. Contemplating his arrival in Guadeloupe in 1826, Sue states the
central paradox of modern slavery with succinct profundity: "Fortifying my
resolve, I am going to see slaves in a free country, in a province of France."[9]
But under the tutelage of a planter, Sue's reservations about slavery seem
to melt away: "The Negroes seemed healthy and happy to me. . . . Their
gaiety astounds me" (14). Before long Sue has bought into the utopian myth
of plantation society, and he sounds much like Roger in *Kelédor*: "A settler
[*colon*] isolated with his family, far from the ostentation of the cities, completely occupied by farming and working in his mills and by taking care of
his blacks — with the continual spectacle of the beauties of nature, which el-
evates the soul and expands one's thinking — [such a man] cannot be fundamentally cruel or mean. He must feel the need for others' affections and the
need to base his own greater happiness on the happiness of those who surround him."[10] At the end of the day Sue observes the master and his slaves
bowing down in silent worship of the Creator: "Men, women, and children
assembled in the most profound silence at the foot of a cross, where the
planter and his family were kneeling. The stars sparkled. . . . Under a dome
of green, master and slave prostrated themselves before the Creator." (We
will see that Sue re-creates this scene, using a very different tone, in *Atar-
Gull.*) Thus once again, as in *Kelédor*, and as partially reflected in Ourika's
dream, a writer during the Restoration offers the image of the colonial plantation as an agrarian utopia ruled over by a just patriarch (whose point of
view is the only one represented here). The passage above provokes a caveat
from the editors in a footnote: Sue's liberal opinions are too well known,
they say, for anyone to take this as a "plea in favor of slavery" (which it
nonetheless gives every appearance of being).

Sue officially launched his literary career in 1829, which was of course
Mérimée's *année miracle*, the year of "Tamango." Sue had previously co-
authored several plays and published some fragments of narrative fiction.
He now attracted notice with the publication of the first maritime novels in
French. In March 1830 Sue published *Kernok le pirate*, a short novel whose
eponymous antihero prefigures the slave trader Brulart in *Atar-Gull*.[11] This
was followed several months later by *El Gitano*, also a maritime novel, like
Atar-Gull built on the theme of vengeance but, oddly, featuring a ship's crew
made up entirely of *mute* blacks. These two works then appeared together
under the title *Plik et Plok* early in 1831. In the preface Sue made it clear

that he wanted to remedy France's "insouciance" with regard to the sea by depicting the "piquant" manners of maritime life. By then he had earned the title of "the French [Fenimore] Cooper." When *Atar-Gull* appeared later that same year, Sue's status as the creator of the French maritime novel was established. There were twenty-one editions of *Atar-Gull* between 1831 and 1875; the novel grew in popularity over the decades.[12] If no one reads Sue in English anymore (as Allan Nevins has suggested), he remains well known in France, although nowhere near as popular as Mérimée or Hugo.

By taking French narrative to sea, Sue opened the door for others to exploit the high drama of the illegal slave trade in literature. Corbière's *Le Négrier* followed quickly, as did Auguste Jal's yarn "Un Négrier," Aténor de Caligny's "Une Ruse de négrier," and the play *La Traite des Noirs* by Desnoyers and Alboize (mentioned in connection with piracy earlier in this study).[13] In many of these narratives the moral tension of the slave trade competes for the reader's attention with a literary commodity labeled and advertised as "adventure." Thus a story published in 1833 was entitled "The Frigate and the Slave Trader: An Adventure at Sea" (*La Frégate et le négrier: Aventure de mer*).[14] In this corpus of stories of the 1830s the slave-trading sea captain was solidified as an ambiguous, sexy, dangerous romantic hero.[15] In 1843 Alexandre Dumas included the themes of the slave trade in his tale of race and slavery in the Indian Ocean, *Georges*.

277

MARITIME HOMOSOCIALITY

> The comeliness and power, always attractive in masculine conjunction, hardly could have drawn the sort of honest homage the Handsome Sailor in some examples received from his less gifted associates.
>
> —MELVILLE, *Billy Budd*

No one mentions the word *abolitionism* in connection with Sue's name; no one tries to pass *Atar-Gull* off as abolitionist. Yet Sue wrote this tale of the slave trade at a crucial moment in its history: its "end." The first fragments of the novel appeared in the *Revue des deux mondes* in the same month, March 1831, in which the French slave trade was finally, effectively, and almost entirely put out of business. The law of March 4, in tandem with a new agreement with the British, imposed real enforcement on the high seas and truly criminalized the slave trade. From then on, the French slave trade was severely limited and "episodic."[16] (By coincidence, Sue propounds a theory of literature that is also episodic.)

Atar-Gull is thus the first "retrospective" look at the slave trade in French literature. But it was published well before the launching (in 1834) of the new campaign to abolish slavery itself, so *Atar-Gull* floats between one abolition and another, with no obvious linkage to either. The novel thus has a peculiar relation to the ills it represents. How had the subject of the slave trade changed in the short time that had elapsed since "Tamango" — a period that nonetheless included a new revolution, the rise to power of abolitionists like Broglie and Auguste de Staël, and, finally, an effective ban on the slave trade? In a preface Sue issues some very interesting guidelines for the interpretation of his novel and the evil that it depicts.

The preface is addressed to James Fenimore Cooper, who, having been kicked out of Yale, took to the sea and wrote of it in novels. Known as the quintessential American author, Cooper was also, to a very significant degree, an Atlanticist: after his time as a sailor he lived in and was much influenced by France and England; he told tales of the Atlantic; and his readership spanned the ocean. With *The Pilot* (1824) he believed he had invented a new genre, the novel of the sea — responding to Sir Walter Scott's *The Pirate* and surpassing it in authenticity.[17] Within four months of its original appearance in English, *The Pilot* was translated into French, then repeatedly reissued in France throughout the nineteenth century. Riding on the great success of *The Last of the Mohicans*, Cooper returned to the maritime novel in 1827 with *The Red Rover*, published in Paris, London, and Philadelphia. This novel is incidentally concerned with, and disapproving of, the American slave trade out of Newport, Rhode Island, in the eighteenth century. With some irony Cooper's characters debate whether "slavers" (slave-trading vessels) are "honest" (having proper papers) or not. A woman passenger asks of the eponymous, mysterious Red Rover, "Is it possible that such a man, can traffic in human beings!"[18] Thus from its beginnings in American literature, the maritime novel — led by Cooper, the first major American novelist — touched on and combined the themes of slave-trading and piracy. This may stem from the fact that Cooper wrote *The Red Rover* entirely in France during the time of the slave-trade abolitionist debates that we have seen. It is also useful to note that Cooper was an important creator of interracial homosocial paradigms in literature.[19]

Living in France in the late 1820s as an American consul, Cooper became a sort of literary godfather to Sue. Cooper's *The Pilot* is cited as the inspiration not only for Sue's maritime novels but for Corbière's works and Dumas's *Le Capitaine Paul* as well.[20] Addressing himself to Cooper in the preface to *Atar-Gull*, Sue warns of the "horror" that is to come, thereby whetting the reader's appetite. Using Cooper as an intermediary, Sue implies a contract between himself and his readers:

> You may find, Sir, that I have, in *Atar-Gull*, abused the license that you have granted us to commit flagrant and atrocious murders in order to excite the readers' sensibilities. But I floundered in vain under the fatal influence of the horrific subject that I had embraced, and, like Shakespeare's *Macbeth*, my *ferocity* had no bounds, because one crime was the consequence, the logical deduction of another crime.
>
> Thus, Sir, I have a terrible fear of looking like an *abominable man*, making horror for pleasure [*faisant de l'horreur à plaisir*].
>
> And yet, for the purpose of this too-exact (I think) depiction of the slave trade and of slavery and its results, I did not want to raise a spurious and shopworn polemic [*une polémique bâtarde et usée*] about rights that are contested by many; rather I wanted to propose facts and figures upon which each adverse party might prepare its balance-sheet [*établir ses comptes*]. The arithmetic [or reckoning: *addition*] alone remains to be done.[21]

Sue has laid out his strategy for navigating the paradox at hand, the tension between entertainment and morality. Readers will get both "pleasure" and "horror" — a flower of evil. Within this contract another important promise is made: that of realistic representation. The slave trade "and its results" will be depicted only "too" exactly. Realism will thus enable readers to justify both their horror and their pleasure; both derive from the "real." How all of this will work out — what it all might mean for anyone's view of the slave trade or slavery — is left as an unsolved equation and an explicit challenge. A direct language of calculation and economics runs through the entire narrative, beginning with this invitation to all sides of the debate on slavery to establish their accounts. What this contract fails to mention, however, is a wild card that will become apparent: irony. The effects of Sue's ironic or parodic rhetoric on the "realistic" equations in *Atar-Gull* remain to be seen.

Sue also propounds a theory of the maritime novel in this preface. In his vision the genre seems to be intrinsically homosocial but not in the way one might think. It might be assumed that the framework for relations between (white) men in such novels would be the ship itself and the close,

279

prolonged contact that the sea imposed. This might also involve deep, *interracial* friendships and even "cosy, loving" relationships and paramarriages (as Melville described the rapport between Ishmael and Queequeg) — with or without sex, about which we cannot know.[22] (We will see extensive evidence of that kind of relationship in Corbière's *Le Négrier* and in another look at Equiano's *The Interesting Narrative*.) This homosociality among seamen, based on prolonged and continuous contact, was the model established by Cooper. *The Pilot* was dedicated to "the recollection of those with whom I once lived in close familiarity with peculiar interest" onboard ship, to "our intimacy." In *The Red Rover* Cooper makes a thesis statement about shipboard relationships: "One hour of the free intercourse of a ship can do more towards softening the cold exterior in which the world encrusts the best of human feelings, than weeks of the unmeaning ceremonies of the land. He who has not felt this truth, would do well to distrust his own companionable qualities. It would seem that man, when he finds himself in the solitude of the ocean, most feels his dependancy on others for happiness. . . . A community of hazard makes a community of interest."[23] The homosociality among the seafaring characters of *The Pilot* is projected onto Cooper's

reading public, when the author suggests that his novel "could scarcely be a favourite with females. The story has little interest for them." It is a man's world in *The Pilot*, filled with manly men like the commander, who, under the "inquisitive gaze of [a] young lieutenant," is described as a "singular being . . . muscular and athletic, exhibiting the finest proportions of manly beauty."[24] The homosocial thus shades into the "homoesthetic," although with no hint of the unthinkable, the unthought — or at least the unnamed: the homosexual.[25]

In his preface (which is addressed to Cooper) Sue promulgates a theory of the maritime novel that is based on something quite different, although it arrives at a similar goal. Instead of a continuity of relations among men onboard ship, he explores the idea of episodic encounters between seamen and men on land. He asks Cooper if he has ever encountered by chance a man whose "physiognomy struck [him]" in such a way that he had to look at him with "a curious attention" (xvi). (This echoes Cooper's "peculiar interest.") By way of example, he tells of having met a pale, dark-eyed young priest in Saint-Pierre, Martinique. This man was so remarkable — conversing brilliantly, writing books, composing and performing music, inventing improved machines for refining sugar — that Sue would always remember him. The maritime novel should be built around such random encounters with exceptional men, who are like meteors, "which burn bright for an instant and then fade away" (xviii–xix). In other words, these novels will not be defined by continuous relations among shipmates so much as by episodic encounters with other men along the way: "the sudden apparition of an extraordinary man whom one sees only once and remembers forever." The seaman-narrator will "cruise" (the pun is inevitable here) in search of such men: the homosocial is linked to an episodic narrative structure. In maritime novels, it's "farewell to the unity of interest" (xix). Readers must therefore be prepared for the abrupt kind of substitution that occurs in *Atar-Gull* when the pirate captain, Brulart, replaces the slave-trading captain, Benoît.

The episodic nature of *Atar-Gull* was signaled by the editors of the *Revue des deux mondes* when they announced the prepublication of two of its chapters; they described the forthcoming novel by the author of *Plik et Plok* as "new maritime scenes under the title of *Atar-Gull*" (editors' note in Sue, "Arthur et Marie," 437n1). The groundwork is already laid for Sue's immense success as a serial novelist.

Before we begin any analysis of these phenomena, we should note that we have entered a universe from which women are almost entirely excluded. The sea is a man's world. It can be no coincidence that the invention of maritime literature coincides with the "hostile takeover" of French literature by males.[26] But as the homosocial shades into the homoesthetic and the homoerotic in these books by Sue and Corbière, the insistence on masculinity begins to take on an ironic light. Also in the preface to *Atar-Gull*, Sue's discussion of Greece, where he met another "extraordinary man," may be a coded invitation to think along homoerotic lines.[27]

ATAR-GULL'S IRONIC FRAME

> Do I have any power to help myself,
> now that success has been driven from me?
>
> — *Job* 6:13

The novel begins with stylistic clues suggesting irony and parody: the first two paragraphs begin with orders to the reader: "See!" and "Listen!" The third paragraph begins with "Oh!" The slave ship *Catherine* is introduced along with her captain, "Monsieur Benoît (Claude-Borromée-Martial)," whose physical shortcomings are catalogued along with those of his wife.

She looks out from a portrait on the wall, and the ship is named after her. Any thought of taking this all in utter seriousness must end when Sue punctuates his description of the portrait this way: "What a portrait! What a woman! What a child! What a rose! What a cat!" Sue follows by inserting the rapier directly: "All of it [was] colorless and white, false and heavy, ugly, strained, feigned," even if it was "not without charm" (*AG*, 148). A rhetoric of satire has been established. Sue's (unidentified) narrator loves to address himself directly both to the reader ("Picture a man . . .") and to the characters ("Sleep in peace, brave Captain . . ."). Sue also uses indirect discourse heavily, thus channeling a multiplicity of voices and viewpoints into his narrative. How will the moral freight of the slave trade be handled within such a cacophony of tones? Who is really speaking? How are we to read, for example, the title of one chapter: "That the Good Lord Punishes You for Trading in Slaves"?[28] This problem of irony in the handling of the slave trade runs parallel to the one I analyzed in my reading of Staël: the juxtaposition of the registers of sentiment and society.

Already, then, we are surrounded in *Atar-Gull* by echoes of Mérimée's "Tamango," and we are faced with challenges that closely resemble some that we saw earlier. Sue's slave trader is named Benoît (blessed) instead of Ledoux (sweet); he is also from Nantes. But there the resemblance ends. Benoît is in this business only out of love for his wife, even at the risk of his soul. He reflects the image of the respectable, "honest," bourgeois slave trader — the picture that Joseph Mosneron sought to give of himself, for his children's edification, in his memoirs. Benoît practices the slave trade "with as much conscience and integrity as it is possible to put into one's business"; he feeds his captives well, and as a result, "except for the *garbage* [that is, the jettisoning of dead or ailing captives], which couldn't be avoided, the cargo always got to the colonies" (*AG*, 158). The slave trade is thus described, with unmistakable irony, as a dull affair.

The dumpy and unattractive Benoît, with his receding chin and doughy cheeks, will soon be displaced by a very different avatar of French manhood, the pirate Brulart, who seizes the *Catherine*, its crew, and its cargo of slaves. Brulart happens to be a paragon of manly beauty and strength. The Byronic Brulart, in stark contrast to Benoît, will be up to the task of facing a reincarnation of Tamango and Bug-Jargal, an African superman named Atar-Gull. Sue's "curious attention" to male appearances — to the elements that make a man handsome or virile, or not — is thus evident from the beginning.

In this reading I want to focus on what differentiates *Atar-Gull* from its precursors: first, Sue's radical expansion of the homosocial relationship between the white and black protagonists and, second, his complex moral economics (or "reckoning") of the slave trade and the Atlantic triangle. On both of these scores *Atar-Gull* goes beyond the earlier texts, of which it is neither a pale imitation nor a cheap parody.

To summarize the novel: Benoît successfully purchases a load of slaves, including the exceptional Atar-Gull, on the coast of southern Africa. The pirate Brulart seizes the slave ship *Catherine* and delivers Benoît and crew over to African cannibals. He sets the ship on fire, blocking the passage of a British warship that is pursuing his own ship, *La Hyène*. Brulart then undertakes the Middle Passage with his stolen cargo of slaves. Atar-Gull emerges as one of those remarkable men who is worthy of "curious attention," Brulart's equal and counterpart. Surprisingly, there is no shipboard slave rebellion. In Jamaica Brulart sells Atar-Gull to the planter Wil, who, despite his kindly nature, has been persuaded by hard-line slaveholders to cash in on the value of an old and unproductive slave. He can do this by having the slave, Job, executed for murder or theft, then collecting a compensation from the government. (The biblical Job, a righteous man who is trifled with by God, is thus invoked.) Wil proceeds to falsely accuse Job and has him executed. It turns out that Job was Atar-Gull's father. From then on Atar-Gull has a single purpose: vengeance, which becomes the sole currency in the "reckoning" that the reader was invited to do in the preface. With the patience of, well, Job, Atar-Gull exacts his revenge. He ingratiates himself to Wil and then causes the deaths of Wil's daughter and wife and the ruin of his plantation. Wil is struck mute by the trauma. Atar-Gull travels with Wil as his "faithful" servant to England and then to Paris (completing the Atlantic triangle), where they live in squalor. Then Atar-Gull finally closes his net: he tells the dying Wil that he alone caused his misery and ruin. The ironic capstone to the novel comes when Atar-Gull is awarded a prize for his virtue. The moral is, "For a good son, VENGEANCE IS VIRTUE" (295).

283

HOMOSOCIAL PAIRINGS

The plot is thus structured by a succession of male-to-male relations that occur in a connected yet episodic sequence. Benoît buys Atar-Gull; Benoît meets Brulart; Brulart meets Atar-Gull; Atar-Gull meets Wil. Those four relationships form the signifying chain of the narrative.[29] Each of these pairings seems designed to explore a particular problem. We saw that Benoît was presented as a soft and unattractive bourgeois. Atar-Gull appears like the Tamango of Berry's film (not the Tamango of Mérimée's tale): a rebellious and powerful captive. The broker from whom Benoît buys Atar-Gull sees him as "one of the finest blacks I've sold in my life; see, he's strong as a bison, tall as a giraffe, but so stubborn!" He is a "young recalcitrant bull," full of "stoical dignity" (*AG*, 169). After this initial presentation Atar-Gull disappears below decks as the face-off between Benoît and Brulart takes center stage.

The pirate captain is first seen through Benoît's eyes, which are full of "curious attention." Brulart is part Byron, part Tarzan:

> Picture a man of athletic stature, with a pale and leaden face, a crinkled brow, a long and thin nose, thick, jade-black eyebrows, and pale, glassy blue eyes with an unbearable stare . . . ; a mouth with thin and pale lips shaken by an almost continual convulsive trembling which let you see — *why not admit it?* [*pourquoi ne l' avouerait-on pas?*] — his beautiful, perfectly straight teeth. His only clothing was a rough, half worn-out blue shirt that he usually wore around his waist with a bit of yarn. So *Benoît was able to admire at his leisure the enormous power of Brulart's muscular, dark, hairy limbs* [*aussi Benoît put-il admirer à son aise la force puissante de ses membres musculeux, bruns et velus*]. Only his hands, even though they were dirty and black, bore witness by their long and slender form and by the refinement of their contours, to a certain distinction of breeding [or race]. (*AG*, 183; emphasis added)

The hands are thus a tantalizing sign of Brulart's rumored aristocratic status, for he is in all likelihood a noble count who killed his wife in a crime of passion, then fled (the backstory that is told in chapter 8).[30] In the passage above, the phrase "why not admit it?" is an interesting gesture: Benoît's admiration for the pirate, which is channeled through indirect discourse here, has something shameful (or at least slightly embarrassing) about it.[31] Before Benoît has any idea to what extent the pirate will humiliate and torture him, it is as if Brulart's beauty and virility were themselves degrading to Benoît. What Benoît must "admit" to himself is the fact of his attraction to Brulart, who surpasses him by every measure. J.-A. Beaucé's illustration of Brulart invites the reader to "admire" Brulart in turn (see figure 12). The whole crew of the *Hyène* surpasses that of the *Catherine* in masculinity: "What men! Or rather, what devils!" With their rough appearance and crude jokes, they give "goose-bumps to honest Benoît" (*AG*, 180). Is Benoît gay?

The twenty-first-century reader may have a hard time reading these pas-

12 J. A. Beaucé, illustration "Le
Commandant Brulart," in *Oeuvres
illlustrées d'Eugène Sue par J.-A.
Beaucé* (Paris: n.p., 1850), 1:1.
Reproduced courtesy of Tulane
University Library.

sages in *Atar-Gull* as anything but gay. But sexuality, gender, and the body   285
were thought about differently in the nineteenth century, and we must resist
the temptation to project our own sexual assumptions onto the past.[32] My
aim here is therefore not to "queer" Marie-Joseph Sue or his characters—
not exactly. What we can say with assurance is that there is some kind of
homosocial and homoesthetic, if not homoerotic, attraction that is being
described here. We cannot possibly know, because Sue does not tell us,
whether any genital excitement was a part of this; we can only continue to
observe this relationship as it unfolds, in the terms that Sue gave us. (Corbière's *Le Négrier* will allow us to explore these questions more explicitly.)

In the ninth chapter of *Atar-Gull* the "interview" between a hogtied Benoît and his pirate captor is colored by Brulart's salty language, perverse humor, and gleeful sadism, for he is "a manufacturer of widows and orphans"
(*AG*, 197). Benoît begs in vain to be left on a safe part of the African coast,
where he and his crew won't be eaten. This must be God's punishment for
"the way I make my living," weeps Benoît, even though he always tried to
be humane. As a last gesture of humiliation, the pirate makes jokes about
the portrait of Benoît's wife (*AG*, 199). These jibes are not quoted; they don't
need to be because, as we saw, the narrator already made them. Here, then,
is homosocial horror as pleasure: the reader is induced to share a pirate's

delight in the mockery and murder of the hapless slave trader Benoît. The reader is complicit. Following the logic of episodic encounters outlined in the preface, we are told, "No one knows what became of Benoît and his companions." But it seems clear that they made a fine meal for Little Namaquas who surrounded them, "with delirious joy," on the shore. (In real life the crews of slave ships captured by pirates were sometimes marooned in desolate places and left to die.)[33]

This is a funny kind of homosociality, to be sure. Benoît's admiration for Brulart has nothing erotic about it—at least not that we can possibly know of—but it is nonetheless a very compelling form of attention, corresponding to the riveting attraction that Sue described in his preface. It is also humiliating, because the man that Benoît admires so avidly is also his torturer; the whole scene suggests sadomasochism. The very ordinary Benoît is a device for introducing Brulart, who is extraordinary; once Benoît has served this purpose, he is discarded. Benoît's "curious attention" for Brulart becomes the reader's.

The contrast between the two men is played for laughs, but it is drawn almost entirely along the scale of manliness, a quality that will be further explored in the next homosocial pairing, between Brulart and Atar-Gull. Now the contrast will work across the line of race. Virility is thus a part of the general calculus pertaining to the slave trade in *Atar-Gull*, but only the next episode will begin to show how these pieces fit together.

Brulart's eye now brings his own curious attention to bear on the "male section" of his new cargo, and "the slave trader contemplated with curious eagerness these vast chests, these sinewy arms, these broad and well-defined shoulders, these supple loins, proportioned and muscular" (*AG*, 203). Brulart sees in these captives some of what Benoît saw in him, but now these qualities are of course quantifiable in terms of the money that they will bring on the auction block. He singles out Atar-Gull for special attention and notices the "two rows of beautiful white teeth" (like Brulart's own, the reader might recall) on this "tall young Negro" (*AG*, 204). Brulart and Atar-Gull are counterparts, of equal size, strength, and beauty, but facing each other across the color line—as represented in the illustration from an English edition of the novel (see figure 13).

Brulart's attention for Atar-Gull is different from Benoît's attention for Brulart; now the look is cast from physical equal to equal, real man to real man, and with a commercial eye. But Sue and his readers might well have known that there was something homoerotic in pirate culture, that hy-

13 Unattributed illustration: Atar-Gull and Brulart. *Atar Gull: A Nautical Tale*, trans. William Henry Herbert (New York: W. F. Burgess, 1849), 44. Courtesy of the Yale University Library.

permasculinity was not a guarantee against same-sex attraction, and that homosexual practices may have been "almost universal" among pirates.[34] Brulart and Atar-Gull have the potential to become one of those interracial homosocial "couples" that nineteenth-century literature generated: Natty Bumppo and Chingachook (well known in France), Ishmael and Queequeg, Huck and Jim.[35] As if to dispel any hint of homoeroticism between Brulart and Atar-Gull, and to keep this sort of coupling at bay, Sue has Brulart move on quickly to look at the women captives onboard the ship. In them he sees a distinctly "erotic tableau" (*AG*, 205). The erotic is thus neatly segregated from the homosocial and the potentially homosexual.

Brulart selects two women and is having them led away, presumably so that he may rape them, when his "attention" is "excited" again by Atar-Gull. The slave is covered with blood; he opened his veins with his own teeth — a fact that is emphasized with three exclamation marks (*AG*, 207). As Atar-Gull is carried away to be bandaged, the narrator addresses the question of the comparison between the two supermen; this passage goes to the heart of homosociality as Sue conceives it and leads us almost to the point of homo-eroticism:

> [Atar-Gull] was, as it has been stated, a man of tall proportions and powerful stature; in a word, as much a colossus in his own *species/race* [son *espèce*] as Brulart was in his. . . .
>
> Between these two men there was I know not what hidden affinity, what secret connection, what bizarre sympathy, stemming from their physical conformation [*naissant de leur conformation physique*]. Involuntarily, *they admired each other*, for each of them bore in all his features the prototype of vigor, or strength, and of indomitable character which is the ideal of beauty among savages.
>
> These two men had to love each other or hate each other: to love, not with that timid and false friendship that we witness in our brilliant salons, which can be purchased with a bit of gold but which shrivels when faced with a word, an infidelity, or a slap on the face; but with that large and powerful affection which gives blow for blow, blood for blood, which shows itself in the midst of murder and carnage, when the cannons roar and the sea bellows, and which prompts kissing [or, to downplay the translation slightly: embracing], lips black with gunpowder and arms red with gore [*qui veut qu'on s'embrasse les lèvres noires de poudre* . . .]. . . . Thus it is that Atar-Gull and Brulart were destined to love or to hate each other, even unto death [*devaient s' aimer, s'aimer ainsi ou se haïr à la mort*] — for all must be extreme with these two men. (208; emphasis added)

So the "bizarre" and "secret" relation between the two has its origins in their "physical conformation," their *equally* colossal stature, in spite of their different "species" (or race). Their mutual admiration is narcissistic; each *recognizes* himself in the other. ("Recognition" in the context of slavery is a question that I will explore below.) This instance of homosociality is thus different from the one we saw between Benoît and Brulart, which was based on differences and was not reciprocal. Brulart and Atar-Gull must either love or hate each other; but their love (or friendship) will be manly, even as they kiss with gunpowder-blackened lips. It is contrasted to relations among men in salon society, which are clearly characterized as effeminate.

Brulart and Atar-Gull, by their very sameness, pose a challenge to the question of race and the drama of the slave trade. Benoît leveraged Brulart into position by virtue of the extreme contrast between the two characters; now Brulart leverages Atar-Gull through this comparison of equals across the color line. How will their equality be factored into the equation of

the slave trade? The answer is simple: as counterparts, like Ledoux and Tamango, they are perfectly set up for a confrontation. This is a standard plot
device, heightening dramatic tension. Everything is prepared for a slave revolt and a battle between Brulart and Atar-Gull . . . which does not happen.
Atar-Gull deviates from the plot that it has prepared, perhaps because it was
already the plot of "Tamango," the plot that readers might be expecting.
Instead, Atar-Gull channels his rebelliousness intelligently through "long
and obscure detours." *Dissimulation* will be his watchword, and it gives him
an "immense advantage" over Brulart (*AG*, 209); but that advantage is never
exploited in a shipboard revolt. The face-off between him and Atar-Gull
has been another episodic encounter, again as described in the preface, and
again leading up to a change of subject as attention shifts.

Thus Brulart turns his attention to committing atrocities: throwing
a baby overboard, beating a woman captive, torturing a sailor and then
throwing him overboard in a cage with two cadavers. Brulart then retires
into the artificial paradise of an opium stupor (chapter 13). A British frigate approaches, as in "Tamango"; its officers are represented as effeminate
fops; one addresses the other in jest as "Madame" (223, 228). Brulart takes
the best fifty captives, including Atar-Gull, onboard the *Hyène* and blows up
the *Catherine* with one or two dozen captives remaining onboard. Two days
later, Brulart sells his cargo in Jamaica to the planter Tom Wil.

Thus the pairing of Brulart and Atar-Gull is suspended without any real
drama having been staged, for now. Their relationship is not consummated
in any way. Following the episodic logic outlined in the preface, we move
on to the next encounter; as Sue said in the preface: "farewell to the unity
of interest." Thus the narrator announces: "Brulart left, and for some time
he was not heard from" (*AG*, 233). In fact, he will be an object of obsession
for Atar-Gull and will return later in the plot to be hanged. For the moment,
though, the effect of this interruption is rather strange. The emphasis that
Sue placed on the homosocial relation between Brulart and Atar-Gull seems
disproportionate; all that we take away from it is a strong dose of a certain
cult of manliness, along with a characterization of the slave, and knowledge
of his patience. The reader, too, must be patient, waiting to see what it all
adds up to.

On Wil's plantation Atar-Gull sees his lover's arm severed in the sugar-
mill (an accident that occurred frequently); he is whipped for no reason.
From then on, "he lived off two very distinct hatreds: Brulart and the
planter" (*AG*, 235). He plots and plans patiently, ingratiating himself with

the master. The new relation between Atar-Gull and Wil is not based on physiques or physiognomies; we don't even learn what Wil looks like. The novel turns increasingly to an explicit consideration of economics, both literal and moral.

MORAL ECONOMICS 101

> But what becomes apparent from the start and comes back constantly in the author's first works is the expression of a bitter skepticism, which stubbornly attributes to all human actions only one motive, vanity, and one goal, self-interest.
>
> —*Larousse du XIXe siècle*, "Sue, Eugène."

The chapter entitled "Father and Son" (chapter 17) begins with an epigraph from Jean-Baptiste Say's *Traité d'économie politique* of 1803. It states in part: "There is a big difference, you see, between productive capital and unproductive capital" (*AG*, 240). Sue parodies the discourse of cold economic calculus that was inherent in the slave system: executing a prisoner, Wil is told, "will get rid of your *unproductive capital*, after which the clerk of the court will *reimburse* you for the hanged man in cold, hard cash" (*AG*, 242). The old slave Job, Atar-Gull's father, is executed by Wil's order because he is unproductive, and at that point something strange happens in the language of the narrative. The hypocritical master, his family, and his slaves gather to mourn for Job, and the description reads like a parody by Sue of his own report from Guadeloupe, written in 1826 and published in the *Revue des deux mondes* only one year before *Atar-Gull*. In the novel Sue writes:

> On the day following the execution . . . the Blacks had fallen on their knees at the last stroke of the bell, for M. Wil, his wife and his daughter had given them an example by beginning the common prayer aloud.
>
> And it was a great and noble spectacle to see the master and the slave equal before the Creator, bowing together, praying the same prayer under the azure dome of the firmament, sparkling with the fire of the stars. (*AG*, 243)

What was apparently sincere in the "Lettres sur la Guadeloupe" — the same scene, using some of the same words, making slight changes to others — has now been turned into bitter irony, a dramatization of Wil's hypocrisy. Did Sue change his mind about slavery between 1826 and 1831? It is possible, but

290

that is not really the question. The shift from piety to heavily ironic parody in the representation of this tableau may result from purely literary motivations, including the appeal and marketability of irony itself. Drawing on his recollections of a plantation on Guadeloupe, Sue was able to create this situation of extreme moral bankruptcy on the part of Wil. In turn, this advances the plot by giving Atar-Gull a new purpose in life: revenge against Wil. From this point forward, Wil joins Brulart as an object of Atar-Gull's obsessive calculus of vengeance.

Alone later that night, Atar-Gull is able to "drop his mask of low and humble submissiveness, his sweet and tender smile" (*AG*, 243). When he puts it back on, Sue describes it as "that stereotyped smile that you are familiar with"—a surprising statement for 1831, perhaps meant to remind readers of blacks (or blackface performances) in the French theater. At this point, Atar-Gull finally speaks at length: "A father for me is a dead body hanging from a gibbet! . . . For me life is slavery, work, and beatings. . . . Oh! But I also have a joy of my own: to hold in my enslaved hands the brilliant and happy destinies [of Wil's daughter and her fiancé], at the end of my knife! To be able to say right now, if I want, that I shall make a coffin out of their nuptial bed" (*AG*, 248). Atar-Gull thus plots a "Hegelian" power reversal: he will enslave his own master.

HEGEL, INEVITABLY

Hegel, infamous for his dismissal, in *The Philosophy of History*, of Africa as a place without history, culture, or self-consciousness, was bound to come up in the course of this study. That passage haunts any consideration of Hegel's thoughts on slavery, which were most enduringly expressed in the famous section on "lordship and bondage"—more commonly known as the master and the slave—in *Phenomenology of Spirit*. Any consideration of a role reversal between master and slave brings these pages of Hegel's to mind: he shows how mastery and slavery can each "pass into the opposite of what it immediately is."[36] In a seminal essay Susan Buck-Morss has suggested that when Hegel wrote his famous text about slavery, between 1805 and 1807, Haiti, and not just other philosophies, had to have been on his mind.[37] Despite his use of the archaic, soft-focus word *Knecht*, instead of the more pointed *Sklave*, modern slavery and the only successful revolution mounted against it can now be seen as integral to Hegel's thinking.[38] This German philosopher was thus no different from other Europeans of his time, including so many of the French writers that we have seen — struggling to understand the impact of the Haitian Revolution.

In the section of *The Phenomenology of Mind* on the master and the slave, the slave is defined as a thing, existing only for "another," dependent, and therefore deprived of *recognition* (the main subject of Hegel's attention).[39] The master/slave relationship is an instance of failed or nonreciprocal recognition: the master is recognized by the slave but does not recognize the slave; the slave recognizes the master (he is coerced and has no choice) but is not recognized by him. (In *Atar-Gull*, the master literally does not know who Atar-Gull is, who Atar-Gull's father is.) The relationship is unstable from the beginning because it is nonreciprocal and based on the "phony recognition" of the master by the slave.[40] Buck-Morss shows how closely Hegel's description of slavery follows the Code Noir, where the slave is defined as moveable property ("Hegel and Haiti," 847). The dialectical reversal of the roles of master and slave begins when the slave realizes that the master is completely dependent on his, the slave's, labor. The master is in fact enslaved, "something quite different from an independent consciousness" (*PS*, 116–17). The slave then can see himself as an agent and a subject, capable of transforming the world. A "life-and-death struggle" takes place between two self-consciousnesses (*PS*, 114), although Hegel does not use the words that most logically come to mind at this point: revolt and revolution.[41] It is nonetheless clear, as Buck-Morss puts it, that for Hegel "freedom cannot be granted to slaves from above" (as it has been persistently represented with regard to the emancipations of both 1794 and 1848 in official French culture).[42] "It is," Hegel writes with heavy resonances of the Haitian Revolution, "only through staking one's life that freedom is won" (*PS*, 114). Liberation is self-liberation, which alone can bring "recognition as an independent self-consciousness" (*PS*, 114). Bondage will "be transformed into a real and true independence" (*PS*, 117, AT). This really does sound like an allegory of the Haitian Revolution.

Fanon commented famously, "What [the master] wants from the slave is not recognition but work."[43] What does the slave — Atar-Gull — want? In Hegelian terms Atar-Gull is seeking recognition; revenge, we will see, is the form of recognition that he has plotted for himself. Hegel's term (*recognition*) and Sue's term (*revenge*) will thus converge in a word that we have seen as essential to the Atlantic triangle: *return*. Atar-Gull's recognition will come from revenge, which he effects by "returning" to France the pain it has caused its slaves. *Un juste retour des choses.*

If, for Hegel, the slave comes into consciousness "through work," the power that Atar-Gull has just discovered in himself is the power of a certain kind of "work." With knife and poison as his technology, he will be able to radically change the equation of slavery. But if, in Hegel, freedom comes from work, and if, in Marxist terms, the slave might free himself by seizing the means of production, in Sue's gothic fiction, change comes from a calculated violence that is both physical and psychological. As in Hegel's paradigm, in *Atar-Gull*, the slave's gratification must be delayed; he must labor patiently, waiting for his moment of recognition. "Through this delayed gratification," writes an interpreter of Hegel, "the slave negates his thralldom, transforms himself, and overcomes his servility."[44] That is Atar-Gull's plan.

Despite their vast and obvious differences, Hegel and Sue echo one another in intriguing ways: both wrote with the specter of Haiti over their shoulders, and both describe the master/slave relation as unstable. Sue offers the scenario of power reversal not as philosophy but as an ironic and perverse literary *divertissement*. Now I want to go back to the question as Sue himself framed it in *Atar-Gull*, as a question of an economic calculus, but Hegel's vocabulary will remain useful in the reading that remains to be done.

293

RECKONING (OR REPARATION) AND RECOGNITION

Sue appends a long footnote to the title of his next chapter, "The Poisoners," explaining a "sect" that existed in the Antilles "still in 1822," devoted to vengeance against whites and dispensing poisons to be used against them (*AG*, 252). What we are about to read, Sue tells us, comes directly from legal proceedings in Martinique. Atar-Gull calls the "terrible and certain vengeance of the poisoners down upon his master" so that "justice might be done." Atar-Gull screams with "infernal joy" (*AG*, 255–56). When Wil's daughter Jenny dies from a snakebite, the slave laughs: he had "calculated right; hatred rarely makes a mistake" (*AG*, 262–63). Wil's wife then dies of grief, advising her husband to abandon the island. His livestock has been devastated by poison, as have some of his slaves, causing him "enormous losses." He should "cash in the little that [he has] left" and go to Europe. Just before dying, she sees a flash of joy on Atar-Gull's face and realizes his "atrocious hypocrisy," but too late (*AG*, 264–65).

The economics of vengeance dominates the rest of the novel (Gautier found that a vengeance "surpassing . . . all human proportions" motivated all of Sue's heroes).[45] Wil is struck dumb (his muteness could be seen as a return and reversal of the condition of the black crew in *El Gitano*). With his "devoted friend" Atar-Gull by his side, Wil sails for England aboard the same British ship that had pursued the *Hyène* off the coast of Africa. The Atlantic triangle, with its linkages and coincidences, is therefore brought back to mind. So, following the logic of reappearances that was such a hallmark of nineteenth-century popular fiction, it is not surprising when Brulart turns back up, adrift in a launch. Atar-Gull remains "faithful to his system . . . calm and cool" (*AG*, 267). Brulart is tried for his previous crimes (the sailor he threw overboard in a cage is present as a witness) and condemned. Justice is rendered, and that account is closed. Now Atar-Gull contemplates his final act: "The time is near for me to complete my vengeance. Oh! It will be terrible and above all long. . . . Death would be an incredible blessing [*bienfait*] compared to the life I am preparing for him [Wil]" (*AG*, 275).

In Paris, where they have settled because it is supposed to be cheaper than London, the two live in urban squalor. *Atar-Gull* is thus the first triangular text that we have seen to make the connection between Atlantic African slavery and the domestic exploited class in the metropole, explicitly labeled by Sue as the proletariat. (The comparison we saw previously, made by Gouges, was between slaves in the colonies and women in the metropole.) Years before it became his trademark in his social(ist) novels, Sue was trying his hand at representing "the mysteries of Paris," the "work and fatigue" of "a republic of industrious proletarians" in the rue Tirechape (*AG*, 277).[46] The closing of the Atlantic triangle also sets the stage for the moral and financial reckoning (or return) that is to come: by having this drama play itself out in Paris, Sue brings the slave trade and its consequences right to the heart of France. The "returns" on the investments of slave traders, which were destined to come back to France in the completion of the triangular trade, are now parodied in this gothic moral comedy.

The Hegelian ambiguities of the master-slave relationship come to the fore and play themselves out within the walls of the room that Atar-Gull and Wil share. Surrounded by those who might be seen as his laboring counterparts—members of the urban proletariat—Atar-Gull attracts admiration for his devotion to his master. The neighbors notice the reversal of roles: "He's a good kid, the Negro, to stay on like that, as a servant to an old skinflint like that who doesn't give him anything; *in fact it's reversed, it's the servant who is feeding his master* [*c'est au contraire le domestique qui nourrit son maître*]" (*AG*, 278). So Atar-Gull has seized the means of production, and the master is entirely dependent on the slave. Sue has neatly dramatized a Hegelian reversal of roles. Living in tidy misery, Atar-Gull gazes on Wil with "an inconceivable expression of joy and of fulfilled hatred! . . . His vengeance was complete" (*AG*, 280). After a further bankruptcy makes their situation even more dire, Atar-Gull runs errands for hire and makes enough to get by. Wil writes his memoirs, in which he heaps praise on his slave's devotion. In the last chapter of the novel the final reckoning—a "horrible and inconceivable scene"—takes place. Atar-Gull begins speaking to Wil: "Listen, white man . . ." and goes on to tie all the threads together. Atar-Gull compares his exquisite hatreds for Brulart and Wil respectively: "If I had to compare the hatred that I bore toward the slave-trader who was hanged to that which I carried for you, Tom Wil, I would have to say that I loved him like a brother. . . . And yet my heart leapt with joy as I watched his execution" (*AG*, 283).

The homosocial bonding between Atar-Gull and Brulart thus enters into this, the final calculation of slavery and the slave trade that Sue promised us at the beginning. That bond is null within the larger framework, the insurmountable crime that Wil committed: "For gold, you sold my blood," in other words, his father's life. By telling Wil how he killed off the planter's family and caused his ruin, Atar-Gull gives himself the exquisite pleasure of watching his master writhe in silent pain—"for I will be constantly by your side." Wil must now *recognize* Atar-Gull for who and what he is: the son of his victim Job, the murderer of his family, and the despoiler of his fortune. Atar-Gull's revenge comes from Wil's recognition of him. At this point the slave's Hegelian struggle for recognition has stopped precisely where it needs to: just "short of death," just before killing the other whose recognition the slave seeks.[47]

Wil therefore lives another six months after this, as Atar-Gull's captive and victim, sinking deeper into dementia, while "Monsieur Targu" is praised as a "model of virtue and heroism" (*AG*, 287). This is the period of Atar-Gull's full recognition and freedom; he later wishes it had lasted longer and that his victim hadn't escaped him through death (*AG*, 295). In the lie of Atar-Gull's pseudocaring relationship with Wil, the truth of slavery—the "phony recognition" on which it is based—is revealed.

After Wil's death Atar-Gull is baptized and receives "the prize for virtue established by the late Monsieur Montyon"—ten thousand francs (*AG*, 291).[48] The long encomium to this "devoted" slave that is read before the "elite of Parisian society" seems to be a satire of abolitionist discourse, which is depicted as both naive and condescending. Duped by Atar-Gull, the speaker condemns the slave trade, "this infamous traffic," because of the "development and intelligence" of Atar-Gull, who has been "well-behaved, submissive, and laborious" (*AG*, 291–92). Actually, Atar-Gull's perverse self-liberation, through revenge, has made a mockery of the speaker's sentiments. It is as if Sue were convinced, intuitively, of a logic that also happens to be Hegel's: that the only valid liberation is self-liberation, that forms of emancipation handed down from on high are false.[49]

The engraving of the prize ceremony has a similar structure to the one we saw earlier representing Ourika, listening to the two French ladies debate the consequences of her racial status (see figure 14). In both engravings the black subject listens from behind a barrier, as discourse about him or her is pronounced by whites. The screen and the curtain symbolize exclusion. But Ourika and Atar-Gull are in very different positions: she is learning for the first time that she is excluded from European society; he never assumed anything but exclusion, and he is enjoying the irony of his acceptance by a society that he rejects. (Earlier, Atar-Gull peered out from behind another curtain as young Jennie Wil was killed by the snake that he unleashed [*AG*, 262–63]).

As Léon-François Hoffmann points out, truth is stranger than fiction: the year after *Atar-Gull* was published, the Montyon Prize was given to a "Good Negro" who had sided with and saved his white owners at the time of the Haitian Revolution. Sue had parodied this event in advance.[50]

Atar-Gull sums up the accounts at the end of the novel:

> After having bought my father as a beast of burden, they hung my father as a thief, because he was old, because he could no longer earn his bread by his labor. . . . I had both his life and his death to avenge. For a good son, VEN-GEANCE IS VIRTUE. Now examine the motivation of my actions, *weigh* my life as a slave, *count up* my tortures, and you will see that the *prize* is well *earned* and well granted [*pesez ma vie d'esclave, comptez mes tortures, et vous verrez que le prix est bien gagné et bien donné*]. (*AG*, 295–96, emphasis added)

Soon Atar-Gull dies, "homesick and Christian." All accounts are therefore reckoned, balanced, and closed at the end. Atar-Gull has avenged himself not only against Wil but, he says, against "society at large" (*cette société tout entière* [295]); France as a whole is explicitly at stake. What Atar-Gull effected was a form of *reparation*, a concept that will merit further examina-

Le prix de vertu.

14 Beaucé illustration of *Atar-Gull* (1850), 1:33: "Le Prix de vertu" (The Prize for Virtue). Reproduced courtesy of the Tulane University Library.

297

tion later in this study; that is what this revenge is. The master was forced to repay the debt of pain that he had so callously incurred in his relations with his slave. The prize money was simply an outward manifestation of the moral reparation that Atar-Gull seized by and for himself.

The reader can only smile at the end, not only at the tidiness of the conclusion but also at the perfection of the final irony. As Sue promised in his preface, we have been treated to horror, pleasure, and even some measure of realism. Now the reader must, following Sue's instructions, do the math (*l'addition*, as Sue called it in the preface) regarding the slave trade. That calculus still contains an undefined x: Sue's irony. Whether his irony can be translated into a serious message that moves beyond the novel's obvious spirit of entertainment is a question that remains open to debate. Any reduction of *Atar-Gull* to a thesis statement risks violating the episodic logic that Sue posited in his preface, ignoring his "farewell to the unity of interest" and the sheer "delirium" of his writing.[51] Edouard Corbière, the subject of the next chapter, found Sue to be "more brilliant than true, more of a colorist than a thinker, more of a skeptic than a philosopher." Sue's seafaring novels, according to Corbière, didn't "smell enough of tar."[52]

But even in this context of irony, skepticism, and entertainment, the

Hegelian dimensions of Sue's plot can lead, quite plausibly, to an abolition-ist reading of *Atar-Gull*. Beyond the smiles and perhaps the chills that it pro-vokes, and beyond the satire of do-gooder abolitionists that is so evident in the prize testimonial, this novel does reveal something about a slave's life-and-death quest for recognition and about the inherent instability of slavery. Sue staged all of this, for whatever purpose and to whatever effect, within an Atlantic triangle that he depicted as an *economy*, as an integrated system. In his view, that economy was animated by a quest for and an exchange of values, morals, and recognition. Sue manipulated all the elements in his plot according to a logic of return: what goes around (exploitation, cruelty, and moral depravity) comes around. In *Atar-Gull* he radically expanded on the idea that I called Atlantic or colonial "blowback" in my discussion of Staël's *Histoire de Pauline*: the notion that the sins of the slave trade will return to haunt France and its "society at large." Sue was no philosopher, but I think there is a method to his madness after all: *Atar-Gull* makes a genuine, if twisted, contribution to our understanding of the slave trade.

ATAR-GULL AND AFRICAN AMERICAN FICTION

> The big planters . . . buy Negroes, that is, free men, removed by ruse or by force from their homeland, and turned by violence into the goods, the property of their fellow men.
>
> —VICTOR SÉJOUR, "Le Mulâtre" (1837)

In another turn of the Atlantic triangle Sue's novel of a slave's revenge lurks within the beginnings of African American literature. The "earliest known work of African American fiction,"[53] Victor Séjour's "Le Mulâtre," was printed in Paris in 1837, in the abolitionist *Revue des colonies*. Born in New Orleans and classified as a "free quadroon," Séjour moved to France for his education in 1836; he stayed and became a successful poet and playwright. His "Le Mulâtre," now thought to be, as Werner Sollors puts it, "the first published short story by an author of African ancestry born in the United States,"[54] owes much to *Atar-Gull*. The noble and devoted slave Georges turns vengeful after the sexual abuse and execution of his virtuous wife, Zé-lie, at the hands of "the sultan of the Antilles," the master Alfred. Georges "raised the curtain that hid the crime of his master," who is also, unbeknownst to Georges, his father. In a moment of gothic melodrama that out-does Sue, Séjour puts reckoning and recognition together. Georges learns of his paternity only as he severs his father's head, gaining his revenge against a cruel master; the second syllable of the word "father" is murmured by Alfred's head as it rolls across the floor. What a moment of recognition! Georges then kills himself.

Set in Saint-Domingue before the Revolution, written by an African American from Louisiana, published within an abolitionist context in France, "Le Mulâtre" is a sign of evolving Atlantic complexities.[55] It fore-shadows the coming of new reflections on the slave trade from the descendants of those who were enslaved. Whereas so many French authors looked back on Saint-Domingue only with abhorrence, Séjour uses its plantation system to illustrate the horrors and injustices of slavery and the slave trade. The chills of gothic literature are offered to the reader, but a liberationist agenda is also served: Georges's revenge is not a mere entertainment; it is effected in the name of "Africa and liberty" ("Le Mulâtre," 71). With something at stake personally, Séjour took Sue's example to a new level. Any contribution of *Atar-Gull* to the abolitionist cause would have been incidental and haphazard, but in "Le Mulâtre" an actual impetus for change is printed in black and white.

299

EDOUARD CORBIÈRE, "MATING," AND MARITIME ADVENTURE

CORBIÈRE, SEAFARING, AND LIBERALISM

Edouard Corbière's status within this study is unique: he is the only French novelist who is alleged to have once participated in the slave trade himself. We have encountered numerous authors who have had various degrees of involvement and complicity in the triangular economy but none who are reputed to have physically participated in the actual slave trade. In his novel *Le Négrier* Corbière is thought to have depicted things that he either witnessed or did himself during his career as a merchant lieutenant in 1821 and as a captain between 1824 and 1828 — thus precisely during the period of the illegal French slave trade. Was Corbière a real-life Ledoux or Brulart? Whether he, as he said, merely witnessed the slave trade or, alternatively, actually participated in it is a question to be explored here. His public position about the colonies, slavery, and the slave trade, we will see, was somewhat ambiguous. And *Le Négrier* is one of the most curious literary artifacts of the French slave trade.

In literary terms Corbière is Eugène Sue's only rival as originator of the French maritime novel; for partisans of the former, the latter's works are ersatz.[1] That, we will see, was very much the way that Corbière himself wanted the comparison to be made. If he is now known mostly as the father of his more famous son Tristan, a *poète maudit*, Corbière was nonetheless a fairly successful writer in his day, mostly because of *Le Négrier*. In our times his work is almost entirely absent from academic discussions, but the ongoing popularity of *Le Négrier* is demonstrated by its regular republication, with seven editions since 1952, two currently in print. One of those recent editions markets the novel as pirate adventure literature, with a cartoonish drawing on the front and a back cover that promises "rough heroes, at once corsairs and slave traders," their "sudden passions," and their "orgies."[2]

Born in Brest in 1793, Corbière had two separate careers at sea before settling on land permanently. He enrolled in the French navy and went to sea at the age of eleven, as a cabin boy. After four years a Napoleonic battle at sea made him a prisoner of the British for fourteen months, furnishing him with graphic materials about prison life that he later exploited in *Le Négrier*. Released and repatriated in 1812, Corbière continued his naval career, making his first voyage to Martinique in 1814. But a purge of the navy in 1816 expulsed all officers suspected of antiroyalist sentiments, including Corbière, already known for his liberal opinions. His career ruined at the age of twenty-two by this arbitrary exercise of power, Corbière's disdain for the Restoration was redoubled, and he took up the pen. Starting in 1818, when he founded the newspaper *La Guêpe* in Brest, Corbière became one of the first provincial journalists to generate antigovernmental, anticlerical polemics. Instead of spying on the population, Corbière opined, shouldn't the imperial police busy themselves with projects that might improve community welfare? Brittany was full of illiterate "savages" (as he called them) who didn't even speak French; shouldn't the church and the state do something to improve these people? If not exactly a Jacobin, Corbière was certainly a liberal universalist, espousing, in effect, the colonization of France's least assimilated region, in which Brest was a French enclave. He was a republican when possible, an admirer of Napoleon, in whose navy he had served, and a child of Voltaire, the Enlightenment, and the Revolution. He strongly preferred the tricolor to the fleur-de-lis. As with Mérimée, Hugo, Auguste de Staël, Musset, and other young liberals, Corbière's time would come with the July Revolution in 1830, in which he participated. Like Mérimée and Sue, Corbière became both a writer and a bourgeois — a recipient of the Legion of Honor in 1831, president of a chamber of commerce later in life. Corbière said himself that he had joined the "literary bourgeoisie."[3] But in the meantime, how could such a person become a slave trader — if he did?[4]

An anticlerical pamphlet earned Corbière an indictment in 1819; although he was acquitted, it was only a matter of time before his writings would land him in jail. In 1821 he may have taken to the sea on a merchant vessel that sailed to Africa; if so, his contact with the slave trade may date from this period.[5] In 1822 Corbière moved to Rouen and became editor of another liberal newspaper, *La Nacelle*; an offending article quickly put him in prison for a month in 1823 and closed down the publication. Released from prison

301

(but still owing a large fine), he took to the sea again, as a merchant. Backed by a friend's father, an outfitter of Le Havre who provided a ship, Corbière was suddenly his own captain. It is in the context of this second career at sea that he is most often alleged to have traded in slaves. But this question is almost as murky as the riddle of Rimbaud's supposed slave trading in Africa later in the century.[6]

The facts are inconclusive but suggestive. An unfriendly contemporary wrote of Corbière: "Despite his liberalism, Corbière practiced the slave trade; he only abandoned it when it became dangerous and when, finally, the profits were reduced."[7] Corbière was captain of two ships in succession, *La Nina* and *Le Royal Louis*, both of which plied the *commerce en droiture* between France and the slave islands. Did his ships go beyond that route, along other axes of the triangle, thereby making slave trading more likely? It is true that Corbière ended his career at sea just as the French slave trade and the traditional Atlantic triangle were fading away, but that may be a coincidence. Many assertions about Corbière the slave trader are in print, but no documentation has been offered.[8] Neither of Corbière's ships appears in the definitive catalogue of the French slave trade of this period, Serge Daget's *Répertoire*, nor in *The Trans-Atlantic Slave Trade: A Database on CD-ROM*, so there is no readily apparent "smoking gun."[9] Still, working the Atlantic between 1824 and 1828, with his principal destination the Antilles, Corbière was at the least a participant in the Atlantic triangle, helping to recover the "returns" of the slave trade and of slave labor. He was without doubt a witness to the slave trade and to the fact of slavery on the islands: as he said himself, "I lived with slave traders."[10] It cannot be stated with any assurance that he was a slave trader himself, but he would appear to be the only French novelist who had extensive, detailed, direct knowledge of the slave trade.

In June 1823, while working on the appeal of his prison sentence, thus just a few months before he became a merchant captain, Corbière published a volume of poetry called *Elégies brésiliennes*, which included a "Précis sur la traite des Noirs" (Remarks on the slave trade).[11] This text has been mentioned, but never discussed, by the few critics who have written about *Le Négrier*. In 1823 Corbière could well have been torn between, on the one hand, his maritime background and ambitions (the author is identified on the title page of the *Elégies brésiliennes* as a "former naval officer"), which could have drawn him into sympathy for the slave trade, and, on the other hand, his liberal beliefs. Slave-trade abolitionism was rising among French liberals. Clarkson was published in French in 1821. In 1822 the Société de la Morale Chrétienne organized its anti-slave-trade committee, the Duc de Broglie documented and denounced the continuing French slave trade in the Chambre des Pairs, and the French Academy announced its poetry contest on the subject of the slave trade. Corbière's "Précis" begins with echoes of that abolitionist thunder: the slave trade is "the most awful violation of peoples' rights and the trade which most humiliates the human species." The balance of the text suggests no unique or intimate knowledge of the slave trade on Corbière's part; all of its information could have been gleaned from previous publications.[12] But if Corbière had indeed sailed to Africa and Brazil in 1821, he might well have seen the things he describes in these pages.

Possibly confirming that theory, near the end of the "Précis," Corbière weaves a personal narrative into his comments. He tells the story of a slave revolt that took place on the island of São Tomé in the Gulf of Guinea when, Corbière says, he was there; he offers no further information about his presence there. The island was a hub of the transatlantic slave trade, a frequent stopover for vessels about to undertake the Middle Passage: "During my stay on the small island of São Tomé [*la petite île de San-Thomé*], situated in the Gulf of Guinea, a slave-trader from Bahia had his whole crew slaughtered by slaves driven to revolt by the prospect of an awful captivity. The guilty did not attempt to disavow the acts that condemned them to die. They marched to the gallows, satisfied with having avenged themselves and with escaping through death the implacable barbarism of their masters" (95).

For Corbière this brief account is an example of justified resistance and revolt. But the text takes a different turn in its conclusion, preparing the ground for *Le Négrier*, which Corbière will write ten years later. Having elicited the "pity of our readers for the sad condition of the wretched Africans," the author turns his attention to the slave traders' moral and economic position. Since "the destiny of the slave is almost always chained to that of his master," attention to both is warranted. When "slave-trading sailors" succeed in defying the bans on their livelihood, Corbière writes, they go to "the island of Saint-Thomas" to spend, "among pirates and corsairs," the gold they have "acquired at the cost of [their] honor." Their earnings are "justified [*légitimé*], if it is possible, by their sacrifices and the dangers they have run" (97). If this "Saint-Thomas" is a reference to the African island that he previously called "San-Thomé," then we can surmise that São Tomé was full of pirates and corsairs (which is quite likely) and that contact with this culture in 1821 may have provided Corbière with knowledge and memories that he exploited in *Le Négrier*. (If he is referring to Saint Thomas in the Virgin Islands, which was a famous haven for pirates, the same observation would apply.)[13] But, more important, in this narrow window of sympathy for slave-trading sailors, closely associated with pirates and corsairs, we see the moral and narrative space in which Corbière will create his novel. The question of whether the earnings of slave traders can "possibly" be justified has been opened and left open. In *Le Négrier* the formulation will be very different: the slave trade will *not* be condemned, and the titillating moral ambiguity of the pirate will dominate. Corbière's "Précis" belies one statement that has been made about him: that he was "the only writer [in France] who did not oppose" slavery or the slave trade.[14] Could anyone have written this "Précis sur la traite des Noirs" and then have participated in the slave trade himself? It is certainly "possible."

Corbière left himself room to drift between his loyalty to the men of the sea on the one hand and his liberal principles on the other. As editor of *Le Journal du Havre* in the late 1820s, he was an "energetic and persistent defender of colonial interests," which of course included slavery.[15] He wanted the "tie that binds the colonies to the metropole to be kept intact." [16] In 1829 he published "Le Capitaine de négrier" (The Slave-Trading Captain) in the nautical review *Le Navigateur*; here he gave voice to a slaver who is thrilled with the exciting and manly life he leads. This captain closely prefigures the narrator of *Le Négrier*.[17]

After the July Revolution, and with his career at sea over, Sue began to translate his exotic experiences into literary form. Cooper was propelled to create a maritime novel that would be more authentic than Sir Walter Scott's *The Pirate*; Corbière had the same reaction to Sue's work (who had taken Cooper as his sponsor).[18] Finding Sue inadequate (as we saw), Corbière set out to create maritime novels that would soak the reader with the sea spray of authenticity. In a preface to the original edition (not reprinted in any of the modern editions), Corbière clears space for himself as a writer by elbowing his competitors aside: "Some writers, strangers to the sea, have ventured to write about men whose character, profession, and habits they know only imperfectly. . . . Leafing through some pages of these novels that are called *maritime*, I was struck by a desire to depict, in my own fashion, the true manners [*mœurs*] of sailors." (*Mœurs* was often a code word for sexual morals.) Even Cooper, a "great master," is insufficient because he represents only American sailors, who are very different from French sailors. The "pre-

304

ciosity" (*afféterie*) of some maritime novelists "disgusts" Corbière (*N 1832*, i–ii, v). A few remarks about his qualifications as an author are designed to silence any potential critics: "I was a sailor, a cadet, a prisoner of war; I have commanded merchant vessels. I have known the freebooters about whom I write under assumed names. *I have lived with slave-traders. I have sojourned in the colonies; I have traded there.*" Everything is "historical." "The maneuvers that I have described are things that I know: I have seen them done and I have ordered them to be done" (*N 1832*, ix–x; emphasis added). Corbière will write what he knows, with a vengeance.

Starting with *Le Négrier*, Corbière produced a dozen maritime novels over the next fourteen years. *Le Négrier* appeared in two installments: the first in March of 1832 and the second in May. The author continued to revise the text until and after the last edition of his lifetime, published in 1855, which he amended by hand (again).[19] In order to keep within the historical context that is most relevant here—the immediate aftermath of the abolition of the French slave trade—I will analyze the text as it was published and republished in the 1830s.

PIRACY AND *MATELOTAGE*

Corsairs seem to me the only real men; the rest are little women [*des femmelettes*].

—EDOUARD CORBIÈRE, *Le Négrier*

This is a mariner's family: a shipmate and a cabin boy [*un matelot et un mousse*].

—CHARLES DESNOYER and J. ALBOIZE,
La Traite des Noirs (1835)

Le Négrier is presented as the diary of a slave-trading sailor who dies in Martinique in 1818 of a disease he caught on the coast of Africa.[20] The narrator who receives "this document, as bizarre as the events that produced it," says that he put it into better "order" as he sailed back and forth across the ocean a dozen times (like Corbière). The old literary convention of the "authentic" discovered diary is thus given a fresh coat of sea salt, and the narrative is launched. As if to one-up his competitors in maritime literature, Corbière has his hero, Léonard, literally born at sea, as his father brings his Creole mother back home to Brest from Saint-Domingue (*N*, 9). Like Corbière himself, Léonard is enrolled in the navy as a cabin boy at a tender age. But failing a test for promotion, Léonard signs on with a corsair—a state-sponsored pirate ship—the *Sans-Façon*, and the sea quickly becomes his "fatherland" (*patrie*; *N*, 20). Colorful sights, characters, and events now come thick and fast: an English vessel bringing colonial products home from India is attacked; knives are wielded and blood flows into the sea; booty is divided in equal portions for the state, the outfitters, and the crew (*N*, 64). Sea tales are told, with the call of "cric!" and the response "crac!" that became the hallmark of Creole oral traditions. Among the colorful effects that Corbière reports (or creates) are elements that we saw in *Atar-Gull* and now need to explore in more detail: issues of gender and sexuality.

Leslie Fiedler wrote in his famous essay on same-sex relations in literature: "The buggery of sailors is taken for granted among us."[21] In the last chapter I insisted that we should not infer homosexuality from homosociality. But now Corbière takes us over the line, from homosociality to explicit homosexuality (without the name, of course). What relation these themes—which would *appear* to concern only those above-decks and not the captives in the hold—might have to the slave trade is a question to which we will have to return. But from the outset we should bear in mind that historically—though not in Corbière's novel—many pirates were African; the color line is anything but clear.[22]

Despite its title, *Le Négrier* is a novel about piracy, not the slave trade, for its entire first half.[23] Issues and images of manliness are foregrounded, starting with the narrator's name, Léonard, which his father thought was "male" and "martial."[24] Early in the novel, we are informed that the pirate captain, Arnaudault, is handsome, with dark, curly hair and an exposed hairy chest. (Beaucé's illustration of Sue's Brulart [figure 12] could serve as a portrait of Arnaudault as well.) The captain has brought two of his sons with him on this voyage, and he has a curious way of bringing them up: "as young ladies." His reason for doing this is even more curious: "so that they will later become, [the captain] said, *proper* freebooters" ("des flibustiers *comme il faut*" [*N*, 20]). (The strange gendering of the captain's sons was removed from later editions by Corbière; in the 1855 edition he wrote that Arnaudault had taken his sons "out of college" so that he might oversee their becoming proper freebooters.)[25]

Corbière offers no immediate explanation, but if any credence can be given to one somewhat controversial historian, "proper freebooters" might be very queer indeed. B. R. Burg describes "almost universal homosexual involvement among pirates" of the Caribbean in the seventeenth century: "Sexual relations between pirates were an ordinary activity, condemned by no one among them and denigrated only by those classes [on land] with whom they had little contact and less familiarity." Pirates established communities where "homosexual contact was the ordinary form of sexual expression." Women were "a rare and exotic feature of their lives." If "masculinity was not diminished by homosexuality among buccaneers," there was nonetheless "no impediment" to the bending of gender barriers.[26] Other historians claim that Burg has exaggerated, but Corbière's text, even though it represents a different century, paints a *very* queer picture of pirate life.[27]

The sailors' life in prison replicates the sexual universe of the ship, with *matelotage* designating dominant and submissive partners. On the seas Captain Arnaudault addresses his crew as "my beloved ones" (*mes amoureux*) in later editions of the novel.[28] And on another corsair, in the Caribbean in chapter 9 of *Le Négrier*, in a long scene that is part Gilbert and Sullivan, part Monty Python, the entire crew dons women's clothes simply because they found them; in drag these "belles dames" then attack a very surprised British ship (*N*, 136–39). On shore afterward, a mock-lesbian "orgy" takes place at the "cabarets of the colony," Martinique, between the sailors in their torn silk dresses and the local "girls of color" (*N*, 141).

A note of caution should enter this analysis. Discussing "bold sailor-boys" skipping about as if in a "ballet" (in Charles Warren Stoddard's account of a journey to Tahiti), Jonathan Ned Katz warns us that "most nineteenth-century readers would not have seen any link between gender and erotic deviance."[29] That is, reading about sailors in drag did not necessarily raise questions of homosexual activity in the nineteenth-century mind. But in the context that Corbière created in *Le Négrier*—of maritime life and of piracy in particular—gender bending, erotic "deviance," and actual homosexuality (*avant la lettre* and without a name) all are clearly and explicitly in play. Corbière was inviting his readers to make a connection that they might not have perceived as automatically as many would now: the link between gender deviation and homosexual activity.

On the *Sans-Façon* a second gender-bender soon follows: a "pretty little novice" (*un joli petit novice* [*N*, 26]) named Jacques, with delicate hands, who is "protected" by one of the officers and shares his bunk, turns out to be a woman, Rosalie. Léonard uncovers the travesty through a linguistic ruse, tricking the novice into describing herself in the feminine (*fainéante*). She

307

is in fact the officer's "wife," who must pass as his male protégé and bunk-mate in order to stay onboard.[30] The key term in the for-show, male-to-male relationship as it is presented to the crew is *amateloté* (25, 26). The officer and "Jacques" are in a relationship of ostensible *matelotage*; Jacques sees it as tyranny (36). Defined here in the novel (25) and in nineteenth-century dictionaries, the term *matelotage* describes two sailors who share a bunk (although, as the narrator quickly points out, normally not at the same time, since their watches alternate). They are known as each other's *matelot*. The original meaning of *matelot*, the French word for sailor, was "bed mate." (The *Petit Robert*, like the narrator of *Le Négrier*, is anxious to point out that this bed-mating was done out of necessity, since there was "only one ham-mock" for every two sailors.)[31] The nineteenth-century *Larousse* defined *matelotage* as "friendship, bond [*lien*] that exists between sailor comrades, who are each other's *matelot*," going on to say that, among freebooters, these unions were "intimate and indissoluble."[32] The English term *mate*, which seems to come from the same Dutch root, encompasses a similar combina-tion of maritime and matrimonial senses, including sexual union. Accord-ing to Burg *matelotage* (alternately called *amatelotage*) among pirates was "an institutionalized linking of a buccaneer and another male — most often a youth — in a relationship with clearly homosexual characteristics." *Matelots* could be "no more than slaves"; they were often men who had sold them-selves for food, protection, or to pay off debts.[33] What is stated in *Le Négrier* is the following: "This *amatelotage* of sailors among themselves, this *ham-mock comraderie*, establishes a type of solidarity and a commonality of inter-ests and of goods between each man and his *matelot*."[34] So this institution could variously combine friendship, brotherly love, servitude, and perhaps even sex; we cannot exclude any of these possibilities. To the extent that one *matelot* could be the possession of the other, *matelotage* had the potential to blur the line between the sailors above decks and, when they were present, the captives in the hold. When pirates (like Brulart in *Atar-Gull* and now Arnaudault in *Le Négrier*) take over slave ships, all these aspects of *matelo-tage* can come together. This is precisely the context that Corbière evoked.

Alternatively, pairs of *matelots* could simply be lovers or friends with a deep emotional commitment to each other, as the bosun Bibi and his mate are depicted to be in Berry's film *Tamango*. Corbière describes a case of ap-parently egalitarian *matelotage* that happens to be interracial in a short nar-rative of the sea he wrote called "The Wish of the Two Sailors" (or mates, *matelots*). A mulatto is the *matelot* of a white Frenchman; before undertaking

308

together a dangerous task in the rigging, the two shake hands and embrace (or kiss) each other.[35] In general, *matelots* often entered into a mutual pact in which they were heirs to each other's property. Signs of these relationships span the Atlantic in time and space. The earliest description of them that I have seen comes from Jean-Baptiste Du Tertre, the early chronicler of life on the new French islands of the Caribbean in the mid-seventeenth century, and it is worth quoting at length:

> There are two kinds of families on the Islands: the first are composed of married persons, and the others of certain bachelors who live together, which they call *matelotage* in the usage of this place. In their house they have equal authority over the servants, everything is jointly owned, and they get along well with each other. When one of the two gets married, they separate, dividing the servants, both the indentured French ones and the Negro slaves. The plantation is readied, and the partner to whom it will now belong is obliged to pay half its value to the other. These separations, which would be the cause of endless litigation in France, are done without furor or quarrel. Previously, they did not even separate, and the one who was not married continued to live with his *Matelot*; but the jealousy that entered the land, and the unfortunate accidents that arose from the indiscretion of the *Matelot* or from the imprudence of the women, obliged the governors to forbid this practice. They no longer permitted a man to live in the house of his *Matelot* after getting married. All the best families that are now present on the Islands started out this way.[36]

The sexual ambiguity that Du Tertre describes (without of course mentioning sex itself) is revealed by the telltale sign of jealousy. Some men clearly were reluctant to give up their *matelot* even after marriage. This, along with the "cric/crac" of the oral tradition, points to the influence of seafaring culture on the early settlers of the islands.[37]

A century or more later, and in a different language, a compelling first-person account of *matelotage* was written by none other than Olaudah Equiano. Early in his *The Interesting Narrative*, the enslaved Equiano is sent from Virginia to England—like Ourika to France—as "a present" for friends of his master, and he tells of a deep bond he shared with a young white man:

> There was on board the ship a young lad who had never been at sea before, about four or five years older than myself: his name was Richard Baker. He was a native of America, had received an excellent education, and was of a most amiable temper. Soon after I went on board he shewed me a great deal of partiality

309

and attention, and in return I grew extremely fond of him. We at length became inseparable, and, for the space of two years, he was of very great use to me, and was my constant companion and instructor. Although this dear youth had many slaves of his own, yet he and I have gone through many sufferings together on shipboard; and we have many nights lain in each other's bosums when we were in great distress.

Richard Baker, fifteen years old, had "discovered a mind superior to prejudice."[38] The fact of the two boys lying together and clinging to each other in times of stress need not be seen in sexual terms; on the other hand, such relations cannot be ruled out. Another sign of informal *matelotage* (which has no English-language equivalent) is the fact that a distraught Equiano inherits Baker's goods after his death.[39] What is of interest here, alongside Corbière's version of these relationships, is Equiano's testimony about *matelotage* across the color line in the eighteenth-century Atlantic.

By bringing *matelotage* into the picture in *Le Négrier*, Corbière found a way to discuss the ambiguities of shipboard male bonding with impunity: since Jacques is really a woman, sexualized same-sex *matelotage* is avoided but broadly hinted at, even as the general institution is described. While the question of the slave trade is held at bay until later in the novel, the ambiguity of gender and sexuality among the French pirates continues as a prominent theme. Léonard's attraction to Jacques grows, and their relationship is, grammatically, same-sex ("mon ami petit Jacques . . . ce joli petit être" [*N*, 38]). When Jacques is "outed" as a woman, one of the sailors tells the inquiring captain that Jacques is "either" a woman or a young man, "as you like, it's up to you" (*N*, 41).[40]

In his depiction of the British prison where Léonard and his shipmates find themselves, Corbière goes beyond ambiguous gender bending into an open and direct discussion of homosexuality. The narrator represents it as "depravity," a "shameful vice, whose very name is an outrage to decency . . . [which] reigned with frenzy in the prisons."[41] Homosexuality in this prison is all-encompassing, with even "acts of marriage, gravely written out and signed by the parties to the contract in places where there was only one sex." The narrator witnesses fights to the death over men called "mistresses." "There was, after all, in prison, love, marriage, rivalries, infidelities, and adulteries; and yet, as I already pointed out, there was only one sex."[42] (In 1834 he added an exclamation point to that statement.)[43] Corbière's "shocked" description of these diverse, formalized same-sex relationships is remarkably precocious, coming as it does thirty-seven years before the term *homosexuality* was coined, thus well before the "homo/hetero divide."[44] If nineteenth-century readers had no fixed terms like *homosexual* or *heterosexual* through which they could process the information that Corbière is providing, the author seems nonetheless inclined to break through the limitations imposed by the language of his times and to make a full range of same-sex relationships real. His invocation of love, and not just sex, is itself remarkable in this context.[45] He describes a homosexual subculture that, despite its lack of name, cannot be mistaken for anything else. *Le Négrier* needs to be seen within the history of the literature of the slave trade but also within the history of literary homosexuality in France. With "no organized expression" and "no body of concepts for this dangerous subject matter," homosexuality is assumed to occupy "only the smallest of space" in French literature "at least up to 1880," according to Jean-Paul Aron and Roger Kempf.[46] Corbière's novel (from fifty years earlier than 1880) supports Graham Robb's more recent theory about the status of homosexuality in nineteenth-century discourse: "the unmentionability of the 'nameless sin' was mentioned all the time."[47]

In this prison the strong rule the weak in bonded relations that clearly reproduce *matelotage*. Léonard's burly friend Ivon secures a dominant position through combat and is consequently able to offer protection against sexual predators to his "little rabbit." Because of this, Léonard was never "insulted" (molested), "despite being 15 years old, with curly hair and a pretty face." Ivon is "everything" for Léonard; Ivon is explicitly Léonard's *matelot*.[48] (Graham Robb reports that a riot broke out in a French prison in 1848 when one prisoner was separated from his boyfriend, the equivalent of his *matelot*.)[49] The prison commissioner's wife also has an eye for "pretty" young men and takes Léonard on, apparently as a sex toy (Ivon is jealous). To amuse herself, she dresses him in women's clothes, which hide his "muscular charms"; he takes advantage by escaping. Thus the prison episode ends.[50]

For the weaker prisoners conditions are, we can see, much the same as those suffered by captives in the hold of a slave ship: "lying entirely naked on the ground or on rough boards, as close to each other as possible in order to be less cold, they [all] rolled over at once, at certain hours of the night, at the blowing of a whistle . . ." (*N*, 89). Rations are ghastly and scarce. Is Corbière's graphic depiction of this *univers concentrationnaire* preparing the reader, as it could, for a comparison between, on the one hand, French cor-

311

sairs in British captivity and, on the other, Africans enslaved by the French?[51] Will the author of the "Précis sur la traite des Noirs" actually make that comparison? Will this novel heap the same opprobrium on the treatment of Africans by French slave traders that it does on conditions among French prisoners in British captivity? At this point in the novel (the fourth and final chapter in the first volume of the original edition), the slave trade is still unmentioned.

Picaresque adventures continue in the second volume (which has ten more chapters), now onboard a class of ship appropriately called an *aventurier*, a type of armed merchant vessel (similar to a corsair). The ship that picks up Léonard and Ivon, commanded by an old friend of theirs, is headed for Martinique, a "new theater" for the hero's exploits (*N*, 107). This, then, will be the conduit between their own captivity in prison and their contact with Africans enslaved on the French islands. First, the new, one-armed captain, like everyone else in the story, falls in a sort of love with Léonard — "took him into his heart" (*me prendre en affection* [*N*, 108]). His "esteem" takes a "bizarre," gruff form that Léonard breaks through with seductive maneuvers, forcing the old captain to declare his affection openly and tearfully (*N*, 109). During the crossing toward the Antilles, Corbière fills his narrative with depictions of life onboard ship (including the traditional ceremony for the crossing of the tropics) and advice to prospective passengers on how they should behave at sea.

A first sign of how Corbière will handle the question of slavery comes when he describes the Antilles as "the tomb of so many Europeans" (*N*, 125). It is strange to see the idea of the "white man's grave" applied to islands that we now think of as tourist paradises; the frequent mention of yellow fever in accounts of the Antilles explains this. In *Le Négrier*, Martinique is "somber" and threatening, with "terrifying" volcanic origins; it is "wild," "sinister," and "desolate" (*N*, 126). There is a bitter irony in Corbière's focus on the deaths of Europeans on these islands, where so many African slaves were literally worked to death (but Raynal had warned that the climate of the islands was dangerous for Europeans, "even Creoles").[52] The narrator's first mention of slavery comes by way of explaining the smoke that is seen rising among the hills: a sign of the camps of marooned slaves, "who feed themselves like real pigs, so they don't have to work . . . !" (*N*, 126). The ship is capsized while under attack by a British cruiser, and many drown. On the streets of Saint-Pierre, Ivon explains to Léonard that the odor of "fried onions" comes from *la négraille*, the "blacktrash." (These terms set off a reverberation with Césaire's *Cahier*.)[53] This provokes Ivon to offer a primer on the slave trade to his young colleague, who "still had no idea what it was" (*N*, 133). What Ivon says is not reported, but the effect of his speech on Léonard is far from moral revulsion:

> Ivon's information and comments on this type of industry made such a vivid impression on me that I can still remember it. I no longer looked upon a fine Negro without attempting to estimate his price and to evaluate him, not for the services that he could perform, but for the price that he might have drawn at auction. I have heard many Europeans, newly arrived from France, mouthing fine phrases about the immorality of a commerce that trades in human flesh, which nonetheless did not prevent them from buying blacks and beating them on occasion. But I admit, perhaps to my shame, I did not feel these sublime philanthropic inspirations when I arrived in the colonies. I saw these blacks, big and fat, lazy and gay [*gros et gras, paresseux et gais*], traipsing around the streets all day [*balander toute la journée*]; they seemed to me a lot happier than our laborers in Europe, and happier than sailors, who sleep only half the time and eat only a ration of biscuit as the recompense for exertions that exhaust their miserable and agitated lives so quickly.[54]

313

This is a remarkable statement about the slave trade and slavery in relation to other forms of hardship, namely those that dominated the lives of millions of Europeans in the eighteenth and nineteenth centuries. Earlier in this study, we considered Patrick Manning's pertinent question about life in the interior of Africa during the time of the slave trade: what must it have been like to see all other human beings as potential objects to be appraised and sold? In this passage Léonard takes to that calculating mentality like a fish to water. And it is specifically the economics of the slave trade, not the productivity of slave labor, that attracts him. He takes a quick swipe at abolitionists' "sublime" misgivings and offers a standard justification of slavery: that it was no worse than other forms of labor; in fact it was much better. As a sailor, this narrator is in a position to relativize the slave trade (although he has not yet seen it) with the authority that his readers would grant him. It was known that Corbière himself was a retired seaman, lending further credence to the testimony of his spokesman, Léonard. This passage runs parallel to the article that Sue published about his 1826 visit to Guadeloupe, with its comforting image of happy slaves. We saw how that passage was turned on its head in *Atar-Gull*. As *Le Négrier* finally turns toward the subject of its title, is Corbière preparing any such ironic reversal?

ATROCITY AND ADVENTURE

Léonard's first taste of slave trading comes when he sells two free blacks who had ferried him and his mate back to Martinique. He gains "owner-ship" of them by falsely claiming it on arrival; when they protest that they are free and cannot be sold, he whips them (*N*, 155). A planter buys them for thirty ounces of gold. This miraculous transformation of value gains Léonard something out of nothing. Ivon, now known as Livonnière, declares, "Heaven must have molded you specially to be a slave merchant" (*N*, 155). Even with Martinique in the hands of the British, the colonies are now a "far better theater than Europe is for sailors inclined to make their fortune by bold strokes" (*N*, 157). First the two *matelots* rent a slave to help them in a counterfeiting operation (*N*, 158). After Ivon/Livonnière dies and Léonard is reunited with Rosalie, Léonard quickly becomes an expert in the interisland slave trade, returning from each voyage to a perfect domestic existence with Rosalie. (With Ivon's death, references to same-sex desire disappear from the novel, which is now almost exclusively devoted to the subject that its title announced, the slave trade.)[55] This new "bourgeois" life is too con-straining for Léonard's pirate spirit. When 1814 brings the Restoration and the return of Martinique to France, it also restores, as we have seen, the con-ditions necessary for the now-illegal transatlantic slave trade. If "the slave trade is forbidden," says Léonard, "so much the better, I'll do it, and I'll add the joy of breaking the law to the pleasure of undertaking a perilous form of commerce" (*N*, 168). Thus, when the slave trade was outlawed, outlaws joined the slave trade, as Corbière said in his 1832 preamble to the novel: the "slave-trading captains who inundated the Antilles after the peace of 1814 had almost all been corsairs in Europe during the war" (*N* 1832, x).

The *Rosalie* is quickly outfitted for the slave trade, and the novel is now, in the eleventh out of fourteen chapters, finally in accord with its title. Léo-nard is now a slave-trading captain, and, in his "splendor," he will "trade with . . . Negro kings . . . on an equal basis" (*N*, 169). The trade that is now depicted in *Le Négrier* is not triangular in the sense that was mandated by the old *Exclusif*, with exchanges moving counterclockwise from France to Africa to the islands and back to France. The new system consists of an il-licit, bilateral trade operating directly between the islands and Africa. Trade goods like cloth, hardware, and guns come from France to Martinique, carried by merchant seamen like Corbière; rum and tobacco produced by slaves on the islands complete the cargo that will be exchanged for new captives on the coast of Africa. So all three points on the old triangle are still in play but in a different configuration. Daget's roster of the illegal trade shows dozens of such expeditions leaving Martinique and Guadeloupe in the years of the Restoration. Léonard is thrilled at the idea of "converting all of that"—his cargo—"into Negroes that [he] would sell for a high price" (*N*, 170).

On the African coast, following the formula established by Mérimée and Sue (and reflecting history), this *négrier* encounters a British cruiser but evades it.[56] The crew of the *Rosalie* witnesses human sacrifices that are performed by Africans onboard pirogues, explained by King Pepel of Bonny (Nigeria) as necessary for appeasing a god; this sets the tone for Corbière's depiction of Africans as "barbaric" (*N*, 171). The first night, Captain Léonard muses at the thought of "these men that I am going to buy and chain in my hold, who are resting peacefully in these huts or singing gaily on this tranquil coast!" (*N*, 172). In the negotiations with Pepel the next day, as in Mérimée's "Tamango," a portrait of Napoleon finds its way into the narrative: Léonard offers the king a bauble that contains the image of the emperor, which the king covers with kisses. The king wants more, but Léonard can only offer pictures of Louis XVIII, to which the king responds, "Lououis Zuit pas, no, no potate, potate!" In a note Corbière adds that "all these details," including the contemptuous term *potate* for Louis XVIII, "are historical, and I have reason to believe that the underlying truth will excuse the vulgarity of the form" (*N*, 174; see *N 1990*, 287). Using a mouthpiece that he represents as clownish, Corbière has found a way to express his Bonapartist and anti-Bourbon sentiments. It is under the tricolor, not the fleur-de-lis, that Léonard prefers to fight (*N*, 177). His stated reason for this is his love of freedom—for himself, not of course for the Africans he now wants to buy.

As Léonard waits for an extended period, basking in the king's hospitality and the admiration of the villagers, he describes in greater detail some of the horrors of Africa, including diseases and gruesome methods of execution. The king is slow in producing the "fine shipment of blacks [Léonard] was expecting from the interior" (*N*, 176). A British attack, part of their repression of the slave trade, is repulsed, and the captives are soon produced, Léonard's three hundred "new guests": "in a whirlwind of sand, several files of Negroes attached by the neck to long poles. This was my cargo" (*N*, 177). As the *Rosalie* outruns British pursuit in a squall, the captives "piled" in the hold "utter awful cries"(*des hurlements affreux*)—this is the only sign of their humanity that is reported (*N*, 178). (Such cries will be

315

taken up and amplified as the "true cry" of Césaire's *Cahier*.) This French narrator, like most of the others we have seen, sums up the Middle Passage in a few phrases:

> Following the violent experiences that I had just had, a crossing is quite monotonous [*une traversée est bien monotone*], even when you think the enemy is on your heels, and Negroes who are always ready to revolt and eat you [*des nègres toujours prêts à se révolter et à vous manger*[57]]. Tiring calms to put up with, foul air to breathe, some dead slaves to throw into the sea, almost all of the nights spent on the bridge, sick people to take care of; this, in a few words, is the story of almost all crossings from the coast of Africa to America. (223)[58]

"This is the story": whose story? The rhetoric of a monotonous list creates the sense of routine; the deaths of slaves are noted only as one more chore for the crew. "Nothing remarkable" about the Middle Passage, as Joseph Mosneron wrote. On shore in Martinique the slaves are baptized (with the priest collecting a fee for each one) and sold at an "enormous profit" (N, 180); Léonard is rich. He offers two slave children to Rosalie as a present. Corbière's depiction of the slave trade is matter-of-fact and, as he puts it, "historical." The impression created by this first voyage is, most important, that Africans deserve enslavement and may well benefit from it, since their homeland is so benighted, and that the illegal slave trade is enormously profitable. The second expedition will, however, be somewhat different.

316

This time, Léonard takes advantage of his American point of embarkation by taking on a crew that includes slaves that he has "rented in order to go buy on the Coast other black slaves like themselves" (N, 182). Less subject to the diseases of Africa, these sailors represent a good value. On this voyage, for the first time in French fiction, we see an explicit breakdown of the assumed color bar between captors and captives. Though the black members of this crew are slaves, they will nonetheless act to enslave new captives. On the coast at Old Calabar Léonard receives expert and "guileless" caresses from an African princess, Fraïda (N, 184). To spare her from being executed, Léonard must marry her. He accepts the nuptial blessing of a marabout, while mocking African religious practices. During the passage across the Atlantic, Fraïda pays him back by acting as a spy, warning him that the captives may be concealing poison; she eavesdrops and detects a plot. But this voyage is doomed. Becalmed in the middle of the ocean, the crew and captives both are stricken with ophthalmia—a disease that often plagued the slave trade, leaving captives and crew blind. Crew members begin to commit suicide. The second in command suggests throwing over-board any captive who becomes ill, in order to staunch the spread of infec-tion and save supplies; but it is not clear that Léonard accepts this horrific proposal. In this context Corbière turns his narrative into an indirect com-mentary on the British repression of the slave trade.[59]

A British ship approaches the *Rosalie*, pausing to retrieve a captive from the water. Léonard recognizes the slave "all too well," knowing what this will mean for him: "It was some of our blind [but still living] Negroes, who *were thrown overboard* in the night and who had managed to stay afloat till daybreak" (*N*, 190; emphasis added).[60] The passive voice is significant. What Léonard realizes is that he will be prosecuted—or summarily hanged—for murder. (In the 1834 edition Corbière added a phrase suggesting that the "indignation" of the British when faced with this spectacle would only be "too just"—but this idea disappears from later editions.)[61] The situation is thus similar to that of the British slaver the *Zong* or the French *La Jeune Estelle*: captives have been discarded *alive*, murdered, in order to preserve the finances of the expedition. Léonard had apparently accepted the pro-posal; we now learn that fifty captives "had been" thrown overboard the day before. The passive construction hides Léonard's agency and responsi-bility. How many might have been alive at the time is not stated, as if it were not significant. The British try to retrieve some "other slaves who were still swimming." In another piratical *coup de théâtre*, the crew members of the *Rosalie* frighten the British by rubbing themselves with saffron to make it look like they have yellow fever; as the British begin to bombard the French vessel, the wind miraculously rises, and the *Rosalie* slips away. If this were a film, the music would shift from comical to triumphant.[62]

Thus an atrocity—the murder of captives, with strong resonances in real incidents that had been publicized by abolitionists—is represented by Cor-bière but quickly converted into an entertaining tale of adventure, clever-ness, and derring-do. A trace of abolitionist, "just" indignation appears in the 1834 edition but then fades away. This passage, with its abrupt transition from crime to comedy, is practically unreadable in our times. No passage in French literature of the slave trade seems more alien than this one.

The voyage is not over yet. The crew, including Léonard, is incapaci-tated by illness. With more echoes of "Tamango" the captives "finally be-came masters of the ship, which was almost sinking and almost out of sus-tenance" (*N*, 192). Their first idea is "to massacre" the crew, but Léonard's lover Fraïda saves him by brandishing a *grigri*; his loyal dogs destroy a slave

317

who attempts to kill Léonard. Finally the *Rosalie* is rescued by a British ship. Now Léonard is under arrest. Ever loyal and resourceful, Fraïda paints Léonard black and helps him to escape from the British island of Dominica to neighboring Martinique, where he will be free and she will be both replaced by Léonard's wife, Rosalie, and possibly enslaved. Gothic horror mounts when Fraïda poisons Rosalie in order to put an end to an untenable love triangle. Fraïda simply disappears from the narrative; her murder of Rosalie, by proscribing her socially, quickly dissolves the problem of representing a free and noble African woman, Léonard's "liberator," within a French slave society.

Revived by the counseling of a priest who is eager to baptize newly imported slaves, Léonard is persuaded to go back to sea, to the slave trade, which is more "honorable" than the mere transporting of sugar or cattle (*N*, 249). (In his final version Corbière changed "honorable" to "noble"; *N 1990*, 320). His new ship was made in Nantes "for getting Negroes, like a young girl is made for love" (*N*, 249). Two more expeditions to Africa ensue. Léonard's lusts are now exhausted, and his life is "a long and cold suicide" (*N*, 259). Defending his own story, Léonard admits that trading in slaves amounts to "always acting toward the same goal and always contracting with the same men." To practice the slave trade, "isn't it to obtain merchandise with money and to transport it, *like any other cargo*, to a place where its sale will be the most advantageous?" It is only when "terrible incidents" arise that the life of the mariner transcends routine: his life "greatens" (*s'agrandit*), and the "importance of the scene is raised" (*N*, 205; emphasis added). It is these moments, Léonard says, that make a story worth telling. In other words, the slave trade alone is not interesting enough to recount. It is the incidents of high drama — of pursuits and battles at sea, of disease, starvation, revolt, and rescue — that make the seafaring hero "a special being" (*un être à part*). In this passage Léonard has thus explained narratologically why his memoirs of the slave trade needed to be combined with tales of piracy: in order to make a better story. The reader, he implies, would not be interested in the "mundane" slave trade on its own terms. It is as if Corbière himself were justifying his departure from what he had actually experienced — maritime commerce, perhaps including the slave trade — and his ventures into the fantastic realms of the pirate tale.

What is encapsulated here, then, is the blindness of a French narrator to the drama of what we now call the Middle Passage for each and every African captive. None of those in the hold, if their point of view could be

318

recaptured (as twentieth-century Francophone writers will attempt to do), would describe the slave trade as a simple and routine series of transactions, in need of melodramatic embellishments. The last one of these flourishes comes when Léonard tragically kills his own long-lost brother in a battle at sea. Thus is concluded the narrative of "an infernal existence that I condemn!" (*N*, 219). Later, Corbière changed this to the milder "infernal existence that [death] will have too belatedly cut off" (*N 1990*, 354).

Corbière gives us every reason to think that this final condemnation by Léonard of his own existence is *not* supposed to reflect on the slave trade, which has not been renounced at any point in *Le Négrier*. The context makes clear that the narrator regrets his life simply because, in its final act, he killed his own brother. The killings of innocent captives, thrown overboard alive because they were sick, were not put on the same moral plane and do not enter into this final reckoning. The abolitionist slogan "Am I not a man and a brother?" haunts the ending of *Le Négrier*.

In the 1830s readers would have brought their own knowledge and perspective to this novel. Those familiar with the arguments and the documents of abolitionists—including Corbière's own "Précis sur la traite des Noirs"—might well have deplored the atrocities committed against Africans in the pages of *Le Négrier*, just as they could have in reading Mérimée's "Tamango." But, as with that close precursor, any abolitionist reading would have come more from the reader than from the writer or the text itself. *Le Négrier* never repudiates or condemns the slave trade. This novel remains in print, in the early twenty-first century, as the most striking text in French literature that passes the slave trade off as entertainment. In fact, a thin but direct lineage connects *Le Négrier* to the present: a twentieth-century tradition of using the slave trade as a backdrop for tales of adventure, in a *littérature populaire négrière*.[63] Some of these texts will influence Francophone writers like Boubacar Boris Diop, Ousmane Sembene, and Edouard Glissant.

319

✦

I remain somewhat nonplussed by the irruption of homosocial and homoerotic themes in the French literature of the slave trade. It did not occur to me that readings in *littérature négrière* would lead me to an important, if little-known, novel that should occupy a prominent position in the history of what we now call gay literature: *Le Négrier*. Perhaps I should not have been surprised, since France, like other European nations, brought itself and its evolving discourse of sexuality onto the oceans and into the slave trade. The slave trade, homosociality, and sexuality were facts of the sea, so it is not by aberration that they come up side by side in works like *Atar-Gull* and *Le Négrier*. It is less the slave trade than seafaring itself that produced the conditions of *matelotage* and same-sex love that were described so vividly in *Le Négrier*. On the sea heteronormativity was not, so to speak, all that normal; *matelotage* was a form of "homonormativity" among sailors.

How do these themes—the slave trade and sexuality—really relate to each other? I organized my readings of French authors in this book, first, according to the gender of the author, and we examined some of the questions raised by that factor. The question of sexuality and sexual orientation has come up among male authors writing later than their female counterparts and in a film from the mid-twentieth century. In Sue and Corbière we certainly found new ways of discussing sexuality; in both *Atar-Gull* and *Le Négrier* the implosion of the master-slave dialectic is juxtaposed to disturbances in what we now call heteronormativity. The intense homosociality of *Atar-Gull* brought us to the brink of a nearly unthinkable revolution on the high seas: Brulart and Atar-Gull, wrote Sue, "had to love each other or hate each other." What if they had loved each other (with or without sex)? To put it in Hegelian terms, what if the hate between them "passed into its opposite," love?[64] We could then imagine a moment of double liberation in which master and slave are freed from slavery even as they throw themselves into same-sex love. Present-day readers might then be tempted to extrapolate from this a more general paradigm of liberation, in which slavery and heteronormativity are both overturned.

But in the nineteenth century, we should remind ourselves, men experiencing love or sex with each other on the high seas was not "liberation" or the embracing of a suppressed identity; it was simply a fact. And Berry's film reminds us of something that must have been a frequent occurrence but which remains, to my knowledge, completely undocumented: homosexual rape of male captives by slave traders. That small moment in one film can serve to remind us that, on a more general plane of analysis, same-sex bonding among slave traders was a means of dominance rather than liberation. As illustrated in *Le Négrier* in particular, homosociality was a potent force, enabling French men to better oppress their captives.[65]

The only trace we have seen of true same-sex love across the color line *and* the line between master and slave is the relationship between Richard Baker (a slave owner) and Olaudah Equiano (then a slave), who were "extremely fond" of each other and "inseparable." We can assume that other such relationships occurred, even if none left a visible narrative trace in French. But here again, even within a supposedly "almost utopian, micro-cosmic alternative to the slavery-infested greater world," devoid of racial prejudice—the British merchant marine[66]—love does not conquer all. In this relationship one boy remained a master and the other a slave (even if Equiano was not owned by Baker, and even though Baker was himself a servant). Their relationship did not erase slavery.

Servitude and sexuality are thus distinct, with only occasional moments of overlap. There is no underlying or overarching *general* narrative of liberation to be found here in the transition from the eighteenth to later centuries; we should restrain ourselves from conflating what might appear to us, now, as two symmetrical forms of liberation: from slavery and from heteronormativity. Just as gender turned out to be less than fully congruent with abolitionism, sexuality, a subject of great interest in narratives of the slave trade, remains a category of its own.

→►◄←

The roughly one-hundred-year gap that now follows in this study, between the publication of *Le Négrier* in 1832 and that of Césaire's *Cahier* in 1939, does not signal either an end of all slave trading or a genuine abolition of servile labor. Hundreds of thousands of Africans and South Asians were brought to the plantation regions (almost 140,000 indentured Indians to the French islands alone) in the late nineteenth century.[67] And, in the wake of the Congress of Berlin, as the deep, modern colonization of Africa took hold, new regimes of forced labor were widely imposed. In 1927 Albert Londres famously exposed the abuses he had seen in a four-month tour of French Africa. He witnessed the nearly genocidal abuse of laborers building the Congo-Ocean railroad, where each tie is said to represent one dead worker. He called his book *Terre d'ébène (La Traite des Noirs)* (Land of Ebony: The Slave Trade).[68]

4

THE
TRIANGLE
FROM
"BELOW"

CÉSAIRE, GLISSANT, CONDÉ

Reimagining the Atlantic

CÉSAIRE'S ATLANTIC SUBSTITUTION

Aimé Césaire's great poem *Cahier d'un retour au pays natal* has been a touchstone throughout the course of this study. No other text, before or since, has done so much to review and rethink the French Atlantic. In my fourth chapter I sketched out an interpretation of this poem that I now want to develop further: the idea that the *Cahier* both inhabits the oppressive logic of the Atlantic triangle and suggests a way out of it. In chapter 9 I explored the relation between Césaire's text and Mérimée's classic short story "Tamango." That reading will remain useful here, though I will not repeat it. The rethinking of linkages to Africa—inevitably implicating the history of the slave trade—is a capital question in the works of Antillean writers throughout the twentieth century. This chapter will examine texts by three authors whose new transatlantic glance leads them to ask questions about the history of the slave trade: Césaire, Maryse Condé, and Edouard Glissant.

As his poetic work ages, and as his politics (long unscrutinized) come under new critiques, Césaire's reputation seems to be shrinking.[1] His status as the inventor of the term *négritude* is a mixed blessing. Everyone acknowledges the historical significance of the Negritude movement, but post-colonial interpreters now tend to see it, somewhat condescendingly, as an instance of "strategic essentialism." Most therefore agree with Sartre's pre-emptive, rather oracular, judgment of Negritude (which appeared physically just *before* Negritude itself, as the preface to the first anthology of Negritude poetry): that it was "the weak moment in a dialectic," soon to fade away.[2]

We now live in the post-Negritude era that Sartre prophesied. It is as if all of Negritude were now the "old negritude" described at one point in the *Cahier*, "progressively cadaverizing."[3] In the 1960s Edouard Glissant asserted that the only possible extension of Negritude was "the act by which it is surpassed," for it ends when "self-possession" begins.[4] Since the mid-1980s the critiques of the Créoliste group—Martinican writers Patrick Chamoiseau, Raphaël Confiant, and Jean Bernabé—have propelled this devaluation of Césaire's intellectual reputation; they have displaced earlier "hagiologies" of Césaire, largely written by non-Martinicans.[5]

The most stinging criticism came from Confiant in his biography, *Aimé Césaire: Une Traversée paradoxale du siècle*, which broke the "taboo" on frank discussions of Césaire and remains a milestone in Césaire studies. According to Confiant's indictment Césaire substituted one false mother, Africa, for another, France.[6] This is part of a pattern that Confiant condemns as Césaire's "plunge into a preserved African unconscious, merely the sweet reverie of a poet" (*Aimé Césaire*, 134). Writing together with one voice in their history of Caribbean literature, Confiant and Chamoiseau concede that "Negritude gave Africa back to us." But they allege that "Negritude, even if it did not intend to, replaced one illusion with another illusion, exchanging Europe for Africa. [Negritude] ignored the realities of Creole culture, in favor of a *strange black world* [*un étrange monde noir*]."[7]

We should stay with that allegation for a moment. Leaving aside the negative judgment it reflects, we must not miss the significance of this gesture: by this account Césaire rewrote the French Atlantic from the Caribbean point of the triangle. In the context of this study we should be in a position to appreciate the importance of his substitution: according to Confiant and Chamoiseau, Césaire switched the axis of desire so that the attention of the French Antilles moved from France to Africa. Bearing in mind that the slave trade made the bottom axis of the Atlantic triangle into a one-way thoroughfare, both physically and culturally—leading exclusively from east to west and almost never back—this is no mean accomplishment. Fanon actually made this same point about Césaire's Atlantic "substitution" long before Confiant and Chamoiseau, though his tone was different. In an essay first published in 1955, he credited Césaire with a great paradigm shift that occurred within "the Antillean," a shift of identification from white to black. Fanon argued, "Until 1939"—the date of the *Cahier*'s first appearance and of Césaire's actual return to Martinique from France—"the Antillean lived, thought and dreamed (as I showed in my book *Black Skin White*

Masks), wrote poems and novels exactly as a white man might have done.
. . . Before Césaire, Antillean literature was a literature of Europeans." After
Césaire's intervention, the Antillean turns toward Africa and sees himself as
"the transplanted son of slaves; he feels the vibration of Africa in the depths
of his body." Fanon describes this, hyperbolically, as nothing less than "a
total remolding [*refonte*] of his world, a metamorphosis of his body." But
Fanon's conclusion puts a funny spin on the praise he has been heaping on
his former lycée teacher: "It therefore seems that the Antillean, after the
great white error, is now living the great black *mirage*."[8] That last word,
clearly suggesting the pitfalls of Negritude, is like a time bomb that will
go off later, in the work of Maryse Condé and the Créolistes, who work to
undermine the Afrocentrism of their literary father. With that conclusion
Fanon is working his way from his initial fidelity to Negritude in *Black Skin*
(where he protests against Sartre's characterization of it as a passing phase)
to his more radical position in *The Wretched of the Earth* (where he aligns
himself with Sartre's view, implying that Negritude is merely a stepping-
stone on the path toward national literature).[9] To go back to the fundamental point here: Césaire is credited with (or blamed for) substituting Africa
for France in French Caribbean culture.

327

Césaire's substitution, made from the Caribbean point on the Atlantic
triangle, shifts attention from the European point to the African point,
leaving one obvious question: what about Caribbean attention to the Caribbean itself? That is the Créolistes' query. In the Créoliste view Césaire was
afflicted with "presbyopia"—an unhealthy far-sightedness that made it easier for him to see, as Confiant rightly points out, a "man of Calcutta" in the
Cahier than to see the Indian immigrants present on his island, including his
own childhood *da* or nurse. For Confiant this is part of a larger problem in
the "Césairian psyche," "the *return* to by-gone worlds [*arrière-mondes*], to
original worlds rather than to the here and now that underpins Creoleness
within a discredited colonialism."[10] Return indeed: primarily to Africa. But
I want to ask how fair Confiant's characterization—which boldly encompasses Césaire's entire political and literary life—might be when applied to
the text of the *Cahier* alone. The extent to which Césaire actually, textually
effected this Atlantic substitution in the *Cahier*, to the supposed exclusion of
all other vectors, is something that remains to be tested. The poem is widely
reputed to be a "manifesto" of return to Africa. That idea too needs to be
examined with care; it is vital in the context of this study, since it is obviously related to the heritage of the slave trade.

In fact, Césaire was hardly the first or only intellectual in the Caribbean to suffer from presbyopia. That condition had been diagnosed by an earlier theoretician of Caribbean culture, who himself advocated a certain focus on Africa. In 1928, during the American occupation of his country, the Haitian physician, diplomat, and amateur ethnographer Jean Price-Mars published *Ainsi parla l'oncle*. His diagnosis of the problem in Haiti was "collective bovarysm"—a pathological quest for status and meaning just over the horizon, never close to home: in his own words, "the propensity of a society to see itself as different from what it is," leaving it with "a borrowed soul."[11] Yet Price-Mars, like Césaire shortly after him, turned to Africa: "Our only chance to be ourselves is to repudiate no part of our ancestral heritage. For eight-tenths of us this heritage is a gift from Africa!"[12] Price-Mars therefore outlined something like the Atlantic substitution, of Africa for France, that Fanon and others have since attributed to Césaire. (In their version of literary history, Chamoiseau and Confiant cite only Price-Mars's focus on Haiti, not his acknowledgment of Africa.)[13] The solution that Price-Mars proposed allows for a comprehensive vision of the full Atlantic triangle: by repudiating "no part of our heritage," Antilleans can acknowledge Africa (and even France) without presbyopia.

The other gloss that needs to be applied to Césaire's Atlantic substitution derives from a condition that I mentioned in the first part of this study. The end of the slave trade, the rise of beet sugar in Europe, and the eventual call for laborers of color to work in France all contributed to a condition that has been almost universally recognized: the obliteration of the Caribbean. Walcott's "brilliant vacuity," Naipaul's "nothing," and Glissant's "canvas of nothingness" are alternative versions of the "inertia" and emptiness that Césaire describes and deplores at the beginning of the *Cahier*.[14] If Césaire's Negritude substituted one distant object for another, it was in reaction to this condition, which he was far from alone in perceiving.

There are multiple Césaires. For many Westerners, in a tradition beginning with Sartre, Césaire has been variously a convenient vehicle of romantic otherness, a herald of liberation, and now a vehicle of hybridity.[15] Alternatively, J. Michael Dash claims that Césaire himself "always insisted on an essentialist approach to culture and on the transcendent values of the Caribbean's African legacy."[16] Widely held views of Césaire make him much more like Senghor than he should be. Lumping these two "Negritude poets" together has tended to harden the reputation of the *Cahier* as an ideological statement. Thus one reads in the *Times Literary Supplement* that Césaire "turned a just cause into poetry" in a "fit of youthful ideology"; his poems are dismissed as a "speech-maker's songs"; the *Cahier* is a "manifesto."[17] An anthology of postcolonial theory warns that Césaire's Negritude "has been much criticized for its essentialist view of identity."[18] And a prominent recent volume, *Black Imagination and the Middle Passage*, denounces the "racial essentialism of negritudinists such as Aimé Césaire and Léopold Sédar Senghor," ordering them both now to "defer to hybrid theoretical perspectives."[19] Essentialism, with its deterministic identitarianism, is of course the cardinal sin of postcolonial studies, the kryptonite, the poison pill. And the essentialist *c'est toujours l'autre*.

From all of this one could infer the image of a Césaire stuck inside an Afrocentric reverie, obsessed with "return," blind to the non-African elements of Caribbean culture ("fantasizing over a far-off, forever lost and probably never-existent African paradise," as Burton paraphrases Confiant, in "Two Views of Césaire," 144). His Negritude, even in the text of the *Cahier*, is described by Abiola Irele as a form of "hyper-romanticism," "a vision of restitution to wholeness of experience promised by a reconnection to the life-enhancing values of an ideal Africa, the peasant continent par excellence."[20] That is very much Césaire's reputation, but I will argue that it is not sustained by a reading of the *Cahier*. It is not an *entirely* false impression, however. When Césaire himself said that he was "an African poet," he fueled such views.[21] What is easy to forget now is that Césaire was "correcting" the condition left in place by the slave trade and the *Exclusif*: the repression of Africa in French Caribbean culture, the impossibility of return. Now the Créolistes (and Maryse Condé in her brilliant novel *Hérémakhonon* [1976]) "correct" Césaire, by turning away from Africa and focusing on their own islands. Chamoiseau and Confiant, in fact, credit Condé for "breaking" the "African mirror in which many Antillean intellectuals had looked at themselves." A "more adult, detached, and realistic relation emerged."[22] Glissant played a role in this process with his notion of *Antillanité*.[23]

But Confiant, for one, takes the process of turning back away from Africa one step too far: he simply reproduces the pre-Negritude "myth of the Negro past," the erasure of Africa, by making some astonishingly retrograde assertions about the aftermath of the slave trade.[24] For Confiant the "hold of the slave ship is a womb . . . which will expulse a new-born, . . . a survivor." That much is unexceptionable. But Confiant goes on to say that this survivor has suffered an "irremediable loss" and will experience "amnesia with regard to Africa." He is the proverbial blank slate. Mere "traces" of his old unconscious will remain. But then Confiant excludes even that possibility: "In opposition to what Césaire postulates, [the slave] was not able to preserve in the depths of his being *any* grain of Africanity."[25] None. The "African slave does not speak; he moans, groans, and suffers," until such time as he is reborn speaking Creole (133). With this stroke of Confiant's pen, any possibility of authentic self-expression in either an African language or French (the language in which he is writing) is excluded; Negritude, inseparable from its Francophone means of expression, is obviously out of the question. For Confiant the Antillean is the "ABSOLUTE VICTIM" (134) of both African and European slave traders; the New World point on the triangle must repudiate *both* of the other points. As a cultural program, what Glissant called a "taking into account of the new land," is an entirely worthwhile correction to Negritude's focus on Africa.[26] But Confiant's revival of an absolute rupture between Africa and the New World is less than constructive, not to mention historically untenable. One can only hope for a world without taboos, in which all points on the Atlantic triangle can be acknowledged without being made into fetish objects. As Price-Mars wrote: repudiate "no part."

330   What risks getting lost among the characterizations and caricatures of Césaire is the textual complexity of his most important contribution to literature and culture, his *Cahier d'un retour au pays natal*.[27] For once, and against my own instincts, I want to argue for a separation between a literary work and the politics of its author, for each deserves a reading on its own terms. To do this is not, *pace* Confiant, to go back to a view of Césaire as "two entirely different persons in one body" (*Aimé Césaire*, 35); it is simply to take Césaire's most important literary text on its own terms, leaving the "paradox" of the larger person to others; it is to see these *two* bodies (the man and the text) for what they are: different objects in the world. Confiant totally conflates the "I" of the man Césaire with the "I" of his poems, in a classic error of reading (see *Aimé Césaire*, 99). For Confiant the politics of Césaire's party "never budged an inch: Negritude, always Negritude, nothing but Negritude."[28] Negritude as a movement in poetry and politics is of course long since dead; it is an artifact of the mid-twentieth century, poorly served by Léopold Sédar Senghor's truly essentialist propagandizing. But underneath all of that, the text of the *Cahier*—where Negritude "stood up for the first time" and said its name—remains available, readable. And the poem is anything but "essentialist."[29] (No such luck! Essentialism might be easier to read.)

AFRICA IN THE *CAHIER*

Since the beginning of this book we have observed the significance of the word *retour*. The third, Caribbean point on the Atlantic triangle was the site where the meaning of return split along racial lines: return to France (with returns on their investment) was the logical economic completion of the triangle for the French officers and crew onboard a slave ship, but for the slaves, return became an impossible dream. What return is evoked in the title of Césaire's *Cahier d'un retour au pays natal?* Critics have often pointed out two different possibilities: on the one hand, return is return *to* the Caribbean, from Europe; on the other hand, return is return to Africa *from* the Caribbean.[30] The former view is partly fueled by biographical information: Césaire first wrote the poem in France, starting in 1936, contemplating his return to Martinique, which would come only after eight years in Paris.[31] But the text supports this view as well, in ways that are crucial to understanding the poem as a whole.

In the sequence that follows the narrator's declaration of a departure ("Partir," stanza 33), he quickly *returns* to "this land of mine" and speaks to it, saying, "'I have wandered for a long time and I am coming back to the deserted hideousness of your sores'" (*je reviens vers la hideur désertée de vos plaies*). It is at this point that the narrator finds his voice and declares his mouth to be "the mouth of those calamities that have no mouth." It is clear in this context that the native land to which he has returned is an island in the Caribbean, still unnamed, but certainly not the continent of Africa. The place he comes home to he calls "my nonfence island" ("mon île non-cloture"); it floats in a "polynesia," an archipelago — the Antilles — that "separates one America from another," while the Atlantic leads toward *both* Europe and Africa. His island is coyly identified only by its proximity to Guadeloupe (with which it is twinned) and to Haiti:

> What is mine, these several thousand deathbearers who spin in the calabash of an island and mine too, the archipelago arched with an anguished desire to negate itself, as if from maternal anxiety to protect this impossibly delicate tenuity separating one America from another; and these loins which secrete for Europe the good liquor of a Gulf Stream, and one of the two slopes of incandescence between which the equator tightropewalks toward Africa. And my nonfence island [*mon île non clôture*], its brave audacity standing at the stern of this polynesia, before it, Guadeloupe, split in two down its dorsal line and equal in

331

poverty to us, Haiti where negritude stood up [*se mit debout*] for the first time and stated that it believed in its humanity and the funny little tail of Florida where the strangulation of a nigger is being completed, and Africa gigantically caterpillaring up to the Hispanic foot of Europe, its nakedness where Death scythes in wide rows. (*Cahier* 10/*Notebook* 47, AT)

An entirely Atlantic geography is described here, in this passage where Negritude appears in print for the first time. The first sentence encompasses the Atlantic world of slavery, with "deathbearers" spinning in a dance of death within the calabash crucible of an island. Césaire evokes the *commerce en droiture*, which "returned" the products of the slave trade and of slave labor back to Europe via the Gulf Stream: its "good liquor" is also rum. He also suggests that the tenuous path leading back to Africa, along the reverse path of the Middle Passage, will be a "tightropewalk."

In the second sentence the narrator's home island emerges as the vantage point for an Atlantic consciousness. It is not isolated, not fenced-in. Here, many pages before the climatic revolt on the slave ship that will liberate the people of Negritude and leave them "standing and free," this island is already audaciously "standing." The narrator's attention follows a *reverse* Atlantic triangle, moving from the New World back to Africa, and *then* to Europe. And this movement seems propelled by an awareness of history (the Haitian Revolution) and of contemporary atrocities (lynchings in the American South). Awareness of the slave trade is made explicit just after this passage, when the narrator recites the names of the principal slave-trading ports of Europe: Bordeaux, Nantes, and Liverpool. To go back to my first point here: it is a return to his island in the Caribbean that begins the narrator's process of consciousness-taking. Africa is mentioned, and eventually regained, only within a fully Atlantic frame—a vision of the historical, slave-based triangle—that the poem establishes here.

On the other hand, return in the *Cahier* is indeed a movement "back to Africa," reversing the Middle Passage. This reading dominates, for obvious reasons: it supports the view of Césaire as an ideological "negritudinist," devoted to a cult of Africa. Only by reducing the meaning of "return" to that single movement—and occluding both the return to the Caribbean and the new Atlantic consciousness that comes out of that return—can interpreters make the *Cahier* into a simplistic "manifesto" of an "essentialist" Negritude. Of course there are *hints* of return to an idealized Africa in the *Cahier*. Just before the departure examined above, the narrator dreams of an intimate other (*toi*) in whom he can "discover" a "land where all is free and fraternal, my land." This land (*terre*, not *pays*) is "a thousand times more native and made golden by a sun that no prism divides" (*Cahier*, 8; *Notebook*, 45, AT). The narrator is a reverse Columbus, "discovering" a golden land, but the land is not yet named; it is not yet Africa. The idea of being "a thousand times more native" is intriguing in its hyperbole; it reads almost like a parody of nativism. The continent is labeled for the first time in the passage that I discussed above ("the Equator tightropewalks toward Africa"). So the *need* for an idealized land is stated before Africa is mentioned by name, which raises the question: *is* Africa that golden, fraternal, supernative land? Will the *Cahier* depict such a place, and perhaps say that it is Africa, or only speculate about it?

Africa is evoked numerous times in the rest of the poem, as a whole or in parts. "By thinking so much of the Congo / I have become a Congo rustling with forests and rivers," the narrator says in a passage loaded both with Baudelairean resonances and with allusions to violent colonial history.[32] Next he sees himself as a recalcitrant colonial subject, "wearing out the patience of missionaries . . . worshipping the Zambezi [River]." He embraces "the breadth of my perversity" and "the horrible leap of my Pahouin ugliness" (*Notebook*, 53). This invocation of Africa is thus already implicated in the embrace and acceptance of negativity that will become one of the hallmarks of the *Cahier* and its brand of Negritude. It is in this spirit that the principal statement about Africa is made:

> I refuse to pass off my puffiness [*mes boursouflures*] for authentic glory.
> And I laugh at my former childish fantasies.
>
> No, we were never Amazons of the king of Dahomey, nor princes of Ghana with eight hundred camels, nor wise men in Timbuktu under Askia the Great, nor architects of Djenne, nor Mahdis, nor warriors. (*Cahier*, 18; *Notebook*, 61, AT)

Painfully, tenuously rediscovered African history—the existence of which was denied by Hegel and ignored by Western institutions—enters the *Cahier*, backwards. The narrator does not deny the existence of these African glories; he just says they have nothing to do with his people. As Ronnie Scharfman explains, "Africa has been violently alienated" from the narrator; "colonialism . . . has erased the very possibility of the kind of African identification [the narrator] liked to use to [his] own destructive ends."[33] In other words, there is no more "Africa" to go home to.

333

The famous dependence of Césaire and Senghor on romantic European Africanists like Frobenius has thus produced quirky results here.[34] The narrator goes on to "admit that we were at all times pretty mediocre dishwashers, shoeblacks without ambition, at best conscientious sorcerers and the only unquestionable record that we broke was that of endurance under the chicotte [whip]." So much for ethnic boosterism! Is this the "far-off, forever lost and probably never-existent African paradise" (Confiant) that is supposed to be Césaire's obsession, the object of his "ardent nostalgia" (Michel Leiris)?[35] Since the poem just dismissed such fantasies as "puerile," support for that allegation would have to lie elsewhere.

In the remainder of the poem there is only one major passage devoted to Africa, and it comes shortly before the "cracking" of the slave ship and the final revolt. In this often-quoted section the narrator mentions African ancestors: "I now see the meaning of this trial by fire: my country is the 'lance of night' of my Bambara ancestors" (*Je tiens maintenant le sens de l'ordalie: mon pays est la 'lance de nuit' de mes ancêtres Bambaras* [*Cahier*, 29; *Notebook*, 77]). This is the closest the poem comes to an embrace of Africa. The quotation marks, however, make clear that this is an explicitly literary connection, mediated by some mixed-up anthropology ("lance of night" is apparently a mistranslation from Bamanankan).[36] Again essentialism strikes out. The nostalgic, idealized Africa for which Césaire is famous is not to be found in his *Cahier*.

It is in his evocations of the generalized people of Negritude, the people of the African diaspora, that Césaire indulges in a more celebratory "racial sentiment" (Irele, *Cahier*, 1). These are "the eldest sons of the world, porous to all the breathing of the world," "those without whom the earth would not be the earth" (22–23/67–69). Still, these, the most positive statements of racial sentiment in the *Cahier*, come just before and after Negritude itself is rather strangely "defined" — "My negritude is not a stone . . . is not a leukoma . . . is neither a tower nor a cathedral." So what is it? The poem does not say; rather it goes on to say what Negritude *does*: "it takes root in the red flesh of the soil." What could be more existential and less essential?[37]

THE *CAHIER* AND THE SLAVE TRADE

Having distanced himself from Africa, the narrator engages with a history that *is* his, that of the slave trade. "This land," which is clearly France, treated us like "walking manure hideously promising tender cane and silky

334

cotton. . . . We slept in our excrement and they sold us on the town square," the narrator says in a stanza that sets up a more specific consideration of the transatlantic slave trade and the Middle Passage:

Nous vomissure de négrier
Nous vénerie des Calebars
quoi? se boucher les oreilles?
Nous, soûlés à crever de roulis, de risées, de brume humée
Pardon tourbillon partenaire!

J'entends de la cale monter les malédictions enchaînées, les hoquettements des mourants, le bruit d'un qu'on jette à la mer . . . les abois d'une femme en gésine . . . des raclements d'ongle cherchant des gorges . . . des ricanements de fouet . . . des farfouillis de vermine parmi des lassitudes . . .

Rien ne put nous insurger jamais vers quelque noble aventure désespérée.
Ainsi soit-il. Ainsi soit-il.

We the vomit of slave ships
We the venery of the Calebars
what? plug up our ears?
We, so drunk on jeers and inhaled fog that we rode the roll to death
Forgive us fraternal whirlwind!

I hear coming up from the hold the enchained curses, the gasps of the dying, the noise of one thrown into the sea . . . the baying of a woman in labor . . . the scrape of fingernails seeking throats . . . the sneerings of the whip . . . the seethings of vermin amid the weariness . . .

Nothing could ever lift us toward a noble hopeless adventure.
So be it. So be it.
(*Cahier*, 18; *Notebook*, 61–63)

335

The history of the French slave trade and of its literary representations has shown us exactly what Césaire is talking about in this passage, which reverberates with representations of the Middle Passage that go back to Equiano's *The Interesting Narrative*, the original notebook on the loss of "my native land." We know that these atrocities took place, and we have seen them turned into literature. But the contrast between, say, Corbière's *Le Négrier* and this poem could not be greater. Césaire surveys this history with powerfully condensed images, while suggesting in his suspension points that he is leaving much out. (The first stanza here is much more powerful than the 1939 stanza that it replaced.)[38] His narrator, like a latter-day Olympe de Gouges, is an "earwitness" to the ills of the Atlantic: it is through hearing that the horrors of the slave trade are described. Equiano, too, reported the sounds of the hold: "The shrieks of the women, and the groans of the dying, rendered the whole a scene of horror almost inconceivable." Curiously, Césaire's narrator must himself already be up on the deck of the ship: he hears the sounds "coming up from the hold."

In the second line above, something strange happens. Césaire metaphorically and lexically conflates the African continent with the slave ship. His made-up word *Calebars* does this all by itself: Cal*a*bar is a place on the coast of Nigeria, a former slave-trading post; *cale* in French is the hold of a ship, the word that Césaire will use as the staging ground for his slaves' revolt.[39] Why "venery of the Calebars"? It is as if Césaire wanted to hint, obscurely, at African complicity in the slave trade. The plural *Calebars* sounds like an African people, and *their* art of hunting (venery) produces slaves. It becomes clear that this implication was no accident when one sees, in the 1939 edition of the *Cahier*, how Césaire extended this association between the continent and the ship in another metaphor: "the polyrigging of dark forests" (*la polymâture de forêts sombres*). In the later versions the poem takes us instantaneously from the shore to the nauseating roll of the ship.

Earlier we looked at the *Cahier* in the context of a discussion on "concatenation" and solidarity. At this point in the poem the narrator has gone beyond declaring himself the spokesman of his people; he moves from "I" to "we" (and back and forth in the passage quoted above). But this invocation of group solidarity is steeped in the horrors of the Middle Passage. The sheer repulsive negativity of vomit as a self-identification ("We the vomit") connects back to the narrator's earlier embrace of ugliness and to the "beneficial internal revolution" that has allowed him to "honor" his "repulsive ugliness" (17/61, AT). The slaves are thus objects expelled by the slave ship, like *Vomito Negro*, a medical term for the vomiting of dark blood (used by Césaire in his poem "Avis de tir").[40] Yet, as Mireille Rosello has demonstrated, vomit also relates to the idea of revolt.[41] Similarly, the volcanic eruption whose absence is deplored at the beginning of the poem will now take place, in the form of a slaves' revolt bursting forth out of the ship's hold. The passive acceptance of impotence — reminding us of Dorothy Dandridge's Ayché in the first reels of the film *Tamango* — expressed at the end of this passage is merely a phase. The slaves *will* be lifted up, and their adventure will

336

not be completely "hopeless"; we saw in chapter 9 how that comes to pass. The narrator's presence "above" the hold may foreshadow this. (We should remember that hope was a central issue in the Tamango scenario, aboard the *Espérance*.)

The revolt leaves the slaves "standing and free." But they do not sail back to Africa and live happily ever after. What return, then, has been effected? We have seen that a simplistic back-to-Africa movement, even a metaphorical one, is not what Césaire suggested in the *Cahier*. After the revolt it is unclear where the poem leaves the revolted slaves, since the rhetoric shifts away from narration to a highly abstract level of representation. They are "spinning in [their] perfect drift," and that motion anticipates the spin of the poem's last word, *verrition*. Working toward that ending, in rising ecstasy, the narrator "surrenders" to his interlocutor/reader a new "conscience [or consciousness] and its fleshy rhythm," along with something that sums up the role that the slave trade has played in the poem: "the intourist of the triangular circuit" (32/83).[42] Referring to the agency that supervised tourists inside the Soviet Union, Césaire (who resigned from the French Communist Party in 1956) surreally and ironically compares two forms of totalitarianism: the slave trade was like an authoritarian "tourist agency," conducting Africans across the Atlantic.[43] Along with the chain gang and the swamp (previously described as bloody), these are objects of memory that the narrator deeds over to the reader. Where is the narrator going? He is being assumed into some higher, *darker* state of consciousness, a "great black hole" containing further mysteries:

337

monte lécheur de ciel
et le grand trou noir où je voulais me noyer l'autre lune
c'est là que je veux pêcher maintenant la langue maléfique de la nuit en son
    immobile verrition!

rise sky licker
and the great black hole where a moon ago I wanted to drown
it is there I will now fish the malevolent tongue of the night in its
    immobile veerition! (33/85, AT)[44]

The final oxymoron, as I mentioned in the first part of this study, suggests a logic that both encompasses and supersedes the old Atlantic triangle. *Verrition* has kept critics busy. Césaire said that he made it out of the Latin verb *verri*, to sweep, to scrape a surface, or to scan.[45] It also resembles *vérine* (or *verrine*): in maritime terminology a hook-rope used for anchors. But *verrine* is also a binnacle-lamp, which illuminates a ship's compass. An Old French word, also *verri*, means diaphanous or translucent.[46] These various resonances might be combined to suggest the sweeping movement of radar, scanning the horizons, seeking a sense of direction, grasping for the anchor of identity. Wielding the "miraculous weapons" of literary modernism, the "malevolent," dark power of language — brandishing neologisms that make his points both compelling and opaque — Césaire created a new way to look at the slave trade and the world it created. Although the history of slavery and the slave trade has been deeply explored and acknowledged in the *Cahier*, the narrator's quest has not produced a definitive "return" that ends in one place. The narrator and his country, alienated from each other at the beginning of the poem, are now "standing" together; that is clear and highly significant. But after that, he says there is still "another sea to cross" (28, 32/77, 81); the quest must continue. The restoration for which Negritude is rightly famous — rebuilding the broken trajectory from the New World back to Africa — is effected by the *Cahier* but not, as we have seen, in any simple, straightforward, final, or "essentialist" way. The *Cahier* is an epic not just of that celebrated return but of other movements as well, spanning the entire Atlantic and beyond.[47] As Césaire wrote in one of the most powerful passages of the poem:

> it is not from hatred of other races
> that I force myself to be a digger for this unique race
> that what I want
> is for universal hunger
> for universal thirst. (24–25/71, AT)

The vectors of the *Cahier* — which we can now call movements of veerition — are complex, cross-hatching the Atlantic triangle and spiraling around and beyond it.[48] The *Cahier* works within and beyond the Atlantic, "coming back," as Roger Bastide wrote, "to a new version of the old 'triangular voyages.'"[49] It does this by seizing language — the French language, as it happens, and as Césaire explained, as it could only be at the time.[50] One phrase in the poem sums this up: "I and I alone take language / contact with the latest anguish" (*C'est moi rien que moi / qui prends langue avec la dernière angoisse* [*Cahier*, 14; *Notebook*, 59]). *Prendre langue* means to make contact. Appropriating language is, in this French figure of speech and in the poem as a whole, synonymous with establishing connections, which is all the *Ca-*

338

hier does. The word *négritude* itself is the prime example of this: it seizes language by inventing a word, and that word establishes contact throughout the African diaspora.

I do not dispute the Créolistes' contention that the *Cahier* and Césaire's politics were both insufficiently Creole, by their definition; but I do not agree with their reading of the poem as a closed, narrowly Afrocentric book nor with the widely held Anglophone view of the work as "essentialist." At the end the narrator is still looking, fishing, peering into a radar screen. Other notebooks and other returns will follow.[51]

THE *CAHIER* IN AFRICA

Whatever its cultural content might be, and despite the challenges posed by its dense language, the *Cahier* has been a phenomenon in the Francophone countries of Africa since the 1950s. No one is a prophet in his own land, but Césaire's poem is a touchstone of African culture. In 2005 a student reports from a classroom at the Université Cheikh Anta Diop in Dakar that, on the prompting of the professor, an amphitheater filled with students recites a passage from the *Cahier* in unison.[52] Almost fifty years earlier, this phenomenon was already so well established that Présence Africaine built it into their advertising for the poem: "Did you know that . . . entire passages of this avant-garde song are recited in French Africa by young people who are sometimes barely literate but eager and thirsty for it? Did you know about the fervor and the hope that this strange masterpiece provokes within the local elites in Africa?"[53] The importance of the *Cahier* in African classrooms caused Lilyan Kesteloot to produce a reading guide specifically aimed at African students.[54] The critic Emile Snyder attributed to Césaire an "African notion of language."[55] An Ivorian critic wrote an influential study of Césaire in the 1970s, looking at Césaire as a "poète négro-africain" (thus within a category that spans and in fact erases the Atlantic—the category created by Negritude) and as a writer "who uses a European language to express *African* speech." Confiant derides this interpretation in his book on Césaire.[56] In Abderrahmane Sissako's *La Vie sur terre*, a beautiful, understated film on daily life in rural West Africa at the dawn of the new millennium, the *Cahier* is a constant leitmotif, returning contrapuntally through a voice-over recitation of its verses.[57]

Edouard Glissant was among the first to comment on the Africanization of the poem. First he seemed to warn against an alienation of the poem from its proper *terroir* in the Caribbean; then, as his thinking evolved toward the valorization of movement and migrancy, he saw the *Cahier*'s fortunes in Africa as an illustration of his own key concept of Detour: "It is understandable that, if Monsieur Césaire is the most famous of Martinicans, his work is less frequently read at home than in Africa." The *Cahier* "will soon be more popular in Senegal than in Martinique." This form of "Detour" is also a "camouflaged or sublimated variation of the Return to Africa."[58] If the *Cahier* and its author are now somewhat discredited in their own *pays*, they have found a new homeland in Africa. Richard Watts has systematically examined this Africanization of the *Cahier* and the consequent removal of the poem from its Caribbean context (as I said above, the favoring of one "return" over another). Watts's conclusion is relevant not just to the paratextual marketing of the poem but to its reception as well: "Whereas the 1942 [Cuban] edition immediately establishes the *Cahier* as a text that stands at the crossroads of Europe, Africa, and the Caribbean [thus as an Atlantic work], the paratexts to the editions from the 1950's through the 1970's make the poem a product and a reflection of Africa, which is only part of the story."[59]

340

GLISSANT, RETURN, AND DETOUR

Glissant's riff on Césaire in Africa quickly moves us into the thickets of Glissant's own thinking about the Atlantic, the African diaspora, and the question of return that has been central to so much of the literature that we have been examining. With full cognizance of the history of the slave trade, Glissant critiques the concept of return and adds a rhyming complement to it: to *retour* he adds *détour*. In one of the richest chapters of his *Discours antillais* Glissant initiates an attack on simplistic notions of "Return," described as the "first impulse of a transplanted population." Return is a fixation on "the old order of values," and it takes the form of "an obsession with Oneness" (*l'obsession de l'Un*) (30). He immediately cites the establishment of Liberia by Americans as a gesture of racist expulsion and "strange barbarism." Return is misguided because the emancipated slaves in question "*are no longer African*" (30). Glissant moves forward with this statement: "The populations transshipped by the slave trade were not able to maintain the impulse of Return for long." That impulse "will be gradually extinguished in a rising acknowledgment of the new land" (*s'éteindra peu à peu dans la prise en compte de la terre nouvelle"*) (31). Glissant clearly valorizes this acknowledgment or seizure of consciousness. In his own Martinique that process has not been "effective," according to Glissant, but the community has tried to "exorcize impossible Return through what I call a practice of Detour" (31–32). His Detour is rather postmodern. It is associated with ruse. Glissant's prime example of Detour is the Creole language itself, in which he sees a "permanent exercise of turning away from transcendence" — from the transcendence of the putative source of Creole: French. Then he cites the example of the *Cahier* in Africa.[60]

I think that Glissant's concept of Detour is closely related to the movements that we saw in the *Cahier*. The "spin" of the slaves who have liberated themselves is detour; veerition is detour. But Glissant's chapter offers one more, crucial lesson about the relation between Return and Detour: "Detour is a profitable ruse only when it is fertilized by Return: not by a return to the original dream, to the immobile Oneness of Being, but return to the point of imbrication, from which one had been forced to turn away. That is where we must finally put the elements of Relation to work, or perish" (36). Leaving aside for the moment some of the complexities contained in this, we can see that return with a little *r* is thus for Glissant a nondelusional, nonromantic act of consciousness *and that return and detour need each other.* Surely that is the form of return (not Return) that we saw in the *Cahier*.

341

GLISSANT'S INDIES

> It seems to me that I have always known [the sea], the route and dumping-ground of the slave traders, depths of the unconscious, or a pit of suffering.
>
> —EDOUARD GLISSANT, *La Cohée du Lamentin*

Like Césaire, Glissant is a monumental poet-essayist. His works are created in impressive form and number; his oeuvre is Nobel-ready. An understanding of the slave trade and its consequences underpins everything he writes, and he has produced some of the most memorable pages on the subject ever written in French. As Ian Baucom has demonstrated, Glissant has long been haunted by images that are specific to the slave trade: the bodies of Africans weighed down by chains and jettisoned, alive, under the pursuit of British cruisers — the central atrocity of the illegal trade during the French Restoration. Glissant invokes this scene in both *Le Discours antillais* (1981) and *Poétique de la relation* (1990).[61] A discussion of the slave trade opens the latter volume; the hold of the slave ship is an "abyss" that is also a "womb." The second abyss is the ocean into which live bodies are thrown. Glissant may have been thinking of the *Zong*, infamous in the Anglophone Atlantic; or he may have been alluding to French atrocities that we have seen, like those of *La Jeune Estelle* or *La Vigilante* (and, in fiction, those in Corbière's *Le Négrier*). Channeling the thoughts of the captives in free indirect style, Glissant evokes the "asceticism" of loss, far from the "Land-Before," followed by a life of "Relation" and poetry. What is remarkable in this section of *Poétique de la relation* is the density and rapidity of Glissant's coverage; this all happens in five pages.[62] This pattern of glancing attention to the slave trade can be seen in *Le Discours antillais*: "Everything begins of course with the first African raided [*razzié*] on the Gold Coast. The ocean of trade was our new country. The land of the other side (our land) thus appeared to us as an unbearable moment [i.e., a temporary condition]. But the traded population reconstituted itself as a people on this land. Here is where the real dispossession took place" (58). The slave trade disappears rather quickly here, as it does in most of Glissant's writings. The slave trade was not the subject of any truly extended narrative or analysis written by Glissant until his recent novel *Sartorius: Le Roman des Batoutos*. In each case before that, the subject was discussed somewhat briefly: it was an essential point of reference for Glissant but not, apparently, a matter for extended analysis or narration. Africa, by association, was far removed; it could not be represented in depth or at length.

Quantity and length should not be mistaken for importance, however. I will propose here a reading of Glissant's three principal narratives of the Middle Passage: the first in his poem *Les Indes* (1955), the second in his novel *Le Quatrième siècle* (1964), and the third in *Sartorius* (1999). My initial argument will be that Glissant's relatively short treatment of the slave trade and the Middle Passage in *Le Quatrième siècle* is one of the finest representations of the subject in French, surpassing the effectiveness of his earlier epic poem. Then I will look at the extensive and curious treatment of the slave trade in *Sartorius*.

Les Indes is a nearly book-length poem; by that fact alone, as well as by its epic, Atlantic subject material, it invites comparison to Césaire's *Cahier*. But Glissant's poem is in fact far more conventional than Césaire's and has little of the creative linguistic energy of the older poem. *Les Indes* is tightly structured, with six chapter divisions or "songs," each with its own title, a prose introduction, and numbered stanzas. The rhetoric is classical, declamatory, and sententious, with multiple old-fashioned apostrophes addressed to various figures of the Atlantic: "O the sea salt . . . O sailors! . . . O land!"[63]

This poem takes us back to a question I asked in our reading of Gouges: what is an "Indie"? Glissant frames the question in this way: "Indies! it was thus, by your name nailed upon madness, that the sea began" (*LI*, 72/70). Glissant's Columbus, finding himself not in the India he expected, names the new place West Indies, in order, he says, "to restore my dream" (97/84). The ambition of *Les Indes* is to encompass within one poetic statement both the conquest of the Americas and the coming of the slave trade. Early in this study I mentioned how closely related these two phenomena were, how Columbus brought with him the seeds of a plantation system that had been previously elaborated on the Canary Islands. So, as Elisabeth Mudimbe-Boyi has said, Glissant is comparing a voyage (of "discovery") with an "anti-voyage" (of forced migration).[64] The Discoverers are empowered by their art of navigation ("the compass, and other works under sail" [69/69]); but the ocean "feeds off its own flesh" (73/71). Quickly, in the first chapter, an allusion to Toussaint ("thrown into the white sea of the Jura" [74/72]) has two effects: it suggests the links between conquest, slavery, and revolt; and it makes this poem seem rather derivative of the *Cahier*. The second chapter, "The Voyage," launches Columbus on his first Atlantic crossing and asks, "Who can, O sailors, fall out of love with [or: avoid] the Indies [*se déprendre des Indes*]?" (82/76).[65] "The Conquest" describes the "covetous and insanely mystical furor" (89/80) of colonialism and its genocide, how men made themselves into God by killing people and sprinkling holy water (99/84). Then comes the need to repopulate. Consequently, it is announced: "I know a people down there in whom I shall trade" (*Je sais là-bas un peuple, dont je ferai commerce* [100/85]). The slave trade is introduced.

The third song of *Les Indes*, "The Slave Trade," is distinct from all the others: it is the only chapter written in (poetic) prose form. As Jeff Humphries points out in introducing his translation, the use of prose serves "to accentuate the unique horror" of the slave trade.[66] "Horrible things, harsh prose," writes Glissant in the second stanza of this chapter (104/86, AT). His introduction to this song invokes the slave trade as that which "shall never

343

be erased from the face of the sea" and describes its transformative effect on the islands, now "the Indie of suffering, after the Indies of dreams" (AT). The Indies of "insanity, . . . of man's rape and of suicides" bring "a new reason" (104/87, AT; 101/86).[67] Then Glissant takes up what is for him a difficult task: the representation of Africa. Like Césaire, he attempts to present a positive image of the continent without lapsing into nostalgia:

> I know, I who address you, O star, that they were bloody and naked! They found joy on the road, like a rock. . . . They also knew the avenues of the plain, the solstices. Their streets, in the open, followed the river of your fires. Their capitals studded [*étoilaient*] other forests, but whose roofs were of azure. And they annotated with great ease the work of those who inebriated the universe. . . . I do not say, I who speak to you: behold the great ones of the past [*voici d'hier les ensoleillés*]. I do not say that they were alone, or that the altar belonged to them. (*Les Indes*, 105/87)

"No, we were never Amazons of the king of Dahomey," wrote Césaire: the overglorification of African roots is avoided by both poets. Glissant gives Africa credit for its civilization, but briefly, and he explicitly rejects mystification. Glissant plays on Africa's position between East and West Indies: Africans are now "deported from East to West, for which Indies, did you know?" The ocean "says nothing" (106/88). The poem now addresses itself to a figure that Glissant will come back to in later decades, in the discussions of the slave trade that I mentioned above, the abyss: "How many times, how many days will you offer yourself, abyss, to the patience of the migrating herd [*transhumants*]?" The abyss is the ocean that swallows living and dead captives, and it is the hold of the ship, with its "odor of cramped-up death" (107/88). The Indies are now "the market of death" (108/89). The Middle Passage is represented by invoking the sufferings of individual captives: one jumps overboard to commit suicide; one hears his wife dying in chains near him, though he cannot see her; another hears his wife leaving on a slave ship as he stays behind (an abolitionist topos); a child kills himself by swallowing his tongue (108–9/89–90). "After the crossing, . . . we are the sons of those who survived," on "a field of sumptuous lands, of poverty and fires, and of hurled black blood" (110/90). This section of *Les Indes* has thus made a major, if dense and brief, addition to literature on the slave trade written in French.[68] As in the *Cahier*, in the closing sections of Glissant's poem the Haitian Revolution provides dramatic relief from the stasis of slavery. The title of the last chapter, "La Relation," introduces a theoretical concept that will be central in Glissant's future works. Here, as in the *Cahier*, new crossings and new returns—to new Indies—are evoked.

LE QUATRIÈME SIÈCLE

In Glissant's novels the main objects of attention are, initially, the figure of the marooned slave and, later, theoretical concepts such as Relation, detour, and finally the Deleuzean rhizome.[69] It is what happens on land after the Middle Passage that preoccupies Glissant for decades: the dichotomy between, on the one hand, the hills (*mornes*), with their maroons, and, on the other hand, the plains, peopled by slaves. That sociopolitical divide is, in fact, at least as important in *Le Quatrième siècle*, even in the first chapters, as the distinction between the slave traders and the captives.

The ocean becomes a nearly insurmountable wall that imposes forgetfulness: "there is not one of us who knows what happened in the country over there beyond the ocean."[70] There are hints of an "old treachery on the other side of the ocean," beyond "the shame of forgetting" (*QS*, 40/32). As Chris Bongie puts it, "a veil is cast over Africa in *Quatrième siècle*: the continent functions as an absent origin to which the reader is given no access."[71] *Veil* is precisely the right term, but a veil does allow *some* access: it is a diaphanous, semipermeable curtain, and not a brick wall, that Glissant draws over Africa, and the process of putting it in place is something that he explicitly describes. In the novel the past is described as "a mountain" (47/40). "All history" can be read in a landscape, if you know how (47/39–40).

A narrative of the slave trade and the Middle Passage unfolds in fragments, mostly within the first two chapters of the novel. It comes from Papa Longoué, of the fourth generation out of Africa (born in 1872), a *quimboiseur* or sorcerer who reminds his listener, Mathieu Béluse, of the sixth generation (born in 1926), that he, Mathieu, does not know either the sea or the "country-before" (*le pays d'avant*), nor what was in the *Rose-Marie* slave ship. That opaque screen, which Mathieu is eager to penetrate (see *QS*, 46/39), is much emphasized, even as Longoué's command of oral history is foregrounded. Glissant has said elsewhere that this old man is "the repository of a suppressed collective memory."[72] In the novel he "knows everything," in fact (40/33, AT). He knows the thoughts and feelings of his African ancestor, knows how "the first to stand on the deck of the slave ship"

345

(24/16) felt about the Middle Passage: it "nourished his hatred" (47/40, AT). Papa Longoué can even smell the foul odor of the slave ship; it was passed down to him through the oral tradition of his family (23–24/16). Cilas Kemedjio rightly calls *Le Quatrième siècle* a "staging of the transmission of knowledge, a novelistic meditation on the conditions under which transmission can take place."[73] The central role given to the storyteller in his novel thus fills the void that the Créolistes saw in Césaire's Negritude: now Creole orality is foregrounded (and the Créolistes approve).[74]

The descriptions of the horrors of the Middle Passage in the first chapter are clear and straightforward: the stench of the hold where the captives are kept like "living manure" (as in the *Cahier*); the torture; the "vomit, blood, and death" (21/14, 23/16). A revolt is feared by the officers, but the "turmoil" turns out to be "a brawl among the Negroes" (25/18): thus the incipient feud between the Longoués and the Béluses, between the future maroons and the future field slaves, already overshadows the opposition between the slave traders and the captives. No revolt will take place on the *Rose-Marie*. The ship's captain, like Mérimée's Ledoux, is *un homme humain* (QS, 32/24). Glissant, like his former lycée teacher Césaire, thus alludes to "Tamango." The trading expedition of the *Rose-Marie* in 1788 is highly efficient; the ship pulls up to a barracoon that is already full and ready to discharge its captives.[75] This is because the "entire country had been swept. Mothers sold their children, men their brothers, kings their subjects, the friend sold his friend for rum made without sugar cane" (33/25). There is a pause as Longoué reflects on his "long speech," which in fact was not so long. Then — telescoping rapidly through the Middle Passage — "When they saw the new land, there was no longer any hope; going back was impossible." Here Glissant is employing familiar tropes from the literature of the slave trade, discourse that descends from Equiano, Mérimée, and others. Strangely, he also seems to have conflated two periods in the history of the slave trade: on the one hand, the French Revolution, with talk of the Estates-General and an incipient uprising in Saint-Domingue (QS, 48/41, 51/44), and on the other hand, as if simultaneously, the Restoration, with its illegal slave trade, flight from British cruisers, and the atrocity of throwing captives overboard when under pursuit (QS, 20/12, 42/35). The original Longoué, bought and whipped, "put off until later any settlement of accounts," much like Atar-Gull (QS, 27/20). (But, for reasons that remain obscure, Longoué's hatred is as much for his countryman Béluse as it is for his new master, La Roche.)

Longoué then revisits the scene of the ship, in a passage of remarkable, poetic, delirious free-indirect style that alters the way the Middle Passage has been written about in French (which I reproduce in French and in English translation):

> Car il eût préféré ô gabarre moi gabarre et il moi sur le ventre la poudre moi bateau et cogne sur le dos le courant et l'eau chaque pied moi corde glisser pour et mourir la rade pays et si loin au loin et rien moi rien rien pour finir tomber l'eau salée salée salée sur le dos et sang et poissons et manger ô pays le pays ("la certitude que tout était fini, *sans retour*: puisque la gabarre et les barques s'éloignaient du bateau, qu'il n'était même plus permis de s'accrocher au monde-bateau flottant fermé mais provisoire; qu'il faudrait maintenant fouler la terre là-bas qui ne bougerait pas; et dans le vide et le néant c'était comme un souvenir des premiers jours du voyage, une répétition des premiers jours quand la côte, maternelle, familière, stable, s'était éloignée *sans retour*; oui le bateau regretté, *malgré l'enfer de l'entrepont*, parce qu'il n'était certes pas apparu comme un lieu irrémédiable, jusqu'à ce moment où il avait fallu le quitter") . . .

> For he would have preferred, O barge I the barge and he I on my belly the powder I the boat and beating on my back the current and the water under each foot I the rope sliding for and dying the harbor country and so far faraway nothing I nothing nothing to end falling the water salty salty salty on the back and blood and fish and eating O country the country ("the certainty that it was all over, *without return* because the barge and the skiffs were pulling away from the ship; that it was no longer even possible to cling to the closed but temporary floating boat-world; that now they would have to set foot on land there and it would not move; and in the emptiness and nothingness it was like a memory of the first days of the voyage, a repetition of the first days when the maternal, familiar, and stable coast grew *distant without return*; yes, nostalgic for the boat, *despite the hell of the [slaves'] hold*, because it had certainly not seemed a fatal or hopeless place, right up to this moment when they had to leave it") . . . (QS, 35–36/27–28, AT; emphasis added)

347

This is a fictional slave narrative, an attempt by Glissant to fill in the missing French-language, first-person testimony of slaves born in Africa. Papa Longoué is a fictionalized Francophone Equiano, but he is channeling three generations of oral tradition. And in his insistence on the fact that his young listener "do[es] not know this, [has] no idea of what went on in the country beyond the sea" (QS, 33/25), Papa Longoué seems to redraw the barrier that he has only partially erased. It is as if Longoué stands alone against a wall of forgetfulness: "it was no wonder that everybody in this country had forgotten the *Rose-Marie*, to say nothing of the sea she crossed and the country she came from where she picked up her cargo of flesh. Yes. All that gone and forgotten into each day that went by" (*QS*, 31/23).

In the passage quoted above, Glissant has chosen to focus on a coda of the Middle Passage: the enslaved ancestor, after being whipped for fighting with his rival Béluse, is lowered into a launch that will take him from the *Rose-Marie* to the land of Martinique, to "an inconceivable existence" (36/28). The ancestor's stream of consciousness (interrupted by a detached narrator, in quotation marks) makes this short trip into a reflection on the entire Middle Passage. The style used here sends a message of its own: this experience *cannot be represented in transparent language*.[76] Normal grammar cannot do it justice. Instead, words pile on top of each other: the phrase "he me" physically reproduces the "tight packing" of the captives in the hold. "Order and thought are for today," not for the time of the Middle Passage (*QS*, 47/40). Yet clear impressions emerge: violence, agony, the impossibility of return. Glissant takes the representation of the Middle Passage into the language of modernism, where opacity flourishes and enjoys credibility. The barrier — the veil — will remain in place, even as Glissant shows how much can be divined through it, about an experience that was "mute" (*QS*, 61/54).

On land Glissant quickly makes the Longoué-Béluse rivalry into an opposition between, respectively, "the ones who refused" and "the ones who accepted" slavery (*QS*, 57/50). The original Longoué escapes from slavery immediately and becomes the archetypal maroon, the figure that anchors Glissant's work for decades.[77] The "wake" of the slave ship is "gradually obliterat[ed]," until Mathieu takes an interest in reviving history, by getting Papa Longoué to speak out of "that whirlwind of death from which we have to pull memory" (57/50, 59/52). But even Longoué cannot actually find "the country back there across the ocean," the unnamed Africa (59/53). Other Middle Passages will occur: a last slave-trading voyage is made by the *Rose-Marie* in 1848 (182–87/184–90); René Longoué is transported to fight for France in World War II in the "hold" of a ship — *la cale* (240/244). In this narrative and in Glissant's contemplation of the possibility of narrating the slave trade and the Middle Passage, a painstaking recalibration of *return* can be seen. Papa Longoué is the only vector of return, and Glissant has carefully circumscribed how much the *quimboiseur* can do.

In *Le Quatrième siècle*, then, an intricate interdependence of Return and

Detour is already visible. But there is unresolved tension between the old and new worlds rather than any happy formula for remembrance. After all, "who here can remember the boat?" (247/250). At the end, Africa, still unnamed, is heavily veiled: "indeed the infinite country back there beyond the ocean was no longer that marvelous place those who were deported had dreamed of, but the irrefutable evidence of the old days, the source of a revived past, the repudiated portion that would in turn repudiate the new land, its population and its work" (287/293). (Price-Mars's voice echoes here: "Repudiate no part.") Memory has "taken root in the new land" (285), but memory has shown itself to be a daunting challenge.[78] This is what Baucom calls "an antimelancholic politics of memory."[79] Africa, the "country before," will be something to "invent," to "dream," Glissant writes a decade after *Le Quatrième siècle*.[80]

My reading of Glissant's early work thus ends, as it were, at the water's edge, short of but not detached from the larger and more modern problems that he goes on to raise. Nationalism ("saying the truth of one's land"), by means of *marronage*, and nomadology ("the thought-process of the wanderer"), also by means of marronage, lie ahead, with all their attendant ambiguities.[81]

349

SARTORIUS

This novel emerges from deep within Glissant's late period of Deleuzean nomadology, of his trademarks *errance* and *Tout-Monde*. In that idiom, which tends toward utopianism and the erasure of inequalities, what can be said about the slave trade, the ultimate inequality? *Sartorius: Le Roman des Batoutos* has partially filled a void in world literature: the need for a major, modern novel in French that is principally concerned with the slave trade, like a French or Francophone *Middle Passage* (Charles Johnson) or *Sacred Hunger* (Barry Unsworth) or *Feeding the Ghosts* (Fred D'Aguiar).[82] Written in a disarmingly direct, oral style, Glissant's novel "of" an African people reads like a fable of origin in its early pages; its style is sometimes reminiscent of René Maran's primitivist *Batouala* of 1921 (another representation of Africa by a Martinican).

It is the seventeenth century in the interior of West Africa, and we meet the Batoutos, a people who live somewhere near the Peul, the Wolof, and the Bambara (106). But the "of" in Glissant's title (*Sartorius: The Novel of the Batoutos*) does not imply transparency; Africa remains partially veiled. The

Batoutos are an "enigma"; no one sees them; their "imperceptible history" cannot be described without "betrayal" (37, 38). They are thus resistant to traditional representation. Africa, consequently, remains distant from the Antilles: Glissant, echoing Maryse Condé, gently critiques the impulse to look "in the mirror of wounded Africa for ancestors, cousins"—as if there were not an "unknowable abyss" in the Atlantic (again, an abyss), whose bottom the Batoutos "labored" (61–62; see also 118).

The Batoutos sometimes speak in quaint aphorisms ("Speech is the crack in silence; silence is the cauldron where all speech is burned" [47]). Their strength is "to not appear strong." "Their splendor is to have no splendor" (61, 344). Many Batoutos were victims of the slave trade but "not their community," which remained unperceived, recorded under other names like Ibo (49). This novel will thus tell a secret, repressed history. *Sartorius* is kaleidoscopic, adhering to the "fractal" poetics that Glissant sees as Creole: bouncing around the globe and back and forth in history, with flashes of autobiography, winks to the author's friends, snippets of anthropology, and gleanings from history—but still, continually returning to the story of the Batoutos.[83] A transatlantic ethnography runs through *Sartorius*: how certain African names and customs have been conserved in Brazil, in Haiti, and "among Black Americans," for example (132; see also 199). Glissant folds this novel into the history of slave-trade literature by quoting the *Cahier*, transposing its allusion to a "fatal triangular calm" into "the figure of a snake god" (53), and, as we will see, by again alluding to "Tamango." The slave trade has left the peoples of the former slave islands adrift, "descendents of those who were traded," wandering, still looking for "other islands" (62)—in other words, precisely in the situation described at the end of both the *Cahier* and *Les Indes*. The function of the Batoutos in *Sartorius* is similar to that of the Allmuseri in Charles Johnson's novels *The Ox-Herding Tale* and *Middle Passage*: these tribes run the risk of being nothing but figments of their authors' respective theoretical convictions.[84] The Batoutos' gods "favor the passage to multiplicity," offering "the astonishing pleasure of diversity" (91); they "explode in mixed diversity" (98). The Batoutos are figures of Detour and Relation; the "invisible" is their "mark" (216). But I am not sure that the Batoutos are nothing but Trojan horses of (Deleuzean) philosophy, and I want to return to this question later.

Odono is the first Batouto to be captured by the "head hunters" and, as had been prophesied, sold across the ocean.[85] He initially follows an itinerary that resembles Olaudah Equiano's: first made a domestic slave in Africa, he is then taken to the sea, where he pronounces himself "dead." "He barely saw but he saw" the horrors taking place at the point of embarkation for the Middle Passage, yet he is somehow impervious himself; his skin bears no trace of scarring. (In fact, all Batoutos will "accept to submit and endure," while retaining their sense of community [*Sar*, 137].) The narrative then makes an astonishing leap: "Then they were disembarked." The Middle Passage is skipped, as we follow Odono to Martinique, where he is sold and then taken to North America; there he escapes and wanders the continent for a year (*Sar*, 110–20). He mingles with many different Indian groups and comes away as some kind of spokesman (as in the *Cahier*, a "mouth of those who have no mouth"): "I have gathered their cries and I bring them to you" (*Sar*, 121). Then the narrative takes us back to Africa, where Odono is now eight years old, and the slave trade can only be "divined" (*Sar*, 130).

Although he does not always cite his sources, Glissant sometimes demonstrates a method of historical bricolage that is transparent. In the middle of *Sartorius* he tells of the shipwreck of an illegal slave-trading vessel off Diamond Rock on the southern tip of Martinique in 1830. This is not *exactly* the same as the wreck of an anonymous slave ship that is now so magnificently memorialized there, at L'Anse Caffard, but that historical event is clearly Glissant's inspiration.[86] He may have gleaned information from the memorial itself or from a small book called *Les Ibos de l'"Amélie,"* by Françoise Thésée, which he does not mention. The real wreck took place on the night of April 8, 1830; Glissant changes this to April 30 of that year; the other facts are mostly the same. The vessel was thought to be French. Eighty-six captives survived—far more women than men because the men were in chains (the novel poses the disproportion as a mystery, whereas Thésée's book explains it).[87] Some were Ibo or Ibo-speaking (and we will see what Glissant does with that). Six of the survivors were taken to a nearby plantation; Glissant does not mention that its owner, who added these slaves to his own, was an *homme de couleur libre* (who also happened to be blind).[88] Some of the others, according to contemporary witnesses, caused "grave concern" among the planters by wandering among local plantations, pronouncing "maxims" that represented a "danger." (The historical Ibos here thus act like Glissant's fictive Batoutos!) To avoid creating a "strange" class of semienslaved, semifree persons of color, and thus destabilizing slavery on Martinique, the remaining sixty-seven survivors were sent to Cayenne.[89]

Glissant then takes off, folding this history into the fiction of *Sartorius*:

351

these Ibos were actually Batoutos who sank the ship on purpose in order to protect "their women" (*Sar*, 141). The story quickly becomes another post-"Tamango" tale of the illegal French slave trade of the 1820s, with many familiar elements: a crafty captain, named Ingleberk, a self-described "honest and conscientious artisan" who throws "cargo" overboard when pursued by English cruisers. The ship — it is now revealed with a wink to readers of *Le Quatrième siècle* — is named the *Marie-Rose*. The captain prides himself on his ability to identify, in any group of captives, the potential leader: the Tamango, the Atar-Gull, the Spartacus. But this time he cannot, so he tries mass torture. With Martinique in sight, the captives revolt, in an "enormous suicide" (*Sar*, 149). In an old-fashioned novelistic twist, the leader of the revolt is revealed to be none other than Odono, our Batouto hero. Now we know why the novel, so surprisingly, skipped over the Middle Passage earlier (as if it were "nothing remarkable"); this tale was being saved. It is obvious that Glissant takes a certain creative joy in the process of mixing history and fiction; for example, when the narrator intuits that Equiano, an Ibo, must really have been a "Batouto" (*Sar*, 184–85). So was Wilhelm Anton Amo (*Sar*, 215–24).

In the process of doing all this, Glissant also enfolds another work of art within his novel: a memorial to the victims of the Anse Caffard shipwreck. On the exact site of the tragedy, Martinican artist Laurent Valère created a magnificent memorial, called *Cap 110*, in 1998, for the commemoration of the 1848 abolition of slavery by France (see figure 15). Rising out of the soil where the drowned captives were buried, these fifteen figures — with their heads bowed in respect and mourning, their arms along their sides suggesting both captivity and tremendous potential energy — stand in a symbolically triangular grouping. Their whiteness is the African color of mourning. They overlook the water in which so many drowned, and they look "back" toward Africa. (The title *Cap 110* refers to the direction or "heading" of the figures — 110 degrees on the compass, east-southeast, looking toward Africa.) Panels alongside the memorial tell what happened to the doomed slave ship and put this event in the context of the larger triangular trade.[90]

Glissant both piggybacks on Laurent Valère's memorial — by incorporating a description of it into *Sartorius* — and builds on it in ways unique to literature:

> The fifteen statues, gathered into a triangle whose apex points to the open water, exactly on the latitude of the Gold Coast in Africa, rise out of the earth, cap-

15 Laurent Valère, *Cap 110* Memorial, Anse Caffard, Martinique.
Photograph by Christopher L. Miller.

353

tured in the rock that continues out under the water, with moving restraint and
dignity. Their arms held at their sides, heads slightly bent, they would evoke the
statues of Easter Island if they were not looking with such intensity, it seems,
towards the sea where so many ships stuffed with enchained slaves capsized. . . .
After so many furies, the pale softness of this contemplation. . . . Small groups
endlessly visit these stone giants, whose scale is so human. The visitors are grave
and silent like the statues; kids play around them; the poet comes again and
again to confer with these witnesses and to meditate with them on the memory
of the immense Waters. (*Sar*, 162–64)

Clearly, Valère's *lieu de mémoire*—a triumph of site-specific art and of memorialization—aided and inspired Glissant to create a new memorial of his
own in this novel. The statues, these mute and artificial "witnesses," as Glissant calls them, speak without words. Glissant converts their silent testimony into language.

↠⋗⋖↞

Ultimately, how can Glissant, who in his later phase so valorizes movement
and relation, come to terms with the slave trade: a movement, and there-

fore subject to valorization in the Deleuzean scheme of things, but a movement of suffering and death? Glissant and Chamoiseau addressed this very
question, together, during a panel discussion, entitled "From Slavery to the
Tout-Monde," in 1998. Their logic runs like this: slavery and the slave trade
were a "foundational crime" (*un crime fondateur*); from this crime "creolization was born in America," and that creolization "prefigured the creolization of the contemporary world," the coming of the Tout-Monde (Glissant).
Slavery is thus a "foundational matrix," a "horror" within which humanity
was nonetheless able to "produce something new" that is "valid for everyone" (Chamoiseau).[91] The slave trade, it can therefore be said, caused the
"mobilization of the Diverse" (Chamoiseau).[92] This thinking reflects a reversal of something Glissant wrote in *Le Discours antillais*: that the slave
trade forces its descendants to call all universals into question.[93] Now the
slave trade is the very precondition of a "universal" (though not using that
tainted word) — something "valid for everyone." Within their new logic,
can Glissant and Chamoiseau avoid implying that the slave trade was a good
thing?

At one point, a voice in *Sartorius* approaches the dangerous hypothesis
of a "happy" Middle Passage: "Weren't they *privileged* to be able to cross —
even if it was in so much suffering — the desert and the sea?" (*Sar*, 190; emphasis added). Oko and Odono "freely chose their routes, so as to prepare
[*prévenir*] all those paths of slavery and to make possible all the paths that
would come after" (*Sar*, 191). The Batoutos are thus like guardian spirits of
the slave trade, mythic figures who pass imperceptibly through the crucible
of the Middle Passage and slavery, emerging unscathed, invisible, and "singular" wherever they go. In the fiction of the Batoutos' existence Glissant
can finesse the difference between the slave trade and nomadology. But this
does not amount to saying that the slave trade was a good thing; that would
be absurd, and it is not what Glissant suggests in *Sartorius*. Instead, what he
has made up is a new way to look at the consequences of the slave trade and
to celebrate survival. The Batoutos are a metaphor for that.

Thus at the end of the novel "all the space of the world is now open,"
and Onkolo, the Batouto homeland, can be "built everywhere, with words
and dreams" (*Sar*, 335). The world is now flat and uniform — a Deleuzean
smooth space — ready for (of all things) "the thought of return" (small *r*) —
because "they were all leaving for that same destination in time" (*ils par-
taient tous dans ce même temps*, [*Sar*, 336]). The Deleuzean influence that

Glissant has been carrying for many years now is thus very present; an epigraph from Deleuze himself opens *Sartorius* (and seems to conjure up "a people yet to come and still hidden"). In a book of essays published after the novel, *La Cohée du Lamentin*, Glissant discusses this quotation, which asserts that "health, like literature, like writing, consists of inventing a missing people." Glissant stipulates that inventing a people must not be an act of "comfortable nationalism or populism." In other words, it must be postidentitarian. Sure enough, adhering to Deleuze, Glissant says that any people one invents must be a "becoming-people" (*un devenir-peuple*)—thus related to all the "becomings" in Deleuze's and Guattari's philosophy. The Batoutos in *Sartorius* are virtual, but unlike the nomads in Deleuze's and Guattari's *A Thousand Plateaus*, the Batoutos are wholly fictional, not real people pressed into the service of philosophy. The void that this people should fill is a void in "the world-totality" or the "Tout-Monde." This is "a world where human beings, animals and landscapes, cultures and spiritualities, mutually contaminate each other. But contamination is not dilution." (The Tout-Monde, by the way, is "the highest object of literature and poetry that can be found.")[94]

Glissant goes on to describe a vision of connectedness that takes us back to Voltaire's vision of the winds that link Africa to Europe: "This opening," writes Glissant, "from place to place—all equally legitimated, and each of them in life and *in connection with all the others*, and none of them reducible to anything—is that which informs the Tout-Monde."[95] (Earlier in the same volume, Glissant seemed to be echoing Voltaire: "The wind from Africa hauled on the Atlantic and makes us an offering" [*Cohée*, 107]). This is a perfectly Deleuzean scheme, claiming immunity from "fixedness [*fixité*], because our realities are mobile." The problems of such thinking have been explored.[96] This interconnected world is a global utopia in which, supposedly, no marginal peoples are lost or crushed; "multiplicity" and "singularity," Glissant asserts, are *not* in contradiction with each other (*Cohée*, 140). As with the quotation from Voltaire that I examined at the beginning of this study, such thinking can be both ethically admirable and blind to the reality of the particular. Its danger lies, as Peter Hallward explains, in its flattening, smoothing "singularity." Ostensibly devoted to the Diverse, and speaking a language of difference, the later Glissant nonetheless prescribes, by Hallward's account, "a totality of inter-folding equivalencies . . . an infinite variety of voices, all singing the same music."[97] Thus it is not surprising to

355

see Glissant inquire if we might not now "be close to a *demultiplied* Imaginary of the Tout-Monde" (*Cohée*, 124; emphasis added)—which is "all the sudden heres and all the times and spaces of all the peoples of the world" (*Cohée*, 236). Getting lost in that is the risk; the danger of the singular totality lurks. But Glissant's stated purpose, as it emerges in *Sartorius* and in *La Cohée du Lamentin*, is rather different. It is not to homogenize or "demultiply" but to fill in the missing "Imaginary of so many forgotten peoples." That task may be, in Glissant's larger scheme, merely preliminary to the advent of the Tout-Monde, but I think it is important nonetheless to focus on the merits of his work along the way to and *short of* that ill-conceived goal.

I am not convinced that *Sartorius* is, like other texts by Glissant, "an expression of the totality itself" (Hallward, 122) nor a manifesto of the emergent Tout-Monde. To read it as such would be reductionist. Perhaps because I admire this novel, and because it has important things to say about the slave trade, I would like to "save" it, so to speak, from Glissant's own theorizing—from the homogenization of the Tout-Monde.[98] I want to do this because I fear that the significance of what *Sartorius* says about the slave trade risks getting lost in the Tout-Monde machine. I can only do this by isolating the novel, to a certain extent, from Glissant's wider body of theory—by building what the French call *garde-fous*. This can be justified on the grounds that *Sartorius* is, after all, fiction and not philosophy (a material, discursive difference). In this spirit one might let the novel have the last word: "Don't lock [the Batoutos] up in the mechanism of global prehensions [apprehending]; they will just escape" (*Sar*, 324). More important, unlike Voltaire, Glissant has visibly *not* surrendered his ability to see differences and tragedies (what Hallward calls the specific), the ability to hear different voices singing different tunes. That is why the novel ends with an evocation of the Rwandan genocide of 1994, why Glissant worries about groups that have been set aside by globalized communications networks,[99] and why *Sartorius* is one of the most remarkable treatments of the slave trade written in French.

A coda on Glissant: in 2004 the seventy-five-year-old writer announced his sponsorship of a maritime expedition by a group of twelve writers. Aboard a three-masted schooner, the writers—including Patrick Chamoiseau, J. M. G. Le Clézio, and Alain Borer—were to roam for two years, calling on "peoples of the water" who can only be visited by boat. The itinerary included Mauritania, where slavery persists.[100]

356

CONDÉ'S *HÉRÉMAKHONON*,
AGAJA, AND TEGBESU

Here means peace (in Mandekan). Condé's Guadeloupean protagonist, Véronica, goes "back" to Africa looking for the solace that might come with
a sense of rootedness; what she finds is something quite different. I have
alluded to Condé's *Hérémakhonon* numerous times in this study, and, although it has been well analyzed by numerous critics, I want to explore
its significance briefly here.[101] It remains one of the most important post-
Césaire interventions in the French/Francophone Atlantic. Years before the
Créolistes burst onto the scene, Condé's novel deconstructed the myth of
return to Africa, rebutting Alex Haley's *Roots* (also published in 1976) with
a vengeance (Glissant says he "never liked . . . *Roots*").[102] What has gone
unexamined in Condé's "diaspora literacy"[103] is a rather obscure but very
meaningful series of allusions to the slave trade that punctuate certain parts
of *Hérémakhonon*.

"Incessant to-ings and fro-ings" (*va-et-vient incessants*) characterize the
original novel, which met a "total lack of success" on the literary market
when it first appeared in 1976. During the rise of Francophone literature in
the 1980s, Condé unfortunately chose to "prune" some of those movements
out of the new edition, with its more accessible title *En attendant le bonheur*
(a translation of the word *heremakhonon*, although substituting "happiness"
for "peace").[104] Plenty of movement remains in the second edition, but the
loss of complexity is regrettable. I will therefore use the original novel as
the object of my comments here.

Hérémakhonon is ostensibly a novel about Africa, but the peripatetic shifts
of the narrator's consciousness — whose thoughts totally dominate the narration, to the exclusion of any other point of new — take the reader around
the Atlantic triangle in a whirl, from West Africa to Guadeloupe, to France,
and so on. The swirling motion of the novel ultimately throws Véronica out
of Africa and back to France. One characteristic of the narrative has persistently confused critics: the absence of any direct quotations from Véronica in the text — along with the dominance of her internal monologue — has
been seen by many as a "failure" of engagement, as an "inability" to speak
or a "lack of enunciation."[105] It is not; as I have argued elsewhere, Véronica's
enunciations work very effectively, if indirectly, to critique postcolonial Africa and to undermine the myth of Return.[106] *Hérémakhonon* is, according to

H. Adlai Murdoch, "an interrogation of the disabling social and cultural du-
alities which figure the desire to construct a functional postcolonial Caribbean identity-structure." Murdoch also suggests that Véronica "establishes
an interpellative triangle whose operative poles are Guadeloupe, France,
and Africa," reworking the Atlantic triangle of the slave trade.[107] That point,
which Murdoch does not pursue further, is obviously of most interest here.
Hérémakhonon is structured by a series of "flights" around the triangle —
the word *fuite* is often used — punctuated by various scenes of separation in
airport lounges (where *fuite* becomes *vol*).[108] The narrative moves in three
principal ways: psychologically, inside and outside of Véronica's consciousness; temporally, between past and present; and geographically, around the
Atlantic triangle.[109]

I alluded earlier to Condé's critical differentiation between "Négritude
césairienne" and "Négritude senghorienne." That essay was published two
years prior to *Hérémakhonon*, and it sets the stage for Condé's novelistic intervention in the Atlantic triangle. In the essay Condé finds one gigantic
failure in Césaire's *Cahier*: the poem is based on something that "does not
exist" — the idea of "the Negro." *Le Nègre* is a European myth, says Condé,
and to found a poetry on it is to "accept Europe even in the worst errors of
its culture." Negritude thus constitutes "a ghetto . . . a trap . . . a lie." Césaire
has at least had the good taste to abandon it, unlike Senghor. So, Condé concludes, let's thank Negritude for the most beautiful poem to come out of colonialism, the *Cahier*; then let's "relegate" the whole project to the dustbin
of history.[110] I do not want to suggest that *Hérémakhonon* is merely this anti-
Negritude argument by other means, but the novel is related to the essay
and certainly flows out of a similar set of concerns.

Condé has described *Hérémakhonon* as "a book of rage" and "refusal"
that was equally "disliked" all around the Atlantic triangle: in France, in the
Antilles, and in Africa.[111] Véronica's flashbacks to her childhood in Guadeloupe are anything but flattering to the petit-bourgeois class of the island.
As for Africa, Condé rightly credits herself as one of the first to denounce
the abuses of Sékou Touré's repressive regime in Guinea, the country that
can clearly be divined in the narrative.[112]

The opening passages of the novel quickly set the narrative veering and
spinning around the Atlantic: from the immediate scene of Véronica's arrival
in Africa, back to Guadeloupe, with her parents seeing her off at the airport
the first time she left for France (not to go "home" for nine years), then back
to the present in Africa. Warmly welcomed "back" to her "racial" home —

358

by an African, Véronica thinks sarcastically: "Great! With one word, he has wiped out three centuries and a half." The conflation of space (the axis of the Middle Passage) and time (the 350 years since the beginning of the slave trade) is Véronica's central conundrum.[113] How can contemporary Africans be her "ancestors"?

The challenging nature of the novel can be gauged by the lines that follow immediately, without transition, in Véronica's stream of consciousness: "Instead of riding the new coach and practicing scales, Tegbesu and Agaja have positioned their men at strategic points. They are driving the whites back into the sea. It is red with their blood. The slave ships in Nantes and Liverpool have been set on fire. No more need for them" (*H*, 13–14/4, AT). An important episode in the history of the Atlantic slave trade is evoked, obscurely, in this passage. This is hardly a transparent detour through African history; Agaja and Tegbesu are not household names, so it is interesting to see that Maryse Condé chose these as the signposts of the slave trade in *Hérémakhonon*. The allusion to Agaja and Tegbesu returns four more times in the novel, marking shifts in Véronica's thinking.

Agaja, the "father of Dahomey," reigned from 1708 to 1732 and is well known in the history of the slave trade: he was a conqueror of territory, extending the power of his inland kingdom to the sea, conquering first Allada and then Whydah. He became a shrewd player in the Atlantic economy. He was an absolute monarch, a student of the West, greatly interested in both material goods and literacy, with a particular affinity for the French. The English slave trader William Snelgrave attested to Agaja's taste for luxuries.[114] After the death of Agaja in 1732, his son Tegbesu became the sixth king of Dahomey and reigned until 1774 — selling into slavery or executing anyone who threatened his power or got too rich. Tegbesu's proclivity for "liquidating all rivals"[115] foretells the repressions of Sékou Touré, the historical basis of *Hérémakhonon*. I have found no confirmation of the kings' interest in keyboard instruments, although Agaja was known to be very fond of European goods.[116]

Agaja's relation to the slave trade is a subject of controversy among historians. Did the Dahomeans fight their way to the sea in order to better engage in the slave trade, eliminating middlemen, or, on the contrary, to "put an end to the overseas trade in slaves"?[117] Was their intervention an African rebellion against the Atlantic slave trade itself, or was it more like the OPEC oil embargo of the 1970s, an attempt to renegotiate trade but certainly not to abolish it? Agaja proposed in a letter to King George I the establishment

359

of sugar, cotton, and indigo plantations in Africa. Was his motivation "abolitionist—as Baron Roger's would be nearly a century later—or was he, again, simply interested in increasing the efficiency of his own slave economy and maximizing his own profits? (In either case, his plan would have diminished the Atlantic slave trade.) In Walter Rodney's influential *How Europe Underdeveloped Africa*, Agaja is described as Dahomey's "greatest king," who "looted and burned European forts and slave camps," reducing "the trade from the 'Slave Coast' to a mere trickle." (Rodney may be the source of this passage in *Hérémakhonon*.) Later, says Rodney, Agaja "had to" agree to "the resumption of slave trading."[118] This makes Agaja sound like another supposedly reluctant monarch, Louis XIII.

In *Hérémakhonon* Véronica echoes Rodney's thesis: the Dahomeans disrupted the slave trade, causing slave-trading ships in Nantes and Liverpool to be burned as junk. A contemporary English observer, the abolitionist naval surgeon John Atkins, first promoted the image of Agaja as an opponent of the slave trade, although other facts make this assessment seem dubious. Agaja quickly reentered the trade, and his son Tegbesu is estimated to have sold nine thousand slaves a year into the Atlantic trade, mostly to the French and the Portuguese. This made him richer than any trader in Nantes or Liverpool; he had seven palaces.[119] Tegbesu took the slave trade to new levels of organization and efficiency, doing much to accommodate his European clients.[120] Both kings of Dahomey and their successor, Kpengla, "played a decisive part" in the slave trade in the eighteenth century.[121]

What does this controversy about the slave trade in the eighteenth century have to do with Véronica's checking into her hotel in Africa in 1960? Here at the beginning of the novel, even if she is cynical about erasing three and a half centuries of distance between herself and the continent, Véronica's mind is steeped in history. By lending credence to a theory of African resistance to the slave trade, she shows that she is open to a form of solidarity along the southern axis of the triangle—the bonded identity that she has come to seek among her "ancestors," her "brothers and sisters." So a few pages later she thinks, diasporically, "We're all related. All coming out of the same slave ship's belly. We all look alike" (*H*, 24/10, AT). But already there is a sign that genealogy will not work here: a character named Birame III is so called not because he is the son and grandson of men with that name but because he is one of three classmates with that name (21/8). Later, as the political situation deteriorates and her lover is named head of a Committee of Public Safety, the exploitation of genealogy by African nobles will bother

Véronica more and more. Ultimately, the genealogical model will be discredited, because her "ancestors . . . play a dirty trick on [her]," forcing her "to choose between the past and the present" (*H*, 287/161) — that is to say, forcing her to choose a place on the Atlantic triangle. No more Return from the diaspora, no "roots." Return in *Hérémakhonon* can take Véronica only back to Paris (*H*, 285/160, 312/176). Véronica has learned not to conflate space and time — that by traveling to Africa she does not meet her ancestors, but rather . . . Africans.

In Véronica's early days in Africa as a professor of philosophy, her students ask where she comes from; this makes her think, not surprisingly, of the slave trade that took her ancestors to Guadeloupe:

> "Mademoiselle, what country are you from?"
>
> Once again my first lecture here is going to be on the Antilles. The slave ships set off again from the Bight of Biafra. All that blood on the glazed eye of the sea. And those jolly sharks, jolly ancestors of the Ku Klux Klan.
>
> "Hunt the nigger!" . . .
>
> [The students] are trusting and naïve. Basically, that was our downfall: trust and naiveté. The whites arrived with their glass beads and we gave them gold. Or men. Well, that's one version. I don't really believe it. There were crooks [*roublards*] like Tegbesu who profited from the situation. He realized where it would take us [*où cela allait nous mener*]. (*H*, 44/21)

The idea of African kings resisting the Atlantic slave trade has obviously receded here, as the image of a profiteering tyrant begins to rise. The parallel to modern dictators soon comes into sharper focus. Mwalimwana, the head of state, "our father," "threw the whites into the sea" (*H*, 56/27) — just like Agaja, as she thought to herself before. But Véronica now thinks: "Something that Tegbesu and his kind were unable to do. Now that the whites are in the sea, though, his people continue to die of hunger. They are free, though. Apparently this is very important." The president himself greets Véronica as "one of the children that Africa lost," to which she replies (silently): "Sold, Mwalimwana, sold. Not lost. Tegbesu got 400 pounds sterling per boat load" (*H*, 64–65/32).

Véronica's dilemma worsens as she realizes that her lover, the minister Ibrahima Sory, is not quite what she was hoping for. Her attraction to him — and the very label she uses for him ("Negro with ancestors") — suggests that he represents to her *the unenslaved*: one whose lineage, unlike hers, has been neither ruptured nor tainted by "social death"; one who has

361

retained all the privileges of African genealogy, as celebrated by the griots. Worse, he is something like a *néo-esclavagiste*. He comes from the class of slave traders, like the Saïfs in Yambo Ouologuem's *Le Devoir de violence* — not from the enslaved. His father, Ibrahima Sory brags, "had the power of life and death over hundreds of men" (*H*, 140/76, AT). By virtue of his noble bloodlines, his family's long collaboration with the colonizers, and his current political power, he is a "master" and even a "Master" (*H*, 210/117, 270/151, AT). He dismisses the idea of equality between master and slave (*H*, 140/76). Ibrahima Sory's predecessors Agaja and Tegbesu thus return at a crucial moment, as Véronica is coming to a new realization: that Ibrahima Sory, in a new, reversed *Exclusif*, refuses to "share" his ancestors with her because she is, like Ayché in the film *Tamango*, "the white man's whore" (*H*, 273/152). There is no shared status of *nègre*, no Negritude: "Ramatoulaye removes her heavy wig, which makes her look like one of the Supremes. Her hair emerges, rose-plaited. Now here is someone who niggrifies herself for pleasure! Shall I warn her? That's how it all began. Tegbesu's apparently innocent desire to be carried by porters. Agaja's wish to play the organ. It didn't look like much. And then everything got messy [*tout a été foutu*]. Europe must be kept at a distance at any price!" (*H*, 218/122, AT). The taste for luxury and pleasure of the kings of Dahomey leads to a "mess," the slave trade, and its historic consequences. Europe is largely to blame. Yet at the end of *Hérémakhonon* there is nowhere for Véronica to go but back to Europe, to Paris. The experiment in rooted identity — her project of "extreme" heritage tourism — has failed. "Yet another flight" is undertaken (*H*, 312/176).

Hérémakhonon is a correction. A proper response to the suppression of Africa in the New World, Condé suggests, is not some misguided Return. On the simplest level the ancestors you seek may turn out to be Agaja and Tegbesu; your lover may turn out to be an "assassin." Furthermore, the novel articulates a deeper objection to the conflation of time and space. Seeking to recapture the past, to find your own ancestors or those of mankind in general, by traveling in the present — a classic mind-set of Europeans in Africa — is delusional. The "mess," the broken southern axis of the Atlantic triangle, cannot be miraculously repaired.[122] "The Middle Passage can only be navigated once," declared Maryse Condé more recently.[123]

Still, if Véronica's identity experiment has failed, because it was built on false suppositions, the novel itself has not: a less naive, more disabused, more historical vision of Africa and the Atlantic can now emerge.[124] Thus

362

it is not surprising to see that Maryse Condé went on to produce several other novels that deal with Africa, including *Ségou*, a historical narration of slavery, the rise of Islam, and the dawn of French colonialism in West Africa, with glances across the Atlantic to Jamaica and Brazil. *Ségou* shows how slavery and the slave trade both profited and ruined an African kingdom.[125]

AFRICAN "SILENCE"

No (Francophone) African novel has matched the vivid historical depiction of slavery that Maryse Condé created in *Ségou*, according to Madeleine Borgomano.[1] Earlier in this study, I described the relative "silence" of Francophone African writers on the subject of the slave trades. But if there is silence, it is what Sony Labou Tansi once called *un silence métissé*, a half-caste silence, interrupted by some significant creative sound. It is a silence that has a particular shape. In this chapter my purpose is neither to describe nor to refute the idea of an African literary "silence" on the subject of the slave trade but rather to feel out the borderlines between silence and utterance in certain works of Francophone African literature and film that are concerned with the slave trade.

SEMBENE'S *BLACK DOCKER*: FRANCOPHONE LITERATURE ON TRIAL

The first novel written by Ousmane Sembene, one of Africa's most prominent authors and filmmakers, not only represents the slave trade, it also encompasses the question of literary representation itself in its narration. It therefore provides a perfect context in which we can contemplate not only an exception to the putative silence of African literature with regard to the slave trade but also the conditions that may have created such a silence. *Le Docker noir*, translated as *Black Docker*, has been disparaged since its first appearance in 1956 by a veritable who's who of literary critics: everyone from René Maran and Lamine Diakhaté through Lilyan Kesteloot and Abiola Irele has found it deficient.[2] But *Black Docker* is in fact a highly innovative work that explores the most important questions about Africa's relation to France and about the very possibility of Francophone literature—even as it makes an important contribution to and revision of *la littérature négrière*. The novel is plotted around the homicide in Paris of a famous French novelist, Ginette Tontisane, by a Senegalese dockworker, Diaw Falla. *Black Docker* is set within the larger context of colonial oppression: in the wake of a massacre in Côte d'Ivoire, one character points out, Diaw has "only got one murder on his conscience, the white people have just massacred dozens of men, and they won't even be tried. Nobody asks them to account for their behavior."[3] Tontisane's murder provokes a racist diatribe in a Marseilles newspaper, calling for the expulsion of all the "uncivilized" Africans and Arabs—all those who "call themselves sailors [*navigateurs*] but know nothing about the workings of modern machines" (*DN*, 28/11, AT). Issues of race, labor, crime, and "know-how" in the form of navigation—with deep roots in the history of the slave trade—thus come together in the basic setup of this novel.

Black Docker begins as a whodunit, although the crime being investigated is not simply the murder of Ginette Tontisane but also the alleged piracy of a novel entitled *The Last Voyage of the Slave Ship "Sirius"* ("*Le Dernier voyage du négrier 'Sirius'*"). Diaw claims to be (and is) the author of this work, which he found impossible to publish in France. During an interrogation that lasts twenty-four hours, Falla "sticks with his story, that he is the true author" of this work—as if much of the questioning had been devoted to that topic rather than to the murder (*DN*, 29/11, AT). The French press is incredulous: the idea that an African dockworker could write a novel seems far-fetched. But with the publicity coming from the crime and the trial, *The Slave Ship "Sirius"* has become a bestseller. It won a prize when it first appeared, as a novel by Ginette Tontisane. Royalties are going neither to Diaw Falla nor to (the estate of) Tontisane, pending the outcome of the trial, which will adjudicate not only the crime of murder but also of literary piracy.

Sembene has set up a hall of mirrors, in which both real and fictional issues of authorship bounce off each other. Like Diaw, Sembene was himself a dockworker in Marseilles when he began to write. Readers thus hold in their hands a book that must be like *The Last Voyage of the Slave Ship "Sirius"* in some way that remains to be seen. Also, although it is not often discussed, the novel that Sembene wrote just after *Black Docker* raised issues of authorship and plagiarism that resonate with the disputed authorship of

The Slave Ship "Sirius" in *Black Docker*: his *O pays, mon beau peuple* (1957) contains passages that are identical to parts of Haitian author Jacques Roumain's 1947 novel *Gouverneurs de la rosée*.[4] In the pages of *Présence Africaine*, Lamine Diakhaté accused Sembene's *Black Docker* of plagiarizing a tale by Birago Diop.[5] In fact, Dominic Thomas has found that certain passages in *Black Docker* reproduce the 1947 French translation of Richard Wright's *Native Son*.[6] On the level of wordplay, it must be noted that the word *nègre* in French means ghostwriter as well as Negro and slave; by stealing Diaw's work, Ginette Tontisane makes him into her involuntary *nègre* in the sense of ghostwriter.[7] A general crisis of ownership redounds both within and around this text.

As he is led to the courtroom in chains, Diaw thinks of the "slaves in his book. 'Why did I write it? Aren't I just like them?'" he wonders (*DN*, 42/19). The publisher of *The Slave Ship "Sirius"* testifies and seems less than wholly certain about its authorship. A detective asserts that Diaw admitted to hitting the victim but nothing more. Diaw himself testifies that he had come to Paris to see the French novelist because she had stolen his work, after he entrusted it to her, and he wanted a "reparation" or redress of this grievance (*DN*, 56/26). Under questioning from the judge, the topic shifts from the facts of the homicide to the authorship of *The Slave Ship "Sirius."* Diaw is asked to recite part of the book from memory as proof of his authorship, and as he performs the last chapter, the slave trade enters this fictive Parisian courtroom — thus through the back door, as fiction — even as it enters Francophone African literature for a rare appearance.

What Diaw recites is a portrait of the horrors of the Middle Passage: the putrescence, the vomit, the rape, the amalgamation of peoples who lose their ethnic identities. Onboard the *Sirius* a revolt takes place; the captives then control the stern while the masters are confined to the bow. As a storm approaches, the ship drifts — shades, once again, of "Tamango."[8] As the *Sirius* sinks, all racial differences are superseded by the fear of death, which claims all onboard. This "last" slave ship is declared a total loss at Nantes on December 4, 1824 (*DN*, 59–63/28–31).[9] When Diaw finishes his recitation, *silence* fills the courtroom.

This is a silence that is worth thinking about. It is, to begin with, the opposite and counterpart of the silence that supposedly characterizes the treatment of the slave trade in African literature: here is an African literary text that has presented (a text about) the slave trade within its own pages, thus rupturing the "silence" of a literature that was then just getting under way. Within the courtroom drama that Sembene has created, it is unclear to what extent the silence of the spectators is due to the horrors of the slave trade and how much of it comes from Diaw's stunning act of memory and its implications for the murder trial. (If he is the true author of the book, is his crime mitigated?) Two forms of memory are thus at play here: the remembrance of forgotten crimes against humanity on the one hand and, on the other, the oral recitation of a written text. Like its close contemporary the film *Tamango*, *Black Docker* revives images of the slave trade before the French public; it does this by creating the fiction of a trial in which the crimes of the French are aired *as fiction, as literature*. So, as "testimony" about the slave trade is being heard inside an institution of the French state, French participation in the trade is not erased (as it was in the film) or silenced. The silence is broken *by fiction and in fiction*.

The silence in the courtroom is then interrupted by the prosecutor, who dismisses *both* acts of memory by accusing Diaw of having simply memorized Tontisane's work. In his closing arguments the prosecutor puts the charge of literary piracy on the same plane as murder: "This monster claims to be the author of *The Slave Ship 'Sirius'*! This insult to our literature is also a crime." Now he demands a "reparation" (countervailing the one Diaw had sought from Tontisane) in the name of the French literature and French civilization (*DN*, 69–70/34, AT). Diaw's lawyer is thus obliged to defend not only his client but all of African civilization, precisely as it is represented by African literature—the very possibility of which is on trial.[10]

Sembene's use of the word *réparation*, in a novel that deals with the slave trade, is of course startling to the early-twenty-first-century reader. Writing long before the current debate on reparations for slavery and the slave trade, Sembene does not suggest any such notion per se. Rather he invokes the more general idea of moral calculus that we saw in such perverse form in Sue's *Atar-Gull*. Like Atar-Gull, Diaw goes to Paris to seek his redress. Diaw wants a reparation from Tontisane, which he does not receive; by convicting Diaw, the French state wants to repair both her murder and an "insult" to its literature. But the idea of moral calculus is most apparent on the more general plane of analysis that is implicit in *Black Docker*: modern colonial labor is morally comparable to slavery—an idea that Sembene now goes on to develop.

As Sembene exposes Diaw's backstory in the second part of the novel, the larger parallel between the slave trade and colonial labor comes into focus. His description of the "little Harlem of Marseilles," reproduces the

367

rhetoric that was used to describe the ethnic diversity of the slave ship in part 1 (see *DN*, 77–78/41–42 and 59–61/28–29). On the slave ship "all ethnic groups were found" (*DN*, 59/28); in Marseilles, "all origins, all ethnic groups are represented" (*DN*, 78/41, AT). The implication is clear: African immigrants in France are comparable to the slaves of previous centuries in terms of both the ethnic blending to which they were subjected and the labor they were required to perform.[11] That comparison is expanded as more information about the lives of African laborers slowly comes forward. To be a sailor (*navigateur*) is to live in poverty (*DN*, 82/44). The labor of the dockworkers "sapped the vital strength from their muscles," leaving them in "tatters," unable to keep up the machinelike pace that is required of them (*DN*, 128–29/69–70, AT). "When the sun had gone down and the day was well and truly over, the holds disgorged this human bile from their bowels" [*les cales vomissaient de leurs entrailles cette scorie humaine*] (*DN*, 130/71, AT). Sembene worked on the docks in Marseilles after his service in the Second World War, even as he taught himself to be a writer, and he suffered serious injury in the process; here he makes his comparison of dockworkers to slaves most explicit.[12] He borrows the discourse of the slave trade (not of slavery itself), using terms we saw in Césaire's *Cahier*. Now the *vomito negro* is an urban, immigrant proletariat, and instead of rising up in a volcanic revolt, they will organize. First there is a work stoppage, led by Diaw, a spontaneous strike against the bosses who "want to own us" (*DN*, 146/80). In this context a union man tells Diaw that he must believe in something if he is going to be a good writer; he must defend a cause (*DN*, 149/81–82). In fact, Diaw traveled to Paris the first time not only to seek the publication of his novel but also as a delegate of his community, to demand help from the elected representatives of "Overseas France" — the colonies; he gets no redress (*DN*, 86/46, 103–4/58).

368

As he awaits word from Paris about the publication of *The Slave Ship "Sirius,"* Diaw leads a double life, seeking work but banned from the docks, finding satisfaction only in the novel he is writing (his second). It is then that he learns with consternation of the publication of his novel under Ginette Tontisane's name: he goes to Paris and confronts her. "Centuries of hatred" between the two races rise to the surface. In an "uncontrollable rage" he attacks her; she hits her head falling over and dies. Diaw learns of her death from the newspapers (*DN*, 193–94/105–6). As the narrative switches back to the present, Diaw is sentenced to life at hard labor. In a letter to his uncle Diaw describes himself as a "slave of [his] own mental wanderings" and a "captive of society." His missive turns into a homily on African society and politics, on the need for reform, self-reliance, and integrity. This letter at the end of *Black Docker* is Sembene's first statement in a novel of the themes that he insisted on throughout his career in literature and film. Despite his crime, Diaw is a new "mouth of those who have no mouth."[13] But his conviction stands as a cautionary tale: those Africans who trample on French territory—and, especially, on the French Republic of Letters—may encounter treachery and repression. But Francophone literature has an important role to play nonetheless: it *can* represent a history like that of the slave trade, at least partially.

Black Docker is one of the most significant and explicit considerations of the world the French slave trade left behind. The novel does not trace a narrative line connecting the past of the slave trade to the present of colonialism directly; it works mostly by comparison: modern immigrant labor is *like* slave labor (the simile that will be developed in *La Noire de* . . .). That comparison is very powerful and provocative, and it of course implies that a *continuous* history of exploitation and oppression has taken place. As in the film *Tamango*, the slave trade is invoked both on its own terms, historically, and for contemporary purposes, as a political allegory. The thrust of that allegory in *Black Docker* bears on issues of labor as they were taking shape during the period of "decolonization"—the 1950s and 1960s. As the demand for immigrant labor began to bring ever-increasing numbers of African, North African, and Antillean workers to the metropole, *Black Docker* initiated the comparison of these workers to slaves. That comparison was carried forward by others; it became almost commonplace.[14] Its literary manifestations include a work by a Fanonist playwright from Martinique, Daniel Boukman: his play *Les Négriers* describes the BUMIDOM program that imported labor to France in a "twentieth-century slave trade."[15] Far more famous is Sembene's own continuation of this line of thought in his novella *La Noire de* . . . (1962) and his marvelous film of the same name (1966).[16]

Sembene's treatment of the slave trade in *Black Docker* leaves much unsaid. There is a "silence" remaining here, the contours of which are defined by the excerpts of the slave-trade novel that we do see. The novel that Sembene wrote is, after all, *Black Docker*, not *The Slave Ship "Sirius."* The latter novel remains virtual and fictional within the pages of the novel that does exist, *Le Docker noir*. If *The Slave Ship "Sirius"* existed in full, it would be of tremendous importance within emerging Francophone African literature and the evolving history of *littérature négrière*. It would be the missing Francophone African novel that gives comprehensive attention to the Atlantic slave trade. Sembene suggested the importance of such a text by staging an imaginary performance of one chapter inside an imaginary French courtroom, making this doubly literary representation into a matter of state. (Which it will in fact become, only much later, on May 10, 2001, when the National Assembly votes to acknowledge that the slave trade and slavery were crimes against humanity.) But by disclosing only part of this virtual novel, he implies that the representational capacities of Francophone writing are limited. Perhaps that is why Sembene did not write *The Slave Ship "Sirius"* itself; perhaps the slave trade was too important to be written about comprehensively in French. A certain skepticism about Francophone writing is thus already visible in Sembene's first novel; it will soon propel him toward cinema.[17] In *Black Docker* Sembene both interrupted and recontoured Africa's "silence" about the slave trade.

CEDDO: SLAVES IN THE FAMILY

In his recourse to cinema as a means of reaching people who do not read, in his act of founding African cinema, Sembene, it can be said without exaggeration, renewed the representation of Africa. Film partially solves — or at least shifts — the language and literacy problem, the severe limitations of Francophone writing. Does this mean that everything can now be said and revealed? Does cinema spell the end of silence?

Ceddo was the first African film to shine a light on slavery and the slave trade inside Africa.[18] Yet its complex and ambiguous attention to these issues is generally overshadowed by its controversial critique of Islam. Completed in 1976 at a cost of $500,000 and released to international critical praise, *Ceddo* encountered resistance and censorship at home, in Senegal. President Léopold Sédar Senghor denounced Sembene as a "Marxist-Leninist" who refused "to obey the law" — the law on the spelling of Wolof.[19] The film was banned until Senghor's resignation in 1981. In fact the dispute over orthography served as a smoke screen for official resistance to Sembene's disruption of the Senegalese national-historical-religious consensus.[20] Senegal's population is overwhelmingly Muslim. An African film that depicts Islam as an alien imposition — like Christianity — is bound to be controversial in Senegal and beyond, perhaps even more so in the early-twenty-first century than in the late 1970s. *Ceddo* was at the time of its release "the most critical artistic scrutiny to date of the history of Islam in Senegalese society," and

it has hardly been superseded since then.[21] "Africans have been deperson-
alized by their conversion to Islam," Sembene has said with characteristic
bluntness. "It was forced upon them and they lost their traditional identity."[22] More recently, Sembene has observed that *Ceddo* can now be seen as
an early warning against Islamic fundamentalism.[23]

The time frame of *Ceddo* is overdetermined: it seems to be the seventeenth
or early eighteenth century — the time of La Courbe and Labat; the film may
be based on a "war of the marabouts" that began in the Senegal river valley
in 1645 and led to other wars in the eighteenth and nineteenth centuries (including the jihad that is the background of Baron Roger's *Kelédor*).[24] It has
also been interpreted as a reflection on the demise of the Joloff state "at the
hands of Islam" in the nineteenth century.[25] But *Ceddo* is in fact even more
transhistorical than that: in a vision sequence it flashes forward to the twentieth century. Also, the third element in Africa's "triple heritage" plays an
intriguing role. Christianity is represented by a priest, whose approach to
conversion is the opposite of the imam's: he merely waits. (His companions
were killed by the warrior Saxewar.) This pacific approach seems to be symbolically rewarded in the "flash-forward" vision sequence, which depicts a
fully Africanized, modern Roman Catholic mass. The slave trader and the
priest are the only Europeans in the film, and they never speak. The white
trader appears to be the sole slave trader in the area, although it is unclear
to whom the imam sells his captives — those who fail to convert. The priest
is associated with the slave trader by race and sits beside him at assemblies
but otherwise is not complicit with the slave trade. This is no Father Labat
or Demanet. By keeping the priest innocent of the slave trade, Sembene pre-
pares room for the model of Africanized Roman Catholicism that he holds
up against Islam, as an implied reproach.

Further hints of an Atlantic dimension come several times in the film,
especially in Sembene's startling and repeated recourse to African American
gospel music as he shows slaves in Africa; the transatlantic and transhistorical link is clear. But, as in *Black Docker*, Sembene leaves the viewer to decide
exactly what connects the past to the present. As we see the abject captives in
Ceddo, and watch them writhe in pain as they are branded with the fleur-de-
lis, a song is heard (extradiegetically), saying in English, "I'll make it home
someday." Sembene uses the song as a signature of the slave trade throughout the film. African American in style and language, Arthur Simms's song
seems to invoke New World dreams of return to Africa, "home."[26] But its
effect is ambiguous: this home is a place where we are watching Africans sell

371

other Africans to a white trader. What are we supposed to deduce from this juxtaposition of sight and sound? The effect is highly ambiguous; Sembene "keeps turning the impetus back on his audience."[27] We are far from *Roots*.

The film begins with dramatic images of the slave trade inside Africa. Two captives, attached to each other by a yoke, are led by an African man into a European trader's compound. The trader shows off a breech-loading rifle (suggesting that this is new technology and that we are in the nineteenth century). The two captives are exchanged for one rifle. Slave trading therefore sets the stage for the beginning of the plot: a princess has been taken hostage. The king's daughter, Dior Yacine (Tabara Ndiaye), was kidnapped by the *ceddo*, or "outsiders," to press their demand that Islam be resisted and tradition respected. The spokesman for the *ceddo* states their grievances to the king: they are tired of being sold, as infidels, into slavery by the converted Muslim nobles. Their rights within an old social contract have been eroded. As if to demolish any notion of slavery as a benign institution within African societies, Sembene shows the warrior Saxewar (Nar Modou Sene), a representative of the dwindling non-Muslim nobility, brutalizing a slave girl who offers him water. As the girl cowers on the ground, the griot Jaraaf (Oumar Gueye) tells Saxewar, "Decide. She is a slave. You have the power of life and death over her." Saxewar is outraged by Dior's kidnapping because he had much invested in his marriage contract with her father: "I had accepted the conditions of the bride-price, making them [the assembled *ceddo*] into slaves by bartering them for rifles with that man with red ears."

Islam is represented by a short, brutal, and doctrinaire imam (Gouré).[28] This religious zealot, followed by a group of sycophants, eventually displaces the old order by usurping the throne; then he enforces the conversion of the people to Islam and imposes Sharia. He will marry Princess Dior in order to preserve the royal line, now under Islamic control. But at the end of the film Dior shoots the imam, killing him, then confidently walks away. She seems to be staking her future (and Africa's) with those who resist. Dior is the film's largely silent center and its final emblem, but what exactly does she represent?[29] She has defeated the imam, but any future role she might play is highly ambiguous. She is not the leader of the *ceddo*, nor is she opposed to slavery. Why, as it is widely assumed, are the *ceddo* supposed to "identify" with her?[30] At the beginning of the film Dior said contemptuously to her *ceddo* captor, "Except for animals, only slaves are tied up. And you're the only slave here." Nothing later in the film suggests that she changes her point of view, although some transformation of her character is suggested.[31] Her ascendancy at the end could just as well be taken as a sign of restoration of the royal power that was usurped by the imam. Thus the freeze-frame on Dior at the end cannot be taken as a simple emblem of heroic, popular nationalism.

Ceddo is widely seen as a defense of indigenous peoples who resist the impositions of Islam and Christianity. But this is not a clear-cut socialist allegory in which "the people" are both innocent and heroic. Both of these monotheistic religions were of course historically associated with slave trading, and each justified the enslavement of "pagans." Sembene makes that clear in *Ceddo*. But he also shows that those who refused both religions, remaining faithful to their "fetishes," also traded in slaves. Historically, *ceddo* status bears a complex relation to slavery. *Ceddo* were originally crown slaves, then became "an aristocratic class of professional warriors."[32] Earlier in this study, in the chapter on Roger's *Kelédor*, we saw an example of a secular *ceddo* regime of the late eighteenth century, that of the Damel of Cayor, Amari Ndeela. In Senegalese national culture the *ceddo* have become symbols of fierce independence, "repositories of the ideals and the ethics of a people," and "legendary heroes."[33] Sembene's own home in Dakar bears the legend "Galle Ceddo," the house of the *ceddo*.[34] But *ceddo* remain ambiguous figures, heroes with feet of clay, prone to slave trading and alcohol by some accounts.[35] The *ceddo* in the film, as we will see, hold slaves and trade in slaves: these "outsiders" are not outside the African system of slavery, and their purpose is not to resist slavery per se. So how can this film be, as the novelist Ayi Kwei Armah calls it, "an exquisitely framed meditation on the theme of liberation"?[36] Liberation for whom?

373

The film is built around the premise that the *ceddo* want to resist enslavement — their own enslavement. Yet when they decide to oppose Islam through armed combat, they are faced with a momentous decision that has been largely ignored by critics: whether or not to sell their own families as chattel to the white slave trader in exchange for the guns they need. The scene in which this decision is made is long and portentous; the link between resistance to Islam and involvement with the slave trade is carefully examined. The choices available to the *ceddo* are identified as:

1   conversion to Islam
2   selling their families as slaves in exchange for guns
3   exile.

Some in this (all-male) council opt for conversion and leave the meeting. One man offers moral hesitations: "Sacrificing one's children so as to survive oneself, that is a hard test for a father." The white man and the nobles are both deplored as "ticks feeding on our blood." But the second option is followed by the majority, one of whom says, "We will proceed as follows: one adolescent, one girl, for one rifle and powder; one adult for two rifles and powder" (see figure 16). Only one man fully opts out of the slave system on behalf of his community, which is called Seneen; they will go into exile so that they may neither be nor have slaves. The decision is made by a vote of the remaining *ceddo*. The leader concludes the council by setting a meeting time for that night, "with our families" — to sell them. Thus the scene chillingly concludes. Sembene has dramatized an answer to a question that I took from Patrick Manning earlier in this study: what would it have been like to live in a place where every person, including one's own family, was a potential object of commerce?

Sembene chose not to depict what happens the next day: the sale of those family members. If he had, the center of gravity of the film might have shifted away from the liberation (of some) and toward its cost, the enslavement (of others); resistance to Islam might not be the perceived subject of the film, and the *ceddo* might no longer be plausible figures of liberation. As it is, the subtext of *Ceddo* that is concerned with slavery and the slave trade stands as a warning about the cost of freedom.[37] That warning is, however, partially *silent* and must be inferred by the viewer, who is nonetheless given ample means to do so.[38] The film cuts away to show the war that was made possible only by the sale of family members, a sale that remains unseen. In that cut the boundary between silence and disclosure can be detected. As Mamadou Diouf puts it, *Ceddo* "leaks noise."[39] Slavery is not a guilty secret in this film: Sembene invites the viewer to look this price of "independence" in the face and to see some, but not all, of its consequences.

Sembene's vision of Sahelian history in *Ceddo* can be compared to Yambo Ouologuem's in his infamous novel of 1968, *Le Devoir de violence* (*Bound to Violence*). Both convey a radically antiromantic vision: an Africa ruled by "fire and blood," in which "conflict is endemic."[40] Slaving is central to the novel and to the film, both of which locate slave trading at the violent intersection of West Africa's "triple heritage," where ancient indigenous cultures entered into contact with Islam and Christianity. Yet *Bound to Violence* says out loud some things that *Ceddo* either implies or does not include:

16 The ceddo decide to sell their families: "One adult for two rifles and some powder . . ." From Ousmane Sembene's *Ceddo*.

To maintain this ostentation and satisfy his craving for glory and new lands, Saïf [the ruler of a fictive African empire], thanks to the complicity of the southern chiefs, accelerated the slave trade, which he blessed like the blood-thirsty hypocrite he was [*en sanguinaire doucereux*]. Amidst the diabolical jubilation of priest and merchant, of family circles and public spheres, Negroes—who unlike God have arms but no soul—were clubbed, sold, stockpiled, haggled over, adjudicated, flogged, bound and delivered, with attentive, studied, sorrowful contempt, to the Portuguese, the Spaniards, the Arabs (on the east and north coasts), and to the French, Dutch, and English (west coast), and so scattered to the winds.[41]

Ouologuem goes on to describe the Middle Passage as "the Christian incognito of ships' holds" [*l'incognito chrétien de l'entrepont*] and life at its other end as "nameless suffering" (12). But his novel, like *Ceddo*, soon turns its attention elsewhere, since it is concerned with the slave trade only as a foreshadowing of modern colonialism. *Ceddo* and *Bound to Violence* devote limited but crucial and revolutionary attention to the slave trade inside Africa.

THE ETHIC OF SILENCE

A rapid discussion of three films, one from each point on the Atlantic triangle, will serve to end this chapter and this book.[42] The word *from* is of course an oversimplification. Cinema, especially cinema that speaks for the less wealthy places on Earth, is an international endeavor. Sembene's films are certainly African, though his financial backing comes from multiple sources in Europe. (It is often said, half jokingly, that the credits of an African film have to be as long as the movie itself, because there are so many people to

375

thank—and only thanks to give them.)[43] The three films that I want to discuss here are all international in some sense and are all concerned with the slave trade. *Le Courage des autres* (*The Courage of Others*, 1983) was filmed in Burkina Faso by a French director who was working there, teaching at a film institute. Starring a young Sotigui Kouyaté (now one of the most recognizable faces in African cinema, seen in *Kéita: L'Héritage des griots*, *Little Senegal*, and many other films), *Le Courage des autres* was written by Christian Richard. It is, to this day, the only film directed by a Frenchman "that has been produced entirely by an African country!"[44] Is this a "French" film because of the passport of its director, or is it something else because of its sponsorship by an African state—something more hybrid? To the extent that it is French, it is the *only* serious French film ever devoted to the slave trade, the only oasis in a vast "desert" of silence.[45] Until recently, it could be seen only by appointment at a specialized cinematheque in Paris.[46] *Passage du milieu* (*The Middle Passage*, 1999) is French according to the passports of both its director, Guy Deslauriers, and its screenwriter, the novelist Patrick Chamoiseau. But both are from Martinique, which is to say France but not France. Roger Gnoan M'Bala's film *Adanggaman* (2000) was written and directed by Ivorians but was coproduced by entities from Côte d'Ivoire, France, Switzerland, and Burkina Faso, with some of its seven-million French franc budget coming from the French ministry of foreign affairs.[47] I don't intend to parse the national status of these films; the point is the diasporic, Atlantic provenance of each. Discussing films automatically makes this chapter on "African silence" intercontinental, taking us around the Atlantic triangle again.

Both *Le Courage des autres* and *Adanggaman* provoked intense controversy when they were released, for one simple reason. They broke an ethic of silence on African participation in the slave trade. I call this an "ethic" of silence because those who wish to enforce it do so more out of a moral concern than out of a sense of being offended. Their concern is that *any* attention to African complicity in the slave trade will distract from what should be the main focus: European profiteering and European responsibility; if Africans are seen as partially responsible, they fear there can be no discussion of European guilt whatsoever.[48] This is a faulty premise; clearly, if the truths of the slave trade are to be faced, there must be room for a careful assessment of actions taken and not taken in all sectors of the Atlantic triangle. The three films in question here—like their predecessors, the works

376

of Sembene that we just examined—all disrupt the ethic of silence. But in doing so, they, like Sembene, use silence as a tool.

The controversial nature of *Le Courage des autres* and *Adanggaman* was heightened by one provocative fact: in both films no white person is seen. The slave trade is visualized entirely as a black-on-black crime, even though the force of the Atlantic trade is felt and occasionally discussed (quite explicitly in *Adanggaman*). By leaving white faces out, these two films add fuel to the fire and invite the kind of dissent that they have received, for they may—inaccurately, in my view—be seen as absolving European responsibility.

↠⌖↞

Le Courage des autres is practically a silent film. The sound is live and synchronous, but barely a phrase is spoken. This approach bears a remarkable resemblance to the one used by Guy Deslauriers in *The Middle Passage*, where there is a complete absence of live speech: no character speaks on camera; a voice-over narration is the only speech that is heard.[49] But *Le Courage des autres* does not even have a voice-over. Practicalities may partially account for this silence: with almost no language being spoken, there is no language barrier, no need for subtitles or dubbing, and no obstacles for those who don't read. For a film made on a shoestring budget, this is an advantage. The images and actions must speak for themselves. But (unprompted by me) Christian Richard has explained his technique in the following terms, which situate his film perfectly within the theme of this chapter: "As I was writing the scenario, I deliberately chose to leave dialogue out and to leave room for silences: the silent humiliation and submission of the captured slaves; the silence of the slave-drivers and of their violence; and finally the silence of the African landscape where the drama takes place."[50] In *The Middle Passage*, the restriction of speech to an extradiegetic narrator facilitated the film's adaptation to other languages and paved the way for its broadcast on HBO in the United States. In both cases a certain silence seems to have made it possible to tell a story of the slave trade.

In the opening frames of *Le Courage des autres* three old men watch impassively as an escaped captive is gunned down by slave traders. Vultures circle overhead. The film's title appears; the need for courage is already apparent. Scenes of pillaging and enslavement follow: Africans gathering and marching other Africans toward, we assume, the unseen Middle Passage.

377

The character played by Sotigui Kouyaté is captured and shackled to another man, a handsome young village chief who becomes his friend and
silent interlocutor. The caravan advances across the barren landscape; as
captives die, they are cut loose from their chains. Kouyaté's eyes have a far-
away, visionary cast, even as his fellow captives sleep. He is stung by a scor-
pion, passes out, and is abandoned. Cared for by strangers, he recovers and
sets off on horseback in pursuit of the slave coffle. His powers as a sorcerer
are now revealed, as he manipulates thunder and scorpions and kills three
slave traders. He enables the chief to lead a revolt among the captives, who
escape. As the film concludes, the mysterious sorcerer hands a bronze scor-
pion — a symbol of resistance to enslavement — to his friend. This description cannot give a sense of the film's power, which derives from its purely
visual language and from the acting skills of Sotigui Kouyaté. In the vast
space of the Sahel, this film tells a tale that can be compared to traditional
West African epics like *Sunjata*: in both cases adversity must be overcome.
But *Le Courage des autres* took the brazen step of placing slavery — a scant
but clearly readable subtext in the epics[51] — at the center of its concerns,
thus representing the courage of those enslaved rather than the heroism of
the dynastic rulers, nearly all of them *esclavagistes*.

378

→−←

The critique of power that is implicit in *Le Courage des autres* is pressed
into highly explicit form by Roger Gnoan M'Bala in *Adanggaman*, which he
describes as "pure fiction coming from an endogenous point of view." His
purpose is to expose "that essential link between slavery and power"; he
insists on the liberty of fiction while admitting that he included "winks" to
African rulers like Samory and King Béhanzin of Dahomey (although Agaja
seems even more relevant). To do this, Gnoan M'Bala says, is to interrupt an
enormous silence concerning Africa's relation to slavery, because "the griots and the epics [*les grands récits*] erase it systematically," in an act of "purposeful . . . forgetfulness."[52] The silence and forgetting are of course not
limited to Africa. Thus the *New York Times* reviewer found that the images
of Africans enslaving other Africans in *Adanggaman* were so "rare" as to
be "a shock and [to] linger in your mind for days afterward."[53] The general
taboo on representing the slave trade in the French Atlantic may take its
purest form in Africa, as the reception of *Adanggaman* demonstrates. When
the film was finally screened in Côte d'Ivoire in 2002, some viewers were reportedly ready to "lynch the director."[54] Clearly Gnoan M'Bala's interven-

tion, designed to fill in the image deficit that the *New York Times* reviewer felt, has not been a smooth process.

Set "somewhere in Africa" at the end of the seventeenth century, *Adanggaman*, like *Ceddo* and *Le Courage des autres* before it, begins with images of Africans enslaving Africans. In a gripping sequence a captive struggles as he is entangled in nets, shackled and muzzled, while he protests: "I am not a slave. I am as free as my heart."[55] After the credits the scene shifts to a village, where a young man and woman flirt. In a transgressive move, the young man, a hunter named Ossei (Honoré Gooré Bi Ziablé), wants to marry a slave girl. He is brutally refused by his father: "The bad blood of that slave will not tarnish our noble blood." The village is raided and burned by Amazon soldiers of a neighboring king, Adanggaman (Rasmane Ouedraogo). Ossei's father and girlfriend are killed, and his mother, Mô Akassi (Albertine N'Guessan, in an outstanding performance), is enslaved. Ossei sets off in pursuit of the slave caravan to rescue her; he must elude a violent Amazon who tries to kill him along the way. Meanwhile, King Adanggaman demands fealty and tribute from his subject chiefs: "Only Adanggaman captures slaves, sells them and buys them." He inspects his captives, baring their teeth; he drinks from a cask of rum marked "Liverpool" and finds it unsatisfactory. With delightful impudence, Mô Akassi delivers an eloquent speech in the king's face: "You are insatiable, for gold, injustice, slaves. Who are you to suppress the lives and freedom of others? Pretending you have the power over life and death [as alluded to in both *Hérémakhonon* and *Ceddo*] by selling human lives! . . . You monkey around with the Whites for rum and guns. . . . You sell your own flesh and blood. You are selling your soul." Ossei encounters a helper who explains that the strongest captives are set aside for "the dreaded voyage across the ocean. The weaker who would never survive are sold to rich locals." Ossei wants to take his mother's place, thus to volunteer knowingly for the Middle Passage. The helper, Sory (Soro Zié), throws cowry shells to divine the future: "The death traders will get richer. . . . We will suffer a humiliation which no other people has known. Despair weaves an immense web around our lives. Here we are again, thrown into the depths of horror." Defying this fate, Ossei presents himself to Adanggaman and offers his freedom in exchange for his mother's. The king replies glibly, echoing European slave traders of the eighteenth century, "You cannot bargain with a freedom you do not have." Adanggaman is a caricature of power, declaring himself to be "the only voice" and "the law." Ossei will be sold to the Dutch.

379

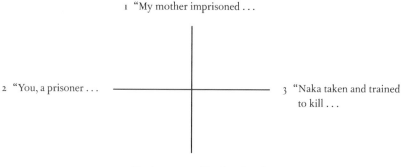

1 "My mother imprisoned . . .

2 "You, a prisoner . . .   3 "Naka taken and trained
                                              to kill . . .

4 "And me, your friend, a slave."

17   *Adanggaman*: The crossroads at which Ossei and Sory meet.

The plot, which has been a straight line so far, now reaches a crossroads. Sory's daughter, it turns out, is the same violent Amazon who pursued Ossei earlier. The daughter, Naka (Mylène-Perside Boti Kouamé), was taken away by slave hunters fifteen years earlier, when she was seven, and made into an Amazon.[56] (Female warriors were a hallmark of the kingdom of Dahomey under Agaja and his successors.)[57] Ossei draws in the sand "this odd crossroads" that has brought him and Sory together (see figure 17).

These two axes, each reflecting the havoc wreaked by the slave trade inside Africa, will come together in the film's idealized dénouement, as Ossei and Naka fall in love. After Sory dies, Naka, with "a cry of revolt," renounces her life as an Amazon in the service of the slave trade and frees Ossei. They set off together seeking "freedom and happiness." They live a brief idyll before being attacked and captured by Amazons, who tell Ossei, "You are a slave and always will be."

The film ends with a voice-over epilogue—spoken in Baule with a printed text in French—that puts a familiar twist on this innovative story of the slave trade: the tables are turned; Adanggaman is enslaved. In the symbolic year of 1685 (the year of the Code Noir), the king is sold by one of his own courtiers. Renamed Walter Brown, he dies a few years later at "Saint-Louis" (Missouri?), where he was a cook, of tuberculosis—an obvious allusion to Tamango.[58] Ossei, however, is shipped across the Atlantic and survives as "John Stanford," the slave of a rich planter in the American South; married with children, he lives to the age of seventy "without ever regaining his status as a free man." The words of this epilogue zoom the film out of Africa and across the Atlantic, supplying the perspective that some

380

(wrongly) find lacking in Gnoan M'Bala's approach. He represents the slave trade in Africa as closely and explicitly linked to the Atlantic and its economy: what happens in Africa is not caused entirely by Africans and does not stay in Africa. Thus it is significant that, as the epilogue is recited, the background is a sweeping pan of the Atlantic as seen from the shore. This film looks at Africa with a critical eye, then looks beyond. I would compare this last movement of the camera in *Adanggaman* to the sweeping, circum-Atlantic scan that ended Césaire's *Cahier*, the gesture of veerition.

→ ← ←

The Middle Passage begins where *Adanggaman* leaves off, on an Atlantic shore, but this time on the opposite side, as a modern boy looks out from a Caribbean shore. Then the narrator takes us back to his time, to Africa in the early nineteenth century. The film will then launch us across the Atlantic (one last time).[59] If Condé's *Hérémakhonon* is the anti-*Roots*, Deslauriers's *The Middle Passage* is the anti-*Amistad*. It breaks away from the Hollywood conventions of Spielberg's film in everything from its use of sound (as I discussed above) to its absence of individuated characters. But if there is one characteristic that most sets this film apart, it is its unrelenting, punishing tone. No easy redemption is offered; no white heroes intervene on behalf of the slaves as a sop to the viewer's conscience. Djimon Hounsou's voice-over narration (the English version written by Walter Mosely) is like a dirge, ponderous and devastating.[60]

Deslauriers has defined *The Middle Passage* as a "docu-fiction," "combining a documentary story-line with a fictional story-line," thus adding drama to "reality." The film is "a story that comes from the hold [*la cale*]. It is the omniscient story of a slave and the reconstitution of scenes viewed from the hold." The result is "a progressive descent into hell." The maritime scenes were filmed onboard an old sailing ship that was taking children on a re-creation of the triangular voyage from Nantes to Gorée to the Antilles and back to Nantes. The ship's hold was reconstructed on Martinique and is supposed to become a central exhibit in a new museum of slavery.[61] *The Middle Passage* produced images barely seen on film since Berry's *Tamango*, bringing the French slave trade back to cinematographic life.

It is interesting that *The Middle Passage*, although it puts considerable blame on Africa, has not been nearly as controversial as *Le Courage des autres* and *Adanggaman*. The narrator says that "Agaja, the king of Dahomey, sold me to the French," thus taking us back to Dahomey and to the king

381

that was mentioned numerous times in *Hérémakhonon*. *The Middle Passage* identifies Agaja as a seller of his fellow Africans but within a larger system of exploitation. Against images of a burning village that resemble those in *Ceddo* and *Le Courage des autres*, the narrator explains, "My story is not only of a slave ship, but also of a land that is surrendering its own children to the four winds. . . . Abduction was instituted as an economic system to satisfy the slave traders' appetite for human flesh." He also deplores the forgetfulness of succeeding generations of Africans: "We have already begun to fade in the memory of Africa. This is our greatest loss. Soon we will cease to exist in the minds and hearts of our people. . . . King Agaja, you are the symbol of our demise, our ancestral traditions violated by the slave trade. . . . The kings of Africa betrayed their people and their continent."

The use of sound in *The Middle Passage* produces a number of paradoxes. When the film wants to represent the Césairian "cry" from the depths of the ship's hold—which in film could be *presented* through synchronized image and sound—instead it *represents* that cry: the narrator *tells* the viewer that "a great cry rose up throughout the hold." But what we see and hear don't fit together neatly. The captives shake their chains, and we hear the (post-synchronous) noise of chains rattling; we see an open mouth, but we hear no cry. The actual cry remains unvoiced, unrecorded. The moving figures on the screen remain silent. The reviewer for *Le Monde* saw this technique as "a defeat of the image by the word," in a film that has a hard time going beyond the status of "illustrated text." This critique is not unreasonable, especially within the context that the reviewer recognizes: a deplorable absence of the slave trade in "the visual memory of mankind," a "void" that Deslauriers tries to fill, by "showing the unshowable," as best he can, with limited resources.[62] Image and sound thus remain estranged in *The Middle Passage*, and the voice-over dominates. Deslauriers and Chamoiseau, who wrote the film together, chose "not to try to say everything" about slavery.[63] In a promotional interview with HBO Deslauriers said that his subject was "still taboo."

The Middle Passage, like Glissant's *Sartorius*, bears a peculiar relation to history. Deslauriers says that Chamoiseau "did not want to rely exclusively on his own imagination; [he also wanted to make use of] exact facts: thus [they did] significant archival research on the slave trade, especially at Nantes, where we found the necessary material." The film is set in the early nineteenth century, the classic period for representations of the French slave trade, on which a good amount of documentation is available. Why, then, did the authors of the film not stick closer to historicity, using a real and documented slaving voyage, for example, as the basis of their story? A truly historical film — telling, for example, the story of *La Vigilante* — is something that the world needs; but perhaps that would cost more than the market is willing to provide. Films translate funding into narratives, making the best of the resources that are available. Deslauriers could not make (and probably did not want to make) a full costume drama, a *Master and Commander* of the slave trade. In order to maximize the impact of his film, he thus veers away from narrow historical specificity, toward something more general: instead of naming a particular ship, the narrator refers to "many such ships," with names *like "La Fortuna, The Queen of Angels, The Grand Duke, The Saint Anne*, and *The King of Dahomey."*

The film quickly leaves the African shore and begins its depiction of the Middle Passage, which unfolds as an unspeakable horror. *The Middle Passage* probably goes further than any other film in its attempt to represent the full horror of this subject. The treatment of the captives is close to genocidal. Half of the captives die during the crossing; many are thrown overboard when they fall sick. Seventeen captives commit suicide in the hold. A revolt is mounted, but fails, and many are killed. In any case, "none of us knew how to navigate their vessel."[64]

Statements made about Agaja at the end of the film veer *The Middle Passage* away from its partial documentary status, taking it into pure fiction, in a way that is somewhat troubling. "Today the Middle Passage is abandoned," says the narrator, "but its waters remain cursed. Take King Agaja of Dahomey, who was *carried across into slavery after he was forced to abdicate by the French"* (emphasis added). Djimon Hounsou, who is from the former Dahomey (Bénin), by way of explaining how much he learned from the film, says in a promotional interview with HBO, "one of my kings [Agaja] was also enslaved." No he wasn't. What Deslauriers and Chamoiseau seem to have done here is to conflate Agaja (who died in 1732) with his distant successor Béhanzin, who in 1894 was forced into *exile* (not slavery) in Martinique by the French — precisely the subject of another film by Deslauriers, *L'Exil du roi Béhanzin* (1994, also with a screenplay by Patrick Chamoiseau). It is hard to see how *The Middle Passage* benefited from this distortion of history. Why should the deficit of representations of the slave trade in the media be even partially filled by something that is patently false and mythological? Ahistoricity is, however, later turned to advantage at the film's end, as we see a modern cruise ship docked at a Caribbean shore, then steaming

383

away, as the same modern boy looks on: a reminder of ongoing inequalities expressed on the ocean, and a productive way to *not* "let the past be the past."

The last words of *The Middle Passage* harken back to the classic topos of French *littérature négrière*: the slave ship adrift: "Will justice ever be done? Until this dark history is brought to light, our world will be haunted by an ill-fated slave ship. On that ship, the crew is not made up of European sailors but of bushy-haired Negroes, raising their broken chains to the sky. With no knowledge of sailing, they roam endlessly on the ocean of our eternal night." The echoes of *Tamango* here are heavily mediated by the spirit of the *Cahier*. As in that poem, the fact of being adrift is embraced as a paradoxical sign of hope. The roaming, scanning motion of the revolted slaves is also an ascent into blackness, the promise of a new life.

→><←

In each of the four films seen in this chapter, there has been some deflection, some partial turning away from a complete and fully "realistic," fully historical representation of the slave trade and the Middle Passage. A certain silence has lingered, even as its dimensions are reduced and reshaped by these works of art. The full measure of the captives' experience can of course not be represented; what is interesting is how each director has built that impossibility into the structure of his work.

CONCLUSION
RECKONING, REPARATION, AND
THE VALUE OF FICTIONS

It is both usual and imperative to end studies of the slave trade by pointing out that slavery and human trafficking persist in the modern and post-modern world. At the end of part 3 of this book I indicated briefly how systems of forced labor and coerced migration morphed, but did not disappear, with the end of the French Atlantic slave trade. In our times uncounted numbers of people around the globe remain in various forms of servitude.[1]

As I worked to conclude this book, a "memory war" about the slave trade and colonialism simmered in France. Right-wing politicians had passed a law in 2004 that mandated a "positive" representation of French colonialism in schoolbooks. An attempt by the socialists to repeal this law failed in the fall of 2005; a poll found that two out of three French citizens approved of it.[2] The debate was renewed for a time. Arguments made by the neoconservative writer and politician Max Gallo shed light on the ideas behind this law. In an essay published in *Le Figaro* he contended that history and memory are not the same; that identity politics based on a revival of colonial memory threatens the very substance of the Republic and the integrity of "national history." Bad memories should not be revived because they might "establish communities hostile to the Republic in function of [the] colonial past." Forget memories, he implies, if they are not good for the universal, unitary state. Why wallow in "penitence"?[3] This was written after Paris (the suburbs, that is) had already burned in the riots of 2005; the colonial past had already come home to roost. The bankruptcy of Gallo's argument — which is merely the old wine of colonial assimilationism in new bottles — is now more evident than ever.

Meanwhile, elements of the left attacked someone who should be their own ally. The historian who has arguably done more to advance awareness of the French slave trade than any other in recent years, Olivier Pétré-Grenouilleau, was sued in November for having claimed in an interview that "the slave trades were not genocides."[4] Redounding through the echo chamber of the Internet, much of the outrage was justified, since the remark appeared to minimize the horror of the trade; yet some of the reaction seemed to come from the shock felt by readers of French who were learning for the first time, through Pétré-Grenouilleau's book *Les Traites négrières*, about research on slavery that had been widely circulated and accepted in the English-speaking world, and even among specialists in France, for some time.[5]

"Memory wars" take place when the past and the present cannot be reconciled. The French consensus on the slave trade consisted mostly of silence. The law passed in 2001 recognizing slavery and the slave trade as crimes against humanity marked a turning point. This act was followed by the establishment of the committee on memory, Le Comité pour la Mémoire de l'Esclavage, chaired by Maryse Condé. In its 2005 report the committee outlined a program for "historical reparation"—for the repairing of France's amnesia about its past as a "great enslaving power" (*une grande puissance esclavagiste*).[6] One day a year—the choice of which was highly controversial—will be reserved for commemoration (the first one was observed on May 10, 2006); an inventory will be made of all materials related to slavery and the slave trade; research and scholarship will be encouraged. Unfortunately the committee did not call for the one thing that is most glaringly needed in France: a comprehensive national museum of slavery and the slave trade, located on the soil of the "hexagon," in Paris, Nantes, or Bordeaux. Such a museum might finally achieve—long after the fact—the abolitionists' goal, making the reality of slavery and the slave trade visible inside France. A large memorial project is in fact now planned for the quays of Nantes, to be completed in 2009, and space in the city's renovated museum is now devoted to the slave trade.[7] Edouard Glissant chairs a commission dedicated to the establishment of a research center on slavery and the slave trade.[8]

As a result of the heated debate in December 2005, the prime minister of France found it in his vocabulary to speak of the slave trade, and the president of the Republic called for a commission on colonial memory so that "minds might be calmed."[9] The consensus of silence now seems to have been shattered (or perhaps merely interrupted); one can hope for a wave of reforms, perhaps based on the recommendations of the Condé committee. But that will only happen if France can finally get over a hurdle that it has never passed before, the obstacle that Françoise Vergès describes as France's "inability to integrate its colonial past [including slavery and the slave trade] into its national past." Gallo's remarks make clear that resistance to that integration is resolute, couched as it is in a defense of French universalism. But the need to recognize the colonial past is, Vergès says, a "test" for the Republic.[10] Celebrations of the admirable values of the Republic must be alloyed with explicit acts of recognition and reckoning. Projects now under way, including permanent museum exhibits and memorials, may finally bring the face of slavery and the slave trade into French consciousness for the first time since the abolitionist movement.[11] Or, plausibly, such displays may be deemed "divisive," and silence will return and prevail.

This book has concerned itself with the past. By reading history, literature, and film, I have attempted to reckon with and to recognize the past. I believe that such accounting should be one element in a wider process of redress; but I fear that the past, unlike the present, cannot be "repaired." As Aimé Césaire said in 2004, "The term 'reparation' . . . implies that there can be reparation. . . . For me, [the past] is irreparable."[12] Only our representations and readings of the past can be changed. Thus when Condé's committee on memory called for "historical reparation," it sought the repairing of France's most significant *lieu d'oubli*. In this book I have tried to read and interpret certain holes and distortions in the representations of the French slave trade and to foreground the importance of the trade in places where it has been forgotten or repressed. We have seen that the boundaries between silence and disclosure, between forgetfulness and memory, are not always what they appear to be. And we have seen the astounding abilities of certain authors and filmmakers to alter those boundaries. In their creativity lies the hope for justice. What can be done with the past? These authors and filmmakers offer exemplary answers to that question.

But what about reparations in the more concrete sense?[13] What is wrong with some approaches to the question of reparations is the idea that the past provides a just prescription for the present, that an accurate reading of historical wrongs will necessarily lead to justice in our times. But what if it does not? What if, as the record shows, some Africans traded other Africans into the Atlantic slave market?[14] Does that mean that a *lesser* measure of economic justice is now due to Africa? Or none at all? Who could establish the algorithm that would derive genuine justice in the present out of the injustice of the past?[15] No: the past is not a perfect allegory or template for the present; time and space can't be collapsed. We should indeed "let the past be the past," and read it as such. We shouldn't demand that representations of the past conform to the needs of the present. Otherwise, disputes about the interpretation of the past will filibuster the urgent, *current* needs of the African continent, of the former slave colonies (including Haiti), and of the immigrant communities in France.

As Maryse Condé's Véronica finds out, we are not our ancestors. Like her, even with full cognizance of history, we are "forced to choose" between the past and the present. Thirty years after she wrote *Hérémakhonon*, in her new capacity as chair of the Committee for the Memory of Slavery, the same Maryse Condé called for a "historical reparation" of memory. Does this reflect either a contradiction or a change of heart about the past on Condé's part? Neither, I think. The repair that she now calls for is a simple and accurate recognition of the past as the past. Even Véronica might agree with that.

388   I do not mean to advocate barriers between past and present—quite the opposite. Lucidly, we should see both, and we should find new ways to shuttle between the two, like Sembene's camera in *Ceddo* and Véronica's stream of consciousness in *Hérémakhonon*. The best we can hope to do, faced with a past that is both horrid and distant, is—to use a phrase from a recent novel by Tierno Monénembo—*rafistoler la mémoire*: to repair memory in a rough sort of way, to patch it together as best one can—with the realization that it will probably fall apart again.[16] That practice is exactly what we have seen in the works of Césaire, Condé, Glissant, Sembene, Gnoan M'Bala, Laurent Valère, and others. Even the perverse, rough "justice" of Sue's *Atar-Gull* and the gothic, "adventurous" horror of Mérimée's "Tamango" and Corbière's *Le Négrier* can add immeasurably to contemporary discussions of the past. In Gouges's plays and in the shadows of Staël's *Histoire de Pauline* are the early flickerings of some post/colonial reckoning. In short, literature and film need to be part of any debate about the slave trade, precisely because of the ambiguities and refractions that they project.

The dearth of contemporary French "hexagonal" literature and film devoted to slavery and the slave trade remains a problem. The absence of the deeply thought reflections that such works can offer impoverishes debate and exacerbates the "memory wars." Also, if the works of the past like those studied in this book were more commonly taught and discussed in France, they might contribute to a broader and more nuanced discussion. Instead, *Ourika*, for example, is far better known in the United States than in France. An encapsulation of the problem in contemporary France: the article on the triangular commerce and the slave trade in the French version of the online encyclopedia *Wikipédia* listed only one work of fiction in its bibliography, François Bourgeon's *Bande dessinée Les Passagers du vent*.[17]

For my part, I wish someone could "commission" first-rate French novels and films related to the slave trade: such works might do more for the promotion of memory than all the rest combined. With dozens of clever French novelists practicing their craft these days, sometimes rewriting literary classics from a different point of view (like that of "Mademoiselle Bovary," Emma's daughter, in two different novels), why can't they turn their talents to the undertold stories of the slave trade? Numerous real events and fictitious characters deserve the kind of attention that fine literature and film — creative *fictions* — can provide:

> The true and tragic stories of *La Jeune Estelle* and *La Vigilante*
>
> A fictive life of the enslaved African character Fraïda in Corbière's *Le Négrier*, her life with Léonard in Martinique (if she survived)
>
> A parallel-universe Ourika who was *not* purchased by the Chevalier de Boufflers but instead made the Middle Passage and lived through the Haitian Revolution

389

What is lacking in France is the equivalent of a Barry Unsworth, whose *Sacred Hunger*, through the power of literature, makes the involvement of Liverpool in the Atlantic slave trade (fictively) real and compelling.[18] As long as the slave trade remains the "responsibility" only of those descended from slaves — as long as only Caribbean writers like Glissant care enough to write about it — a problem will remain, and the heritage of the French Atlantic triangle will be continuing inequality and a failure of reckoning.

On May 10, 2007, the second annual day of commemoration of slavery and the slave trade in France, a statue was inaugurated in the Jardin du Luxembourg, near the Senate, by the outgoing president, Jacques Chirac. Entitled *Le cri, l'écrit* (The cry, the written), this sculpture by Fabrice Hyber brings the iconography of slavery and survival to the heart of the French capital in a small but new and significant way. The statue — like the Taubira Law of 2001, declaring slavery and the slave trade to be crimes against humanity — represents a genuine act of acknowledgment by the French state. Through initiatives like this one and others (such as programs in schools) propelled by the Committee for the Memory of Slavery, the slow but steady growth of a new public awareness of slavery and the slave trade can be anticipated in France—unless the newly elected president, Nicolas Sarkozy, successfully fulfills a campaign promise to *end* the era of "repentance."[19]

NOTES

PREFACE

1 See Farid Laroussi and Christopher L. Miller, editors' preface, in "French and Francophone: The Challenge of Expanding Horizons," special issue, *Yale French Studies* 103 (2003): 1–6. On the question of human "species" and its implications for abolitionism see chapter 6 of this volume.

2 Michaël Hajdenberg, "Esclavage: Bordeaux refuse de noircir son image," *Libération*, May 24, 2005, 16.

3 This myth was mentioned and discredited in an early work on the French slave trade, Emmanuel Bourcier's *Le Bois d'ébène* (Paris: Librairie des Champs-Elysées, 1934), 10–11. The historian cited by Hajdenberg, Eric Saugera, author of the definitive study on Bordeaux as a slave-trading city, documents the presence of African slaves there but says nothing about any captives "transiting" through French ports on their way to the Antilles. See Eric Saugera, *Bordeaux port négrier: Chronologie, économie, idéologie, XVIIe-XVIIIe siècles* (Paris: Karthala, 1995), 288–92.

4 See Pierre Nora, ed., *Les Lieux de mémoire*, 7 vols. (Paris: Gallimard, 1984). And see Marc Ferro, ed., *Le Livre noir du colonialisme: XVIe–XXIe siècle, de l'extermination à la repentance* (Paris: Robert Laffont, 2003), 103–131.

5 In this, France's memory of slavery is somewhat like that of the older northern states of the United States. Until recently these states thought of themselves as innocent of slavery and the slave trade; now a movement of renewed historiography has begun to change that misperception. The conference "Yale, New Haven, and American Slavery," organized by the Gilder Lehrman Center for the Study of Slavery, Resistance, and Abolition at Yale University, September 26–28, 2002, addressed this issue, as did the exhibit at the New York Historical Society, "Slavery in New York," October 7, 2005–March 5, 2006. But one fundamental difference remains between the northern U.S. states and France: there were "no slaves in France." On this theme see chapter 2. For a comprehensive overview of French perspectives on the slave trade see Françoise Vergès, "Les Troubles de mémoire: Traite négrière, esclavage et écriture de l'histoire," in *Cahiers d'études africaines* (forthcoming). The report issued by the Comité pour la mémoire de l'esclavage, of which Maryse Condé is

president and Vergès vice president, was a major event in the new movement toward collective memory in France. See www.comite-memoire-esclavage .fr and the published report, Comité pour la mémoire de l'esclavage, *Mémoires de la traite négrière, de l'esclavage et de leurs abolitions: Rapport à monsieur le premier ministre* (Paris: La Découverte, 2005).

1 INTRODUCTION

1 I had not seen the term "French Atlantic" anywhere in print before using it during the early stages of my work on this subject; since then, Bill Marshall has published work using the term. See his edited volume *France and the Americas: Culture, Politics, and History* (Santa Barbara: ABC-Clio, 2005). And see Kenneth J. Banks, *Chasing Empire across the Sea: Communications and the State in the French Atlantic, 1713–1763* (Montreal: Queen's University Press, 2002), which unfortunately neglects Africa in its conception of the French Atlantic.

2 See Charles Piot, "Atlantic Aporias: Africa and Gilroy's Black Atlantic," *South Atlantic Quarterly* 100, no. 1 (winter 2001): 168.

3 "Trafic triangulaire: trafic maritime et commercial opéré au XVIIe et surtout au XVIIIe siècle, principalement par les négriers des ports anglais et français de l'Atlantique" (*Grand Larousse* [1960]). The phrase "commerce circuiteux" is also used frequently. Explicit references to a triangle (named as such) in both French and English seem to begin only in the twentieth century. See Walter Minchinton, "The Triangular Trade Revisited," in *The Uncommon Market: Essays in the Economic History of the Atlantic Slave Trade*, ed. Henry A. Gemery and Jan S. Hogendorn (New York: Academic Press, 1979), 332–34.

4 Richard D. E. Burton demonstrates the power of "family images" in Martinique in his *La Famille coloniale: La Martinique et la mère patrie, 1789–1992* (Paris: L'Harmattan, 1994).

5 Aimé Césaire, quoted in annotations of his *Cahier d'un retour au pays natal*, 2nd ed., ed. Abiola Irele (Columbus: Ohio State University Press, 2000), 44.

6 Clayton Eshleman and Annette Smith say that Césaire revealed this etymology to them: Aimé Césaire, *The Collected Poetry*, trans. Clayton Eshleman and Annette Smith (Berkeley: University of California Press, 1983), 26. Irele cites the root as *vertere* in his edition of *Cahier d'un retour au pays natal*, 150.

7 In a similar, but more postmodern, gesture Edouard Glissant states that the slave trade "obliges the 'traded' population to call into question all ambitions for a generalizing universal" (*Le Discours antillais* [Paris: Seuil, 1981], 28).

8 See Fernand Braudel, *The Perspective of the World*, vol. 3 of *Civilization and Capitalism, 15th–18th Century*, trans. Siân Reynolds (New York: Harper and Row, 1984), 21–24.

9 Giovanni Arrighi, *The Long Twentieth Century: Money, Power, and the Origins of Our Times* (London: Verso, 1994), 52.

10 The passage from "Chaîne ou génération des événements" is in a context where Voltaire is commenting on the "système de la nécessité et de la fatalité ... inventé de nos jours par Leibnitz" (voc 18:126). This leads him into a discussion of interlocking circumstances surrounding the treaty of Utrecht, and then to the passage I have cited.

11 See Roger Mercier, *L'Afrique noire dans la littérature française: Les Premières images, XVIIe–XVIIIe siècles* (Dakar: Université de Dakar, Faculté des Lettres et des Sciences Humaines, 1962), 185. And see Arthur O. Lovejoy, *The Great Chain of Being: A Study of the History of an Idea* (Cambridge, Mass.: Harvard University Press, 1974).

12 Orlando Patterson, *Slavery and Social Death: A Comparative Study* (Cambridge, Mass.: Harvard University Press, 1982): viii–ix.

13 Jean-Jacques Rousseau, *Du contrat social* (1762; Paris: Garnier, 1975), 303.

14 Cowries were apparently in use in West Africa, but not as currency, before the Portuguese first brought them by ship in the sixteenth century; cowries immediately became associated with the slave trade and "in purely quantitative terms overshadow[ed] all other" forms of currency in that trade (Jan Hogendorn and Marion Johnson, *The Shell Money of the Slave Trade* [Cambridge: Cambridge University Press, 1986], 1, 106, 109). Cowries constituted "the most widespread currency zone" in Africa (Paul E. Lovejoy, "Slavery in the Context of Ideology," in *The Ideology of Slavery in Africa*, ed. Paul E. Lovejoy [Beverly Hills: Sage, 1981], 107). Jean-Baptiste Labat reported that cowries were "the primary and most important article" in the merchandise loaded into a slave-trading ship before its departure (Jean-Baptiste Labat, *Voyage du Chevalier des Marchais en Guinée, isles voisines, et à Cayenne, fait en 1725, 1726 & 1727* [Paris: Chez Saugrain, 1730], 1:30). On cowries see also Robert Harms, *The Diligent: A Voyage through the Worlds of the Slave Trade* (New York: Basic Books, 2002), 81.

393

15 See Patrick Manning, *Slavery and African Life: Occidental, Oriental, and African Slave Trades* (Cambridge: Cambridge University Press, 1990), 22; henceforth abbreviated *SAL*. See Boubacar Barry, *Senegambia and the Atlantic Slave Trade*, trans. Ayi Kwei Armah (Cambridge: Cambridge University Press, 1998), 117; henceforth abbreviated *SAST*. As for the United States, I grew up in an area of what was then rural New Jersey, never dreaming (nor being taught) that slavery had ever existed on the local farms. Recent work by a historian reveals that slaves and slavery were an integral and very significant part of the economy there, well into the nineteenth century. See Kenneth E. Marshall, "Work, Family, and Day-to-Day Survival on an Old Farm: Nance Melick, a Rural Late Eighteenth- and Early Nineteenth-Century New Jersey Slave Woman," *Slavery and Abolition* 19, no. 3 (1998): 22–45.

16 See *SAL*, 9–12, 20–22. One of the rare works to bring the various slave trades together, in a risky attempt to compare them, is Olivier Pétré-Grenouilleau, *La Traite des Noirs*, 2nd ed. (Paris: Presses Universitaires de France, 1997); henceforth abbreviated PG. Pétré-Grenouilleau greatly expanded on his

comparative work in his book *Les Traites négrières: Essai d'histoire globale* (Paris: Gallimard, 2004). A controversy exploded around Pétré-Grenouilleau in 2005 after he said in an interview that "the slave trades were not genocide" (interview by Christian Sauvage, "Un Prix pour *Les Traites négrières*," *Le Journal du Dimanche* 3049 [June 12, 2005]). For "contesting a crime against humanity" he was sued in French court, under the Taubira Law, by an association dedicated to the memory of slavery: Le Collectif des Antillais, Guyanais, et Réunionnais (see Didier Arnaud and Hervé Nathan, "Un Historien pour-suivi," *Libération*, November 30, 2005 (see www.collectifdom.com). The Col-lectif also sought to have Pétré-Grenouilleau suspended from his position as a professor, for "revisionism" (for an overview see Luc Daireaux, "L'Affaire Olivier Pétré-Grenouilleau: Élements de chronologie," www.clionautes .org/article.php3?id_article=925). The suit was dropped in February 2006. Pétré-Grenouilleau's remarks were poorly chosen and highly insensitive (he also accused descendants of slaves of "choosing among their ancestors"), but there is some irony in attempting to silence the historian who has probably done more to bring the history of the French slave trade to light than anyone before him. How much bearing the author's remarks in an interview have on the substance of his written work is a matter for debate. For a nuanced critique of *Les Traites négrières*, with attention to the pitfalls of comparing one trade to another, see Marcel Dorigny, "Traites négrières et esclavage: Les Enjeux d'un livre récent," *Hommes & libertés* 131 (July–September 2005): 51–53.

17 See Immanuel Wallerstein, *World-Systems Analysis: An Introduction* (Dur-ham: Duke University Press, 2004).

18 Ian Baucom, "Globalit, Inc.; or, The Cultural Logic of Global Literary Studies," *PMLA* 116, no. 1 (January 2001): 160.

19 Braudel, *The Perspective of the World*, 22.

20 François Renaud and Serge Daget, *Les Traites négrières en Afrique* (Paris: Karthala, 1985), 69.

21 See Joseph Roach, *Cities of the Dead: Circum-Atlantic Performance* (New York: Columbia University Press, 1996); Christopher L. Miller, *Nationalists and Nomads: Essays on Francophone African Literature and Culture* (Chicago: University of Chicago Press, 1998), 152–70.

22 Gilles Deleuze and Félix Guattari, *Anti-Oedipus: Capitalism and Schizophre-nia*, trans. Robert Hurley, Mark Seem, and Helen R. Lane (New York: Viking Press, 1977), 28.

23 See Judith Butler, *Subjects of Desire: Hegelian Reflections in Twentieth-Century France* (New York: Columbia University Press, 1999), 205.

24 I put quotation marks around the word *economy* here (just this once) to indi-cate that I make no promise to engage in any systematic way with the con-temporary discipline of economics. I have been informed by the economic analyses of the slave trade that I have read, but my use of the term *economy*

will usually adhere to one of these two more general definitions of economy taken from the *OED*: "7. The structure, arrangement, or proportion of parts, of any product of human design. 8. In wider sense: The organization, internal constitution, apportionment of functions, of any complex unity."

25 The *Trésor de la langue française*, s.v. *traite*, agrees with this etymology: "Subst. au fém. du part. passé de *traire*, 'tirer du lait.'" In the usage of slave traders, however, the verb *traiter* was often used to describe what they were doing: they would write, for example, of "les captifs que j'ai traités." See Abbé Demanet, *Nouvelle histoire de l'Afrique françoise* (Paris: Chez la Veuve Duchesne, 1767), 1:264: "je traitai moi-même un autre captif sans le secours des Interprétes." This common usage, no doubt stimulated by the similarity between *traiter* and *traite*, corresponds to another meaning of the verb *traiter*: to deal, buy or sell (*Dictionnaire de l'Académie Française*, 8th ed., 1932, s.v. *traiter*, "Entrer en négociation pour vendre, acheter, affermer, etc."). For perspective on the terms *traite* and *traite négrière* see Pétré-Grenouilleau, *Les Traites négrières*, 19–20.

26 Joseph A. Miller, "History and Slavery as Problems in Africa," David Brion Davis Lecture Series in the History of Slavery, Race, and Its Legacies, Yale University, February 8, 2005.

27 Jean Barbot, "Journal d'un voyage de traite en Guinée, à Cayenne et aux Antilles fait par Jean Barbot en 1678–1679," ed. Gabriel Debien, Maurice Delafosse, et G. Thilmans, *Bulletin de l'Institut Fondamental d'Afrique Noire* 40, no. 2 (April 1978): esp. 272–76. Barbot was a French Huguenot who became English in 1686 (238).

28 See Catherine Coquery-Vidrovitch, "The Colonial Economy of the Former French, Belgian, and Portuguese Zones, 1914–1935," in *General History of Africa*, vol. 7, *Africa under Colonial Domination, 1880–1935*, ed. A. Adu Boahen (Paris: UNESCO, 1985), 353.

29 One also sees the word *traite* used as a synonym for the slaves themselves: "fait danser la traite"; "notre traite, effrayée, se précipita dans la cale." These quotes are from a nineteenth-century log book kept by one P. Michaud on a voyage in 1821, quoted in Léon Vignols, "Une expédition négrière en 1821," *Revue de l'histoire des colonies françaises* 16 (May–June, 1928): 291, 299.

30 *Trade* in English used to have this meaning, according to the *OED*: "a course, way, path . . . the course trodden by a person, or followed by a ship." The term *trade winds* reflects this.

31 Ronald Findlay, "The 'Triangular Trade' and the Atlantic Economy of the Eighteenth Century: A Simple General-Equilibrium Model," Essays in International Finance, Department of Economics, Princeton University, no. 177 (March 1990): 20; Eric Saugera, "De Sidoine à Sophie Raphel ou les lettres d'un capitaine négrier à sa femme pendant la traite illégale, 1824–1831," in *La Dernière Traite*, ed. Hubert Gerbeau and Eric Saugera (Paris: Société Française d'Histoire d'Outre-Mer, 1994), 59–60; see Orlando Patterson, *Slavery*

and *Social Death: A Comparative Study* (Cambridge, Mass.: Harvard University Press, 1982), 162; and Herbert S. Klein, *The Atlantic Slave Trade* (Cambridge: Cambridge University Press, 1999), 71.

32 See Findlay, "The 'Triangular Trade' and the Atlantic Economy," 2.

33 Daget says there is good reason to think that Columbus took Africans to Hispaniola in 1493; see Serge Daget, *La Traite des Noirs: Bastilles négrières et velléités abolitionnistes* (Rennes: Editions Ouest-France Université, 1990), 36; henceforth abbreviated D. Hugh Thomas speculates on this but says there is no proof; see *The Slave Trade: The Story of the Atlantic Slave Trade, 1440–1870* (New York: Simon and Schuster, 1997), 87; henceforth abbreviated T.

34 W. E. B. Du Bois, *The World and Africa: An Inquiry into the Part Which Africa Has Played in World History* (New York: International Publishers, 1965), 44.

35 Arrighi, *The Long Twentieth Century*, 49.

36 Barbara L. Solow, "Slavery and Colonization," in *Slavery and the Rise of the Atlantic System*, ed. Barbara L. Solow (Cambridge: Cambridge University Press, 1991), 21.

37 Roach shows how, in "triangular encounters, at least one of the parties seems fated to disappear from the selective memory of another" (*Cities of the Dead*, 121). It is now recognized that the New World was far more heavily settled by Africans than by Europeans until the middle of the nineteenth century; see David Eltis, *The Rise of African Slavery in the Americas* (Cambridge: Cambridge University Press, 2000); henceforth abbreviated E. Eltis shows that slaves made up around 60 percent of all migrants between 1580 and 1700, then 75 percent from 1700 to 1760; "In the 1820's . . . , 90% of those coming across the Atlantic were African, not European" (11–12).

38 Eric Williams, "Economics, Not Racism, as the Root of Slavery," in *The Atlantic Slave Trade*, ed. David Northrup (Lexington, Mass.: D. C. Heath, 1994), 11.

39 On white servitude see ibid., 5–11; see also Winthrop Jordan, *White over Black: American Attitudes toward the Negro, 1550–1812* (New York: Norton, 1968). On white servitude in the French colonies see Robert Louis Stein, *The French Slave Trade in the Eighteenth Century: An Old Regime Business* (Madison: University of Wisconsin Press, 1979), 9–10; henceforth abbreviated S. And see Gabriel Debien, *Le Peuplement des Antilles françaises au XVIIe siècle: Les Engagés partis de La Rochelle* (Cairo: Les Presses de l'Institut français d'archéologie orientale du Caire, 1942).

40 Abdoulaye Ly, *La Compagnie du Sénégal* (Paris: Présence Africaine, 1958), 32–33, 42–43.

41 John Thornton, *Africa and Africans in the Making of the Atlantic World, 1400–1680* (Cambridge: Cambridge University Press, 1992), 6–7.

42 Arthur L. Stinchcombe, *Sugar Island Slavery in the Age of Enlightenment: The Political Economy of the Caribbean World* (Princeton: Princeton University Press, 1995), 67.

43 The Maréchal de Castries, secretary of the navy, wrote in 1784: "Il faut . . .

au moins trois cargaisons de sucre pour absorber les fonds d'une cargaison de Noirs" (quoted in Liliane Crété, *La Traite des nègres sous l'ancien régime: Le Nègre, le sucre et la toile* (Paris: Librairie Académique Perrin, 1989), 26, 29; henceforth abbreviated C. Harms says it took "the unused cargo space of approximately two direct trading voyages to carry back the excess sugar from a single slave trading voyage" (*The Diligent*, 75).

44 From the early days of the slave trade, the absence of cash was noted, and it was described as an advantage to traders by Jacques Savary, in *Le Parfait negociant* (Paris: Chez Jean Guignard fils, 1675), 136.

45 Lucien Peytraud, *L'Esclavage aux Antilles françaises avant 1789 d'après des documents inédits des archives coloniales* (Pointe-à-Pitre: Emile Désormeaux, 1973), 129.

46 Ibid., 180.

47 Olaudah Equiano, *The Interesting Narrative of the Life of Olaudah Equiano, or Gustavus Vassa, the African, Written by Himself* (New York: Norton, 2001), 36; henceforth abbreviated OE.

48 "At the time of the greatest extent of slavery and the slave trade, we must imagine a situation in which everybody knew the value, as a captive, of everyone he or she met. . . . People were forced to think of how much they could get for selling a neighbor, or [how] much they would pay to ransom a loved one" (*SAL*, 123).

49 Michel Jajolet de la Courbe, *Premier voyage du Sieur de La Courbe fait a la coste d'Afrique en 1685*, ed. P. Cultru (Paris: Edouard Champion, 1913), 126; William B. Cohen, *The French Encounter with Africans: White Response to Blacks, 1530–1880* (Bloomington: Indiana University Press, 1980), 38; henceforth abbreviated WC. Barbot's notes of a voyage from 1678 to 1679 report the sale of slaves to Guadeloupe at a price of five thousand pounds of sugar (Barbot, "Journal d'un voyage de traite en Guinée," 254).

50 Describing his experiences in Africa in the mid-eighteenth century, Pruneau de Pommegorge explains how highly certain purebred horses were valued in the Senegal River valley: "J'ai vu vendre un des ces chevaux à un roi négre; il le paya cent captifs, cent boeufs, & vingt chameaux" (Antoine Edme Pruneau de Pommegorge, *Description de la Nigritie par M. P. D. P.* (Amsterdam: Chez Maradan, 1789), 17. Boubacar Barry states that in the early years of the slave trade (the fifteenth to the seventeenth centuries), "what the people of Senegambia received in exchange [for slaves] was . . . horses, each horse being valued at between eight and fifteen slaves" (*SAST*, 40). Jean René Antoine Verdun de la Crenne reports in his *Voyage fait par ordre du roi en 1771 et 1772* (Paris: Imprimerie Royale, 1778) that a horse was worth six prime slaves (1:140).

51 Pierre Pluchon, *La Route des esclaves: Négriers et bois d'ébène au XVIIIe siècle* (Paris: Hachette, 1980), 147. On particular forms of cheating see Banks, *Chasing Empire across the Sea*, 178–79.

52 Jean-Baptiste Du Tertre, *Histoire générale des Antilles habitées par les Fran-*

çois (Paris: Thomas Iolly, 1667): "des jeunes gens engagez, qu'ils [merchants] vendoient aux habitans, pour les servir trois ans *comme des esclaves* . . . ce detestable negoce . . . leur faisant croire mille merveilles du pays, où ils les alloient reduire *a l'esclavage.* . . . ce detestable commerce" (2:464–65, 525; emphasis added). Olivier Pétré-Grenouilleau erroneously quotes this reference to "honteux commerce" as a condemnation of the African slave trade (*Les Traites négrières*, 72). On the African slave trade Du Tertre uses milder, though still critical, language: "Je ne scay ce que cette nation a fait; mais c'est assez que d'estre noir, pour estre pris, vendu, & engagé à une servitude facheuse qui dure toute une vie" (2:494). Despite this language (very much ahead of its time), Du Tertre agrees with the harsh treatment of black slaves, because they are "proud" and "arrogant" (2:465). On Du Tertre see Doris Garraway, *The Libertine Colony: Creolization in the Early French Caribbean* (Durham: Duke University Press, 2005), 49–56, 71–74, 119–29.

53 Quoted in Hubert Deschamps, *Histoire de la traite des Noirs de l'antiquité à nos jours* (Paris: Fayard, 1971), 78.

54 Paul Gilroy, *The Black Atlantic: Modernity and Double Consciousness* (Cambridge, Mass.: Harvard University Press 1993), 213.

55 This voyage is far from clear. Thomas does not cite any source (T, 153), and Alfonce's own *Voyages avantureux* (c. 1536) and *Cosmographie* (1544) describe no such itinerary. The first description published in French, of a voyage linking Africa to the New World, and therefore completing the Atlantic triangle, seems to be in André Thévet's *Les Singularités de la France antarctique* (1557). Having gone down the coast of Africa to the Cape of Good Hope, Thévet writes: "L'autre voie de notre grand cap tire à dextre pour aller à l'Amérique, laquelle nous suivîmes, accompagnés du vent qui nous fut fort bon et propice" (quoted in Frank Lestringant, *Le Brésil d'André Thévet: Les Singularités de la France antarctique [1557]*) (Paris: Editions Chandeigne, 1997), 106. Lestringant comments: "Il fallait une 'histoire-cadre' qui pût refermer la diversité de ces matériaux glanés sans ordre, un canevas spatial et chronologique en forme de récit de voyage *avec un aller par l'Afrique et un retour par les Indes Occidentales*" (21; emphasis added; see also 26). Thus the triangle was apparently written into Thévet's influential *Singularités* in order to make a good story, as part of an argument in support of France's colonial adventure in Brazil. On Alfonce's nationality see Roger Schlesinger and Arthur P. Stabler, *André Thevet's North America: A Sixteenth-Century View* (Kingston: McGill-Queen's University Press, 1986), xxviii, note.

56 See Deschamps, *Histoire de la traite des Noirs*, 62; Gabriel Debien, *Les Esclaves aux Antilles* (Basse Terre: Société d'histoire de la Guadeloupe, 1974), 252; and Eric Saugera, *La Traite des Noirs en 30 questions* (La Crèche: Geste Editions, 1998), 14. Thomas repeats the story, citing Labat as its only source (T, 452, 841n). See also Jérôme Gautheret, "Traites négrières, esclavage: Les Faits historique," *Le Monde*, January 10, 2006.

57 Montesquieu, *The Spirit of the Laws*, trans. Anne M. Cohler, Basia Caro-

lyn Miller, Harold Samuel Stone (Cambridge: Cambridge University Press, 1989), 249; Montesquieu, *Oeuvres complètes de Montesquieu*, ed. André Masson (Paris: Nagel, 1950), 1:329: "[Louis XIII] se fit une peine extrême de la loi qui rendoit esclaves les nègres de ses colonies; mais, quand on lui eut bien mis dans l'esprit que c'étoit la voie la plus sure pour les convertir, il y consentit."

58 On Labat see Pluchon, *La Route des esclaves*, 129, 152, 240; and Garraway, *The Libertine Colony*, esp. 97, 130–45. On his plagiarism see WC, 29. Labat's influence is revealed both by Montesquieu's reliance on him and by the forty-two citations of him in the *Encyclopédie* (counted using the ARTFL database).

59 Jean Baptiste Labat, *Nouveau voyage aux isles de l'Amérique* (Paris: Chez Guillaume Cavelier fils, 1722), 4:114. This volume, which can be downloaded from the BNF Web site, will be referred to as Labat, *Nouveau voyage*.

60 Sue Peabody states, "I have not been able to corroborate this anecdote in any earlier source" (*"There Are No Slaves in France": The Political Culture of Race and Slavery in the Ancien Régime* [New York: Oxford University Press, 1996], 176n71). Numerous historians refer to a decree by which Louis XIII supposedly authorized the slave trade, but no one cites or quotes any such text directly. See, e.g., Robin Blackburn, who gives an erroneous date of 1648 (five years after the death of Louis XIII) for the edict in his *The Making of New World Slavery: From the Baroque to the Modern, 1492–1800* (London: Verso, 1997), 281. Historians of French law also traffic in this myth, repeating Labat's words in paraphrase; for example, Paul Viollet, *Précis de l'histoire du droit français* (Paris: L. Larose et Forcel, 1884), 1:283. Ibrahim Boukari Amidou repeats the thesis of Louis XIII as authorizer of the French slave trade in "Evolution de la représentation de l'Afrique et des Africains dans l'*Encyclopédie* de Diderot et au cours du siècle des Lumières, 'Tamango' de Mérimée, *Le Roman d'un spahi* de Pierre Loti, *Le Voyage au Congo* de Gide: Humanisme, exotisme, et colonialisme" (Ph.D. diss., University of Cincinnati, 2002), 69–70. Amidou's (cited but unquoted) source on this is Joseph Morenas, an intriguing abolitionist writer of the Restoration period, but Morenas specifically says that Louis XIII did *not* authorize the slave trade; it was Morenas who exposed the myth. See Joseph Elzéar Morenas, *Précis historique de la traite des Noirs et de l'esclavage colonial* (1828; Geneva: Slatkine Reprints, 1978). Refuting Labat, Morenas writes that "le cardinal de Richelieu protecteur [des] compagnies, toléra la traite et l'emploi d'esclaves noirs, *sans qu'il ait jamais existé, sous le règne de Louis XIII, aucun acte qui permette ce trafic.* Ce n'est qu'en 1670, sous Louis XIV, que la traite a été légalement autorisée en France" (206; emphasis added). Lucien Peytraud writes of "diverses inexactitudes au sujet du commencement de la traite française. . . . La traite [in its early decades] n'a que l'approbation tacite du gouvernement" (*L'Esclavage aux Antilles françaises*, 33, 34). But generations of historians have ignored Morenas's rectification, choosing instead to repeat the Labat/Montesquieu myth. "Lettres patentes" granting privileges to the settlers of Saint-Christophe in March 1642 — while placing emphasis on the "conversion des peuples barbares" of the Ameri-

cas—make no mention of slavery or the slave trade (Clairambault ms, fol. 61, Bibliothèque Nationale de France, transcribed by Kenneth Loiselle; see Albert Isnard and Suzanne Honoré, *Catalogue général des imprimés de la Bibliothèque Nationale: Actes royaux* [Paris: Imprimerie Nationale, 1938], 2:634. No edict on the slave trade appears in the listings devoted to Louis XIII in this compendium of royal decrees. There is no sign of a decree that actually authorizes the slave trade per se.

The myth of Louis XIII and the slave trade is repeated in literature as it is in historiography; for example, in Joseph La Vallée's *Le Nègre comme il y a peu de blancs* (Madras: Buisson, 1789), 1:336, "On lui représenta que [l'esclavage] étoit l'unique moyen de tirer les Africains de l'idolâtrie, . . . Louis le Juste se rendit." I am grateful to Philip Boucher for help with this question about Louis XIII. Thanks also to Kenneth Loiselle for help with research at the Bibliothèque Nationale.

61 See Victor Tapié, *France in the Age of Louis XIII and Richelieu* (Cambridge: Cambridge University Press, 1984); Gilles Henry, *Louis XIII le Juste* (Paris: France-Empire, 1948).

62 See Clairambault ms. 385 cited in note 60 above.

63 Ly, *La Compagnie du Sénégal*, 67; Peytraud, *L'Esclavage aux Antilles françaises*, 34; Gaston Martin, *Histoire de l'esclavage dans les colonies françaises* (Saint-Pierre-de-Salerne, France: Gérard Monfort, 1978), 8. Peytraud documents the beginnings of the French slave trade and state sponsorship of it, inaugurated by Colbert (*L'Esclavage aux Antilles françaises*, 34–38).

64 Simone Berbain, *Le Comptoir français de Juda (Ouidah) au XVIIe siècle* (Paris: Larose, 1942), 35.

65 On the Jews exiled from Brazil see Stein: "In 1654, the Portuguese expelled the Dutch and Jewish settlers from Brazil, an event of capital importance for the Antilles. Many of the exiles arrived in the French islands, bringing with them the secrets of successful sugar cane treatment" (s, 7). Others suggest it was one group of Dutch Jews. A video presentation at the Habitation Fond Saint-Jacques (Labat's base) in Martinique, produced by Patrick Sardi and dated September 1986, stressed that it was a group of Jews expelled from Brazil who brought the secret of refining sugar to the French islands. There is a bitter irony in this: once a highly profitable sugar-slave system was in place and in need of regulation, thirty years after the arrival of these immigrants from Brazil, the Code Noir was promulgated; its first article expelled Jews from the French colonies.

66 See Jacques Proust, *L'Encyclopédie Diderot et d'Alembert: Planches et commentaires* (Paris: Hachette, 1985), 43–45.

67 Peytraud, *L'Esclavage aux Antilles françaises*, 7.

68 See T, 173, including Donnan quote.

69 Yves Bénot, "Les Amis des Noirs et les 'déclamations' de Diderot," in *Esclavage et abolitions: Mémoires et systèmes de représentation*, ed. Marie-Christine

Rochmann (Paris: Karthala, 2000), 223. See also Patricia Gravatt, *L'Eglise et l'esclavage* (Paris: L'Harmattan, 2003).

70   See Peabody, *"There Are No Slaves in France"*; and Christopher L. Miller, *Blank Darkness: Africanist Discourse in French* (Chicago: University of Chicago Press, 1985), 102–3.

71   The *Histoire naturelle et morale des Antilles* (1665) by Charles de Rochefort, as interpreted by Keith Sandiford, is a significant example of a discourse that promotes both power and enlightenment; see Sandiford, *The Cultural Politics of Sugar: Caribbean Slavery and Narratives of Colonialism* (Cambridge: Cambridge University Press, 2000), 43, 53.

72   Peytraud, *L'Esclavage aux Antilles françaises*, 15. See also C, 185; S, 9–10; and Gabriel Debien, *Le Peuplement des Antilles françaises au XVIIe siècle: Les Engagés partis de La Rochelle* (Cairo: Notes d'histoire coloniale II, 1942), 43–52.

73   Deschamps, *Histoire de la traite des Noirs*, 62; WC, 39; C, 24, 26. The epigraph for this section is drawn from "Lettre du Ministre à M. de Reynaud, Commandant en Chef par intérim, sur les Armements directs aux Isles pour les Côtes d'Afrique," in Moreau de Saint-Méry, *Loix et constitutions des colonies françaises de l'Amérique sous le vent* (Paris: Chez l'auteur, chez Moutard, 1784), 6:112.

74   Banks, *Chasing Empire across the Sea*, 42. Unfortunately, Banks's taxonomy of French Atlantic sea routes encompasses only the *commerce en droiture*: voyages back and forth between France and its New World colonies (68). The Africa trade (the "motor of all the others" according to Choiseul) is thus marginalized. Banks does discuss the slave trade but separately (see 78–79).

401

75   E, 9; S, 23; T, 370; D, 171; and Philip Curtin, *The Atlantic Slave Trade: A Census* (Madison: University of Wisconsin Press, 1969), 170.

76   David Eltis et al., *The Trans-Atlantic Slave Trade: A Database on CD-ROM* gives a total of 1,178,173 slaves embarked by the French, with 1,006,417 disembarked, for a mortality rate of 13.2 percent. Only 456 voyages are recorded outside the eighteenth century.

77   David Geggus, "The French Slave Trade: An Overview," *William and Mary Quarterly*, 3rd series, 58, no. 1 (January 2001): 121–22.

78   Edward Reynolds, *Stand the Storm: A History of the Atlantic Slave Trade* (London: Allison and Busby, 1985), 73.

79   Michel-Rolph Trouillot, *Silencing the Past: Power and the Production of History* (Boston: Beacon Press, 1995), 17; he takes this from Curtin, *The Atlantic Slave Trade*. Trouillot notes that the disproportion is explained by the greater birth rate among slaves in the United States.

80   See Deschamps, *Histoire de la traite des Noirs*, 74–75; and Ly, *La Compagnie du Sénégal*, 4–6.

81   Chevalier Stanislas de Boufflers, *Lettres d'Afrique à Madame de Sabran* (Paris: Actes Sud, 1998), 170, 156, 162.

82 Le Sieur Froger's relation of a slave-trading journey to Africa starting in 1695 describes how a French vessel on the coast of Africa, charged with taking English prisoners back to France, "devoit *passer par* Cayenne pour y porter une partie de nos Negres" (Froger, *Relation du voyage de Mr. De Gennes au detroit de Magellan* [Paris: Chez N. de Fer, 1698], 37; emphasis mine).

83 Paul Roussier, *L'Etablissement d'Issinie, 1687–1702* (Paris: Larose, 1935), vi.

84 A search of Eltis et al., *The Trans-Atlantic Slave Trade*, using all French ports as the point of disembarkation produces only three ships — one from 1679, one from 1680, and one from 1738 — bringing a combined total of only seventy-one slaves to France, temporarily; they were all then sent to the Americas.

85 See Geggus, "The French Slave Trade," 122.

86 Edouard Glissant, *Le Quatrième siècle* (Paris: Seuil, 1964), 33.

87 Guillaume-Thomas (Abbé) Raynal, *Histoire philosophique et politique des établissemens et du commerce des Européens dans les deux Indes*, 3rd ed. (Geneva: Chez Jean-Léonard Pellet, 1780), 3:90. This four-volume edition, which includes additions and corrections made by Diderot, can be downloaded from the Bibliothèque Nationale de France. I will henceforth refer to this text as *Histoire des deux Indes*. On editions of this work (including an "identical but differently paginated" ten-volume version of the same third edition), see Srinivas Aravamudan, *Tropicopolitans: Colonialism and Agency, 1688–1804* (Durham: Duke University Press, 1999), 401n2.

88 Robert Stein may be mistaken to refer to the large amount of direct trade between France and its islands as "relatively independent of the slave trade" (s, 52), if it is true that that trade was necessary to complete the balance of payments for slaves imported from Africa. Pierre Pluchon offers a convincing counterargument: "La traite négrière et le commerce colonial direct sont étroitement imbriqués. . . . Dès lors, peut-on, à la suite d'une discrimination intellectuelle trop abstraite, dissocier ce qui, dans les faits, constitue un ensemble soudé? Peut-on dire valablement où commencent et où finissent les bénéfices de la navigation en droiture et ceux du trafic triangulaire? Non, et les armateurs ne s'y trompaient pas, qui avaient une stratégie globale. Les historiens n'ont pas retenu cette manière de voir et, par réflexe rationaliste, ont introduit des catégories là où la pratique n'en avait pas établies" (*La Route des esclaves*, 281).

89 Montesquieu, *The Spirit of the Laws*, book 21, ch. 21, p. 391, AT. On the *Exclusif* see Jean-Pierre Pousson, Philippe Bonnichon, and Xavier Huetz de Lemps, *Espaces coloniaux et espaces maritimes au XVIIIe siècle: Les Deux Amériques et la Pacifique* (Paris: SEDES, 1998), 141–46.

90 Cabuzel Andréa Banbuck, *Histoire politique, économique et sociale de la Martinique sous l'Ancien Régime (1635–1789)* (Fort-de-France: Société de Distribution et de Culture, 1972), 259, 261.

91 J. B. Dubuc (who wrote in favor of the rights of colonial planters), quoted in c, 177; see also Deschamps, *Histoire de la traite des Noirs*, 83.

92 Laurent Dubois, *Avengers of the New World: The Story of the Haitian Revolution* (Cambridge, Mass.: Harvard University Press, 2004), 20.

93 J. Tramond, quoted in Banbuck, *Histoire politique*, 260. Banks shows how merchants and the French state did not necessarily follow the same rules and how the state's ability to control the colonies and trade was limited (*Chasing Empire*, 153–83, 220).

94 "In the years 1801 to 1825, 12 percent of expeditions set out from the Caribbean, and in the following quarter century, as the French trade withered, that proportion rose to 43 percent, with another 7 percent of French vessels leaving from Brazil" (Geggus, "The French Slave Trade," 122). See also Josette Fallope, "Négriers de la Guadeloupe sur la côte africaine au début du XIXe siècle," in *L'Afrique entre l'Europe et l'Amérique: Le Rôle de l'Afrique dans la rencontre de deux mondes (1492–1992)*, ed. Elikia M'Bokolo (Paris: UNESCO, 1995), 103–16.

95 Christiane Taubira, introduction to *Codes noirs de l'esclavage aux abolitions*, ed. André Castaldo, (Paris: Dalloz, 2006), xxxiii–xxxiv.

96 On the history of slave labor in sugar production see Sidney Mintz, *Sweetness and Power: The Place of Sugar in Modern History* (New York: Penguin, 1985), 29, 43.

97 Ibid., 189; Blackburn, *The Making of New World Slavery*, 295; T, 275.

98 Mintz, *Sweetness and Power*, 174.

99 Abbé Henri-Joseph Dulaurens, quoted in Mercier, *L'Afrique noire dans la lit-térature française*, 99.

100 Sugar is among the commodities used in trading for slaves on the coast of Africa, enumerated by the Abbé Demanet in his *Nouvelle histoire de l'Afrique françoise* (Paris: Chez la Veuve Duchesne, 1767), 1:253.

101 For information on how this evolved in Nantes, starting in the 1720s, see T, 252–53. The *indiennes* first came from Asia, but this defeated a principle of mercantilism, so French imitations were manufactured, thus stimulating industry in the metropole; see Deschamps, *Histoire de la traite des Noirs*, 81. According to Crété, *indiennes* were not made in France until 1759, and it was forbidden to sell them in France (C, 75–76).

102 C. L. R. James, *The Black Jacobins: Toussaint L'Ouverture and the San Domingo Revolution*, 2nd ed. (New York: Vintage Books, 1989), 47; see also ix, 57.

103 Quoted in C, 31. More famously, Voltaire wrote in chapter 23 of *Candide*: "Vous savez que ces deux nations [France and England] sont en guerre pour quelques arpents de neige vers le Canada; et qu'elles dépensent pour cette belle guerre beaucoup plus que tout le Canada ne vaut" (VOC 7:196).

104 Jean Tarrade, *Le Commerce colonial de la France à la fin de l'Ancien Régime: l'évolution de "l'Exclusif"* (Paris: Presses Universitaires de France, 1972), 7.

105 It should be noted that the colonies of the future United States were an exception to this rule; there the slave population was maintained and increased with fewer imports; see Patterson, *Slavery and Social Death*, 3; Trouillot, *Silencing the Past*, 17.

106 Du Tertre, *Histoire générale des Antilles*, 2:524: "Il meurt une infinité de Négres."

107 Raynal, *Histoire des deux Indes*, 3:181.

108 Blackburn, *The Making of New World Slavery*, 585.

109 Du Bois cited in D, 169; Manning cited in D, 122.

110 See PG, 54; and Pétré-Grenouilleau, *Les Traites négrières*, 140–41.

111 See PG, 163–64. These figures reflect totals between 1519 and 1867 for the
entire Atlantic slave trade.

112 The first three articles are thus consonant with the spirit of the Revocation of
the Edict of Nantes and the idea of "une foi, un roi, une loi." To that doctrine,
Roach points out, the Code Noir added one more: "un sang" (Joseph Roach,
"Body of Law: The Sun King and the Code Noir," in *From the Royal to the
Republican Body: Incorporating the Political in Seventeenth- and Eighteenth-
Century France*, ed. Sara E. Melzer and Kathryn Norberg [Berkeley: University of California Press, 1998], 115). Joan DeJean points out that the timing of
the Code is indicative of growing centripetal forces in France, an increased
sense of "national entitlement"; the Code appeared within three years of the
founding of the first school for "Frenchness." See Joan DeJean, *Ancients and
Moderns: Culture Wars and the Making of a Fin de Siècle* (Chicago: University of Chicago Press, 1997), 130–34. On the Code, see also WC, 50–56; and
Blackburn, *The Making of New World Slavery*, 290–92. On some planters'
resistance to the Code see Dubois, *Avengers*, 30–31.

113 Du Tertre, *Histoire générale des Antilles*, 2:527.

114 Louis Sala-Molins, *Le Code Noir ou le calvaire de Canaan* (Paris: PUF, 1987), 9;
Paul Gilroy, *The Black Atlantic: Modernity and Double Consciousness* (Cambridge, Mass.: Harvard University Press, 1993), 213.

115 Roach, "Body of Law," 113.

116 Erick Noël, *Etre noir en France au XVIIIe siècle* (Paris: Tallandier, 2006), 95.

117 Cilas Kemedjio, *De la Négritude à la Créolité: Edouard Glissant, Maryse Condé
et la malédiction de la théorie* (Hamburg: Lit Verlag, 1999), 144.

118 See Ambroise Kom and Lucienne Ngoué, *Le Code Noir et l'Afrique* (Ivry:
Nouvelles du Sud, 1991); Werner Sollors, *Neither Black nor White yet Both:
Thematic Explorations of Interracial Literature* (New York: Oxford University
Press, 1997), chap. 6, "Code Noir and Literature"; and Joan Dayan, "From
the Plantation to the Penitentiary: Chain, Classification, and Codes of De-
terrence," in *Slavery in the Caribbean Francophone World: Distant Voices,
Forgotten Acts, Forged Identities*, ed. Doris Y. Kadish (Athens: University of
Georgia Press, 2000), 191–210.

119 Froger, *Relation du voyage de Mr. De Gennes*, 150; emphasis added.

120 Reynolds, *Stand the Storm*, 78; see also James, *The Black Jacobins*, 55–56.

121 There is a discrepancy between Thomas's figure and the figure of 456 voyages
outside the eighteenth century, which I quoted earlier from the Eltis CD-ROM
database.

122 Philip Curtin had suggested the figure of 9.5 million: *The Atlantic Slave Trade:*

A Census (Madison: University of Wisconsin Press, 1969), 87. Barry raises serious questions about the reliability of Curtin's figures and accuses Curtin of being "predisposed to minimize the importance of the trans-Atlantic slave trade" (*SAST*, 67). On the total French trade see s, 211; c, 109–10.

123 See Peter Linebaugh and Marcus Rediker, *The Many-Headed Hydra: Sailors, Slaves, Commoners, and the Hidden History of the Revolutionary Atlantic* (Boston: Beacon Press, 2000), 7. I am transposing the authors' terms to the French context, which they do not discuss. There is a fundamental flaw in Linebaugh and Rediker's otherwise fascinating book: they expect us to believe in a *singular* (albeit diverse and mobile) "Atlantic proletariat" made up of slaves, sailors, and commoners. They utterly fail to acknowledge the role of slave-trading sailors as *agents* of enslavement, and this weakens the credibility of their thesis, which David Brion Davis says "reads like a parody of highly romanticized Marxism" (see David Brion Davis, "Slavery—White, Black, Muslim, Christian," *New York Review of Books*, July 5, 2001, 53). Some slave-trading sailors may have been, individually or as a class, revolutionaries for themselves, but the labor they performed was not for the benefit of their African captives. The example, discussed later in this chapter, of Jacques Proa—an ordinary sailor who took delight in his share of the profits of the slave trade—is surely not exceptional. What Rediker wrote in his earlier book, *Between the Devil and the Deep Blue Sea: Merchant Seamen, Pirates, and the Anglo-American Maritime World, 1700–1750* (Cambridge: Cambridge University Press, 1987), 405 is true: "Seamen in the slave trade, themselves the captors of slaves, were at the same time the captives of their own merchants and captains" (50). But that does not give seamen and slaves the same status. The Haitian Revolution and its relation to the French Revolution of course provide counterexamples, cases of solidarity in liberation across racial boundaries: "In March 1791 troops of French soldiers arrived [in Saint-Domingue] spreading the revolutionary message of freedom and equality." (Kadish, introduction to *Slavery in the Caribbean Francophone World*, 4).

124 Banks, *Chasing Empire across the Sea*, 99. Banks does not include Saint-Domingue in this sentence, but the observation seems to apply nonetheless.

125 c, 225. Blackburn, in *The Making of New World Slavery*, notes that "the [French] planters . . . became notorious for their preference for contraband dealings with English, Dutch or North American traders" (446). Labat offers a definition of interlope in his *Voyage du Chevalier des Marchais*, 3:53–54. See also Banks, *Chasing Empire across the Sea*, 84, 184–216.

126 Tarrade, *Le Commerce colonial*, 95, 83–112.

127 See Julius S. Scott, "Crisscrossing Empires: Ships, Sailors, and Resistance in the Lesser Antilles in the Eighteenth Century," in *The Lesser Antilles in the Age of European Expansion*, ed. Robert L. Paquette and Stanley L. Engerman (Gainesville: University Press of Florida, 1996), 135.

128 D, 138. For a general survey of sources in French see Liliane Chauleau, "Quelle histoire possible de l'esclavage? Quelle parole de l'esclave?" in Rochmann,

Esclavage et abolitions, 21–32; see also Sylviane Diouf, ed., *Fighting the Slave Trade: West African Strategies* (Athens: Ohio University Press, 2003).

129 See S. E. Ogude, "Facts into Fiction: Equiano's Narrative Reconsidered," *Research in African Literatures* 13, no. 1 (spring 1982): 31–43. Ogude asserts that the narrative is "to a large extent fictional"; that Equiano's "account of his early life cannot bear close scrutiny . . . [and] is an imaginative reorganization of a wide variety of tales about Africa from an equally wide range of sources" (including William Snelgrave, Thomas Astley, and other European travel writers); that the author had a "nearly total dependence on other sources for what he claimed to be his personal experience" (31, 32, 36). Vincent Carretta, in "Olaudah Equiano or Gustavus Vassa? New Light on an Eighteenth-Century Question of Identity," *Slavery and Abolition* 20, no. 3 (December 1999): 96–105, provides considerable archival evidence that complicates the question of Equiano's birthplace—which may have been South Carolina, as indicated on his baptismal record in England—and of his identity. Carretta judiciously observes: "If he was a native of Carolina, his account of Africa may have been based on oral history and reading [such as the sources named by Ogude], rather than on personal experience" (103). Even if Equiano/Vassa was born in South Carolina and produced a semifictional autobiography—in which he projected himself back to an Africa that he knew only through the testimony of his fellow slaves, augmented by readings of European travel writers—*The Interesting Narrative* would still remain one of the few *indirect* but *proximate* sources of insight into the African experience of enslavement and the Middle Passage. In my use of this text I will assume it to be a composite source, combining voices under the control of the author. Vincent Carretta makes an appropriate statement when he admits that he as a modern reader accepts Equiano's assertion of his African birth "in part because I want it to be" (Carretta, *Unchained Voices: An Anthology of Black Authors in the English-Speaking World of the Eighteenth Century* [Lexington: University Press of Kentucky, 1996], 16n13). But in his newer biography of Equiano, Carretta concludes that Equiano "probably invented an African identity" and that his account of Africa and the Middle Passage is "probably fictitious" (Carretta, *Equiano the African: Biography of a Self-Made Man* [Athens: University of Georgia Press, 2005], xv, xvi). Adam Hochschild, defending the authenticity of *The Interesting Narrative,* speculates that Equiano may have claimed an American birth and long avoided use of his African name for reasons of prudent self-protection; see Hochschild, *Bury the Chains: Prophets and Rebels in the Fight to Free an Empire's Slaves* (Boston: Houghton Mifflin, 2005), 369–72. See also Jennifer Howard, "Unraveling the Narrative," *Chronicle of Higher Education,* September 9, 2005, http://chronicle.com/free/v52/i03/03a01101.htm (accessed September 8, 2005).

Equiano was not translated into French before the publication of *La Véridique histoire d'Olaudah Equiano, Africain, esclave aux Caraïbes, homme libre,* trans. Claire-Lise Charbonnier (Paris: Editions Caribbéennes, 1983); the editor states that this is the first French translation (iv, n2). A second translation, with a critical apparatus, was done by Régine Mfoumou-Arthur: *Olaudah Equiano ou Gustavus Vassa l'Africain: Le Passionnant récit de ma vie* (Paris: L'Harmattan, 2002). The sole sign of any influence of Equiano in France during the time of slavery is not a negligible one: the section devoted to him in the Abbé Grégoire's *De la littérature des Nègres* (Paris: Maradan, 1808), 245–52.

130 A more comprehensive treatment of discourse than I can do here would include nonnarrative texts of many genres (speeches, reports, letters) that emanated from the Caribbean and that spoke for the interests of the enslaved in the Revolutionary period. Leaders like Toussaint Louverture, the insurgent Jean-François, and Louis Delgrès of Guadeloupe wrote or dictated many such texts, which reflected on and altered the French Atlantic. In this study L'Ouverture's memoirs will serve as a small example of such productions. A multiplicity of these texts are reviewed and interpreted by historians such as Carolyn E. Fick, *The Making of Haiti: The Saint Domingue Revolution from Below* (Knoxville: University of Tennessee Press, 1990); and Laurent Dubois in his two books, *A Colony of Citizens: Revolution and Slave Emancipation in the French Caribbean, 1787–1804* (Chapel Hill: University of North Carolina Press, 2004) and *Avengers of the New World*.

131 Robin Law and Paul E. Lovejoy, introduction, Mahommah Gardo Baquaqua and Samuel Moore, *The Biography of Mahommah Gardo Baquaqua: His Passage from Slavery to Freedom in Africa and America*, ed. Robin Law and Paul E. Lovejoy (Princeton: Marcus Wiener, 2001), 8. The phrase that may best reveal the structure of shared narrative authority in this text comes at the point where Moore introduces a new first-person passage by writing: "We will give the matter in *nearly* his own words" (136; emphasis mine).

132 Relying largely on oral sources in contemporary Ghana, Anne C. Bailey makes a significant addition to literature on this subject in her *African Voices of the Atlantic Slave Trade: Beyond the Silence and the Shame* (Boston: Beacon Press, 2005).

133 Quobna Ottobah Cugoano, "Thoughts and Sentiments on the Evil and Wicked Traffic of the Slavery . . . ," in *Black Atlantic Writers of the Eighteenth Century: Living the New Exodus in England and the Americas*, ed. Adam Potkay and Sandra Burr (New York: St. Martin's, 1995), 136. Cugoano was translated into French (Hochschild, *Bury the Chains*, 136).

134 Osei Bonsu, "Views of the King of Asante, 1820," in Northrup, *The Atlantic Slave Trade*, 92–94.

135 Harms, *The Diligent*, 176.

136 Moira Ferguson, "The Literature of Slavery and Abolition," in *The Cambridge History of African and Caribbean Literature*, ed. F. Abiola Irele and Simon Gikandi (Cambridge: Cambridge University Press, 2004), 1:245.

137 Toussaint L'Ouverture, *Mémoires du Général Toussaint-L'Ouverture écrits par lui-même* (Port-au-Prince: Bélizaire, 1951). On his life as a slave Toussaint

says only, "J'ai été esclave, j'ose l'avouer, mais je n'ai jamais essuyé même des reproches de la part de mes maîtres" (94). See Daniel Désormeaux, "The First of the (Black) Memorialists," *Yale French Studies* 107 (2005): 131–45. Toussaint L'Ouverture's son Isaac Louverture wrote a memoir that gives a mythic account of the enslavement and Middle Passage of Toussaint's father, said to be the son of an African king; but the memoir says nothing about Toussaint's time as a slave. See "Mémoires et notes d'Isaac Louverture," in Antoine Métral, *Histoire de l'expédition des Français à Saint-Domingue sous le consulat de Napoléon Bonaparte (1802–1803)* (Paris: Karthala, 1985), 227–340, esp. 325–26.

138 On *Le More-Lack* see Dubois, *A Colony of Citizens*, 71–72.

139 Mercier, *L'Afrique noire dans la littérature française*, 87; see Edward D. Sypher, *Anti-Slavery Opinion in France during the Second Half of the Eighteenth Century* (New York: Greenwood Press, 1969), 22.

140 Abbé Prévost, *Le Pour et le contre: Ouvrage périodique d'un goût nouveau . . .* (Paris: Didot, 1735), 6:340–53.

141 Sala-Molins, *Le Code Noir*, 209n; his comments on Lecointe-Marsillac's *Le More-Lack* (1789) are relevant (see also Mercier, *L'Afrique noire dans la littérature française*, 174–75). Other scholars agree that there are no slave narratives in French: see Lydie Moudileno, "Retrouver la parole perdue: Edouard Glissant et le récit d'esclave reconstitué," *Romanic Review* 90, no. 1 (January 1999): 84; and Lydie Moudileno, *L'Ecrivain antillais au miroir de sa littérature: Mises en scène et mise en abyme du roman antillais* (Paris: Karthala, 1997), 116. See also Léon-François Hoffmann, "Présence et absence de l'esclave dans les lettre haïtiennes," in Rochmann, *Esclavage et abolitions*, 176. Jean-Pierre Sainton of the Université des Antilles-Guyane writes: "In my knowledge, in the French Caribbean (Martinique and Guadeloupe) there are not slave narratives as in English or in the Spanish-speaking Caribbean" (H-Caribbean Discussion List [H-Caribbean@H-Net.MSU.EDU], April 26, 2001). Chauleau discusses another source of exceptional testimonies coming from slaves: court records, many of which were burned by order in 1787 ("Quelle histoire possible de l'esclavage?" in Rochmann, *Esclavage et abolitions*).

142 Edouard Glissant says in a novel—*Mahagony* (Paris: Seuil, 1987), 21—that literacy in the French islands was a capital crime in the 1830s. Fouchard makes no mention of this; the only *ordonnance* that has been cited mandates twenty lashes for slaves who tried to learn reading and writing, but Fouchard casts doubt on the authenticity of that order. He believes, plausibly, that the very real interdictions on literacy in the United States may have influenced perceptions of the French colonies (Fouchard, *Les Marrons du syllabaire*, 66).

143 See Antoine Gisler, *L'Esclavage aux Antilles Françaises (XVIIe-XIXe siècle): Contribution au problème de l'esclavage* (Paris: Karthala, 1981), 56–57. Labat claimed, however, that at the time of his stay in the French West Indies (1693–1705), "Le catéchisme . . . se fait en commun soir et matin dans les mai-

sons bien réglées, comme sont presque toutes les habitations des îles du Vent" (*Nouveau voyage*, 145).

144 Quoted in Peytraud, *L'Esclavage aux Antilles françaises*, 192 (emphasis added); see his chapter "Religion des esclaves," 165–92. The priest Du Tertre wrote that he and his fellow missionaries in the Antilles taught their "Négres" to read and to serve at mass but that the *habitans* (planters) preferred to keep them "dans une crasse ignorance de toutes choses" (*Histoire générale des Antilles*, 2:511).

145 Villaret, *capitaine général* of Martinique, quoted in Gisler, *L'Esclavage aux Antilles Françaises*, 89.

146 Jean Fouchard, *Les Marrons du syllabaire: Quelques aspects du problème de l'instruction et de l'éducation des esclaves et affranchis de Saint-Domingue* (Port-au-Prince: Henri Deschamps, 1953). Fouchard's book seems to have been unjustly neglected; many recent scholars pondering the problem of the slaves' "silence" have failed to cite Fouchard. See Liliane Chauleau, "Quelle histoire possible de l'esclavage? Quelle parole de l'esclave?" in Rochmann, *Esclavage et abolitions*, 21–32; and T, 798. What Rochmann (in her introduction to *Esclavage et abolitions*, 7) calls the "absence de tout apport testimonial direct issu de la population servile des Antilles" needs to be modified in light of the evidence Fouchard brought to light, even if most of it is not totally "direct." Joan Dayan is an exception, making good use of Fouchard in her section on theater in Saint-Domingue: *Haiti, History, and the Gods* (Berkeley: University of California Press, 1995), 182–86. Doris Y. Kadish cites *Les Marrons du syllabaire* but says its materials "add up more to a tantalizing set of bits and pieces than a coherent picture" (preface to *Slavery in the Caribbean Francophone World*, xii). See Kadish's discussion of literacy and the absence of slave narratives (xii–xiii).

147 "Où donc trouva-t-il le Syllabaire, cet esclave indien nommé Pierre, 'de petite taille, 23 ans, ayant la peau rouge, les jambe fluettes, le genou un peu en devant, des cicatrices de coups de fouet sur le dos' et dont M. Marty, Trésorier de la Marine à Saint-Marc [Saint-Domingue] dénonçait la fuite le 3 mai 1769 avec ce signalement suggestif: 'Comme il sait lire et un peu écrire, on présume qu'il pourrait bien être porteur de quelque billet'" (Fouchard, *Les Marrons du syllabaire*, 98–99). The first and most obvious source of literacy for some slaves, Fouchard points out, was an Islamic education acquired in Africa and retained in the New World (see ibid., 5–18).

148 Quoted ibid., 118.

149 Quoted in Chauleau, "Quelle histoire possible de l'esclavage?" 30. On revolutionary slave letters in Martinique in 1789, also using a discourse of nationalism, see Catherine Reinhardt, "French Caribbean Slaves Forge Their Own Ideal of Liberty in 1789," in *Slavery in the Caribbean Francophone World*, ed. Doris Y. Kadish, 24–30. David Geggus explains that the word *nation* in a similar context is "employed in a local, particularist sense. Just as French colo-

409

nists referred to different African ethnic groups as *nations*, the slaves on St. Pierre [Martinique] used the phrase 'the entire nation' to refer to themselves and also applied the term separately to whites and free coloreds" (Geggus, "The Slaves and Free Coloreds of Martinique during the Age of the French and Haitian Revolutions," in *The Lesser Antilles in the Age of European Expansion*, ed. Robert L. Paquette and Stanley L. Engerman [Gainesville: University Press of Florida, 1996], 287).

150 Saugera, "De Sidoine à Sophie Raphel," 119; Olivier Pétré-Grenouilleau, *Nantes au temps de la traite des Noirs* (Paris: Hachette, 1998), 245.

151 Renault and Daget, *Les Traites négrières en Afrique*, 70.

152 See Rochmann, introduction to *Esclavage et abolitions*, 9. To the partial extent that it is French, John Berry's film *Tamango* is an exception to this; see chap. 9. And Christian Richard's *Le Courage des autres*, if it is French, is an exception; see chap. 14. The *bandes dessinées Le Comptoir de Juda* and *Le Bois d'ébène* by François Bourgeon (Brussels: Castermann, 1994 [both volumes]) continue the nineteenth-century tradition of representing the slave trade as a form of adventure romance; slaves are depicted with sympathy but are given almost no speaking parts; soft pornography characterizes the iconography. For an overview of French representations of slavery and the slave trade, including pedagogical materials, see Comité pour la mémoire de l'esclavage, *Mémoires de la traite négrière, de l'esclavage, et de leurs abolitions: Rapport à Monsieur le premier ministre* (Paris: n.p., April 12, 2005), 34–40, 56–60.

410

153 Comité pour la mémoire de l'esclavage, *Mémoires de la traite négrière*, 21.

154 Ibid., 12.

155 Edouard Glissant, *Ormerod* (Paris: Gallimard, 2003), 217–18.

156 A similar incident, in which a statue commemorating slavery was vandalized, took place in Saint Denis de La Réunion in the same year, 1998, reports Françoise Vergès, in *Abolir l'esclavage: Une Utopie coloniale: Les Ambiguïtés d'une politique humanitaire* (Paris: Albin Michel, 2001), 207. On the change of heart of the city government of Nantes, from an initial refusal to sponsor a conference on the slave trade in 1985 to support for the Anneaux de la mémoire exhibition in 1992, see Saugera, *La Traite des Noirs en 30 questions*, 62–63.

157 See www.lesanneauxdelamemoire.com and more recent information in my conclusion.

158 Serge Daget, "Une mémoire sans monument: La Traite," in *La Dernière traite: Fragments d'histoire en hommage à Serge Daget*, ed. Hubert Gerbeau and Eric Saugera (Paris: Société Française d'Histoire d'Outre-Mer, 1994), 284. The project for a memorial to slavery in Paris has reportedly met with official indifference (see Bruno Masi, "Noirs désirs: médias, culture, éducation, les minorités réclament plus de visibilité. Enquête," *Libération*, May 24, 2000). But on May 10, 2001, the French parliament voted to recognize slavery and the slave trade as crimes against humanity.

159 See Pap Ndiaye, "Noirs, il y a de l'espoir," *Libération*, February 28, 2005, article 278757.

160   See Comité pour la mémoire de l'esclavage, *Mémoires de la traite négrière*, 3. By *réparation historique*, the Committee seems to mean the repairing of history, the end of silence and neglect; see 8–9, 32, 51. A rival committee of descendants of slaves proposed May 23 as a day of remembrance; see www.cm98.org (accessed May 16, 2005).

161   Martin Klein, *Slavery and Colonial Rule in French West Africa* (Cambridge: Cambridge University Press, 1998), 246.

162   Curtin, *The Atlantic Slave Trade*, 6, 87. There is some irony in the fact that Curtin, in his work that first brought the number down from fifteen million, does not cite a sentence in another work by Du Bois that was already in line with Curtin's revised figure: in *The Negro* (New York: Henry Holt, 1915), Du Bois wrote, "Certainly it seems that at least 10,000,000 Negroes were expatriated" (155).

163   See Ralph Austen, "The Slave Trade as History and Memory: Confrontations of Slaving Voyage Documents and Communal Traditions," *William and Mary Quarterly* 58, no. 1 (January 2001): 229–44.

164   Djibril Tamsir Niane, *Soundjata: Epopée mandingue* (Paris: Présence Africaine, 1960), 153. Cf. Manning: "In the wake of imperialistic condemnations of slavery and of African life generally, the memory of the African sacrifice to the evolving Atlantic economy was lost" (*SAL*, 109).

165   Glissant, *Le Quatrième siècle*, 61.

166   Patrick Chamoiseau, *L'Esclave vieil homme et le molosse* (Paris: Gallimard, 1997), 17.   411

2   AROUND THE TRIANGLE

1   *Les Anneaux de la mémoire*, catalogue of exposition, Château des Ducs de Bretagne, Nantes, 1992–94 (Nantes: Corderie royale, 1993), 68. For an analysis of the European merchandise that was traded for slaves, see D, 86–99; C, 73–78; S, 71–72. On the term *pacotille* (often misunderstood as meaning goods of little worth) see D, 92–93.

2   Olivier Pétré-Grenouilleau, *La Traite des Noirs*, 2nd ed. (Paris: PUF, 1997), 81; henceforth abbreviated PG.

3   See T, 304. On names see Hubert Deschamps, *Histoire de la traite des Noirs de l'antiquité à nos jours* (Paris: Fayard, 1971), 80. "Le Franklin" appears in the following notice published in *La Gazette du jour* (a daily newspaper of Le Cap Français, Saint-Domingue), number 15 (November 15, 1790): "La corvette *le Franklin*, capitaine Durard, est arrivé de Gorée & Sénégal le 6 mars, avec une belle cargaison de Noirs à l'adresse de MM. Lory, Le Houx, fils, & Compagnie, qui en ouvriront la vente le 21 du courant" (59).

4   Philip Curtin has attacked what he calls the "hoax" and "scam" of the Slave House on Gorée, calling it "architecturally one of the finest houses on Gorée, certainly not a place where slaves would be kept" (H-Africa Usenet, July 31, 1995, www2.h-net.msu.edu/~africa/, Gorée thread, posting 1). See also

the replies, many of which rightly insist on the continuing symbolic value of Gorée and of the Slave House; see esp. Achille Mbembe's posting, August 8, 1995.

5 There were nonetheless times when European vessels were able to embark hundreds of captives at once; see Boubacar Barry, *Senegambia and the Atlantic Slave Trade*, trans. Ayi Kwei Armah (Cambridge: Cambridge University Press, 1998), 64; henceforth abbreviated *SAST*.

6 D, 145–46. On this voyage see Alain Yacou, *Journaux de bord et de traite de Joseph Crassous de Médeuil, de La Rochelle à la côte de Guinée et aux Antilles (1772–1776)* (Paris: Karthala, 2001), 219–77.

7 Mahommah Gardo Baquaqua and Samuel Moore, *The Biography of Mahommah Gardo Baquaqua: His Passage from Slavery to Freedom in Africa and America*, ed. Robin Law and Paul E. Lovejoy (Princeton: Marcus Wiener, 2001): 153.

8 James Green, "The Publishing History of Olaudah Equiano's *Interesting Narrative*," *Slavery and Abolition* 16, no. 3 (December 1995): 362.

9 Manning lists the mechanisms of capture in the following order of significance: "warfare, in which slaves resulted as prisoners of war and booty; razzia or raids, aimed particularly at the capture of slaves [thus corresponding to what Orlando Patterson argues]; kidnapping on an individual level [to which Equiano was subjected]." Any of these may be followed by various judicial decisions and by self-enslavement in cases of famine or epidemic (*SAL*, 88–89). Herbert S. Klein downplays the importance of the slave trade in causing wars in Africa but says that "in no known instance did warfare [in Africa] not lead to the sale of slaves" (Herbert S. Klein, *The Atlantic Slave Trade* [Cambridge: Cambridge University Press, 1999], 72, 116). Boubacar Barry emphasizes that "domestic slavery in Africa developed on a large scale, to become an extension of the trans-Atlantic trading system"; that system "everywhere [in Africa] reinforced arbitrary rule and the centralization of monarchical power" (*SAST*, 58). Alongside all the scholarly debate about the relation between war and the slave trade in Africa, it is instructive to read this sentence in the journal of a French slave trader, Jacques Proa, in Africa in 1777: "Le vainqueur vendant les prisonniers qu'il a faits, en sorte que *c'est nous qui allumons la guerre par l'appât du gain*" (Jacques Proa, journal, quoted in Régis Antoine, "Aventures d'un jeune négrier français d'après un manuscrit inédit du XVIIIe siècle," *Notes africaines* 141 [January 1974]: 52; emphasis added).

10 Raynal, *Histoire des deux Indes* (Geneva: Chez Jean-Léonard Pellet, 1780), 3:198. Raynal (or possibly his editor and cowriter Diderot) refutes that last claim with a statement that resoundingly rejects the alibi of metaphorical, political slavery: "the condition of these unfortunates is *not* the same as ours" (200; emphasis added). Voltaire, in his *Essai sur les mœurs*, appears to agree with the defense of slavery: "Nous n'achetons des esclaves domestiques que chez les nègres. On nous reproche ce commerce: un peuple qui trafique de ses enfants est encore plus condamnable que l'acheteur; ce négoce démontre

notre supériorité; celui qui se donne un maître était né pour en avoir" (VOC 13:177–78). Cordorcet, the abolitionist, who edited Voltaire's works, hurries to rectify this incriminating statement by Voltaire, in a footnote that seems to reverse the burden of guilt and to remove any defense of enslavement: "Cette expression doit s'entendre dans le même sens qu'Aristote disait qu'il y a des esclaves par nature. . . . Certainement le roitelet nègre qui vend ses sujets, celui qui fait la guerre pour avoir des prisonniers à vendre, le père qui vend ses enfants, commettent un crime exécrable; mais ces crimes sont l'ouvrage des Européens . . . ceux-ci sont les vrais coupables" (VOC 13:178). See Edward Derbyshire Seeber, *Anti-Slavery Opinion in France during the Second Half of the Eighteenth Century* (New York: Greenwood Press, 1969), 66.

11 See Jacobus Elisa Johannes Capitein, *The Agony of Asar: A Thesis on Slavery by the Former Slave*, trans. Grant Parker (Princeton: Markus Wiener, 2001), 113, 131; for a comparison of Capitein and Equiano see ibid., 17–19.

12 *SAST*, 61.

13 Maryse Condé, "Négritude césairienne, Négritude senghorienne," *Revue de littérature comparée* 48, nos. 3–4 (July–December 1974): 418.

14 "Nous l'avons déjà observé, en achetant des Négres en Guinée, on ne leur ôte pas leur liberté, ils n'en jouissent plus, on ne les fait point esclaves, on les trouve tels" (Jean Bellon de Saint-Quentin, *Dissertation sur la traite et le commerce des Négres* [Paris: n.p., 1764], 61).

15 John Thornton, *Africa and Africans in the Making of the Atlantic World, 1400–1680* (Cambridge: Cambridge University Press, 1992), 74.

16 I have interpolated the word *no* in the second sentence, following the Gates edition, *The Classic Slave Narratives*, ed. Henry Louis Gates Jr. (New York: New American Library, 1987), 19. This makes better sense in the context.

17 There were many African societies in which "captives" and their children were gradually enfolded into the family structure of the free person who owned them, but anthropologist Claude Meillassoux nonetheless records an example of the alternative, showing slavery among the Wolof to be a form of "social death" characterized by extraneity, alterity, reification, and negative stereotyping (even in present-day Senegal, long after abolition). See Claude Meillassoux, *Anthropologie de l'esclavage: Le Ventre de fer et d'argent* (Paris: Presses Universitaires de France, 1986), 68–78, 99–116, 308.

18 See Ismail Rachid, "'A Devotion to the Idea of Liberty at Any Price': Rebellion and Antislavery in the Upper Guinea Coast in the Eighteenth and Nineteenth Centuries," in *Fighting the Slave Trade: West African Strategies*, ed. Sylviane Diouf (Athens: Ohio University Press, 2003), 132–51.

19 Baquaqua underwent a similar evolution, from high status as the privileged assistant of a king, using the king's slaves in his work, to captive and slave, sold into the Atlantic slave trade; about this he says: "The loss of my liberty *and honorable position with the king*, grieved me very sorely" (Baquaqua and Moore, *The Biography of Mahommah Gardo Baquaqua*, 137; emphasis mine; see 137–52).

20 See *SAL*, 142–43. Manning names Kano and Sinsani, Old Calabar, Asante, Abeche, and Mangbetu as such centers. "During the nineteenth century (and in some areas during the late eighteenth century), the scope and intensity of African slavery expanded greatly. Slavery became, then, not just a social status accorded to some, but a way of life, a mode of production, and a social system. It was set in place at the beginning of the century, then destroyed in the course of the European conquests at the end of the century" (*SAL*, 19). In his assertion that there was for a time a slave mode of production in Africa, Manning directly contradicts the earlier prescriptions of Jean Suret-Canale, *Essais d'histoire africaine: De la traite des Noirs au néo-colonialisme* (Paris: Editions Sociales, 1980), 27–28. Barry states that "the Atlantic slave trade, which dominated the region from the sixteenth century, intensified slave-master relationships in all areas of Senegambian life" (*SAST*, 113).

21 Paul E. Lovejoy, *Transformations in Slavery: A History of Slavery in Africa*, 2nd ed. (Cambridge: Cambridge University Press, 2000), 283, 21.

22 Le Sieur de La Courbe, *Premier voyage du Sieur de La Courbe fait a la coste d'Afrique en 1685*, ed. P. Cultru (Paris: Edouard Champion, 1913), 51–52. James Searing explains that nakedness marks the condition of enslavement, in his *West African Slavery and Atlantic Commerce: The Senegal River Valley, 1700–1860* (Cambridge: Cambridge University Press, 1993), 113. Thomas Hale discusses this passage from La Courbe for its significance as an early European reflection on griots (about whom La Courbe offers a great deal of information and puzzled observations), but Hale does not point out that the workers described here are likely slaves (he calls them "villagers"). See Thomas Hale, *Griots and Griottes: Masters of Words and Music* (Bloomington: Indiana University Press, 1998), 87. See also Klein, *The Atlantic Slave Trade*, 8: "Several of the Wolof states had agricultural slaves who produced for local consumption as well as for export." Labat appropriated this passage in his *Nouvelle Relation de l'Afrique occidentale* (Paris: Théodore Legras, 1728), 2:308.

23 See *SAL*, 163, 139. On the institutions of slavery in Africa see also Martin Klein, *Slavery and Colonial Rule in French West Africa* (Cambridge: Cambridge University Press, 1998); Searing, *West African Slavery and Atlantic Commerce*; and Meillassoux, *Anthropologie de l'esclavage*.

24 Joseph A. Miller, "History and Slavery as Problems in Africa," David Brion Davis Lecture Series in the History of Slavery, Race, and Its Legacies, Yale University, February 8, 2005. See also François Renault and Serge Daget, *Les Traites négrières en Afrique* (Paris: Karthala, 1985), 95.

25 Klein, *The Atlantic Slave Trade*, 9; Olivier Pétré-Grenouilleau, *Les Traites negrières: Essai d'histoire globale* (Paris: Gallimard, 2004), 147. See also Orlando Patterson, *Slavery and Social Death: A Comparative Study* (Cambridge, Mass.: Harvard University Press, 1982), 157–59. Renault and Daget suggest that the two slave-exporting systems, Atlantic and "Oriental," may have dealt in an equal number of captives—from twelve million to fourteen

million in each case (François Renault and Serge Daget, *Les Traites négrières en Afrique* [Paris: Karthala, 1985], 229).

26 David Brion Davis, *Slavery and Human Progress* (New York: Oxford University Press, 1984), 61.

27 Manning asserts that "a single force—the New World demand for slaves—conditioned the development and differentiation of slavery throughout African society" (*SAL*, 126); see also Searing, *West African Slavery and Atlantic Commerce*, 199; and Lovejoy, *Transformations in Slavery*.

28 "Je regarde ce commerce comme le mobile de tous les autres, et je verrai avec regret la moindre partie de ce trafic passer en d'autres mains" (quoted in P. Dieudonné Rinchon, *Pierre-Ignace-Liévin Van Alstein, capitaine négrier: Gand 1733–Nantes 1793* [Dakar: IFAN, 1964], 98n1; emphasis mine). On Choiseul's Africa policy Guy Chaussinand-Nogaret writes in *La Vie quotidienne des Français sous Louis XV* (Paris: Hachette, 1979), 213: "Plus imaginatif que la plupart de ses contemporains que les îles à sucre hypnotisaient exclusivement, Choiseul ne perdait pas l'Afrique de vue. . . . Il tenta de jeter les premiers fondements d'une audacieuse politique africaine." The Chambre de Commerce of Nantes stated in 1784: "Le commerce d'Afrique est le plus intéressant [in the sense of advantageous, profitable] du royaume, la source la plus abondante des richesses qui entrent dans l'Etat; sans lui l'Amérique privée d'esclaves deviendrait infructueuse. *La traite des Noirs est la base de toute notre navigation*" (quoted in Suret-Canale, *Essais d'histoire africaine*, 73; emphasis added). Raynal reflects differently on this same point: "Les travaux des colons, établis dans ces isles long-tems méprisées, sont l'unique base du commerce d'Afrique; étendent les pêcheries & les défrichemens de l'Amérique Septentrionale; procurent des débouchés avantageux aux manufactures d'Asie; doublent, triplent peut-être l'activité de l'Europe entiere. *Ils peuvent être regardés, comme la cause principale du mouvement rapide qui agite l'univers*" (*Histoire des deux Indes*, 3:604; emphasis added). See James A. Rawley, *The Transatlantic Slave Trade: A History* (New York: Norton, 1981), 120.

29 Eric Saugera, *Bordeaux port négrier: Chronologie, économie, idéologie, XVIIe–XVIIIe siècles* (Paris: Karthala, 1995), 62.

30 Quoted in Jean Fouchard, *Les Marrons du syllabaire: Quelques aspects du problème de l'instruction et de l'éducation des esclaves et affranchis de Saint-Domingue* (Port-au-Prince: Henri Deschamps 1953), 42; emphasis added.

31 It should be noted, however, that at the time of Columbus there was less of a distinction in Europe between slavery and other forms of servitude. See Patterson, *Slavery and Social Death*, 6–7. Gradually the idea of race would insert a wedge, until the point (in the nineteenth century) when *nègre* and slave are synomymous in French (see *Larousse du XIXe siècle*, "nègre").

32 Jacques Savary, *Le Parfait negociant, ou instruction générale pour ce qui regarde le commerce* (Paris: Chez Jean Guignard fils, 1675), 140; Roger Mer-

415

cier, *L'Afrique noire dans la littérature française: Les Premières images, XVIIe-XVIIIe siècles* (Dakar: Université de Dakar, Faculté des Lettres et des Sciences Humaines, 1962), 86.

33 Quoted in c 93.

34 Jean-Baptiste Labat, *Nouveau voyage aux isles de l'Amérique* (Paris: Chez Guillaume Cavelier fils, 1722), 4:116–17.

35 See c 121; and Pierre Pluchon, *La Route des esclaves: Négriers et bois d'ébène au XVIIIe siècle* (Paris: Hachette, 1980), 147, 289.

36 See Renault and Daget, *Les Traites négrières en Afrique*, 88.

37 Robin Blackburn, *The Making of New World Slavery: From the Baroque to the Modern, 1492–1800* (London: Verso, 1997), 386.

38 Jean-Baptiste Labat, *Voyage du Chevalier des Marchais en Guinée, isles voisines, et à Cayenne, fait en 1725, 1726 & 1727* (Paris: Chez Saugrain, 1730), 1:32.

39 In Antoine, "Aventures d'un jeune négrier," 54.

40 Pluchon, *La Route des esclaves*, 151.

41 OE, 39. The fear was, of course, mutual, and a European sailor like Joseph Mosneron feared being eaten: "Nous connaissions le caractère de ces féroces cannibales qui sans pitié nous auraient exterminés jusqu'au dernier pour nous dévorer ensuite" (Olivier Pétré-Grenouilleau, ed., *Moi, Joseph Mosneron, armateur négrier nantais /1748–1833/* [Rennes: Editions Apogée, 1995], 69; henceforth abbreviated *MJM*).

42 Jacques Savary, *Le Parfait negociant, ou instruction générale pour ce qui regarde le commerce . . .* (Paris: Chez Jean Guignard fils, 1675), 140.

43 Labat, *Voyage du Chevalier des Marchais*, 3:53. See Gaston Martin, *Nantes au XVIIIe siècle: L'Ère des négriers (1714–1774)* (Paris: Lélix Alcan, 1931), 111; and т, 412.

44 Clarkson quoted in *OED*, 2nd ed., s.v. "middle passage." Vincent Carretta cites James Ramsay's *An Inquiry into the Effects of Putting a Stop to the African Slave Trade . . .* (1784) as the first occurrence of the phrase. See Vincent Carretta, *Equiano the African: Biography of a Self-Made Man* (Athens: University of Georgia Press, 2005), 17.

45 See c, 137. *The Encyclopedia Britannica* gives another, more recent interpretation: that Middle Passage refers to "the middle part of the slave's journey" ("Middle Passage," www.britannica.com). Using the *OED* 2nd ed. online, a quotations search for "middle passage" turns up only usages that suggest the point of view of the slavers: "The Round Trip . . . was commonly divided into three 'passages.' . . . Slaves . . . were shipped to America and the West Indies on the notorious Middle Passage" C. Lloyd, *The Navy and the Slave Trade* (1949) (see http://jeeves.library.yale.edu/cgi-bin/oed/oed-idx.pl). It seems clear that this phrase has shifted lexically from an initial, implied point of view that was white to one that is now black; it has been appropriated, and rightly so, by African Americans, to reflect the experience of their ancestors.

46 Edouard Glissant, *Tout-Monde: Roman* (Paris: Gallimard, 1993), 92–93. See

Joan Dayan, "Paul Gilroy's Slaves, Ships, and Routes: The Middle Passage as Metaphor," *Research in African Literatures* 27, no. 4 (winter 1996): 7–14. There was of course "hybridity" on slave ships, but not of a benign sort, if only in the form of rape; Pluchon reports that women captives were made to serve as concubines and as spies (*La Route des esclaves*, 255); see also C, 138; and Edward Reynolds, *Stand the Storm: A History of the Atlantic Slave Trade* (London: Allison and Busby 1985), 50–51.

47 Klein, *The Atlantic Slave Trade*, 128.

48 The balance of interpretation that I am trying to strike in this description of the Middle Passage is quite different from the idea of an "Atlantic proletariat," uniting white and black sailors, and white and black slaves and commoners, described in compelling but less than wholly credible terms by Peter Linebaugh and Marcus Rediker in their *The Many-Headed Hydra: Sailors, Slaves, Commoners, and the Hidden History of the Revolutionary Atlantic* (Boston: Beacon Press, 2000).

49 As Raina Croff has pointed out to me, some slave owners were themselves the interracial *signares* of the Senegalese coast: rich women, born from liaisons between French men and African women.

50 Reynolds, *Stand the Storm*, 53; T, 411.

51 See Geneviève Fabre, "The Slave Ship Dance," in *Black Imagination and the Middle Passage*, ed. Maria Dietrich, Henry Louis Gates Jr., and Carl Pedersen (New York: Oxford University Press, 1999), 33–46; C, 136; Pluchon, *La Route des esclaves*, 153; Martin, *Nantes au XVIIIe siècle*, 116–17.

52 Antoine, "Aventures d'un jeune négrier," 53.

53 These are the dimensions for the *Brookes*; see Malcolm Cowley and Daniel P. Mannix, "The Middle Passage," in *The Atlantic Slave Trade*, ed. David Northrup (Lexington, Mass.: D. C. Heath, 1994), 101.

54 Rev. John Newton, quoted in Cowley and Mannix, "The Middle Passage," 100.

55 On conditions of *entassement* on French vessels see D, 152–57.

56 On diseases see C, 147–50; and Pluchon, *La Route des esclaves*, 222–27. See also Eric Williams's comments on the conditions of the Middle Passage: "The transportation of these white servants shows in its true light the horrors of the Middle Passage—not as something unusual or inhuman but as a part of the age. The emigrants were packed like herrings" (Eric Williams, "Economics, Not Racism, as the Root of Slavery," in *The Atlantic Slave Trade*, ed. David Northrup [Lexington, Mass.: D. C. Heath, 1994], 8).

57 Wilson Harris, *History, Fable, and Myth in the Caribbean and the Guianas* (Wellesley, Mass.: Calaloux, 1995), 20. Edouard Corbière's novel *Le Négrier*, to be discussed in a later chapter, dramatizes the theme of blindness on slave-trading voyages.

58 Blackburn, *The Making of New World Slavery*, 392.

59 Klein, *The Atlantic Slave Trade*, 150–51.

60 T, 424; Herbert S. Klein reports only 313 rebellions out of a sample of 24,259

voyages (*The Atlantic Slave Trade*, 159). David Richardson suggests that "as many as 10 percent" of ships experienced an insurrection (David Richardson, "Shipboard Revolts, African Authority, and the Transatlantic Slave Trade," in Diouf, *Fighting the Slave Trade*, 201).

61 La Courbe, *Premier voyage du Sieur de La Courbe*, 273.

62 Robert Durand, *Journal de bord d'un négrier, 1731–1732*, General Ms. vol. 7, Beinecke Rare Book Library, Yale University, 67. See Harms, *The Diligent: A Voyage through the Worlds of the Slave Trade* (New York: Basic Books, 2002), 268–70. The Durand manuscript can be seen online at www.vcdh.virginia .edu/xml_docs/durand/.

63 Pluchon, *La Route des esclaves*, 188.

64 La Courbe, *Premier voyage du Sieur de La Courbe*, 272.

65 Even the former captive Abu Bakr Al-Siddiq, in his very short narrative about his enslavement, says only, "We continued on board ship, at sea, for three months, then came on shore in the land of Jamaica" (Philip D. Curtin, ed., *Africa Remembered: Narratives by West Africans from the Era of the Slave Trade* [Madison: University of Wisconsin Press, 1967], 162).

66 *MJM*, 138–39. There is only one other utterance by an African in his journal, the only direct quotation: a very strong male captive tells the sailors that he can break his chains; they ask him to show them, and he does, swearing loyalty: "Si . . . vous me débarrassez de mes entraves, je serais fidèle et reconnaissant. On prit confiance en lui et il ne cessa de se comporter avec autant de zèle que d'intelligence et force" (*MJM*, 74).

67 "Silence" here is of course the usual and slightly deceptive metaphor for the absence of a *written* record. We would do well to remind ourselves that the captives in the hold were in all likelihood very far from silent. See T, 798.

68 After obtaining 221 barrels of white sugar, 15,699 pounds of coffee, and 1,197 pounds of indigo, he still had more than half of his credit to spend (C, 212).

69 Klein, *The Atlantic Slave Trade*, 128.

70 Gaston Martin, *Nantes au XVIIIe siècle*, 373.

71 Quoted in Madeleine Borgomano, "La Littérature romanesque d'Afrique noire et l'esclavage: 'Une mémoire de l'oubli'?" in *Esclavage et abolitions: Mémoires et systèmes de représentation*, ed. Marie-Christine Rochmann (Paris: Karthala, 2000), 103.

72 Edouard Glissant, *Le Discours antillais* (Paris: Seuil, 1981), 18. For Glissant the "impulse" for return (*pulsion de Retour*), associated with a nostalgia for Oneness, fades away and is (or should be) replaced by a rising consciousness of the new land, the New World (*une prise en compte de la terre nouvelle*) (ibid., 31). He observes, however, that too often the old dream of an (impossible) return to Africa is replaced with a new dream of France, French citizenship, etc. (ibid., 105).

73 "Diasporas usually presuppose longer distances and a separation more like exile: *a constitutive taboo on return*, or its postponement to a remote future"

(James Clifford, "Diasporas," *Cultural Anthropology* 9, no. 3 [August 1994]: 304; emphasis added).

74 Desertion could reach as high as 15 percent of the crew (Pluchon, *La Route des esclaves*, 268). On the problem of the deserters' "libertinage" see *Ordonnance du Roy, au sujet des Matelots qui desertent dans les Colonies* (Paris: December 23, 1721): Bibliothèque Nationale de France call number F-23622 (554).

75 Via ARTFL database. Cf. *Trésor de la langue française*, s.v. "retour": "2. *vieilli*. Biens, profits obtenus au terme d'une expédition coloniale, d'une entreprise."

76 Antoine, "Aventures d'un jeune négrier," 53. Proa calculates his personal profits, aside from his wages, this way: "Ma pacotille [the goods he brought to Africa to sell himself] avait aussi très bien produit: j'avais de la poudre d'or, de l'ivoire, et un nègre que j'avais eu la permission d'acheter. En sorte que avec mille francs que j'avais en marchandises de France, j'avais bien trois mille francs non compris environ 1,500 francs qui me revenaient de mes appointements et des par-tête sur les nègres" (ibid.).

77 Ibid.

78 Patterson, *Slavery and Social Death*, viii–ix.

79 *SAST*, 115, 116.

80 Patterson, *Slavery and Social Death*, 342.

81 The notion of sacrifice is aptly chosen by Manning as a general theme in his book (*SAL*).

82 Herbert S. Klein complains of a "myth of the so-called triangular trade," the myth being that the whole triangle was completed by each single ship; he writes, "There is little question that this trade can be considered to have had a triangle-style relationship, but the slave ships, for all intents and purposes, really made a significant impact only on the outbound to Africa and the Africa to American legs of the trip" (Klein, *The Atlantic Slave Trade*, 97).

83 Pluchon, *La Route des esclaves*, 86.

84 VOC, 12:417. This remark about prices comes in the middle of a passage that is one of Voltaire's strongest condemnations of slavery, and I will quote more of the passage below. The initial period of time that Voltaire refers to here, the 1740s, was two decades after he was known to have extensive investments in the slave trade through the Compagnie des Indes (see below).

85 Reynolds, *Stand the Storm*, 109. See Chaussinand-Nogaret, *La Vie quotidienne des Français sous Louis XV*, 195. Among those who lost money in the trade was René-Auguste de Chateaubriand — father of François-René and a slave-trading captain working out of Nantes. He suffered losses so heavy, due to a sudden drop in the prices of slaves in 1756, that he carried a huge debt with him to his grave thirty-eight years later. His son, writes Crété, "projeta de recouvrer la fortune insaisissable que les gens de Saint-Domingue devaient au défunt armateur; mais la Révolution compromit sa mission aux *Iles du Bonheur*" (C, 215).

86   c, 7–8. David Eltis asserts that "the slave trade formed such a tiny share of the Atlantic trade of any European power that . . . its contribution to the economic growth . . . was trivial" (E, 265). But his statistics at this point are strictly British, and, more important, the real question is not just the impact of the trade but of the trade and slave labor taken together, as one aggregate machine. The latter is a point that Robert Harms rightly emphasizes: "Like the French, the British understood that the real profits lay not in the slave trade itself, but in the products produced by slaves in the New World colonies" (Harms, *The Diligent*, 142).

87   C. L. R. James, *The Black Jacobins: Toussaint L'Ouverture and the San Domingo Revolution*, 2nd ed. (New York: Vintage Books, 1989), 47. His thesis seems to repose on profit margins of 15 or 20 percent that have since been called into question.

88   S, 181; see also c, 43.

89   Martin, *Nantes au XVIIIe siècle*, 164; see also 429.

90   See Gilles Bienvenu and Françoise Lelièvre, "L'Hôtel Grou," in *Les Anneaux de la mémoire*, 55.

91   Ibid., 135.

92   Sue Peabody, *"There Are No Slaves in France": The Political Culture of Race and Slavery in the Ancien Régime* (New York: Oxford University Press, 1996).

93   See Saugera, *Bordeaux port négrier*, 296–97. *Nantes, archéologie de la mémoire*, also known as *Les Anneaux de la mémoire*, film by Kitia Touré (France, 1994).

94   Louis Sala-Molins, *Le Code Noir ou le calvaire de Canaan* (Paris: Presses Universitaires de France, 1987), 220; William B. Cohen, *The French Encounter with Africans: White Response to Blacks, 1530–1880* (Bloomington: Indiana University Press, 1980), 111; henceforth abbreviated WC.

95   It seems possible that the high figure of five thousand was the result of inflation by authorities anxious to impose the ban of 1777 (see WC, 315n29). Cohen also points out that the situation in England was very different: "in England blacks represented 20,000 out of 8 million inhabitants" (WC, 112)—a small group, but far larger than in France. See also Erick Noël, *Etre noir en France au XVIIIe siècle* (Paris: Tallandier, 2006), 95.

96   Olivier Pétré-Grenouilleau, *Les négoces maritimes français: XVIIe–XXe siècle* (Paris: Belin, 1997), 109.

97   Gloria Bigot-Legros, "Postface: Un Exil de trois siècles," in Saugera, *Bordeaux port négrier*, 348.

98   James, *The Black Jacobins*, 48.

99   According to some late-eighteenth-century estimates, as much as a quarter of the French population depended on the Atlantic slave trade to some extent: see Pieter Emmer, "Capitalism after Slavery? The French Slave Trade and Slavery in the Atlantic, 1500–1900," *Slavery and Abolition* 14, no. 3 (December 1993): 239. While this figure may be hard to believe, Emmer points out that in

any case the proportion of dependence on the trade in France must have been higher than it was in other European slave-trading nations (ibid.).

100   *SAST*, 121.

3   THE SLAVE TRADE IN THE ENLIGHTENMENT

1   Gaston Martin, *Nantes au XVIIIe siècle: L'Ère des négriers (1714–1774)* (Paris: Lélix Alcan, 1931), 429; see also *MJM*, 19.

2   See Gaston Martin, "Les 'Chambres littéraires' de Nantes et la préparation de la Révolution," *Annales de Bretagne* 37 (1925–26): "Leur bibliothèque est avant tout librairie de techniciens. Les écrits de Voltaire, de Rousseau, de Montesquieu, de Bayle y sont à l'honneur, et c'est tout naturel. Mais à côté, et plus nombreux, ils ont groupé les livres d'informations" (356). For an analysis of libraries as a cultural artifact within the class masquerade of the *armateurs*, see Olivier Pétré-Grenouilleau, *L'Argent de la traite: Milieu négrier, capitalisme et développement: Un Modèle* (Paris: Aubier 1996), 132–48.

3   See Claudine Hunting, "The Philosophes and Black Slavery: 1748–1765," *Journal of the History of Ideas* 39, no. 3 (July–September 1978): 405–18.

4   See Rodolphe Damon, *Joseph Crassous de Médeuil, 1741–1793: Marchand, officier de la Marine royale et négrier* (Paris: Karthala, 2004), 161. Crassous's library also included Labat's works.

5   See www.lib.uchicago.edu/efts/ARTFL/projects/encyc/. This article moved beyond other, more ambiguous treatments of slavery in the *Encyclopédie*, such as the long article "Esclave" by Boucher d'Argis, which is quite matter-of-fact about the institution and does not condemn it in any way; the article "Nègres, considérés comme esclaves dans les colonie d'Amérique," by M. le Romain says that "Ces hommes noirs, nés vigoureux & accoutumés à une nourriture grossière, trouvent en Amérique des douceurs qui leur rendent la vie animale beaucoup meilleure que dans leur pays"—and the article provides comparative ratings of different types of Africans as slaves; the article "Sucrerie," also by Le Romain, issues warnings about the "vicieuse" character of slaves and gives advice about how to get them to work. Jaucourt's articles (thirteen of them bearing on slavery or the trade according to Jean Ehrard's analysis) are very different and show no tolerance for slavery. The best quantitative perspective on the *Encyclopédie* is provided by Jean Ehrard, who found that the seventy-two thousand articles of the *Encyclopédie* contained only thirty-three references to slavery or the slave trade. Ehrard writes: "Sur la petite cinquantaine d'articles étudiés dont le sujet pouvait appeler la mention de l'esclavage des Noirs, quinze s'abstiennent d'en parler, vingt l'évoquent de façon neutre—silence pesant sur une telle question!—, dix le condamnent avec plus ou moins de vigueur, et trois l'approuvent" (Jean Ehrard, "L'Esclavage devant la conscience morale des Lumières françaises: Indifférence, gêne, révolte," in *Les Abolitions de l'esclavage: De L. F.*

Sonthonax à V. Schoelcher, ed. Marcel Dorigny [Paris: Presses Universitaires de Vincennes, 1995], 143, 146).

6   David Brion Davis, *Slavery and Human Progress* (New York: Oxford University Press, 1984), 107.

7   Edward Derbyshire Seeber, *Anti-Slavery Opinion in France during the Second Half of the Eighteenth Century* (New York: Greenwood Press, 1969), 56.

8   Roger Mercier, *L'Afrique noire dans la littérature française: Les Premières images, XVIIe–XVIIIe siècles* (Dakar: Université de Dakar, Faculté des Lettres et des Sciences Humaines, 1962), 68.

9   Montesquieu, *Lettres persanes*, letter 34 (Paris: Garnier, 1975), 74.

10   Ibid., letter 118, 249; *Persian Letters*, trans. C. J. Betts (New York: Penguin Books, 1973), 213.

11   Before the nineteenth century the Spanish did not practice the slave trade in Africa themselves but granted lucrative *asientos* to other nations and companies, licensing them to provide slaves to the Spanish colonies. The French Compagnie de Guinée held the asiento from 1702 to 1712, agreeing to provide either thirty-eight thousand slaves (if there was war in Europe) or forty-eight thousand (if there was peace) to the Spanish colonies (see "Assiente ou assiento," in the *Encyclopédie*). See C, 23; and Robin Blackburn, *The Making of New World Slavery: From the Baroque to the Modern, 1492–1800* (London: Verso, 1997), 141, 203, 212, 294, 495.

12   Montesquieu, *The Spirit of the Laws*, trans. Anne M. Cohler, Basia Carolyn Miller, and Harold Samuel Stone (Cambridge: Cambridge University Press, 1989), 249.

13   See Madeleine Dobie, *Foreign Bodies: Gender, Language, and Culture in French Orientalism* (Stanford, Calf.: Stanford University Press, 2001), 37; and Léon-François Hoffmann, *Le Nègre romantique: Personnage littéraire et obsession collective* (Paris: Payot, 1973), 63.

14   See Hunting, "The Philosophes and Black Slavery," 417; and Michèle Duchet, "Voltaire et les sauvages," *Europe* 361–362 (May–June 1959): 97.

15   Montesquieu, *Spirit of the Laws*, 252, AT; *L'Esprit des lois*, 332, 333.

16   Montesquieu, *Spirit of the Laws*, 261–62; *L'Esprit des lois*, 345. See David Brion Davis, *The Problem of Slavery in Western Culture* (Ithaca: Cornell University Press, 1966), (henceforth abbreviated DBDI), 397.

17   VOC, 18:604; but Voltaire criticizes Montesquieu for suggesting that Africans sell themselves into slavery. In his "Commentaire sur *L'Esprit des lois*" (1777) Voltaire writes: "Si quelqu'un a jamais combattu pour rendre aux esclaves de toute espèce le droit de la nature, la liberté, c'est assurément Montesquieu" (VOC, 30:445). In *L'A, B, C*, (1762), the figure "C," who opposes slavery, says that Montesquieu's chapter is "bien comique; il triomphe en s'égayant sur notre injustice" (VOC, 21:355). On Montesquieu's positions on slavery see Pierre Pluchon, *La Route des esclaves: Négriers et bois d'ébène au XVIIIe siècle* (Paris: Hachette, 1980), 32; Seeber, *Anti-Slavery Opinion in France*, esp. 61–63; DBDI, chap. 13; Michèle Duchet, *Anthropologie et histoire au siècle*

des lumières (Paris: Flammarion, 1977), 132; and τ, 465–66. Crété describes Montesquieu's judgment of slavery as condemnation "avec sursis" (c, 258). Claudine Hunting sees in the irony of the philosophes "a brilliantly effective weapon against slavery" (Hunting, "The Philosophes and Black Slavery," 418). Her article is, however, problematic: in her unconvincing defense of all the philosophes (whom she groups together with little attention to their differences) and their position on slavery, she says that *L'Esprit des lois* "dealt vigorously with the black question" (407n4). Hunting would have us believe that a "fight" against the slave trade and slavery was "fundamental" to (all) the philosophes' intentions—that it was even "their primary objective" (408). The evidence does not support such a conclusion.

18 Abbé Antoine Pluche, *Le Spectacle de la nature ou entretiens sur les particularités de l'histoire naturelle . . .* (1735; Paris: Frères Estienne, 1780), 3:208–209. See Mercier, *L'Afrique noire dans la littérature française*, 88.

19 Pluchon, *La Route des esclaves*, 32.

20 Jean-Jacques Rousseau, *La Nouvelle Héloïse* (Paris: Hachette, 1925), part 4, letter 3, 309; *Julie or the New Heloise*, trans. Philip Stewart and Jean Vaché, in *The Collected Writings of Rousseau* (Hanover: University Press of New England, 1997), 6:340.

21 Having missed these few lines (which I found through the ARTFL database), Louis Sala-Molins alleges that Rousseau wrote "not one word" condemning the enslavement of Africans; this is nearly true. See Sala-Molins, *Les Misères des Lumières: Sous la raison, l'outrage* (Paris: Robert Lafont, 1992), 97; and *Le Code Noir ou le calvaire de Canaan* (Paris: Presses Universitaires de France, 1987), 246. This oversight takes *almost* nothing away from Sala-Molins's larger point: "Rousseau mérite mille fois le titre de pourfendeur de la servitude et de l'asservissement des citoyens par les couronnes. Mais il a usurpé celui de contempteur de l'*esclavage* au sens des pratiques qui lui furent contemporaines. Son silence à leur propos est révoltant" (*Le Code Noir*, 253). See also Same Kolle, "Le Code Noir et les Lumières françaises: Le Paradoxe d'un silence psychohistorique," in *Le Code Noir et l'Afrique*, ed. Ambroise Kom and Lucienne Ngoué (Ivry: Nouvelles du Sud, 1991); and Christian Delacampagne, *Une Histoire de l'esclavage: De l'antiquité à nos jours* (Paris: Librairie Générale Française, 2002), 174–200.

22 Jean-Jacques Rousseau, *Emile ou de l'éducation*, in *Oeuvres complètes* (Paris: Gallimard, 1969), 4:266–67: "Un françois vit en Guinée et en Laponie; mais un négre ne vivra pas de même à Tornea, ni un samoyéde au Benin. Il paroit encore que l'organisation du cerveau est moins parfaite aux deux extrêmes. Les négres ni les lapons n'ont pas le sens des européens."

23 Mercier, *L'Afrique noire dans la littérature française*, 68; Jean-Baptiste Labat, *Nouvelle Relation de l'Afrique occidentale* (Paris: Chez Théodore Le Gras, 1728), 1:i.

24 Pruneau de Pommegorge, himself a complicated case, makes a scathing attack on Labat's reliability at the beginning of his *Description de la Nigritie*

(Amsterdam: Chez Maradan, 1789): "Le pere Labat n'a écrit que d'après les questions qu'il faisoit aux matelots nègres, qui venoient à bord de son navire, & qui, pour avoir un verre de vin ou d'eau-de-vie, lui débitoient chacun ce qui leur venoit en tête. . . . De là, on doit juger du cas que l'on doit faire de son ouvrage" (vi–vii).

25 On the status of knowledge about Africa in general see Christopher L. Miller, *Blank Darkness: Africanist Discourse in French* (Chicago: University of Chicago Press, 1985); on Labat see Mercier, *L'Afrique noire dans la littérature française*, 53–68; and on Demanet, ibid., 117–20.

26 See Mercier, *L'Afrique noire dans la littérature française*, 82.

27 Benjamin-Sigismond Frossard, *La Cause des esclaves nègres et des habitans de la Guinée* (Lyon: Aimé de La Roche, 1789), 194.

28 Jean-Jacques Rousseau, *Du Contrat social* (Geneva: C. Bourquin, 1947), 186.

29 Jean-Jacques Rousseau, *Discours sur l'origine et les fondements de l'inégalité parmi les hommes*, in *Oeuvres complètes*, 3:191. In *Du Contrat social*: "de vils esclaves"; "il est esclave, il n'est rien" (298, 307). The main statement of this idea in *Du Contrat social* is the following: "Les esclaves perdent tout dans leurs fers, jusqu'au désir d'en sortir: ils aiment leur servitude comme les compagnons d'Ulisse aimoient leur abrustissement" (177). See Rousseau, *La Nouvelle Héloïse*, 1:245: "un lâche esclave sans force et sans courage, qui va traînant dans l'ignominie sa chaîne et son désespoir."

30 *Du Contrat social*, 302, 237.

31 David Brion Davis writes: "Rousseau's very extremism [in opposition to slavery] led to certain paradoxes. . . . [Slavery was] an act of dehumanization to which only a madman could consent" (DBD1, 414).

32 In *Du Contrat social* see Rousseau's remarks on Sparta (309), and on Rome (298).

33 Rousseau, *Emile*, in *Oeuvres complètes*, 4:253.

34 Rousseau, *Discours sur l'origine*, in *OC*, 3:193.

35 The general problem here is put in perspective by Duchet in *Anthropologie et histoire*, 14. Michel-Rolph Trouillot writes: "'Slavery' was at that time an easy metaphor, accessible to a large public who knew that the word stood for a number of evils *except perhaps for the evil of itself*. . . . This metaphorical usage permeated the discourse of various nascent disciplines from philosophy to political economy up to Marx and beyond" (Michel-Rolph Trouillot, *Silencing the Past: Power and the Production of History* [Boston: Beacon Press, 1995], 85, 86; emphasis added). Srinivas Aravamudan puts the question of metaphorization in context: "One function of anticolonial rhetoric was to metaphorize wrongs abroad in order to radicalize democratic aspirations in France even while escaping censorship" (Srinivas Aravamudan, *Tropicopolitans: Colonialism and Agency, 1688–1804* [Durham: Duke University Press, 1999], 298).

36 A nineteenth-century view, critiqued by David Brion Davis, suggested that after reading Montesquieu, Voltaire, and Rousseau, "there was not one chance in a thousand that any man who had once made any considerable number of

these ideas his own could ever support slavery"—Andrew Dickson White (1862), quoted in David Brion Davis, *The Problem of Slavery in the Age of Revolution, 1770–1823* (Ithaca: Cornell University Press), 165; henceforth abbreviated DBD2. Nor did being "steeped" in Rousseau prevent Moreau de Saint-Méry, a Creole from Martinique and a revolutionary in 1789, from defending slavery and the slave trade. See DBD2, 164–212, esp. 187–88.

37 Pétré-Grenouilleau writes: "Joseph Mosneron Dupin s'initie à la lecture et prend goût à celle de Rousseau. On pourrait penser qu'il en retire une vision critique de l'ordre social. Elle le confirme dans son désir de défendre la famille et la religion, et, finalement, nourrit une pensée conservatrice" (Pétré-Grenouilleau, *L'Argent de la traite*, 109).

38 Chevalier Stanislas de Boufflers, *Lettres d'Afrique à Madame de Sabran* (Paris: Actes Sud, 1998), 148–49.

39 Edouard Glissant, *Poétique de la relation* (Paris: Gallimard, 1990), 17n. Was there a text onboard, or did the crew reinvent the play based on someone's memory? Mosneron does not say. Thanks to Julia Prest for raising this question.

40 A. Owen Aldridge, *Voltaire and the Century of Light* (Princeton: Princeton University Press, 1975), 97. It should be pointed out that one year earlier, Americans and other exotic figures were lavishly represented, and with some sympathy, in Jean-Philippe Rameau's opera-ballet *Les Indes galantes* (first performed August 23, 1735). A performance of this work by Les Arts Florissants at the Palais Garnier in Paris in September 2003 made it clear how toe-tappingly seductive was Rameau's depiction of colonialism. Like *Alzire*, *Les Indes galantes* expresses, at moments, what seems to be genuine sympathy for the demise of other civilizations at the hands of European imperialism; an early form of cultural romanticism emerges. A sign of the near oblivion into which *Alzire* fell comes in A. J. Ayer's biography, *Voltaire* (London: Weidenfeld and Nicolson, 1986); Ayer refers to it as "a melodrama set in Paris" (15). Seminar research by Susannah Carson (April 2005) shows that numerous plays featuring the theme of "primitivism" and representing Native Americans preceded *Alzire*.

41 Jeanne Monty, "Le Travail de composition d'*Alzire*," *French Review* 35, no. 4 (February 1962): 384, including the quotation from Voltaire. Jean Orieux subscribes to the theory that Le Franc plagiarized *Alzire*; see his *Voltaire*, trans. Barbara Bray and Helen R. Lane (Garden City, N.Y.: Doubleday, 1979), 115.

42 Georg Brandes, *Voltaire* (New York: Albert and Charles Boni, 1930), 1:355.

43 Raynal established the prize in 1780 (Mercier, *L'Afrique noire dans la littérature française*, 159; see also Duchet, *Anthropologie et histoire*, 21). But Saint-Lambert had asked the same question in his *Les Saisons* in 1769 (Mercier, *L'Afrique noire dans la littérature française*, 125).

44 VOC, 12:398, 402. The composition of the *Essai sur les mœurs*, which took definitive form only in 1769, apparently began around 1740, seven years after *Alzire* was first written. Voltaire's version of the history of Peru is in chapter

425

148 of the *Essai sur les mœurs*: "On ne sait si on doit plus admirer le courage opiniâtre de ceux qui découvrirent et conquirent tant de terres, ou plus détester leur férocité: la même source, qui est l'avarice, produisit tant de bien et tant de mal" (VOC, 12:400). In this chapter Voltaire attacks what he sees as Spanish Catholic fanaticism, while at the same time revealing his belief in the natural "supériorité" "en tout" of the Europeans (ibid.). On possible sources for *Alzire* see Jean-Pierre Sanchez, "Voltaire et sa tragédie américaine *Alzire* (1736)," *Caravelle* 58 (1992): 17–38; and Merle L. Perkins, "The Documentation of Voltaire's *Alzire*," *MLQ* 4, no. 4 (December 1943): 433–36.

45 Voltaire, *Alzire, ou les Américains: Tragédie en cinq actes et en vers*, in VOC, 3:388; *Alzire*, in *The Works of Voltaire*, trans. William F. Fleming (New York: E. R. Dumont, 1901), 17:7–8. The translation is loose, abridged, and problematic, so I have translated missing lines and corrected mistranslations (indicated by the abbreviation AT). (The name Montèze is egregiously mistranslated as Montezuma, and all references to "America" are removed.) Further references to *Alzire* will be abbreviated *A*, followed by the page number of the original, then of the translation. The original text of *Alzire* is available online from the Bibliothèque Nationale de France.

46 Responding to critics, Voltaire protests (too much) in a footnote at this point: "une conversion subite serait ridicule" (*A*, 435n1).

47 Voltaire, quoted in Monty, "Le Travail de composition d'*Alzire*," 384.

48 Theodore E. D. Braun, "Subject, Substance, and Structure in *Zaïre* and *Alzire*," *Studies on Voltaire and the Eighteenth Century* 87 (1972): 186, 187.

49 See Duchet, *Anthropologie et histoire*, 262–63: Voltaire "pose le problème en termes juridiques, et ne met pas en cause le principe meme de l'esclavage, mais seulement ses modalités." See Guy Vermée, "Avancées et limites des discours antiesclavagistes et anticolonialistes des philosophes des Lumières," in Association française d'amitié et de solidarité avec les peuples d'Afrique, *Esclavage, colonisation, libérations nationales, de 1789 à nos jours*, (Paris: L'Harmattan, 1990): "Raynal et les autres ne soumettront jamais rien d'autre que de rester aux colonies tout en essayant d'aménager et d'humaniser les modes d'exploitation" (38); "Pas un seul penseur du [18e] siècle n'échappe à la tentation de croire que la civilisation des peuples sauvages constitue la tâche la plus urgente à accomplir" (41).

50 VOC, 12:401. See Herbert S. Klein, *The Atlantic Slave Trade* (Cambridge: Cambridge University Press, 1999), 22: "Already by the mid-1550s there were some three thousand African slaves in the Peruvian viceroyalty, with half of them in the city of Lima."

51 See Braun, "Subject, Substance, and Structure in *Zaïre* and *Alzire*," 195, 187, 181, 188.

52 "Assimilé à une bête de somme aux colonies, le Noir faisait simplement partie du décor dans l'Orient que l'imagination collective s'était créé" (Léon-François Hoffmann, *Le Nègre romantique*, 63).

53 See VOC, 21:223–33.

54 VOC, 12:416–17; emphasis added.

55 *Dictionnaire philosophique* (1764), in VOC, 18:602–3.

56 The ambiguity of Voltaire's position(s) may best be reflected in his *L'A, B, C* (1762), a dialogue in which some of the defenses of slavery are contested, but with little force (especially by comparison to Raynal's version of the same exercise, discussed below). See in *L'A, B, C,* "A": "'Nous n'avons pas, à la vérité, le droit naturel d'aller garrotter un citoyen d'Angola pour le mener travailler à coups de nerf de boeuf à nos sucreries de la Barbade . . . mais nous avons le droit de convention. Pourquoi ce nègre se vend-il? ou pourquoi se laisse-t-il vendre?'" "B" then responds: "'Quoi! vous croyez qu'un homme peut vendre sa liberté?, qui n'a point de prix?'" (VOC, 21:355). The trade is implicitly defended—through fictionally non-European mouthpieces, the device used in *Les Lettres persanes*—in *Lettres d'Amabed* (1769), in which an Asian Indian voyager makes disparaging remarks about Hottentots ("cette race ne peut avoir la même origine que nous" [VOC, 21:459]) and witnesses the slave trade in Angola: "Le capitaine a acheté, sur un rivage qu'on nomme Angola, six nègres qu'on lui a vendus pour le prix courant de six boeufs. . . . Comment une si abondante population s'accorde-t-elle avec tant d'ignorance?" (ibid., 462).

57 Quoted in Duchet, *Anthropologie et histoire*, 235.

58 *Essai sur les mœurs*, in VOC, 12:381; emphasis added. On Voltaire's "polygenist" anthropology see Duchet, *Anthropologie et histoire*, 229–63; on Voltaire and the slave trade see Pluchon, *La Route des esclaves*, 32. Hunting is able to make Voltaire into a pure opponent of slavery only by dismissing the thorough and convincing analysis of his work by Duchet (Hunting, "The Philosophes and Black Slavery," 413n11). Voltaire's curiosity extends to what he sees as the limit cases of the human species, and he wonders about the "missing link." See "Chaîne des êtres créés," in his *Dictionnaire philosophique* (VOC, 18:124). In the *Essai sur les mœurs* he mentions a creature who seems close to being the missing link, in Voltaire's mind: an African albino brought to Paris by a slave merchant. He describes this African as one of "ces animaux ressemblants à l'homme" (VOC, 12:367–68).

59 VOC, 30:445–47. Voltaire's discussions of slavery often turn their focus toward the analogous problem of the serfs, especially those in the service of the Church. For polemical purposes Voltaire erases any distinction between serfdom and slavery, calling the serfs of the Church slaves: "On appelle les moines eux-mêmes *gens de mainmorte*, et ils ont des esclaves. . . . Disons donc que les moines ont encore cinquante ou soixante mille eslaves mainmortables dans le royaume des Francs" (VOC, 18:603, 606; this article, "Esclaves," appeared in the *Questions sur l'"encyclopédie"* [1771]). It is understandable that Voltaire would be very concerned about the condition of serfs in France. Haydn Mason writes: "At Saint-Claude, not far from Ferney, he discovered that a chapter of twenty monks was holding twelve hundred peasants in conditions of serfdom. . . . From the late 1760s . . . he waged the

427

battle for the serfs' liberation. . . . [This may have been] the most important of all the philosophe's campaigns in its wider political significance" (Haydn Mason, *Voltaire: A Biography* [Baltimore: Johns Hopkins University Press, 1981], 118–19). It was not until the Revolution that this form of servitude was finally banned. This, then, is the true struggle to which Voltaire committed himself—not the abolition of African slavery and the Atlantic slave trade (*pace* Hunting).

60 According to an ARTFL search, *esclave* and *esclavage* appear in *Alzire* eighteen times. In many cases the usage is metaphorical, such as "esclave d'un coup d'oeil" (6) or "esclave de la crainte" (4).

61 Both 1736 editions have *fierté* (pride) instead of *fureur*. *Alzire, ou les Américains* (Paris: Chez Jean-Baptiste-Claude Bauche, 1736), 58; and *Alzire, ou les Américains* (Amsterdam: Chez Etienne Ledet, 1736), 67.

62 The problem of Voltaire's investments in the slave trade is full of dead ends and false information. It is commonly stated in France that he had investments in the trade, and some historians have repeated that claim, with varying degrees of confirmability; numerous statements have been made without any bibliographical reference or proof. Thus Michèle Duchet: Voltaire "a des intérêts dans le commerce des Antilles et des actions dans plusieurs compagnies de navigation" ("Voltaire et les sauvages," 95–96)—with no documentation; Liliane Crété writes: "Il semble que Voltaire, malgré ses belles paroles sur les méfaits de l'esclavage, ait pris des parts dans une société négrière nantaise" (c, 258); Crété's source is Hubert Deschamps, who writes: "Voltaire lui-même semble bien avoir pris des actions d'une société négrière" (*Histoire de la traite des Noirs de l'antiquité à nos jours* [Paris: Fayard, 1971], 167), with no documentation. In turn, Guy Chaussinand-Nogaret writes, "Voltaire—dérision!—figure au rang des actionnaires du négrier Montaudoin" (*La Vie quotidienne des Français sous Louis XV* [Paris: Hachette, 1979], 198). No proof emerges from any of these sources. Further in the background, allegations about Voltaire's investments in the slave trade appear to have emerged in the nineteenth century as part of a religious attack on the Enlightenment. Thus Eugène de Mirecourt published a letter that he claimed was written by Voltaire—as Seeber points out "with no indication of its source" (Seeber, *Anti-Slavery Opinion in France*, 65n)—in which "Voltaire" gloats over gains from the slave trade. See Eugène de Mirecourt, *Voltaire: Ses hontes, ses crimes, ses oeuvres* (Paris: Bray et Retaux, 1877), 127. This rumor was then repeated; but the title of Mirecourt's book gives his show away. Clarification of the entire issue comes from Emeka Abanime, "Voltaire antiesclavagiste," *Studies on Voltaire and the Eighteenth Century* 182 (1979): 237–51. In an authentic letter (D104 in Besterman's edition, 1:117) dated April 1722, Voltaire states that a good part of his wealth is invested in the Compagnie des Indes, which for a long time had a monopoly on the trade in slaves. His actual investments in the slave trade thus appear to have been through the Compagnie, which traded in many things, including slaves. Voltaire could not have been unaware of

428

this, yet he held on to his shares in the Compagnie for more than fifty years. The Compagnie did stop trading in slaves in midcentury but continued to be deeply involved in colonial, and thus slave-based, commerce. (On the Compagnie des Indes and the slave trade see Stein, *The French Slave Trade*, 18–21). On Voltaire's attitudes Abanime concludes: "Voltaire donne l'impression d'être plus touché par le sort des 'esclaves' français que par celui des esclaves noirs" ("Voltaire antiesclavagiste," 243); the enslavement of Africans seemed more justifiable to him than the serfdom of peasants in France (244); he seemed to see slavery as "un mal nécessaire" (247). In 1775 his shares in the Compagnie were still making money for him: see Jacques Donvez, *De quoi vivait Voltaire?* (Paris: Deux Rives, 1949), 161. I am grateful to Catherine Labio for help with my research on this topic.

63   T, 465. Voltaire wrote a letter to Jean Gabriel Montaudoin on June 2, 1768: "Puisque vous daignez donner mon nom à un de vos vaisseaux, je défierai désormais toutes les tempêtes. Vous me faites un honneur dont je ne suis pas certainement digne, et qu'aucun homme de lettres n'avait jamais reçu" (*The Complete Works of Voltaire*, ed. Theodore Besterman et al., [Geneva: Institut et Musée Voltaire, 1974], 117:374). The Montaudoin family — "the greatest [name] in this trade in Nantes" (T, 251) — was the leading slave-trading clan in Nantes (see C, 48–49); they sent out more expeditions than any other family in France (S, 153). The Montaudoin name was virtually synonymous with the slave trade. "Le Voltaire" does not appear in Jean Mettas's *Répertoire des expéditions négrières françaises au XVIIIe siècle*, ed. Serge Daget (Paris: Société Française d'Histoire d'Outre-Mer, 1984), 2 volumes. This suggests that it was not used in the actual slave trade. Voltaire's eager acceptance of this "investment" of his famous *name*, in what could only have been an enterprise closely tied to the slave trade, strikes me as more significant than his financial investments, discussed above.

64   This may be because Voltaire saw Peru as "la nation la plus policée et la plus industrieuse du Nouveau Monde" — and the only "primitive" nation having a religion that does not "offenser notre raison" (see above, n. 39; see also Duchet, *Anthropologie et histoire*, 247, 248).

65   Jean Fouchard, *Artistes et répertoire des scènes de Saint-Domingue* (Port-au-Prince: Imprimerie de l'Etat, 1955), 96, 120, 136, 144, 194, 195. I say "at least" because Fouchard's listings are not considered to be exhaustive.

66   Robert Cornevin, *Le théâtre haïtien des origines à nos jours* (Montréal: Leméac, 1973), 22, 26.

67   Quoted in Jean Fouchard, *Le Théâtre à Saint-Domingue* (Port-au-Prince: Henri Deschamps, 1988), 19.

68   S. J. Ducoeur-Joly, *Manuel des habitans de Saint-Domingue* (Paris: Lenoir, 1802), 2:80.

69   Fouchard, *Le Théâtre à Saint-Domingue*, 198, 235–38.

70   For further analysis of theater in Saint-Domingue, including the interesting case of an anonymous play (*Le Héros africain*, 1797) that "returns" to Africa,

see Sibylle Fischer, *Modernity Disavowed: Haiti and the Cultures of Slavery in the Age of Revolution* (Durham: Duke University Press, 2004), 206–213. Fischer says that *Le Héros africain* "shifts the focus of cultural exchange from the routes used by the colonizers to the routes used by the slave traders — from Europe's America to America's Africa" (213).

71   See www.ibiblio.org/laslave. Another important sign of the continuing popularity of Voltaire's play is the appearance of Verdi's opera *Alzira* in 1854, based on the play. In Edouard Corbière's novel *Le Négrier* (Paris: Klincksieck, 1990), Alzire is the name of a female slave, a *capresse*, who is destined for a seraglio (243).

72   Arthur Young, quoted in Olivier Pétré-Grenouilleau, *Nantes au temps de la traite des Noirs* (Paris: Hachette, 1998), 127.

73   Etienne Destranges, *Le Théâtre à Nantes depuis ses origines jusqu'à nos jours, 1430–1901* (Paris: Librairie Fischbacher, 1902), 21–22. Destranges identifies him only as "Mosneron," whom I take to be Joseph's father, Jean (1701–73).

74   Camille Mellinet, *Notice historique sur le théâtre de Nantes* (Nantes: A la Librairie de Mellinet-Malassis, 1825), 19.

75   Fouchard, *Le Théâtre à Saint-Domingue*, 192. A statue of Voltaire now graces the entrance of the Théâtre Graslin in Nantes. Graslin was one of the merchants who invested in 1770 along with Mosneron (Destranges, *Le Théâtre à Nantes*, 21).

76   Mellinet displays this thought pattern in his "Prologue en vers, pour l'ouverture de l'année théâtrale 1825," in *Notice historique sur le théâtre de Nantes*: "Dérobons-nous aux fers que portaient *nos* ancêtres" (38; emphasis added).

77   Raynal, *Histoire des deux Indes* (Geneva: Chez Jean-Léonard Pellet, 1780), 3:177; emphasis added. On the attribution of this passage to Diderot see Yves Bénot, "Diderot, Pechmeja, Raynal, et l'anticolonialisme," *Europe* 41 (January–February 1963): 140.

78   René Pomeau, *D'Arouet à Voltaire, 1694–1734* (Oxford: Voltaire Foundation, 1985), 340. Rousseau reports this experience in a letter to Mme de Warens, September 13, 1737.

79   See Anne C. Vila, *Enlightenment and Pathology: Sensibility in the Literature and Medicine of Eighteenth-Century France* (Baltimore: Johns Hopkins University Press, 1998), 182–84.

80   I am grateful for Vilashini Cooppan's comments on this anecdote.

81   Bulfinch Lambe was a slave trader who was enslaved in Africa in 1722; see Harms, *The Diligent*, 166. This turning of the tables becomes a common theme in a subgenre of American drama at the end of the eighteenth century and in the early nineteenth century. American sailors were enslaved by Barbary pirates; see Benilde Montgomery, "White Captives, African Slaves: A Drama of Abolition," *Eighteenth-Century Studies* 27, no. 4 (summer 1994): 615–30. A similar narrative in French, set in North Africa (brought to my attention by Jessica Nyamugusha) is Pierre-Joseph Dumont, *Histoire de l'esclavage en Afrique (pendant trente-quatre ans)* (Paris: Chez Pillet ainé, 1819).

82 VOC, 21:131.

83 We have already seen hints of answers to this question: there were profits to be made; Africans enslaved each other, didn't they?; they are better off with us, in the islands, where they can be productive; sugar has become a necessity; the "enslavement" of modern man in European society is a more pressing concern. Each of these rationales had influence.

84 Destranges, *Le Théâtre à Nantes*, 21.

85 Ibid., 24.

4 THE VEERITIONS OF HISTORY

1 Michèle Duchet, *Anthropologie et histoire au siècle des lumières* (Paris: Flammarion, 1977), 136.

2 See Adam Hochschild, *Bury the Chains: Prophets and Rebels in the Fight to Free an Empire's Slaves* (Boston: Houghton Mifflin, 2005); C, 279; Herbert S. Klein, *The Atlantic Slave Trade* (Cambridge: Cambridge University Press, 1999), 186–87.

3 Duchet, *Anthropologie et histoire*, 138.

4 Roger Mercier, *L'Afrique noire dans la littérature française: Les Premières images, XVIIe–XVIIIe siècles* (Dakar: Université de Dakar, Faculté des Lettres et des Sciences Humaines, 1962), 98.

5 "Esclavage" and "Traite des nègres," by the Chevalier de Jaucourt, are both antislavery; Boucher d'Argis's article "Esclave" is neutral; Le Romain's article "Nègres, considérés comme esclaves dans les colonies de l'Amérique" defends slavery. On the *Encyclopédie* and slavery see DBDI, 415–17. According to an analysis of the fifty articles in the *Encyclopédie* that might have said something about slavery, fifteen don't mention it; twenty discuss it neutrally; ten condemn it; and three approve of it. See Jean Ehrard, "L'Esclavage devant la conscience morale des Lumières françaises: indifférence, gêne, révolte," in *Les Abolitions de l'esclavage: De L. F. Sonthonax à V. Schoelcher*, ed. Marcel Dorigny (Paris: Presses Universitaires de Vincennes, 1995), 143–52.

6 Raynal, *Histoire des deux Indes* (Geneva: Chez Jean-Léonard Pellet, 1780), 3:204; on music see ibid., 182–83. This third edition "suppresses the explicit reference to Spartacus" that was included in previous editions (Srinivas Aravamudan, *Tropicopolitans: Colonialism and Agency, 1688–1804* [Durham: Duke University Press, 1999], 405n17). Raynal may also have had investments in the trade (T, 483). Mercier places Raynal, in spite of his ambiguities and contradictions, at the beginning of a "revolution" of abolitionist thought in France (Mercier, *L'Afrique noire dans la littérature française*, 121, 129–46). Duchet provides an analysis and critique of Raynal's sources and of his evolving and contradictory positions on slavery (Duchet, *Anthropologie et histoire*, 143–48). See also Michel-Rolph Trouillot, who interprets the Spartacus passage as a warning to the planters (Trouillot, *Silencing the Past: Power and the Production of History* [Boston: Beacon Press, 1995], 81–85).

431

7   See C. L. R. James, *The Black Jacobins: Toussaint L'Ouverture and the San Domingo Revolution* (New York: Vintage Books, 1989), 25. Fouchard reports doubts about this story in *Les Marrons du syllabaire: Quelques aspects du problème de l'instruction et de l'éducation des esclaves et affranchis de Saint-Domingue* (Port-au-Prince: Henri Deschamps, 1953), 159n148. Trouillot says it's both unproven and beside the point (*Silencing the Past*, 170n22). Aravamudan explores the implications of this possibly apocryphal scene of reading in *Tropicopolitan* (292–325).

8   See Edward Derbyshire Seeber, *Anti-Slavery Opinion in France during the Second Half of the Eighteenth Century* (New York: Greenwood Press, 1969), 82; and Yves Bénot, "Diderot, Pechmeja, Raynal, et l'anticolonialisme," *Europe* 41 (January–February 1963): 149, 153. But Trouillot says that one should see behind the apparent radicalism of Diderot (and Raynal) merely an effort to better manage the colonies, not to abolish them (*Silencing the Past*, 81).

9   Marie-Jean-Antoine-Nicolas de Caritat, Marquis de Condorcet, *Oeuvres complètes* (Paris: Chez Henrichs, 1804), 11:124.

10 John Claiborne Isbell, "Voices Lost? Staël and Slavery, 1786–1830," in *Slavery in the Caribbean Francophone World: Distant Voices, Forgotten Acts, Forged Identities*, ed Doris Y. Kadish (Athens: University of Georgia Press, 2000), 40.

11 Antoine Edme Pruneau de Pommegorge, *Description de la Nigritie par M. P. D. P.* (Amsterdam: Chez Maradan, 1789), 108–9. The leaders are executed with cannons, which Pruneau says is "une suite nécessaire du commerce infâme que presque tous les européens font dans ces contrées" (ibid.). Later, onboard ship during the Middle Passage, the same group revolts again; 230 of them are killed, and 7 whites die (113–18). This would have taken place sometime before 1765, when Pruneau returned to France. See Raymond Mauny, "Révoltes d'esclaves à Gorée au milieu du XVIIIe siècle d'après Pruneau de Pommegorge," *Notes africaines* 141 (January 1974): 11.

12 Seeber, *Anti-Slavery Opinion in France*, 160.

13 Catherine Reinhardt, "French Caribbean Slaves Forge Their Own Ideal of Liberty in 1789," in *Slavery in the Caribbean Francophone World: Distant Voices, Forgotten Acts, Forged Identities*, ed. Doris Y. Kadish (Athens: University of Georgia Press, 2000), 22.

14 Lawrence C. Jennings, *French Anti-Slavery: The Movement for the Abolition of Slavery in France, 1802–1848* (Cambridge: Cambridge University Press, 2000), 3.

15 I am grateful to Laurent Dubois for bringing this point into focus for me.

16 Laurent Dubois makes the counterargument: "les fondements politiques et militaires du décret d'émancipation de 1794 se trouvaient aux Antilles, dans les insurrections d'esclaves." *Les Esclaves de la République: L'Histoire oubliée de la première émancipation, 1789–1794* (Paris: Calmann-Lévy, 1998), 12.

17 "Historically, the Negro steeped in the inessentiality of servitude was set

free by his master. *He did not fight for his freedom*" (Frantz Fanon, *Peau noire, masques blancs* [Paris: Seuil, 1952], 178; emphasis added); Frantz Fanon, *Black Skin, White Masks*, trans. Charles Lam Markmann (New York: Grove Press, 1967), 219. See Nigel Gibson, "Dialectical Impasses: Turning the Table on Hegel and the Black," *Parallax* 8, no. 2 (2002): 30–45.

18   Françoise Vergès, *Abolir l'esclavage: Une Utopie coloniale: Les Ambiguïtés d'une politique humanitaire* (Paris: Albin Michel, 2001), 105.

19   Jennings, *French Anti-Slavery*, 1, 3.

20   Laurent Dubois, *A Colony of Citizens: Revolution and Slave Emancipation in the French Caribbean, 1787–1804* (Chapel Hill: University of North Carolina Press, 2004), 373.

21   Mercier, *L'Afrique noire dans la littérature française*, 213.

22   Robin Blackburn, *The Making of New World Slavery: From the Baroque to the Modern, 1492–1800* (London: Verso, 1997), 570.

23   Jennings, *French Anti-Slavery*, 60, 286. The titles of some of Jennings's chapters reveal much about the nature of French abolitionism: "Procrastinations, Consultations, and Interpellations," "Stalemate and Regression," "Crisis and Further Setbacks," and "Toward Immediatism."

24   Edouard Glissant, *Le Discours antillais* (Paris: Seuil, 1981), 495.

25   See Pieter Emmer, "Capitalism after Slavery? The French Slave Trade and Slavery in the Atlantic, 1500–1900," *Slavery and Abolition* 14, no. 3 (December 1993): 245.

26   Josette Fallope, "Esclavage en Guadeloupe au XIXe siècle: Organisation sociale et mutations," in *Esclavage et abolitions: Mémoires et systèmes de représentation*, ed. Marie-Christine Rochmann (Paris: Karthala, 2000), 345; see also, in the same volume, Marie-Christine Rochmann, "Les Représentations de l'abolition de 1848 dans la littérature de Martinique et Guadeloupe," 195.

27   Daniel Maximin, "Allocution d'ouverture," in Rochmann, *Esclavage et abolitions*, 17–18. On this dialectic see Fallope, "Esclavage en Guadeloupe au XIXe siècle," 345, 346.

28   It seems hard to see in the rise of European beet sugar, which began to rival Caribbean cane sugar, a mere coincidence with abolition. See William B. Cohen, *The French Encounter with Africans: White Response to Blacks, 1530–1880* (Bloomington: Indiana University Press, 1980), 192; henceforth abbreviated WC; and Dale W. Tomich, *Slavery in the Circuit of Sugar: Martinique and the World Economy, 1830–1848* (Baltimore: Johns Hopkins University Press, 1990), 63, 74. In the glossary to his *Discours antillais* Glissant writes: "BETTERAVE. C'est étonnant comme ce tubercule a dominé invisible l'histoire des Antilles francophones. Ce qui s'est passé dans les plaines brumeuses du nord de la France a changé le paysage tropical de la Martinique" (*Le Discours antillais*, 496).

29   T, 797. On abolition as the putative triumph of Republican ideals in France (and other myths) see Christopher L. Miller, "Unfinished Business: Colonial-

433

ism in Sub-Saharan Africa and the Ideals of the French Revolution," in *The Global Ramifications of the French Revolution*, ed. Joseph Klaits and Michael H. Haltzel (Cambridge: Cambridge University Press, 1994), 105–126.

30 Emmer, "Capitalism after Slavery?" 243.

31 Derek Walcott, *The Antilles: Fragments of Epic Memory (The Nobel Lecture)* (New York: Farrar, Straus and Giroux, 1992), 11, 14; V. S. Naipaul, *The Middle Passage: Impressions of Five Societies—British, French and Dutch—in the West Indies and South America* (New York: Vintage Books, 1981), 29; Glissant, *Le Discours antillais*, 11. Naipaul cites the British historian James Froude, who famously wrote in 1887: "There are no people there [in the Caribbean] in the true sense of the word, with a character and a purpose of their own" (quoted in Naipaul, *The Middle Passage*, 10).

32 "L'éloignement géographique, l'indifférence avec laquelle la France traite les Vieilles Colonies—une fois conquis les territoires comme l'Algérie—et leur abandon aux pouvoir des potentats locaux prolongeront la situation paradoxale dans laquelle les a placées l'abolition" (Vergès, *Abolir l'esclavage*, 185).

33 Richard D. E. Burton, *La Famille coloniale: La Martinique et la mère patrie 1789–1992* (Paris: L'Harmattan, 1994).

34 Vergès, *Abolir l'esclavage*, 184.

35 Jeffrey Herbst, *States and Power in Africa: Comparative Lessons in Authority and Control* (Princeton: Princeton University Press, 2000), 11; Joseph Ki-Zerbo, "La Route mentale de l'esclave: Brèves réflexions à partir de la condition présente des peuples noirs," in *La Chaîne et le lien: Une vision de la traite négrière*, ed. Doudou Diène (Paris: UNESCO, 1998), 175; Barbara Crossette, "Aid from West Drops Sharply," *New York Times*, July 3, 2001, A7.

36 Howard W. French, "China in Africa: All Trade, with No Political Baggage," *New York Times*, August 8, 2004, A4.

37 See Yves Bénot, "De la traite négrière au sous-développement," in Diene, *La Chaîne et le lien*, 129.

38 See Thomas: "Like slaves in antiquity, African slaves suffered, but the character of their distress may be more easily conveyed by novelists such as Mérimée than chronicled by a historian" (T, 798). Mérimée seems a particularly poor choice, as I will explain later in this study.

39 Wilson Harris, *History, Fable, and Myth in the Caribbean and the Guianas* (Wellesley, Mass.: Calaloux, 1995), 29.

40 But note the persistence of the opposite claim by some Caribbean intellectuals. See Dany Bébel-Gisler, "Le Passé inachevé de l'esclavage: L'Héritage culturel africain dans le réel, l'inconscient et l'imaginaire social guadeloupéen," in Diène, *La Chaîne et le lien*, 296.

41 Patrick Chamoiseau, *L'Esclave vieil homme et le molosse* (Paris: Gallimard, 1997), 17.

42 See Madeleine Borgomano's survey of this question: "La Littérature roma-

nesque d'Afrique noire et l'esclavage: 'Une Mémoire de l'oubli'?" in Rochmann, *Esclavage et abolitions*, 99–126.

43 Matar Gueye, "Les Mémoires oublieuses de l'esclavage," in Rochmann, *Esclavage et abolitions*, 90.

44 See Lamine Senghor, *La Violation d'un pays* (Paris: Bureau d'Edition, de Diffusion et de Publicité, 1927).

45 See Martin Klein, *Slavery and Colonial Rule in French West Africa* (Cambridge: Cambridge University Press, 1998); Trevor R. Getz, *Slavery and Reform in West Africa: Toward Emancipation in Nineteenth-Century Senegal and the Gold Coast* (Athens: Ohio University Press, 2004).

46 Aminata Sow Fall, *Le Jujubier du patriarache* (Dakar: Editions Khoudia, 1993), 18; Ahmadou Kourouma, *Monnè, outrages et défis* (Paris: Seuil, 1990), 20.

47 See Christopher L. Miller, *Theories of Africans: Francophone Literature and Anthropology in Africa* (Chicago: University of Chicago Press, 1990), 110–13.

48 Bassori Timité's *Grelots d'or* (Abidjan: CEDA, 1983) depicts the slave trade that continued inside Africa after the end of the transatlantic trade. I am grateful to Samba Gadjigo for bringing this novel to my attention.

49 Ibrahima Ly, *Les Noctuelles vivent de larmes* (Paris: L'Harmattan, 1988); Roger Gnoan Mbala, *Adanggaman* (Côte d'Ivoire, 2000).

50 The few exceptions include Thomas Hale, "From Afro-America to Afro-France: The Literary Triangle Trade," *French Review* 49, no. 6 (May 1976): 1089–96; revised version, "Pre-*Roots*: The Literary Triangle Trade," *Minority Voices* 1, no. 1 (1977): 35–40; and Vèvè Clark, "Developing Diaspora Literacy and Marasa Consciousness," in *Comparative American Identities: Race, Sex, and Nationality in the Modern Text*, ed. Hortense J. Spillers (New York: Routledge, 1991), 40–61.

435

5 GENDERING ABOLITIONISM

1 Paul Auster, *The Book of Illusions* (New York: Henry Holt, 2002), 69. See François Chateaubriand, *Mémoires d'outre-tombe* (Paris: Gallimard, Bibliothèque de la Pléiade, 1951), 1:167.

2 David Patrick Geggus, "Slavery, War, and Revolution in the Greater Caribbean," in *A Turbulent Time: The French Revolution and the Greater Caribbean*, ed. David Barry Gaspar and David Patrick Geggus (Bloomington: Indiana University Press, 1997), 2.

3 A reversal has taken place: we now think of physical transfer as a metaphorical translation and of linguistic translation, the *OED*'s second definition, as literal.

4 The *Dictionnaire de l'Académie Française* of 1798 (5th ed.) lists the first definition of *traduire* as "Transférer d'un lieu à un autre. Il ne se dit que des personnes" (860). The 8th edition (1932) retains this as the first definition. But

a recent *Petit Robert* (CD-ROM, 2001) gives the first definition as "citer, dé-
férer."

5   Jean Pierre Plesse, *Journal de bord d'un négrier* (1762; Paris: Editions Le Mot
et Le Reste, 2005), 123.

6   For the period stated in the title of *Translating Slavery*—1783 to 1823—the
male authors named above are unconvincing cases in support of this point:
Mérimée's *Tamango*, which Massardier-Kenney rightly cites as an example of
male insensitivity to the cause of abolitionism, was published in 1829, thus
beyond the bounds of the volume. Hugo is slightly closer to a fair comparison—although only his first, short, anonymous version of his *Bug-Jargal* was
printed in this period, in 1820, when Hugo was sixteen years old. The expanded, definitive version was not published until 1826.

7   Some of these figures are mentioned in *Translating Slavery*, but only Grégoire
is (briefly) acknowledged as a contributor to the tradition of abolitionist
"translation" (by Kadish, *TS*, 43). Frossard and Morenas are not mentioned,
but Condorcet, Brissot, Broglie, and Auguste de Staël are included.

8   "Readers are thus often left with the impression that most writing about
slavery by Europeans was negative, if not altogether racist. This volume attempts to correct that impression by showing, starting with [Aphra] Behn,
the existence of a more positive and emancipatory intertextual tradition of
women writing about slaves" (Kadish, "Translation in Context," in *TS*, 28–29;
emphasis added).

9   According to Kadish, Behn is at the origin of the "positive and emancipatory intertextual tradition of women writing about slaves" (*TS*, 29). Kadish
complains of "French literary historians" and their neglect of the female tradition to which *TS* is devoted (beginning with Aphra Behn), but at this point
(*TS*, 28n9) she cites only Régis Antoine's *Les Ecrivains français et les Antilles*,
not mentioning the most important work on the representation of blacks in
French literature, Léon-François Hoffmann's *Le Nègre romantique: Personnage littéraire et obsession collective* (Paris: Payot, 1973). Hoffmann gives considerable attention to the influence of Behn's *Oroonoko* in France, including
its visible impact on Saint-Lambert's *Ziméo* (see Hoffmann, *Le Nègre romantique*, 86–87). Behn is of course at the origin of a female literary-abolitionist
tradition—ironic in light of the largely proslavery stance taken in the novella. See Elliot Visconsi, "A Degenerate Race: English Barbarism in Aphra
Behn's *Oroonoko* and *The Widow Ranter*," *ELH* 69 (2002): 687. But Behn also
sets off a long tradition of *men* writing about slaves, many of them in fact
inspired by Behn and imitating her. That tradition begins quickly in England,
with Thomas Southerne's highly successful tragedy *Oroonoko* of 1695, which
may have been, ironically, more feminist than Behn's novel. See Janet Todd,
introduction to Aphra Behn, *Oroonoko, The Rover and Other Works* (London:
Penguin Books, 1992), 19. Behn's influence therefore crossed both gender
lines and the English Channel; she is at the beginning of the long tradition of
derivative, translated abolitionism in France. Antislavery discourse, even as

it derived some of its basic philosophy from the French Enlightenment, was largely imported from England to France, to such an extent that it was always suspected of being a stalking horse for perfidious Albion. See William B. Cohen, *The French Encounter with Africans: White Response to Blacks, 1530–1880* (Bloomington: Indiana University Press, 1980), 202; henceforth abbreviated WC. Kadish discusses the importance of translation from English to French for the abolitionist movement (*TS*, 37–38).

10   On the readership of *Oroonoko* see Mercier, *L'Afrique noire dans la littérature française*, 91. See also Edward D. Seeber, *Anti-Slavery Opinion in France during the Second Half of the Eighteenth Century* (New York: Greenwood Press, 1969), 27. *Oroonoko* was translated into French in 1745, to wide acclaim (Seeber, *Anti-Slavery Opinion in France*, 27). References to Behn's *Oroonoko* as "abolitionist" need to be tempered by the observation made decades ago by Wylie Sypher: "Mrs. Behn is repelled not by slavery, but by the enslaving of a prince. . . . Her disgust is not with slavery, but with the treachery of the white man" (Wylie Sypher, *Guinea's Captive Kings: British Anti-Slavery Literature of the XVIIIth Century* [1942; New York: Octagon Books, 1969], 110, 113). Kadish gives detailed attention only to the distortions and compromises of Behn's abolitionism that were perpetrated by her French translator, Pierre-Antoine de La Place—an important subject, of course (*TS*, 26–35). But this analysis should have been augmented by attention to other French literary texts that, despite those distortions and compromises of Behn, continued to inject a genuine abolitionism, clearly derived from Behn, into French culture. Kadish creates the impression that French male authors all either ignored or sabotaged the abolitionism that Behn spawned. An enlightening recent discussion of *Oroonoko* is in Srinivas Aravamudan's *Tropicopolitans: Colonialism and Agency, 1688–1804* (Durham: Duke University Press, 1999), 29–70.

437

11   There is an exception that proves the rule here: Kadish mentions Joseph Lavallée's novel *Le Nègre comme il y a peu de blancs* (1789) as a "work which bears many resemblances to the literary works presented in this volume"— but only in function of the fact that it was translated by Phillis Wheatley (*TS*, 38). The porous border of gender is thus approached but not crossed. In the same essay Kadish acknowledges Grégoire as a male abolitionist "translator" (43).

12   I use the term *takeover* here in anticipation of an argument that I will make later, borrowing terms from Margaret Cohen, *The Sentimental Education of the Novel* (Princeton: Princeton University Press, 1999).

13   Jean-François de Saint-Lambert, *Contes américains: L'Abenaki, Ziméo, Les Deux amis* (1769; Exeter: University of Exeter Press, 1997), 11, 13–19. Aphra Behn's description of Oroonoko can clearly be seen behind Saint-Lambert's description of Ziméo (cf. *Oroonoko*, 80–81). *Ziméo* is also reprinted in Youmna Charara, *Fictions coloniales du XVIIIe siècle* (Paris: L'Harmattan, 2005), 49–63.

14   Charara, *Fictions coloniales*, 29.

15 Saint-Lambert is not an appropriate name to cite among authors who may have left the impression "that most writing about slavery by Europeans was negative, if not altogether racist" (*TS*, 28). Hoffmann is right to point out the reformist rather than abolitionist implications of *Ziméo*'s plot. Still, the last sentence cited ("votre argent ne peut vous donner le droit . . .") is categorically abolitionist.

16 Mailhol is not mentioned in *Translating Slavery*.

17 Gabriel Mailhol, *Le Philosophe nègre et les secrets des Grecs* (London: n.p., 1764), 66–67.

18 *Etudes de la nature*, in *Oeuvres complètes* (Paris: P. Dupont, 1826) 5:16; 5:396n.

19 WC, 138.

20 See Chris Bongie, *Islands and Exiles: The Creole Identities of Post/colonial Literature* (Stanford: Stanford University Press, 1998), 16. *Paul et Virginie* was first published as an addition to the third edition of *Etudes de la nature* (1788).

21 Jacques-Henri-Bernardin de Saint-Pierre, *Paul et Virginie*, in *Oeuvres complètes*, 6:120: "fidèles serviteurs." Elsewhere, Saint-Pierre makes clear his disdain for what he calls "la stupide Afrique" and for "Nègres sans prévoyance et sans police" (*Etudes de la nature*, in *Oeuvres complètes*, 5:329, 119).

22 See Mercier, *L'Afrique noire dans la littérature française*, 170–71. For Mercier, *Paul et Virginie* is "l'oeuvre décisive, dans laquelle les Nègres obtinrent enfin droit de cité dans la littérature française" (169).

23 Ibid., 171.

24 Carolyn Vellenga Berman, *Creole Crossings: Domestic Fiction and the Reform of Colonial Slavery* (Ithaca: Cornell University Press, 2006), 79. Berman's overall approach could well be applied to the texts by Staël that I will discuss.

25 See Berman, *Creole Crossings*, 80.

26 This poetry competition is barely mentioned in *Translating Slavery* (185).

27 Only five of the poems were published, all by men. There is no mention of female poets in the scholarship on the subject. The honorable mention went to Anne Bignan, a man (target of a satirical drawing by Victor Hugo, "M. Bignan recevant le prix de poésie à l'Académie").

28 See Hoffmann, *Le Nègre romantique*, 155–61.

29 See Gouges, *Les Droits de la femme* (N.p.: N.p., n.d. [1791]), 5: "Cherche, fouille et distingue, si tu peux, les sexes dans l'administration de la nature. Partout tu les trouveras confondus, partout ils coopèrent avec un ensemble harmonieux à ce chef-d'œuvre immortel." This text is commonly referred to as the "Déclaration des droits de la femme et de la citoyenne." Like many other writings by Gouges, it is available for download on the Gallica Web site of the Bibliothèque Nationale de France (http://gallica.bnf.fr/ark:/12148/bpt6k426138).

30 I am referring to the suggestion, made and repeated by Kadish, that "French

438

women" (without qualification, as if possibly in great numbers) fought against slavery and for women's rights. Kadish says in her introduction that the period from 1783 to 1823 "delineate[s] an especially active period in which French women resisted the joint oppression of slaves and women" (2). Kadish then writes in her essay on translation: "A century after *Oroonoko*, French women will see themselves very clearly 'in the place of the African slave' and will push the mutuality between women and slaves to new emancipatory lengths" (*TS*, 35). Which French women? How many, beyond the three authors in the volume? Sophie Doin could have been included but is not mentioned in *Translating Slavery*; her works were later edited by Kadish: Sophie Doin, *La Famille noire, suivie de trois nouvelles blanches et noires* (Paris: Harmattan, 2002).

6 OLYMPE DE GOUGES,
"EARWITNESS TO THE ILLS OF AMERICA"

1   The epigraph with which I open this section is drawn from *Le Départ de M. Necker et de Madame de Gouges*, in *Ecrits politiques, 1788–1791* (Paris: Côté-Femmes, 1993), 1:18. Further references to these two volumes of Gouges's writings will be abbreviated *EP*. Information on Gouges' life comes from Olivier Blanc, *Olympe de Gouges: Une humaniste à la fin du XVIIIe siècle* (Paris: René Viénet, 2003); henceforth abbreviated *ODG*. This biography seems intended to replace Blanc's earlier work, *Olympe de Gouges* (Paris: Syros, 1981). Blanc cites a work by Charles Monselet, *Les Oubliés et les dédaignés* (Paris: Poulet-Malassis et de Broise, 1859), which includes Gouges. Blanc's *ODG* is the only real biography of Gouges, and it is well researched and crafted. There are some causes for reservation, however, starting with his apparent but unclear disavowal of his first book on Gouges (*ODG*, 12). He also tends toward hagiography and seems preoccupied with defending his subject against all accusations of moral compromise or self-promotion. He tolerates no reproach of Gouges; she is for him simply "l'amie des minorités et des opprimés" (*ODG*, 39).

2   Joan Wallach Scott, *Only Paradoxes to Offer: French Feminists and the Rights of Man* (Cambridge, Mass.: Harvard University Press, 1996), 19–56. Scott's essay first appeared as "French Feminists and the Rights of Man: Olympe de Gouges's Declarations," *History Workshop* 28 (1989): 1–21. Blanc shows total hostility to Scott's work, without any sign of having tried to understand it.

3   On Gouges's haste in writing and its relation to literary quality see Roland Bonnell, "Olympe de Gouges et la carrière dramatique: 'Une passion qui porte jusqu'au délire,'" in *Femmes et pouvoir: Réflexions autour d'Olympe de Gouges*, ed. Shannon Hartigan, Réa McKay, and Marie-Thérèse Seguin (Moncton, N.B.: Editions d'Acadie, 1995), 83–85. Gouges claimed that she wrote her play *Mirabeau aux Champs Elysées* in four hours (88). I think that Gouges's disclaimers are more than a mere "*topos* de modestie" (DeJulio, in

439

TS, 327n6). See Brissot's remark: "Quoiqu'elle ait enrichi la scène de plusieurs pièces de théâtre qui n'étaient pas sans mérite, cependant elle manquait des connaissances les plus indispensables à tout écrivain; elle savait à peine écrire" (quoted by Blanc in the preface to Olympe de Gouges, *EP*, 1:19).

4   Marie-Pierre Le Hir, "Feminism, Theater, Race: *L'Esclavage des Noirs*," in *TS*, 66, 68.

5   These two quotations are from Brown's first publication on Gouges, "The Self-Fashionings of Olympe de Gouges, 1784–1789," *Eighteenth-Century Studies* 34, no. 3 (2001): 395, 384.

6   Ibid., 394.

7   Gregory S. Brown, *A Field of Honor: Court Culture and Public Culture in French Literary Life from Racine to the Revolution* (New York: Columbia University Press, 2002), 5/98, 114. Further references to this e-book, available via www.gutenberg-e.org, will be abbreviated *FH*, followed by the chapter and paragraph numbers. Le Hir makes a statement similar to Brown's (see *TS*, 78). On the Amis see David Brion Davis, *The Problem of Slavery in the Age of Revolution: 1770–1823* (Ithaca: Cornell University Press, 1975), 95–100; henceforth abbreviated D B D 2.

8   Brissot wrote: "Admise dans notre société [des Amis des Noirs], les premiers essais de sa plume furent consacrés aux malheureux que tous nos efforts ne pouvaient arracher à l'esclavage" (quoted in *ODG*, 91). Blanc describes Gouges elsewhere as an "assiduous" participant in meetings of the Amis (*EP*, preface, 1:20). Jacques-Pierre Brissot de Warville (1754–1793) was the leading founder of the Société des Amis des Noirs and a Girondist in the Revolution. He was a friend of Gouges; the Comtesse du Barry is reported to have introduced Brissot to Voltaire in 1778. See Joan Haslip, *Madame du Barry: The Wages of Beauty* (London: Weidenfeld and Nicolson, 1991), 131.

9   Such a conflation is visible in Joan Scott's jumbled reference to "*Zamore et Miʒrah* [sic], *ou l'esclavage des nègres*" (30); no such play exists. Le Hir also conflates the two plays, referring to "*Zamor* [sic] *et Mirʒa*—as *L'Esclavage des Noirs* was first called" (*TS*, 69). Le Hir does not cite or quote the published versions of *Zamore et Mirʒa*, although one of them appears in the bibliography of *TS* (331). Roland Bonnell also states that *L'Esclavage des Noirs* is *Zamore et Mirʒa* "sous un nouveau titre" ("Olympe de Gouges et la carrière dramatique," 86). Gouges herself began this tradition of conflating the two plays by retroactively calling *Zamore et Mirʒa L'Esclavage des Noirs* (e.g., *EP*, 2:175). I will refer to the three printed versions of the play as follows: (1) *Zamore et Mirʒa, ou l'heureux naufrage: Drame indien, en trois actes et en prose* (Paris: Chez l'Auteur et Chez Cailleau, [August] 1788), abbreviated *ZM1*; (2) *Zamore et Mirʒa, ou l'heureux naufrage: Drame indien, en trois actes et en prose*, in *Oeuvres de Madame de Gouges*, tome 3 (Paris: Chez l'Auteur et Chez Cailleau, [September] 1788), abbreviated *ZM2*; and (3) *L'Esclavage des Noirs, ou l'heureux naufrage: Drame en trois actes, en prose* (Paris: Chez la Veuve Duchesne, Chez Bailly, [March] 1792), abbreviated *EN*. The latter is the text that

is reproduced in *TS*. I have consulted all three original editions. The texts of *ZM1* and *ZM2* appear to be identical, with the same pagination and typesetting; however, *ZM2* includes a preface. Since the pagination is the same, I will cite the play simply as *ZM*. I have not seen the manuscript "copie de souffleur" of *Zamore et Mirza* that Brown discusses; he says it dates from December 1789 and "is slightly revised from the first printed edition" (*FH*, 5/118).

10   Olympe de Gouges, *Projet d'un second théâtre et d'une maternité*, quoted in Bonnell, "La carrière dramatique," 80.

11   On Benjamin Frossard, Davis writes: "Since Negro slaves lived so far away, he argued, their sufferings could not arouse an immediate authentic compassion. When Europeans read accounts of the slave trade, their emotions were as fleeting as those evoked by a sentimental romance. It was therefore necessary for writers to make direct appeals to reason and conscience" (*DBD2*, 258n). What we have seen, however, suggests that those appeals were often channelled through the emotions and even invocations of the body itself.

12   Bonnell, "La Carrière dramatique," 70–71.

13   Quoted ibid., 75; the number of women authors, 76.

14   Olympe de Gouges, "Lettre au littérateurs français," in *EP*, 1:139.

15   On Emmanuel-Félicité de Durfort, Duc de Duras (1715–89), "premier gentilhomme de la Chambre du roi" (who was also a member of the Académie Française and a contributor to the *Encyclopédie* on military science) and his role in the proposed arrest of Gouges, see *ODG*, 73, 87. See also *Dictionnaire de biographie française* (Paris: Letouzey et Ané, 1970), 12:729. His grandson was Amédée-Bretagne-Malo de Durfort, the last duc de Duras (1771–1838), who married Claire de Kersaint in 1797. See Yves Durand, *La Maison de Durfort à l'époque moderne* (Fontenay-le-Comte: Imprimerie Lussau, 1975), 302–4. On the elder duke's role in the colonial lobby known as the Club Massiac see *ODG*, 91. On the role of the First Gentlemen of the Royal Bedchamber see *FH*, glossary, under Institutions, First Gentlemen.

16   Olympe de Gouges, *Les Comédiens démasqués ou Madame de Gouges ruinée par la Comédie Françoise pour se faire jouer* (Paris: Imprimerie de la Comédie Françoise, 1790), 11.

17   Henry Weber, *La Compagnie française des Indes (1604–1875)* (Paris: Arthur Rousseau, 1904), 450. The *syndics* were appointed by the king. The Compagnie's colonial empire was ruined, Weber reports, by the end of the Seven Years' War in 1763 (449). See Jean Mettas, *Répertoire des expéditions négrières françaises au XVIIIe siècle* (Paris: Société Française d'Histoire d'Outre-Mer, 1978 and 1984), 1:530 (ref. no. 917).

18   The date 1767 is from Erica Harth, *Cartesian Women: Versions and Subversions of Rational Discourse in the Old Regime* (Ithaca: Cornell University Press, 1992), 213; Thiele Knobloch says "around 1768" in her preface to Olympe de Gouges, *Théâtre politique* (Paris: Côté-Femmes, 1993), 2:27. Blanc reports that Gouges had achieved the status of "dame de la société" by 1776 (*ODG*,

441

57), but he is oddly silent in *ODG* about the date of Gouges's arrival in Paris. In his preface to volume 1 of *EP* he says that she arrived "at the very end of the reign of Louis XV," which would mean 1774 (7).

19 Gouges, preface to *Zamore et Mirза*, consisting of an exchange of letters with the Comédie Française, with some additional commentary by Gouges (*ZM2*, 1, 23, 8, 22, 6).

20 The phrase "Fauteurs du despotisme américain" is from an article Gouges published in the *Chronique de Paris* (December 19, 1789), quoted in *ODG*, 95. After the debacle of *EN* at the Comédie, Gouges continued to attack the "cabale de quelques colons" and "l'opposition des planteurs," whom she blamed, along with the Comédie itself, for the play's economic failure. Gouges, *Les Comédiens démasqués*, 48, 47. See also Bonnell, "La carrière dramatique," 73.

21 Olympe de Gouges "Aux auteurs du Journal," *Le Journal de Paris* 362 (December 28, 1789): 1700; in *EP*, 1:133.

22 Olympe de Gouges, letter to *Chronique de Paris*, December 20, 1789, in *EP*, 1:130; emphasis added.

23 See *ODG*, 96–99, 137.

24 Martine Reid, "Language under Revolutionary Pressure," in *A New History of French Literature*, ed. Denis Hollier (Cambridge, Mass.: Harvard University Press, 1989), 574–75. It should also be noted that writers would gain ground over the old privileges of the Comédie Française soon thereafter, in 1791 (see *ODG*, 102).

25 Olympe de Gouges, "Adieux aux Français," in *EP*, 1:162.

26 Quoted in Graham Robb, *Strangers: Homosexual Love in the Nineteenth Century* (New York: Norton, 2003), 176. On the "emancipation" of the Jews and its relation to slavery see Ronald Schechter, *Obstinate Hebrews: Representations of Jews in France, 1715–1815* (Berkeley: University of California Press, 2003), 156–60.

27 Olympe de Gouges, *Le Bonheur primitif de l'homme* (Paris: Chez Royer et Chez Bailly, 1789), 104.

28 My page references for "Réflexions" are to *TS*, although the version printed there is not complete. The text of "Réflexions" in *TS* is taken from the Groult edition of Gouges's *Oeuvres* (83–87). Groult indicates that the text dates from February 1788, but she unfortunately gives no information about its provenance. The full version of "Réflexions" was printed at the end of *Zamore et Mirза* (in both editions, *ZM1* 92–99 and *ZM2* 92–99). Thus *TS* does not include most of several concluding paragraphs (*ZM1*, 98–99; and *ZM2*, 98–99) that attack the actors of the Comédie with increased bitterness and self-pity.

29 On the number of blacks in France see William B. Cohen, *The French Encounter with Africans: White Response to Blacks, 1530–1880* (Bloomington: Indiana University Press, 1980), 315n29; henceforth abbreviated WC. I am assuming, perhaps wrongly, that there would have been significantly fewer

blacks in France in the 1750s than in the 1770s (when a census reported, perhaps with exaggeration, five thousand). See Sue Peabody, *"There Are No Slaves in France": The Political Culture of Race and Slavery in the Ancien Régime* (New York: Oxford University Press, 1996): "France's black population was disproportionately small compared to that of England." For now, she says, the exact number of French blacks remains "elusive" (4). Jules Mathorez claims that parts of France during the Ancien Régime had too many black servants to count, but the only places he names are seaports associated with the slave trade (Lorient, Nantes, Le Havre). See Jules Mathorez, *Les Étrangers en France sous l'Ancien Régime* (Paris: Edouard Champion, 1919), 1:399–400. See also Hans Werner Debrunner, *Presence and Prestige: Africans in Europe* (Basel: Basler Afrika Bibliographien, 1979), 87–91. These sources are now supplanted by Erick Noël, *Etre noir en France au XVIIIe siècle* (Paris: Tallandier, 2006); see his chapter 8.

30 Brown sees Gouges in "Réflexions" "present[ing] the slaves as the reason she had become a writer" ("The Self-Fashionings of Olympe de Gouges, 1784–1789," 392); his interpretation of the text is more prosecutorial than mine. Focusing on Gouges's "self-fashioning," he does not give credit to Gouges for the creativity of this statement about race. He sees what I have called Gouges's retrofitting of abolitionism as self-promotion: "she repeatedly equated her efforts to have the play performed with the efforts of the Société to abolish the slave trade, presenting both as necessary steps towards 'liberty' for the French people" (*FH*, 5/114). It is true that Gouges's jump-cutting between, on the one hand, promoting her own play and, on the other, discussing the plight of the slaves, is disconcerting. As Brown suggests, it is as if the two issues were of equal importance to Gouges. But Brown's judgment seems too harsh. Of course Gouges was promoting her play in "Réflexions": she needed to, since the play was being held hostage by the Comédie. And it was, after all, in its fashion, an abolitionist play: performance of the play would advance the cause of abolition (as the reaction of the colonial lobby made clear). 443

31 See Christopher L. Miller, *Blank Darkness: Africanist Discourse in French* (Chicago: University of Chicago Press, 1985), 21–22; and wc, 9–13, 80–84.

32 On Gouges's social relations with Condorcet see *ODG*, 130.

33 Marie-Jean-Antoine-Nicolas de Caritat, Marquis de Condorcet, *Réflexions sur l'esclavage des Nègres*, in *Oeuvres complètes* (1781; Paris: Henrichs, 1804) 11:124.

34 Ibid., 109, 123. This is not the only time that Gouges would follow Condorcet's lead: his feminist manifesto "Sur l'admission des femmes au droit de cité," although it is less radical than Gouges's, dates from 1790 (*Oeuvres de Condorcet* [Paris: Firmin Didot, 1847], 10:121–30). Gouges's "Declaration of the Rights of Women" came one year later (see *ODG*, 130; and Harth, *Cartesian Women*, 221). Condorcet's male feminism is another case of gender-bending that is ignored in *Translating Slavery*. His "Réflexions" are mentioned in a

footnote by Kadish (*TS*, 320–21n26), but not in connection to Gouges's "Réflexions." Condorcet's position on women's rights is mentioned in a footnote by Maryann DeJulio (*TS*, 327n15), but the fact that Gouges's text followed Condorcet's is not discussed. See also *ODG*, 152.

35 I do not subscribe to DeJulio's rationale for changing Gouges's vocabulary by way of translating it. For example, it seems to me simply a distortion to omit the value-laden qualifier *fade* (dull) in this sentence, in order "to rid the color system that was in place of affective qualifiers" (*TS*, 326 n1). To do so is not to translate but to rewrite.

36 Catherine Nesci, "La Passion de l'impropre: Lien conjugal et lien colonial chez Olympe de Gouges," in *Corps/Décors: Femmes, orgie, parodie*, ed. Catherine Nesci (Amsterdam: Rodopi, 1999), 45–56.

37 See Christian Delacampagne, *Une Histoire de l'esclavage: De l'antiquité à nos jours* (Paris: Librairie Générale Française, 2002), 194.

38 Quoted in Yves Benot, "Diderot, Pechmeja, Raynal et l'anticolonialisme," *Europe* 405–6 (January–February 1963): 140. See Cohen's discussion of polygenism (*WC*, 85).

39 See Dominique-Harcourt Lamiral, *L'Affrique et le peuple affriquain considérés sous leurs rapports avec notre Commerce & nos Colonies* (Paris: Chez Dessenne, 1789), 394; and his argument about the color line (ibid., 379).

40 "Tout concourt donc à prouver que le genre humain n'est *pas* composé d'especes essentiellement différentes. La différence des blancs aux bruns vient de la nourriture, des mœurs, des usages, des climats; celle des bruns aux Noirs a la même cause. . . . Il n'y a donc eu originairement qu'une seule race d'hommes" (Diderot, in *Encyclopédie*, s.v. "Humain," subarticle "Humaine espèce"; emphasis added). See also Marc A. Christophe, "Changing Images of Blacks in Eighteenth-Century French Literature," *Phylon* 48, no. 3 (fall 1987): 187.

41 Polygenism was "literally" radical in that it posited different roots or origins for different types of humans. In translating "Réponse," Maryann DeJulio downplays the meaning of *espèce* by rendering it as "class" (*TS*, 122). DeJulio has a rationale for doing this (see *TS*, 130–31), but I think it is an excessively presentist translation of that term.

42 See Raynal, *Histoire des deux Indes* (Geneva: Chez Jean-Léonard Pellet, 1780), 3:122–72).

43 See my *Blank Darkness*, 6–8.

44 *Encyclopédie*, s.v. "Indes" (8:662).

45 See Madame de Duras, *Ourika: Nouvelle édition revue et augmentée*, ed. Roger Little (Exeter: University of Exeter Press, 1998), 68; and *WC*, 64. On the confusion of Africans and Indians see also Wylie Sypher, *Guinea's Captive Kings: British Anti-Slavery Literature of the XVIIIth Century* (New York: Octagon Books, 1969), esp. 105–8.

46 *ZM*, 19. Masson states that *Zamore et Mirza* is about "esclaves indiens d'Amérique" ("Anti-Esclavagiste," 154). I have reservations about Brown's

view that *ZM* is "set in a romanticized version of the French colony of Isle de France (in the Indian Ocean)" (*FH*, 5/98). That island (now Mauritius) was indeed an important element in the French Empire in the Indian Ocean, but it was described in the *Encyclopédie* (s.v. *Maurice*) as "île d'Afrique" (10:211). (Its association with Africa is clear in Dumas's novel *Georges* [1843]). Brown's interpretation is thus not consistent with Gouges's description of the setting as "dans l'Inde." Still, the possibility cannot be ruled out, either as a figment of the author's rather loose geographical imagination or as a reflection of the geopolitics of her times. On the latter, Claude Wanquet points out: "Entre les îles [the Mascarenes, including Ile de France/Maurice] et les comptoirs français de l'Inde, c'est d'abord la notion de communauté qui s'impose, à l'intérieur d'un ensemble géopolitique, celui des colonies orientales françaises" ("Les Iles Mascareignes, l'Inde et les Indiens pendant la Révolution française," in *Compagnies et comptoirs: L'Inde des Français, XVIIe-XXe siècle* [Paris: Société Française d'Histoire d'Outre-Mer, 1991], 32).

47 "GUINÉE, s.f. (Commerce.) toile de coton blanche plûtôt fine que grosse, qui vient de Pondichery. . . . Ces toiles sont bonnes pour la traite qu'on fait sur les côtes d'Afrique; c'est-là ce qui les a fait appeller guinées" (*Encyclopédie*, 7:1009).

48 Binita Mehta argues that the loss of the Indian colonies in the mid-eighteenth century accounts for rising French intellectual interest in India: "it is precisely because of this loss that India continued to hold such a sway in the imagination of French dramatists." Although Mehta does not mention Gouges, *Zamore et Mirza*, in its purely *nominal* depiction of the Indian subcontinent, belongs within that history. See Binita Mehta, *Widows, Pariahs, and "Bayadères": India as Spectacle* (Lewisburg, Pa.: Bucknell University Press, 2002), 14.

445

49 Deryck Scarr, *Slaving and Slavery in the Indian Ocean* (New York: St. Martin's, 1998), 114. Robert Louis Stein reports that merchants from the Mascarene Islands "occasionally" sought slaves in India in addition to their usual sources, the east coast of Africa and Madagascar; but slaves from India were thought to be "lazy" (Stein, *The French Slave Trade in the Eighteenth Century: An Old Regime Business* [Madison: University of Wisconsin Press, 1979], 122).

50 Stein, *The French Slave Trade*, 124.

51 Scarr, *Slaving and Slavery*, 42.

52 Louis-Sébastien Mercier, "Petits Nègres," in *Tableau de Paris, nouvelle édition* (Amsterdam: n.p., 1783), 253–54.

53 Arsène Houssaye wrote in his article on Du Barry in the *Grande Encyclopédie* (Paris: H. Lamirault, 1886): "Zamore, ce joli nègre, qui avait pris son nom dans l'*Alzire* de Voltaire et sa fortune dans la poche de Louis XV" (5:512). The unsigned article in the *Grand Dictionnaire universel du XIXe siècle* (Paris: Larousse, 1867) describes him as "son hideux négrillon, ce fameux Zamore, créature grotesque qu'elle habillait de soie, d'or et de pierreries" (2:271). See also Mathorez, *Les Etrangers en France*, 1:401. Alexandre Dumas depicted Za-

more in his novel *Joseph Balsamo* (1846–48). Two recent French novels resurrect Zamor. In *Zamor: Le Nègre de la du Barry* (Paris: L'Harmattan, 1997), Gérard Saint-Loup acknowledges in a postface that "Le Zamor historique était Indien" but makes him into a Martinican slave of African origin. In Eve Ruggieri's *Le Rêve de Zamor* (Paris: Plon, 2003) Zamor is from Pondicherry but is referred to as "le nègre Zamor" (197; see also 133) and as "un enfant noir issue de l'esclavage" (68). A portrait of Zamor by Jacques Antoine Marie Lemoine, "Louis Benoît Zamor, page de Mme du Barry" (1785) depicts him with clearly African features, as does an anonymous portrait: see illustrations in Erick Noël, *Etre noir en France au XVIIIe siècle* (Paris: Tallandier, 2006): after page 160. As for "Mirza," Brown points out that it is a Persian name that Montesquieu made famous in his *Lettres persanes* (Brown, "Self-Fashioning," 398n14); it will be reused by Madame de Staël.

54 Haslip, *Madame du Barry*, 81. Haslip's depiction of Zamor is unrelentingly racist; she sees him as an ungrateful traitor to the countess who "adored him" (90). He had the audacity to grow "from an amusing little blackamoor [*sic*] . . . into an ugly, misshapen sixteen-year-old" (114).

55 On Zamor as a reader of Rousseau see Philip M. Laski, *The Trial and Execution of Madame Du Barry* (London: Constable, 1969), 75.

56 *Alzire* is, to my knowledge, mentioned in only one study of Gouges: Catherine Masson, "Olympe de Gouges, anti-esclavagiste et non-violente," *Women in French Studies* 10 (2002): 153–65. Brown says the earliest instance of the use of "Zamor" in fiction is a novel from 1755, which *Alzire* obviously predates (Brown, "Self-Fashioning," 398n14).

57 Gouges, *Le bonheur primitif de l'homme ou les rêveries patriotiques* ("Amsterdam" [Paris]: Chez Royer et Chez Bailly, 1789), 109.

58 Brown, *Field of Honor*, 5/117. By way of contrast, Gisela Thiele Knobloch constructs a perfectly smooth, "resolutely modern" version of Gouges's engagement with the problem of slavery and race, devoid of internal tensions, in her preface to Gouges, *Théâtre politique* (Paris: Côté-Femmes, 1991), 1:12–13.

59 See *Encyclopédie*, s.v. "Habitant" (8:17). In *Zamore et Mirza*, *habitants* (also spelled *habitans*) are Indian; the European colonists are referred to as European or French.

60 Zamore's response to Mirza's question (which remains the same in *L'Esclavage des Noirs* [*TS*, 91/237]) is, "Cette différence est bien peu de chose, elle n'existe que dans la couleur." This echoes the quip supposedly made by Louis XIV to his African guest Aniaba: "Il n'y a donc plus de différence entre vous et moi que du noir au blanc" (see my *Blank Darkness*, 32).

61 In the *Encyclopédie*, Jaucourt was not equivocal about the geographical location of "Sauvages" in his article of that title (14:729): "Tous les peuples indiens qui ne sont point soumis au joug du pays, & qui vivent à-part. . . . Il se trouve plusieurs nations sauvages en Amérique." No other part of the world

is mentioned. In *Les Indes galantes*, the *entrée* called "Les Sauvages" takes place among American Indians.

62 Gouges changes *sauvage* to *nègre* a number of times from one play to the other: see *ZM*, 63/*EN* in *TS*, 255. In *EN* Azor says that he and his father were "bought on the coast of Guinea" (*TS*, 101/246). For an example of the change from *esclaves* to *Noirs* see *ZM*, 43/*TS*, 252).

63 "Divertissement (Belles-Lettres) . . . n'est qu'une fête, un mariage, un couronnement, &c. qui ne doit avoir que la joie publique pour objet" (*Encyclopédie*, 4:1069). The *divertissement* is included in both *ZM1* and *ZM2*.

64 See Brown, *FH* 5/119; Mercier, *L'Afrique noire dans la littérature française*, 187. Maryann DeJulio says that Gouges "confuses American Indians and Africans" (*TS*, 327n10); Cohen says the same (*WC*, 64).

65 The translation of *L'Esclavage des Noirs* in *Translating Slavery* erases the lingering confusion of Gouges's geography by making Saint-Frémont governor of an island "in the Indies," therefore consistent with the stated setting (*TS*, 90).

66 Masson, "Anti-Esclavagiste," 155.

67 Olympe de Gouges, letter written in prison, July 20, 1793, in *EP*, 2:13.

68 In act I, scene 1 Zamor says to Mirza: "Peut-être avant peu notre sort va changer. Une morale douce et consolante a fait tomber en Europe le voile de l'erreur. Les hommes éclairés jettent sur nous des regards attendris: nous leur devrons le retour de cette précieuse liberté, le premier trésor de l'homme, et dont les ravisseurs cruels nous ont privés depuis si longtemps" (*TS*, 92/238).

69 "White men, seeking to save brown women from brown men . . ." (Gayatri Chakravorty Spivak, "Can the Subaltern Speak?" in *Colonial Discourse and Postcolonial Theory*, ed. Patrick Williams and Laura Chrisman [New York: Columbia University Press, 1994], 101).

70 Gouges, *Les Comédiens démasqués*, 48 (and quoted in *TS*, 76, AT).

71 See Masson, "Anti-esclavagiste."

72 Le Hir, in *TS*, 70.

73 In *Translating Slavery* an apparent effort to make Gouges more admirable for our times leads Le Hir to suggest that, in spite of what we have just seen, Gouges was "radical." Le Hir deduces this from a passage spoken by the governor in *L'Esclavage des Noirs*, in which he appeals to monarchs to "render their Peoples happy." Le Hir sees in this an "ultimatum" and "a radical departure from the old patriarchal order. The king's absolute political authority is being questioned and his role entirely redefined" (*TS*, 75). This is a wild exaggeration. The king's authority is, if anything, reinforced by the act of benevolence that he is asked to perform; by altering the social orders *beneath* him, including that of the slaves, he would simply confirm his own authority. As Le Hir herself rightly explains, this comes after various earlier sections of the play have floated the image of a "new ideal sociopolitical framework. . . .

447

The important role granted to the father [governor] in acts II and III therefore seems to cancel the democratic ideal presented in act I and to indicate a return to the patriarchal order" (*TS*, 72).

74   The wedding of Zamor and Mirza, which is not in the printed text of *EN*, is confirmed by an account of the play in the newspaper *Le Moniteur*, quoted in *ODG*, 97.

75   This encomium is at odds with the account that Gouges gave in *Les Comédiens démasqués*, where she makes no mention of the ballet. I have not been able to find any passage in *Les Comédiens démasqués* where Gouges, according to Le Hir, discusses the actors' supposed refusal to paint their faces black (*TS*, 80). The text of the "ballet" printed in 1792 suggests the opposite. There is evidence that, before the actual performance, the Comédie resisted "putting that color [black] on its stage," as Gouges put it in her "Préface sans caractère" of 1789 (quoted in Brown, "Self-Fashioning," 400n49).

76   Abbé Grégoire, *Mémoires de Grégoire* (Paris: J. Yonet, 1840), 1:391.

77   s, 181, 182. On the styling of Jean-Baptiste's name see Blanc's explanation of the "de" in Gouges's adopted name (*ODG*, 33).

78   *MJM*, 14, 18, 100n. Jean-Baptiste Mosneron later authored *Le Vallon aérien ou relation du voyage d'un aéronaute dans un pays inconnu jusqu'à présent* (Paris: Chaumerot, 1810), an account of a journey in the Pyreenees by balloon.

79   *MJM*, 100n.

80   "Lettre de M. Mosneron de L'Aunay, Député du Commerce de Nantes auprès de l'Assemblée nationale, à M le Marquis de Condorcet, Président de la Société des amis des Noirs," *Journal de Paris*, supplement to no. 362 (December 28, 1789): 1701, 1704. On this see Brown, *FH* 6/84. The Mosneron name is misspelled in Brown's book, as "Monseron," although it is correct in the article "Self-Fashioning" (393).

81   In January 1790 — thus just after the performances of *L'Esclavage des Noirs* — rumors of a potential move by the Amis des Noirs to abolish the slave trade provoked vehement reactions from Jean-Baptiste Mosneron and other members of the colonial lobby; the triangular trade was in jeopardy. On January 24 Jean-Baptiste published another defense of slavery in a Paris newspaper; see Gabriel Debien, *Les Colons de Saint-Domingue et la Révolution: Essai sur le Club Massiac* (Paris: Armand Colin, 1953), 179–80. Two days later he gave a speech that made him famous, defending the slave trade and the colonial system; see *MJM*, 18.

82   David Patrick Geggus, *Haitian Revolutionary Studies* (Bloomington: Indiana University Press, 2002), 228n12.

83   I base my attribution of the pamphlet on Brown, *FH*, 6/82. The pamphlet is listed as anonymous in André Martin and Gérard Walter, *Catalogue de l'histoire de la Révolution Française* (Paris: Bibliothèque Nationale, 1955) 4.2.418, #8283. I subscribe to Brown's attribution because it seems perfectly plausible, given the style and content of the pamphlet when compared to Mosneron's signed publications; also his authorship of the pamphlet makes

sense in the sequence of events. I am grateful to Gregory Brown for his generous help with this question.

84   "Lettre à Mme de Gouges, en réponse à celle insérée dans *La Chronique de Paris*, no. CXVIII, du dimanche 20 décembre, et datée du 19 du même mois," in *EP*, 1:131. The letter is signed "Un Colon très aisé à connaître" and dated in Paris December 25, 1789. I consulted what appears to be an original print of this pamphlet in the New York Public Library (KVR1714), and I quote it as it is printed there (including the emphasis, which is missing in *EP*).

85   Brown writes: "[On] 28 December 1789, the day of the premiere, she published letters in two prominent newspapers, identifying herself and her new play with the campaign of the Société des Amis des Noirs for abolition" ("Self-Fashioning," 393).

86   A text by Gouges that dates from the previous month, December 1789, "Adieux aux Français," cited above, contains some of the ideas that one finds here in "Réponse." In the earlier text she wrote, "Je vais allumer la guerre entre les champions américains et les vrais chevaliers français."

87   *TS*, 122/268–69, AT. DeJulio translates *espèce* as "class," which I think distorts the degree of difference implicit in that word; my translation as "species" may well err on the other side, overstating difference. "Race" might in fact be the best translation.

88   Jean Fouchard, *Artistes et répertoire des scènes de Saint-Domingue* (Port-au-Prince: Imprimerie de l'Etat, 1955). Fouchard comments: "Entre l'année 1791 et l'année 1797, les gazettes de la colonie ne mentionnent pas de spectacles" (270n).

89   Pierre-Ambroise-François Choderlos de Laclos, "Des Femmes et de leur éducation," in *Oeuvres complètes* (Paris: Gallimard, Bibliothèque de la Pléiade, 1979), 390, 391. I translated *susceptible d'éducation* as "educable." For Laclos, as for Rousseau, slavery is "vile" (420).

90   Preface to *The Philosopher Corrected*, quoted in Marie Josephine Diamond, "The Revolutionary Rhetoric of Olympe de Gouges," *Feminist Issues* 14, no. 1 (spring 1994): 3–23.

91   Gouges, "Le Bonheur primitif de l'homme," quoted in Scott, *Only Paradoxes to Offer*, 31.

92   Since only a short excerpt from the "Déclaration des droits de la femme et de la citoyenne" is included in *TS*, my references are to the text in volume 1 of *EP*. Page numbers provided parenthetically in the text are to this version, and translations are my own.

93   Madelyn Gutwirth, "The Rights and Wrongs of Woman: The Defeat of Feminist Rhetoric by Revolutionary Rhetoric," in *Representing the French Revolution: Literature, Historiography, and Art*, ed. James A. W. Heffernan (Hanover: University Press of New England, 1992), 158.

94   See Nesci's interpretation of this passage, "La Passion de l'impropre," 51–53.

95   The translation of the "Declaration" in *Women in Revolutionary Paris, 1789–1795* by Darline Gay Levy, Harriet Branson Applewhite, and Mary Durham

Johnson (Urbana: University of Illinois Press, 1979) contains some large mistakes. "La résistance qu'on *lui* oppose [lui = père]" becomes "the resistance opposed to *them*"; "la contraindre avec violence [la = résistance]" becomes "To constrain (blood) violently" (96; emphasis added). There is often a problem of pronoun antecedents in Gouges's writing, part of what Vanpee rightly describes as her oral style: some passages are "full of deictic markers that point to unnamed referents"—but there is no confusion about the antecedents I just quoted. See Janie Vanpée, "Taking the Podium: Olympe de Gouges's Revolutionary Discourse," in *Women Writers in Pre-Revolutionary France: Strategies of Emancipation*, ed. Colette H. Winn and Donna Kuizenga (New York: Garland, 1997), 305.

96   See Florence Gauthier, "Périssent les colonies plutôt qu'un principe! De Jaucourt à Marx en passant pas Robespierre et Desmoulins," in *Périssent les colonies plutôt qu'un principe! Contributions à l'histoire de l'abolition de l'esclavage, 1789–1804*, ed. Florence Gauthier (Paris: Société des Etudes Robespierristes, 2002), 91–103; and DBD2, 143.

97   Harth, *Cartesian Women*, 229, 233. On the "Declaration" and the loss of the empire see also Joan B. Landes, *Women and the Public Sphere in the Age of the French Revolution* (Ithaca: Cornell University Press, 1988), 124.

98   Gouges, *Le Bonheur primitif*, 65. The idea of equality is circumscribed in Gouges's mind, as Harth demonstrates in *Cartesian Women* (225–26).

99   See ODG, 151; and Scott, *Only Paradoxes to Offer*, 36.

100   Gouges, quoted in Scott, *Only Paradoxes to Offer*, 23: "I am a woman and I have served my country as a great man." See also E. Lairtullier, *Les Femmes célèbres de 1789 à 1795*, quoted in Scott, *Only Paradoxes to Offer*, 33.

101   Scott, *Only Paradoxes to Offer*, 33.

102   Her friend Brissot, meanwhile, was arguing for the equal rights of blacks and mulattoes who were *already* free in the colonies, precisely so that the slaves could be kept at work (DBD2, 146).

103   Grégoire, quoted in DBD2, 148; the characterization of this abolition as an "aberration" is Davis's (150). I am indebted to one of my anonymous readers for clarification on this point and for my phrasing here.

7   MADAME DE STAËL, MIRZA, AND PAULINE

1   Quoted in Comtesse Jean de Pange, "Madame de Staël et les nègres," *La Revue de France* 14, no. 50 (September–October 1934): 439.

2   André Lang, "L'Extraordinaire histoire du mariage de Germaine Necker et d'Eric Staël de Holstein," *Les Oeuvres libres* 123, no. 349 (August 1956): 160.

3   Necker (1769), quoted in Weber, *La Compagnie des Indes*, 605; see also 600–602.

4   Necker, *De l'administration des finances de la France*, quoted in Liliane Crété, *La Traite des nègres sous l'Ancien Régime* (Paris: Perrin, 1989), 260. On slave-

ship names see Mettas, *Répertoire des expéditions négrières françaises au XVIIIe siècle*, 1:741, 2:119, 537; and on expeditions of the Compagnie from Lorient, 1744–1791 see ibid., 2:611–24. On the Compagnie des Indes and the slave trade see s, 18–21.

5 Yvan Debbasch, "Poésie et traite: L'Opinion française sur le commerce négrier au début du XIXe siècle," *Revue française d'histoire d'outre-mer* 172–73 (January 1963): 328.

6 On the arrangement of Germaine's wedding, the most detailed account is Lang, "L'Extraordinaire histoire." See also Helen B. Posgate, *Madame de Staël* (New York: Twayne, 1968), 30–31; B. d'Andlau, *La Jeunesse de Madame de Staël (de 1766 à 1786)* (Geneva: Droz, 1970), 87–101 (on Saint-Barthélémy, 94); Maria Fairweather, *Madame de Staël* (New York: Carroll and Graf, 2005), 52–53, 56. On Saint-Barthélémy see т, 450, where it becomes apparent that this transfer of ownership in 1785 was part of a larger treaty between France and Sweden. The island deal was part of an effort on Eric's part to demonstrate that he was worthy of being named permanent ambassador to France, the position that would secure his marriage contract with the Neckers. Lang quotes King Gustave III writing to Madame de Boufflers: "C'est à M. de Staël, par la suite, par ses services et le succès de ses négotiations, de mériter un titre plus considérable . . . l'ambassade de Paris" (Lang, "L'Extraordinaire histoire," 178–79). The ceding of Saint-Barthélémy, arranged by Eric, was part of that process: see Lang, "L'extraordinaire histoire," 186. See also Georges Bourdin, *Histoire de Saint Barthélémy/History of St. Barthelemy* (Pelham, N.Y.: Porter Henry, 1978), 154–67. Bourdin reports the population as 458 whites and 281 blacks (161); exports (mostly of cotton) from the island seem to have been very slight (163), but the potential was more fully realized by the Swedes (169). On Sweden's trade with Africa, including the slave trade, see т, 172, 176, 222–24.

7 See Thérèse de Raedt, "Ourika en noir et blanc: Une Femme africaine en France" (Ph.D. diss., University of California, Davis, 2000), 80. The Maréchale de Beauvau's touching account of Ourika's death and the grief it provoked is in Madame Standish, ed., *Souvenirs de la Maréchale Princesse de Beauvau* (Paris: Léon Techener, 1872), 147–50. According to David O'Connell the text of these memoirs was available and known to Claire de Duras (O'Connell, "Ourika: Black Face, White Mask," *French Review*, special issue no. 6 [spring 1974]: 47–56 [here quoting 50n12]).

8 On the dating of *Mirza* see d'Andlau, *La Jeunesse de Madame de Staël*, 108. See also Chevalier de Boufflers, *Lettres d'Afrique à Madame de Sabran* (Paris: Actes Sud, 1998), 170; and Léon-François Hoffmann, *Le Nègre romantique: Personnage littéraire et obsession collective* (Paris: Payot, 1973), 132–33.

9 Staël, *Correspondance générale*, 1:141. This passage in her letter rehearses the themes of *Mirza*. See d'Andlau, *La Jeunesse de Madame de Staël*, 108; and Comtesse de Pange, "Madame de Staël et les nègres," 429. Boufflers, despite his lamentations, participated in the slave trade in Africa: see Nicole Vaget

451

Grangeat, *Le Chevalier de Boufflers et son temps: Étude d'un échec* (Paris: Nizet, 1976), 69–70. Staël reported in another letter that Boufflers "n'a autre chose à faire que de favoriser la traite des nègres, et il faut convenir qu'un philosophe n'est pas ravi d'une semblable commission . . ." (Staël, *Correspondance générale*, 1:104).

10 See *TS*, 41. The only source that Kadish cites on the existence of this slave is a personal communication with Simone Balayé (*TS*, 321n40). Balayé makes no mention of this in her preface to Madame de Staël, *Oeuvres de jeunesse* (Paris: Desjonquières, 1997), 7–18 (henceforth abbreviated *OJ*); nor in her *Madame de Staël: Lumières et liberté* (Paris: Klincksieck, 1979).

11 For a comprehensive overview of Staël's engagement with abolitionism see John Claiborne Isbell, "Voices Lost? Staël and Slavery, 1786–1830," in *Slavery in the Caribbean Francophone World: Distant Voices, Forgotten Acts, Forged Identities*, ed. Doris Y. Kadish (Athens: University of Georgia Press, 2000), 39–52.

12 Madame la Baronne Staël de Holstein, *Recueil de morceaux détachés* (Lausanne: Chez Durand, Ravanel et Cie. Libraires, and Paris: Chez Fuchs, Libraire, 1795), 65n (henceforth abbreviated *RMD*). Consulted at the Houghton Library, Harvard University. For convenience I will continue to refer to the printing of the preface and *Mirza* in *TS*, although I will correct the quotations to reflect the original text. *RMD* is completely and accurately reproduced, with modernized spelling, in *OJ*.

13 See Margaret Cohen, *The Sentimental Education of the Novel* (Princeton: Princeton University Press, 1999), 6.

14 See de Raedt, "Ourika en noir et blanc," 64; and Vaget Grangeat, *Le Chevalier de Boufflers et son temps*, 69. "Souvenirs vivants" is from Jules Mathorez, *Les Etrangers en France sous l'Ancien Régime* (Paris: Edouard Champion, 1919), 402.

15 *Azor* was a hugely popular name for slaves in Louisiana, with 195 records in the *Afro-Louisiana History and Genealogy* database from 1790 to 1820. As we saw earlier in this study, *Alzire* was also a name that was used, with twenty-four occurrences. See www.ibiblio.org/laslave.

16 Her other Atlantic fiction, another *oeuvre de jeunesse*, is entitled *Zulma*. It represents an idealized "Orénoque" where "nulle distinction n'est établie par la loi [et] il semblait se créer la royauté du génie" (*OJ*, 110).

17 "Cette anecdote est fondée sur des circonstances de la traite des nègres, rapportée par les voyageurs au Sénégal" (*RMD*, 65). *OJ* (159n) and the editions of Staël's complete works cited below all read "rapportées" (referring to "circonstances" instead of "rapportée" for "anecdote"). This important footnote, appended to the middle of the first sentence of *Mirza* in the original edition (after the word *voyage*), is not included in *TS*, although it is found in the edition that the editors followed (see *TS*, 271n): *Oeuvres complètes de Madame la Baronne de Staël-Holstein* (Geneva: Slatkine, 1967), 1:72, which is in turn a facsimile of *Oeuvres complètes de Madame la Baronne de Staël-Holstein* (Paris:

Firmin Didot, 1861), 1:72. Subsequent references to this edition of Staël's complete works will be abbreviated SOC. The footnote is included in *OJ*, 159. In these editions of Staël's complete works the *Recueil des morceaux détachés* is not mentioned as such; its component parts, including the "Essai sur les fictions" and "Trois nouvelles," are reproduced separately. *OJ* reproduces the *Recueil* exactly except that it modernizes the spelling and corrects occasional errors in the text. For consistency I will cite *Mirza* and its translation by Françoise Massardier-Kenney in *TS*; but I have corrected the text to reflect the original in *RMD*, and I have altered the translation when necessary.

18 Boufflers, *Lettres d'Afrique*, 60, 370, 354. The child referred to in his letter of February 8, 1786, would appear to be a different girl, destined to be a gift to the Duchesse d'Orléans. See de Raedt, "Ourika en noir et blanc," 63n104.

19 Jean-François de Saint-Lambert, *Ziméo*, in *Contes américains: L'Abenaki, Ziméo, Les Deux amis* (1769; Exeter: University of Exeter Press, 1997), 11. See also Cohen, *The French Encounter with Africans: White Response to Blacks, 1530–1880* (Bloomington: Indiana University Press, 1980), 92; henceforth abbreviated WC.

20 Massardier-Kenney in *TS*, 135, 143. My main quarrel with Massardier-Kenney's interpretation of *Mirza* derives from this statement: "Staël does not depict 'real' Africans any more than she would later depict 'real' Germans. She is using the depiction of the other, of the foreigner, to bring out particularities and deficiencies in her own culture" (*TS*, 141). If the other is not really being represented but is rather an abstraction, then what kind of translation can be taking place? Also, this seems to contradict the other claim, that Staël is "engaged in the representation of different modes of thinking and speaking."

21 See Boubacar Barry, *Senegambia and the Atlantic Slave Trade*, trans. Ayi Kwei Armah (Cambridge: Cambridge University Press, 1998), 94–106; henceforth abbreviated *SAST*.

22 See Béatrice Didier, *Madame de Staël* (Paris: Ellipses, 1999), 38. If the title *Corinne, ou l'Italie* suggests an "analogy between gender and national culture," as Sarah Maza suggests, then Africa is also aligned with the feminine by Staël (as I have indicated in my parodic title "*Mirza* ou l'Afrique," above). See Sarah Maza, "Women's Voices in Literature and Art," in *A New History of French Literature*, ed. Denis Hollier (Cambridge, Mass.: Harvard University Press, 1989), 625. Massardier-Kenney points out that even the male protagonist, Ximéo, is "feminized" in *Mirza* (*TS*, 143–44).

23 Hoffmann sees Mirza as feminist (*Le Nègre romantique*, 132), as does Massardier-Kenney (*TS*, 142); the Comtesse de Pange describes her as "Mme de Staël elle-même" and as "une négresse bas bleu" ("Madame de Staël et les nègres," 430).

24 Isbell, "Voices Lost?" 41.

25 This plot device is repeated by Joseph Lavallée in *Le Nègre comme il y a peu de blancs* ("Madras" and Paris: Buisson, 1789), 1:17–18.

453

26 See *RMD*, 84–85. The phrase "sans doute" is missing in TS (279) and in SOC, 1:76.

27 Massardier-Kenney rightly emphasizes the importance of Mirza's gender in this abolitionist speech, which reduces men to silence.

28 The original text reads: "[J]'aurais cru que j'avais rêvé ton inconstance; mais maintenant pour anéantir ce souvenir, il faut percer le coeur dont rien n'a pu l'effacer" (*RMD*, 88–89; *OJ*, 171). TS (280) and SOC (1:77) have "rien ne peut l'effacer." Massardier-Kenney proposes an alternative motive for Mirza's suicide, "the impossibility for the independent woman to owe her life and her freedom to a European colonialist" (*TS*, 142). That proposition is intriguing but presentist and unsupported by the text.

29 Staël, *Histoire de Pauline*, in *OJ*, 199. I have compared the text in *OJ* to the original edition in *RMD*, and I will note the few slight deviations from the original.

30 The word *Nègres* is capitalized in the original text (*RMD*, 143) but not in *OJ*.

31 Saint-Domingue is mentioned (only once) as a source of a *fortune considérable* (the same phrase as in Staël's *Histoire de Pauline*), in another *Histoire de Pauline*, attributed to Choderlos de Laclos, signed "M.C.D.L.," and published in the *Mercure de France* (May 30, 1789): in *Anthologie du conte en France, 1750–1799*, ed. Angus Martin (Paris: 10/18, 1981), 349–63. In both stories an innocent young woman named Pauline, described as *malheureuse*, *sensible*, and *infortunée* in both stories, is victimized by corrupt men and ultimately dies. If Staël did write her *Histoire de Pauline* before 1786, as she said, one might wonder if Laclos had had access to it and was influenced by it. In both stories Saint-Domingue is synonymous with the acquisition of wealth, but Laclos shows no sign of the moral condemnation of slavery that can be inferred in Staël's tale. I am grateful to Susannah Carson for bringing the Laclos story to my attention.

32 On syphilis see Joyce Carol Oates, introduction to Charlotte Brontë, *Jane Eyre* (New York: Bantam Books, 1981), viii.

33 Edward Said, *Culture and Imperialism* (New York: Knopf, 1993), 74; see also 62. My reading of *Histoire de Pauline* is of course aligned with the project that Said prescribed: within "the entire archive of modern and pre-modern European and American culture . . . to draw out, extend, give emphasis and voice to what is silent or marginally present or ideologically represented . . . in such works" (66).

34 In *Histoire de Pauline* see, e.g., *dégrader* (216), *supplice* (216, 226), *torts* (217, 218), *honte* (218, 224), *barbare* (221).

35 See Condorcet, *Réflexions*: *maux* (87), *tort* (93), *crimes* (94, 123, 189), *supplice* (95), *barbare* (119, 130, 193).

36 On the history of this anxiety about contamination between revolutionary Saint-Domingue and metropolitan France see Laurent Dubois, *Avengers of the New World: The Story of the Haitian Revolution* (Cambridge, Mass.: Harvard University Press, 2004), 77.

37 Carolyn Vellenga Berman, *Creole Crossings: Domestic Fiction and the Reform of Colonial Slavery* (Ithaca: Cornell University Press, 2006), 81.

38 On this theme see Christopher L. Miller, *Blank Darkness: Africanist Discourse in French* (Chicago: University of Chicago Press, 1985), 93–107.

8 DURAS AND HER OURIKA, "THE ULTIMATE HOUSE SLAVE"

1 Richard Switzer, "Mme de Staël, Mme de Duras and the Question of Race," *Kentucky Romance Quarterly* 20, no. 3 (1973): 304.

2 On the history of *Ourika*, its editions, and its reception see Thérèse de Raedt, "Ourika en noir et blanc: Une Femme africaine en France" (Ph.D. diss., University of California, Davis, 2000), 245–74; Madame de Duras, *Ourika: Nouvelle édition revue et augmentée*, ed. Roger Little (Exeter: University of Exeter Press, 1998), 96–106; and Lucien Scheler, "Un Best-seller sous Louis XVIII: *Ourika* par Mme de Duras," *Bulletin du bibliophile* 1 (1988): 11–28.

3 See De Raedt, "Ourika en noir et blanc," 11.

4 *Dictionnaire de biographie française*, 1:1443–46. See also Cabuzel Andréa Banbuck, *Histoire politique, économique et sociale de la Martinique sous l'Ancien Régime (1635–1789)* (Fort-de-France: Société de Distribution et de Culture, 1972), 95; and www.ghcaraibe.org/bul/ghco85/p1713.html.

5 A photograph of the masters' house of La Frégate can be seen in Jean-Luc de Laguarigue, *Les Habitations: Livre cartes postales, Martinique maisons créoles* (Le Pallet, France: Editions Traces, 2003).

6 Agénor Bardoux, *La Duchesse de Duras* (Paris: Calmann Lévy, 1898), 49; and Pailhès, *La Duchesse de Duras*, 33–34. Bardoux says that mother and daughter "left America" on June 16, 1796 (28 Prairial, An IV) (51). But that is *after* they are reported to be established in London.

7 Charles-Augustin Sainte-Beuve, "Madame de Duras," one of the "Portraits littéraires," in *Oeuvres* (Paris: Gallimard, 1951), 2:1045; emphasis added. Claire was not "truly" an orphan: her mother did not die until 1815. Another early biographer claims that Claire and her mother sought "refuge" in Martinique (see M. G. Duplessis, "Notice sur la vie et les écrits de Madame la Duchesse de Duras," in *Oeuvres de Madame la Duchesse de Duras* [Paris: Passard, 1851], xv).

8 See Massardier-Kenney in *TS*, 186: "Claire de Kersaint . . . was ready to embark for Martinique with her mother to recover 'a great fortune she had inherited' and she later managed this fortune herself in Martinique, her mother 'being sick and weak of mind.'" The quotations embedded in this run-on sentence are from Denis Virieux's edition of Duras's *Olivier* (Paris: Corti, 1971), 63. But Virieux, who herself cites no source on this point, does not say that Duras "managed this fortune herself in Martinique." Virieux wrote: "C'est [Duras] qui décida le voyage en Amérique, qui géra ensuite la fortune *ramenée de la Martinique*" (63; emphasis added). Elsewhere in *TS*, Kadish

455

states without documentation that Duras lived in Martinique "for several years" (48). Without citing any source, De Raedt writes that mother and daughter "s'arrêtèrent brièvement à Philadelphie et allèrent ensuite à la Martinique où Claire, très jeune, réclama légalement la propriété de sa mère" ("Ourika en noir et blanc," 12; see also 102n162). Joan DeJean repeats the idea that Claire went to Martinique in her introduction to *Ourika: The Original French Text*, ed. Joan DeJean (Paris: Modern Language Association of America, 1994), vii. The idea appears in Jean Giraud's introduction to *Ourika suivi de Edouard* (Paris: Stock, 1950), 9n; in Grant Crichfield's chronology in *The Three Novels of Madame de Duras: "Ourika," "Edouard," "Olivier"* (The Hague: Mouton, 1975), 1; and in Brigitte Galtier, "Les Maux étranges d'Ourika," in *Esclavage, libérations, abolitions, commémorations*, ed. Christiane Chaulet-Achour and Romuald-Blaise Fonkoua (Paris: Séguier, 2001), 154. See also David O'Connell, "*Ourika*: Black Face, White Mask," *French Review* 47, special issue no. 6 (spring 1974): 48. Little refers to Duras's "expérience de la Martinique," although earlier, in his narrative of her life, he does not say she went there—rather that Claire and her mother "stayed only a few months in the New World" (Duras, *Ourika*, 102, 36). Deborah Jenson called the myth of Claire's visit to Martinique into question, describing it as "apparently erroneous," in her *Trauma and Its Representations: The Social Life of Mimesis in Post-Revolutionary France* (Baltimore: Johns Hopkins University Press, 2001), 101.

9 Bardoux, *La Duchesse de Duras*, 49–51. Mrs. [Catherine Mary Charlton] Bearne, in her version of these events in *Four Fascinating Frenchwomen* (London: T. Fisher Unwin, 1910), follows and cites Bardoux, mentioning no trip to Martinique (180–81). In a letter to a prefect dated 15 Brumaire An X (November 6, 1801), Claire says that her mother "se trouve actuellement aux Iles" (quoted in Pailhès, *La Duchesse de Duras*, 86).

10 "On relève la présence de la mère et de la fille à Philadelphie le 15 juin 1794; et après un séjour en Suisse, Claire et Mme d'Ennery, sa tante, se retrouvent à Londres, en 1795" (Pailhès, *La Duchesse de Duras*, 34).

11 The British attacked Martinique on February 6, 1794, four months before the Kersaint women are known to have been in Philadelphia. The island had been in upheaval during the French Revolution. The abolition that was declared in Paris two days before the British invasion of Martinique would never be applied there; France reclaimed the island in 1802, when Napoleon reestablished slavery.

12 Virieux says that their return from America took place in 1794 (*Olivier*, 17); Bardoux documents them in Philadelphia (*La Duchesse de Duras*, 49).

13 Another source makes the 1794 trip to Martinique seem dubious. In her memoirs Henriette-Lucie, Marquise de La Tour du Pin, a lifelong friend of Claire de Duras, recollected that Claire talked of a voyage to the island after her marriage, during the time in England, apparently in 1799. The purpose of the journey was "to look after certain affairs of her mother, who had gone to

Martinique to sell the plantation that she owned there." Thus the reason for going in 1794 still existed in 1799, suggesting that they had not gone in 1794. See Henriette-Lucie (Dillon) de La Tour du Pin de Gouvernet, *Journal d'une femme de cinquante ans, 1778–1815* (Paris: Berge-Levrault, 1930), 2:190. The voyage was, La Tour du Pin explains, proposed as a "pretext" for Madame de Duras to be absent when her husband went into service as Premier Gentilhomme de la Chambre of Louis XVIII (still in exile in Germany). Since Admiral Kersaint had participated in the trial of Louis XVI, causing a "stain" on the family's reputation, Louis XVIII refused to receive the daughter, Claire. For a fuller account of how funds from the sale of Claire's mother's plantation in Martinique went toward the purchase of the château of Ussé, see La Tour du Pin, *Journal d'une femme de cinquante ans*, 2:235.

As this book was going to press, I learned about another source of information (which I was not able to consult) on the Alesso d'Eragny-Kersaint family and on the sojourn of Madame de Kersaint and her daughter in Philadelphia. Professor Heather Brady, in a forthcoming essay, cites the correspondence of Madame de Rouvray, the sister of Madame de Kersaint (and Claire's aunt), which covers this period and includes one letter from Madame de Kersaint to Madame de Rouvray, along with much information about the family's dealings and holdings in Martinique and Saint-Domingue. That correspondence is found in Laurent François Le Noir, marquis de Rouvray, *Une correspondance familiale au temps des troubles de Saint-Domingue: Lettres* [457] *du marquis et de la marquise de Rouvray à leur fille, Saint-Domingue—États-Unis, 1791–1796* (Paris: Société de l'histoire des colonies françaises, 1959). Professor Brady concurs with me that Claire and her mother likely did not reach Martinique; she informs me that this correspondence places the date of the Kersaints' departure from Philadelphia and return to Europe in 1796 (correcting Pailhès, who said they reached London in 1795: *La Duchesse de Duras*, 34). See Heather Brady, "Recovering Claire de Duras's Creole Inheritance: Race and Gender in the Exile Correspondence of Her Saint-Domingue Family," *L'Esprit créateur*, forthcoming. I am grateful to Professor Brady for sharing her research with me.

14 Chantal Bertrand-Jennings, *D'un siècle l'autre: Romans de Claire de Duras* (Jaignes, France: La Chasse au Snark, 2001), 10. Edith E. Lucas wrote, "Mme de Duras qui avait connu cette race infortunée pendant son séjour en Amérique, affirme qu'elle est capable d'un large développement intellectuel" (Lucas, *La Littérature anti-esclavagiste au dix-neuvième siècle: Étude sur Madame Beecher Stowe et son influence en France* [Paris: E. de Boccard, 1930], 20–21).

15 See Bardoux, *La Duchesse de Duras*, 87. According to Maurice Levaillant and Georges Moulinier, the Durases bought Ussé in 1807 (*Mémoires d'outre-tombe*, index, 2:1287). See Jérémy Côme and Marie-Laure de Clermont-Tonnerre, "Casimir de Blacas: Bienvenue chez la Belle au bois dormant," *Gala* 625 (June 1, 2005): 54–57.

16 Pailhès, *La Duchesse de Duras*, 26. Pailhès proposes a reading of the melan-

choly in Duras's works along "absolutely biographical" lines (28). That is, Ourika is for him a projection of Claire de Duras, thus neither a reflection of the historical Ourika nor a meditation on larger problems like race: "Le roman est le véridique récit des épreuves de l'auteur" (303).

17 Sainte-Beuve, "Portraits littéraires," 1048; Pailhès, *La Duchesse de Duras*, 314, 313.

18 See Switzer, "Mme de Staël," 315. Little makes a similar point in his edition of *Ourika*, 69.

19 See Cohen, *The Sentimental Education of the Novel*, 120–21.

20 O'Connell pinpoints the message that is conveyed by this narrative tactic: "The reader was thus exhorted to affirm a theoretical adherence to the notion of black equality without being forced to posit it as a right for all blacks" (O'Connell, "*Ourika*," 51).

21 I owe this characterization of Ourika to Raina Croff.

22 Citations of *Ourika* will refer to the text as it is printed in *TS*. I have in all cases checked the text using Little's critical edition.

23 Chevalier de Boufflers, *Lettres d'Afrique*: "Tout ce que j'*apporte* (et ce n'est pas grand-chose), meurt autour de moi. . . . Il me reste une perruche pour la reine, un cheval pour M de maréchal de Castries, *une petite captive* pour M. de Beauvau" (169–70; emphasis added). By contrast, he uses the verb *ramener* when he reports that he is bringing another African girl back to France in 1787 (264).

24 O'Connell, "*Ourika*," 52.

25 Roger Little, preface to Duras, *Ourika*, x.

26 Outside the frame of this fiction it is interesting that the real Chevalier de Boufflers, on the return trip to France that he made with his Ourika, was blown halfway across the Atlantic. As I noted earlier in this study, this voyage nearly took the ship to America, where some of the crew suggested they go, so as to then be taken "straight" to Europe by the winds. See Boufflers, *Lettres d'Afrique*, 156.

27 Margaret Waller, introduction to Duras, *Ourika*, xv.

28 On that propaganda see André Cabanis and Michel L. Martin, "L'Indépendance d'Haïti devant l'opinion publique française sous le Consulat et l'Empire: Ignorance et malentendus," in *Mourir pour les Antilles: Indépendance nègre ou esclavage (1802–1804)*, ed. Michel L. Martin and Alain Yacou (Paris: Editions Caribéennes, 1991), 221–37.

29 The Marquis de Fénelon complained of these practices in a 1764 report, quoted in Gabriel Debien, *Les Esclaves aux Antilles françaises (XVIIe–XVIIIe siècles)* (Basse-Terre: Société d'Histoire de la Guadeloupe, 1974), 362, 363.

30 Bernard Moitt, *Women and Slavery in the French Antilles, 1635–1848* (Bloomington: Indiana University Press, 2001), 80, 84; the priest quoted is the abbé Castelli, quoted by Moitt, 84; see also 35. Jennifer L. Morgan, *Laboring Women: Reproduction and Gender in New World Slavery* (Philadelphia: University of Pennsylvania Press, 2004), 68, 150. Arlette Gautier documents what

she calls a "double abandon des politiques de constitution de couples et de christianisation"; she asserts that, on the French islands, "les mariages sont très rares." Marriage among slaves was slightly more frequent on Martinique but still "quite rare" (Gautier, *Les Sœurs de solitude: La Condition féminine dans l'esclavage aux Antilles du XVIIe au XIXe siècle* (Paris: Editions Caribéennes, 1985), 82, 103.

31 Using ARTFL, I checked "compagnon" in the *Encyclopédie*, the *Dictionnaire de L'Académie Française*, 5th ed. (1798) and 6th ed. (1832–5), and the *Trésor de la langue française*. The 5th edition of the *Dictionnaire* says, "On dit proverbialement, Qui a compagnon a maître; et cela se dit De toutes les personnes qui vivent ensemble en société, et principalement d'un mari et d'une femme" (273). The sense and phrasing that Duras employs is listed in the *Trésor* only in the twentieth century: "Spéc. Celui qui passe sa vie auprès d'une femme. Le compagnon de sa vie: 'Mère se retourna, toute raide, et considéra longuement ce compagnon extraordinaire, l'homme de sa vie, l'homme dont elle était devenue, pour toujours, l'ombre fidèle.' G. Duhamel, *Chronique des Pasquier, Le Notaire du Havre*, 1933, p. 233."

32 Quoted in Gautier, *Les Sœurs de solitude*, 8.

33 Moitt, *Women and Slavery in the French Antilles*, 89–90.

34 Ibid., 96 (Moitt's paraphrase of the doctor's findings). The suggestion of fertility here heightens the drama of Ourika's inability to reproduce in France and the implications of infertility in her very name: see Michelle Chilcoat, "Civility, Marriage, and the Impossible French Citizen: From *Ourika* to *Zouzou* and *Princesse Tam Tam*," *Colby Quarterly* 37, no. 2 (June 2001): 130; and Martine Delvaux, "Le Tiers espace de la folie dans *Ourika, Juletane*, et *L'Amant*," *Mots pluriels* 7 (1998): 3. On the name *Ourika*, see also Roger Little, "Le Nom et les origines d'Ourika," *Revue d'histoire littéraire de la France* 98, no. 4 (July–August 1998): 633–37. Little's thesis that *Ourika* must have been a Peul name, "Ouri Ka," is plausible, but the name could also have come from a valley of that exact name and spelling in Morocco.

459

35 Gautier, *Les Sœurs de solitude*, 95, 96.

36 For a discussion of Duras's views on translation see Massardier-Kenney in *TS*, 185–93.

37 Françoise Thésée, "La Révolte des esclaves du Carbet à la Martinique (octobre–novembre 1822)," *Revue française d'histoire d'outre-mer* 301, no. 4 (1993): 551–84.

38 Edouard Glissant, *La Case du commandeur* (1981; Paris: Gallimard, 1997), 131–37.

39 *Ourika* therefore runs parallel to another novel by Duras, *Olivier, ou le secret* (1822), in which the "secret," teased out by Duras, is homosexuality. Graham Robb interprets *Olivier* as "the first sympathetic novel in modern literature about a homosexual man" (Robb, *Strangers: Homosexual Love in the Nineteenth Century* [New York: Norton, 2003], 86).

40 Duras's phrase "chaîne des êtres" is significant since it evokes an important

current in eighteenth-century thought: the idea that beings each have a specific place in an ordered and hierarchical universe and that all are interconnected. We will see how that idea is reflected in Baron Roger's image of the perfect plantation: each worker has his or her exact role, in which he or she must be happy. On the great chain of being see Arthur O. Lovejoy, *The Great Chain of Being: A Study of the History of an Idea* (New York: Harper and Row, 1960).

41 Chilcoat points out that "'Ourika' resembles the ancient Greek noun . . . [for] mule . . . and a closely resembling verb . . . meaning 'to mark out by boundaries' or 'to define'" ("Civility, Marriage, and the Impossible French Citizen," 130).

42 See Delvaux, "Le Tiers espace." I would dispute Delvaux's idea that Ourika "regains" her identity in religion (3). And see Werner Sollors, *Neither Black nor White yet Both: Thematic Explorations of Interracial Literature* (New York: Oxford University Press, 1997): the "tear-jerking strategy" of *Ourika* can be taken both as "an affirmation of essential racial difference" and as a critique of that difference (346–47).

43 On the similarities between Ourika and Zouzou see Chilcoat, "Civility, Marriage, and the Impossible French Citizen," 125–44. Miriam Warner-Vieyra tells a similar story in a postcolonial frame, but still within the French Atlantic triangle, in her novel *Juletane* (1982).

44 See Lucas, *La Littérature anti-esclavagiste au dix-neuvième siècle*, 20.

45 *L'Affaire de "La Vigilante," batiment négrier de Nantes* (Paris: Imprimerie de Crapelet, 1823), 1–4. David Eltis et al., *The Trans-Atlantic Slave Trade: A Database on CD-ROM* contains a special feature on the *Vigilante* (including the sketch that I have reproduced from the original brochure here).

46 On the *Zong* see Ian Baucom, "Specters of the Atlantic," *South Atlantic Quarterly* 100, no. 1 (2001): 61–82. Baucom shows how an event like that of the *Zong* has been imprinted on the work of Edouard Glissant. For Baucom's complete treatment of the Zong affair, see his book *Specters of the Atlantic: Finance Capital, Slavery, and the Philosophy of History* (Durham: Duke University Press, 2005). See also Fred D'Aguiar's novel *Feeding the Ghosts* (London: Chatto and Windus, 1997).

47 T, 622; see also Serge Daget, *Répertoire des expéditions négrières à la traite illégale (1814–1850)* (Nantes: Centre de Recherche sur l'Histoire du Monde Atlantique, 1988), 135.

CONCLUSION TO PART TWO

1 Liliane Crété, *La Traite des nègres sous l'Ancien Régime*, 245.

2 See Mettas, *Répertoire des expéditions négrières françaises au XVIIIe siècle*, 1:794 (ref. no. 1423).

3 Cohen, *The Sentimental Education of the Novel*, 13, 6, 136n48, 20–25.

9 TAMANGO AROUND THE ATLANTIC

1   By many standards, Mérimée's "Tamango" itself is canonical: it has been constantly available to the French public from the time of its initial publication, and it has undoubtedly been very widely read. Mérimée's status as a canonical author is beyond dispute. Still, it is other texts of his that clearly form the backbone of his reputation, especially *Colomba* and *Carmen*. The fame of "Tamango" is due in part to its frequent inclusion in volumes that headlined Mérimée's more-popular works like those. Thus "Tamango" was included in *Colomba, suivi de La Mosaïque et autres nouvelles* (Paris: Charpentier, 1842; new edition, 1874); and in *Colomba* (Paris: Gautier-Languereau, 1932)—an edition that could have been available to Césaire. I will review other such editions below. The arbiter of the French canon, Gustave Lanson, counted Mérimée among "nos grands prosateurs simples" (quoted in Martine Jey, *La Littérature au lycée* [Paris: Klincksieck, 1998], 155).

2   See Benedict de Spinoza, *The Ethics*, www.gutenberg.org/dirs/etext97/5spne10.txt (accessed March 18, 2007). I am indebted to Yves Citton's use of this term in the conference he organized at the University of Pittsburgh, November 15–16, 2002. Citton's lecture was "The Great Chain of Nations: Globalization in a Spinozist Context." Citton translated Spinoza's Latin *concatenandi* to the English "concatenate," in the sentence, "We have the power to arrange and concatenate the affections of our body." See Yves Citton, "ConcatéNations: L'Écriture du corps mondialisé dans la tradition spinoziste," *Textuel* 44 (2004): 85–107. The term *concatenation* has a number of advantages, beginning with its relative unfamiliarity. It is free from the connotations and the cant that sometimes resound in phrases like "the people," "the masses," "proletariat," etc. Its greatest felicity in this context, however, comes from its clear etymological associations: the idea of linkage (*con*), the image of the chain (*catena*), and the fortuitous suggestion of the "nation." The other terms that I will use in this chapter to describe the question of collectivity and connectivity will come from the works themselves: *conjuration* (conspiracy, from Mérimée's "Tamango"); crowd (from Césaire's *Cahier*); the "many" (from Shakespeare's *Coriolanus*). Michael Hardt and Antonio Negri describe Spinoza's philosophy (in terms that echo their own) as "affirming the democracy of the multitude as the absolute form of politics" (see Michael Hardt and Antonio Negri, *Empire* [Cambridge, Mass.: Harvard University Press, 2000], 77). My work here will remain agnostic on that question.

3   Richard Follett, email announcement on H-NET List on the History of the Atlantic World, 1500–1800, July 15, 2003; emphasis added. The Spinozist model of concatenation propounded by Yves Citton abjures a priori valorizations: see Citton, "ConcatéNations," 91. This stands in contrast to the Voltairean model of connectedness that we saw at the beginning of this book.

4   As Yves Citton explained in his remarks at the "Concatenations" conference,

461

the chain might hold the slave, but the slave can pull on the chain; the meta-phor allows for power — perhaps unequal, perhaps reversible — at both ends.

5 David Richardson, "Shipboard Revolts, African Authority, and the Trans-atlantic Slave Trade," in *Fighting the Slave Trade: West African Strategies*, ed. Sylviane A. Diouf (Athens: Ohio University Press, 2003), 211.

6 Prosper Mérimée, "Tamango," in *Théâtre de Clara Gazul, romans et nouvelles* (Paris: Gallimard "Bibliothèque de la Pléiade," 1978), 480. Translation: *"Carmen" and Other Stories*, trans. Nicholas Jotcham (Oxford: Oxford University Press, 1989), 73. Further references to the Pléiade text will be abbreviated PM; page references to the translation will follow after a slash.

7 It is interesting to note that Mérimée repeats this description later in the story, with reference to the governor of Jamaica, and that Edouard Glissant uses the same phrase to describe the captain of the slave ship *Rose-Marie* in *Le Quatrième siècle* (Paris: Seuil, 1964), 32.

8 "Révolte sur un négrier," unsigned, *La France Maritime* 2 (1852): 336. For an explanation of the date of publication of this version (which he says is actu-ally 1837, not 1852), and a summary of the revisions, see Léon Vignols, "Une Version remaniée et inconnue du 'Tamango' de Mérimée," *Revue d'histoire littéraire de la France* 34 (1927): 208–9. Mallion and Salomon say that this version is not attributable to Mérimée (PM, 1345). Pierre Trahard and Pierre Josserand say, however, that the modifications were made with Mérimée's "authorization," if not by his own hand (*Bibliographie des oeuvres de Prosper Mérimée* (Paris: Librarie Ancienne Honoré Champion, 1929), 50.

9 André Billy, *Mérimée* (Paris: Flammarion, 1959), 44. Cf. P.-A. Buisine: "La nouvelle de Prosper Mérimée est un ardent plaidoyer contre l'esclavage" ("Tamango: Premier film en France de Dorothy Dandridge," *La Cinématographie française* 1728 [July 13, 1957]: 21).

10 The authoritative Frank Paul Bowman saw in "Tamango" an "anti-slavery at-titude," despite Mérimée's generally "reactionary" politics (Frank Paul Bow-man, *Prosper Mérimée: Heroism, Pessimism, and Irony* [Berkeley: University of California Press, 1962], 40). Adele King writes, "Mérimée invented the character of Tamango, and used his story to support the anti-slavery move-ment in nineteenth-century France" (Adele King, *"Le Temps de Tamango*: Eighteen Hundred Years of Solitude," *Komparatistische Hefte* 12 [1985]: 85). In a detailed chapter on "Tamango," Ibrahim Boukari Amidou asserts, "Nous pouvons dire en toute légitimité que l'ouvrage de Mérimée se prête bien à la propagande anti-esclavagiste par ses descriptions d'évènements historiques qui marquent le voyage des Noirs vers les Iles des Caraïbes" (Ibrahim Bou-kari Amidou, "Evolution de la représentation de l'Afrique et des Africains dans *L'Encyclopédie* de Diderot et au cours du siècle des Lumières, *Tamango* de Mérimée, le *Roman d'un spahi* de Pierre Loti, et *Voyage au Congo* de Gide: Humanisme, exotisme, et colonialisme" (Ph.D. diss., University of Cincin-nati, 2002), 134.

11 "Mateo Falcone," in *Nouvelles*, ed. Françoise Rio (Paris: Larousse, 2000), 166.

12 Nicholas Jotcham, introduction to Mérimée, *"Carmen" and Other Stories*, xx.

13 A. W. Raitt, *Prosper Mérimée* (London: Eyre and Spottiswoode, 1970), 130. Cf. Antonia Fonyi, introduction to "Tamango" in Mérimée, *"Tamango," "Mateo Falcone" et autres nouvelles* (Paris: Flammarion, 1983): "la nouvelle n'est pas mise au service d'une cause humanitaire . . ." (80).

14 Eric Gans, "Un Pari contre l'histoire: Les Premièrs nouvelles de Mérimée (*Mosaïque*)," *Archives des lettres modernes* 9, no. 141 (1972): 25, 30.

15 Mérimée, quoted in "Contextes" section of Mérimée, *"Tamango," "Mateo Falcone" et autres nouvelles*, 17.

16 Quoted in Alan Spitzer, *The French Generation of 1820* (Princeton: Princeton University Press, 1987), 4.

17 See Tzvetan Todorov, "Freedom and Repression during the Restoration," in *A New History of French Literature*, ed. Denis Hollier (Cambridge, Mass.: Harvard University Press, 1989), 617–23.

18 Doris Kadish, introduction to Sophie Doin, *La Famille noire* (Paris: L'Harmattan, 2002), xxi. On the indemnification of the former planters of Saint-Domingue see my chapter 10.

19 Rémusat's play was influential in spite of the fact that it was never performed; see Spitzer, *The French Generation of 1820*, 125.

20 See Yvan Debbasch, "Poésie et traite: L'Opinion française sur le commerce négrier au début du XIXe siècle," *Revue française d'histoire d'outre-mer* 172–73 (1961): 311–52; and Léon-François Hoffmann, *Le Nègre romantique: Personnage littéraire et obsession collective* (Paris: Payot, 1973), 155–61. On possible uses of some of the 1823 poems by Mérimée see G. Hainsworth, "West-African Local Colour in *Tamango*," *French Studies* 21, no. 1 (January 1967): 21–22.

21 On "exoticism" and "ugliness" in this context see Billy, *Mérimée*, 29, 31.

22 I am referring to the various works published in the volume *Le Théâtre de Clara Gazul* (1825), to *La Guzla ou choix de poésies illyriques recueillies dans la Dalmatie, la Croatie et l'Herzégovine* (1827), as well as to "Mateo Falcone" and "L'Enlèvement de la redoute" (both 1829). I am not aware of any work of Mérimée's from before 1830 that represents metropolitan, "hexagonal" France, as, for example, *La Double méprise* will in 1833.

23 In fact, "Tamango" will remain the only one of Mérimée's works "dealing 'overtly' with his own culture." See Corry Cropper, "Mérimée's *Columba* and the July Monarchy," *Nineteenth-Century French Studies* 29, nos. 1–2 (fall–winter 2000–2001): 35.

24 Mérimée's preface to an 1842 reprinting of *La Guzla*, quoted in Pierre Josserand, introduction to Mérimée, *Colomba et dix autres nouvelles* (Paris: Gallimard, 1964), 12.

25 See Spitzer, *The French Generation of 1820*, 126.

26 Robert L. A. Clark, "South of North: *Carmen* and French Nationalisms," in

East of West: Cross-Cultural Performance and the Staging of Difference, ed. Claire Sponsler and Xiaomei Chen (New York: Palgrave, 2000), 189. Note that *Gazul* and *Guzla* are anagrams.

27 See Raitt, *Prosper Mérimée*, 131. Mallion and Salomon, however, state that the corrections were minor (PM, 1313).

28 Raitt, *Prosper Mérimée*, 123.

29 Quoted ibid., 393; see also 32, 43.

30 Ibid., 393.

31 Emile Henriot, "L'Imagination de Mérimée," *Le Temps* (October 10, 1933): 3.

32 Thus a Corsican peasant shoots his own son to death in cold blood ("Mateo Falcone"); a despotic Swedish king sees the prophetic apparition of a gruesome decapitation (*La Vision de Charles XI*); a French soldier describes the carnage of a battle in the Russian campaign ("L'Enlèvement de la redoute"); a brutal slave-trading sea captain and his crew are ravaged by captive Africans who are even more brutal ("Tamango"); a debauched Neapolitan nobleman bargains with Jesus Christ, lives 180 years as a gambler, and nonetheless talks his way through the Pearly Gates at the end (*Federigo*).

33 Charles-Augustin Sainte-Beuve, "*Théâtre de Clara Gazul*: Nouvelle édition," *Le Globe*, January 24, 1831, 96. In this article, Sainte-Beuve is commenting on the entirety of Mérimée's oeuvre to date, including "Tamango," not just on *Clara Gazul.*

34 Raitt, *Prosper Mérimée*, 122, 36.

35 See ibid., 76.

36 Léon Laleau, "Trahison," in *Anthologie de la nouvelle poésie nègre et malgache de langue française*, ed. Léopold Sédar Senghor (Paris: Presses Universitaires de France, 1948), 108.

37 This is what I described as the "anthropological" dimension of Francophone African literature in my book *Theories of Africans*. Mérimée's most explicit use of an ethnographic mode of writing within his fiction must be the heavy-handed last section of *Carmen*, a disquisition on the culture of gypsies, which he added in 1846.

38 The current Larousse edition follows this pattern, which goes back at least as far as the publication of *"Mateo Falcone," "Tamango," "L'Enlèvement de la redoute"* (London: Rivingtons, 1890).

39 "C'est cette manière de taillis fourré que l'on nomme mâquis" (PM, 451/54, AT).

40 The *Grand Robert* dictionary (2nd ed., 2001) attributes the first usage of the word in French to Mérimée in "Mateo Falcone." *Macchia*, from the Latin *macula* (mark or stain), refers to the appearance created on the hillsides by these areas of dense regrowth.

41 "Le laboureur corse, pour s'épargner la peine de fumer son champ, met le feu à une certaine étendue de bois: tant pis si la flamme se répand plus loin que besoin n'est" (PM, 451/54, AT). We should not forget what this microcosm of

"Corsican manners" consists of: the murder of a son by a father, heavy with implications of a primitive sense of honor.

42 Of course the big difference between the metaphorically "enslaved" words and the genuinely enslaved Africans is that the former, not the latter, actually travel to the metropole and become French (perhaps in the way that Ourika did; and they are still marked by their difference); the slaves do not.

43 On local color in Mérimée and in romanticism in general see Jan Willem Hovencamp, *Mérimée et la couleur locale: Contribution à l'étude de la couleur locale* (Nijmegan, Netherlands: Drukkerij De Phoenix, 1928); on *mœurs* see p. 1.

44 See, e.g., Sembene Ousmane's treatment of the words *mama*, *moké*, and *n'gounou* in his novel *Les Bouts de bois de Dieu: Banty mam yall* (Paris: Presses Pocket, 1960), 19, 28–29, 77, 81. The first time he uses these African words, he italicizes them and translates them in a footnote. The second occurrence of the word, even several pages later, is in roman type, as if the word has been assimilated to French, naturalized. Ahmadou Kourouma updates this technique in *Les Soleils des indépendances*, using quotation marks instead of italics and parenthetical explanations of African terms instead of footnotes; but the process remains the same. See his treatment of the word *tara* in *Les Soleils des indépendances* (Paris: Seuil, 1970), 158.

45 PM, 1650. With the exception of *maghzen*, all of those Arabic words are found in the current *Petit Robert* dictionary, as French vocabulary. On *maghzen* see PM, 1656.

46 Mérimée uses the seventeenth-century form of the word, *guiriot*, as it appeared for the first time in French, in Alexis de Saint-Lo's *Relation du voyage du Cap-Verd* (1637), as opposed to the modern form, *griot*, which Hugo, for example, had used in *Bug-Jargal* (in the second, expanded version of 1826). See Victor Hugo, *Bug-Jargal ou la révolution haïtienne* (Fort-de-France: Désormeaux, 1979), 253; Hugo also uses the term *balafo* (255). *Guiriot* is used by Labat, whom Mallion and Salomon say Mérimée "certainly" read (PM, 1343). In a passage that is heavily indebted to (in fact a wretched paraphrase of) La Courbe's manuscript, which we encountered in the first part of this study (although Labat attributes the information to André Brüe), Labat describes how Brüe (in fact it was La Courbe) went to a festival, called a *folgar*, at which *guiriots* entertained. See Jean-Baptiste Labat, *Nouvelle relation de l'Afrique occidentale* (Paris: Théodore Le Gras, 1728), 2:276–80; *folgar* is defined by Labat as "une espèce de bal public, où toute la jeunesse du Village & des environs se rend avec empressement, pour témoigner par leurs danses, leurs chansons, leurs luttes & autres exercices, le plaisir qu'ils ont de voir ceux à qui leur Prince veut donner du divertissement" (3:17). *Folgar* is "a Portuguese and Luso-African word that passed into Franco-African usage as a general term for celebrations with music and dancing" (George Brooks, *Eurafricans in Western Africa* [Athens: Ohio University Press, 2003], 216). Thanks to Philip J. Havik and Peter Mark for help with this. The *balafo* is given a

precise description and a full-page illustration in Labat's work (2:332). We should note also that Mérimée describes another West African instrument, the *kora*, without mentioning it by name ("des guitares faites avec des moitiés de calebasses," 488). On the relations among Saint-Lô, La Courbe, and Labat see Thomas Hale, *Griots and Griotes: Masters of Words and Music* (Bloomington: Indiana University Press, 1998), 84–86; and see William B. Cohen, *The French Encounter with Africans: White Response to Blacks, 1530–1880* (Bloomington: Indiana University Press, 1980), 18; henceforth abbreviated WC, 18. Hainsworth argues that all of these elements could have come to Mérimée from a reading of Prévost's compendium (which incorporated information from many sources, including Labat), *Histoire générale des voyages* (as well as Park) (Hainsworth, "West-African Local Colour in *Tamango*," 16–17).

47   "Nègre jouant du balafo," in Labat, *Nouvelle relation de l'Afrique occidentale*, 2:332.

48   Thus he writes "*guiriot* ou magicien" (reflecting the false impression among Europeans that West African griots were magicians). The only annotations that Mérimée added to the text of the story are explanations of "trafiquants de bois d'ébène" ("nom que se donnent eux-mêmes les gens qui font la traite" [479]); and of "Tamango entonnait le chant guerrier de sa famille" ("Chaque capitaine nègre a le sien" [491]). The only other italicized term in "Tamango" refers to "ces fers que l'on nomme, je ne sais pourquoi, *barres de justice*" (480); this terminology of the slave trade apparently came to Mérimée from the testimony of the Baron de Staël, published in the pages of the *Journal de la Société de la Morale Chrétienne* (see PM, 1348n11).

49   Mungo Park, *Travels in the Interior Districts of Africa* (first published 1799), ed. Kate Ferguson Marsters (Durham: Duke University Press, 2000), 92–93. Park finds that he must travel back from Africa to England via the West Indies, on a slave-trading vessel from South Carolina, where the "mode of confining and securing Negroes . . . made these poor creatures to suffer greatly" (305). Hainsworth points out that two earlier accounts of Mumbo-Jumbo were also available: in Prévost (1747) and in an article devoted to this subject in the *Encyclopédie* (Hainsworth, "West-African Local Colour in *Tamango*," 18–19). See "Mumbo-Jumbo," in *Encyclopédie* 10:860. For an amusing psychoanalytic interpretation of Mérimée's change of "Mumbo-Jumbo" to "Mama-Jumbo," see Jacques Chabot, *L'Autre moi: Fantasmes et fantastique dans les nouvelles de Mérimée* (Aix-En-Provence: Edisud, 1983), 71–78.

50   Robert Baschet, *Du Romantisme au Second Empire: Mérimée (1803–1870)* (Paris Nouvelles Editions Latines, 1958), 55.

51   Raitt, *Prosper Mérimée*, 130.

52   The Société had nine committees, including one, headed by the Baron de Staël, devoted to the abolition of the slave trade. This committee "played the leading role in French slave-trade abolitionism in the 1820's" (Lawrence C. Jennings, *French Anti-Slavery: The Movement for the Abolition of Slavery in France, 1802–1848* [Cambridge: Cambridge University Press, 2000], 12). Jen-

nings credits Staël's committee with "launch[ing] the movement for the second abolition of French colonial slavery" (13).

53 Ibid., 10.

54 Nelly Schmidt, *Abolitionnistes de l'esclavage et réformateurs des colonies, 1820–1851: Analyse et documents* (Paris: Karthala, 2000), 37.

55 This seems to be the logic used by Pierre Trahard: "On aimerait à croire que *Tamango* aida à la libération des Noirs; dix-huit mois après sa publication, la loi du 4 mars 1831 met fin à la traite des esclaves" (Pierre Trahard, *La Jeunesse de Prosper Mérimée, 1803–1834* [Paris: Edouard Champion, 1925], 78). David O'Connell writes that "there can also be no doubt that *Tamango* is a pro-abolitionist work. Mérimée, an anti-clerical liberal, was wholeheartedly devoted to the cause of black emancipation just as the monarchist Hugo had been" (David O'Connell, "The Black Hero in French Romantic Fiction," *Studies in Romanticism* 12, no. 2 [spring 1973]: 518). But I have seen nothing that supports the claim that Mérimée was devoted to such a cause. O'Connell's idea of a Mérimée who hides his true abolitionist feeling behind "a veritable ironical smokescreen" (518) in "Tamango" is therefore dubious.

56 An Englishwoman who observed French society and its salons at this precise moment in history, and who wrote about Mérimée in this context, Lady Sydney Morgan, said nothing about abolitionism (even after visiting a meeting of the Société de la Morale Chrétienne) and in no way associated the very "liberal" Mérimée with it. Her chapter "Public Opinion in 1829" includes no discussion of slavery, the slave trade, or abolition. See Lady Sydney Morgan, *France in 1829–1830* (New York: J. and J. Harper, 1830), 1:136–37, 171–93. The agenda for the meeting of the société that she attended includes, as its last item, "Rapport sur le résultat du Concours sur l'Abolition de la Traite des Noirs et de l'Esclavage, par M. Edouard Thayer" (2:130).

57 Jean Mallion and Pierre Salomon, "Approche de Mérimée," introduction to PM, xlviii. Fanny Wright was a counterexample, a nonreligious abolitionist; see Celia Morris Eckhardt, *Fanny Wright: Rebel in America* (Cambridge, Mass.: Harvard University Press, 1984), 243.

58 Abbé Henri Grégoire, *De la Traite et de l'esclavage des Noirs et des Blancs par un ami des hommes de toutes les couleurs* (Paris: Adrien Egron, 1815), 23.

59 Duc de Broglie, "Discours prononcé par M le Duc de Broglie à la Chambre des Pairs le 28 mars 1822 sur la Traite des Nègres" (Paris: Société de la Morale Chrétienne, Comité pour L'Abolition de la Traite des Nègres, 1822), 59.

60 Debbasch, "Poésie et traite," 333n4.

61 T, 584; Serge Daget, "Les mots esclave, nègre, Noir, et les jugements de valeur sur la traite négrière dans la littérature abolitionniste française de 1770 à 1845," *Revue française d'histoire d'outre-mer* 60, no. 221 (1973): 546.

62 *L'Affaire de "La Vigilante," batiment négrier de Nantes* (Paris: Crapelet, 1823), 6. This pamphlet has been cited as a source of Mérimée's "Tamango" (see, e.g., PM, 1341).

63 See Debbasch, "Poésie et traite," 315; Paule Brasseur, "Libermann et l'abolition

de l'esclavage," *Revue française d'histoire d'outre-mer* 73, no. 272 (1986): 336; and Serge Daget, "France, Suppression of the Illegal Slave Trade, and England, 1817–1850," in *The Abolition of the Atlantic Slave Trade: Origins and Effects in Europe, Africa, and the Americas*, ed. David Eltis and James Walvin (Madison: University of Wisconsin Press, 1981), 194. The pattern of French indifference to things *outre-mer* will reappear with eerie familiarity in the era of French imperialism in the early twentieth century; see Christopher L. Miller, *Nationalists and Nomads: Essays on Francophone African Literature and Culture* (Chicago: University of Chicago Press, 1998), 65.

64   David Geggus, "Haiti and the Abolitionists: Opinion, Propaganda, and International Politics in Britain and France, 1804–1838," in *Abolition and Its Aftermath: The Historical Context, 1790–1916*, ed. David Richardson (London: Frank Cass, 1985), 118.

65   Francis Arzalier, "Les Mutations de l'idéologie coloniale en France avant 1848: De l'esclavagisme à l'abolitionnisme," in *Les Abolitions de l'esclavage: De L. F. Sonthonax à V. Schoelcher*, ed. Marcel Dorigny (Saint-Denis: Presses Universitaires de Vincennes, 1995), 300.

66   See Debbasch, "Poésie et traite," 346.

67   Broglie, "Discours prononcé par M le Duc de Broglie," 95. Paule Brasseur cites the sequence of laws that were passed in 1817 and 1818 to enforce the 1815 ban on the slave trade, but the application of those laws was less than effective. See Paule Brasseur "Le Sénégal et sa lente intégration au mouvement abolitionniste," in *Rétablissement de l'esclavage dans les colonies françaises: 1802*, ed. Yves Bénot and Marcel Dorigny (Paris: Maisonneuve and Larose, 2003), 377. On France's abolitionism, forced by Britain after Waterloo, see Herbert S. Klein, *The Atlantic Slave Trade* (Cambridge: Cambridge University Press, 1999), 187.

68   Serge Daget, "L'Abolition de la traite des Noirs en France de 1814 à 1831," *Cahiers d'études africaines* 11 (1971): 28–29; quoted in WC, 187.

69   The information and quotations about Surcouf are from T, 588.

70   Serge Daget, "The Abolition of the Slave Trade by France: The Decisive Years, 1826–1831," in *Abolition and Its Aftermath: The Historical Context, 1790–1916*, ed. David Richardson (London: Frank Cass, 1985), 142; and Serge Daget, *Répertoire des expéditions négrières à la traite illégale (1814–1850)* (Nantes: Centre de Recherche sur l'Histoire du Monde Atlantique, 1988), 101.

71   Daget, *Répertoire des expéditions négrières à la traite illégale*, 455–541; Olivier Pétré-Grenouilleau, "Cultural Systems of Representation, Economic Interests and French Penetration into Black Africa, 1780s–1880s," in *From Slave Trade to Empire: Europe and the Colonisation of Black Africa, 1780s–1880s*, ed. Olivier Pétré-Grenouilleau (New York: Routledge, 2004), 183n.

72   Daget, *Répertoire des expéditions négrières à la traite illégale*, 69, 70. The Pléiade edition is thus wrong to say: "Aucun des navires négriers du port de Nantes ne s'appelait à cette époque *L'Espérance*" (PM, 1347n3).

73 Hoffmann, *Le Nègre romantique*, 483n1.

74 See Daget, "The Abolition of the Slave Trade by France," 160–62.

75 Jacques Ducoin, "Les pirates noirs, le négrier nantais *La Concorde*, et le pirate anglais Edward Teach, dit Blackbeard," *Cahiers des anneaux de la mémoire* 4 (2002): 92. Marcus Rediker says that pirates were usually more interested in the ships than in their cargoes of slaves (Marcus Rediker, *Villains of All Nations: Atlantic Pirates in the Golden Age* [Boston: Beacon Press, 2004], 138; see also 189n31). He also argues that pirates' interference in the (British) slave trade on the coast of Africa provoked a crackdown that led to the death of piracy by 1734 (144). See also T, 311, 430; and Robert Harms, *The Diligent: A Voyage through the Worlds of the Slave Trade* (New York: Basic Books, 2002): 326–27. For a narration of an encounter between a slave-trading vessel and a pirate ship see Jean-Baptiste Labat, *Voyage du Chevalier des Marchais en Guinée, isles voisines, et à Cayenne, fait en 1725, 1726 & 1727* (Paris: Chez Saugrain, 1730), 3:59–62. See also Abdoulaye Ly, *La Compagnie du Sénégal* (Paris: Présence Africaine, 1958), 33.

76 Doris Garraway, *The Libertine Colony: Creolization in the Early French Caribbean* (Durham: Duke University Press, 2005), 98.

77 Edouard Corbière, *Le Négrier: Aventures de mer* (Paris: Denain, 1832), x.

78 See François Roudaut, introduction to Edouard Corbière, *Le Négrier* (Paris: Klincksieck, 1990), xxii. Roudaut says that piracy disappeared in the 1830s (xxiv).

79 Charles Desnoyer and J. Alboize, *La Traite des Noirs* (1835), in *Magasin théâtral* (Paris: Marchant, 1843), 5:19. The debt to Corbière's novel is visible also in the name of an African woman character, Fraïda.

80 Louis Enault, quoted in P. W. M. Cogman, "Mérimée and His Sources: A Note on *Tamango* and *Oroonoko*," *French Studies Bulletin* 45 (winter 1992–93): 7; Henriot, "L'Imagination de Mérimée," 3. Cf. Pierre Trahard: "Il est prouvé que Mérimée n'invente rien" (Trahard, *La Jeunesse de Prosper Mérimée*, 75–76).

81 Pierre Josserand, introduction to *Colomba et dix autres nouvelles* (Paris: Gallimard, 1964), 12.

82 Clarkson said that nine out of ten Europeans who go to Africa are only interested in the slave trade; see Thomas Clarkson, *An Essay on the Impolicy of the African Slave Trade* (London: J. Phillips, 1788), 8. This text was translated into French by the Société des Amis des Noirs as *Essai sur les désavantages politiques de la Traite des Nègres*, trans. Gramagnac (Paris: n.p., n.d).

83 Louis Narcisse Baudry Deslozières, quoted in Claude Wanquet, "Un Réquisitoire contre l'abolition de l'esclavage: *Les Egarements du nigrophilisme* de Louis Narcisse Baudry Deslozières," in *Rétablissement de l'esclavage dans les colonies françaises: 1802*, ed. Yves Bénot and Marcel Dorigny (Paris: Maisonneuve and Larose, 2003), 36, 37.

84 See Thomas Clarkson, *The Cries of Africa, to the Inhabitants of Europe; or, A Survey of that Bloody Commerce Called the Slave-Trade* (London: Harvey and

Darton, n.d.), 42; and Broglie "Discours prononcé par M le Duc de Broglie," 88.

85 Madame de Staël, "Appel aux souverains réunis à Paris, pour en obtenir l'abolition de la traite des nègres," quoted in Brasseur, "Libermann et l'abolition de l'esclavage," 335.

86 Charles de Rémusat, "Sur la colonie de Sierra-Léone," *Journal de la Société de la Morale Chrétienne* 1 (1822): 212.

87 Martial Barrois, *L'Abolition de la traite des Noirs* (Paris: Firmin Didot, 1823), 5.

88 Edouard Alletz, *L'Abolition de la traite des Noirs* (Paris: Delaunay, 1823), 4.

89 J. J. V. Chauvet, *L'Abolition de la traite des Noirs* (Paris: Firmin Didot, 1823), 1. A poem from three years later echoes this image of an edenic Africa: "... Humains, hospitaliers, / Accueillant la fortune, accueillant l'indigence, / De l'heureux âge d'or ils rappelaient l'enfance" (Louis-Marie Fontan, "Les Nègres et le négrier," in *Odes et épîtres* [Paris: Auguste Imbert, 1826], 77). Similar images of Africa before the slave trade will be used by twentieth-century African nationalists like Lamine Senghor; see my *Nationalists and Nomads*, 25.

90 Ange-Benjamin Marie du Mesnil, *L'Esclavage* (Paris: Firmin Didot, 1823), 18. In footnotes to the poem, Marie du Mesnil cites Park and Clarkson as his sources of information about Africa. Debbasch shows how the clichés of the noble savage in these poems derived from Clarkson and Wilberforce: "Du coup, le vieux mythe, vérifié et comme appelé à la réalité par les observateurs les moins suspects [Mungo Park and Sylvanian de Golbéry, who were in turn the sources cited by Clarkson and Wilberforce], y gagnait une seconde jeunesse" (Debbasch, "Poésie et traite," 343). See also my commentary on the 1823 poems (Christopher L. Miller, *Blank Darkness: Africanist Discourse in French* [Chicago: University of Chicago Press, 1985], 125–27).

91 The first version of *Bug-Jargal* was written in 1818 and published in 1820.

92 Chauvet, *L'Abolition de la traite des Noirs*, 8.

93 E. Barbier-Vemars, "L'Abolition de la traite des Noirs," quoted in Hoffmann, *Le Nègre romantique*, 158.

94 Although they are not listed among the identified sources of "Tamango," other narratives of slave traders (both European and African) who are themselves enslaved are certainly part of the background. Voltaire's *Histoire de Scarmentado* (1756), which I mentioned earlier in this study, is such a text.

95 See Srinivas Aravamudan's fine analysis of *Oroonoko*, "Petting Oroonoko," in his *Tropicopolitans: Colonialism and Agency, 1688–1804* (Durham: Duke University Press, 1999), 29–70. See also Roger Little, "*Oroonoko* and *Tamango*: A Parallel Episode," *French Studies* 46, no. 1 (January 1992), 26–32. On *Oroonoko* in France see Hoffmann, *Le Nègre romantique*, 59–62. See Aphra Behn, *Oroonoko, or the Royal Slave, A True History* (New York: Penguin Books, 1992), 126.

96 Daniel Defoe, *The Life, Adventures, and Piracies of the Famous Captain Sin-*

gleton (New York: Jenson Society, 1907), 206–20. In turn, Defoe's source may have been John Esquemeling's *The Buccaneers of America* (1685); see A. J. Roche, "La Source du *Tamango* de Mérimee," *Revue de littérature comparée* 14 (1934): 549–54.

97   Louis-Marie-Joseph Ohier de Grandpré, *Voyage à la côte occidentale d'Afrique* (Paris: Dentu, 1801), 1:xii, xvi, xvii–xx.

98   Auguste de Staël, "Rapport verbal, présenté au Comité pour l'abolition de la Traite," in *Assemblé générale annuelle de la Société de la Morale Chrétienne* (April 13, 1826), 44, 60, 52. Staël also reported to the society in an unsigned letter to its journal, *Journal de la Société de la Morale Chrétienne* 6 (1826): 185–92.

99   The 1781 case of the British slave ship *Zong* represents perhaps the most famous question of insurance in the history of the slave trade; see Ian Baucom, "Specters of the Atlantic," *South Atlantic Quarterly* 100, no. 1 (2001): 61–82. The massacre of captives aboard the *Zong* is the subject of Fred D'Aguiar's novel *Feeding the Ghosts* (London: Chatto & Windus, 1997).

100 Balthazard-Marie Emerigon, *Traité des assurances et des contrats à la grosse*, ed. P. S. Boulay-Paty (Rennes: Molliex, 1828): "Il paraît donc impossible qu'un être si excellent, qui tient le milieu entre le créateur et les choses créées, pour qui tout ce qui est matière a été fait, puisse devenir une chose, un animal semblable à la jument, une marchandise susceptible d'achat et de vente! . . . Mais la traite des nègres a été autorisée par les ordonnances du royaume. L'art. 44 du Code noir déclare les nègres être meubles. Ils peuvent par conséquent devenir la matière de l'assurance maritime" (1:208, 210).

471

101 Of the three vessels bearing the name *Comte d'Estaing* in Daget's *Répertoire des expéditions négrières françaises au XVIIIe siècle* (Paris: Société Française d'Histoire d'Outre-Mer, 1978 and 1984), 2 vols. (see Daget's numbers 768, 830, and 2391), none corresponds to this case.

102 Serge Daget, "J. E. Morenas à Paris: L'Action abolitionniste, 1819–1821," *Bulletin de l'Institut Fondamental d'Afrique Noire* 31, no. 3 (July 1969): 877. Brasseur says that Morenas was Grégoire's "agent" ("Libermann et l'Afrique," 336).

103 Morenas, quoted in Daget, "J. E. Morenas à Paris," 878; see also 875, 878, 881, 882.

104 Ibid., 881.

105 Broglie had nonetheless been hostile to Morenas in 1820; see Debbasch, "Poésie et traite," 325n1.

106 Joseph Elzéar Morenas, *Précis historique de la traite des Noirs et de l'esclavage colonial* (Paris: Firmin Didot, 1828), i.

107 Although Françoise Vergès does not discuss Morenas, his abolitionism is marked by the utopian dimension that she analyzes in abolitionist discourse, in *Abolir l'esclavage: Une Utopie coloniale: Les Ambiguïtés d'une politique humanitaire* (Paris: Albin Michel, 2001). On Morenas see Serge Daget, "The Abolition of the Slave Trade by France," 157–58.

108 "Undeniably" comes from the Larousse edition, quoted above (note 15); see also Amidou, "Evolution," 134.

109 Amidou interprets "Tamango" as a philosophical tale and sees Mérimée's irony as precisely balanced between the whites and the blacks; Tamango is "identique à Ledoux" ("Evolution," 132, 121).

110 The degeneration and regeneration of Africa was a key subject of debate among those eager to colonize; see Alyssa Goldstein Sepinwall, "Les Paradoxes de la régénération révolutionnaire: Le Cas de l'abbé Grégoire," *Annales historiques de la Révolution française* 3 (2000): 69–90; and François Manchuelle, "The Regeneration of Africa: An Important and Ambiguous Concept in 18th and 19th Century French Thinking about Africa," *Cahiers d'études africaines* 144, no. 36 (1996): 559–88.

111 The translator in this case seems to have chosen to make Mérimée's language less offensive for the modern reader: he translated "stupide désespoir" as "abject despair."

112 See Francis Marcoin, "Mérimée l'incorrect," in *Esclavage, libérations, abolitions, commémorations*, ed. Christiane Chaulet-Achour and Romuald-Blaise Fonkoua (Paris: Séghier, 2001), 163–78. Marcoin's well-argued point is quite the opposite of mine. In what must be considered a manifestation of the continuing French fascination with and assault on American "political correctness," Marcoin defends Mérimée "the incorrect," citing many of the same elements in the tale that I do here. Marcoin concedes that the condition of the revolted slaves, adrift and unable to steer themselves, does not look good, and he acknowledges that Mérimée "negates the possibility of an epic" in "Tamango" (176). But he attributes this to the "énigmaticité" (163) of the text, although there is nothing enigmatic about this image at all. He also attempts to dilute the effect of this image by suggesting that European literature is full of such "bateaux fous"—as if the stakes were the same in Rimbaud as in Mérimée's "Tamango"; but only in the latter is an entire race indicted and its emancipation mocked. Marcoin goes on to posit a dimension in "Tamango" that is utterly vague and inconsequential in comparison to the image of the boat gone adrift: "l'étrange attraction du 'sauvage' chez un auteur qui va bien plus loin que le pittoresque alors de mode et qui s'interroge sans cesse sur l'écart entre le sauvage et le civilisé, mais aussi sur leur points de rencontre." Marcoin also discusses the film *Amistad* as a pure fiction, ignoring its historical base—and as a representative of "une fiction [*sic*] bien-pensante dont se méfiait Mérimée" (177).

113 See Margaret Cohen, "Traveling Genres," *New Literary History* 34, no. 3 (summer 2003): 486.

114 Corbière, *Le Négrier: Aventures de mer* (Paris: Nouvelles Editions Baudinière, 1979), 111. (The previously cited Klincksieck edition uses different phrasing.)

115 For discussion of this theme in Mérimée see Khama-Bassili Tolo, *L'Intertextualité chez Mérimée: L'Étude des sauvages* (Birmingham, Ala:

Summa Publications, 1998), 234–39. Tolo points out that one sees "savages" unable to steer boats elsewhere in Mérimée's works: in *Les Espagnols en Danemark* (1825, Mérimée's first play and part of *Le Théâtre de Clara Gazul*) a shipwreck is briefly recounted, but Don Juan's inability to steer the launch is explained (and therefore excused): "Mais vous n'êtes pas marin . . ." (PM, 29). In Mérimée's treatment of other, European "savages" there is nothing like the indictment of Africans in "Tamango."

116 See W. Jeffrey Bolster, *Black Jacks: African American Seamen in the Age of Sail* (Cambridge, Mass.: Harvard University Press, 1997), esp. chap. 2, "African Roots of Black Seafaring." The French trader Dominique-Harcourt Lamiral reported on extensive use, in the slave trade itself, of *slave sailors* along the Senegambian coast in the late eighteenth century: "nous avons des bateaux & des esclaves matelots que nous envoyons jusques à Galam traiter des Noirs que nous vendons ensuite à des Marchands Européens au Sénégal" (Lamiral, *L'Affrique et le peuple affriquain considérés sous leurs rapports avec notre Commerce & nos Colonies* [Paris: Chez Dessenne, 1789], 19; see also 24–25 on the use by the Compagnie du Sénégal of slave sailors for "navigation"). It should also be pointed out that in the most famous case of a successful shipboard slave rebellion, the Africans onboard the *Amistad* anticipated the problem of navigation and dealt with it during their revolt by keeping one of the Spanish navigators alive to steer the ship; he, however, took the ship on a zigzag path that led to their capture. See Howard Jones, *Mutiny on the "Amistad": The Saga of a Slave Revolt and Its Impact on American Abolition, Law, and Diplomacy* (New York: Oxford University Press, 1987), 26.

117 Eric Saugera, *Bordeaux port négrier: Chronologie, économie, idéologie, XVIIe–XVIIIe siècles* (Paris: Karthala, 1995), 297.

118 Gaspard Théodore Mollien, *L'Afrique occidentale en 1818* (Paris: Calmann-Lévy, 1967), 146.

119 Raynal, *Histoire des deux Indes* (Geneva: Chez Jean-Léonard Pellet, 1780), 3:202. See also Aimé Césaire, *Toussaint Louverture: La Révolution Française et le problème colonial* (Paris: Présence Africaine, 1961), 309.

120 See Abbé Henri Grégoire, *De la littérature des Nègres* (Paris: Perrin, 1991), 161–63.

121 Mademoiselle de Palaiseau, *Histoire de Mesdemoiselles de Saint-Janvier, les deux seules Blanches conservées à Saint-Domingue* (Paris: J.-J. Blaise, 1812). I am grateful to Sue Peabody for bringing this text to my attention.

122 My interpretation thus differs somewhat from Doris Kadish's reading of "Tamango," in which she sees a refusal "to acknowledge Saint Domingue as an historical subtext." I would say that it is precisely as a subtext—but only as a subtext—that Saint-Domingue *is* acknowledged; "Tamango" may have spoken all the more loudly on the subject this way. But I agree with Kadish about one of the effects that Mérimée produces: he "tends to build a myth around the violence that occurred in the colonies rather than dealing with the social conditions from which it arose or the effects it produced" (Doris Y. Kadish,

"The Black Terror: Women's Responses to Slave Revolts in Haiti," *French Review* 68, no. 4 [March 1995]: 675).

123   Honoré de Balzac, *Lettres à Madame Hanska* (Paris: Les Bibliophiles de l'Originale, 1971), 4:323. The editor explains: "Balzac compare les révolutionnaires de 1848 aux esclaves révoltés incapables de diriger le navire dont ils se sont emparé."

124   The obvious debt that this description owes to a passage in Hugo's *Bug-Jargal* is pointed out by Mollien and Salomon (PM, 1349n4).

125   Shakespeare, *Coriolanus*, all in act 3, scene 1.

126   The extent to which Tamango may be an ironic reflection on Napoleon, who also ended up defeated, on an island, in the hands of the British, and perhaps in a uniform, is a question that has been discussed by James S. Patty, "Neither Black nor White: An Interpretation of *Tamango*," *French Literature Series* (University of South Carolina) 2 (1975): 73. Napoleon is alluded to in the story: "le capitaine, pour mettre Tamango en belle humeur, lui fit présent d'une jolie poire à poudre en cuivre, ornée du portrait de Napoléon en relief" (PM, 482). This representation of Napoleon's face, embedded within the scene of slave trading, silently invokes the emperor's role in the reestablishment of slavery and the slave trade.

127   Hainsworth, "West-African Local Colour in *Tamango*," 19.

128   See "Le Négrier," in Doin, *La Famille noire*, 71–82. Doris Kadish suggests that "Le Négrier" is an exception to Doin's overall style, to the extent that it uses a simple and direct narrative style. Kadish acknowledges the obstacle posed by Doin's "fioritures d'un style néo-classique . . . [ce qui] d'un point de vue contemporain . . . rend le style de Doin artificiel, démodé, par trop indirect et sans franchise" (introduction to *La Famille noire*, xxviii). In *TS* Kadish rightly called attention to the dangers of "applying aesthetic criteria that serve to dismiss the legitimacy of women's writing" (*TS*, 54).

129   Francis Marcoin, "Mérimée, entre Voltaire et Shakespeare," in *Prosper Mérimée: Écrivain, archéologue, historien*, ed. Antonia Fonyi (Paris: Droz, 1999), 220.

130   Amidou correctly points out the thematic linkage between *Les Vêpres siciliennes* and "Tamango" but mistakenly discusses Verdi's opera of the same title, which dates from 1855, instead of Delavigne's play, which is the work alluded to by Mérimée (Amidou, "Evolution," 114n58).

131   Casimir Delavigne, *Les Vêpres siciliennes: Tragédie en cinq actes* (Paris: Barba, 1820), 52; emphasis added. See also in *Les Vêpres siciliennes*: "Sans doute un grand complot, prêt à s'exécuter, / Avait besoin d'un chef pour oser éclater" (51); "indignés d'un honteux *esclavage*, . . . nous comptons des rois parmi nos *conjurés*" (4; emphasis added).

132   See Patrick Berthier, "Théâtre néo-classique ou théâtre du juste-milieu? Situation de Casimir Delavigne," *L'Etat des études françaises dans le monde* 50 (May 1998): 160. Delavigne's *Les Vêpres siciliennes* was the basis for an opera of the same name, in French, by Verdi, with a libretto by Eugène Scribe

(1855). See Mario Hamlet-Metz, "La Destinée théâtrale des *Vêpres siciliennes*," *Nineteenth-Century French Studies* 4, no. 3 (spring 1976): 233–43.

133   See Pierre H. Dubé, *Bibliographie de la critique sur Prosper Mérimée: 1825– 1993* (Geneva: Droz, 1997), 18. Among editions including "Tamango" that were available in the 1920s and 1930s (the years of Césaire's youth and education) were two editions of Mérimée's complete works: *Oeuvres complètes*, ed. Pierre Trahard and Edouard Champion (Paris: Honoré Champion, 1927–33), with "Tamango" in vol. 14, dated 1933, featuring an illustration of the infamous slave ship the *Brookes* (p. 48); and *Oeuvres complètes* (Paris: Le Divan, 1927–31). Seven editions of Mérimée's collected works published between 1924 and 1935 included "Tamango." Césaire arrived in Paris in 1931 at the age of eighteen to study at the Lycée Louis-le-Grand and then at the Ecole Normale Supérieure; he stayed for eight years, at the end of which the *Cahier* was published.

134   Aimé Césaire, *Cahier d'un retour au pays natal*, ed. Abiola Irele (Columbus: Ohio State University Press, 2000), 30.

135   Ibid., 31; Aimé Césaire, *The Collected Poetry*, trans. by Clayton Eschleman and Annette Smith (Berkeley: University of California Press, 1983), 81, AT. I have printed the verses exactly as they appeared in what A. James Arnold calls the "pre-original" edition of the poem: Aimé Césaire, "Cahier d'un retour au pays natal," *Volontés* 20 (August 1939): 49. See Arnold, "Césaire's *Notebook* as Palimpsest: The Text before, during, and after World War II," *Research in African Literatures* 35, no. 3 (fall 2004): 133.

136   I am referring to the *Oeuvres complètes* (Paris: Honoré Champion, 1933), vol. 14 (entitled *Mosaïque*).

137   Césaire, quoted in Lilyan Kesteloot, *Comprendre le "Cahier d'un retour au pays natal" d'Aimé Césaire* (Issy les Moulineaux: Les Classiques Africains, 1982), 100.

138   As with so many things in the *Cahier*, this is ambiguous: does *folle* refer to an autonomous "madwoman," as the Eschleman/Smith and Rosello/Pritchard translations both have it? The latter translation adds a word that can be inferred in the French: "not *like* a poor madwoman" (Aimé Césaire, *Notebook of a Return to My Native Land*, trans. Mireille Rosello and Annie Pritchard [Newcastle Upon Tyne: Bloodaxe Books, 1995], 131). Or, alternatively, is *folle* an adjective modifying *la négraille* (as Irele reads it)? Along with the translators, I subscribe to the former interpretation. The old Emile Snyder translation in the bilingual Présence Africaine edition — *Cahier d'un retour au pays natal/Return to My Native Land* (Paris: Présence Africaine, 1971) — has "madman" (148). For Irele's interpretation see Césaire, *Cahier d'un retour au pays natal*, 143. The antecedence of *sa* in *sa liberté* compounds the problem: I read this as "her," referring to the madwoman; Irele and Rosello/Pritchard read it as "its," referring to "Negridom" (Rosello and Pritchard's translation of *la négraille*). Smith and Eschleman changed their translation of this line. Their first translation, cited and quoted above, is the one I agree with: "no

longer a poor madwoman in *her* maritime freedom and destitution." This was changed to "no longer a poor madwoman in *its* maritime freedom and destitution" (Aimé Césaire, *Notebook of a Return to the Native Land* [Middletown, Conn.: Wesleyan University Press, 2001], 48).

139 Thus corresponding to this sense of the word *parfait*: "Qui répond exactement, strictement à un concept; *absolu, complet, total*" (*Petit Robert*). This verse has, I believe, been subject to differing interpretations based on a scansion or lineation that varies from edition to edition. Gregson Davis has commented on this problem: in the absence of a "definitive scholarly edition" the lineation of the poem has been left to the decisions of typesetters (Gregson Davis, *Non-Vicious Circle: Twenty Poems of Aimé Césaire*, trans. Gregson Davis [Stanford: Stanford University Press, 1984]: 24–25). Daniel Delas describes the *Cahier* as "non versifié . . . [et] spatialisé sans modèle fixe" (*Aimé Césaire* [Paris: Hachette, 1991]: 31). The collection of Césaire's poetry edited by Daniel Maximin and Gilles Carpentier, *La Poésie* (Paris: Seuil, 1994), is the same as the original 1939 edition, except that the following line is merged "en la dérive parfaite et la / voici . . ." (55). The scansion in the long-extant, bilingual Présence Africaine edition is consistent with my reading (*Cahier d'un retour au pays natal/Return to My Native Land*, 149). In the Irele edition that I have cited—and only in that edition—the words *girant en la parfaite dérive* stand as their own line, creating the impression that they constitute an autonomous verse, not governed by the *non point* that precedes them—an impression that Irele reinforces in his annotations, referring to the "positive nature" of the *dérive parfaite* as part of "the moral victory." Irele writes: "The poet . . . stresses the lucid disposition of the slaves (*non point folle*, referring to *la négraille*) in their precarious freedom (*dans sa liberté et son dénuement maritimes*) and the positive nature of this drifting (*dérive parfaite*) both in the sense of the moral victory it represents and that of its spiritual significance, made clear in the next stanza" (143). I read *girant en la dérive parfaite* as part of the negative counterexample, associated with the madwoman who is free but destitute—what we might call the "Tamango" scenario. "Drift" is associated with that negative moment, not with the moral triumph that nonetheless occurs; *la voici*, in my view, then takes the reader back to *la négraille*. The loose versification and lexical complexity of the *Cahier* leave the poem open to this type of debate.

140 See Robert Harms, "The Transatlantic Slave Trade in Cinema," *Black and White in Colour: African History on Screen*, ed. Vivian Bickford-Smith and Richard Mendelsohn (Athens: Ohio University Press, 2007), 59–81. I am grateful to Harms for sharing this essay with me before its publication. The only earlier film that I know of which represents the slave trade is *Slave Ship* (1937), directed by Tay Garnett, based on a novel by George S. King, with the "story" of the film by William Faulkner. *Slave Ship*, in two separate sequences, shows Africans being brutally whipped as they are forced into the hold of the eponymous ship, which operates illegally out of Salem, Massa-

chusetts, in the late 1850s. Berry's *Tamango* owes some of its visual representation of the hold in which the slaves are kept, and of the slaves' attempts to rise up, to this film. Remarkably, too, decades before Spielberg's *Amistad* and Deslauriers's *Middle Passage*, *Slave Ship* showed captives being thrown overboard in chains. As in historical and fictional cases that we have seen, this is done in order for the slavers to evade arrest and hanging at the hands of the British. The American hero (Gary Cooper) of another film from 1937, *Souls at Sea*, directed by Henry Hathaway, works with British authorities to suppress the slave trade in the 1840s; Africans' experience of the slave trade is only briefly, but graphically, represented.

141 Quoted in Robert K. Lightning, "Dorothy Dandridge: Ruminations on Black Stardom," *Cineaction Performance* 44 (1997): 34. See Donald Bogle, *Dorothy Dandridge* (New York: Amistad, 1997). Gary Daupin refers to Dandridge as "the first truly integrated Black goddess" (quoted in Gwendolyn Audrey Foster, *Captive Bodies: Postcolonial Subjectivity in Cinema* [Albany: State University of New York Press, 1999], 180).

142 Michel Duran, "Les Films qu'on peut voir à la rigueur cette semaine," *Le Canard enchaîné*, January 29, 1958, 1. This is confirmed by Jacques Doniol-Valcroze, "Le Cinéma: 'Tamango,'" *France Observateur*, January 30, 1958, 23: "*Carmen Jones* (toujours inédit en France)." The suit was brought by the heirs of Bizet's librettists, who asserted that the film was a travesty (*détournement*) of the original: see www.dvdclassik.com/crititiques/dvd_carmenjones.htm (accessed November 11, 2005). Henri Lopes mentions this "affaire" in his novel *Le Lys et le flamboyant* (Paris: Seuil, 1997), 301.

143 E. L., "Aiche menu," *Cahiers du cinéma* 14, no. 80 (February 1958): 61.

144 Paulin Soumanou Vieyra, *Le Cinéma et l'Afrique* (Paris: Présence Africaine, 1969), 63.

145 John Berry, interview by Patrick McGilligan, in Patrick McGilligan and Paul Buhle, *Tender Comrades: A Backstory of the Hollywood Blacklist* (New York: St. Martin's Griffin, 1997), 82.

146 See http://history.sffs.org/films/ (search: Tamango).

147 Foster, *Captive Bodies*, 180. This claim is hard to justify in relation to *Tarzan's Peril*.

148 See Dina Sherzer, *Cinema, Colonialism, Postcolonialism: Perspectives from the French and Francophone Worlds* (Austin: University of Texas Press, 1996), 5–6.

149 "Movie of the Week: 'Tomango,'" [*sic*] *Jet Magazine*, August 27, 1959, 65. Darcy DeMille, while allowing that *Tamango* "presents a good and wonderful case AGAINST racial discrimination," opined that "Negroes from all walks of life . . . will intensely dislike 'Tamango,'" because "they too go to the theatre to be entertained." The story, though true, is "especially hard to take at this point of the 20th century" and "should never have been filmed" (Darcy DeMille, "'Tomango' [*sic*] Shouldn't Have Been Made," *Los Angeles Sentinel*, October 8, 1959, 2c).

150 Little more information is available about Alex Cressan; see Lightning, "Ru-minations," 37. Cressan is identified as Martinican in *Jet Maga₹ine*, August 27, 1959.

151 Ephraim Katz, *The Film Encyclopedia* (New York: Putnam, 1979), 115.

152 "Filmmaker John Berry to Shed Light on Hollywood Blacklist at the Virginia Film Festival," press release, 1997, www.vafilm.com/1997/berry.html; Mc-Gilligan and Buhle, *Tender Comrades*, 55–57.

153 Berry refers to blacklisted movies as "black pictures," in McGilligan and Buhle, *Tender Comrades*, 82. He points out that the blacklist was no longer in force when *Tamango* was released in the United States.

154 See Howard Fast, "*Spartacus* and the Blacklist," introduction to his *Spartacus* (Armonk, N.Y.: North Castle Books, 1996), vii–viii. For particularly trans-parent passages, in which slavery obviously stands in for modern oppression, see 170–71, 214, and 254. Another point of comparison is Guy Endore's novel *Babouk* (New York: Monthly Review Press, 1991), first published in 1934. En-dore, an American leftist, uses the eighteenth-century French slave trade and slavery in Saint-Domingue as an allegory of modern racism in the United States (he makes this explicit [53]).

155 Jehan Mousnier, *Journal de la traite des Noirs* (Paris: Editions de Paris, 1957). This volume was one of very few on the French slave trade that were pub-lished in this period. It includes excerpts from ships' documents, slave-traders' journals, a glossary, and, most important, a version of Mérimée's "Tamango" (237–54). Strangely, Mousnier prints the version of the story that was published in *La France Maritime* in 1837 and 1852, without Mérimée's name, and with altered names of the main characters (see above, note 6). Mousnier wrongly identifies this as the original version of "Tamango," and he adds a first-person preface to the narrative that appears to be apocryphal. Also in 1957, the same publishing house put out a new edition of Mérimée, with "Tamango," exceptionally, leading the title: *Tamango, Carmen, Colomba* (Paris: Les Editions de Paris, 1957); the volume includes numerous photo-graphs from Berry's film.

156 Berry interview in McGilligan and Buhle, *Tender Comrades*, 82. I have been able to view the French version only once, at the Cinémathèque Française, but came away with the strong impression that Dorothy Dandridge was speaking her own lines in French; her lips are certainly moving to the French words, the voice sounds like hers, and the American accent sounds authen-tic.

157 See Tyler Stovall, *Paris Noir: African Americans in the City of Light* (Boston: Houghton Mifflin, 1996), 190, 201. But awareness of the limitations of French liberalism toward "their" Africans was given voice as early as the late 1920s by Claude McKay in his novel *Banjo: A Story without a Plot* (1927–28; New York: Harcourt, Brace, Jovanovich, 1957).

158 J. Hoberman, "Film: Tamango," *Village Voice*, July 1, 1997, 89. Other ex-amples of this include Jules Dassin's *Uptight* and Herbert Biberman's *Slaves*.

159 See Norman Collins, *Black Ivory* (New York: Pocket Books, 1948); Harold Calin, *Black Cargo* (New York: Lancer Books, 1969).

160 *Tamango*, dir. John Berry (Les Films du Cyclope, 1957). Video from Ivy Classics Video (Charlotte, N.C., 1992).

161 Women captives were often allowed to go about unchained on slave ships.

162 The film's Ayché meets all of the six conditions defining the "Tragic Mulatto complex" that Werner Sollors derives from Sterling Brown's original usage of the term: she is derived from texts more than from life; she is not "statistically representative"; she is "exceptionally beautiful but . . . doomed"; she is tortured by her own "warring blood"; "the whole desire of her life [until the ending] is to find a white lover, and then go down, accompanied by slow music, to a tragic end" (Brown); and she is the creation of white writers. See Werner Sollors, *Neither Black nor White yet Both: Thematic Explorations of Interracial Literature* (New York: Oxford University Press, 1997), 223–26. But in Berry's film Ayché overcomes some of these conditions by joining her fate to that of the black slaves. She is more than the mere embodiment of a ready-made stereotype.

163 There is one exception to this: Ayché, in the women's quarters below decks, passes on advice through the wall to the male captives as to where they can hide the body of the bosun, killed by Tamango.

164 Frantz Fanon, *Les damnés de la terre* (Paris: Gallimard, 1991), 135; *The Wretched of the Earth*, trans. Constance Farrington (New York: Grove Press, 1963), 199.

165 Sollors, *Neither Black nor White yet Both*, 6.

166 Foster, *Captive Bodies*, 183; emphasis added. Foster does not seem to have considered the "counterhegemonic" potential of the in-between, biracial position in *Tamango*; she mentions it only as "the trope of the tragic mulatto" (with reference to a different film) in opposition to "the real" (184). Marguerite H. Rippy describes *Tamango* as "one of the few films that depicts Dandridge in final solidarity with, rather than in deviation from, *her race*. . . . Aiche's dilemma echoes Dandridge's own subject position" (Marguerite H. Rippy, "Commodity, Tragedy, Desire: Female Sexuality and Blackness in the Iconography of Dorothy Dandridge," in *Classic Hollywood, Classic Whiteness*, ed. Daniel Bernardi (Minneapolis: University of Minnesota Press, 2001), 199; emphasis added. It is interesting to note that the forced assimilations of the mulatto to the black come from the United States and from the lone African commentator I have found, more than from the French. *Le Figaro* more accurately observed that Ayché joined "her slave brothers" (January 25, 1958); although *France Observateur* said that it was the "voice of blood" (that is, of race) that called Ayché. What is most significant about this is the suppression of the third, in-between term: in the film and in the discussions of the film Ayché's biracialism is eradicated.

167 Rippy, "Commodity, Tragedy, Desire," 189. The phrase "mixed American" is from an autobiography of dubious authenticity that was published after

479

Dandridge's death; it is not clear to what extent the text reflects her own thoughts: Dorothy Dandridge and Earl Conrad, *Everything and Nothing: The Dorothy Dandridge Tragedy* (New York: Abelard-Schuman, 1970). "If I am in any way a symbol, it stems from my being a 'mixed American.' The melting pot characteristics are written into my features. By parental and grandparental relationships on both sides, I am one-fourth English, one-fourth Jamaican (which is often a mixture of Indian, English, and African), one-fourth American Negro, one-eighth Spanish, and one-eighth Indian. . . . All that has happened to me in life seems in mystical ways related to this genetic inheritance. . . . If it is true that the American Indian was of Asiatic origin, then my physiological composition is about as international as possible" (19). "What was I? That outdated 'tragic mulatto' of earlier fiction? Oddly enough, there remains some validity in this concept, in a society not yet integrated. I wasn't fully accepted in either world, black or white." (178). On the status of this text see Rippy, "Commodity, Tragedy, Desire," 187.

168 This reading of Ayché aligns her with other reinterpretations of the *mulâtresse* within national romances as a "republican companion"; see John Garrigus, "Race, Gender, and Virtue in Haiti's Failed Foundational Fiction," in *The Color of Liberty: Histories of Race in France*, ed. Sue Peabody and Tyler Stovall (Durham: Duke University Press, 2003), 81.

169 See Jean Barbot, "Journal d'un voyage de traite en Guinée, à Cayenne et aux Antilles fait par Jean Barbot en 1678–1679," presented and annotated by Gabriel Debien, Marcel Delafosse, and Guy Thilmans, *Bulletin de l'Institut Fondamental d'Afrique Noire* 40, no. 2 (April 1978): "sont peu traitables . . . aussi traitables que beaucoup d'autres . . ." (272, 273).

170 I do not agree completely with Marguerite H. Rippy's interpretation of Ayché as the object of *equal* and opposite instances of violence coming from the captain and Tamango respectively. Rippy associates Tamango with a "doctrine of violent black separatism" (197–98), which is a strange and inaccurate way to describe a slave uprising. She seems to see this as the moral counterweight and equivalent to "Captain Reinker's doctrine of white capitalistic exploitation" (198). I agree with Rippy that Ayché is "trapped, literally between two spaces" and that the film offers her nothing but a binary choice. But the slaves' space is in the film not merely a second space of "masculine violence" as Rippy describes it: it is the space of a revolt from below, led by a man but shared by both sexes.

171 See Aravamudan, *Tropicopolitans*, 61.

172 Sollors, *Neither Black nor White yet Both*, 131.

173 "Et même si nous mourons, nous gagnerons. Parce qu'on peut vendre des hommes vivants, mais non des hommes morts. Moi, ils ne me vendront jamais."

174 Howard Fast's Spartacus says, "Even if we fail today, we did a thing that men will remember forever" (Fast, *Spartacus*, 289).

175 See Vito Russo, *The Celluloid Closet: Homosexuality in the Movies* (New York: Harper and Row, 1981).

176 See my *Nationalists and Nomads*, 118–51.

177 My point is not that there was no such thing as a direct Spanish slave trade with Africa but that it was little and late in comparison to the trade of other powers, including France. "The division of the world into Spanish and Portuguese spheres of influence first by a Papal Bull of 1493 and then by the Treaty of Tordesillas in 1494 meant that Spain was denied direct access to the coast of Africa and thus deprived of owning slave factories herself. She was forced to rely on foreigners to supply slaves to meet the great demand for servile labor in her American colonies" (David R. Murray, *Odious Commerce: Britain, Spain, and the Abolition of the Cuban Slave Trade* [Cambridge: Cambridge University Press, 1980], 2). The papal ban would of course be violated by Spanish traders: by the late eighteenth century there was some direct Spanish slave trading on the coast of Africa, and by the 1820s and 1830s, there seems to have been considerable Spanish-Cuban activity. (The *Amistad*, we should recall, was a coastal Spanish schooner sailing from Havana to Puerto Principe in Cuba, not a transatlantic vessel; the captives had made the Middle Passage onboard the *Teçora*, a Portuguese vessel operated by Spanish slave traders from Cuba, with an American captain.) Spain banned its Atlantic slave trade in 1817. See Jones, *Mutiny on the "Amistad,"* 14–16; and William A. Owens, *Black Mutiny: The Revolt on the Schooner "Amistad"* (New York: Penguin Plume, 1968), 25. By having the *Esperanza* set sail for Havana, the film *Tamango* actually introduces a plausible element of history: in the period depicted, Cuba was "the major destination" for illegal slave traders working out of Nantes (Murray, *Odious Commerce*, 9). The French also traded illegally with Puerto Rico in this period; see Joseph C. Dorsey, *Slave Traffic in the Age of Abolition: Puerto Rico, West Africa, and the Non-Hispanic Caribbean, 1815–1859* (Gainesville: University Press of Florida, 2003), 49.

178 Natalie Zemon Davis, *Slaves on Screen: Film and Historical Vision* (Cambridge, Mass.: Harvard University Press, 2000), 136.

179 We can disregard the fact that the film shows a tricolor, the emblem of the French Republic, inaccurate in the context of the Restoration.

180 See Daget, "France, Suppression of the Illegal Slave Trade, and England," 194. Daget explains that renewed enforcement was insisted on by the British, but only in 1823, producing better results (198–99).

181 Vieyra, *Le Cinéma et l'Afrique*, 61.

182 The video box mistakenly says the film was "banned in France."

183 Davis (*Slaves on Screen*, 65) points out this same procedure in Tomás Gutiérrez Alea's *The Last Supper* (*La Ultima Cena*). In the telefilm *Roots* the captives in the hold of the slave ship are seen learning each other's languages so that they can communicate.

184 A counterexample to this is provided by one of the precursor texts, Defoe's

481

Captain Singleton, in which the revolted slaves must learn English before they can tell their story (213–14).

185 Friends and colleagues of mine from various parts of Africa have agreed that this chant does not appear to be in any real African language.

186 "Like Aiche, caught between black and white male worlds of violence, Dandridge ultimately chose self-destruction as her form of authorship" (Rippy, "Commodity, Tragedy, Desire," 200).

187 I am thinking of a question—perhaps the most powerful one—raised by Edward Said in his *Orientalism* (New York: Pantheon, 1978): "Can one divide human reality, as indeed human reality seems to be genuinely divided, into clearly different cultures, histories, traditions, societies, *even races*, and *survive the consequences humanly?*" (45; emphasis added).

188 David Bellos kindly pointed out to me that Perec's *La Vie: Mode d'emploi* (Paris: Hachette, 1978) contains a chapter that is concerned with "the shell money of the slave trade," cowries (chapter 13)—although Perec does not mention the slave trade in that chapter. The bibliography to that chapter contains fake sources (e.g., *The Cauri System and African Banking*) by real authors (David S. Landes) and fake sources by fake authors ("R. Rorschash" et al.) (75–76). Diop's practice of pseudodocumentation and parahistoriography owes something to Perec; see Marcel Benabou, "Vraie et fausse érudition chez Perec," in *Parcours Perec*, ed. Mireille Ribière (Lyon: Presses Universitaires de Lyon, 1990), 41–47.

189 Adele King, "*Le Temps de Tamango*," 77. I am also indebted to John D. Erickson, "Writing Double: Politics and the African Narrative of French Expression," *Studies in 20th Century Literature* 15, no. 1 (winter 1991): 101–22. Erickson's remarks about the interplay of various levels of narration, producing fantastic results, are particularly insightful (107).

190 See Ousmane Sembene, *Le Docker noir* (Paris: Présence Africaine, 1973).

191 Diop first read the novella when he had to teach it as part of the prescribed literature program for a lycée in Senegal in the early 1970s (conversation with Boubacar Boris Diop, New Haven, September 30, 2004).

192 Adele King is right to suggest that Diop's "mockery of literature, history and most attempts to establish a stable point of view on human behavior" has a precursor in Yambo Ouologuem's *Le Devoir de violence* (1968); see King, "*Le Temps de Tamango*," 77.

193 Consonant with this, N'Dongo is later reported to have left behind him the fragments of a novel. Supposedly an exercise in engaged literature, designed to "raise consciousness," it goes *adrift*: "on sent un léger dérapage par rapport à son objectif initial et il apparaît clairement que N'Dongo finit par ériger la divagation systématique en technique d'écriture" (Diop, *Le Temps de Tamango*, 141).

194 Mongo Beti seems to have failed to see the skepticism that Diop is expressing about the postrevolutionary regime; Beti writes in his preface to *Le Temps de Tamango*: "l'auteur situe sa méditation à une époque où nous avons enfin

conquis cette liberté si désirée" (8). As King points out, Diop hardly represents the twenty-first century as a golden age (see King, "*Le Temps de Tamango*," 87).

195 Patoudem's company web site is http://patoufilms.free.fr/pres.htm. In 2007 it listed "Tamango" as "in development."

196 Google reveals that the name *Tamango* lives on as: a dancer (Herbin "Tamango" Van Cayseele) of international fame from French Guiana, a perfume, an African restaurant in Bordeaux, a type of rose . . . and a novel, *Tamango* (set in Africa but having nothing to do with the slave trade), by Jeanine Leconte-Raffalli.

10 FORGET HAITI

1 Michel-Rolph Trouillot, *Silencing the Past: Power and the Production of History* (Boston: Beacon Press, 1995), 73.

2 David Brion Davis, "Impact of the French and Haitian Revolutions," in *The Impact of the Haitian Revolution in the Atlantic World*, ed. David. P. Geggus (Columbia: University of South Carolina Press, 2001), 3.

3 Jean-Pierre Dozon, *Frères et sujets: La France et l'Afrique en perspective* (Paris: Flammarion, 2003), 69. See also Yves Bénot, *La Démence coloniale sous Napoléon* (Paris: La Découverte, 1992), 117–28.

4 Léon-François Hoffmann, *Le Nègre romantique: Personnage littéraire et obsession collective* (Paris: Payot, 1973), 135; Melvin D. Kennedy, "The Bissette Affair and the French Colonial Question," *Journal of Negro History* 45, no. 1 (January 1960), 2. On the Louisiana Purchase and the quotation from Napoleon see Edwidge Danticat, "Ignoring the Revolution Next Door," *Time*, July 5, 2004. Danticat writes that "Alexander Hamilton said Napoleon would not have sold his claims except for the 'courage and obstinate resistance [of the] black inhabitants' of Haiti."

5 Davis, "Impact of the French and Haitian Revolutions," 5.

6 Winston C. Babb, quoted in Dorothy Kadish, introduction to *Slavery in the Caribbean Francophone World: Distant Voices, Forgotten Acts, Forged Identities*, ed. Dorothy Y. Kadish (Athens: University of Georgia Press, 2000): 9.

7 Mademoiselle de Palaiseau, *Histoire de Mesdemoiselles de Saint-Janvier de Saint-Janvier, les deux seules Blanches conservées à Saint-Domingue* (Paris: J. J. Blaise, 1812).

8 Patricia Motylewski, *La Société française pour l'abolition de l'esclavage, 1834–1850* (Paris: L'Harmattan, 1998), 29.

9 Henri Pain, "De la nécessité de l'émancipation consentie par les colons pour éviter un nouveau Saint-Domingue" (1847), quoted in *D'une abolition l'autre: Anthologie raisonnée de textes consacrés à la seconde abolition de l'esclavage dans les colonies françaises*, ed. Myriam Cottias (Marseille: Agone, 1998), 4; emphasis added. See also Henri Pain, "Du souvenir de Saint-Domingue & de la nécessité de l'esclavage," in the same volume, 27.

483

10　Françoise Vergès, *Abolir l'esclavage: Une Utopie coloniale: Les Ambiguïtés d'une politique humanitaire* (Paris: Albin Michel, 2001), 116.

11　These were the conditions imposed on Haiti for its "emancipation" (recognition) by Charles X in 1825; by paying this amount (using loans from France!) the Haitian government thought it was erasing any risk of a new French invasion and takeover. (150 million francs was the equivalent of the budget of France for one year.) The indemnity was later renegotiated down to 90 million. This creation of what we would now call third-world debt was well ahead of its time; it crippled the Haitian economy. See François Blancpain, "L'Ordonnance de 1825 et la question de l'indemnité," in *Rétablissement de l'esclavage dans les colonies françaises: 1802*, ed. Yves Bénot and Marcel Dorigny (Paris: Maisonneuve and Larose, 2003), 221–29; and Gusti Klara Gaillard-Pourchet, "Aspects politiques et commerciaux de l'indemnisation haïtienne," in Bénot and Dorigny, *Rétablissement de l'esclavage dans les colonies françaises*, 233.

12　David Geggus, "Haiti and the Abolitionists: Opinion, Propaganda, and International Politics in Britain and France, 1804–1838," in *Abolition and Its Aftermath: The Historical Context, 1790–1916*, ed. David Richardson (London: Frank Cass, 1985), 128. Among the notable exceptions would be Lamartine's play *Toussaint-Louverture* (1850).

13　Emmanuel Serot, "French Defense Minister Promises to Help Haiti Rebuild," *Caribbean Net News*, April 16, 2004, www.caribbeannetnews.com/2004/04/16/rebuild.htm (accessed March 20, 2007); Joseph Guyler Delva, "Haiti Drops 'Ridiculous' $22 Billion Claim," Reuters, April 19, 2004, www.wehaitians.com/april%202004%20news%20and%20analysis.html (accessed March 20, 2007). See also "Dominique de Villepin à Port-au-Prince," *Le Monde*, March 27, 2004; Elaine Sciolino, "About-Face in France: Government's Out, Then It's In," *New York Times*, March 31, 2004. On the call for reparations see Dionne Jackson Miller, "Aristide's Call for Reparations from France Unlikely to Die," Inter Press Service News Agency (http://ipsnews.org), March 12, 2004.

14　On this point as it pertains to Africa see Boubacar Barry, *Senegambia and the Atlantic Slave Trade*, trans. Ayi Kwei Armah (Cambridge: Cambridge University Press, 1998), 115–16; henceforth abbreviated *SAST*.

15　"Cette Isle précieuse [Saint-Domingue], dont le commerce a élevé dans le Royaume des villes qui étonnent par leur magnificence" (Médéric Louis Elie Moreau de Saint-Méry, *Fragment sur les mœurs de Saint-Domingue* [n.p.: n.p., n.d.]), 14. Microfiche LI113–1 at the Bibliothèque Nationale de France.

16　Victor Hugo, preface to 1832 edition of *Bug-Jargal* (Fort-de-France: Désormeaux, 1979), 132.

17　See Robert Harms, *The Diligent: A Voyage through the Worlds of the Slave Trade* (New York: Basic Books, 2002), 175, 192.

18　William B. Cohen, *The French Encounter with Africans: White Response to Blacks, 1530–1880* (Bloomington: Indiana University Press, 1980), 158; henceforth abbreviated WC. For an overview of the linkage between abolitionism and the colonization of Africa see ibid., 164–66.

19 Abbé Roudaut, *Histoire générale de l'Asie, de l'Afrique, et de l'Amérique*, quoted in WC, 164.

20 Du Pont de Nemours, writing in *Les Ephémérides du citoyen* (1771), quoted in WC, 164. See Olivier Pétré-Grenouilleau, "Cultural Systems of Representation, Economic Interests and French Penetration into Black Africa, 1780s–1880s," in *From Slave Trade to Empire: Europe and the Colonisation of Black Africa, 1780s–1880s*, ed. Olivier Pétré-Grenouilleau (New York: Routledge, 2004), 159.

21 Michèle Duchet, *Anthropologie et histoire au siècle des Lumières* (Paris: Flammarion, 1977), 46–49.

22 François Manchuelle, "Le Rôle des Antillais dans l'apparition du nationalisme culturel en Afrique noire francophone," *Cahiers d'études africaines* 32, no. 3 (1992): 377.

23 Louis-Sébastien Mercier, *L'An 2440: Rêve s'il en fut jamais* (1771; Paris: France Adel, 1977), 2.

24 Raynal, *Histoire des deux Indes* (Geneva: Chez Jean-Léonard Pellet, 1780), 3:201.

25 WC, 165; see also Pétré-Grenouilleau, "Cultural Systems of Representation," 160. In all the arguments in Condorcet's earlier work *Réflexions sur l'esclavage des nègres* (1781), the idea of growing colonial products in Africa does not seem to come up. See Marie-Jean-Antoine-Nicolas de Caritat, Marquis de Condorcet, *Oeuvres complètes* (Paris: Henrichs, 1804) 11:83–198.

26 This was the second abolitionist "Société des Amis des Noirs." It argued that "In their native lands, the Africans are unaware of all the advantage they can draw from their soil and their climate for their own use and that of others." Quoted in Alyssa Goldstein Sepinwall, *Regenerating the World: The Abbé Grégoire, the French Revolution, and the Making of Modern Universalism* (Berkeley: University of California Press, 2005), 152. I am grateful to Alyssa Sepinwall for her assistance. See also Marcel Dorigny, "La Société des Amis des Noirs et les projets de colonisation en Afrique," *Annales historiques de la Révolution française* 3/4 (1993): 421–29. The terms of enlightened self-interest that will be used by Baron Roger are anticipated by a figure quoted in Dorigny's article, Bonnemain, who wrote in 1790: "Mais ne serait-il pas juste, *intéressant*, de *laisser en Afrique* les hommes que la divinité y a placés, et leur apprendre à cultiver une terre dont ils feraient sortir des trésors?" (422; emphasis added).

27 Madame de Staël, "Mirza, ou lettre d'un voyageur," in *Oeuvres de jeunesse* (Paris: Desjonquères, 1997), 162.

28 Louis-Marie-Joseph Ohier de Grandpré, Comte, *Voyage à la côte occidentale d'Afrique dans les années 1786 et 1787* (Paris: Dentu, 1801), 1:vx, 225. The abolitionist Abbé Henri Grégoire argued in 1815: "Certes la France, depuis longtemps, aurait pu et dû apporter la civilisation sur les rives du Sénégal, où,

sans remords, sans dangers, elle formeroit des Colonies prospères sur un sol *luxuriant*, et plus rapproché de la mère-patrie que ces Antilles dont une partie déjà lui est échappée et qui toutes bientôt peut-être échapperont à l'Europe" (Grégoire, *De la traite et de l'esclavage des Noirs et des Blancs* [Paris: Adrien Egron, 1815], 35). Grégoire was a friend of Roger's (WC, 223).

29 Meanwhile, in the United States the American Colonization Society was formed in 1816 "to promote the colonization of free blacks in Africa." David Brion Davis, *The Problem of Slavery in the Age of Revolution: 1770–1823* (Ithaca: Cornell University Press, 1975), 33.

30 Madame de Staël, "Mirza, ou lettre d'un voyageur," 162; emphasis added.

31 Ira Berlin, "The Promised Land," review of *Mississippi in Africa*, by Alan Huffman, *New York Times Book Review*, May 2, 2004, 29.

32 Vincent Carretta, *Unchained Voices: An Anthology of Black Authors in the English Speaking World of the Eighteenth Century* (Lexington: University Press of Kentucky, 1996), 296n62. Olaudah Equiano himself supported the opening of Africa to European, post-slave-trade commerce; in his narrative he looks back on his homeland with "an evaluating, entrepreneurial eye" (Geraldine Murphy, "Olaudah Equiano, Accidental Tourist," *Eighteenth-Century Studies* 27, no. 4 [summer 1994]: 557).

33 Georges Hardy, *La Mise en valeur du Sénégal, 1817–1854* (Paris: Payot, 1921), 117.

34 Ibid., 124.

35 Ibid., 231n.

36 G. Wesley Johnson, *Naissance du Sénégal contemporain* (Paris: Karthala, 1991), 67. On Roger see also Jean-Pierre Biondi, *Saint-Louis du Sénégal: Mémoires d'un métissage* (Paris: Denoël, 1987), 82–90.

37 On Faidherbe see Jean-Loup Amselle, *Vers un multiculturalisme français: L'Empire de la coutume* (Paris: Aubier, 1996), 117–50. Roger foreshadows the role that Amselle attributes to Faidherbe as "le véritable inventeur de la notion d'Afrique noire" (117). Amselle acknowledges Roger's "penchant pour le multiculturalisme" (120). On Delafosse and Clozel see Alf Schwarz, *Colonialistes, africanistes et Africains* (Montréal: Nouvelle Optique, 1979), 9–11. Dozon makes a similar argument about Roger as the person who inaugurates the "administrateur-ethnologue" (*Frères et sujets*, 73).

38 The figure 680 is Philip Curtin's, an average covering the years 1821 to 1830; cited in Paule Brasseur, "Le Sénégal et sa lente intégration au mouvement abolitionniste," in *Rétablissement de l'esclavage dans les colonies françaises: 1802*, ed. Yves Bénot and Marcel Dorigny (Paris: Maisonneuve and Larose, 2003), 385n47. Boubacar Barry gives a figure of "at least . . . 1,000 a year between 1814 and 1831 (*SAST*, 139). Barry has vehemently contested Curtin's overall statistics on the slave trade.

39 Geggus, "Haiti and the Abolitionists," 118.

40 Ibid., 119.

41 See Marcel Dorigny, "Sismondi et les colonies: Un Maillon entre Lumières et théoriciens du XIXe siècle?" in *Rétablissement de l'esclavage dans les colonies françaises: 1802*, ed. Yves Bénot and Marcel Dorigny (Paris: Maisonneuve and Larose, 2003), 475; and Geggus, "Haiti and the Abolitionists," 119.

42 Eugène Sue, "Lettres sur la Guadeloupe" (dated 1826), *Revue des deux mondes* 4 (December 1830): 337.

43 See Hoffmann, *Le Nègre romantique*, 161–63. Geggus writes: "The French government's decision to recognise Haiti came entirely out of the blue, and like most of the achievements of French anti-slavery, seems to have owed little to direct abolitionist influence" ("Haiti and the Abolitionists," 127).

44 Joseph-Joachim-Victor Chauvet, "Avant-Propos," *Haïti, chant lyrique* (Paris: Chez Delaforest, 1825), 4.

45 Hardy, *La Mise en valeur du Sénégal, 1817–1854*, 123.

46 Jacques-François Roger, *Fables sénégalaises, recueillies de l'Oulof et mises en vers français* (Paris: Nepveu, 1828). See also his *Recherches linguistiques sur la langue ouolofe suivi d'un vocabulaire abrégé français-ouolof* (Paris: Librairie Orientale Dondey-Dupré, 1829).

47 William Cohen writes, "One can discount a novel by Baron Roger, *Kelédor* (1828), for, after all, the author was governor of Senegal and had written the book to propagandize his plantation schemes there" (wc, 279). Léon Fanoudh-Siefer offers a balanced assessment of *Kelédor* in *Le Mythe du nègre et de l'Afrique noire dans la littérature française (de 1800 à la 2e Guerre mondiale)* (Paris: C. Klincksieck, 1968), 29–33. See also Kusum Aggarwal, "Les Perspectives africanistes dans l'oeuvre du baron Roger," in *Littératures et colonies*, ed. Jean-François Durand and Jean Sévry (Paris: Kailash Editions, 2003), 183–208.

48 Baron Jacques-François Roger, *Kelédor, histoire africaine* (Paris: A. Nepveu, 1828), 225; henceforth abbreviated к.

49 Roger, quoted in Hardy, *La Mise en valeur du Sénégal, 1817–1854*, 155. The first meaning of the French word *culture* listed in the *Petit Robert* is "the act of cultivating the earth," and by extension (in the plural) "cultivated lands."

50 *SAST*, 137. See the comprehensive treatment of this subject in Boubacar Barry, *Le Royaume du Waalo: Le Sénégal avant la conquête* (Paris: Maspero, 1972), 237–64. According to Dozon the whole plan was originally conceived by Baron Portal, director and then minister of the colonies (*Frères et sujets*, 70–71).

51 Hardy, *La Mise en valeur du Sénégal, 1817–1854*, 146, 233; Barry, *Le Royaume du Waalo*, 253–55. See also François Zuccarelli, "Le régime des engagés à temps au Sénégal (1817–1848)," *Cahiers d'études africaines* 2, no. 3 (1962): 420–61, esp. "la ligne de partage entre la traite des Noirs et l'engagement à temps est bien mince" (438).

52 Barry, *Le Royaume du Waalo*, 254; Martin Klein, *Slavery and Colonial Rule in French West Africa* (Cambridge: Cambridge University Press, 1998), 24;

Trevor R. Getz, *Slavery and Reform in West Africa: Toward Emancipation in Nineteenth-Century Senegal and the Gold Coast* (Athens: Ohio University Press, 2004), 46–51.

53 Quoted in Hardy, *La Mise en valeur du Sénégal, 1817–1854*, 150, 232.

54 Jacques-François Roger, quoted in Abbé David Boilat, *Esquisses sénégalaises* (1853; Paris: Karthala, 1984), 340, 341. Boilat was included in a small group of Senegalese students, male and female, who were sent to France with Roger's sponsorship to continue their education; he followed their progress after his return to France. See Yvon Bouquillon and Robert Cornevin, *David Boilat (1814–1901): Le Précurseur* (Dakar: Les Nouvelles Editions Africaines, 1981), 43. I am grateful to Kelly Duke for bringing this to my attention.

55 Quoted in Hardy, *La Mise en valeur du Sénégal, 1817–1854*, 236 (emphasis added); see also 246, where one of Roger's successors as governor, Brou, is quoted describing the experiment as a false "utopie" and as "un spirituel et séduisant roman."

56 Barry (*SAST*, 138–39) explains the reasons for this failure in more detail: the neighboring African states viewed this French adventure with suspicion and did what they could to create "a climate of insecurity detrimental to agricultural development"; "The inhabitants refused to work on French plantations." And slave traders, still working in the region, did everything to oppose this new form of trade.

57 Biondi, *Saint-Louis du Sénégal*, 90; see also Getz, *Slavery and Reform in West Africa*, 70.

58 See Michael Crowder, *Senegal: A Study of French Assimilation Policy* (London: Methuen, 1967), 12.

59 "Une seconde Antille" is from Barry, *Le Royaume du Waalo*, 245. The phrase "une seconde France" is Hardy's paraphrase of Roger's idea (Hardy, *La Mise en valeur du Sénégal, 1817–1854*, 127).

60 *SAST*, 139. Cf. "par un sort vengeur de l'histoire, au moment où on songea à utiliser la main-d'oeuvre sur place, après trois siècles de traite négrière, il n'y avait plus de bras dans ce vaste réservoir qu'on avait cru inépuisable" (Barry, *Le Royaume du Waalo*, 255).

61 Nelly Schmidt, *Abolitionnistes de l'esclavage et réformateurs des colonies, 1820–1851: Analyse et documents* (Paris: Karthala, 2000), 37; see Lawrence C. Jennings, *French Anti-Slavery: The Movement for the Abolition of Slavery in France, 1802–1848* (Cambridge: Cambridge University Press, 2000), 13.

62 Manchuelle, "Le Rôle des Antillais," 379. Melvin Kennedy says that the deportees were a group of 260 merchants ("The Bissette Affair and the French Colonial Question," 5).

63 Dozon rightly emphasizes the "unprecedented" nature of this "return" (*Frères et sujets*, 76). On Bissette see Chris Bongie, *Islands and Exiles: The Creole Identities of Post/Colonial Literature* (Stanford: Stanford University Press, 1998), 262–87.

64 Aggarwal, "Les Perspectives africanistes," 197.

65 See Cohen's chapter "Scientific Racism," in WC (210–62).

66 See Aggarwal, "Les Perspectives africanistes," 196, 199.

67 [Edme-François] Jomard, "Analyse de l'ouvrage intitulé *Kelédor, histoire africaine*, par M. le baron Roger," *Bulletin de la Société de Géographie* 58 (February 1828): 62, 63, 64.

68 I have analyzed such gestures in Mariama Bâ's *Une si longue lettre* (with specific reference to the epistolary format) in my book *Theories of Africans: Francophone Literature and Anthropology in Africa* (Chicago: University of Chicago Press, 1990), 246–93; and in Ferdinand Oyono's *Une Vie de boy* in my *Nationalists and Nomads: Essays on Francophone African Literature and Culture* (Chicago: University of Chicago Press, 1998), 118–51.

69 Camara Laye, *Le Maître de la parole: Kouma lafôlô kouma* (Paris: Plon, 1976), 29; Djibril Tamsir Niane, *Soundjata ou l'épopée mandingue* (Paris: Présence Africaine, 1960), 7. On these works see Miller, *Theories of Africans*, 68–113.

70 See Hoffmann, *Le Nègre romantique*, 182; and Léon Fanoudh-Siefer, *Le Mythe du nègre*, 30.

71 Robinson cites the novel as "Baron J. Roger, ed. and col., *Kelédor, histoire africaine* (Paris, 1829)" (David Robinson, "The Islamic Revolution in Futa Toro," *International Journal of African Historical Studies* 8, no. 2 [1975]: 206n53). See also Barry, *Le Royaume du Waalo*, 384; and *SAST*, 104.

72 The name *Clédor* exists in Senegal.

73 See Vincent Carretta, "Olaudah Equiano or Gustavus Vassa? New Light on an Eighteenth-Century Question of Identity," *Slavery and Abolition* 20, no. 3 (December 1999): 96–105.

74 See Paule Brasseur, "Les Campagnes abolitionnistes en France, 1815–1848," in *De la traite à l'esclavage*, ed. Serge Daget (Nantes: CHRMA-SFHOM, 1985), 337.

75 According to John Thornton, "60 to 70 percent of the adult slaves listed on inventories [in Saint-Domingue] in the late 1780's and 1790's were Africa born" and came "overwhelmingly" from the Lower Guinea coast region and the Angola coast area, including the Kongo kingdom. Thornton argues that African veterans of wars in Africa "may prove to be the key that unlocks the mystery of the success" of the Haitian Revolution." John Thornton, "African Soldiers in the Haitian Revolution," *Journal of Caribbean History* 25, nos. 1 and 2 (1991): 59, 74; on the Senegalese in Haiti see 72.

76 Barry, *Le Royaume du Waalo*, 384. See also *SAST*, 104. The precise context of the war described in *Kelédor* is analyzed by Barry in *SAST*, 102–6. See also David Wallace Robinson, "Abdul Bokar Kan and the History of Futa-Toro, 1853–1891" (Ph.D. dissertation, Columbia University, 1971): "The best remembered [campaign] and the only sally that can be clearly identified as a declared *jihad* or holy war, was the march against the Damel (king) of Cayor in 1796. . . . The campaign ended in the disaster of Bunguye where many Futanke lives were lost and the Almamy himself was taken prisoner and held for

489

several months before returning to Futa" (37–38). See also Robinson, "The Islamic Revolution in Futa Toro," 185–221.

77 Ousmane Sembene's film *Ceddo* (1976) depicts this context. *Ceddo* regimes "lived by slave raiding and selling slaves for arms and other goods," writes David Richardson, in "Shipboard Revolts, African Authority, and the Transatlantic Slave Trade," in *Fighting the Slave Trade: West African Strategies*, ed. Sylviane A. Diouf (Athens: Ohio University Press, 2003), 211.

78 See Mamadou Diouf, *Histoire du Sénégal: Le Modèle islamo-wolof et ses péripheries* (Paris: Maisonneuve et Larose, 2001): "Ces nouveaux régimes [islamiques] ont été capables de substituer à l'aristocratie traditionnelle, devenue l'alliée des négriers, un nouveau pouvoir capable de résister à la traite et de rétablir la sécurité ainsi qu'une économie agropastorale prospère" (101). And see Ly Djibril, "The Bases of Humanitarian Thought in the Pulaar Society of Mauritania and Senegal," *International Review of the Red Cross* 325 (December 31, 1998): 643–53.

79 Robinson explains, "The Almamy's position on the commerce in slaves was consistent with Islamic law: Muslims could not be enslaved, but non-Muslim prisoners of war or domestic slaves might be sold into the Senegambian trade. . . . The new regime did not oppose the enslavement of non-Muslims" ("The Islamic Revolution in Futa Toro," 201).

80 On the comparison to Buffon and Cuvier see Aggarwal, "Les Perspectives africanistes," 196, 199.

81 Olaudah Equiano, *The Interesting Narrative of the Life of Olaudah Equiano, or Gustavus Vassa, the African, Written by Himself* (New York: Norton, 2001), 39; emphasis added.

82 See Martial Barrois, "L'Abolition de la traite des Noirs" (Paris: Firmin-Didot, 1823); Edouard Alletz, "L'Abolition de la traite des Noirs" (Paris: Delaunay, 1832). On these poems see Hoffmann, *Le Nègre romantique*, 155–63; and my *Blank Darkness: Africanist Discourse in French* (Chicago: University of Chicago Press, 1985), 125–27.

83 Mungo Park, *Travels in the Interior Districts of Africa* (New York: Arno Press, 1971), 332.

84 Françoise Vergès, "The Age of Love and Pity: Slavery and the Politics of Reparation," lecture at Yale University, January 23, 2002. Vergès argued persuasively that humanitarian movements including abolitionism have deployed pity as a motivating tool; but pity occludes perception of the conditions on which an institution like slavery is built, making those conditions ahistorical.

85 Wilberforce was published in French, with a preface by Madame de Staël, in 1814; Clarkson's *The Cries of Africa* was translated in 1821. Alexander Falconbridge, *An Account of the Slave Trade on the Coast of Africa* (London: J. Phillips, 1788); the passage that Roger quotes is on pp. 24–25; I have not located the French translation that Roger seems to be citing. On British dominance in abolitionism see Yvan Debbasch, "Poésie et traite: L'Opinion française sur le

commerce négrier au début du XIXe siècle," *Revue française d'histoire d'outre-mer*, 172–73 (January 1963): 311–52; and Serge Daget, "France, Suppression of the Illegal Slave Trade, and England, 1817–1850," in *The Abolition of the Atlantic Slave Trade: Origins and Effects in Europe, Africa, and the Americas*, ed. David Eltis and James Walvin (Madison: University of Wisconsin Press, 1981), 194.

86   See Khama-Bassili Tolo, *L'Intertextualité chez Mérimée: L'Étude des sauvages* (Birmingham, AL: Summa Publications, 1998), 234–39; and chapter 9 herein.

87   See Sue Peabody, *"There Are No Slaves in France": The Political Culture of Race and Slavery in the Ancien Régime* (New York: Oxford University Press, 1996). To a certain extent the lieutenant's statement may be a projection of the measures (discussed by Peabody) banning or limiting the entrance of slaves into France. Thus, although the lieutenant is going to Spain, he says "Europe," and the reader may well understand that France is being suggested.

88   Gabriel Mailhol, *Le Philosophe nègre et les secrets des Grecs: Ouvrage trop nécessaire* (London: n.p., 1764), 38, 41, 69.

89   "Ces nègres-là ["les sages du Fouta-Toro"] ont agi plus sagement que les Français vingt ans plus tard [thus in 1794]; ils ont senti qu'il y avait trop d'inconvénients, trop de dangers, pour les esclaves eux-mêmes, à l'abolition immédiate de l'esclavage; ils l'ont sagement modifié, et ils ont hâté l'époque de l'affranchissement pour ceux qui, par leur application et les progrès de leur intelligence, s'en montraient plus dignes. . . . Ils sont fiers de nous avoir devancés dans la carrière de la raison, de la justice et de l'humanité" (*K*, 238–39).

90   Vergès, *Abolir l'esclavage*, 118: "En transformant la plantation en espace du mal absolu, où l'ordre est entièrement fondé sur la violence physique, les abolitionnistes préparent, à leur insu, le terrain nécessaire à l'instauration de techniques de discipline et de surveillance. Quoique apparemment moins violentes, celles-ci sont fondées sur la même volonté: obtenir du travail à moindre prix." This description corresponds closely to what we have seen in Roger: the repudiation of one form of discipline (slavery) and the invention of a new form (his "garden" in Africa).

91   The utopian dimensions of abolitionist thought are explored at length by Vergès in *Abolir l'esclavage*. Dozon rightly points out the traces of Fouiérisme and Saint-Simonisme in Roger's experimental and utopian thinking (Dozon, *Frères et sujets*, 73).

92   Cf. René Maran, preface to *Batouala: Véritable roman nègre* (1921; Paris: Albin Michel, 1965): "Tu bâtis ton royaume sur des cadavres" (11).

93   Kelédor's participation in a hunt for marooned slaves resembles a similar event in Mailhol's *Le Philosophe nègre*. Tintillo's master tells him: "Nous ne devons tuer que des Négres Marons" (72).

94   Carolyn E. Fick, *The Making of Haiti: The Saint Domingue Revolution from Below* (Knoxville: University of Tennessee Press, 1990), 206.

95 David Patrick Geggus, *Haitian Revolutionary Studies* (Bloomington: Indiana University Press, 2002), 223.

96 Laurent Dubois, *A Colony of Citizens: Revolution and Slave Emancipation in the French Caribbean, 1787–1804* (Chapel Hill: University of North Carolina Press, 2004), 338.

97 Pierre Pluchon, introduction to Pamphile de Lacroix, *La Révolution de Haïti* (Paris: Karthala, 1995), 17. This book includes the entire text of Lacroix's *Mémoires pour servir à l'histoire de la révolution de Saint-Domingue* (1819). On Toussaint's manumission see Geggus, *Haitian Revolutionary Studies*, 230n30. On his ownership or control of slaves see Gabriel Debien, Jean Fouchard, and Marie Antoinette Menier, "Toussaint Louverture avant 1789," *Conjonction* 134 (June–July 1977): 65–80.

98 Fick, *The Making of Haiti*, 207, 213, 250, 214. See also Geggus, "Haiti and the Abolitionists," 134.

99 Toussaint L'Ouverture, *Mémoires du Général Toussaint-L'Ouverture écrits par lui-même* (1853; Port-au-Prince: Bélizaire, 1951), 29. These memoirs, composed in prison, edited and no doubt corrected by Joseph Saint-Rémy, have been strangely ignored by historians such as Fick and Geggus. See Daniel Désormeaux's welcome study of the memoirs, "The First of the (Black) Memorialists," *Yale French Studies* 107 (2005): 131–45.

100 Victor Schoelcher, *Vie de Toussaint Louverture* (Paris: Karthala, 1982), 401.

101 See Hoffmann's interesting remarks on Lamartine's play, in *Le Nègre romantique*, 211–13. On the early British appropriation of Toussaint as a romantic hero, Adam Hochschild points out that this was largely motivated by glee at Napoleon's defeat in Haiti; see Hochschild, *Bury the Chains: Prophets and Rebels in the Fight to Free an Empire's Slaves* (Boston: Houghton Mifflin, 2005), 294.

102 Fick, *The Making of Haiti*, 213.

103 Lacroix, *La Révolution de Haïti*, 344. In his description of the burning of Le Cap in 1802 (292–96) Lacroix does not say that Toussaint gave the order. (Lacroix offers a more balanced overall appraisal of Toussaint [354–56].) Lacroix is characterized as "unreliable" by Geggus, *Haitian Revolutionary Studies*, 120.

104 See chapter 8 for my discussion of the passage in *Ourika*, in which Madame de Duras evokes the Haitian Revolution.

105 In one of his endnotes Roger assures us that two such expeditions, repatriating Africans from Havana to Africa, took place, in 1819 and 1822 (*K*, 263n5).

106 See François-Xavier Verschave, *La Françafrique: Le Plus long scandale de la République* (Paris: Stock, 1998); Baadikko Mammadu, *Françafrique, l'échec: L'Afrique postcoloniale en question* (Paris: L'Harmattan, 2001); and Dozon's comments on "La Françafrique," in *Frères et sujets*, 339–48.

107 Michel-Rolph Trouillot eloquently describes this process in *Silencing the Past*.

108 "Discussion du projet de loi portant demande d'un crédit extraordinaire de 326,200 Fr. pour le service des colonies," *Revue des colonies* 2, no. 9 (March 1836): 404–5. See Motylewski, *La Société française pour l'abolition de l'esclavage*, 47. By the 1840s Roger would become an immediatist abolitionist (Jennings, *French Anti-Slavery*, 60).

11 HOMOSOCIALITY, RECKONING, AND RECOGNITION IN EUGÈNE SUE'S *ATAR-GULL*

1 Sainte-Beuve, quoted in Francis Lacassin, preface to Eugène Sue, *Romans de mort et d'aventure* (Paris: Robert Laffont, 1993), ii. Quotations from *Atar-Gull* will refer to this edition, abbreviated *AG*. I have also consulted the original 1831 edition of the novel (Paris: C. Vimont, [June] 1831) at the Princeton University Library Rare Books Room. The Laffont edition appears to be virtually identical to the original.

2 Peter Brooks, "The Melodramatic Imagination," in *A New History of French Literature*, ed. Denis Hollier (Cambridge, Mass.: Harvard University Press, 1989), 607; Robert Bezucha, "Discourses on Misery," also in Hollier, *A New History of French Literature*, 689.

3 See Lucienne Frappier-Mazur, "Publishing Novels," in *A New History of French Literature*, ed. Denis Hollier (Cambridge, Mass.: Harvard University Press, 1989), 697. Marx, however, was singularly unimpressed; he derided Sue's role as a politician, claiming that Sue's election made "an April Fool of March 10" (Marx, *The 18th Brumaire of Louis Bonaparte* [London: ElecBook, 2001], 71).

4 "Eugène Sue (1804–1857)," www.kirjasto.sci.fi/esue.htm (accessed February 19, 2007).

5 Parts of *Atar-Gull* appeared as "Arthur et Marie" and "Le Faux Pont," published together in *La Revue des Deux Mondes*, n.s., 1 (March 1831): 437–53. "Arthur et Marie" is presented in the novel and in the *Revue* as "une anecdote, qui, sans se rattacher précisément à son [Brulart's] histoire, y a trait" (*AG*, 187; *Revue*, 437). Another chapter was published in *La Mode* in (May 1831); see Peter Whyte, "Eugène Sue et les paradis artificiels," in *La Culture populaire en France*, ed. Peter Whyte and Christopher Lloyd (Durham: University of Durham, 1997), 17. The first complete edition was the C. Vimont edition of 1831.

6 Nora Atkinson, *Eugène Sue et le roman-feuilleton* (Paris: A. Nizet and M. Bastard, 1929), 85, 83.

7 "Jean-Joseph [Sue] II fit embarquer son fils sur un vaisseau de l'Etat, espérant l'éloigner suffisamment des délices de Paris" (Jean-Louis Bory, *Eugène Sue: Dandy mais socialiste* [Paris: Hachette, 1973], 78). On Baudelaire see Christo-

493

pher L. Miller, *Nationalists and Nomads: Essays on Francophone African Literature and Culture* (Chicago: University of Chicago Press, 1998), 222n7.

8 Eugène Sue, *Histoire de la marine française* (Paris: Au Comptoir des Imprimeurs-Unis, 1844–45). This history ends with the death of Louis XIV, thus before the French slave trade reached its full force. A Dutch voyage to "Goerée" is mentioned, without reference to the slave trade (1:169–70). Sue writes his history in a very novelistic form, with elaborate descriptions and animated dialogues. His paragraphs on the galley system are highly evocative: "c'est la chiourme, les esclaves, les forçats, le bruit des chaînes, le sifflement des fouets, les cris de rage et de douleur . . . la force locomotrice et animale du bâtiment" (1:314). A black galley-slave is described as a "monster"; his nose and ears have been cut off as punishment for attempting to escape — thus showing terms similar to those of the Code Noir (1:457–58). On slaves, incidentally mentioned as merchandise in the Antilles, see ibid., 3:186.

9 "Je m'arme de résolution, je vais voir des esclaves dans un pays libre, dans une province de France" (Eugène Sue, "Lettres sur la Guadeloupe," *Revue des deux mondes*, ser. 2, tome 4 [October–November 1830]: 13). The second installment was published in the same journal in December 1830.

10 "Lettres sur la Guadeloupe" (December 1830): 341; see 343.

11 *Kernok le pirate* was published in three installments in *La Mode* (March 1830) (see chronology in *AG*, 1360). Kernok is a Breton corsair who started his career in the slave trade, taking particular pleasure in the use of the whip. Like Mérimée's Ledoux, he found new ways to fit more slaves in the hold of a ship. Like Brulart, he is a figure of manly beauty and strength, and, like Brulart, he is amoral. But the main action of *Kernok*, concerned with Anglo-French rivalry in the Atlantic, does not involve the slave trade.

12 Sue's first literary work, the anonymous "Première lettre de l'homme-mouche à M. le Préfet de Police," apparently dated from 1826. See Bory, *Eugène Sue*, 74, 93–94; Atkinson, *Eugène Sue*, 83–84; and the bibliography in *AG*, 1365–68. On the rising popularity of *Atar-Gull* see Pierre Orecchioni, "Eugène Sue: Mesure d'un succès," *Europe* 60, nos. 643–44 (November–December 1982): 160. The preface to *Plik et Plok* is in *AG*, 1309–14. Later, Sue reused the Antilles as a literary backdrop for one of his longer novels, *Le Morne-au-Diable* (1842), which features a priest who seems to be modeled on Labat.

13 See Auguste Jal, "Un Négrier," in his *Scènes de la vie maritime* (Paris: Charles Gosselin, 1832), 3:3–51; Aténor de Caligny, "Une Ruse de négrier," *Revue maritime* 2 (1834): 107–11; Charles Desnoyers and M. Alboize, *La Traite des Noirs*, in *Magasin théatral* (Paris: Marchant, 1843), 5:1–32.

14 D. de Tr . . . f, "La Frégate et le négrier: Aventure de mer," *Le Navigateur, journal des naufrages, pirateries, voyages, événemens de mer, etc*, Fifth year, no. 1, tome 8 (1833): 66–78. In this tale of a slaver outrunning a presumably British frigate, vessels enforcing the ban on the slave trade are referred to as "instrumens rapaces d'une philanthropie décevante" (67), and a sailor complains that the slaves in the hold are treated better than the crew (74).

494

15 See Léon-François Hoffmann, *Le Nègre romantique: Personnage littéraire et obsession collective* (Paris: Payot, 1973), 253–54.

16 Serge Daget, *Répertoire des expéditions négrières françaises à la traite illégale (1814–1850)* (Nantes: Centre de Recherche sue l'Histoire du Monde Atlantique, Université de Nantes, 1988), 547. The last year of the "great illegal French slave trade" was 1830, with twenty-seven documented voyages (521); in 1831 the number dropped to six, only one of which was outfitted in a metropolitan French port (544). See also Daget, "The Abolition of the Slave Trade by France: The Decisive Years 1826–1831," in *Abolition and Its Aftermath: The Historical Context, 1790–1916*, ed. David Richardson (London: Frank Cass, 1985), 160.

17 Kay Seymour House, "Historical Introduction," in James Fenimore Cooper, *The Pilot: A Tale of the Sea* (Albany: State University of New York Press, 1986), xxv. Cooper's role in inspiring the French maritime novel, directly through Sue, fits with Margaret Cohen's description of maritime fiction as an international genre in "Traveling Genres," *New Literary History* 34, no. 3 (summer 2003): 481–99.

18 *The Red Rover*, in James Fenimore Cooper, *Sea Tales: The Pilot, Red Rover* (New York: Library of America, 1991), 568, 610; see also 434: "no less true than perplexing, the Merchants of Newport were becoming, at the same time, both slave-dealers and gentlemen." It turns out that the Red Rover (Captain Heidegger) had merely disguised his ship as a "slaver" in order to ensure a warm welcome in Newport (459). *The Red Rover* features a remarkable depiction of an African sailor on an American vessel, a "black jack," known as Guinea. He is described as "a man for whose equal one might look in vain" (856), and his relations with his mates are, at the end, marked by "singular tenderness" (852). For a novel about piracy *The Red Rover* is exceptionally dull. Sue will increase the "gothic" aspects of the maritime novel by a factor of ten.

19 See Chris Packard, *Queer Cowboys and Other Erotic Male Friendships in Nineteenth-Century American Literature* (New York: Palgrave Macmillan, 2005), 19–40.

20 House, "Historical Introduction," xxxiii, xxxv, xxxvi.

21 Eugène Sue, "A Monsieur Fenimore Cooper," dated May 1831, preface to *Atar-Gull* (*AG*, 1315–16).

22 See Jonathan Ned Katz, *Love Stories: Sex between Men before Homosexuality* (Chicago: University of Chicago Press, 2001), 6; and on interracial relationships see Leslie Fiedler, "Come Back to the Raft Ag'in, Huck Honey!" *Partisan Review* 15, no. 6 (June 1948): 664–71.

23 Cooper, *Sea Tales*, 613. Exceptionally, in the context of this quotation, the "interest" of women (passengers) in a seaman is suggested. Cooper's homosociality is expanded in his "Leatherstocking" books: "Natty Bumppo abhorred women and lived isolated from them on the frontier where he was safe from their wiles and could expend his love and devotion on Chingachook, his

495

male Indian associate" (B. R. Burg, *Sodomy and the Pirate Tradition: English Sea Rovers in the Seventeenth-Century Caribbean* [New York: New York University Press, 1995], 134).

24   James Fenimore Cooper, *The Pilot*, in *Sea Tales*, 2, 7, 61.

25   I owe the term *homoesthetic* to Christopher Rivers.

26   See Margaret Cohen, *The Sentimental Education of the Novel* (Princeton: Princeton University Press, 1999), 13.

27   I owe this observation to Tara Golba. On Greece as coded reference to homosexuality see Graham Robb, *Strangers: Homosexual Love in the Nineteenth Century* (New York: Norton, 2003).

28   This is the only difference I have found between the original edition of *Atar-Gull* and the Laffont edition: the original reads "Que le bon Dieu vous punit de faire la traite" (127), whereas the Laffont edition has "Que le bon Dieu nous punit de faire la traite" (*AG*, 193).

29   Other, secondary pairings occur along the way. Benoît's first "mate" in the novel is Simon, a devoted officer: "Simon naviguait avec lui depuis si longtemps! Simon connaissait ses habitudes, lui était dévoué, s'occupait des minutieux détails de l'emménagement des nègres à bord, avec une patience, une humanité qui charmait le capitaine" (158). The slave broker Van Hop, an old friend of Benoît's, is also encountered on the southern coast of Africa (chaps. 3, 4).

30   The pirate who is a renegade aristocrat may be derived from Cooper's *Red Rover*, who is the "favoured mortal son of a Lord" (Cooper, *Sea Tales*, 795).

31   The teeth in this passage are reminiscent of those that Cooper gave to one of his characters in *The Red Rover*, a young sailor with "noble and manly" features including a "firm and manly" mouth, with "a set of glittering teeth, that shone the brighter from being cased in so dark [tanned] a setting" (Cooper, *Sea Tales*, 449).

32   This point is stated eloquently by Katz, in *Love Stories*, 8–12. At the same time, I want to bear in mind the argument made by Graham Robb in *Strangers*: "For a thousand years at least, people have been complaining that sodomites, margeries, homosexuals or gays are more prevalent than ever before" (3). Robb also writes, correctly in my opinion: "There always were people who were primarily or exclusively attracted to people of their own sex" (*Strangers*, 12).

33   Hugh Thomas, *The Slave Trade: the Story of the Atlantic Slave Trade: 1440–1870* (New York: Simon & Schuster, 1997): 240; henceforth abbreviated T.

34   See Burg, *Sodomy and the Pirate Tradition*, 173; see also xxxix: "Among pirates, . . . homosexual acts were not integrated with or subordinated to alernate styles of sexual contact. They were the only form of sexual expression engaged in by members of the buccaneer community." It should be noted that Burg's study is focused on, though not strictly limited to, English pirates of the seventeenth century. But still in the nineteenth century "the Caribbean was full of pirates" (T, 579).

35   See Burg, *Sodomy and the Pirate Tradition*, 134–35. If these examples all come

from American literature, we should nonetheless bear in mind the important influence of Cooper's works that were translated into French. On these partnerships see also Robb, *Strangers*, 267; and Leslie A. Fiedler, *Love and Death in the American Novel* (New York: Criterion Books, 1960), 534–39, 571–74.

36 G. W. F. Hegel, *Phenomenology of Spirit*, trans. A. V. Miller (Oxford: Clarendon Press, 1977), 77; henceforth abbreviated *PS*.

37 Susan Buck-Morss, "Hegel and Haiti," *Critical Inquiry* 26 (summer 2000): 821–65. Buck-Morss suggests that Hegel, who read the newspaper in the morning as if it were an act of "prayer" (844), "knew about real slaves revolting successfully [in Haiti] against real masters, and he elaborated his dialectic of lordship and bondage deliberately within this contemporary context" (844).

38 Nick Nesbitt sees in Hegel's 1821 *Philosophy of Right* "the first great analysis of the Haitian Revolution . . . a philosophical analysis of the Haitian Revolution, . . . defending in the strongest terms the absolute right of slaves to overthrow a slave-holding society" (Nick Nesbitt, "Troping Toussaint, Reading Revolution," *Research in African Literatures* 35, no. 2 [summer 2004]: 25, 23). He adds, "Hegel never actually refers to Haiti by name in the 400-odd pages of the *Philosophy of Right*" (23). Nesbitt points out the switch from *Knecht* in the *Phenomenology* to *Sklaverei* in the *Philosophy of Right*. According to Buck-Morss, Hegel often used the terms interchangeably ("Hegel and Haiti," 846n79).

39 See Buck-Morss, "Hegel and Haiti," 847.

40 See Robert R. Williams, *Hegel's Ethics of Recognition* (Berkeley: University of California Press, 1997), 60, 63–64.

41 As Sybille Fischer puts it: "In Hegel, there is a retreat into silence and obscurity at the very moment when revolutionary slaves might have appeared on the scene" (Sybille Fischer, *Modernity Disavowed: Haiti and the Cultures of Slavery in the Age of Revolution* [Durham: Duke University Press, 2004], 32).

42 Buck-Morss, "Hegel and Haiti," 849. She sees in Hegel's silence on revolt and revolution a tacit awareness of "the next step to revolutionary practice" and argues that "the slaves of Saint-Domingue were, as Hegel knew, taking that step for him" (848n84).

43 Frantz Fanon, *Peau noire, masques blancs* (Paris: Seuil, 1952), 179n9; Frantz Fanon, *Black Skin, White Masks*, trans. Charles Lam Markmann (New York: Grove Press, 1967), 220n. On Fanon's rewriting of Hegel see Nigel Gibson, "Dialectical Impasses: Turning the Table on Hegel and the Black," *Parallax* 8, no. 2 (2002): 30–45.

44 Williams, *Hegel's Ethics of Recognition*, 65.

45 Théophile Gautier, "Histoire de la Marine" (1836), in *AG*, 1341.

46 The comparison between race and class seems to be hinted at in the name of one neighbor in the Paris tenement: "Madame Bougnol," a real French name that happens to resemble the ethnic slur *bougnoul*. But according to the *Petit Robert* and the *Trésor de la langue française*, that word only entered French

497

(from Wolof for "black") in 1890. The rue Tirechape or Tirechappe was in the first *arrondissement*, next to the rue de la Monnaie; it was eliminated during the Second Empire, becoming part of the rue du Pont-Neuf. An evocative photograph of the street, taken by Charles Marville in 1860, can be seen at www.getty.edu/art/collections/objects/068586.html.

47 "If the other is simply eliminated, his death is an abstract total negation that produces the opposite of what is desired. For what each seeks is not the death of the other so much as his recognition. Consequently some way has to be found to stop the struggle for recognition short of death" (Williams, *Hegel's Ethics of Recognition*, 61).

48 Jean-Baptiste Antoine Auget, Baron de Montyon, established two prizes within the Académie Française in 1782: the "Prix de la vertu," for "le Français pauvre ayant accompli l'action la plus vertueuse," and the "Prix pour l'ouvrage littéraire le plus utile aux mœurs."

49 See Nesbitt's further examination of this idea in Hegel's *Philosophy of Right* (Nesbitt, "Troping Toussaint, Reading Revolution," 26–27).

50 See Hoffmann, *Le Nègre romantique*, 208.

51 *Délire* is a term used by Francis Lacassin in his preface to *AG*, p. iv.

52 Edouard Corbière, quoted in Jean Roudaut, "Les Deux Corbière," *Critique* 17, no. 224 (January 1966): 6; Corbière quoted in P. Levot, "Notice biographique sur Edouard Corbière," *Bulletin de la Société Académique de Brest*, ser. 2, tome 3 (1877): 230.

53 Henry Louis Gates Jr. and Nellie Y. McKay, eds., *The Norton Anthology of African American Literature* (New York: Norton, 1997), 286.

54 Werner Sollors, *Neither Black nor White yet Both: Thematic Explorations of Interracial Literature* (New York: Oxford University Press, 1997), 165. Sollors comments on the relation of this story to the Code Noir. The link to *Atar-Gull* is further illuminated by Sollors's mention of Job (167). "Le Mulâtre" was republished by David O'Connell in "Victor Séjour: Écrivain américain de langue française," *Revue de Louisiane/Louisiana Review* 1, no. 2 (winter 1972): 60–75. On the *Revue des colonies* see Chris Bongie, *Islands and Exiles: The Creole Identities of Post/Colonial Literature* (Stanford: Stanford University Press, 1998), 266–87.

55 The frame tale of "Le Mulâtre" is set after the Revolution.

12 EDOUARD CORBIÈRE, "MATING," AND MARITIME ADVENTURE

1 An exposition in 1990 dubbed Corbière "father of the maritime novel in France"; see Jean Berthou, *Edouard Corbière: Père du roman maritime in France, catalogue de l'exposition présentée à Brest (mai–juin 1990) et à Morlaix (juillet–août 1990)* (Paris: Gallimard, 1990). Michel Mollat du Jourdin gives the same honor to Corbière, instead of Sue, in his *L'Europe et la mer* (Paris: Seuil, 1993), 289. Monique Brosse says that Corbière was the first to bring

the "words and the objects" of the sea into French literature ("Le Statut des langues étrangères dans la fiction maritime du romantisme: Ou Babel conjurée," in *Etudes de langue et de littérature française offertes à André Lanly* [Nancy: Université de Nancy, 1980], 435). Jean de Trigon calls Sue a "fabricant de toc," in his *Poètes d'océan: La Landelle, Edouard et Tristan Corbière* (Paris: Emile-Paul, 1958), 19. Philippe Girard calls *Le Négrier* "unique dans la littérature française de l'époque, car il est le seul à montrer dans sa vérité la vie maritime" ("Un Romantique de la mer: Corbière l'Ancien," in *Marceline Desbordes-Valmore & Verlaine: d'Edouard Corbière à Louis II de Bavière* [Paris: A Rebours, 1986], 55–56).

2   Edouard Corbière, *Le Négrier* (Saint-Malo: L'Ancre de Marine, 2002). This is apparently a reissue of an edition that first appeared in 1990.

3   Edouard Corbière, "Dédicace de 1865," in *Les Pilotes de l'Iroise* (Paris: José Corti, 2000), 40.

4   On Corbière's life see P. Levot, "Notice biographique sur Edouard Corbière," 220–34; Yves Le Gallo, "Corbière père et fils," in *Etudes sur Edouard et Tristan Corbière, Cahiers de Bretagne Occidentale* 1 (1976): 3–17; Louis Le Guillou, "*La Guêpe* d'Edouard Corbière," in *Etudes sur Edouard et Tristan Corbière, Cahiers de Bretagne Occidentale* 1 (1976): 37–47; and Jacques-Remi Dahan, "Chronologie," in Corbière, *Les Pilotes de l'Iroise*, 23–38.

5   François Roudaut asserts: "Il s'embarque [in 1821] à bord d'un navire marchand et gagne, comme second, les côtes d'Afrique et du Brésil" ("Sommaire biographique," in Edouard Corbière, *Le Négrier* [Paris: Klincksieck, 1990], xlv; henceforth abbreviated *N 1990*). Other sources of information on Corbière's life do not confirm this episode at sea in 1821, but the testimony that he offers in his "Précis sur la traite des Noirs," which I will discuss below, lends credence to this theory.

6   See Christopher L. Miller, *Blank Darkness: Africanist Discourse in French* (Chicago: University of Chicago Press, 1985), 161–64.

7   Jean-François Brousmiche, writing in 1844 or 1845, quoted in Yves Le Gallo, "Corbière père et fils," in *Etudes sur Edouard et Tristan Corbière, Cahiers de Bretagne Occidentale* 1 (1976): 16. Le Gallo comments, "Il nous est difficile de confirmer ou d'infirmer la participation d'Edouard Corbière à la traite des noirs. Il est vraisemblable qu'il la pratique: l'un des meilleurs arguments à cet égard est la sûreté d'information de J.-F. Brousmiche" (34n39). Jean de Trigon writes in *Poètes d'océan*, "Sans doute a-t-il vu de près la traite des noirs" (26). There is thus disagreement on the question of Corbière's active participation or mere eyewitnessing of the slave trade.

8   Le Gallo writes, without explanation, of *Le Royal Louis* that its "destinations n'étaient pas seulement les Antilles" ("Corbière père et fils," 12). Alain Buisine says that Corbière commanded his two ships "entre la France, l'Afrique, et les Antilles," thus around the full triangle, but he offers no documentation. See Buisine, "Sans rime ni marine," *Revue des sciences humaines* 49, no 177 (January–March 1980): 141. Also without documentation Michel Dansel

499

says that Corbière commanded the two ships "entre la France, l'Afrique et les Antilles. . . . Aucun corbiériste ne s'est prononcé sur la nature des marchandises qui occupaient les cales de *La Nina* et du *Royal Louis*" (introduction to Edouard Corbière, *Le Négrier: Aventures de mer* [Paris: Nouvelles Editions Baudinière, 1979], 10). A leading authority on Corbière, François Roudaut, in his edition of *Le Négrier*, can only say that the author sailed for six years between Le Havre and the Antilles, probably venturing to Africa and Brazil, and that "he probably participated slightly in the slave trade" (*sans doute se livre-t-il un peu à la traite des Noirs*) (*N 1990*, xvii). Roudaut also says that Corbière went to Africa and Brazil as second in command of a merchant vessel in 1821; he does not give the name of the ship. This, rather than the period of his captaincy starting in 1823, may have been Corbière's firsthand experience of the slave trade.

9   Serge Daget, *Répertoire des expéditions négrières à la traite illégale, 1814–1850* (Nantes: Centre de Recherche sur l'Histoire du Monde Atlantique, 1988); David Eltis et al., *The Trans-Atlantic Slave Trade: A Database on CD-ROM* (Cambridge: Cambridge University Press, 1999).

10 Edouard Corbière, untitled preface to *Le Négrier: Aventures de mer* (Paris: Denain, [1832]), 1:ix; further reference to this, the original edition of the novel, abbreviated *N 1832*.

11 Edouard Corbière, *Elégies brésiliennes, suivies de poésies diverses, et d'une notice sur la traite des Noirs* (Paris: Plancher, Brissot-Thivars, [July] 1823). I have also consulted the edition available in the Bibliothèque Nationale de France, which bears the same title and lists the same Paris publishers but adds Béchet and Bureau de *la Nacelle* in Rouen and Chapelle in Le Havre (dated June 1823). In both editions the title printed at the beginning of the text itself is "Précis sur la traite des Noirs."

12 Corbière's use of the word *cacique* in reference to African chiefs or kings suggests the limitations of his knowledge. *Cacique* was used almost exclusively with reference to New World leaders; the *Encyclopédie* mentions the Incas and Cuba. The dictionaries of the French Academy associate the term with Mexico and "some regions of America," including (as of the 1932–35 edition) the Antilles, but do not mention Africa. See www.lib.uchicago.edu/efts/ARTFL/projects/dicos.

13 In the late eighteenth and early nineteenth centuries, Saint Thomas (then Danish) was a "transit market" in the slave trade; it had long been a haven for pirates. See T, 526–27; and B. R. Burg, *Sodomy and the Pirate Tradition: English Sea Rovers in the Seventeenth-Century Caribbean* (New York: New York University Press, 1995), 98.

14 François Roudaut counts Corbière as "le seul écrivain qui ne s'oppose pas à cette pratique [l'esclavage]," in his introduction to *Le Négrier* (*N 1990*, xlv).

15 P. Levot, "Notice biographique sur Edouard Corbière," *Bulletin de la Société Académique de Brest*, ser. 2, tome 3 (1875–76): 228.

16 Charles Levavasseur, "Notice sur Edouard Corbière" (Rouen: H. Boissel,

n.d.), 9 (transcription by Kenneth Loiselle at Bibliothèque Nationale de France).

17 "Et crois-tu que ce ne soit pas quelque chose de délicieux que de se montrer avec supériorité au milieu d'une peuplade de nègres . . . ? . . . Et puis cette mâle satisfaction de commander à un équipage d'homme aventureux que j'avais conduits, à travers tant de dangers, sur des côtes où les croiseurs nous poursuivaient encore" (Edouard Corbière, "Le Capitaine de négrier," in his *La Mer et les marins: Scènes maritimes* [Berrien: Morvran, 1978], 41). See also Hoffmann, *Le Nègre romantique*, 254.

18 Like Sue, Corbière pays homage to the mastery of James Fenimore Cooper, while enjoining himself not to "copy [Cooper] with servility" (Corbière, preface, *N 1832*, iii).

19 Those final corrections and alterations are reflected in *N 1990*. As François Roudaut points out, *N 1990* (the Klincksieck edition prepared by Roudaut) is a version of the novel that has never been printed before: it is based on the 1855 edition but also includes previously unpublished corrections that Sue added to a copy of that edition; see *N 1990*, lxviii. (Roudaut, wrongly in my view, counts Mérimée as an opponent of slavery.)

20 Edouard Corbière, *Le Négrier: Aventures de mer* (Paris: Nouvelles Editions Baudinière, 1979), 69; further references to this edition abbreviated *N*. This edition comprises the 1834 edition of the novel (according to Roudaut, *N 1990*, lxvii); I have found that the text of the novel in this edition conforms, with rare exceptions, to the 1832 original and to the 1834 edition—*Le Négrier: Aventures de mer* (Paris: A.-J. Dénain et Delamare, 1834), 2 vols.—now available online through the Gallica Web site of the Bibliothèque Nationale de France. I will cite *N* (the 1979 edition) rather than Roudaut's more recent and more scholarly edition (*N 1990*; see above) because I am interested in the novel as an artifact of the 1830s rather than of the 1850s (which *N 1990* is). I have consulted what seems to be the only extant copy of the original 1832 edition of the novel (*N 1832*) in the Rare Books Room of the Princeton University Library. (Remarkably, both volumes of *N 1832* bear a stamp inside the front cover: "Bibliothèque de Tsarksoe Selo," the czars' country retreat.) The original edition contains one important element that has not been reprinted in any modern edition, an untitled preface by the author, cited earlier, in which he explains his motivations and qualifications for writing *Le Négrier*. The most recent edition, *Le Négrier* (Saint-Malo: L'Ancre de Marine, 2002) is also based on the text of 1832. I will note revisions that Corbière made after 1832 when they are pertinent, through references to *N 1990*. I have also consulted *Le Négrier: Aventures de mer* (Paris: Club Bibliophile de France, 1953), abbreviated *N 1953*.

21 Leslie Fiedler, "Come Back to the Raft Ag'in, Huck Honey!" *Partisan Review* 15, no. 6 (June 1948): 669. He goes on to argue that maritime homosexuality may not be circumstantial; men may become sailors in order to seek "male encounters."

22 See W. Jeffrey Bolster, *Black Jacks: African American Seamen in the Age of Sail* (Cambridge, Mass.: Harvard University Press, 1997), 13–15, 51.

23 In his preface to the 1855 edition Corbière claims that he published the first part of the novel without thinking about the second (*N 1990*, 4–5). But the original edition makes it clear that this could not have been the case: in his preamble to the first volume Corbière announces the subject matter of the second volume, explaining how the narrative in the second volume will belatedly justify the title of the novel: "Dans la seconde partie de l'ouvrage, je m'occuperai de retracer la vie modifiée de nos marins, dans les colonies, et faisant la traite sur les côtes d'Afrique. Cette seconde partie justifiera le titre de NEGRIER, que j'ai donné au héros du roman, dès le premier volume" (*N 1832*, x). *N 1832* also lists the chapters of the forthcoming second volume, "pour paraître incessamment" (announcement facing the title page).

24 In the 1832 (*N 1832*, 6) and 1979 editions (*N*, 16) the name is described as "sonore," "marin," and "martial." "Mâle" was added to the 1855 edition (*N 1990*, 14).

25 See *N 1990*, 24. In this passage Corbière not only removed the feminine outfitting of the two sons; he also added the qualifier *mâle* to his description of the captain's face (*sa large et mâle figure*). See also the variant, *N 1990*, 360.

26 Burg, *Sodomy and the Pirate Tradition*, 173, 172, 171, xl, 170.

27 Hans Turley writes, in his *Rum, Sodomy, and the Lash: Piracy, Sexuality, and Masculine Identity* (New York: New York University Press, 1999), that the pirate was "a sexual transgressor." (2); "the piratical subject can be connected to the newly emergent sodomitical subject" (75), even if "the homosocial world of the pirate cannot be defined as explicitly homoerotic" (5). Turley describes Burg's work as "notable but problematic" (45). Marcus Rediker echoes Turley's note of caution about Burg's close association of piracy and sodomy; see Marcus Rediker, *Villians of All Nations: Atlantic Pirates in the Golden Age* (Boston: Beacon Press, 2004), 74.

28 See Roudaut, "Les Deux Corbière," 11. *N* reads "Voyons, mes fils" (30), which conforms to *N 1832*, 55. *N 1990* has "mes amoureux" (42).

29 Jonathan Ned Katz, *Love Stories: Sex between Men before Homosexuality* (Chicago: University of Chicago Press, 2001), 185.

30 The full story of the relationship between Jacques/Rosalie and the *capitaine d'armes* is recounted (*N*, 43–44).

31 In modern nautical parlance *matelotage* refers to the art of tying knots. *Matelot* came from the Middle Dutch *mattenoot*, meaning bunk mate. The *Dictionnaire de l'Académie Française*, 6th ed. (1835) defines the verb *amateloter*: "Mettre, classer deux à deux tous les hommes d'un équipage, pour qu'ils s'aident ou se remplacent mutuellement dans le même service, dans le même emploi." In his *Contes de bord* (Paris: Lecointe et Pougin, 1833), Corbière uses the word *matelotage* to refer to the skills of sailing (19). But in the same work he also offers an explanation (similar to the one in *Le Négrier*) of *matelotage* as the bonding of two sailors, with an anecdote illustrating the closeness of

their emotional ties: as in the film *Tamango*, a sailor's death provokes the inconsolable grief of his mate, his *matelot* (25–31). On matelotage see Doris Garraway, *The Libertine Colony: Creolization in the Early French Caribbean* (Durham: Duke University Press, 2005), 126–27.

32   Larousse, *Grand dictionnaire universel du XIXe siècle*, s.v. *matelotage*.

33   Burg, *Sodomy*, 128. See also Katz on "chickens" in nineteeth-century American sailor slang (*Love Stories*, 138–39). *Matelotage* bears some resemblance to a "medical" condition described in *The Lancet* in 1836: "Adhesiveness. I knew two gentlemen whose attachment to each other was so excessive, as to amount to a disease. When the one visited the other, they slept in the same bed, sat constantly alongside of each other at table, spoke in affectionate whispers, and were, in short, miserable when separated" (quoted in Graham Robb, *Strangers: Homosexual Love in the Nineteenth Century* [New York: Norton, 2003], 52).

34   *N*, 25; emphasis added. In *N 1990* Corbière adds: ". . . une communauté d'existence bien plus intime encore que celle qui unit à l'armée un soldat à son camarade de lit" (33).

35   Edouard Corbière, "Le Voeu des deux matelots," in *La Mer et les marins*, 64.

36   Jean-Baptiste Du Tertre, *Histoire générale des Antilles habiteés par les François* (Paris: T. Jolly, 1667–71), 2:452–53. I am grateful to Ryan Poynter for bringing this passage to my attention.

37   See Edouard Corbière, *Cric-crac: Roman maritime* (Paris: Librarie spéciale pour les cabinets de lecture, 1846).

38   Olaudah Equiano, *The Interesting Narrative of the Life of Olaudah Equiano, or Gustavus Vassa, the African, Written by Himself* (New York: Norton, 2001), 46. I am not aware of any discussion of this relationship as an example of *matelotage* in the literature on Equiano. Sue Peabody called attention to the larger, unexplored question of Equiano's sexuality, in an online forum ("The Homosocial World of Equiano," H-Caribbean-net, www.h-net.org/~carib/ [March 10, 2003]).

39   See Equiano, *The Interesting Narrative*, 58.

40   In *N 1990* Corbière added the word *hermaphroidique* to this dialogue; the phrase "comme vous voudrez"—quite startling with regard to the question of gender—is changed to "je vous en répons" (61).

41   *N*, 87. In 1855 Corbière added even more force to his rhetoric on this point: "Un vice, le plus infâme de tous, celui que l'on ne peut nommer décemment dans aucune langue . . . régnait avec frénésie dans les prisons" (*N 1990*, 141).

42   *N*, 87; the text is identical in *N 1832*, 253–54. An exclamation point was added to the last sentence in some later editions (see, e.g., *N 1990*, 141); and the phrase "parties to the contract" (*les contractants*) was changed to *les fiancés* (*N 1990*, 141).

43   *N 1834*, 2:104.

44   *Homosexual* was coined in 1868 and 1869 by Karl Maria Kertbeny in a let-

503

ter and then in a pamphlet that advocated the repeal of Prussia's sodomy laws (Robb, *Strangers*, 67). The "homo/hetero divide" is Katz's phrase (*Love Stories*, 10). I say "alleged" simply to avoid implying that before a certain date there was literally no difference between homosexuality and heterosexuality.

45 In the detailed table of contents at the beginning of this chapter in *N 1834* (2:97): "Vices et amours des Prisons."

46 Jean-Paul Aron and Roger Kempf, "Triumphs and Tribulations of the Homosexual Discourse," in *Homosexualities and French Literature: Cultural Contexts/Critical Texts*, ed. George Stambolian and Elaine Marks (Ithaca: Cornell University Press, 1979), 141, 142.

47 Robb, *Strangers*, 91. Robb demonstrates that homosexuality, despite the absence of that word, existed and that some men led "quite openly" homosexual lives in Restoration France (ibid., 88).

48 *N*, 92, 100, 146. The fact that *matelotage* did not exclude having sex with women is made clear in passages like this one: "Mon matelot Livonnière [Ivon] était enchanté de ses faciles conquêtes [des plus jolies filles de couleur de la Basse-Terre]" (*N*, 146). See other uses of the expression *mon matelot*: *N*, 149, 150, 152, 157; see also "mon compagnon" (153). When Ivon/Livonnière dies in chapter 11, the narrator sums up their relationship in a way that echoes the grief-stricken mourning of Bibi's lover in the film *Tamango*: "Il n'avait vu que moi, que son cher Léonard, en expirant, et mon avenir avait été sa dernière pensée . . . J'éprouvai après sa mort, pour la première fois, ce que c'est qu'une douleur de l'âme et un déchirement du coeur . . . Je sentais que je venais de perdre une partie de moi-même . . . Je fus anéanti" (*N*, 161). In *N 1990* Corbière backed away from the physicality of the relationship between Léonard and Ivon, changing "il me protégea de toute la largeur de son corps" (*N*, 38) to "il me couvrit de toute l'ampleur de sa colossale individualité" (*N 1990*, 55). "Mon ami Ivon" (*N*, 55) is changed to "Le philosophe Ivon" (*N 1990*, 83).

49 Robb, *Strangers*, 179.

50 *N*, 103. On the prison as "univers concentrationnaire," and for a homophobic view of the homosexuality that Corbière depicts, see Jean Roudaut, "Les Deux Corbière," *Critique* 22, no. 224 (January 1966): 10–11.

51 The French prisoners are described as *captifs* (*N*, 89, 93), a word that was commonly used for Africans taken into the slave trade, especially before they were taken onboard ships for the Middle Passage. Roger used the term in *Kélédor*. Recounting the slave trade later in the novel, however, Corbière will use a different vocabulary for African captives, avoiding the word *captif*: Africans are described as *nègres, mes nègres, noirs, cargaison*, and *traite*.

52 Guillaume Thomas Raynal, *Histoire des deux Indes* (Geneva: Chez Jean-Léonard Pellet, 1780), 3:233.

53 The *Cahier* contains this verse: "La négraille aux senteurs d'oignon frit retrouve dans son sang répandu le goût amer de la liberté" (Aimé Césaire, *Ca-*

hier d'un retour au pays natal, ed. Abiola Irele, 2nd ed. [Columbus: Ohio State University Press, 2000], 31).

54 *N*, 133. *N 1990* (222) has "le prix qu'on avait pu en tirer en le livrant à l'encan" (the price that he *had* drawn . . .), whereas *N*, quoted here, has "le prix qu'on aurait pu en tirer . . ." (the price that he *might have* drawn . . .).

55 I owe this observation to Tara Golba.

56 *Le Négrier* echoes *Tamango* in the dress of the ambassador of the king of Boni, which is like Tamango's when he is first seen: "Cet ambassadeur, grotesquement recouvert d'un débris de manteau . . ." (*N*, 171).

57 In *N 1990* Corbière changed this to: "des nègres toujours prêts à sortir de la cale pour vous manger" (294).

58 In what may be an error, *N* has "de la côte d'Afrique et d'Amérique," while *N 1832* reads "de la côte d'Afrique en Amérique."

59 In Corbière's short story "Un Négrier: Superchérie" (in his *Contes de bord*), French slavers, in a reversal of roles, rise up in revolt against British sailors who have taken over their ship (145–61).

60 *N 1832* is, as elsewhere, identical to *N* in this passage. In the slightly revised second edition (*N 1834*) Corbière changed part of this passage to the singular: "C'était *un* de nos nègres" (*N 1834*, 4:115; see also *N 1953*, 239).

61 "Ce que j'avais à redouter *de leur trop juste indignation*" (*N 1834*, 4:115; emphasis added; see *N 1990*, 310). The phrase in italics is not found in *N 1832*.

62 The "ruse" of faking yellow fever by applying saffron is also used by Aténor de Caligny (another naval officer) in his short story "Une Ruse de négrier," *Revue maritime* 2 (1834): 107–11. Pursued by a British frigate, the captain in this story rejects, on purely practical grounds, the option of jettisoning captives, which Léonard exercised: "Car il ne faut pas penser à effacer les traces de la cargaison, en jetant à la mer les noirs et leurs fers: la disposition du navire et, encore bien plus, une odeur de nègre qu'aucun parfum ne pourrait enlever, trahiraient toujours" ("Une Ruse de négrier," 109).

63 See, e.g., Théodore Canot, *Les Aventures d'un négrier*, trans. (from the English) Marthe Nouguier (Paris: Plon et Nourrit, 1931); Maurice Magre, *Pirates, flibustiers et négriers* (Paris: Bernard Grasset, 1934 [the ninth edition of this work]); Roger Vercel, *Ange-Marie, négrier sensible* (Paris: Albin Michel, 1938); Louis Garneray, *Voyages, aventures, et combats: Pirates et négriers* (Paris: Editions de la Nouvelle France, 1944), published in a series called "La Vie exaltante." On this tradition see János Riesz, "'Le Dernier voyage du négrier *Sirius*': Le Roman dans le roman dans *Le Docker noir* d'Ousmane Sembene," in *Sénégal-Forum: Littérature et histoire*, ed. Papa Samba Diop (Frankfurt: IKO, 1996), 186–87. A contemporary manifestation of this tradition is found in a series of *bandes dessinées* on the theme of the slave trade: François Bourgeon, *Les Passagers du vent*, vol. 3, *Le Bois d'ébène* (Paris: Casterman, 1994) and vol. 5, *Le Comptoir de Juda* (Paris: Casterman, 1994).

64 In fact Atar-Gull claims at the end to have "loved [Brulart] like a brother. . . . And yet my heart leapt with joy as I watched his execution" (*AG*, 283).

65 For the workings of this pattern in the American expansion into the West see Chris Packard, *Queer Cowboys and Other Erotic Male Friendships in Nineteenth-Century American Literature* (New York: Palgrave Macmillan, 2005), 19–40.

66 Vincent Carretta, *Equiano the African: Biography of a Self-Made Man* (Athens: University of Georgia Press, 2005), 72.

67 Olivier Pétré-Grenouilleau, *Les Traites négrières: Essai d'histoire globale* (Paris: Gallimard, 2004), 284.

68 Albert Londres, *Terre d'ébène (La Traite des Noirs)* (Paris: Albin Michel, 1929). See also Emmanuel Dongala's depiction of this episode in his novel *Le Feu des origines* (Paris: Le Serpent à Plumes, 2001).

13 CÉSAIRE, GLISSANT, CONDÉ

1 See Raphaël Confiant, *Aimé Césaire: Une Traversée paradoxale du siècle* (Paris: Stock, 1993); Roger Toumson and Simonne Henry-Valmore, *Aimé Césaire: Le Nègre inconsolé* (Paris: Syros, 1993). In 2006 *Le Monde* stated: "En France, Aimé Césaire reste aussi méconnu que ses Antilles natales" ("Aimé Césaire au présent," unsigned article, March 17, 2006). The pendulum will no doubt swing back after Césaire's death.

2 Jean-Paul Sartre, "Orphée noir," preface to Léopold Sédar Senghor, *Anthologie de la nouvelle poésie nègre et malgache de langue française* (Paris: PUF, 1948), ix–xliv.

3 Aimé Césaire, *Cahier d'un retour au pays natal*, ed. Abiola Irele, 2nd ed. (Columbus: Ohio State University Press, 2000), 30; *Notebook of a Return to the Native Land*, in Aimé Césaire, *The Collected Poetry*, trans. Clayton Eshleman and Annette Smith (Berkeley: University of California Press, 1983), 79, AT. Further references to the *Cahier* will cite the page numbers of Irele's edition, followed by those of this translation. Some of the mistakes in this original California translation (like translating "Afrique" as "Europe," 46–47) were corrected in the new edition: Aimé Césaire, *Notebook of a Return to the Native Land*, trans. Clayton Eshleman and Annette Smith (Middletown, Conn.: Wesleyan University Press, 2001). Unless otherwise noted, I have not necessarily reproduced the line breaks of verses that are printed as prose (see chapter 9). Irele's introduction and annotations of the poem are extremely helpful, even if a reader need not agree with each of his interpretations. It should be kept in mind that the first, shorter version of the *Cahier* was printed in 1939, in a French journal: *Volontés* 20 (August 1939): 23–51; henceforth referenced as *Cahier* 1939. I referred to the history of the poem's subsequent editions in chapter 9.

4 Edouard Glissant, *L'Intention poétique* (Paris: Seuil, 1969), 148.

5 On this see Richard D. E. Burton, "Two Views of Césaire: *Négritude* and *créolité*," *Dalhousie French Studies* 35 (1996): 135.

6 See Confiant, *Aimé Césaire*; on the "taboo" see 38. Confiant writes: "Au lieu d'arrimer la Martinique aux Amériques, et en particulier aux Caraïbes, n'a-t-il

pas longtemps, trop longtemps, nourri une chimère d'Afrique?" (18). Burton semifacetiously summarizes Confiant's biography as a nine-point indictment ("Two Views of Césaire," 143–45). It should be noted that other critiques of Césaire preceded Confiant's; see, e.g., Christian Filostrat, "La Négritude et la 'conscience raciale et révolution sociale' d'Aimé Césaire," *Présence franco-phone* 21 (1980): 119–30. Filostrat claims that Césaire's Negritude "resulted in nothing valid for the Antilles" (130).

7 Patrick Chamoiseau and Raphaël Confiant, *Lettres créoles: Tracées antillaises et continentales de la littérature, 1635–1975* (Paris: Hatier, 1991), 127. In their manifesto *Éloge de la créolité* (Paris: Gallimard, 1989), Jean Bernabé, Patrick Chamoiseu, and Raphaël Confiant write: "la Négritude fit, à celle d'Europe, succéder l'illusion africaine" (20). Europe and Africa are memorably described as "deux monstres tutélaires" (18).

8 Frantz Fanon, "Antillais et Africains," *Esprit* 23 (February 1955): 268, 266, 269; emphasis added.

9 Frantz Fanon, *Peau noire, masques blancs* (Paris: Seuil, 1952), 107–8; *Black Skin, White Masks*, trans. Charles Lam Markmann (New York: Grove Press, 1967), 132–33; *Les Damnés de la terre* (Paris: Gallimard, 1991), 268; *The Wretched of the Earth*, trans. Richard Philcox (New York: Grove Press, 2004), 158–59. Fanon does not mention Negritude by name here, but it clearly belongs in his second or "precombat" phase of literature. On "the substitution of Africa for France" in Haiti see C. L. R. James, *The Black Jacobins: Toussaint L'Ouverture and the San Domingo Revolution*, 2nd ed., revised (New York: Vintage Books, 1989), 395.

10 Confiant, *Aimé Césaire*, 70, 72; emphasis added. The word *presbyopia* is used by Burton ("Two Views of Césaire," 147). Confiant gets around the problem of Césaire's considerable emphasis on Haiti—the birthplace of Negritude according to the *Cahier*—by claiming that Haiti "in [Césaire's] mind" is simply "a substitute for Africa" (*Aimé Césaire*, 89). One wonders who is doing the substituting here.

11 "Un *bovarysme collectif*, c'est-à-dire la faculté que s'attribue une société de se concevoir autre qu'elle n'est . . . une âme d'emprunt" (Jean Price-Mars, *Ainsi parla l'oncle . . . : Essais d'ethnographie* [Compiègne: Imprimerie de Compiègne, 1928], ii, iv).

12 Price-Mars, *Ainsi parla l'oncle*, 220; emphasis added. See Lilyan Kesteloot, *Black Writers in French: A Literary History of Negritude*, trans. Ellen Conroy Kennedy (Philadelphia: Temple University Press, 1974), 27. See also James, *The Black Jacobins*: "[In the wake of the American occupation] Haiti's image of itself had changed. . . . [There was a] substitution of Africa for France" (395).

13 Chamoiseau and Confiant, *Lettres créoles*, 88.

14 Note that for Chamoiseu and Confiant "la perspective de néantisation crainte par Edouard Glissant dans *Le Discours antillais* ne s'est jamais produite" (*Lettres créoles*, 66). Richard D. E. Burton accuses Glissant of creating the "non-

histoire" that he, Glissant, describes (*Le Roman marron: Études sur la littérature martiniquaise contemporaine* [Paris: L'Harmattan, 1997], 80).

15 For a critique of this see J. Michael Dash, *The Other America: Caribbean Literature in a New World Context* (Charlottesville: University Press of Virginia, 1998), 40–41. For a "postmodern" Césaire, who "required" his partisans "to abandon fixed ideas of settled identity and culturally authorized definition . . . even during the heat of struggle," see Edward Said, "Representing the Colonized: Anthropology's Interlocutors," *Critical Inquiry* 15, no. 2 (winter 1989): 225.

16 J. Michael Dash, "Postcolonial Caribbean Identities," in *The Cambridge History of African and Caribbean Literature*, ed. F. Abiola Irele and Simon Gikandi (Cambridge: Cambridge University Press, 2004), 2:788.

17 Clive Wake, "A Speech-Maker's Songs," *TLS*, July 19, 1985, 792.

18 Patrick Williams and Laura Chrisman, introduction to part 2, in *Colonial Discourse and Post-Colonial Theory: A Reader* (New York: Columbia University Press, 1994), 129.

19 Maria Diedrich, Henry Louis Gates Jr., and Carl Pedersen, "The Middle Passage between History and Fiction: Introductory Remarks," in *Black Imagination and the Middle Passage*, ed. Maria Diedrich, Henry Louis Gates Jr., and Carl Pedersen (New York: Oxford University Press, 1999), 9. Irele argues that any distinction between a "radical" Césaire and a "conservative" Senghor is "specious," but these are not the only options in my view: Senghor is indisputably conservative, but Césaire's *Cahier* can be seen as *neither* radical nor essentialist. See Irele, introduction to *Cahier d'un retour au pays natal*, xlix. Critics would do well to read an essay by Maryse Condé that suggests some of the vast differences between the two poets: "Négritude césairienne, négritude senghorienne," *Revue de littérature comparée* 48 (1974): 409–19. Daniel Delas describes the two versions nicely in his *Aimé Césaire* (Paris: Hachette, 1991), 47; as does Gloria Saravaya, in her *Le Thème du retour dans le "Cahier d'un retour au pays natal"* (Paris: L'Harmattan, 1996), 82. Césaire himself once insisted on the difference between himself and his Senegalese friend in rather blunt terms: "Senghor est un patricien noir" (quoted in Cilas Kemedjio, *De la Négritude à la Créolité: Edouard Glissant, Maryse Condé et la malédiction de la théorie* [Hamburg: Lit Verlag, 1999], 166).

20 Irele, introduction to *Cahier*, 1–li.

21 Césaire, quoted in Aliko Songolo, "Césaire's Surrealism and the Quest for Africa," *Ba Shiru* 7, no. 2 (1976): 32.

22 Chamoiseau and Confiant, *Lettres créoles*, 152.

23 For Glissant's definition of *Antillanité* (which includes mention of the concept of *Créolité*) see Wolfgang Bader, "Poétique antillaise, poétique de la Relation: Interview avec Edouard Glissant," *Komparatistische Hefte* 9/10 (1984): 97–98.

24 See Melville J. Herskovits, *The Myth of the Negro Past* (1941; Boston: Beacon Press, 1958). Specifically, Confiant reinvents Herskovits's third "myth":

"Since the Negroes were brought from all parts of the African continent [and] spoke diverse languages . . . no least common denominator of understanding or behavior could have possibly been worked out by them" (1). Henry Louis Gates Jr. rejects this myth of total erasure as an "odd . . . fiction" (Henry Louis Gates Jr., *The Signifying Monkey: A Theory of Afro-American Literary Criticism* [New York: Oxford University Press, 1988], 4).

25 Confiant, *Aimé Césaire*, 131; emphasis added.

26 Glissant, *Le Discours antillais* (Paris: Seuil, 1981), 31.

27 I agree with Gregson Davis's argument against the reductionism to which the poem has been subjected: "Our account of négritude as it is obliquely articulated on the pages of *Cahier* sees it as multivocal. The history of the poem's reception, however, is replete with accounts that read it as largely univocal" (Gregson Davis, *Aimé Césaire* [Cambridge: Cambridge University Press, 1997], 60).

28 Confiant, *Aimé Césaire*, 71.

29 Even Burton allows for the possibility that the *Cahier* might be, exceptionally in Césaire's otherwise "existentialist" oeuvre, essentialist (Burton, "Two Views of Césaire," 146).

30 Thomas Hale, *Aimé Césaire: His Literary and Political Writings with a Bio-Bibliography* (Ann Arbor: University Microfilms, 1974): "The first *partir* refers to a departure from Martinique, rather than from Europe, while the second *partir* refers to the projected departure from Europe to return to the island" (27). Quoted in A. James Arnold, *Modernism and Negritude: The Poetry and Poetics of Aimé Césaire* (Cambridge, Mass.: Harvard University Press, 1981), 155–56. My reading of the *Cahier* is influenced by Ronnie Scharfman, *"Engagement" and the Language of the Subject in the Poetry of Aimé Césaire* (Gainesville: University of Florida Press, 1980); and by John Erickson, "Le *Cahier* d'Aimé Césaire et la subversion du discours magistral," in *Soleil éclaté: Mélanges offerts à Aimé Césaire à l'occasion de son soixante-dixième anniversaire*, ed. Jacqueline Leiner (Tübingen: G. Narr, 1984), 125–36.

31 Delas, *Aimé Césaire*, 13.

32 *Cahier*, 12; *Notebook*, 51; see Irele's gloss on this passage, *Cahier*, 79–80. See also Charles Baudelaire, "Le Poème du hashich," in *Oeuvres complètes* (Paris: Gallimard, 1975), 1:419–20.

33 Scharfman, *"Engagement,"* 44.

34 On Frobenius and Negritude see Dominique Combe, *Aimé Césaire: "Cahier d'un retour au pays natal"* (Paris: PUF, 1993), 29–32; Christopher L. Miller, *Theories of Africans: Francophone Literature and Anthropology in Africa* (Chicago: University of Chicago Press, 1990), 16–20; and Sandra Adell, *Double Consciousness, Double Bind: Theoretical Issues in Twentieth-Century Black Literature* (Urbana: University of Illinois Press, 1973), 31–34.

35 Michel Leiris, "Qui est Aimé Césaire?" in Lilyan Kesteloot and Barthélémy Kotchy, *Aimé Césaire: L'Homme et l'oeuvre* (Paris: Présence Africaine, 1973), 16. In *Lettres créoles* Chamoiseau and Confiant stipulate what Césaire's Negri-

tude "would have had to do" to satisfy them but allegedly failed to do (127). But in my view everything they list *can* be seen in the *Cahier*, with only one exception: the relation to the oral tradition.

36 See Irele in *Cahier*, 137. On the anthropological "mistake" reflected in the phrase "lance de nuit," see Lilyan Kesteloot, *Comprendre le "Cahier d'un retour au pays natal" d'Aimé Césaire* (Issy les Moulineaux: Les Classiques Africains, 1982), 96.

37 A case for an essentialist Césaire can be attempted by analyzing his uses of the image of blood in the *Cahier*. Blood is of course the key metaphor for theories of race, and Césaire uses the image generously in the poem. Irele cites the verse "Sang! Sang! tout notre sang ému par le coeur mâle du soleil" as a "controversial" declaration that might be "stretched" to suggest "biologism" (*Cahier*, 1[roman num. 50]). I agree that it would be a stretch. Blood is many things in the poem, including, in a signal gesture, the material of words themselves ("Des mots? . . . ah oui, des mots! mais des mots de sang frais" [15/57]). Like other key metaphors in the *Cahier* (such as the sun), blood moves from an initial association with oppression and horror ("Ma mémoire est entourée de sang. Ma mémoire a sa ceinture de cadavres!" [16/59]), to be recuperated as a sign of solidarity (as above, "tout notre sang ému" and "terres consanguinaires"). This shift can be seen in condensed fashion in the single line: "Terres rouges, terres sanguines, terres consanguines" [10/47]). But the narrator/hero of the *Cahier* is not the nationalist messiah that the Rebel of Césaire's *Et les chiens se taisaient* (Paris: Présence Africaine, 1958) will declare himself to be: "Que de mon sang / je fonde ce peuple" (62). On the theme of blood see René Hénane, *Aimé Césaire, le chant blessé: Biologie et poétique* (Paris: Jean-Michel Place, 1999), 41–76, esp. 59–61.

38 The 1939 stanza reads: "Le négrier! proclame mon sûr et ténébreux instinct, les voiles de noires nuages, la polymâture de forêts sombres et des dures magnificences des Calebars, insigne souvenir à la proue blanchoyant—ce squelette!" ("Cahier d'un retour au pays natal," *Volontés* 20 [August 1939]: 37). The Présence Africaine edition has "Calabars," but the collected edition of Césaire's poetry restores "Calebar"; see Aimé Césaire, *La Poésie* (Paris: Seuil, 1994), 35.

39 The California edition (*Notebook*, 60, 61), following the Présence Africaine edition, wrongly changes the spelling of this to "Calabar," thereby destroying the pun that Césaire created with *cale*. On "Calebars" see Irele, *Cahier*, 101–2. Césaire uses "Calabars" (with an *a* this time) again as if it were the name of a people in "Moi, laminaire" (1982), in *La Poésie*, 405.

40 See Hénane, *Aimé Césaire, le chant blessé*, 23. See also Césaire, "Avis de tir," *Tropiques* 8–9 (October 1943): 13; and Mireille Rosello, *Littérature et identité créole aux Antilles* (Paris: Karthala, 1992), 123. In "Avis de tir," *Vomito Negro* is the name of a pirate ship.

41 Mireille Rosello, *Littérature et identité créole aux Antilles*, 126–34. "Le vo-

missement, . . . effrayant par la violence que le corps subit, sert de modèle à toute activité de refus" (128). See also Rosello's discussion of vomit in Glissant's *Le Quatrième siècle*, 127.

42 *Notebook* egregiously mistranslates this as "nontourist" (83).

43 See Césaire, *Lettre à Maurice Thorez* (Paris: Présence Africaine, 1956). However, this verse appears in 1939 as well; the word is spelled *in-tourist* there (50). I agree with Kesteloot's explication of this phrase: "*l'intourist du circuit triangulaire*, c'est-à-dire le trajet contrôlé et obligatoire du circuit négrier: Europe — Afrique — Amérique" (*Comprendre le "Cahier,"* 103). Just above in the *Cahier*, Césaire evokes a "fatal calme triangulaire," which, as Irele rightly explains, subversively associates the triangle of the Atlantic slave trade with the triangle of the Catholic Church's Holy Trinity (see Irele, *Cahier*, 146).

44 These final verses are lexically identical to their original 1939 form (51); only some punctuation, capitalization, and line breaks changed. It should be noted that in this ending the narrator comes rather close to passing himself off as the nationalist messiah that I earlier said he was *not*.

45 Eschleman and Smith, introduction to *Notebook*, 26. See Liliane Pestre de Almeida, "'Les Structures anthropologiques de l'imaginaire' dans un texte de Césaire," *Présence francophone* 23 (autumn 1981): 155.

46 Hénane, *Aimé Césaire, le chant blessé*, 315.

47 The self-countervailing movements of the poem are well described in Gary Wilder, *The French Imperial Nation-State: Negritude and Colonial Humanism between the Two World Wars* (Chicago: University of Chicago Press, 2005), 289.

48 See the diagram of the *Cahier*'s movements in Kesteloot and Kotchy, *Aimé Césaire: l'homme et l'oeuvre*, 28.

49 Roger Bastide, *African Civilisations in the New World*, trans. Peter Green (New York: Harper and Row, 1971), 223, AT.

50 See Césaire's remarks on Creole and French in Jacqueline Leiner, "Entretien avec Aimé Césaire," *Tropiques* (Paris: Jean-Michel Place, 1978), 1:xii–xiii.

51 A return that I have not considered here is that of the narrator *from* Africa, from a sojourn that might have put him in contact with his roots.

52 Email communication from Sarah Laskow, June 22, 2005.

53 Back cover of 1956 Présence Africaine edition of *Cahier*, quoted in Richard Watts, *Packaging Post/Coloniality: The Manufacture of Literary Identity in the Francophone World* (Lanham, Md.: Lexington Books, 2005), 108. On Césaire's reception in Africa see also Kemedjio, *De la Négritude à la Créolité*, 235–36; and Femi Ojo-Ade, "Caribbean Negritude and Africa: Aspects of Black Dilemma," in *A History of Literature in the Caribbean*, vol. 3, ed. A. James Arnold (Amsterdam: John Benjamins, 1997), 363.

54 Kesteloot, *Comprendre le "Cahier,"* 14.

55 Emile Snyder, "A Reading of Aimé Césaire's *Return to My Native Land*," *L'Esprit créateur* 10, no. 3 (fall 1970): 201.

56 Bernard Zadi Zaourou, *Césaire entre deux cultures: Problèmes théoriques de la littérature négro-africaine d'aujourd'hui* (Abidjan: Nouvelles Editions Africaines, 1978), 11. See also Confiant, *Aimé Césaire*, 126–28.

57 Abderrahmane Sissako, *La Vie sur terre* (Mali, 1998). This quiet film is much concerned with questions of communication and contact, with the difficulties of how to *prendre langue* in Africa. As one character says, "La communication c'est une question de chance."

58 The first interpretation is in Glissant, *L'Intention poétique*, 150; the word *terroir* is mine; he uses the word *pays*. The second is in Edouard Glissant, *Le Discours antillais* (Paris: Seuil, 1981), 35.

59 Watts, *Packaging Post/Coloniality*, 109.

60 For an enlightening reading of Glissant's *retour* and *détour* see Jeannie Suk, *Postcolonial Paradoxes in French Caribbean Writing: Césaire, Glissant, Condé* (Oxford: Clarendon Press, 2001), 57–70.

61 See Ian Baucom "Specters of the Atlantic," *SAQ* 100, no. 1 (2001): 64–65.

62 For a reading of Glissant's comments on the slave trade in both *Le Discours antillais* and *Poétique de la relation* see Baucom, "Specters of the Atlantic," 64–70.

63 Edouard Glissant, *Les Indes, Un Champ d'îles, La Terre inquiète* (Paris: Seuil, 1965), 69, 82, 91; "The Indies," in Edouard Glissant, *The Collected Poems of Edouard Glissant*, trans. Jeff Humphries with Melissa Manolas (Minneapolis: University of Minnesota Press, 2005), 69 (AT), 76 (AT), 80. Further references to the French original, followed by the translation, will be abbreviated *LI*.

64 See Elisabeth Mudimbe-Boyi, "L'Histoire autre: Conquête, désir, jouissance et abjection dans *Les Indes* d'Edouard Glissant," *Protée* 22, no. 1 (winter 1994): 56.

65 The more metaphorical translation of *se déprendre* comes from Glissant, *The Indies*, trans. Dominique O'Neill (Toronto: Editions du GREF, 1992), 29.

66 Jeff Humphries, introduction to Glissant, *The Collected Poems of Edouard Glissant*, xxx.

67 Glissant's invocation of reason can be usefully connected to Paul Gilroy's treatment of "rationality" in *The Black Atlantic: Modernity and Double Consciousness* (Cambridge, Mass.: Harvard University Press, 1993), 213. Later, Glissant defines this new "reason" as creolization and his "Tout-Monde."

68 Some verses of Glissant's poem "Le Sel noir" (1960) are devoted to Africa and the slave trade; see Edouard Glissant, *Le Sel noir* (Paris: Gallimard, 1983), 105–14.

69 See J. Michael Dash, *Edouard Glissant* (Cambridge: Cambridge University Press, 1995); Burton, *Le Roman marron*, 65–103; and Peter Hallward, *Absolutely Postcolonial: Writing between the Singular and the Specific* (Manchester: Manchester University Press, 2001), 66–125.

70 Edouard Glissant, *Le Quatrième siècle* (Paris: Gallimard, 1964), 59; *The Fourth Century*, trans. Betsy Wing (Lincoln: University of Nebraska Press, 2001), 52;

further references abbreviated *QS*, with the page of the translation following that of the original.

71 Chris Bongie, *Islands and Exiles: The Creole Identities of Post/Colonial Literature* (Stanford: Stanford University Press, 1998), 147.

72 Glissant, in Bader interview, "Poétique antillaise, poétique de la Relation," 94 (see note 23 above).

73 Kemedjio, *De la Négritude à la Créolité*, 194–95.

74 See Chamoiseau and Confiant, *Lettres créoles*, 190.

75 Several slave-trading vessels were named *Marie-Rose*: one sailed from Nantes in 1731, bought 460 captives on the coast of Africa (of whom 44 died during the Middle Passage), sold the survivors in Martinique, and returned to Nantes after nineteen months in the triangle. This is number 262 in Jean Mettas, *Répertoire des expéditions négrières françaises au XVIIIe siècle* (Paris: Société Française d'Histoire d'Outre-Mer, 1984), 1:158–59. None named *Rose-Marie* appears. Many ships were named *Marie* and several *Rose* in the period of the illegal trade, but no *Rose-Marie* is listed; see Serge Daget, *Répertoire des expéditions négrières françaises à la traite illégale (1814–1850)* (Nantes: Centre de Recherche sur l'Histoire du Monde Atlantique, Université de Nantes, 1988).

76 Tierno Monénembo's narrator in the novel *Pelourinho* (Paris: Seuil, 1995) echoes this question: "Les cadavres jetés par-dessus bord, les ethnies englouties . . . crois-tu que cela puisse s'écrire et s'enseigner?" (145).

77 For a critique of Glissant's myth of the maroon see Burton, *Le Roman marron*, 65–103.

78 On Glissant's vision of the past and its affinities to Faulkner see Dash, *Edouard Glissant*, 74–78.

79 Baucom, "Specters of the Atlantic," 67.

80 Edouard Glissant, "Le Pays d'avant," in Alain Baudot, *Bibliographie annotée d'Edouard Glissant* (Toronto: Editions du GREF, 1993), 661.

81 Edouard Glissant, *La Lézarde* (Paris: Seuil, 1958), 109; Glissant, *Poétique de la Relation* (Paris: Gallimard, 1990), 27 (*la pensée de l'errance*). On Glissant's shift from nationalism to "singular" nomadology see Hallward, *Absolutely Postcolonial*, 66–125. Glissant deals with the slave trade and the Middle Passage also in his novel *La Case du commandeur* (1981; Paris: Gallimard, 1997). He evokes a primordial, fraternal act of treason, as in *Le Quatrième siècle* (19–20, 79, 141), and the gang raping of women by sailors during the Middle Passage (131–37), discussed earlier in this study (chapter 8). Glissant's novel *Tout-Monde* (Paris: Seuil, 1993) — not to be confused with his collection of essays entitled *Traité du Tout-Monde* — recounts events on the slave ship *Marie-Anne* ("or was it the *Marie-Rose*?" he continually asks) as it "rolls in a crazy triangle" from Nantes to Senegal to the Americas. Part of the chapter called "Un Pied de Térébinthe" (90–102) revisits the Middle Passage of the Longoué and Béluse (feuding) ancestors, previously seen in *Le Quatrième siècle*. Now Glissant adds the story of a proud young female captive named

513

Oriamé, taken in, like Dorothy Dandridge's Ayché, by an officer of the ship. Oriamé describes the different perspective that women captives in her position gain: "We are ahead of you [the male captives]," because the women know firsthand that their captors are merely men. Then she commits suicide by jumping overboard. The slave ship, writes Glissant, "did not drift one inch." This narrative thus complements what Glissant wrote about the Middle Passage in *Le Quatrième siècle* and *La Case du commandeur*, while still adhering to the brevity that characterized his descriptions of the slave trade prior to *Sartorius*.

82 Edouard Glissant, *Sartorius: Le Roman des Batoutos* (Paris: Gallimard, 1999).

83 See Edouard Glissant, *La Cohée du Lamentin: Poétique V* (Paris: Gallimard, 2005), 222: "les poétiques des langues créoles sont avant tout fractales"—because of the ruptured relation to Africa.

84 See Charles Johnson, *The Ox-Herding Tale* (New York: Grove Weidenfeld, 1982); and Charles Johnson, *Middle Passage* (New York: Penguin, 1990). On Johnson see Hallward, *Absolutely Postcolonial*, 151–55.

85 In *Ormerod* Glissant's *datation* situates "Odono, premier Batouto aux Antilles" at the year "1540 environ" (Edouard Glissant, *Ormerod* [Paris: Gallimard, 2003], 362). *Ormerod*, which is full of allusions to Glissant's previous works, makes frequent mention of the Batoutos (see, e.g., 73–76, 168, 219, 254, 350–55), but it is not a novel "of" the Batoutos to the extent that *Sartorius* is. *Ormerod* is mainly concerned with two events: a revolt of marooned slaves on Saint Lucia in 1793, and the coup d'état in Grenada in 1983. Glissant described *Sartorius* as the "first novel I devoted to the Batouto people," so *Ormerod* is the second; see *La Cohée du Lamentin*, 135.

86 The wreck of an anonymous vessel that is memorialized at Anse Caffard happened on April 8, 1830. That memorial is beautifully described in *Sartorius*, 162–64. On the memorial, called "Cap 110," by the artist Laurent Valère, see www.mathnique.com/cap110fa.htm. The memorial can be seen using Google Earth at these coordinates: 14°27′51.40″N, 61°02′47.32″W.

87 See Françoise Thésée, *Les Ibos de l'"Amélie": Destinée d'une cargaison de traite clandestine à la Martinique, 1822–1838* (Paris: Editions Caribéennes, 1986): 92; *Sartorius*, 140. The *Amélie* was not the shipwreck of April 8, 1830; it was a vessel that brought a shipment of captive Ibos to Martinique, illegally, in 1822.

88 Ibid., 90–91.

89 Ibid., 95, 96, 98.

90 I am grateful to J. Ryan Poynter for introducing me to this memorial.

91 This is not an aberrant opinion. Henry Louis Gates Jr. argued in the 1980s that the Middle Passage was, "inadvertently," a precondition "for the emergence of a new African culture [in the New World], a truly Pan-African culture fashioned as a colorful weave of linguistic, institutional, metaphysical, and formal threads" (Henry Louis Gates Jr., *The Signifying Monkey: A Theory*

of Afro-American Literary Criticism [New York: Oxford University Press, 1988], 4).

92 Edouard Glissant and Patrick Chamoiseau, "De l'esclavage au Tout-Monde," in *Poétiques d'Edouard Glissant*, ed. Jacques Chevrier (Paris: Presses de l'Université de Paris-Sorbonne, 1999), 79, 63.

93 Glissant, *Le Discours antillais*, 28.

94 Glissant, quoted in René de Ceccatty, "Edouard Glissant, voyageur du tout-monde," *Le Monde*, July 3, 2004.

95 Glissant, *La Cohée du Lamentin*, 135–37; emphasis added.

96 See Hallward, *Absolutely Postcolonial*, esp. 11–15; and Christopher L. Miller, "Beyond Identity: The Postidentitarian Predicament in Deleuze and Guattari's *A Thousand Plateaus*," in *Nationalists and Nomads: Essays on Francophone African Literature and Culture* (Chicago: University of Chicago Press, 1998): 171–209.

97 Hallward, *Absolutely Postcolonial*, 123–24.

98 My reading thus runs somewhat parallel to that of Nick Nesbitt, who sees in Glissant's later works, despite the "logic of tautology" of the Tout-Monde, "a stealthy, subterranean *continuity* of a *modernist* Glissant" — thus, I would say, a Glissant who still has something to say about a problem like the slave trade. See Nick Nesbitt, *Voicing Memory: History and Subjectivity in French Caribbean Literature* (Charlottesville: University of Virginia Press, 2003), 171.

99 See *Cohée*, 168. For a similar thought within the metaphor of the wind see *Cohée*, 246.

100 See De Ceccatty, "Edouard Glissant, voyageur du tout-monde." Borer is mentioned in *Sartorius* (183). In 2006 Glissant launched a book series based on this idea, called "Peuples de l'eau," with Editions du Seuil.

101 Mireille Rosello questions the narrative that has dominated studies of Condé since her turn away from Africa: that of a "return" to her native land of Guadeloupe after thirty years of absence. As Rosello points out that this view risks replicating a myth that Condé was instrumental in destroying, the myth of Return to wholeness in Africa. See Mireille Rosello, "Caribbean Insularization of Identities in Maryse Condé's Work: From *En Attendant le bonheur* to *Les Derniers rois mages*," *Callaloo* 18, no. 3 (1995): 566–69.

102 Glissant, in "De l'esclavage au Tout-Monde," 76.

103 Vèvè A. Clark, "Developing Diaspora Literacy and *Marasa* Consciousness," in *Comparative American Identities: Race, Sex, and Nationality in the Modern Text*, ed. Hortense Spillers (New York: Routledge, 1991), 40–61.

104 See Condé's *avant-propos*, *En Attendant le bonheur (Heremakhonon)* (Paris: Robert Laffont, 1988), 11.

105 See Françoise Lionnet, *Autobiographical Voices: Race, Gender, Self-Portraiture* (Ithaca: Cornell University Press, 1989), 175, 179; H. Adlai Murdoch, "Divided Desire: Biculturality and the Representation of Identity in *En attendant le bonheur*," *Callaloo* 18, no. 3 (1995): 579, 591.

106 Christopher L. Miller, "After Negation: Africa in Two Novels by Maryse

Condé," in *Postcolonial Subjects: Francophone Women Writers*, ed. Mary Jean Green et al. (Minneapolis: University of Minnesota Press, 1996), 173–85.

107 Murdoch, "Divided Desire," 590.

108 Véronica leaves her parents and her native Guadeloupe for the first time from Le Raizet airport (Maryse Condé, *Hérémakhonon* [Paris: Union Générale d'Editions, 1976], 13, 291; *Heremakhonon: A Novel*, trans. Richard Philcox [Washington, D.C.: Three Continents Press, 1982], 4, 163); further references to the original edition of the novel are abbreviated *H*, followed by the translation. Véronica leaves Paris and her lover Jean-Michel (from Le Bourget) for Africa (*H*, 287/161); she leaves Africa to return to Paris (*H*, 285/160).

109 On *Hérémakhonon* and the Atlantic triangle see Arlette M. Smith, "Maryse Condé's *Hérémakhonon*: A Triangular Structure of Alienation," *CLA Journal* 32, no. 1 (September 1988): 45–54.

110 Condé, "Négritude césairienne, Négritude senghorienne," 413, 414, 407, 419.

111 Maryse Condé, "Notes sur un retour au pays natal," *Conjonction* 176, supplement (1987): 14.

112 Ibid., 15.

113 Mary Gallagher rightly refers to "the time-space that Véronica calls Africa" (Mary Gallagher, *Soundings in French Caribbean Writing since 1950: The Shock of Time and Space* [Oxford: Oxford University Press, 2002], 227).

114 See William Snelgrave, *A New Account of Some Parts of Guinea and the Slave-Trade* (1734; London: Frank Cass, 1971), esp. 79.

115 I. A. Akinjogbin, *Dahomey and Its Neighbors, 1708–1818* (Cambridge: Cambridge University Press, 1967), 117.

116 On Agaja and Tegbusu see Edna G. Bay, "Dahomey," in *Encyclopedia of Africa South of the Sahara*, ed. John Middleton (New York: Charles Scribner's Sons, 1997), 1:392; Robert Harms, *The Diligent: A Voyage through the Worlds of the Slave Trade* (New York: Basic Books, 2002), 165–86, 323–24; Akinjogbin, *Dahomey and Its Neighbors*, 60–140; T, 353–59; Melville J. Herskovits, *Dahomey: An Ancient West African Kingdom* (Evanston, Ill.: Northwestern University Press, 1967), 16–20.

117 Bay, "Dahomey," 392.

118 Walter Rodney, *How Europe Underdeveloped Africa* (1972; Washington: Howard University Press, 1981), 81.

119 T, 354; Akinjogbin, *Dahomey and Its Neighbors*, 136. Akinjogbin asserts that Agaja wanted to "restrict and eventually stop the slave trade" and to substitute other forms of trade with Europeans (*Dahomey and Its Neighbors*, 77); on his relations with the French see 84–86. Bay points out that Dahomey nonetheless quickly "began to engage directly in the slave trade" following its conquests to the sea ("Dahomey," 392). And Akinjogbin concedes that, after Agaja's "conversion" in 1730, slave trading became "the basis of the Dahomean economy" for decades to come (95). See also Patrick Manning, *Slavery, Colonialism, and Economic Growth in Dahomey, 1640–1960* (Cam-

bridge: Cambridge University Press, 1982). Manning says that Akinjogbin's thesis "remains attractive despite the buffeting it has received. . . . Perhaps Agaja had this goal [ending the slave trade] in mind. . . . [But] the evidence gives little support to Akinjogbin's thesis" (40–41).

120 See Akinjogbin, *Dahomey and Its Neighbors*, 134–35.

121 Thomas, *The Slave Trade*, 358.

122 As for magical travel see Simone Schwartz-Bart's novel *Ti-Jean L'Horizon* (Paris: Seuil, 1979). An oral tradition assures the hero that descendants will be welcomed back to Africa "even to the thousandth generation" (65). Ti-Jean magically flies to Africa, to his ancestors' village; but there he finds that the words *nègre* and *frère* are called into question (140). Ti-Jean protests: you sold me, but I am not a stranger or a foreigner here; but he is told to go home (146, 148). Instead he travels to France, then home, completing a reverse triangle.

123 Maryse Condé, quoted in Madeleine Borgomano, "La Littérature romanesque d'Afrique noire et l'esclavage: 'une mémoire de l'oubli'?" in *Esclavage et abolitions: Mémoires et systèmes de représentation*, ed. Marie-Christine Rochmann (Paris: Karthala, 2000), 103.

124 I agree with Arlette Smith's suggestion that *Hérémakhonon* does not represent a "failure." See her "Maryse Condé's *Hérémakhonon*," 52–53.

125 See *Ségou: Les Murailles de terre* (Paris: Robert Laffont, 1984); and *Ségou: La Terre en miettes* (Paris: Robert Laffont, 1985); *The Children of Segu*, trans. Linda Coverdale (New York: Ballantine Books, 1989). On slavery in this novel see Borgomano, "La Littérature romanesque d'Afrique noire et l'esclavage," 102–103.

14 AFRICAN "SILENCE"

1 Madeleine Borgomano, "La Littérature romanesque d'Afrique noire et l'esclavage: 'une mémoire de l'oubli'?" in *Esclavage et abolitions: Mémoires et systèmes de représentation*, ed. Marie-Christine Rochmann (Paris: Karthala, 2000), 103. Among other Francophone African novels that might be considered here are Bassori Timité, *Grelots d'or* (Abidjan: CEDA, 1983); and Ibrahima Ly, *Les Noctuelles vivent de larmes* (Paris: L'Harmattan, 1988). Ly's novel contains a powerful evocation, within an entirely African context, of the feelings of captives as they are stripped of their personhood and their sense of community (see 29, 42, 58).

2 On the reception of *Le Docker noir* see János Riesz, "'Le Dernier voyage du négrier *Sirius*': Le Roman dans le roman dans *Le Docker noir* d'Ousmane Sembene," in *Sénégal-Forum: Littérature et histoire*, ed. Papa Samba Diop (Frankfurt: IKO, 1996), 181–82. Riesz reports having made several attempts to "rehabilitate" the novel (181n1). See also Wilfried F. Feuser, "Richard Wright's *Native Son* and Ousmane Sembene's *Le Docker noir*," *Komparatistische Hefte* 14 (1986): 110–11.

3 Ousmane Sembene, *Le Docker noir* (Paris: Présence Africaine, 1973), 17; *Black Docker*, trans. Ros Schwartz (London: Heinemann, 1986), 4; further references to the novel and the translation, abbreviated *DN*, will appear in that order in parentheses.

4 See Victor O. Aire, "Affinités électives ou imitation: *Gouverneurs de la rosée* et *O pays, mon beau peuple*," *Présence francophone* 15 (fall 1977): 3–10.

5 See Riesz, "Le Roman dans le roman," 182. Despite resemblances between the two works, Riesz argues against the charge of plagiarism (190).

6 See Dominic Thomas, *Black France: Colonialism, Immigration, and Trans-nationalism* (Bloomington: Indiana University Press, 2007), 109–10. The resemblances between *Black Docker* and *Native Son* were explored in Feuser, "Richard Wright's *Native Son* and Ousmane Sembene's *Le Docker noir*," 103–16. But Feuser limits his comments to thematic concerns, overlooking the instances of textual "borrowing" that Thomas documents.

7 See Christopher L. Miller, *Blank Darkness: Africanist Discourse in French* (Chicago: University of Chicago Press, 1985), 225–28; and Thomas, *Black France*. The play on the word *nègre* seems visible in this passage: "Pourquoi n'avez-vous pas essayé de voir ce qui a excité ma colère et occasionné ce crime que je me refuse à reconnaître? . . . Je suis un Nègre!" (*DN*, 214/117). In Spanish, "the primary definition of *plagiario* 'plagiarist' or 'plagiary' in Spain throughout the nineteenth century referred to the Roman term for kidnapping and enslaving a free person" (Lisa Surwillo, "Representing the Slave Trader: *Haley* and the Slave Ship; or, Spain's *Uncle Tom's Cabin*," *PMLA* 120, no. 3 [May 2005]: 779).

8 On *Le Docker noir* and Mérimée's "Tamango" see Riesz, "Le Roman dans le roman," 184–86.

9 According to Daget a slave ship named *Le Sirius*, under a Captain Jouanne, set sail for Africa from Nantes on November 29, 1824. It was known to have traded in Senegal and then gone on to Havana. But then it disappeared and was declared a total loss by the French navy council in November 1827. See Serge Daget, *Répertoire des expéditions négrières françaises à la traite illégale (1814–1850)* (Nantes: Centre de Recherche sur l'Histoire du Monde Atlantique, Université de Nantes, 1988), 354. Sembene's likely source for this information (as Riesz points out, "Le Roman dans le roman," 187) was Louis Lacroix, *Les Derniers négriers: Derniers voyages de bois d'ébène, de coolies et de merles du Pacifique* (Paris: Amiot-Dupont, 1952), 51. Lacroix, who provides general information about the illegal slave trade during the Restoration, says that the *Sirius* called at "San-Thomé." The date given in *Le Docker noir* and in *Les Derniers négriers* as that of its disappearance (December 4, 1824) does not agree with the information in Daget, *Répertoire*, 354. On other works that Sembene could have used for information on the slave trade see Riesz, "Le Roman dans le roman," 186–87.

10 For an insightful analysis of the literary politics of colonialism, including Sembene's concern with the compromises of writing in French, see Cilas Ke-

medjio, *De la Négritude à la Créolité: Edouard Glissant, Maryse Condé et la malédiction de la théorie* (Hamburg: Lit Verlag, 1999), 88–89.

11 For a fuller treatment of this subject within the broader context of African immigration in France see Thomas, *Black France*.

12 On Sembene's life see Samba Gadjigo's forthcoming biography (*Ousmane Sembene: La Formation de l'artiste militant* [Paris: Présence Africaine]); and Samba Gadjigo "Ousmane Sembene: Les Enjeux du cinéma et de la littérature," in *Littérature et cinéma en Afrique francophone: Ousmane Sembene et Assia Djebar*, ed. Sada Niang (Paris: L'Harmattan, 1996), 110–21. Like a worker who is mentioned in *Le Docker noir* (173/95), Sembene fractured his spine while working on the docks.

13 As Thomas points out, this letter fills a void created when Diaw fails to respond to the presiding judge's offered chance to speak before he is sentenced. Thomas writes, "His testimony therefore takes place outside the legal system so as to enable Sembene to record a voice otherwise silenced by dominant conventions" (*Black France*, 98).

14 See Jean-Pierre N'Diaye, *Négriers modernes: Les Travailleurs noirs en France* (Paris: Présence Africaine, 1970).

15 BUMIDOM stands for "Bureau pour les migrations des départements d'outre-mer." See Daniel Boukman, *Les Négriers: Pièce en trois parties* (Paris: Pierre Jean Oswald, 1971), 10. To feed the hunger of the French metropole for labor, "les négriers du XXe siècle" set up "Le DUBIDON" (a marvelous parody of BUMIDOM, suggesting a dubious gift), which imports workers to France "sans retour," emptying the islands (10, 33, 37). Med Hondo's film *West Indies* (1979) was adapted from Boukman's *Les Négriers*. See T. Mpoyi-Buatu, "*Ceddo* de Sembene Ousmane et *West Indies* de Med Hondo," *Présence Africaine* 119, no. 3 (1981): 161.

16 See Thomas's work on *La Noire de . . .* in *Black France. La Noire de . . .* was the first sub-Saharan feature film; see Françoise Pfaff, *Twenty-Five Black African Filmmakers* (New York: Greenwood Press, 1988), 240. A poem that follows the novella *La Noire de . . .* compares the fate of the exploited heroine, Diouana, to that of victims of the slave trade. See "Nostalgie," in Ousmane Sembene, *Voltaïque* (Paris: Présence Africaine, 1962): 175–77.

17 On Sembene's ambivalence about writing in French see Alioune Tine, "Wolof ou français, le choix de Sembene," *Notre Librairie* 81 (1985): 43–50.

18 Mpoyi-Buatu, "*Ceddo* de Sembene Ousmane et *West Indies* de Med Hondo," 158. See also Robert Cancel's useful analysis of *Ceddo*: "Epic Elements in *Ceddo*," *A Current Bibliography on African Affairs* 18, no. 1 (1985–86): 3–19; and Antoine Kakou, "*Ceddo*": *Lecture d'un texte filmique* (Abidjan: Université d'Abidjan Cérav No. 50, n.d.). Sembene Ousmane, *Ceddo*, DVD (Paris: Médiathèque des Trois Mondes, 2002).

19 Léopold Sédar Senghor, letter to *Le Monde*, August 14, 1979, in "dossier de presse" in DVD of *Ceddo* (Médiathèque des Trois Mondes).

20 See Pfaff, *Twenty-Five Black African Filmmakers*, 241–42, 253–55. The offi-

cial government orthographic system for the Wolof language dictated spelling the word *cedo*. (The word can be translated as "the outsiders.") Sembene's deviance from the official spelling was a sign of his larger goal, of "disrupt[ing]/reorganiz[ing] the nationalist discourse" of Senegal (Mamadou Diouf, "History and Actuality in Ousmane Sembene's *Ceddo* and Djibril Diop Mambety's *Hyenas*," in *African Experiences of Cinema*, ed. Imruh Bakari and Mbye B. Cham [London: British Film Institute, 1996], 241). Diouf explains how the film "is built on the ruins of [Senegalese] nationalist history and political itineraries based on patronage," making for "a radical critique of the postcolonial compromise" (244). On the larger history of French and Senegalese censorship of Sembene's films, see [anon.] "Sembene Ousmane and the Censor," *Africa: An International Business, Economic, and Political Monthly* 86 (October 1978): 85. According to that article the Senegalese authorities tried to get Sembene to hand out "a brief written explanation stating that it was a fictitious reconstruction of a historical nature," in other words, to disavow the historicity of his film. Such a statement would have been reminiscent of the paragraph that precedes the credits in the French version of the film *Tamango*, a paragraph that describes France as an abolitionist state.

21 Mbye Boubacar Cham, "Art and Ideology in the Work of Sembene Ousmane and Haile Gerima," *Présence Africaine* 129, no. 1 (1984): 82. See also Cham's "Official History, Popular Memory: Reconfiguration of the African Past in the Films of Ousmane Sembene," in *Ousmane Sembene: Dialogues with Critics and Writers*, ed. Samba Gadjigo, Ralph Faulkingham, Thomas Cassirer, and Reinhard Sander (Amherst: University of Massachusetts Press, 1993), 22–28.

22 Anon., "Sembene Ousmane and the Censor," 85.

23 Ousmane Sembene, in interview, Ousseynou Diop, "L'Organisation traditionnelle africaine ne correspond plus à l'Afrique nouvelle," *Cinébulles* 12, no. 4 (1993): 30.

24 Diouf, "History and Actuality," 243.

25 Cham, "Official History, Popular Memory," 25.

26 Arthur Simms is a black singer-songwriter (coauthor of "That Thang of Yours") who has been active in France, singing in Luc Besson's film *Subway* (1985) and composing the score to Gilles Behat's *Urgence* (1985).

27 Cancel, "Epic Elements," 16.

28 I mention his stature only because this bit of casting on Sembene's part is reminiscent of the short man who played the president (of the chamber of commerce, but clearly an allusion to President Senghor) in his previous film, *Xala* (1974). A satirical effect is created.

29 On Dior's silence see David Uru Iyam, "The Silent Revolutionaries: Ousmane Sembene's *Emitai*, *Xala*, and *Ceddo*," *African Studies Review* 29, no. 4 (December 1986): 81.

30 Ibid., 86.

31 Iyam explains her transformation: "Sembene hypostasizes Dior's character

by immersing her in water to give us a sense of her transformation. Thus sanctified, she attacks her captor soon after, to prepare the audience for the greater task ahead" (ibid., 83).

32 G. Wesley Johnson Jr., *The Emergence of Black Politics in Senegal*, quoted in Iyam, "The Silent Revolutionaries," 81. The Peul-language plural of *ceddo* is *cebbe*, but to avoid confusion I will use the invariable form *ceddo*.

33 Werner Glinga, "La Société *ceddo* dans le Sahel Occidental: Son idéal et ses mythes littéraires," in *Semper Aliquid Novi: Littérature comparée et littérature d'Afrique*, ed. János Riesz and Alain Ricard (Tübingen: Gunter Narr Verlag, 1990), 77, 78. Glinga discusses literary representations of the *ceddo*, including Ousmane Socé's *Karim* and Nafissatou Diallo's *Le Fort maudit*.

34 In Peul language. Samba Gadjigo, personal communication.

35 Mamadou Diouf, *Histoire du Sénégal: Le Modèle islamo-wolof et ses périphéries* (Paris: Maisonneuve et Larose, 2001), 55. See also David Richardson, "Shipboard Revolts, African Authority, and the Transatlantic Slave Trade," in *Fighting the Slave Trade: West African Strategies*, ed. Sylviane A. Diouf (Athens: Ohio University Press, 2003), 211.

36 Ayi Kwei Armah, quoted in Pfaff, *Twenty-Five Black African Filmmakers*, 254.

37 "Black-over-Black slavery and the trade of Black slaves to the White is a central element of the social world [in *Ceddo*], whose validity remains unquestioned and unnoted by any character" (Philip Rosen, *Change Mummified: Cinema, Historicity, Theory* [Minneapolis: University of Minnesota Press, 2001], 296).

38 On Sembene's use of silence see Iyam, "The Silent Revolutionaries."

39 Diouf, "History and Actuality," 245.

40 Ibid., 240.

41 Yambo Ouologuem, *Le Devoir de violence* (Paris: Seuil, 1968), 17–18; Ralph Manheim, trans., *Bound to Violence* (London: Heinemann, 1971), 11–12, AT.

42 Among other relevant films that I was not able to include here are *West Indies: Les Nègres marrons de la liberté*, by Med Hondo (1979); *La Côte des esclaves*, a documentary about Dahomey/Benin, by Elio Suhamy (1994); *Les Anneaux de la mémoire*, a documentary by Kitia Touré (1994); *Asientos*, by François Woukoache (1995). See Olivier Barlet, *African Cinemas: Decolonizing the Gaze*, trans. Chris Turner (London: Zed Books, 2000), 56–61.

43 Flora Gomes, the filmmaker from Guinea-Bissau, made this remark in a discussion at Yale University, April 11, 2005.

44 Christian Richard, email, September 28, 2005.

45 See the editorial comment in *Africultures*: "Concernant l'esclavage et la traite, c'est l'écran noir: le cinéma occidental ne touche pas à 'la chose.' Du côté français, c'est le désert" (Olivier Barlet, "Une Réflexion sur le pouvoir: Entretien avec Roger Gnoan M'Bala," *Africultures* 20 [September 1999]: 40). If there is any (other) exception in French cinema, it might be Bernard Gi-

raudeau's *Les Caprices d'un fleuve* (France, 1995), a strange, narcissistic film that nonetheless contains some striking images of the slave trade. In addition, John Berry's film *Tamango* was of course partially French.

46 A DVD of *Le Courage des autres* was produced by La Médiathèque des Trois Mondes, Paris, in 2007. See www.cine3mondes.com.

47 Brahimia Ouedraogo, "Film on Slave Trade Rekindles Reparations Debate," www.afrol.com/Categories/Culture/cu1013_slavetrade_film.htm. On the budget see Christopher Koffi, "*Adanggaman* ou la responsabilité des Africains dans l'esclavage," AFP: www.mbolo.com/afp/fespaco/09h39.asp.

48 "When *Le Courage des autres* was shown at the opening of the FESPACO in 1983, the debate revolved around the risk of reducing the West's share of the guilt [*déculpabiliser l'Occident*]" (Olivier Barlet, question addressed to director Roger Gnoan M'Bala, in "Une Réflexion sur le pouvoir," 42). Patrick Ilboudo writes, "L'esclavage des Noirs par des Noirs dont il est question dans le film est-il l'esquisse d'une esquisse de justification de la grande Traite des Noirs par les esclavagistes blancs?" (Ilboudo, *Le FESPACO*, 1969–1989: Les Cinéastes africains et leurs oeuvres [Ouagadougou: Editions La Mante, 1988], 113).

49 Deslauriers's more recent film *Biguine* (2004), set in Martinique at the time of the volcanic eruption in 1902, uses a similar technique, with very few instances of characters speaking.

50 Christian Richard, email, September 28, 2005.

51 See, e.g., Djibril Tamsir Niane, *Soundjata ou l'epopée mandingue* (Paris: Présence Africaine, 1960). Sunjata, when he becomes emperor, establishes a new system of peace and justice, protecting the weak from the abuses of the strong (147); but there is no question, of course, of abolishing slavery. Slaves remain in the margins of this epic, barely visible (see 33). The purpose of the struggle is to prevent (the nobles of) the Manding as a whole from being "enslaved" (103).

52 Barlet interview, "Une Réflexion sur le pouvoir," 40.

53 Elvis Mitchell, "Africans Making Slaves of Africans," *New York Times*, July 11, 2001, B5.

54 Alexie Tcheuyap, message posted to H-Aflitcine, February 6, 2004, www .h-net.org/~aflitweb/.

55 Roger Gnoan M'Bala, director, *Adanggaman* (Côte d'Ivoire, 2000), screenplay by Jean-Marie Adiaffi, Roger Gnoan M'Bala, and Bertin Akaffou.

56 Sory recognizes his daughter by the scarification she bears on her arm, which he gave her as a child. In a flashback Sory explains that the scar represents the *sankofa*, a bird "that is the emblem of our people" and whose cry means "all must come to an end." It seems likely that this is an allusion to a very influential film about the slave trade, Haile Gerima's *Sankofa* (1993). On the process of "reconversion" by which a young woman was transformed into an Amazon in Dahomey see Hélène D'Almeida-Topor, *Les Amazones* (Paris: Rochevigne, 1984), 52–53.

57 T, 358; Robert Cornevin, *Histoire du Dahomey* (Paris: Berger-Levrault, 1962): 105–6; and D'Almeida-Topor, *Les Amazones*, which is devoted entirely to Dahomey. John Thornton points out that "the only African state to deploy Amazons was Dahomey" (H-Africa discussion group, February 7, 2004, www .h-net.org/~africa).

58 Mia Mask compares *Adanggaman* to Berry's *Tamango*: "*Tamango* referenced (though it didn't feature) the involvement of African monarchs who happily traded bodies for perishable products" (Mia Mask, "Review: The African King; 'Adanggamman's' [*sic*] Slave Tale Sets Sights on African Complicity," *Indiewire*, www.indiewire.com/movies/rev_010712_Adanggamman.html.

59 Guy Deslauriers, director, *The Middle Passage* (France, 1999), script by Claude Chonville and Patrick Chamoiseau. English-language version, with narration written by Walter Mosely, on HBO.

60 The French voice-over narration is spoken by the Cameroonian actor Maka Kotto. Hounsou played the leader Cinqué in *Amistad*.

61 Olivier Barlet, "Entretien avec Guy Deslauriers" (Paris, March 1998), *Africultures*, www.africultures.com/index.asp?menu=affiche_article&no=384 (accessed May 29, 2007).

62 Thomas Sotinel, "Ressusciter les images de la traite négrière," *Le Monde*, February 14, 2001.

63 Barlet, "Entretien avec Guy Deslauriers."

64 *The Middle Passage* is heavily slanted toward a male point of view. The captives are male. The narrator says, "They raped *our* women and young boys and girls nightly" (emphasis added). This film thus stands in marked contrast to *Ceddo* and to *Adanggaman*, both of which foreground important female roles.

523

CONCLUSION

1 See Dominique Torrès, *Esclaves: 200 millions d'esclaves aujourd'hui* (Paris: Phébus, 1996); Sylvie O'Dy, *Esclaves en France* (Paris: Albin Michel, 2001); Anti-Slavery International, www.antislavery.org; and SOS-Esclaves, www .sos-esclaves.org.

2 Guillaume Perrault, "Deux Français sur trois saluent le 'rôle positif' de la colonisation," *Le Figaro*, December 2, 2005, 8.

3 Max Gallo, "Colonisation: La Tentation de la pénitence," *Le Figaro*, November 30, 2005, 18. See also Paul-François Paoli, interview with Max Gallo, "L'Histoire ne doit pas se confondre avec le devoir de mémoire," *Le Figaro*, November 3, 2005, 3.

4 Interview by Christian Sauvage, "Un Prix pour *Les Traites négrières*," *Le Journal du Dimanche*, June 12, 2005. On this affair see Françoise Vergès, *La Mémoire enchaînée: Questions sur l'esclavage* (Paris: Albin Michel, 2006), 124–30.

5 See above, chap. 1, n. 18. Part of the reaction also comes into focus when one

sees the "relativizing" uses made of Pétré-Grenouilleau's work by Max Gallo in Paoli, interview with Gallo, "L'Histoire ne doit pas se confondre." Gallo cites the existence of slavery and slave trading in Africa as a reason for France not to confront its own history in any manner that smacks of "culpabilisation" or "une conception pénitentielle."

6 Comité pour la mémoire de l'esclavage, *Mémoires de la traite négrière, de l'esclavage, et de leurs abolitions: Rapport à Monsieur le premier ministre* (Paris: n.p., April 12, 2005), 8–9, 12.

7 "Le Mémorial de Nantes," *Sud-Ouest*, May 9, 2006, 2; Thierry Leclère, "Ports d'attaches," *Télérama* no. 2939 (http://forums.telerama.fr/forums/B060620000416.html). On the museum see Didier Arnaud, "Le 10 mai: L'Histoire ne se fait pas en un jour," *Libération*, May 10, 2006, www.liberation.fr/page.php?Article=380884. On Nantes's recent history of memorialization see Robert Aldrich, *Vestiges of the Colonial Empire in France: Monuments, Museums, and Colonial Memories* (Gordonsville, Va.: Palgrave Macmillan, 2005), 80–83.

When the Château des Ducs de Bretagne — the main museum in Nantes — reopened in February 2007, after fifteen years of remodeling, its Web site barely mentioned the slave trade. Although space is allocated to the slave trade in the new museum, the publicity surrounding the reopening downplayed its importance. See www.chateau-nantes.fr (accessed February 8, 2007). Didier Guivarc'h, a member of the museum's advisory board, when asked in an interview how the slave trade was being treated, stated that it would be enfolded in the general history of the city ("inscrite dans l'histoire globale de la ville"); that it was important to avoid all "déploration," "repentance" and "dramaturgie." See "Un Lieu de mémoires vives sans tabous," February 6, 2007, www.nantes.maville.com/actu/re/chateau_detail/actu_10104-374280.

In fact, the museum itself, which I visited on April 30, 2007, just before this book went to press, does a good job of representing the slave trade and the prominent role that Nantes played in it. Eight out of thirty-two rooms in the museum are related to the trade. If the displays lack any compelling representation of the captives' experience before, during, and after the Middle Passage — the point of view remains quite rigorously *nantais* — perhaps it is due to the museum's fear of "dramaturgie." The panel titled "La Traversée" is a model of understatement: the captives "disposent d'un espace restreint." The Liverpool museum takes a broader approach and is more successful. One of the most impressive exhibits in the Musée du Château is the statue that was vandalized on the quays of Nantes in 1998 (referred to earlier in this study), displayed to illustrate the city's former resistance to acknowledging its history.

8 Unsigned article, "M. Chirac invite la France à assumer toute son histoire," *Le Monde*, January 30, 2006. See Edouard Glissant, *Mémoires des esclavages: La Fondation d'un centre national pour la mémoire des esclavages et de leurs*

abolitions (Paris: Gallimard, 2007). Glissant foresees the establishment of a center in Paris, with five thousand square meters of space, a staff of twenty-three, a memorial, and a goal of "transforming the very nature of the study and thinking related to the trans-Atlantic slave trade" (147).

9 "Dans l'histoire de la colonisation, ceux qui ont été jetés dans le ventre des galions, qui ont traversé l'Atlantique pour être amenés au coeur des plantations: ce sont des souvenirs qui sont vivants" (Dominique de Villepin, quoted in "La Polémique sur la loi relative au 'rôle positif' de la colonisation enfle," and in "Polémique colonisation: Chirac annonce la création d'une mission," both in *Le Monde*, December 12, 2005).

10 Françoise Vergès, "Les Troubles de mémoire: Traite négrière, esclavage et écriture de l'histoire," *Cahiers d'études africaines*, forthcoming.

11 At this point it is unclear what permanent exhibition related to slavery and the slave trade may be produced in France. See the site of the Musée des Ducs de Bretagne in Nantes: www.nantes.fr/mairie/services/responsa bilites/dgc/chateau.

12 Aimé Césaire, *Nègre je suis, nègre je resterai: Entretiens avec Françoise Vergès* (Paris: Albin Michel, 2005), 39.

13 My remarks here bear only on the remains of the French Atlantic triangle.

14 As I have stated, I reject the widely accepted notion that any recognition of African involvement in the slave trade automatically "lessens" the crime of the trade or European responsibility for what Europe did. A murderer with an accomplice is no less of a murderer. See Vergès, "Les Troubles de mémoire," 32. For an accessible overview of African involvement in the Atlantic slave trade see Elikia M'Bokolo, "La Dimension africaine de la traite des Noirs," *Le Monde diplomatique* (April 1998), www.monde-diplomatique .fr/1998/04/M_BOKOLO/10269.

15 Such an algorithm is implied in the Dakar Declaration and Programme of Action (the product of a meeting that was held to prepare for the World Conference against Racism, Racial Discrimination, Xenophobia, and Related Intolerance (Durban, South Africa, August 31–September 7, 2001): "an International Compensation Scheme to be set up for the *victims* of the slave trade" (emphasis added). The problem with this is reflected in the very significant ellipsis that that phrasing encompasses: there are no victims of the Atlantic slave trade living now, only *descendants* of those victims. The declaration makes the mistake of conflating past and present. The proposal is thus doubly vexed: it suggests a form of reckoning that would be impossible because it attempts to apply the past directly to the present, and it suppresses the distance between the past and the present in its usage of the term *victims*. (Descendants of victims of the Atlantic slave trade are indeed victims of inequality and exploitation now, but economic and social justice should not be subjected to a genealogical test.) The declaration's second proposal makes more sense to me because it is oriented toward the present and the future: "a Development Reparation Fund to be set up to provide resources for the development pro-

525

cess in countries affected by colonialism." Quoted in United Nations Office of the High Commissioner for Human Rights, *Newsletter of the World Conference against Racism Secretariat* 3 (April 2001), 4. Furthermore, parsing the extent to which Africa's development was inhibited by the slave trade—an important task—will not provide a solution to Africa's contemporary problems, either. The rich nations of the earth should aid Africa *now*—or at least give it a fair shot at helping itself, for example, by reducing subsidies to farmers in the nations of the North—because Africa is poor *now*.

16   Tierno Monénembo, *Pelourinho* (Paris: Seuil, 1995), 150. The same narrator adds, "Je veux rabibocher le présent et l'autrefois" (150).

17   See fr.wikipedia.org/wiki/Commerce_triangulaire (accessed February 21, 2007). I cite *Wikipedia* precisely because it is a reflection of the popular Zeitgeist more than a voice of official academic research. I modified this bibliography on December 8, 2006, adding some of the works of fiction discussed in this study.

18   Barry Unsworth, *Sacred Hunger* (New York: Norton, 1992). The recent French literary efforts that I have seen fall short of the mark—by which I mean a standard of truly *compelling* literature, capable of generating deep insights into the history and culture of the French slave trade: the standard set by works like Glissant's *Le Quatrième siècle* and *Sartorius*. Recent French works include André Coupleux, *Moi, Pierre Tessier, capitaine du "Jason"* (Paris: Belfond, 1983); Jean-Pierre Gourmelon, *Les Crins du négrier* (Rennes: Terre de Brume, 2000); Paul Ohl (a Québecois), *Les Chaînes de Gorée* (Paris: Presses de la Cité, 2000); and Daniel Vaxelaire, *Chasseur de Noirs* (N.p.: Editions Orphie, 2000). *Procès d'un négrier*, by Marc Tardieu (Monaco: Editions du Rocher, 2007), comes closer than any other recent metropolitan French novel that I have found to fulfilling the need for accurate representations of the slave trade. As a purposefully historical novel, it cites real names and events, including the Mosneron family, the affair of the *Vigilante*, and the *Jeune Estelle*. But, classified and sold as a *roman historique*, not very artfully written, and displaying some of the didactic awkwardness of the genre, *Procès d'un négrier* is unlikely to have a broad impact.

19   See Nicolas Sarkozy's speech on the evening of his election, in which he repeated something that he had been saying during his campaign: "Je vais en finir avec la repentance qui est une forme de haine de soi et la concurrance des mémoires qui nourrit la haine des autres" ("Verbatim: La France a choisi le changement," *Le Monde*, May 8, 2007, 4). See also Laetitia Van Eeckhout, "Opposé à la repentance, M. Sarkozy participe à la commémoration de l'abolition de l'esclavage," *Le Monde*, May 10, 2007.

⇥ SELECTED BIBLIOGRAPHY ⇤

Abanime, Emeka. 1979. "Voltaire antiesclavagiste." *Studies on Voltaire and the Eighteenth Century* 182:237–51.

Abernethy, David B. 2000. *The Dynamics of Global Dominance: European Overseas Empires, 1415–1980.* New Haven: Yale University Press.

L'Affaire de "La Vigilante," batiment négrier de Nantes. 1823. Paris: Imprimerie de Crapelet.

Aldridge, A. Owen. 1975. *Voltaire and the Century of Light.* Princeton: Princeton University Press.

Alfonse, Jean (Fontenau, "de Saintonge"). 1559. *Les Voyages avantureux du capitaine Ian Alfonce, Sainctongeois.* Poitiers: Au Pelican.

———. 1904 (first published 1544). *La Cosmographie avec l'espère et régime du soleil et du nord.* Paris: Ernest Leroux.

Alletz, Edouard. 1823. *L'Abolition de la traite des Noirs.* Paris: Delaunay.

Amidou, Ibrahim Boukari. 2002. "Evolution de la représentation de l'Afrique et des Africains dans *L'Encyclopédie* de Diderot et au cours du siècle des Lumières, *Tamango* de Mérimée, le *Roman d'un spahi* de Pierre Loti, et *Voyage au Congo* de Gide: Humanisme, exotisme, et colonialisme." Ph.D. diss., University of Cincinnati.

Amselle, Jean-Loup. 1996. *Vers un multiculturalisme français: L'Empire de la coutume.* Paris: Aubier.

Les Anneaux de la mémoire: Itinéraires de l'exposition. 1993. Catalogue of Exposition, Château des Ducs de Bretagne, Nantes.

Antoine, Régis. 1974. "Aventures d'un jeune négrier français d'après un manuscrit inédit du XVIIIe siècle." *Notes africaines* 141 (Jan.): 51–56.

Aravamudan, Srinivas. 1999. *Tropicopolitans: Colonialism and Agency, 1688–1804.* Durham: Duke University Press.

Armah, Ayi Kwei. 1973. *Two Thousand Seasons.* London: Heinemann.

Arrighi, Giovanni. 1994. *The Long Twentieth Century: Money, Power, and the Origins of Our Times.* London: Verso.

Augeard, Eugène. 1901. *La Traite des Noirs avant 1790 au point de vue du commerce nantais*. Nantes: R. Guist'hau, A. Dugas.

Austen, Ralph. 2001. "The Slave Trade as History and Memory: Confrontations of Slaving Voyage Documents and Communal Traditions." *William and Mary Quarterly* 58, no. 1 (Jan.): 229–44.

Bailyn, Bernard. 2001. "Considering the Slave Trade: History and Memory." *William and Mary Quarterly* 58, no. 1 (Jan.): 245–51.

Banbuck, Cabuzel Andréa. 1972. *Histoire politique, économique et sociale de la Martinique sous l'Ancien Régime (1635–1789)*. Fort-de-France: Société de Distribution et de Culture, 1972.

Banks, Kenneth J. 2002. *Chasing Empire across the Sea: Communications and the State in the French Atlantic, 1713–1763*. Montreal: McGill-Queen's University Press.

Baquaqua, Mohammah Gardo, and Samuel Moore. 2001 (first published 1854). *The Biography of Mahommah Gardo Baquaqua: His Passage from Slavery to Freedom in Africa and America*. Ed. Robin Law and Paul E. Lovejoy. Princeton: Marcus Wiener.

Barbot, Jean (John). 1978. "Journal d'un voyage de traite en Guinée, à Cayenne et aux Antilles fait par Jean Barbot en 1678–1679," ed. Gabriel Debien, Maurice Delafosse, et G. Thilmans. *Bulletin de l'Institut Fondamental d'Afrique Noire* 40, no. 2 (April): 235–395.

Bardoux, Agénor. 1898. *La Duchesse de Duras*. Paris: Calmann Lévy.

Barlet, Olivier. 2000. *African Cinemas: Decolonizing the Gaze*. Trans. Chris Turner. London: Zed Books.

Barrois, Martial. 1823. *L'Abolition de la traite des Noirs*. Paris: Firmin Didot.

Barry, Boubacar. 1972. *Le Royaume du Waalo: Le Sénégal avant la conquête*. Paris: Maspero.

———. 1998. *Senegambia and the Atlantic Slave Trade*. Trans. Ayi Kwei Armah. Cambridge: Cambridge University Press.

Baucom, Ian. 2001. "Globalit, Inc.; or, The Cultural Logic of Global Literary Studies." *PMLA* 116, no. 1 (Jan.): 158–72.

———. 2001. "Specters of the Atlantic." *The South Atlantic Quarterly* 100, no. 1:61–82.

———. 2005. *Specters of the Atlantic: Finance Capital, Slavery, and the Philosophy of History*. Durham: Duke University Press.

Behn, Aphra. 1992. *Oroonoko, The Rover, and Other Works*. London: Penguin.

Bellon de Saint-Quentin, Jean. 1764. *Dissertation sur la traite et le commerce des Nègres*. N.p.: N.p.

Bénot, Yves. 1963. "Diderot, Pechmeja, Raynal, et l'anticolonialisme." *Europe* 41 (Jan.–Feb.): 137–53.

———. 1992. *La Démence coloniale sous Napoléon*. Paris: La Découverte.

Bénot, Yves, and Marcel Dorigny, eds. 2003. *Rétablissement de l'esclavage dans les colonies françaises: 1802*. Paris: Maisonneuve and Larose.

Bernabé, Jean, Patrick Chamoiseau, and Raphaël Confiant. 1993. *Eloge de la créolité*. Paris and Baltimore: Gallimard and Johns Hopkins University Press.

Berry, John. 1957. *Tamango*. Film. France.

Besson, Maurice. 1928. "La Police des Noirs sous Louis XVI en France." *Revue de l'histoire des colonies françaises* 16, no. 21:433–46.

Billy, André. 1959. *Mérimée*. Paris: Flammarion.

Blackburn, Robin. 1997. *The Making of New World Slavery: From the Baroque to the Modern, 1492–1800*. London: Verso.

Blanc, Olivier. 2003. *Olympe de Gouges: Une Humaniste à la fin du XVIIIe siècle*. Paris: René Viénet.

Bogle, Donald. 1997. *Dorothy Dandridge*. New York: Amistad.

Boilat, Abbé David. 1984 (first published 1853). *Esquisses sénégalaises*. Paris: Karthala.

Bolster, W. Jeffrey. 1997. *Black Jacks: African American Seamen in the Age of Sail*. Cambridge, Mass.: Harvard University Press.

Bongie, Chris. 1998. *Islands and Exiles: The Creole Identities of Post/colonial Literature*. Stanford: Stanford University Press.

Boufflers, Stanislas, Chevalier de. 1998. *Lettres d'Afrique à Madame de Sabran*. Paris: Actes Sud.

Boukman, Daniel. 1971. *Les Négriers: Pièce en trois parties*. Paris: Pierre Jean Oswald.

Bourgeon, François. 1994. *Le Bois d'ébène*. Brussels: Casterman.

———. 1994. *Le Comptoir de Juda*. Brussels: Casterman.

Braudel, Fernand. 1984. *The Perspective of the World*. Vol. 3 of *Civilization and Capitalism, 15th–18th Century*. Translated from the French by Siân Reynolds. New York: Harper and Row.

Breteau, Jean, and Marcel Lancelin. 1998. *Des Chaînes à la liberté: Choix de textes français sur les traites négrières et l'esclavage de 1615 à 1848*. Rennes: Éditions Apogée.

Broglie, Achille Charles Léonce Victor, Duc de. 1822. "Discours prononcé par M le Duc de Broglie à la Chambre des Pairs le 28 mars 1822 sur la Traite des Nègres." Paris: Société de la Morale Chrétienne, Comité pour L'Abolition de la Traite des Nègres.

Brooks, George E. 2003. *Eurafricans in Western Africa: Commerce, Social Status, Gender, and Religious Observance from the Sixteenth to the Eighteenth Century*. Athens: Ohio University Press.

Brown, Gregory S. 2002. *A Field of Honor: Writers, Court Culture and Public Theater in French Literary Life from Racine to the Revolution*. New York: Columbia University Press. E-book available through www.gutenberg-e.org.

Buck-Morss, Susan. 2000. "Hegel and Haiti." *Critical Inquiry* 26 (summer): 821–65.

Burg, B. R. 1995. *Sodomy and the Pirate Tradition: English Sea Rovers in the Seventeenth-Century Caribbean*. New York: New York University Press.

Burton, Richard D. E. 1994. *La Famille coloniale: La Martinique et la mère patrie 1789–1992*. Paris: L'Harmattan.

———. 1997. *Le Roman marron: Études sur la littérature martiniquaise contemporaine*. Paris: L'Harmattan.

529

Caligny, Aténor de. 1834. "Une Ruse de négrier." *Revue maritime* 2 (1834): 107–11.

Carretta, Vincent, ed. 1996. *Unchained Voices: An Anthology of Black Authors in the English-Speaking World of the Eighteenth Century.* Lexington: University Press of Kentucky.

———. 1999. "Olaudah Equiano or Gustavus Vassa? New Light on an Eighteenth-Century Question of Identity." *Slavery and Abolition* 20, no. 3 (Dec.): 96–105.

———. 2005. *Equiano the African: Biography of a Self-Made Man.* Athens: University of Georgia Press.

Césaire, Aimé. 1939. "Cahier d'un retour au pays natal." *Volontés* 20:23–51.

———. 1961. *Toussaint Louverture: La Révolution Française et le problème colonial.* Paris: Présence Africaine.

———. 1983. *The Collected Poetry.* Translated by Clayton Eshleman and Annette Smith. Berkeley: University of California Press.

———. 1994. *Cahier d'un retour au pays natal.* Edited by Abiola Irele. Ibadan: New Horn Press.

Chalons, Serge, Christian Jean-Etienne, Suzy Landau, and André Yébakima, eds. 2000. *De l'esclavage aux réparations.* Paris: Karthala.

Chamoiseau, Patrick. 1997. *L'Esclave vieil homme et le molosse.* Paris: Gallimard.

Chamoiseau, Patrick, and Raphaël Confiant. 1991. *Lettres créoles: Tracées antillaises et continentales de la littérature, 1635–1975.* Paris: Hatier.

Charara, Youmna. 2005. *Fictions coloniales du XVIIIe siècle: Ziméo; Lettres africaines; Adonis, ou le bon nègre, anecdote coloniale.* Paris: L'Harmattan.

Chaussinand-Nogaret, Guy. 1979. *La Vie quotidienne des Français sous Louis XV.* Paris: Hachette.

Chauvet, J. J. V. 1823. *L'Abolition de la traite des Noirs.* Paris: Firmin Didot.

Clark, Vèvè A. 1991. "Developing Diaspora Literacy and *Marasa* Consciousness." In *Comparative American Identities: Race, Sex, and Nationality in the Modern Text*, ed. Hortense Spillers, 40–61. New York: Routledge.

Clarkson, Thomas. 1788. *An Essay on the Impolicy of the African Slave Trade.* London: J. Phillips.

———. 1789. *Essai sur les désavantages politiques de la Traite des Nègres.* Trans. M. Gramagnac. Paris: Société des Amis des Noirs.

———. 1821. *Le Cri des Africains contre leurs oppresseurs.* Trans. B. La Roche. London: Société de la Morale Chrétienne.

———. n.d. *The Cries of Africa, to the Inhabitants of Europe; or, A Survey of That Bloody Commerce Called the Slave-Trade.* London: Harvey and Darton.

Cohen, Margaret. 1999. *The Sentimental Education of the Novel.* Princeton: Princeton University Press.

———. 2003. "Traveling Genres." *New Literary History* 34, no. 3 (summer): 481–99.

Cohen, William B. 1980. *The French Encounter with Africans: White Response to Blacks, 1530–1880.* Bloomington: Indiana University Press.

Comité pour la Mémoire de l'Esclavage. *Mémoires de la traite négrière, de l'esclavage*

et de leurs abolitions: Rapport à monsieur le premier ministre. April 12, 2005. www
.comite-memoire-esclavage.fr.

Condé, Maryse. 1976. *Hérémakhonon.* Paris: Union Générale d'Editions.

———. 1982. *Heremakhonon: A Novel.* Trans. Richard Philcox. Washington: Three
Continents Press.

———. 1984. *Ségou: Les Murailles de terre.* Paris: Robert Laffont.

———. 1985. *Ségou: La Terre en miettes.* Paris: Robert Laffont.

———. 1987. "Notes sur un retour au pays natal." *Conjonction* 176, supplement:
7–23.

———. 1988. *En Attendant le bonheur (Heremakhonon).* Paris: Robert Laffont.

———. 1995. "Language and Power: Words as Miraculous Weapons." *CLA Journal*
39, no. 1 (Sep.): 18–25.

Condorcet, Marie-Jean-Antoine-Nicolas de Caritat, Marquis de. 1788. *Réflexions
sur l'esclavage des Nègres par M. Schwartz, pasteur . . . à Bienne.* Neufchatel: Chez
Froullé.

———. 1804. *Oeuvres complètes.* Paris: Chez Henrichs.

———. 1999 (first published 1781). "Reflections on Black Slavery." In *The Enlightenment: Cambridge Readings in the History of Political Thought,* ed. David
Williams, 308–16. Cambridge: Cambridge University Press.

Confiant, Raphaël. 1993. *Aimé Césaire: Une Traversée paradoxale du siècle.* Paris:
Stock.

Cooper, Anna J. 1925. *L'Attitude de la France à l'égard de l'esclavage pendant la Révolution.* Paris: Imprimerie de la Cour l'Appel.

Cooper, James Fenimore. 1991. *Sea Tales: The Pilot, Red Rover.* New York: Library
of America.

Coquery-Vidrovitch, Catherine. 1985. "The Colonial Economy of the Former
French, Belgian, and Portuguese Zones, 1914–1935." In *General History of Africa.*
Vol. 7, *Africa under Colonial Domination, 1880–1935,* ed. A. Adu Boahen, 351–81.
Paris: UNESCO.

Corbière, Edouard. 1823. *Elégies brésiliennes, suivies de poésies diverses, et d'une
notice sur la traite des Noirs.* Paris: Plancher, Brissot-Thivars.

———. 1832. *Le Négrier: Aventures de mer.* 2 vols. Paris: Denain.

———. 1833. *Contes de bord.* Paris: Lecointe et Pougin.

———. 1834. *Le Négrier: Aventures de mer.* 4 vols. Paris: A.-J. Dénain et Delamare.

———. 1846. *Cric-crac: Roman maritime.* Paris: Librarie spéciale pour les cabinets
de lecture.

———. 1978. *La Mer et les marins: Scènes maritimes.* Berrien: Morvran.

———. 1979. *Le Négrier: Aventures de mer.* Paris: Nouvelles Editions Baudinière.

———. 1990. *Le Négrier.* Paris: Klincksieck.

———. 2000. *Les Pilotes de l'Iroise.* Paris: José Corti.

———. 2002. *Le Négrier.* Saint-Malo: L'Ancre de Marine.

Cottias, Myriam, ed. 1998. *D'une abolition l'autre: Anthologie raisonnée de textes con-*

531

sacrés à la seconde abolition de l'esclavage dans les colonies françaises. Marseille: Agone.

Couchoro, Félix. 1983 (first published 1929). *L'Esclave.* Paris: Akpagnon.

Cowley, Malcolm, and Daniel P. Mannix. 1994. "The Middle Passage." In *The Atlantic Slave Trade*, ed. David Northrup, 99–111. Lexington, Mass.: Heath.

Crété, Liliane. 1989. *La Traite des nègres sous l'ancien régime: Le Nègre, le sucre et la toile.* Paris: Librairie Académique Perrin.

Cugoano, Quobna Ottobah. 1995 (first published 1787). *Thoughts and Sentiments on the Evil and Wicked Traffic of the Slavery and Commerce of the Human Species, Humbly Submitted to the Inhabitants of Great Britain, by Ottobah Cugoano, a Native of Africa.* Excerpts. In *Black Atlantic Writers of the Eighteenth Century: Living the New Exodus in England and the Americas*, ed. Adam Potkay and Sandra Burr, 125–56. New York: St. Martin's.

Curtin, Philip D., ed. 1967. *Africa Remembered: Narratives by West Africans from the Era of the Slave Trade.* Madison: University of Wisconsin Press.

———. 1969. *The Atlantic Slave Trade: A Census.* Madison: University of Wisconsin Press.

———. 1998. *The Rise and Fall of the Plantation Complex.* 2nd ed. Cambridge: Cambridge University Press.

Daget, Serge. 1969. "J. E. Morenas à Paris: L'Action abolitionniste, 1819–1821." *Bulletin de l'Institut Fondamental d'Afrique Noire* 31, no. 3 (July): 875–85.

———. 1971. "L'Abolition de la traite des Noirs en France de 1814 à 1831." *Cahiers d'études africaines* 11, no. 1:14–58.

———. 1973. "Les mots esclave, nègre, Noir, et les jugements de valeur sur la traite négrière dans la littérature abolitionniste française de 1770 à 1845." *Revue française d'histoire d'outre-mer* 60, no. 221:511–48.

———. 1978 and 1984. *Répertoire des expéditions négrières françaises au XVIIIe siècle.* Paris: Société Française d'Histoire d'Outre-Mer. 2 volumes.

———. 1985. "The Abolition of the Slave Trade by France: The Decisive Years, 1826–1831." In Richardson, *Abolition and Its Aftermath*, 141–67.

———. 1985. *De la traite à l'esclavage: Actes du colloque international sur la traite des Noirs, Nantes, 1985.* Nantes: CHRMA-SFHOM.

———. 1988. *Répertoire des expéditions négrières à la traite illégale (1814–1850).* Nantes: Centre de Recherche sur l'Histoire du Monde Atlantique.

———. 1990. *La Traite des Noirs: Bastilles négrières et velléités abolitionnistes.* Rennes: Editions Ouest-France.

———. 1994. "Une mémoire sans monument: La Traite." In *La Dernière traite: Fragments d'histoire en hommage à Serge Daget*, ed. Hubert Gerbeau and Eric Saugera, 283–91. Paris: Société Française d'Histoire d'Outre-Mer.

Damas, Léon. 1956. *Black-Label: Poèmes.* Paris: Gallimard.

Damon, Rodolphe. 2004. *Joseph Crassous de Médeuil, 1741–1793: Marchand, officier de la Marine royale et négrier.* Paris: Karthala.

Dash, J. Michael. 1995. *Edouard Glissant.* Cambridge: Cambridge University Press.

————. 1998. *The Other America: Caribbean Literature in a New World Context.* Charlottesville: University Press of Virginia.

Davis, David Brion. 1966. *The Problem of Slavery in Western Culture.* Ithaca: Cornell University Press.

————. 1975. *The Problem of Slavery in the Age of Revolution: 1770–1823.* Ithaca: Cornell University Press.

————. 1984. *Slavery and Human Progress.* Oxford: Oxford University Press.

————. 2001. "Slavery—White, Black, Muslim, Christian." *New York Review of Books,* July 5, 51–55.

Davis, Gregson. 1997. *Aimé Césaire.* Cambridge: Cambridge University Press.

Davis, Natalie Zemon. 2000. *Slaves on Screen: Film and Historical Vision.* Cambridge, Mass.: Harvard University Press.

Dayan, Joan. 1995. *Haiti, History, and the Gods.* Berkeley: University of California Press.

————. 1996. "Paul Gilroy's Slaves, Ships, and Routes: The Middle Passage as Metaphor." *Research in African Literatures* 27, no. 4:7–14.

Debbasch, Yvan. 1963. "Poésie et traite: L'Opinion française sur le commerce négrier au début du XIXe siècle." *Revue française d'histoire d'outre-mer* 172–173 (Jan.): 311–52.

Debien, Gabriel. 1942. *Le Peuplement des Antilles françaises au XVIIe siècle: Les Engagés partis de La Rochelle.* Cairo: Notes d'histoire coloniale II.

————.1953. *Les Colons de Saint-Domingue et la Révolution: Essai sur le Club Massiac.* Paris: Armand Colin.

————. 1974. *Les Esclaves aux Antilles françaises (XVIIe–XVIIIe siècles).* Basse-Terre: Société d'Histoire de la Guadeloupe.

Defoe, Daniel. 1907 (first published 1720). *The Life, Adventures, and Piracies of the Famous Captain Singleton.* Vol. 6 of *The Works of Daniel Defoe.* New York: Jenson Society.

Delacampagne, Christian. 2002. *Une Histoire de l'esclavage: De l'antiquité à nos jours.* Paris: Librairie Générale Française.

Delas, Daniel. 1991. *Aimé Césaire.* Paris: Hachette.

Delavigne, Casimir. 1820. *Les Vêpres siciliennes.* Paris: Barba.

Deleuze, Gilles, and Félix Guattari. 1977. *Anti-Oedipus: Capitalism and Schizophrenia.* Trans. Robert Hurley, Mark Seem, and Helen R. Lane. New York: Viking, 1977.

Demanet, Abbé. 1767. *Nouvelle histoire de l'Afrique françoise.* Paris: Chez la Veuve Duchesne.

De Raedt, Thérèse. 2000. "Ourika en noir et blanc: Une Femme africaine en France." Ph.D. diss., University of California, Davis.

Deschamps, Hubert. 1971. *Histoire de la traite des Noirs de l'antiquité à nos jours.* Paris: Fayard.

Description d'un navire négrier. Undated pamphlet in Bibliothèque Nationale de France, 8-R PIECE-2641.

Deslauriers, Guy. 1999. *Middle Passage (Passage du milieu).* Film. France.

533

Desnoyers, Charles, and M. Alboize. 1843 (debuted 1835). *La Traite des Noirs*. In *Magasin théatral*. Vol. 5:1–32. Paris: Marchant.

Deveau, Jean-Michel. 1994. *La France au temps des négriers*. Paris: France-Empire.

Diène, Doudou, ed. 1998. *La Chaîne et le lien: Une Vision de la traite négrière*. Paris: UNESCO.

Dietrich, Maria, Henry Louis Gates Jr., and Carl Pedersen. 1999. *Black Imagination and the Middle Passage*. New York: Oxford University Press.

Diouf, Mamadou. 2001. *Histoire du Sénégal: Le Modèle islamo-wolof et ses périphéries*. Paris: Maisonneuve et Larose.

Diouf, Sylviane A., ed. 2003. *Fighting the Slave Trade: West African Strategies*. Athens: Ohio University Press, 2003.

Dobie, Madeleine. 2001. *Foreign Bodies: Gender, Language, and Culture in French Orientalism*. Stanford: Stanford University Press.

Doin, Sophie. 2002 (first published 1825 and 1828). *La Famille noire, suivie de trois nouvelles blanches et noires*. Paris: L'Harmattan.

———. 2005 (first published 1824). *La Chaumière africaine, ou histoire d'une famille française jetée sur la côte occidentale de l'Afrique à la suite du naufrage de la frégate "La Méduse."* Paris: L'Harmattan.

Dorigny, Marcel. 1995. *Les Abolitions de l'esclavage: De L. F. Sonthonax à V. Schoelcher*. Paris: Presses Universitaires de Vincennes.

Dozon, Jean-Pierre. 2003. *Frères et sujets: La France et l'Afrique en perspective*. Paris: Flammarion.

Dubois, Laurent. 1998. *Les Esclaves de la République: L'Histoire oubliée de la première émancipation, 1789–1794*. Paris: Calmann-Lévy.

———. 2004. *Avengers of the New World: The Story of the Haitian Revolution*. Cambridge, Mass.: Harvard University Press.

———. 2004. *A Colony of Citizens: Revolution and Slave Emancipation in the French Caribbean, 1787–1804*. Chapel Hill: University of North Carolina Press.

Du Bois, W. E. B. 1915. *The Negro*. New York: Henry Holt.

———. 1965. *The World and Africa: An Inquiry into the Part Which Africa Has Played in World History*. New York: International Publishers.

Ducasse, André. 1948. *Les Négriers ou le trafic des esclaves*. Paris: Hachette.

Duchet, Michèle. 1977. *Anthropologie et histoire au siècle des lumières*. Paris: Flammarion.

Ducoeurjoly, S. J. 1802. *Manuel des habitans de Saint-Domingue*. 2 vols. Paris: Lenoir.

Dumas, Alexandre. 1974 (first published 1843). *Georges*. Paris: Gallimard.

Durand, Robert. 1731. *Journal de bord d'un négrier*. Manuscript, Beinecke Rare Book Library, Yale University.

Duras, Claire de. 1826. *Ourika*. Paris: Ladvocat.

———. 1983 (first published 1825). *Edouard*. Paris: Mercure de France.

———. 1994 (first published 1823). *Ourika: The Original French Text*, ed. Joan DeJean, introd. by Joan DeJean and Margaret Waller. New York: Modern Language Association.

————. 1998. *Ourika: Nouvelle édition revue et augmentée*, ed. Roger Little. Exeter: University of Exeter Press.

Du Tertre, Jean-Baptiste. 1667. *Histoire générale des Antilles habitées par les François*. 3 vols. Paris: Thomas Iolly.

Eltis, David. 2000. *The Rise of African Slavery in the Americas*. Cambridge: Cambridge University Press.

————. 2001. "The Volume and Structure of the Transatlantic Slave Trade: A Reassessment." *William and Mary Quarterly* 58, no. 1 (Jan.): 17–46.

Eltis, David, Stephen D. Behrendt, David Richardson, and Herbert S. Klein. 1999. *The Trans-Atlantic Slave Trade: A Database on CD-ROM*. Cambridge: Cambridge University Press.

Eltis, David, and James Walvin, eds. 1981. *The Abolition of the Atlantic Slave Trade: Origins and Effects in Europe, Africa, and the Americas*. Madison: University of Wisconsin Press.

Emerigon, Balthazard-Marie. 1828. *Traité des assurances et des contrats à la grosse*. Ed. P. S. Boulay-Paty. Rennes: Molliex.

Emmer, Pieter. 1993. "Capitalism after Slavery? The French Slave Trade and Slavery in the Atlantic, 1500–1900." *Slavery and Abolition* 14, no. 3 (Dec.): 234–47.

Endore, Guy. 1991 (first published 1934). *Babouk*. New York: Monthly Review Press.

Equiano, Olaudah. 1983. *La Véridique histoire d'Olaudah Equiano, Africain, esclave aux Caraïbes, homme libre*. Trans. Claire-Lise Charbonnier. Paris: Editions Caribéennes.

————. 2001 (first published 1789). *The Interesting Narrative of the Life of Olaudah Equiano, or Gustavus Vassa, the African, Written by Himself*. Ed. Werner Sollors. New York: Norton.

————. 2002. *Olaudah Equiano ou Gustavus Vassa: Le Passionnant récit de ma vie*. Trans. and ed. Regine Mfoumou-Arthur. Paris: L'Harmattan.

Fabre, Geneviève. 1999. "The Slave Ship Dance." In *Black Imagination and the Middle Passage*, ed. Maria Dietrich, Henry Louis Gates Jr., and Carl Pedersen, 33–46. New York: Oxford University Press.

Faits relatifs à la traite des Noirs, suivis de détails sur la colonie de Sierra-Léone, publiés par un comité nommé par la société religieuse des Amis, pour concourir à l'abolition complète de la traite des Noirs. 1824. Paris: Lachevardière fils.

Falconbridge, Alexander. 1788. *An Account of the Slave Trade on the Coast of Africa*. London: J. Phillips.

Fanon, Frantz. 1952. *Peau noire, masques blancs*. Paris: Seuil.

————. 1967. *Black Skin, White Masks*. Trans. Charles Lam Markmann. New York: Grove Press.

————. 1991 (first published 1961). *Les Damnés de la terre*. Paris: Gallimard, 1991.

————. 2004. *The Wretched of the Earth*. Trans. Richard Philcox. New York: Grove Press.

Fast, Howard. 1996 (first published 1951). *Spartacus*. Armonk, NY: North Castle Books.

535

Ferro, Marc, ed. 2003. *Le Livre noir du colonialisme: XVIe–XXIe siècle, de l'extermination à la repentance*. Paris: Robert Laffont.

Fick, Carolyn E. 1990. *The Making of Haiti: The Saint Domingue Revolution from Below*. Knoxville: University of Tennessee Press.

Findlay, Ronald. 1990. "The 'Triangular Trade' and the Atlantic Economy of the Eighteenth Century: A Simple General-Equilibrium Model." *Essays in International Finance*, no. 177 (March). Department of Economics, Princeton University.

Fischer, Sibylle. 2004. *Modernity Disavowed: Haiti and the Cultures of Slavery in the Age of Revolution*. Durham: Duke University Press.

Foster, Gwendolyn Audrey. 1999. *Captive Bodies: Postcolonial Subjectivity in Cinema*. Albany: State University of New York Press.

Fouchard, Jean. 1953. *Les Marrons du syllabaire: Quelques aspects du problème de l'instruction et de l'éducation des esclaves et affranchis de Saint-Domingue*. Port-au-Prince: Henri Deschamps.

————. 1955. *Artistes et répertoire des scènes de Saint-Domingue*. Port-au-Prince: Imprimerie de l'Etat.

————. 1988. *Le Théâtre à Saint-Domingue*. Port-au-Prince: Henri Deschamps.

Gadjigo, Samba. 1996. "Ousmane Sembene: Les Enjeux du cinéma et de la littérature." In *Littérature et cinéma en Afrique francophone: Ousmane Sembene et Assia Djebar*, ed. Sada Niang, 110–21. Paris: L'Harmattan.

————. Forthcoming. *Ousmane Sembene: La Formation de l'artiste militant*. Paris: Présence Africaine.

Gallagher, Mary. 2002. *Soundings in French Caribbean Writing since 1950: The Shock of Time and Space*. Oxford: Oxford University Press.

Garraway, Doris. 2005. *The Libertine Colony: Creolization in the Early French Caribbean*. Durham: Duke University Press.

Gates, Henry Louis, Jr. 1988. *The Signifying Monkey: A Theory of Afro-American Literary Criticism*. New York: Oxford University Press.

Gauthier, Florence, ed. 2002. *Périssent les colonies plutôt qu'un principe! Contributions à l'histoire de l'abolition de l'esclavage, 1789–1804*. Paris: Société des Etudes Robespierristes.

Gautier, Arlette. 1985. *Les Sœurs de Solitude: La Condition féminine dans l'esclavage aux Antilles du XVIIe au XIXe siècle*. Paris: Editions Caribéennes.

Geggus, David. 1996. "The Slaves and Free Coloreds of Martinique during the Age of the French and Haitian Revolutions." In *The Lesser Antilles in the Age of European Expansion*, ed. Robert L. Paquette and Stanley L. Engerman, 280–301. Gainesville: University Press of Florida.

————. 2001. "The French Slave Trade: An Overview." *William and Mary Quarterly* 58, no. 1 (Jan.): 119–38.

————, ed. 2001. *The Impact of the Haitian Revolution in the Atlantic World*. Columbia: University of South Carolina Press.

————. 2002. *Haitian Revolutionary Studies*. Bloomington: Indiana University Press.

Gerbeau, Hubert, and Eric Saugera. 1994. *La Dernière traite: Fragments d'histoire en hommage à Serge Daget*. Paris: Société Française d'Histoire d'Outre-Mer.

Getz, Trevor R. 2004. *Slavery and Reform in West Africa: Toward Emancipation in Nineteenth-Century Senegal and the Gold Coast*. Athens: Ohio University Press.

Gilroy, Paul. 1993. *The Black Atlantic: Modernity and Double Consciousness*. Cambridge, Mass.: Harvard University Press.

Giraudeau, Bernard. 1995. *Les Caprices d'un fleuve*. DVD. France.

Gisler, Antoine. 1981. *L'Esclavage aux Antilles Françaises (XVIIe–XIXe siècle): Contribution au problème de l'esclavage*. Paris: Karthala.

Glissant, Edouard. 1964. *Le Quatrième siècle*. Paris: Gallimard.

———. 1965. *Les Indes, Un Champ d'îles, La Terre inquiète*. Paris: Seuil.

———. 1969. *L'Intention poétique*. Paris: Seuil.

———. 1981. *Le Discours antillais*. Paris: Seuil.

———. 1993. *Tout-Monde: Roman*. Paris: Gallimard.

———. 1997 (first published 1981). *La Case du commandeur*. Paris: Gallimard.

———. 1999. *Sartorius: Le Roman des Batoutos*. Paris: Gallimard.

———. 2001. *The Fourth Century*. Trans. Betsy Wing. Lincoln: University of Nebraska Press.

———. 2003. *Ormerod*. Paris: Gallimard.

———. 2005. *La Cohée du Lamentin: Poétique V*. Paris: Gallimard.

———. 2005. *The Collected Poems of Edouard Glissant*. Trans. Jeff Humphries. Minneapolis: University of Minnesota Press.

Gnoan M'Bala, Roger. 2000. *Adanggaman*. Film. Côte d'Ivoire.

Golbéry, Silvain-Meinrad-Xavier de. 1802. *Fragmens d'un voyage en Afrique*. Paris: Chez Trettel et Würtz.

Gouges, Olympe de. 1788. *Oeuvres de Madame de Gouges*. Paris: Chez l'Auteur et Chez Cailleau.

———. 1788. *Zamore et Mirza, ou l'heureux naufrage: Drame indien, en trois actes et en prose*. Paris: Chez l'Auteur et Chez Cailleau.

———. 1790. *Réponse au champion américain ou colon très aisé à connaître*. Jan. 18. Paris: n.p.

———. 1792. *L'Esclavage des Noirs ou l'heureux naufrage*. Paris: Chez la Veuve Duchesne.

———. 1993. *Ecrits politiques, 1788–1791*. Paris: Côté-Femmes.

Grandpré, Louis-Marie-Joseph Ohier, Comte de. 1801. *Voyage à la côte occidentale d'Afrique fait dans les années 1786 et 1787*. 2 vols. Paris: Dentu.

Green, James. 1995. "The Publishing History of Olaudah Equiano's *Interesting Narrative*." *Slavery and Abolition* 16, no. 3 (Dec.): 362–75.

Grégoire, Abbé Henri. 1815. *De la Traite et de l'esclavage des Noirs et des Blancs par un ami des hommes de toutes les couleurs*. Paris: Adrien Egron.

———. 1840. *Mémoires de Grégoire*. Paris: J. Yonet.

———. 1991 (first published 1808). *De la littérature des Nègres*. Paris: Perrin.

Hale, Thomas. 1977. "Pre-*Roots*: The Literary Triangle Trade." *Minority Voices* 1, no. 1:35–40.

537

Hallward, Peter. 2001. *Absolutely Postcolonial: Writing between the Singular and the Specific*. Manchester: Manchester University Press.

Hardt, Michael, and Antonio Negri. 2000. *Empire*. Cambridge, Mass.: Harvard University Press.

Hardy, Georges. 1921. *La Mise en valeur du Sénégal, 1817–1854*. Paris: Payot.

Harms, Robert. 2002. *The Diligent: A Voyage through the Worlds of the Slave Trade*. New York: Basic Books.

Harris, Wilson. 1995. *History, Fable, and Myth in the Caribbean and the Guianas*. Wellesley, Mass.: Calaloux Publications.

Hegel, G. W. F. 1977. *Phenomenology of Spirit*. Trans. A. V. Miller. Oxford: Clarendon Press.

Herbst, Jeffrey. 2000. *States and Power in Africa: Comparative Lessons in Authority and Control*. Princeton: Princeton University Press.

Herskovits, Melville. 1941. *The Myth of the Negro Past*. New York: Harper and Brothers.

Hochschild, Adam. 2005. *Bury the Chains: Prophets and Rebels in the Fight to Free an Empire's Slaves*. Boston: Houghton Mifflin.

Hoffmann, Léon-François. 1973. *Le Nègre romantique: Personnage littéraire et obsession collective*. Paris: Payot.

Hogendorn, Jan, and Marion Johnson. 1986. *The Shell Money of the Slave Trade*. Cambridge: Cambridge University Press.

Hugo, Victor. 1979 (first published 1818 and 1826). *Bug-Jargal ou la révolution haïtienne*. Ed. Roger Toumson. Fort-de-France: Désormeaux.

Hunting, Claudine. 1978. "The Philosophes and Black Slavery: 1748–1765." *Journal of the History of Ideas* 39, no. 3 (July–Sep.): 405–18.

Jal, Auguste. 1832. "Un Négrier." In *Scènes de la vie maritime*, 3:3–51. Paris: Charles Gosselin.

James, C. L. R. 1989. *The Black Jacobins: Toussaint L'Ouverture and the San Domingo Revolution*. 2nd ed. New York: Vintage Books.

Jennings, Lawrence C. 2000. *French Anti-Slavery: The Movement for the Abolition of Slavery in France, 1802–1848*. Cambridge: Cambridge University Press.

Johnson, G. Wesley. 1991. *Naissance du Sénégal contemporain*. Paris: Karthala.

Johnson, Lemuel. 1980. "The Middle Passage in African Literature: Wole Soyinka, Yambo Ouologuem, Ayi Kwei Armah." *African Literature Today* 11:62–84.

Kadish, Doris Y., ed. 2000. *Slavery in the Caribbean Francophone World: Distant Voices, Forgotten Acts, Forged Identities*. Athens: University of Georgia Press.

Kadish, Doris Y., and Françoise Massardier-Kenney, eds. 1994. *Translating Slavery: Gender and Race in French Women's Writing, 1783–1823*. Kent, Ohio: Kent State University Press.

Katz, Jonathan Ned. 2001. *Love Stories: Sex between Men before Homosexuality*. Chicago: University of Chicago Press.

Kemedjio, Cilas. 1999. *De la Négritude à la Créolité: Edouard Glissant, Maryse Condé et la malédiction de la théorie*. Hamburg: Lit Verlag.

538

Kesteloot, Lilyan. 1974. *Black Writers in French: A Literary History of Negritude.* Trans. Ellen Conroy Kennedy. Philadelphia: Temple University Press.

———. 1982. *Comprendre le "Cahier d'un retour au pays natal" d'Aimé Césaire.* Issy les Moulineaux: Les Classiques Africains.

Klein, Herbert S. 1999. *The Atlantic Slave Trade.* Cambridge: Cambridge University Press.

Klein, Martin. 1998. *Slavery and Colonial Rule in French West Africa.* Cambridge: Cambridge University Press.

Kom, Ambroise, and Lucienne Ngoué, eds. 1991. *Le Code Noir et l'Afrique.* Ivry: Nouvelles du Sud.

Labat, Jean-Baptiste. 1722. *Nouveau voyage aux isles de l'Amérique.* Paris: Chez Guillaume Cavelier fils.

———. 1728. *Nouvelle relation de l'Afrique Occidentale.* Paris: Théodore Legras.

———. 1730. *Voyage du Chevalier des Marchais en Guinée, isles voisines, et à Cayenne, fait en 1725, 1726 & 1727.* Paris: Chez Saugrain.

———. 1993 (first published 1720). *Voyage aux isles: Chronique aventureuse des Caraïbes, 1693–1705.* Paris: Editions Phébus.

La Courbe, Michel Jajolet, Sieur de. 1913. *Premier voyage du Sieur de La Courbe fait à la coste d'Afrique en 1685.* Ed. P. Cultru. Paris: Edouard Champion.

Lacroix, Pamphile de. 1995. *La Révolution de Haïti.* Paris: Karthala.

Lamiral, Dominique-Harcourt. 1789. *L'Affrique et le peuple affriquain considérés sous leurs rapports avec notre Commerce & nos Colonies.* Paris: Chez Dessenne.

Lavallée, Joseph. 1801 (first French edition 1789). *The Negro Equalled by Few Europeans.* Translated from the French. Philadelphia: William W. Woodward.

Lee, Debbie. 2002. *Slavery and the Romantic Imagination.* Philadelphia: University of Pennsylvania Press.

Linebaugh, Peter, and Marcus Rediker. 2000. *The Many-Headed Hydra: Sailors, Slaves, Commoners, and the Hidden History of the Revolutionary Atlantic.* Boston: Beacon Press.

L'Ouverture, Toussaint. 1951. *Mémoires du Général Toussaint-Louverture écrits par lui-même.* Port-au-Prince: Bélizaire.

Lovejoy, Arthur O. 1964. *The Great Chain of Being: A Study of the History of an Idea.* Cambridge, Mass.: Harvard University Press.

Lovejoy, Paul E., ed. 1981. *The Ideology of Slavery in Africa.* Beverly Hills: Sage.

Lucas, Edith E. 1930. *La Littérature anti-esclavagiste au dix-neuvième siècle: Étude sur Madame Beecher Stowe et son influence en France.* Paris: E. de Boccard.

Ly, Abdoulaye. 1958. *La Compagnie du Sénégal.* Paris: Présence Africaine.

Ly, Ibrahima. 1988. *Les Noctuelles vivent de larmes.* Paris: L'Harmattan.

Mailhol, Gabriel. 1764. *Le Philosophe nègre et les secrets des Grecs.* London: n.p.

Manning, Patrick. 1982. *Slavery, Colonialism, and Economic Growth in Dahomey, 1640–1960.* Cambridge: Cambridge University Press.

———. 1990. *Slavery and African Life: Occidental, Oriental, and African Slave Trades.* Cambridge: Cambridge University Press.

539

Martin, Gaston. 1925–26. "Les 'Chambres littéraires' de Nantes et la préparation de la Révolution." *Annales de Bretagne* 37.

———. 1931. *Nantes au XVIIIe siècle: L'Ère des négriers (1714–1774)*. Paris: Lélix Alcan.

Mason, Haydn. 1981. *Voltaire: A Biography*. Baltimore: Johns Hopkins University Press.

Mathorez, J. 1919. *Les Etrangers en France sous l'ancien régime*. Paris: Librairie Ancienne Edouard Champion.

Meillassoux, Claude. 1986. *Anthropologie de l'esclavage: Le Ventre de fer et d'argent*. Paris: Presses Universitaires de France.

Mercier, Louis-Sébastien. 1783. *Tableau de Paris, nouvelle édition*. Amsterdam: n.p.

———. 1999 (first published 1771). *L'An 2440: Rêve s'il en fut jamais*. Introduction and notes by Christopher Cave and Christine Marcandier-Colard. Paris: La Découverte.

Mercier, Roger. 1962. *L'Afrique noire dans la littérature française: Les Premières images (XVIIIe–XVIIIe siècles)*. Dakar: Université de Dakar, Faculté des Lettres et des Sciences Humaines.

Mérimée, Prosper. 1964. *Colomba et dix autres nouvelles*. Paris: Gallimard.

———. 1978. *Théâtre de Clara Gazul, romans et nouvelles*. Paris: Gallimard, "Bibliothèque de la Pléiade."

———. 1983. *"Tamango," "Mateo Falcone" et autres nouvelles*. Paris: Flammarion.

———. 1989. *"Carmen" and Other Stories*. Trans. Nicholas Jotcham. Oxford: Oxford University Press.

Mettas, Jean. 1984. *Répertoire des expéditions négrières françaises au XVIIIe siècle*. Ed. Serge Daget and Michèle Daget. 2 vols. Paris: Société Française d'Histoire d'Outre-Mer.

Meyer, Jean, Jean Tarrade, Annie Rey-Goldzeiguer, and Jacques Thobie. 1991. *Histoire de la France coloniale des origines à 1914*. Paris: Armand Colin.

Miller, Christopher L. 1985. *Blank Darkness: Africanist Discourse in French*. Chicago: University of Chicago Press.

———. 1998. *Nationalists and Nomads: Essays on Francophone African Literature and Culture*. Chicago: University of Chicago Press.

Minchinton, Walter E. 1979. "The Triangular Trade Revisited." In *The Uncommon Market: Essays in the Economic History of the Atlantic Slave Trade*, ed. Henry A. Gemery and Jan S. Hogendorn, 331–52. New York: Academic Press.

Mintz, Sidney. 1985. *Sweetness and Power: The Place of Sugar in Modern History*. New York: Penguin.

Misrahi-Barak, Judith. 2005. *Revisiting Slave Narratives/Les Avatars comtemporains des récits d'esclaves*. Montpellier: Centre d'Etudes et de Recherches sur les Pays du Commonwealth, Université Monypellier III.

Moitt, Bernard. 2001. *Women and Slavery in the French Antilles, 1635–1848*. Bloomington: Indiana University Press.

Mollien, Gaspard Théodore. 1967. *L'Afrique occidentale en 1818*. Paris: Calmann-Lévy.

Montesquieu, Charles de Secondat, Baron de. 1950. *Oeuvres complètes de Montesquieu*. Ed. André Masson. Paris: Nagel.

Montgomery, Benilde. 1994. "White Captives, African Slaves: A Drama of Abolition." *Eighteenth-Century Studies* 27, no. 4 (summer): 615–30.

Moreau de Saint-Méry, Médéric Louis Elie. 1958 (first published 1796). *Description . . . de la partie française de l'isle de Saint-Domingue*. Paris: Société de l'histoire des colonies françaises.

———. n.d. *Fragment sur les mœurs de Saint-Domingue*. N.p.: Bibliothèque Nationale de France, microfiche LI 113–1.

Morenas, Joseph Elzéar. 1828. *Précis historique de la traite des Noirs et de l'esclavage colonial*. Paris: Firmin Didot.

Morgan, Jennifer L. 2004. *Laboring Women: Reproduction and Gender in New World Slavery*. Philadelphia: University of Pennsylvania Press.

Motylewski, Patricia. 1998. *La Société française pour l'abolition de l'esclavage, 1834–1850*. Paris: L'Harmattan.

Moudileno, Lydie. 1997. *L'Ecrivain antillais au miroir de sa littérature: Mises en scène et mise en abyme du roman antillais*. Paris: Karthala.

———. 1999. "Retrouver la parole perdue: Edouard Glissant et le récit d'esclave reconstitué." *Romanic Review* 90, no. 1:83–91.

Mousnier, Jehan. 1957. *Journal de la traite des Noirs*. Paris: Editions de Paris.

Munford, Clarence J. 1991. *The Black Ordeal of Slavery and Slave Trading in the French West Indies, 1625–1715*. Lewiston, N.Y.: E. Mellen Press.

Murphy, Geraldine. 1994. "Olaudah Equiano, Accidental Tourist." *Eighteenth-Century Studies* 27, no. 4 (summer): 551–68.

Naipaul, V. S. 1981. *The Middle Passage: Impressions of Five Societies — British, French, and Dutch — in the West Indies and South America*. New York: Vintage Books.

N'Diaye, Joseph. 2006. *Il fut un jour à Gorée: L'Esclavage raconté à nos enfants*. Neuilly-sur-Seine: Michel Lafon.

Nesbitt, Nick. 2003. *Voicing Memory: History and Subjectivity in French Caribbean Literature*. Charlottesville: University of Virginia Press.

Niane, Djibril Tamsir. 1960. *Soundjata ou l'épopée mandingue*. Paris: Présence Africaine.

Noël, Erick. 2006. *Etre noir en France au XVIIIe siècle*. Paris: Tallandier.

Northrup, David, ed. 1994. *The Atlantic Slave Trade*. Lexington, Mass.: Heath.

O'Connell, David. 1973. "The Black Hero in French Romantic Fiction." *Studies in Romanticism* 12, no. 2 (spring): 516–29.

Ogude, S. E. 1982. "Facts into Fiction: Equiano's *Narrative* Reconsidered." *Research in African Literatures* 13, no. 1 (spring): 31–43.

Ouologuem, Yambo. 1968. *Le Devoir de violence*. Paris: Seuil.

Pailhès, Gabriel. 1910. *La Duchesse de Duras et Chateaubriand d'après des documents inédits*. Paris: Perrin.

Park, Mungo. 2000 (first published 1799). *Travels in the Interior Districts of Africa*. Ed. Kate Ferguson Marsters. Durham: Duke University Press.

541

Patterson, Orlando. 1982. *Slavery and Social Death: A Comparative Study*. Cambridge, Mass.: Harvard University Press.

Peabody, Sue. 1996. *"There Are No Slaves in France": The Political Culture of Race and Slavery in the Ancien Régime*. New York: Oxford University Press.

Pedersen, Carl. 1993. "Middle Passages: Representations of the Slave Trade in Caribbean and African-American Literature." *Massachusetts Review* 34, no. 2 (summer): 225–38.

———. 1994. "Sea Change: The Middle Passage and the Transatlantic Imagination." In *The Black Columbiad: Defining Moments in African American Literature and Culture*, ed. Werner Sollors and Maria Dietrich, 42–51. Cambridge, Mass.: Harvard University Press.

Pétré-Grenouilleau, Olivier. 1995. *Moi, Joseph Mosneron: Armateur négrier nantais. Portrait culturel d'une bourgeoisie négotiante au siècle des Lumières*. Rennes: Editions Apogée.

———. 1996. *L'Argent de la traite: Milieu négrier, capitalisme et développement: Un Modèle*. Paris: Aubier.

———. 1997. *Les Négoces maritimes français: XVIIe–XXe siècle*. Paris: Belin.

———. 1997. *La Traite des Noirs*. 2nd ed. Paris: Presses Universitaires de France.

———. 1998. *Nantes au temps de la traite des Noirs*. Paris: Hachette.

———. 2004. *Les Traites négrières: Essai d'histoire globale*. Paris: Gallimard.

Peytraud, Lucien. 1973 (first published 1897). *L'Esclavage aux Antilles françaises avant 1789 d'après des documents inédits des archives coloniales*. Pointe-à-Pitre: Emile Désormeaux.

Plesse, Jean Pierre. 2005 (written 1762). *Journal de bord d'un négrier*. Paris: Editions Le Mot et Le Reste.

Pluche, Abbé Antoine. 1780 (first published 1735). *Le Spectacle de la nature ou entretiens sur les particularités de l'histoire naturelle*. Vol. 3. Paris: Frères Estienne.

Pluchon, Pierre. 1980. *La Route des esclaves: Négriers et bois d'ébène au XVIIIe siècle*. Paris: Hachette.

Pomeau, René. 1985. *D'Arouet à Voltaire, 1694–1734*. Oxford: Voltaire Foundation.

Pousson, Jean-Pierre, Philippe Bonnichon, and Xavier Huetz de Lemps. 1998. *Espaces coloniaux et espaces maritimes au XVIIIe siècle: Les Deux Amériques et la Pacifique*. Paris: SEDES.

Prévost, Abbé Antoine-François. 1735. *Le Pour et le contre: Ouvrage périodique d'un goût nouveau*. Vol. 6. Paris: Didot.

Price-Mars, Jean. 1928. *Ainsi parla l'oncle . . . : Essais d'ethnographie*. Compiègne: Imprimerie de Compiègne.

Privileges concédés à Messieurs de la Compagnie des Isles de l'Amérique. 1642 (March). Clairambault ms. 385, fol. 61. Paris: Bibliothèque Nationale de France.

Pruneau de Pommegorge, Antoine Edme. 1789. *Description de la Nigritie par M. P. D. P.* Amsterdam: Chez Maradan.

Rawley, James A. 1981. *The Transatlantic Slave Trade: A History*. New York: Norton.

Raynal, Abbé Guillaume Thomas. 1780. *Histoire philosophique et politique des établissemens et du commerce des Européens dans les deux Indes*. 3rd ed. 4 vols. Geneva: Chez Jean-Léonard Pellet.

Rediker, Marcus. 2004. *Villains of All Nations: Atlantic Pirates in the Golden Age*. Boston: Beacon Press.

Renault, François, and Serge Daget. 1985. *Les Traites négrières en Afrique*. Paris: Karthala.

Reynolds, Edward. 1985. *Stand the Storm: A History of the Atlantic Slave Trade*. London: Allison and Busby.

Richard, Christian. 1982. *Le Courage des autres*. Film. Burkina Faso and France.

Richardson, David, ed. 1985. *Abolition and Its Aftermath: The Historical Context, 1790–1916*. London: Frank Cass.

Riesz, János. 1996. "'Le Dernier voyage du négrier *Sirius*': Le Roman dans le roman dans *Le Docker noir* d'Ousmane Sembene." In *Sénégal-Forum: Littérature et histoire*, ed. Papa Samba Diop, 179–96. Frankfurt: IKO.

Rinchon, P. Dieudonné. 1964. *Pierre-Ignace-Liévin Van Alstein, capitaine négrier: Gand 1733–Nantes 1793*. Dakar: IFAN.

Roach, Joseph. 1996. *Cities of the Dead: Circum-Atlantic Performance*. New York: Columbia University Press.

Robb, Graham. 2003. *Strangers: Homosexual Love in the Nineteenth Century*. New York: Norton.

Rochmann, Marie-Christine, ed. 2000. *Esclavage et abolitions: Mémoires et systèmes de représentation*. Paris: Karthala.

Rodney, Walter. 1981. *How Europe Underdeveloped Africa*. Washington: Howard University Press.

Roger, Jacques-François, Baron. 1828. *Fables sénégalaises, recueillies de l'Oulof et mises en vers français*. Paris: Nepveu.

———. 1828. *Kelédor, histoire africaine*. Paris: Nepveu.

Rosello, Mireille. 1992. *Littérature et identité créole aux Antilles*. Paris: Karthala.

Rousseau, Jean-Jacques. 1925. *La Nouvelle Héloïse*. Paris: Hachette.

———. 1966–69. *Oeuvres complètes*. Paris: Gallimard.

———. 1975 (first published 1762). *Du Contrat social*. Paris: Garnier.

Sainte-Beuve, Charles Augustin. 1951. "Portraits littéraires." In *Oeuvres*, vol. 2. Paris: Gallimard, Bibliothèque de la Pléiade.

Saint-Lambert, Jean-François. 1997 (first published 1769). *Ziméo*. In *Contes américains: L'Abenaki, Ziméo, Les Deux amis*, ed. Roger Little. Exeter: University of Exeter Press.

Saint-Pierre, Jacques-Henri-Bernardin de. 1825. *Oeuvres complètes de Jacques-Henri-Bernardin de Saint-Pierre*. Paris: Chez P. Dupont.

———. 1995. *Empsaël et Zoraïde, ou, Les blancs esclaves des Noirs a[u] Maroc*. Ed. Roger Little. Exeter: University of Exeter Press.

Sala-Molins, Louis. 1987. *Le Code Noir ou le calvaire de Canaan*. Paris: Presses Universitaires de France.

———. 1992. *Les Misères des Lumières: Sous la raison, l'outrage*. Paris: Robert Laffont.

543

Sandiford, Keith A. 2000. *The Cultural Politics of Sugar: Caribbean Slavery and Narratives of Colonialism*. Cambridge: Cambridge University Press.

Saugera, Éric. 1994. "De Sidoine à Sophie Raphel ou les lettres d'un capitaine négrier à sa femme pendant la traite illégale, 1824–1831." In *La Dernière Traite*, ed. Hubert Gerbeau and Eric Saugera, 119–50. Paris: Société Française d'Histoire d'Outre-Mer.

———. 1995. *Bordeaux port négrier: Chronologie, économie, idéologie, XVIIe–XVIIIe siècles*. Paris: Karthala.

———. 1998. *La Traite des Noirs en 30 questions*. Paris: Geste Editions.

Savary, Jacques. 1675. *Le Parfait negociant, ou instruction générale pour ce qui regarde le commerce*. Paris: Chez Jean Guignard fils.

Scarr, Deryck. 1998. *Slaving and Slavery in the Indian Ocean*. New York: St. Martin's.

Schlesinger, Roger, and Arthur P. Stabler. 1986. *André Thevet's North America: A Sixteenth-Century View*. Kingston: McGill-Queen's University Press.

Schmidt, Nelly. 2000. *Abolitionnistes de l'esclavage et réformateurs des colonies, 1820–1851: Analyse et documents*. Paris: Karthala.

Schoelcher, Victor. 1948. *Esclavage et colonisation*. Paris: Presses Universitaires de France.

Schwartz-Bart, Simone. 1979. *Ti-Jean L'Horizon*. Paris: Seuil.

Scott, Julius S. 1996. "Crisscrossing Empires: Ships, Sailors, and Resistance in the Lesser Antilles in the Eighteenth Century." In *The Lesser Antilles in the Age of European Expansion*, ed. Robert L. Paquette and Stanley L. Engerman, 128–43. Gainesville: University Press of Florida.

Searing, James. 1993. *West African Slavery and Atlantic Commerce: The Senegal River Valley, 1700–1860*. Cambridge: Cambridge University Press.

Seeber, Edward Derbyshire. 1969 (first published 1937). *Anti-Slavery Opinion in France during the Second Half of the Eighteenth Century*. New York: Greenwood Press.

Séjour, Victor. 1972 (first published 1837). "Le Mulâtre." In David O'Connell, "Victor Séjour: Écrivain américain de langue française." *Revue de Louisiane/Louisiana Review* 1, no. 1 (winter): 60–75.

Sembene, Ousmane. 1962. "La Noire de . . ." In *Voltaïque*, 149–77. Paris: Présence Africaine.

———. 1966. *La Noire de . . .* Film. France and Senegal.

———. 1973 (first published 1956). *Le Docker noir*. Paris: Présence Africaine.

———. 1976. *Ceddo*. Film DVD. Paris: Médiathèque des Trois Mondes.

———. 1986. *Black Docker*. Trans. Ros Schwartz. London: Heinemann.

Senghor, Lamine. 1927. *La Violation d'un pays*. Paris: Bureau d'Editions, de Diffusion et de Publicité.

Sepinwall, Alyssa Goldstein. 2005. *The Abbé Grégoire and the French Revolution: The Making of Modern Universalism*. Berkeley: University of California Press.

Sherzer, Dina. 1996. *Cinema, Colonialism, Postcolonialism: Perspectives from the French and Francophone Worlds*. Austin: University of Texas Press.

Smith, Arlette. 1988. "Maryse Condé's *Hérémakhonon*: A Triangular Structure of Alienation." *CLA Journal* 32, no. 1 (Sep. 1988): 45–54.

Sollors, Werner. 1997. *Neither Black nor White yet Both: Thematic Explorations of Interracial Literature*. New York: Oxford University Press.

Solow, Barbara L., ed. 1991. *Slavery and the Rise of the Atlantic System*. Cambridge: Cambridge University Press.

Staël, Anne-Louise-Germaine Necker, Madame de. 1795. *Recueil de morceaux détachés*. Lausanne: Chez Durand, Ravanel et Cie. Libraires.

———. 1858 (first published 1786). "Mirza, ou lettre d'un voyageur." In *Oeuvres de Madame la Baronne de Staël-Holstein*, 1:147–59. Paris: Lefèvre.

———. 1967. *Oeuvres complètes de Madame la Baronne de Staël-Holstein*. Geneva: Slatkine. Facsimile of *Oeuvres complètes de Madame la Baronne de Staël-Holstein*. Paris: Firmin Didot, 1861.

———. 1997. *Oeuvres de jeunesse*. Paris: Desjonquières.

Staël, Auguste de. 1826. "Rapport verbal, présenté au Comité pour l'abolition de la Traite," in *Assemblée générale annuelle de la Société de la Morale Chrétienne*. April 13.

Stambolian, George, and Elaine Marks, eds. 1979. *Homosexualities and French Literature: Cultural Contexts/Critical Texts*. Ithaca: Cornell University Press.

Stein, Robert Louis. 1979. *The French Slave Trade in the Eighteenth Century: An Old Regime Business*. Madison: University of Wisconsin Press.

Stinchcombe, Arthur L. 1995. *Sugar Island Slavery in the Age of Enlightenment: The Political Economy of the Caribbean World*. Princeton: Princeton University Press.

Sue, Eugène. 1830 (letters dated 1826). "Lettres sur la Guadeloupe." *Revue des deux mondes*, ser. 2, tome 4 (Oct.–Nov.): 12–20; (Dec.): 331–43.

———. 1831. *Atar-Gull*. Paris: C. Vimont.

———. 1844–45. *Histoire de la marine française*. Paris: Au Comptoir des Imprimeurs-Unis.

———. 1850. *Oeuvres illustrées d'Eugène Sue par J.-A. Beaucé*. Paris: n.p.

———. 1993. *Romans de mort et d'aventure* [including *Atar-Gull*]. Paris: Robert Laffont.

Suk, Jeannie. 2001. *Postcolonial Paradoxes in French Caribbean Writing: Césaire, Glissant, Condé*. Oxford: Clarendon Press.

Suret-Canale, Jean. 1980. *Essais d'histoire africaine: De la traite des Noirs au néo-colonialisme*. Paris: Editions Sociales.

Sypher, Wylie. 1969. *Guinea's Captive Kings: British Anti-Slavery Literature of the XVIIIth Century*. New York: Octagon Books.

Taubira, Christiane. 2006. Introd. to *Codes Noirs de l'esclavage aux abolitions*, ed. André Castaldo. Paris: Dalloz.

Thésée, Françoise. 1986. *Les Ibos de l'"Amélie": Destinée d'une cargaison de traite clandestine à la Martinique, 1822–1838*. Paris: Editions Caribéennes.

Thomas, Dominic. 2007. *Black France: Colonialism, Immigration, and Transnationalism*. Bloomington: Indiana University Press.

545

Thomas, Hugh. 1997. *The Slave Trade: The Story of the Atlantic Slave Trade, 1440–1870*. New York: Simon and Schuster.

Thornton, John. 1992. *Africa and Africans in the Making of the Atlantic World, 1400–1680*. Cambridge: Cambridge University Press.

Timité, Bassori. 1983. *Grelots d'or*. Abidjan: CEDA.

Tomich, Dale W. 1990. *Slavery in the Circuit of Sugar: Martinique and the World Economy, 1830–1848*. Baltimore: Johns Hopkins University Press.

Touré, Kitia. 1994. *Les Anneaux de la mémoire* [also called *Nantes: Archéologie de la mémoire*]. Film. France.

Toussaint Louverture, François Dominique. 1951. *Mémoires du général Toussaint-L'Ouverture, écrits par lui-même, pouvant servir à l'histoire de sa vie*. Port-au-Prince: Bélizaire.

Tr . . . f, D. de. 1833. "La Frégate et le négrier: Aventure de mer." *Le Navigateur, journal des naufrages, pirateries, voyages, événemens de mer, etc*. Fifth year, no. 1, tome 8:66–78.

Trouillot, Michel-Rolph. 1995. *Silencing the Past: Power and the Production of History*. Boston: Beacon Press.

Turley, Hans. 1999. *Rum, Sodomy, and the Lash: Piracy, Sexuality, and Masculine Identity*. New York: New York University Press.

Vercel, Roger. 1938. *Ange-Marie, négrier sensible*. Paris: Albin Michel.

Vergès, Françoise. 2001. *Abolir l'esclavage: Une Utopie coloniale: Les Ambiguïtés d'une politique humanitaire*. Paris: Albin Michel.

―――. 2006. *La Mémoire enchaînée: Questions sur l'esclavage*. Paris: Albin Michel.

Vignols, Léon. 1928. "Une Expédition négrière en 1821 d'après son registre de bord." *Revue de l'histoire des colonies françaises* 16 (May–June): 265–324.

Vila, Anne C. 1998. *Enlightenment and Pathology: Sensibility in the Literature and Medicine of Eighteenth-Century France*. Baltimore: Johns Hopkins University Press.

Vissière, Isabelle, and Jean-Louis Vissière. 1982. *La Traite des Noirs au siècle des lumières (témoignages de négriers)*. Paris: A. M. Métailié.

Voltaire, François Marie Arouet de. 1876–83. *Oeuvres complètes*. Paris: Garnier.

Walcott, Derek. 1992. *The Antilles: Fragments of Epic Memory (The Nobel Lecture)*. New York: Farrar, Straus and Giroux.

Watts, Richard. 2005. *Packaging Post/Coloniality: The Manufacture of Literary Identity in the Francophone World*. Lanham, Md.: Lexington Books.

Williams, Eric. 1984 (first published 1970). *From Columbus to Castro: The History of the Caribbean, 1492–1969*. New York: Vintage Books.

―――. 1994 (first published 1944). *Capitalism and Slavery*. Chapel Hill: University of North Carolina Press.

―――. 1994. "Economics, Not Racism, as the Root of Slavery." In *The Atlantic Slave Trade*, ed. David Northrup, 3–12. Lexington, Mass.: Heath.

Woukoache, François. 1995. *Asientos*. Film. Senegal and Belgium.

Page locators in italics refer to illustrations.

554

CHRISTOPHER L. MILLER is the Frederick Clifford Ford Professor of African American Studies and French at Yale University. He is the author of *Blank Darkness: Africanist Discourse in French* (1985); *Theories of Africans: Francophone Literature and Anthropology in Africa* (1990); and *Nationalists and Nomads: Essays on Francophone African Literature and Culture* (1998).

Library of Congress Cataloging-in-Publication Data

Miller, Christopher L., 1953–
The French Atlantic triangle : literature and culture of the slave trade /
Christopher L. Miller.
p. cm.
Includes bibliographical references and index.
ISBN-13: 978-0-8223-4127-7 (cloth : alk. paper)
ISBN-13: 978-0-8223-4151-2 (pbk. : alk. paper)
1. French literature — History and criticism.
2. Slavery in literature.
3. Slavery in motion pictures.
4. Slave-trade — France. I. Title.
PQ145.6.S38M55 2008
840.9'3552 — dc22
2007033635